EFFECTIVE GROUP DISCUSSION
Theory and Practice

ELEVENTH EDITION

EFFECTIVE GROUP DISCUSSION
Theory and Practice

GLORIA J. GALANES
Southwest Missouri State University

KATHERINE ADAMS
California State University at Fresno

with JOHN K. BRILHART
University of Nebraska, Omaha (Emeritus)

Boston   Burr Ridge, IL   Dubuque, IA   Madison, WI   New York   San Francisco   St. Louis
Bangkok   Bogotá   Caracas   Kuala Lumpur   Lisbon   London   Madrid   Mexico City
Milan   Montreal   New Delhi   Santiago   Seoul   Singapore   Sydney   Taipei   Toronto

Higher Education

EFFECTIVE GROUP DISCUSSION
Published by McGraw-Hill, a business unit of The McGraw-Hill Companies, Inc., 1221 Avenue of the Americas, New York, NY, 10020. Copyright © 2004, 2001, 1998, 1995, 1992, 1989, 1986, 1982, 1978, 1974, 1967, by The McGraw-Hill Companies, Inc. All rights reserved. No part of this publication may be reproduced or distributed in any form or by any means, or stored in a database or retrieval system, without the prior written consent of The McGraw-Hill Companies, Inc., including, but not limited to, in any network or other electronic storage or transmission, or broadcast for distance learning.

Some ancillaries, including electronic and print components, may not be available to customers outside the United States.

This book is printed on acid-free paper.

2 3 4 5 6 7 8 9 0 DOC/DOC 0 9 8 7 6 5 4

ISBN 0-07-284347-0

Publisher: *Phillip A. Butcher*
Sponsoring editor: *Nanette Giles*
Developmental editor II: *Jennie Katsaros*
Producer, Media technology: *Jessica Bodie*
Lead project manager: *Susan Trentacosti*
Production supervisor: *Carol A. Bielski*
Designer: *Sharon C. Spurlock*
Lead supplement producer: *Marc Mattson*
Associate photo research coordinator: *Natalia C. Peschiera*
Associate art editor: *Cristin Yancey*
Cover design: *Lisa Buckley*
Interior design: *Anne Flanagan*
Cover image: *The Heritage Center Museum of Lancaster County, Inc.*
Typeface: *10/12 Garamond*
Compositor: *Shepherd Inc.*
Printer: *R. R. Donnelley and Sons, Inc.*

Library of Congress Cataloging-in-Publication Data

Galanes, Gloria J.
    Effective group discussion : theory and practice / Gloria J. Galanes, Katherine Adams
with John K. Brilhart.—11th ed.
        p. cm.
    Includes index.
    Rev. ed. of: Effective group discussion / John K. Brilhart, Gloria J. Galanes, Katherine
Adams. 10th ed. c2001
    ISBN 0-07-284347-0 (softcover : alk. paper)
    1. Small groups. 2. Communication in small groups. 3. Group problem solving. 4.
Discussion I. Adams, Katherine H., 1954– II. Brilhart, John K. III. Brilhart, John K.
Effective group discussion. IV. Title.
HM736.B75 2004
302.3'4—dc21   2003054068

www.mhhe.com

Brief Contents

Contents

15 Observing and Evaluating Group Discussions   427

Appendix A Making Public Presentations of the Group's Output   A–1

Appendix B Informational Resources for the Small Group   A–7

Preface

The 11th edition was written to help students become more effective small group members and leaders by giving them the research-based tools—both in terms of theoretical understandings and practical suggestions—for effective participation in groups. With these tools, people can understand why one group is satisfying and, perhaps, why another feels like torture. More important, they will understand what they can *do* about it.

Effective Group Discussion focuses on secondary groups, such as work groups, committees, task forces, self-directed work teams, and other small groups with tasks to complete. The text is written for academically prepared beginning students of small group communication and is likely to be most useful to upper-division students who can appreciate the extensive research base that grounds the narrative. It also serves well as a reference source for advanced communication students, consultants, or group leaders.

Overview

Generally, the chapters move the discussion from systems inputs to throughput processes to outcomes. However, after Chapters 1 and 2, the text is designed so instructors have the flexibility to skim or skip chapters or cover them in a different order. For instance, we offer a section that covers basic communication theory for students without a previous course in communication, but this section can be skimmed quickly if it reviews material students already know.

Part I presents an overview of small group theory. Chapter 1 introduces several ideas that are developed in subsequent chapters: the importance of small groups in our lives, types of groups, why diversity is important, and how technology can help a group. Chapter 2 introduces the organizing framework of systems theory.

Part II, "The Foundations of Communicating in Groups," presents a theoretical description of the communication process, placing *communication* at the center of a group's throughput processes. If it is a review for some students, it can be skimmed. Chapter 3 explains the communication process, Chapter 4 concentrates on verbal and nonverbal signals, and Chapter 5 describes the effects of culture and cultural differences on communication in small groups.

Part III focuses on the development of the group as an entity. Chapter 6 discusses the members. Chapters 7 and 8 deal with how members develop from a collection of individuals into a group, with Chapter 7 focusing on structuration and the development of roles and norms, and Chapter 8 on networks, status relationships, cohesiveness, avoiding groupthink, teambuilding, and SYMLOG. Chapter 9 presents theoretical perspectives about leadership, and Chapter 10 offers guidelines for designated small group leaders.

Part IV links throughput processes with outputs as it presents information about effective problem solving. It begins with an overview of problem solving in Chapter 11, moves to a discussion of decision making in Chapter 12, and concludes in Chapter 13 with information about how properly managed conflict can enhance these important small group processes.

Part V contains techniques and tools for evaluating and improving small groups. Chapter 14 presents specific discussion techniques that maximize small group effectiveness. Techniques and tools for observing, analyzing, and evaluating small group communication are presented in Chapter 15.

Finally, the appendices contain information that is important to some instructors but that others do not use. Appendix A covers information about how to make public presentations of a group's work and Appendix B describes the information gathering process group members should use.

When compared to our other small group text, *Communicating* in *Groups, Effective Group Discussion* includes more current research, uses a more extensive vocabulary, and places greater emphasis on connecting application directly to theoretical principles and models. Visual illustrations are incorporated to depict and teach rather than to entertain or capture attention. Students will find their needs for research summaries and theoretical explanations well met. Intersecting with these strong academic underpinnings are numerous practical suggestions for participating effectively in small groups.

Systems theory is the theoretical foundation on which *Effective Group Discussion* is based. We believe it provides the most useful, accessible framework for incorporating all that we know about small groups. We discuss the other major theories that bear on small group discussion, such as structuration, symbolic convergence, and so forth, but systems theory serves to organize what we present in the text and to remind readers of the interdependent relationships among *all* the components of small groups.

Changes to the 11th Edition

This 11th edition of *Effective Group Discussion* extends a series of the changes that was started with the 10th edition. Gloria Galanes and Kathy Adams have assumed primary responsibility for the text, with Jack Brilhart serving as a consultant. For all of us, small group work is too important to be left to chance or conventional wisdom. Thus, the new edition continues to provide a comprehensive survey and interpretation of the small group research literature, accompanied by practical, prescriptive guidance that readers have come to expect of this text.

We pride ourselves on providing a solid research base for readers. As we update each edition with the most current research available, our challenge has always been what to leave out. In this edition, to accommodate increased coverage of technology and diversity, we have streamlined certain sections and removed tangential information. We believe diversity is a critical issue for groups; to emphasize this, we have retained the chapter on intercultural communication, but we have also placed information about group diversity throughout the text. In addition, we have expanded our coverage of technology and groups by including such coverage, where relevant, throughout the text. We have expanded the discussion of structuration theory, to include information about adaptive structuration theory. We have added information about socialization of members into groups, generational differences, and the effects of poor diversity management. We have moved the groupthink section to the decision-making chapter and linked it more closely to decision processes. We also include quotes throughout the text from individuals identified by their peers as being excellent leaders. These quotes came from extensive interviews Gloria completed last year and underscore the messages in the text. Finally, we continue to use examples from our own lives, from media reports, and from stories our students and colleagues have shared with us.

Features

Case Studies: Each chapter begins with a case study that illustrates main points from the chapter. These are usually real-life stories that serve to help students retain key content and understand the relevance and application of the chapter's topic.

Consider This Boxes: Consider This boxes ask the students to apply a concept explicated in the chapter. This feature is designed to help students think more deeply about a concept by asking them to apply it. This not only helps students learn the material but also encourages them to understand how the information is useful in everyday small group situations. *Consider This* boxes can be used to prompt class discussion.

Leader Quotes: Each chapter includes quotes relevant to the chapter's topics. These quotes are taken from interviews with individuals who have been identified by their peers as being excellent leaders, and they reinforce the importance of the topic.

Emphasis on Technology: There are many ways in which technology can be used by groups, and we are just beginning to learn how technology affects group interaction. This information is distributed throughout the text.

Emphasis on Diversity: The importance of diversity and intercultural communication cannot be overemphasized! In addition to a chapter devoted to this topic, relevant information about diversity is distributed throughout the text.

Tables and Figures: Tables and figures are provided to illustrate concepts in the text. They offer a concise, visual summary of information explicated in the text. Several new tables and figures are included in this edition.

Learning Aids: Each chapter includes learning objectives for the chapter; a list of key terms, which are boldface in the text; a chapter summary highlighting the chapter's main points; and exercises that apply the information. The bibliography that accompanies each chapter provides additional reading material should instructors or students wish to pursue chapter information in more depth. The glossary at the end of the text provides definitions of all key terms.

Online Learning Center and Small Group Supersite (www.mhhe.com and www.mhhe.com/smallgroups): McGraw-Hill provides online learning for students that supplements topics in the chapter. An icon at the end of each chapter guides students to relevant tools and activities including interactive quizzes, glossary flashcards, and weblinks.

Resources for Instructors

Instructor's Manual: The manual provides sample syllabi, sample lecture notes, additional exercises, writing assignments, "writing to learn" assignments, suggestions for relevant videos and films that illustrate chapter contents, and a test bank of objective and essay questions to help the instructor.

Videos: Two videos are available with the text. *Communicating Effectively in Small Groups* offers four scenarios that lend themselves to extended analysis. Each scenario focuses on a specific small group topic: leadership, conflict, effective problem solving, and ineffective problem solving. *Communicating in Groups: Short Takes* provides 24 short scenes, each depicting a specific concept discussed in the text.

Websites: The *Online Learning Center* and the *Small Group Website* offer book-specific exercises, quizzes, supplemental content, and up-to-date links to sites with interesting information for both students and instructors.

Gloria J.Galanes
Katherine Adams
John K. Brilhart

Acknowledgments

Wε gratefully appreciate your use of *Effective Group Discussion*. We welcome your written reactions to its content and composition. You can send such comments to us via the McGraw-Hill Company; the Department of Communication and Mass Media, Southwest Missouri State University, Springfield, Missouri; or the Department of Communication, California State University, Fresno, California.

May all your groups be enjoyable and satisfying!

Numerous people contributed to this book; we can name only a few. First, we acknowledge our debt to instructors and writers Freed Bales, Ernest Bormann, Elton S. Carter, B. Aubrey Fisher, Larry Frey, Kenneth Hance, Randy Hirokawa, Sidney J. Parnes, J. Donald Phillips, M. Scott Poole, Marvin Shaw, Victor Wall, and W. Woodford Zimmerman.

The following reviewers were exceptionally helpful in supplying thoughtful, carefully considered suggestions:

Dennis S. Gouran
Pennsylvania State University

Jean-Claude Bruno Teboul
DePaul University

Robert D. Harrison
Gallaudet University

Carol Leeman
University of North Carolina at Charlotte

Sharon Roach
University of Louisiana at Monroe

Claire Sullivan
University of Maine

G. J. G
K. A.
J. K. B.

© Matthew Alan/Corbis

INTRODUCTION TO THE STUDY OF SMALL GROUPS

The two chapters in Part I provide introductory information to focus your study of small groups. Chapter 1 introduces important terms and concepts used throughout the text, and Chapter 2 presents systems theory as a framework for studying and understanding small groups.

THE SMALL GROUPS IN EVERYONE'S LIFE

Central Message

If you want to succeed in modern organizational and social life, you must understand how to communicate effectively as a member of a group.

STUDY OBJECTIVES

As a result of studying Chapter 1 you should be able to:

1. Explain why you need to understand small group communication and to participate productively in small group discussions.
2. Use correctly the terms presented in this chapter, particularly *group*, *small group*, *discussion*, *small group discussion*, and *ethics*.
3. Describe the two major categories of small groups.
4. Describe the five ethical principles most relevant to small group communication.
5. Consciously and intentionally become a participant-observer during group discussions

In the Grimm fairy tale, *The Bremen Town Musicians,* an old donkey, grown too frail for hard labor in the fields, knows his days are numbered.[1] He sets off for Bremen to become a town musician. Along the way, he meets a decrepit dog, too old to hunt, that has run away from the master who plans to kill him. Donkey and Dog soon encounter an ancient cat, escaped from the mistress who plans to drown her because she has become too slow to catch mice. Presently, the three are joined by Rooster, who has discovered his mistress's plan to offer him up as Sunday lunch. On their way to Bremen, the four friends spy a brightly lit cottage in the distance. Hoping the owner will offer them food and shelter for the night, Donkey peeks in the window. He sees robbers getting ready to enjoy a tasty feast. The animals devise a plan to frighten the robbers away. Donkey places his forelegs on the window, Dog stands on his back, Cat climbs on Dog, and Rooster perches on Cat's head. Donkey brays, Dog barks, Cat meows, and Rooster crows. The terrified robbers scatter, leaving the feast for the four friends to devour. Later, with the lights out and the animals sated and sleepy, one robber returns to investigate. His candle makes Cat's eyes look like live coals, which he tries to light. Cat shrieks and claws him. Running away, the robber trips on Dog, who bites him, and stumbles on Donkey, who kicks him. Rooster, aroused by the noise, crows "Cock-a-doodle-doo." The thoroughly petrified robber explains to his cronies that a witch has claimed the cottage. The witch scratched him, a man stabbed him, a monster beat him, and a judge condemned him. The robbers abandon the cottage for good. The four friends decide to forgo becoming musicians in Bremen—they will live happily ever after in the cottage instead.

This fable makes an important point about real-life groups. One person—or animal—alone does not have all the talent, skill, or ideas to accomplish a complex task. But by working together, individuals in a group can achieve far more than individuals working alone. If your idea or project is at all complex, you need others to help carry it out. A small group can help ensure your chances of success.

> You come to the realization, "I can't do it all myself, so I have to depend upon teams."
>
> *J. T., CEO and General Manager, Public Utility*

Small groups—teams, task forces, committees—are the way most work gets done in present-day American society. This is true whether the context is education, business and industry, health care, social services, religion, family life, politics, or government work—small groups are the basic building blocks of our society and are themselves smaller models of the social interaction and interactive processes operating in the society as a whole.[2] We agree with Lawrence Frey, a leading scholar of small group communication, who believes that the small group is *the* most important social formation:

> Every segment of our society—from the largest multinational organization to the political workings of federal, state, city, and local governments to the

smallest community action group to friendship groups to the nuclear and extended family—relies on groups to make important decisions, socialize members, satisfy needs, and the like.[3]

We spend a tremendous amount of our time in formal and informal groups. For example, Cole reported in 1989 that executives spent an average of half their time in business meetings,[4] and Lawren noted that there are an estimated 20 million meetings each day in the United States.[5] When you add to this the amount of time people spend in groups unconnected with work, you begin to understand how pervasive groups are in modern society. Moreover, the ability to work effectively as part of a team requires skills that must be practiced. In a recent national survey of 750 leading American companies, 71.4 percent of respondents mentioned "ability to work in teams" as an essential skill for MBA graduates—more important by far than knowledge of quantitative and statistical techniques.[6] If you want to get anything done—on the job or anywhere else—you must learn how to be a good team member.

To help you with that learning, four important ideas about groups are introduced in this chapter. First, groups exist to meet important human needs, and humans are willing to exchange items of value—time, energy, and money—to participate in groups. Schutz explained that groups meet needs for inclusion, affection, and control: a need to belong and be identified with others; a need for love and esteem from others; and a need to achieve and exert power over others and our environment.[7] We humans cannot meet these needs by ourselves—participation with others is mandatory. In addition, these needs are so important that we willingly give of our own resources, especially time and energy, to participate in groups. For example, many people in Springfield, Missouri, worked to transform a decaying downtown space into Founders Park, a public green space in the city's center. Working in various groups, they selected the design, obtained necessary legal clearances, raised funds, publicized the project, and oversaw the construction. Numerous committee members worked long and hard in groups, not only because the issue was so important to them, but also because they knew the project would succeed only if they worked collectively rather than individually. But participation in groups always requires trade-offs—you get something, but you give up something, too. In return for being included, getting to use your talents, and accomplishing something important to you, you give up some autonomy and the license to do whatever you want, whenever you want.

A second important point about groups is that because the formation of groups is natural to humans, groups are everywhere. List all the small groups in which you participated during the past week, regardless of how briefly— and don't forget to list your family! Students in college classes average about 8 to 10, and sometimes list as many as 24 groups. For example, one student listed the following: family, Bible study, sorority, executive committee of sorority, study group in small group class, project group in marketing class, intramural volleyball team, car pool, and work group of clerks in clothing department. Our faculty colleagues often list even more groups than these. In fact, Goldhaber found that the average tenured faculty member served on six committees simultaneously and spent 11 hours per week in meetings![8]

Does this seem like a lot of groups? Consider this: Reliance on groups in our society is increasing and expected to increase further, perhaps dramatically. American managers are recognizing the value of participative decision making, with the small group as one important vehicle for encouraging employee participation and improving corporate decision making. The Ford Taurus and General Motors Saturn success stories are in large part the stories of successful group work. *Consumer Reports,* for example, praised Saturn for having a much better than average reliability record in its first year of production,[9] a far cry from the poor records of other General Motors cars throughout the 1980s. Years ago, Ouchi, developer of Theory Z management, warned American managers that their ability to counter Japanese competition depended on how well they learned to work in groups.[10] More recently, Waterman identified teamwork as a key element in companies that have kept their competitive edge.[11] It seems that Americans are getting the message.

Why is group work successful? Groups are usually better problem solvers, in the long run, than solitary individuals because they have access to more information than individuals do, can spot flaws and biases in each others' thinking, and then can think of things an individual may have failed to consider. Moreover, if people participate in planning the work of solving the problem, they are more likely to work harder and better at carrying out the solution. Thus, participation in problem solving and decision making helps guarantee continued commitment to decisions and solutions.

> It's a management philosophy to say, "If you get people thinking together, you're going to get a better product."
>
> *J. T., CEO and General Manager, Public Utility*

The third key point about groups is this: Just because we often participate in groups, we cannot assume we participate effectively. Just doing it doesn't mean we do it well! And unless we know something about why a group is unproductive, we won't know what we can do about it and we can't help a group improve. We may laugh at the saying, "A camel is a horse designed by a committee," but when our own group's horse looks suspiciously like a camel, we're often helpless to know what to do about it.

Students often groan when we tell them that a major portion of their grade will be based on a group project. Sorensen calls this **grouphate**—the antipathy many people feel toward working in groups.[12] Interestingly, she found that grouphate is partly caused by lack of training in how to communicate effectively as a group member. We hope to reduce your grouphate by providing you with information about the process of group communication and with education in effective discussion techniques. Strong communication skills are central to effective discussion and productive teamwork. Donald Petersen, former CEO at Ford Motor Company, learned this during his rise at Ford. At first he envi-

Grouphate

The feeling of antipathy and hostility many people have against working in a group, fostered by the many ineffective, time-wasting groups that exist.

sioned his role as that of a solitary engineer designing cars, but later he discovered that a successful company requires interaction and teamwork: "Communication skills are crucial. And I mean that in both directions—not only the ability to articulate . . . in a good fashion, but to listen."[13]

> There's nothing worse—we've been there. You walk out of a meeting just totally exhausted, drained, and depressed.
>
> *L. O., CEO, Health Care Collaborative*

The fourth and final point is that groups provide the vehicle by which the individual can make a contribution to the organization and the society as a whole. Larkin postulated that humans have a motivation to give. The basic ingredient cementing social cohesion is not the satisfaction of needs, but rather the availability for contribution. What best binds individuals to groups may not be so much the pressure to obtain necessities as the opportunities to give of oneself to something beyond merely self-interested acquisition.[14] The dignity of individuals, Lawson states, comes from people's contributions to something greater than themselves. People who give, of their time, money, energy and other resources, live healthier, happier, and more fulfilled lives; they report that their lives are more meaningful than those who do not.[15] For example, legendary baseball pitcher Nolan Ryan remembers the unity and team spirit of the 1969 pennant-winning New York Mets as a high point of his distinguished 27-year career.[16] We believe that the success of work-related committees stems largely from this need to contribute collaboratively with others.

The focus of this book is the communicative behavior of group members—what people say and do in groups. Although we will draw upon findings from other fields, we will concentrate on the process of communication among members, especially in Western cultures such as the United States, and on how you as a group member can influence this process. In psychology, you may have studied how groups modify the behavior of individuals or provide therapeutic benefits, and, in sociology, how groups help establish and maintain social organization. In communication, you will study what happens as members talk and work together, and what you can do to make your own communication as productive as possible. Moreover, we will use as examples groups from a variety of settings. Although groups in business and industry have captured a great deal of attention, group work is fundamental in all arenas of modern life. Thus, our examples come from the educational sphere, political life, sports and entertainment, health care situations, religious settings, social services, and community development organizations as well as the corporate and industrial realms.

Small group discussion, the talk among group members, cannot be reduced to a set of prescriptions; it is far too complex for simplistic rules. Each element of group discussion influences every other element in the group system; we describe this interdependence in depth in Chapter 2. Because the only person you can directly control is yourself, this book is designed to promote your awareness of your own behavior in small groups and its implications for other members. We do give guidelines and suggestions for you to consider, yet we do so with the understanding that you will remember to take into account your group's entire and unique situation as you enact those guidelines.

In the remainder of this chapter, we present definitions of key terms we use throughout the book to reduce the possibility of misunderstanding. We also present information about the types of groups you will encounter in many different kinds of settings, provide a brief discussion of ethical behavior important to effective group functioning in Western cultures, and conclude with a description of the participant-observer perspective we hope you will adopt in your groups.

Important Concepts and Terms

Group

Three or more people with an interdependent goal who interact and influence each other.

Interaction

Mutual influence by two or more people through the communication process.

Group is the first term we must consider. Although a variety of definitions exists, we believe none surpasses Marvin Shaw's: "persons who are interacting with one another in such a manner that each person influences and is influenced by each other."[17] Shaw's conception of a group emphasizes interaction and mutual influence. **Interaction** implies communication, the exchange of signals (words, gestures, and so forth) among people who belong to the group. It also implies that at least some of these signals are perceived and responded to in such a way that each member can potentially affect the other members' behaviors, beliefs, opinions, values, and so on. By this definition, a collection of people in one place would not necessarily constitute a group unless there were reciprocal awareness and influence. Following this logic, group members who are widely scattered geographically, but who interact and mutually influence each other by way of newsletters, telephone conversations, computer networks, closed-circuit TV, or radio *do* constitute a group.

Consider This 1.1

Do group members have to interact face-to-face to be a "real" group? Molly, Gloria's stepdaughter, communicates frequently with her group of high school friends via email and instant messaging, even though group members are scattered in colleges from coast to coast. Molly would argue that this virtual group is just as "real" as when the women saw each other daily in high school, although there are some differences.

What differences do you see between face-to-face (FTF) and computer-mediated (CM) groups? What limitations might FTF groups have over CM groups, and vice versa? Do you think virtual groups are as satisfying as FTF groups? What difference might it make if the virtual group members know each other in FTF context as opposed to knowing each other just online?

The study of groups may include large groupings (e.g., whole societies) or small ones; our focus is on small groups. The notion that "each person influences and is influenced by each other" implies that members are aware of each other, and from this mutual awareness we derive our definition of small as being based on perceptual awareness. A **small group,** therefore, is a group small enough that each member is aware of and able to recall each other group member, know who is and is not in the group, and recognize what role each is taking. We admit that this is fuzzy, but attempts to define small on the basis of number of members have never worked. At the low end, we can certainly perceive all members in a group of three. (We arbitrarily eliminate the dyad, or two-person unit, as a small group because dyads function differently from units of three or more.) At the high end, most of us can take in up to 11 members in a unit and, with training, may learn to handle 12 to 14.[18] But at the end of a semester, even a class as large as 25 may seem small to a teacher.

Some authors differentiate teams from small groups. Lumsden and Lumsden see teams as highly functioning groups where members are committed to the goal, leadership is shared, and the team has forged a strong sense of identity.[19] Harris and Sherblom reserve team for those groups where leadership is shared, such as the problem-solving or self-managed work groups we discuss later.[20] We do not differentiate between teams and small groups and we sometimes use the terms interchangeably in this text. In everyday life, a group may be called a team (e.g., "the management team" or "the red team"), yet function no better than other groups of its type. Like Larson and LaFasto,[21] we are interested in groups that function well, regardless of what they are called, and our intent in this text is to provide you and your fellow group members with the tools you need to achieve top-notch performance.

> The people we bring in to the plant, we have more and more of a need for folks to have small group skills, leadership skills.
>
> *M. I., Human Resource Manager, Manufacturing Company*

One key feature of a group is an **interdependent goal,** meaning that all members succeed or fail together in the accomplishment of the group's purpose. For example, one player on a softball team cannot win while the others on the same team lose. The players' fates are linked—they all succeed or fail as a group. Without an interdependent goal, a collection of people is not a group. The animals in our opening fable have frightening the robbers away as one of their goals, and it took all their combined talents to accomplish that.

Discussion, another term essential to the concept of a group, is the primarily verbal exchange among members through which the work of the group is accomplished. This exchange may be face-to-face or may use communication technology such as a computer or audioconferencing equipment. In this book, **small group discussion** refers to a small group of persons talking with each other (often face-to-face) in order to achieve some interdependent goal, such as increased understanding, coordination of activity, or a solution to a

Small Group

A group of at least three but few enough members for each to perceive all others as individuals, who meet face-to-face, share some identity or common purpose, and share standards for governing their activities as members.

Interdependent Goal

An objective shared by members of a small group in such a way that one member cannot achieve the goal without the other members also achieving it.

Discussion (Small Group Discussion)

A small group of people communicating with each other to achieve some interdependent goal, such as increased understanding, coordination of activity, or solution to a shared problem.

shared problem. We will now "unpack" this definition, which suggests several characteristics of small group discussion:

1. A small enough number of people for each to be aware of and have some reaction to each other (typically 3 to 7, rarely more than 15).

2. A mutually interdependent purpose, making the success of one member contingent on the success of all.

3. Each person having a sense of belonging, of being part of the group.

4. Interaction involving verbal and nonverbal channels, with words conveying the content of the discussion. This definition includes as "verbal" manual languages, such as American Sign Language and typed computer-mediated messages. The *emoticons* used in e-mail messages, such as :) to indicate smiling, count as nonverbal indicators. Members continuously respond to and adapt their actions to each other. The give and take of impromptu communication, rather than prepared speeches, is the essence.

5. A sense of cooperation among members. Although there may be disagreement and conflict, all members perceive themselves as searching for a group outcome that will be as satisfactory as possible to all, so that no one is frustrated at losing to another group member.

Small Group Communication

The scholarly study of communication among members of a small group, among two or more groups, and between groups and larger organizations; the body of communication theory produced by such study.

The term **small group communication** refers to the study of interaction among small group members as well as to the large body of communication theory yielded by such study. Throughout this book, we will examine in detail this body of theory and principles. Communicative behavior of group members is the focus of this book, and its study is a relatively new field. Early researchers, such as Muzafer Sherif, W. F. Whyte, and Robert Bales, were often social psychologists who were particularly interested in how groups influenced individual behavior and how norms developed in groups. Later communication researchers, extending their interest in public speaking, began to examine the communication within groups and to link members' communicative behaviors to group outcomes such as the effectiveness of decisions and the degree of cohesiveness. Now, as the field of communication has matured, researchers have increasingly attended to the process of communication within the group, including how ideas are developed, how the communication creates and maintains group structure, how leadership is enacted by what people say and do, and how groups can best be studied. These trends are expected to continue and are being encouraged as appropriate directions for small group communication scholars.[22]

Types of Small Groups

There are two major categories of small groups, *primary* and *secondary.* Each meets different human needs, but most of the groups to which you will belong contain elements of each category.

Primary groups exist chiefly to satisfy what are termed *primary* needs—needs for inclusion (affiliation, belonging) and affection (love, esteem). They are usually long term. Examples include a nuclear family, roommates, several friends who meet daily around a table in the student center, co-workers who regularly share coffee breaks, and Molly's virtual group of friends, mentioned in Consider This 1.1, who interact via e-mail and instant messaging. Although such groups may tackle particular tasks, they exist mainly to provide personal attention and support for the members. The tasks they perform are less important than their primary purpose of providing affection. Members' talk, which seems disorganized and informal, is the end in itself. More than any other forces in our lives, primary groups socialize and mold us into the people we become; their importance is tremendous. For most of us, the family is our "first" group, where we learn communication patterns, functional and dysfunctional, that can last generations and affect all aspects of our lives.[23] Primary groups are not the main focus of this book; typically, primary groups are studied in interpersonal communication, sociology, and psychology courses. However, the interpersonal relationships at the heart of primary groups are very important to understanding small groups in general.

Secondary groups focus on task accomplishment and are formed for the purpose of doing work—completing a project, solving a problem, making a decision. Secondary groups, such as most work teams and problem-solving groups, meet primarily what are called secondary needs—needs for control and achievement. Such groups enable members to exert power over their environment and others. For example, the teams that worked to create Founders Park in downtown Springfield were secondary groups with a specific performance objective to be attained, and members had to coordinate their efforts in order to achieve that objective. All groups initiated to accomplish some task

Primary Group

A group whose main purpose is to meet members' needs for inclusion and affection.

Secondary Group

A group whose major purpose is to complete a task, such as making a decision, solving a problem, writing a report, or providing recommendations to a parent organization.

" Screws fall out all the time; the world's an imperfect place."
— The Breakfast Club (Judd Nelson)

are more secondary than primary, although many task groups also help members achieve primary needs for socialization and affection.

Consider This 1.2

Were the Bremen Town Musicians, described in the opening story, more primary or secondary? Why do you think so? What factors seem more primary? What factors seem more secondary? To what extent did the group change over time? What primary and secondary groups do you belong to?

As you may have discerned by this point, there are no pure primary or secondary groups. Although groups are classified as primary or secondary according to their major focus, primary groups engage in work, and secondary groups provide affection and belonging to their members. Thus, most groups blend primary and secondary characteristics and meet many human needs in addition to the ones for which they were initially formed. In fact, Anderson and Martin demonstrated that secondary group members are motivated by a number of factors that are more primary than secondary, including desires for pleasure and to escape. Such factors strongly influence secondary group members' communication behaviors, feelings of loneliness, and satisfaction with the group and are worth examining.[24] Figure 1.1 illustrates this blend of interpersonal (primary) and task (secondary) characteristics for a variety of groups.

In addition to the two major classifications just described, there are many other ways to categorize groups. The four categories described below exhibit both primary and secondary characteristics in varying degrees, with the fourth more purely secondary than the first three.

Activity Groups

Activity groups enable members to participate in an activity, both for the sake of doing the activity and for the affiliation provided by doing the activity with others. The following are examples: a book club whose members meet regularly to discuss a preselected book, bridge and poker clubs, road rally clubs, hunting and bird-watching groups, and numerous other interest groups. Members of such groups solve problems and make choices—when and where to meet, how to pay for their activities, how group membership is determined—but enjoyment of the activity and fellowship with others whose interests are similar are the main purposes.

Personal Growth Groups

Therapy and support groups are called collectively **personal growth groups.** They are composed of people who come together to develop personal insights, help themselves and others with personal problems, and grow as individuals from the feedback and support of others. Goal interdependence is low

---

Activity Group

A group formed primarily for members to participate in an activity such as bridge, bowling, hunting, and so forth.

Personal Growth Group

A group of people who come together to develop personal insights, overcome personality problems, and grow personally through feedback and support of others.

FIGURE 1.1   Types of groups and the needs they satisfy.

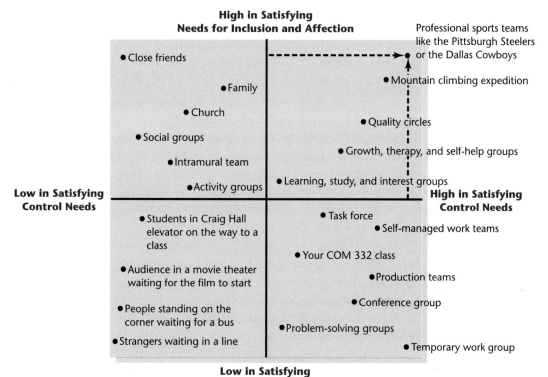

because no purely group goal is sought; rather, members meet their individual needs for personal learning, awareness, and support in the context of the group. Examples include local chapters of 12-step programs such as Alcoholics Anonymous and Al-Anon, mutual support groups like gay or women's rights groups, outpatient groups for clients with personal adjustment problems, support groups for parents whose babies died of SIDS, cancer survivors' support groups, and therapy groups for spouse abusers.

Learning Groups

Learning groups, or study groups, are formed so members can understand a subject more thoroughly by pooling their knowledge, perceptions, and beliefs. For example, local public libraries often organize issue-oriented learning discussions so citizens can become better informed regarding important or controversial issues. In addition to learning about specific subject matter, members of such groups also learn skills of effective speaking, listening, critical thinking, and effective interpersonal communication.

Learning Group (Study Group)

A group discussing for the purpose of learning about and understanding a subject more completely.

Problem-Solving Groups

Problem-solving groups formed to address some condition or problem vary widely in their composition and functioning. Examples we have already mentioned include the Ford Taurus and General Motors Saturn development teams and the various Founders Park committees. Whatever their main function, problem-solving groups are so classified because they are created expressly to solve problems. There are many ways of describing subtypes of problem-solving groups. In this book, we deal with three major subtypes prevalent in modern organizational and social life: committees, quality control circles, and self-managed work groups. We introduce these briefly here and elaborate on them in subsequent chapters.

Committees   **Committees** are groups that have been assigned a task by a parent organization or person with authority in an organization. Committees may be formed to investigate and report findings, recommend a course of action for the parent group, formulate policies, or plan and carry out some action. All these tasks require discussion among members. Boards, councils, and staffs are special kinds of committees. For example, a *board of directors* is often called an *executive committee* and represents a larger organization. It may have extensive power to make and execute policy.

Committees can be classified as either *ad hoc* or *standing*. The **ad hoc** or **special committee**, established to perform a specific task, normally ceases to exist when that task has been completed. Ad hoc committees address all kinds of problems, such as evaluating credentials of job applicants, drafting bylaws, hearing grievances, planning social events, conducting investigations, devising plans to solve work-related problems, advising legislators on what to do about

Problem-Solving Group

A group whose purpose is finding ways to solve a problem or address a particular condition.

Committee

A small group of people given an assigned task or responsibility by a larger group (parent organization) or person with authority.

Ad Hoc or Special Committee

A group that goes out of existence after its specific task has been completed.

A committee discusses the content of a report.

© Mark Richards/PhotoEdit

statewide problems, and evaluating programs and institutions. A *task force* is a type of ad hoc committee with members appointed from various departments of an organization or political body and usually charged with investigating a broad issue, such as how to ensure that rural areas receive needed health care. Once the task force or special committee has reported its action or recommendations, it disbands.

Standing committees are ongoing committees established through the constitution or bylaws of an organization to deal with recurring types of problems or to perform specific organizational functions. The most important standing committee of most organizations is called the executive committee, board, or steering committee. Usually this group is charged with overall management of the organization and can function for the entire organization when general membership meetings are not feasible. Other standing committees encountered commonly go under names such as membership committee, personnel committee, parking and traffic committee, program committee, bylaws committee, and so forth. These groups continue indefinitely, even though the membership changes. Usually, some members of a standing committee are replaced annually so that the group includes both experienced members and those with a fresh perspective. Standing committees often meet regularly, such as the first Tuesday of every month, to resolve a number of problems at a single meeting.

Conference committees are composed of members who represent the interests of two or more other groups. The members serve as representatives of their constituent groups; their primary allegiance is often to the groups they represent rather than the conference committee. For example, a community's arts council may consist of representatives from the community theater, art museum, ballet, symphony, and jazz ensemble, who meet to coordinate their scheduling, marketing, and publicity efforts so that individual events do not compete with each other. Delegates of the U.S. Senate and House of Representatives routinely meet in conference committees to resolve differences in legislation passed by each body. As we write this, a Senate-House conference committee has just recommended a $28.9 billion antiterrorism bill that reconciles differences between the original Senate and House versions. Often, conference committees do not have the authority to resolve matters themselves, but must submit their recommendations to their respective constituent groups for approval.

Quality control circles　A **quality control circle** consists of workers (usually five to seven) in a company who either volunteer or are selected to meet regularly on company time to discuss work-related problems. Sometimes called *continuous improvement teams, cycle time reduction groups,* or just plain *quality circles,* their purpose is to improve some aspect of work life—efficiency, quality of finished products, worker safety, and so forth. Quality circles represent attempts to capitalize on the fact that groups usually make better and more readily accepted decisions about complex problems than

Standing Committee

A group given an area of responsibility that includes many tasks and continues indefinitely.

Conference Committee

A group composed of representatives from two or more groups; members' responsibilities are to represent the interests of their constituents.

Quality Control Circle

A group of employees who meet on company time to investigate work-related problems and to make recommendations for solving these problems (also called a quality circle).

individuals do, and that individuals actually performing the work are in the best position to recommend ways to improve it. We discuss quality circles and the next group, self-managed work groups, in more detail in Chapter 14.

Self-Managed Work Groups **Self-managed work groups,** also called *autonomous work groups* or *peer-led work teams,* are groups of workers given a defined area of freedom to manage their productive work within certain preset limits established by the organization. For example, an automobile assembly team may be responsible for assembling a car from start to finish. It may be given a deadline by which the car must be fully assembled, but within that limit the team members are free to elect their own leaders, plan their work procedures, and schedule individual assignments for the members. Members of self-managed work groups are often cross-trained, so each member can perform several jobs competently. This permits human and other resources to be allocated efficiently and effectively, gives workers the chance to develop a variety of skills, and reduces boredom. In the future, with more employees involved in self-managed work groups and quality control circles, sensitivity to group phenomena and skills in discussion leadership become increasingly important.

In the same way that no group is purely primary or secondary, most small groups you encounter will combine elements of all four group types just described—activity, personal growth, learning, and problem solving. Several years ago, the Springfield City Council established an ad hoc task force to investigate and recommend solutions to the city's solid waste disposal problem. Members had to educate themselves about solid waste, various disposal options, and pros and cons of the options before they could make their recommendations to the city council. They also had to manage their own resources of time and information and be concerned with the comprehensive quality of life in the Springfield area. Thus, this group comprised elements of a learning group, problem-solving group, quality circle, and self-managed work group.

Consider This 1.3

From the types of groups just described, what kind of group would you call the Founders Park group mentioned earlier? Which of the descriptions provided seem to fit that group best?

Ethical Behavior of Group Members

For a group to perform effectively, its leader and members must behave ethically. **Ethics** refer to the "rules or standards for right conduct or practice."[25] Appropriate standards of behavior from the general culture apply also to behavior within groups; however, the unique nature of small groups requires attention, in our Western culture, to special ethical concerns regarding the treatment of speech, of people, and of information. We offer the following five ethical principles to guide group member behavior.

> People, I think, search for ethical guidelines and they love them when they find them, and they love them even more when everyone lives by them.
>
> *J. M., Executive Coach and President, Marketing Agency*

1. **Members should be willing to speak and should not do anything to prevent others from speaking freely.** Groups work because several heads perform better than one, but that advantage will not be realized if group members are unwilling or afraid to speak freely in the group. All members should be willing to share their unique perspectives and help ensure that others feel free to share as well. The field of communication has evolved from what was originally the study of speech. Our field has a long and distinguished tradition, dating from Aristotle, that supports the value of free speech.[26] Each member of a group must feel free to share his or her knowledge, beliefs, and opinions within the group, according to the appropriate discussion rules established in the group.

2. **Group members should embrace diversity within the group.** Member diversity should not only be tolerated but encouraged and supported. Diversity stems from various factors that include, but are not limited to, race, ethnicity, age, religion, sexual orientation.[27] These factors contribute to differences in members' perspectives—the very differences that have the potential to enrich and enhance a group's performance. Groupings such as race, ethnicity, gender, and so forth, form what Orbe calls **co-cultures,** smaller groups that exist "simultaneously within, as well as apart from, other cultures"[28] in the United States. However, group members from such co-cultures run the risk of being marginalized, their perspectives and opinions ignored by members of the dominant culture. Orbe argues that co-culture members employ a number of strategies to have their perspectives heard. In short, they have to work harder to be included and have their opinions considered than do members of the dominant culture. The challenge to group members, particularly ones representing the dominant culture, is to make it possible for *all* members—regardless of co-culture—to contribute equally. Members who marginalize fellow group members both behave unethically and defeat the purpose of the group.

3. **Group members must conduct themselves with honesty and integrity.** Honesty and integrity take various forms. First, and most obviously, group members should not intentionally deceive one another or manufacture information or evidence to persuade other members to their points of view.

Group Ethics

Co-culture

A smaller group that co-exists simultaneously within and separate from other cultures.

Integrity implies that members should support group decisions, which may present challenges for the individual member. Sometimes you may be asked to do something for a group that violates your own personal values, beliefs, morals, or principles. For example, what if a group on which you serve decides to suppress information that is contrary to a decision the group wishes to make, and pressures you to go along? What will you do? Only you can answer that question. You may try your best to persuade the group to see things your way; you may decide to leave the group. But if you choose to stay with the group, make sure you can support, or at least live with, the group's actions and decisions.

Integrity also suggests that you are willing to place the good of the group ahead of your own individual goals. We believe that if groups are to function effectively, members should make public their private agendas so they are not operating from motives unknown to the other members. We have known individuals who are not able to become part of a team because they are unable or unwilling to merge their personal agendas with that of the group. These individuals make poor team members, and the group is better off without them.

4. **Group members should not disconfirm, belittle, or ridicule other members and should make sure they understand members before agreeing or disagreeing with them.** Deetz stresses that ethical interpersonal behavior should strengthen one's personal identity and should have mutual understanding as its goal.[29] Our first goal, as we interact, should be to strive to understand others to their satisfaction. If this happens, we will confirm and support each others' self-concept and identity, even when we disagree strongly.

5. **Group members should be thorough in gathering information and diligent in evaluating it.** Members should make a conscientious effort to find and present to the group all information and points of view relevant to the group's work. They should also set aside personal biases and prejudices when evaluating that information, and refrain from doing anything that short-circuits this process. Many consequential decisions are made in groups, from how best to get children to read to whether or not it is safe to launch a space shuttle in cold weather. These decisions will be only as good as the information on which they are based and the reasoning that members use to assess the information. It is absolutely crucial that group members consider all relevant information in an open-minded, unbiased way by employing the best critical thinking skills they can; to do otherwise can lead to tragedies such as the fatal decision to launch the space shuttle *Challenger*. It follows from this that members must credit or document the sources of information they share with the group, and must not falsify data or information. We will return to the subject of ethical behavior at various points throughout the book.

The Participant-Observer Perspective

A major purpose of this book is to help you develop a participant-observer perspective. A **participant-observer** is a regular member of the group who engages actively in its discussions, but at the same time observes, evaluates, and adapts to the group's processes and needs. Participant-observers direct part of their attention to participating in the group and part to assessing how the group is functioning; they try always to be aware of what the group needs at the moment. For example, if the group seems confused, a participant-observer will try to clarify; if group members seem tired of the task, a participant-observer may suggest a break. Because such members simultaneously pay dual attention to the group's processes and the content of the discussion, they can supply essential information, ideas, procedural suggestions, and interpersonal communication skills when needed.

Don't underestimate the value of knowing how to be a skillful participant-observer or its counterpart, the nonmember *consultant,* which we discuss in Chapter 15. Several former students of ours have landed wonderful jobs because they were able to demonstrate that they were effective team members and also that they were proficient in diagnosing and helping solve group problems. We hope this text gives you the tools you need to do both.

Some members supply valuable information but have little understanding of group processes. As long as the group is operating well, these members contribute needed facts and ideas, but they are of no help in resolving conflicts, reducing misunderstandings, offering procedural suggestions, or helping solve other process problems.

Other people are members in name only; they are **social loafers** who watch and listen but contribute little, satisfied to let the rest of the members carry the workload. We all have experienced groups with social loafers—the committee member who makes no suggestions, the classmate in a discussion group who has not read the assignment to be discussed. This behavior may result from a lack of understanding of group processes or lack of confidence; it is inappropriate and unhelpful in any case.

In contrast to both these types of members, participant-observers who are competent communicators and have extensive knowledge about groups contribute to the quality of both the process and the product of the group. In a recent survey of real-life groups, Broome and Fulbright found, among other things, that members wanted stronger guidance about group methods, procedures, and techniques as well as fellow members skilled in the communication process.[30] To be an all-around valuable member of the group, you need both a participant-observer focus and information and expertise essential to completing the group's task. This is what *Effective Group Discussion* is designed to teach you.

Participant-Observer

An active participant in a small group who at the same time observes and evaluates its processes and procedures.

Social Loafer

A person who makes a minimal contribution to the group and assumes the other members will take up the slack.

SUMMARY

1. Small groups provide a source for our identity, a means for solving complex problems, and a vehicle to satisfy many basic needs. The use of groups in the workplace and throughout society will continue to increase, so learning to operate effectively in small groups is an essential skill worth learning.

2. Small group discussion refers to three or more people, each perceptually aware of the others, interacting in order to achieve an interdependent goal.

3. Primary groups such as families and groups of close friends focus on interpersonal relationships. Secondary groups focus on task accomplishment. Subtypes, which may have both primary and secondary characteristics, include activity, personal growth, learning (study), and problem-solving groups such as committees, quality control circles, and self-managed work groups.

4. Ethical members of groups treat speech, people, and information conscientiously, honestly, respectfully, carefully, and open-mindedly.

5. Participant-observers who can attend to both the content and the process of group discussion are valuable and valued group members.

KEY TERMS

 Test your knowledge of these key terms by visiting the Online Learning Center website at mhhe.com/galanes11

Activity group
Co-culture
Committee
  Ad hoc or special committee:
  Standing committee
  Conference committee
Discussion (small group
  discussion)
Ethics

Group
Grouphate
Interaction
Interdependent goal
Learning group (study group)
Participant-observer
Personal growth group
Primary group
Problem-solving group

Quality control circle
Secondary group
Self-managed work group
Small group
Small group communication
Small group discussion (see
  discussion)
Social loafers

EXERCISES

 Go to self-quizzes on the Online Learning Center at mhhe.com/galanes11 to test your knowledge of the chapter concepts

1. This icebreaker exercise is designed to help you get acquainted with classmates and reduce the tension and formality that exist among strangers. Each of you should take out a blank sheet of paper. Count the number of people in the room and make a grid on your paper with as many squares as there are people in the room. Your instructor will also make a master grid on the board. Your instructor will then hand out one index card to each of you. On this card, without using your name, write down a personal characteristic about yourself that most people in the class would not know. This could be a hobby, an event in your life, a favorite food, and so forth. Pass your card in to your instructor. Your instructor will read each card; as he or she does so, write that characteristic in your grid as the instructor writes it on the master grid on the board.

All of you should stand up, push your desks against the perimeter of the room, and mingle with each other in the middle. Through conversation, try to find out who is linked to each characteristic without directly asking the person a question such as, "Are you the person who owns a rare coin from the Civil War?" When you find someone you think is a match, write that person's name in the appropriate square on your grid. The object is to be the first person to complete one row, column, or diagonal for a "Bingo." The first person to get "Bingo" yells it out loud and activity stops to check the matches. The student who claimed "Bingo" should read off his or her matches; if one is wrong, all someone has to say is "incorrect" and the game continues. If the matches are correct, a winner is declared and you should all go back to your seats to discuss the activity.

2. For the next week, keep a list of all the small groups in which you actively participate. Classify these groups according to the types presented in this chapter. Next, rate your personal satisfaction with each group, from 1 (very dissatisfied) to 7 (very satisfied). Compare your lists in class. What do you conclude? Do your classmates like and dislike the same things in a group that you do? Using these lists, can you develop a list of general principles for having an effective group?

3. If you participate in a virtual group, list all the similarities and differences between that group and any face-to-face group in which you have participated. Share your observations with classmates who have participated in virtual groups. What do you conclude?

BIBLIOGRAPHY

Cathcart, Robert S., and Larry A. Samovar, eds. *Small Group Communication: A Reader.* 6th ed. Dubuque, IA: Wm. C. Brown Publishers, 1992, Sections 1 and 2.

Larson, Carl E., and Frank M. J. LaFasto. *TeamWork: What Must Go Right/What Can Go Wrong.* Newbury Park, CA: Sage, 1989.

NOTES

1. There are several versions of this tale. This one comes from www.bremen.de/info/skp/stadt musikanten/townmusicians.htm. A children's animated version can be found at www.bremen townmusicians.com.
2. Kurt W. Back, "The Small Group: Tightrope between Sociology and Personality," *Journal of Applied Behavioral Science* 15 (1979): 283–94.
3. Lawrence W. Frey, "Applied Communication Research on Group Facilitation in Natural Settings," in *Innovations in Group Facilitation: Applications in Natural Settings,* ed. Lawrence R. Frey (Cresskill, NJ: Hampton Press, 1995): 1–26.
4. Diane Cole, "Meetings That Make Sense," *Psychology Today* (May 1989): 14.
5. Bill Lawren, "Competitive Edge," *Psychology Today* (September 1989): 16.
6. Charles C. DuBois, "Portrait of the Ideal MBA," *The Penn Stater* (September/October 1992): 31.
7. William C. Schutz, *FIRO: A Three-Dimensional Theory of Interpersonal Behavior* (New York: Rinehart, 1958).
8. Gerald Goldhaber, "Communication and Student Unrest" (Unpublished report to the president of the University of New Mexico, undated).
9. "Road Test," *Consumer Reports* (April 1992): 266; (July 1992): 427.
10. William Ouchi, *Theory Z: How American Business Can Meet the Japanese Challenge* (Reading, MA: Addison-Wesley, 1981).
11. Robert H. Waterman, Jr., *The Renewal Factor: How the Best Get and Keep the Competitive Edge* (New York: Bantam Books, 1987).

12. Susan Sorensen, "Grouphate" (Paper presented at the International Communication Association, Minneapolis, May, 1981).

13. Quoted in Lisa Stroud, "No CEO Is an Island," *American Way* (November 15, 1988): 97.

14. T. J. Larkin, "Humanistic Principles for Organization Management," *Central States Speech Journal* 37 (1986): 37.

15. Douglas M. Lawson, *Give to Live: How Giving Can Change Your Life* (LaJolla, CA: ALTI Publishing, 1991).

16. Nolan Ryan, personal interview on the *Today Show* (May 25, 1993).

17. Marvin E. Shaw, *Group Dynamics: The Psychology of Small Group Behavior,* 3rd ed. (New York: McGraw-Hill, 1980): 8.

18. Robert F. Bales, *Interaction Process Analysis* (Cambridge, MA: Addison-Wesley, 1950): viii, 35–39.

19. Gay Lumsden and Donald Lumsden, *Communicating in Groups and Teams: Sharing Leadership* (Belmont, CA: Wadsworth, 1993): 13–15.

20. Thomas E. Harris and John C. Sherblom, *Small Group and Team Communication* (Boston: Allyn and Bacon, 1999): 123–31.

21. Carl E. Larson and Frank M. J. LaFasto, *Team-Work: What Must Go Right/What Can Go Wrong* (Newbury Park, CA: Sage, 1989): 19.

22. Richard E. Sykes, "Imagining What We Might Study if We Really Studied Small Groups from a Speech Perspective," *Communication Studies* 41 (Fall 1990): 200–211.

23. Thomas J. Socha, "Communication in Family Units: Studying the `First' Group," in *The Handbook of Group Communication Theory and Research,* ed. Lawrence R. Frey (Thousand Oaks, CA: Sage, 1999): 475–92.

24. Carolyn M. Anderson and Matthew M. Martin, "The Effects of Communication Motives, Interaction Involvement, and Loneliness on Satisfaction: A Model of Small Groups," *Small Group Research* 26 (February 1995): 118–37.

25. *The Random House Dictionary of the English Language,* 2nd ed. unabridged (New York: Random House, 1987): 665.

26. Ronald C. Arnett, "The Practical Philosophy of Communication Ethics and Free Speech as the Foundation for Speech Communication," *Communication Quarterly* 38 (Summer 1990): 208–17.

27. Brenda J. Allen, " 'Diversity' and Organizational Communication," *Journal of Applied Communication Research* 23 (1995): 143–55.

28. Mark P. Orbe, "From the Standpoint(s) of Traditionally Muted Groups: Explicating a Co-cultural Communication Theoretical Model," *Communication Theory* 8 (February 1998): 2.

29. Stanley Deetz, "Reclaiming the Subject Matter as a Guide to Mutual Understanding: Effectiveness and Ethics in Interpersonal Interaction," *Communication Quarterly* 38 (Summer 1990): 226–43.

30. Benjamin J. Broome and Luann Fulbright, "A Multistage Influence Model of Barriers to Group Problem Solving: A Participant-Generated Agenda for Small Group Research," *Small Group Research* 26 (February 1995): 25–55.

THE SMALL GROUP AS A SYSTEM

Central Message

All components of a small group operate interdependently with one another, and the group itself is interdependent with its environment. To understand a group fully, we must examine the components in relationship to one another, not in isolation.

STUDY OBJECTIVES

As a result of studying Chapter 2 you should be able to:

1. List and explain the major input, throughput, and output variables in a small group system and provide examples of their interdependence.
2. Define the main terms and types of variables pertaining to systems.
3. Describe the characteristics of an effective discussion group.

During one traumatic week, the church board—one minister and three lay people—of a new Unity church faced nearly insurmountable challenges. On Monday the board chair suffered a stroke; on Wednesday the minister died. The remaining members, in shock, recruited three other members to help carry on the work. The board had been working to establish a second Unity church in Springfield, Missouri, following an unpleasant church split two years earlier. The new church had just gotten off the ground when these tragedies occurred, but members, committed to the project, decided to keep the church going. The board elected Bill, a lawyer, as chair. Sally, a widowed secretary whose husband had been a minister, agreed to serve as secretary. The other members included Marina, a college professor; Sunni, director of a university speech and hearing clinic; and Norm, a massage therapist who was also an accomplished musician. No paid employees worked for the church—all the work was accomplished by volunteers, including board members.

Among the challenges board members faced were how to handle Sunday services without a minister, how to pay for the lease they had recently signed on an older building, and how to overcome opposition to the new congregation, both from the denomination's headquarters and the original church's minister. The board quickly decided they needed additional expertise so they soon added two more members: Don, a retired business owner, and Gary, a maintenance worker. The members had diverse experiences and expertise, but they all shared a similar vision for the church and common values to guide them in their work. The board met every week for two years. At the end of that time, members could point to several important accomplishments: Sunday services were held every week and attendance had increased from about 40 members to about 90 members per Sunday; bylaws had been approved by the congregation; the board, originally an informal, self-selected board, was voted in by the congregation; enough money had been set aside to cover a minister's salary for six months; and, most important of all, the formerly renegade congregation had received official approval from the denomination's headquarters and were now "legal."

If you can work in a church, you can work anywhere.

N. T., Senior Communication Associate, State Social Service Agency

We have already discussed how pervasive small groups are in our daily lives and why we should study them. In this chapter we will use the church board we just introduced to illustrate the basic principles of general systems theory, a framework for understanding small groups. We periodically present dialogue from the church board to illustrate how various principles of systems theory may appear communicatively. Once you have a communication-based model for understanding systems principles, you can recognize the principles operating in any group.

The Small Group as an Open System

You have probably noticed that when a new person joins a group, the group changes in some ways. For example, when a new baby is brought into a family, all family relationships will change, including between the parents, between the other children, and between the parents and the children. In addition, new relationships must be accommodated—between everyone else and the new baby. This illustrates the idea of a **system**—a set of relationships among interdependent, interacting components and forces. General systems theory is built upon an analysis of living entities—including groups and organizations—as they attempt to remain in dynamic balance with the environment by making constant adjustments.

Systems theory provides a useful framework to help you keep track of all the individual elements and components of a small group as they interact in a complex whole. In fact Edward Mabry, a communication theorist, has remarked that *systemness* is one of the most used and perhaps most taken-for-granted concepts as it applies to small group communication.[1] Thinking about and researching groups as social systems represented a significant advance in small group communication theory. The assumption that *communication* is what connects the relevant parts of a system together is fundamental to conceptualizing a small group as a system. This moves the role that communication plays in emergent social systems to the forefront of small group theory.

Systems theory's contribution to small group communication research and to our understanding of the process of small group interaction is obvious. However, the theory is not without its detractors. Any theory is a human construction and therefore limited in scope—it gives *a* particular view of a phenomenon not *the* view. Some, for instance, have questioned whether system theory research is merely a philosophical framework, but not a useful explanatory framework.[2] Still others take issue with the system theory assumption of homeostasis, or dynamic balance—the idea that systems are self-maintaining and work toward keeping on track. This emphasis on balance, some argue, draws attention to system stability rather than change. We have chosen systems theory as our theoretical framework because of its centrality in small group research and its focus on patterns and wholes. While our point is not to elaborate on or refute the specific concerns about system theory, we do want you to know that it is but one theory used by theorists to understand small group communication. Let's now take a closer look at some of the underlying principles of this theory.

> The board is like the body. All the parts have to be together and they have to work together and they have to fit, or something's not right. It throws the wheel out of whack.
>
> *D. W., Executive Director, Voluntary Organization*

System

An entity made up of components in interdependent relationship to each other, requiring constant adaptation among its parts to maintain organic wholeness and balance.

Several principles of systems theory are especially relevant to your study of small groups. One of the most important is the principle of **interdependence**, which states that the parts of a system do not operate in isolation but continuously affect each other, as well as the system as a whole. The new baby affects every other family member. Similarly, if the usually cheerful chair of a committee comes to a group meeting in a grouchy mood, the other members will feel uneasy and the group's normally effective decision-making processes may be impaired. In the church board we described, every decision was accomplished through open discussion that emphasized member interdependence. No individual's views (including those of board chair Bill) were treated as more important than another's. Consider the following excerpt from the first board meeting members held after the minister died, at which members were trying to figure out what needed to be done for Sunday services:

Interdependence

The property of a system such that all parts are interrelated and affect each other as well as the whole system.

Bill: Why don't we make a list of all the things that have to be done on Sunday mornings, and see who wants to do what? Does that sound all right to you?

Group: Yes, that's a good idea. That will help. Sounds fine.

Marina: We have to make sure things are cleaned up for Sunday. Gary, if you come in Saturday morning to clean, I'll help you, then I can get Chandra to decorate the sanctuary on Saturday afternoon.

In this fashion, members listed jobs to be done for the next half hour while Sally made a list on a flip chart. Often, the member who presented a task simultaneously volunteered to do it. Members jumped in to claim the "unclaimed" tasks or to recruit someone from the congregation to do them. Even though each member ended up with several unglamorous tasks, she or he recognized that the success of the entire enterprise—having a good Sunday service—depended on everyone doing the jobs effectively. They acknowledged their interdependence with each other, as well as their interdependence with the congregation.

A column by George Will in *Newsweek* dramatically illustrates the principle of interdependence and also reminds us that, because we are all interdependent, actions we take sometimes have unanticipated consequences.[3] When the Lincoln Memorial was illuminated at night, the lights attracted insects, which attracted the spiders that fed on them, which then attracted the birds that fed on the spiders. To keep the monument beautiful for visitors, workers scrubbed the bird droppings and the spider webs that had accumulated, but the act of scrubbing the marble made it susceptible to the exhaust fumes from the traffic in Washington, D.C. Lighting the monument, intended to have a positive effect, also set in motion a chain of events that is contributing to the monument's deterioration. We cannot know in advance all the effects our actions will cause.

Another key principle is the system property of **nonsummativity** (nonadditivity), which states that the whole system is not the sum of its parts. It may

Nonsummativity

The property of a system that the whole is not the sum of its parts, but may be greater or lesser than the sum.

be either greater or less than the sum of its parts, with either positive synergy or negative synergy operating. Imagine a collection of individuals when they first begin to interact and coordinate their efforts to form a competitive basketball team. The team involves much more than the simple addition of the abilities of each player. The group will take on a life of its own and become an identifiable entity. Sports fans know they will lose money on a basketball or football game if they add up the statistics for each player, arrive at team totals, and bet on the team with the higher total. On any given day, a so-called poor team can play beyond its apparent potential (positive synergy), or a terrific team can have an off day (negative synergy). Why? Because each team or group is a living system in which everything is interdependent, and no one can predict precisely how the new system will function during any particular time or how the parts will affect one another.

In other arenas of endeavor, groups frequently design technologies beyond the collective capacities of the individual members. For example, most recent Nobel prizes in science have been given for breakthroughs that required teams of scientists. On the other hand, groups of intelligent, knowledgeable, and committed members sometimes make bad decisions, such as the groups of scientists and managers who decided to launch the space shuttle *Challenger* on its ill-fated trip.

> It's so important for a group leader to do whatever it takes to maximize the effort of the group as a whole. And that's really what you're trying to do.
>
> *S. P., Vice President, Human Resources, Manufacturing Company*

No one can predict whether a group will experience positive or negative synergy. In our classes, we have often had groups composed of bright students whose final products disappointed us. However, Salazar has posited that the amount of ambiguity a group faces plays a major role in process losses and gains.[4] Ambiguity determines the types of obstacles a group will encounter. Whether the obstacles are dealt with in a helpful or disruptive way determines whether a process loss (negative synergy) or gain (positive synergy) will occur. In any case, the communication behavior of the members is the principal determining factor for process gains or losses.

Consider This 2.1

The church board introduced at the beginning of the chapter clearly demonstrates positive synergy—seven ordinary people who, together, accomplished an extraordinary result. What do you think are the factors that helped produce this positive synergy? What effect do you think members' commitment to the task had on the group? How might one member's commitment affect another member's? What does this say about member interdependence?

The systems perspective helps keep us from oversimplifying our understanding of how a group functions and perhaps missing something important. For example, systems theory emphasizes **multiple causation**, the fact that whatever happens in a system is not the result of a single, simple cause, but is produced by complex interrelationships among multiple forces. For example, several factors contributed to the church board's successful efforts, including the board's shared leadership, Bill's democratic coordination, the commitment and expertise of the members, the fact that creation of a new congregation filled a need in the community, and probably some fortuitous factors, such as the availability of an affordable location.

Multiple Causation

The principle that each change in a system is caused by numerous factors.

Variables of a System

The **variables** of a system are its characteristics or dimensions. They may be classified as either *individual-level* or *system-level* features of a group.[5] **Individual-level variables** are properties of the individual members, such as their traits, skills, abilities, expertise, values, attitudes, gender and ethnicity. **System-level variables** are characteristics of the group as a whole, including preexisting societal and cultural norms, the degree of cohesiveness, and procedures the group uses. The individual-level and system-level variables are interdependent within themselves and with each other. For example, a new member may be well informed about a topic the group is discussing (an individual-level variable), but if the group has established a norm that new members should be seen and not heard until they have "paid their dues" (a system-level variable), the group will not benefit from that member's information. In the church board, Sally, whose husband had been a minister, had expertise in the creation of church bylaws—an individual-level variable. But her expertise would not have been made available to the group in open discussion if the board had not developed a democratic structure in which everyone, not just lawyer Bill, got a chance to contribute their expertise—a system-level variable. Thus, individual characteristics and group (system) characteristics mutually influence each other, as well as the group's outputs.

System variables have been classified into three broad categories: *input*, *throughput*, and *output*. In a small group, **input variables** are components from which a small group is formed and that it uses to do its work, including the members; the reasons for the group's formation; resources such as information, expertise, money, and computer technology; and environmental conditions and forces that influence the group. In the church committee, members with their diverse areas of expertise were inputs. For instance, both Sunni and Sally had examples of bylaws from other churches, and Bill knew what to do to incorporate and receive tax-exempt status. All this information, possessed by individuals and shared with the group, served as resource input variables that ultimately affected both the group's deliberations and its success. Consider this exchange, after the minister died:

Variables

Observable characteristics or qualities that can vary.

Individual-Level Variables

Characteristics of the individual members of a group that affect the group's interaction, such as traits, attitudes, values, beliefs, and skills.

System-Level Variables

Features or characteristics of the group as a whole, such as cohesiveness, interaction patterns, norms, roles, and so forth, that affect the group's interaction.

Sunni: I'm in shock from the past week, but I don't want to give up.

Norm: Me, neither. We're just on the verge of creating something that people have been wanting for two years, and I want to see us keep going.

Marina: Me, too. It's really important for me to have a church where I feel comfortable, so I'm willing to give whatever time is necessary to pull this off!

Communicatively, members demonstrate the high level of commitment they bring to this daunting task and their willingness to see it through—important input variables.

Throughput variables of a group involve how the group transforms inputs into final products and are characteristics of how the system functions, what it actually does. Examples include roles, rules, and norms; procedures the group follows; the group's leadership; communication among members; and all the other things that are part of the process in which the group engages as it works toward completing its task. In our church board, observe how certain rules and procedures evolved. First, the members complimented each other and affirmed their commitment to the group's task. This led to a pattern of expressing cohesiveness and mutual respect, which later made it easier for members to contribute freely and frankly. Bill operated as a democratic chair who supported the group's norms of equality and shared leadership. This helped other members feel comfortable to jump in with suggestions or comments. Look at the following exchange:

Bill: Well, here's draft one of the bylaws! They aren't carved in stone. I suggest that everybody take them home, read them carefully, and come prepared with changes next week. Then we can make the changes and have them copied and distributed for the congregation to look at. Sound OK?

Norm: Hang on a second, Bill. We said we were going to give these to Reverend Lacy [minister of another congregation who agreed to give the denomination's perspective] for feedback. That will take longer than one week.

Bill: You're right, I forgot. Let's schedule our discussion of the bylaws after Norm gets Reverend Lacy's perspective.

In this exchange, chair Bill's original suggestion is challenged, politely, by Norm. Bill acknowledges that he made a mistake and backtracks. This illustrates a throughput process that is democratic, where members can contribute without fear of repercussion and the leader has no more power to control events than the others do.

Output variables of a group are the results or products of the group's throughput processes, including the tangible work accomplished (such as written reports, items built, and policies developed), changes in the members (such as increases in commitment and increased self-confidence), the group's effect on its environment, and changes in the group's procedures. The church board's most obvious output to its environment was the formation of a church now serving many people in southwest Missouri. Within the group, though,

---

Input Variables

The energy, information, and raw material used by an open system, which is transformed into output by throughput processes.

Throughput Variables

The actual functioning of a system, or how the system transforms inputs into outputs.

Output Variables

Anything that is produced by a system, such as a tangible product or a change in the system; in a small group, includes such things as reports, resolutions, changes in cohesiveness, and attitude changes in members.

strong bonds of affection, cohesiveness, and pride at a job well done were intangible outputs that developed. In one meeting, after the group had been together for over a year, members articulated their feelings:

Don: As much as we complain about how much work we have to do, look at our finances! We have nearly half a year's salary in the minister's fund.

Bill: I know. At times when I'm swamped and feel like giving up, I think about what we've created and I'm energized again.

Marina: When I get discouraged about all that we *haven't* done and all the things that have fallen through the cracks, I think about how enthusiastic the congregation is, and how wonderful you all are, and I'm overcome with gratitude!

Gary: Speaking of gratitude, I haven't told you all how hesitant I was to be part of this group at first. You all have a lot more education than I do, and I didn't feel like I could express myself as well. But this has been one of the best experiences of my life, and I'm grateful for your encouragement and support.

Clearly, this is a cohesive, supportive group. Gary could admit something like this only if he trusted the others.

Consider This 2.2

The church board was a secondary group with a well-defined task to perform, but its strong primary characteristics made it unique. How did members communicate their commitment to each other and their caring? How were Schutz's (see Chapter 1) human needs of affection, inclusion, and control met in this group? Can any group become this cohesive and productive? Why or why not?

A System and Its Environment

Feedback

A response to a system's output; it may come in the form of information or tangible resources and helps the system determine whether or not it needs to make adjustments in moving toward its goal.

Open systems interact freely with their environments. **Feedback is the environment's response to a system's output. It can come in the form of information or tangible resources and helps the system determine whether or not it needs to make adjustments to reach its goals.** For instance, a car company that sells many cars (outputs) receives money for those cars (response to the outputs). This positive consumer response to the cars also provides the company with the information that it will likely reach its profit goals. One goal of the church board was having its bylaws approved by its denomination's Ministerial Association. To achieve this goal, the board sought feedback:

Sally: I used to know people at the association, but everyone I knew has moved on. The association's approval is critical—if they don't like our bylaws, we won't get official approval as a church.

Sunni: Is there any way we can get a preliminary reaction, before we send our final draft?

Norm: Yes—remember Reverend Lacy, from Columbia? She said she'd help us however she could, and she's on a couple of committees at the association. She could look at the bylaws and tell us how the association is likely to react.

Reverend Lacy did have several suggestions for modifying the bylaws. Her reaction (feedback) to the draft of the bylaws (the output) produced several changes in the bylaws that strengthened them and enhanced their chances of being approved.

As you can see, input, throughput, and output variables are not separable; everything influences and is influenced by everything else. For example, attitudes affect interaction, which in turn affects the outcome.

Just as input, throughput, and output variables are interdependent, so is a group highly interdependent with its **environment**, the setting in which the group exists. Many small group researchers have criticized small group research for ignoring the effect of the group's environment on the group.[6] Some group researchers have implied that the quality of a group's output is entirely or largely within a group's control. They have suggested that as long as the group has skilled and knowledgeable members (inputs) and effective leadership with helpful norms such as a conscientious attitude and good listening behaviors (throughputs), then the group will produce high-quality outputs. This oversimplifies the case because most groups are not self-contained entities but in fact are highly dependent on their environments. For instance, Broome and Fulbright asked real-life group members what factors hurt their efforts.[7] They found that organizational factors beyond a group's control often had strong negative effects on a group's performance. One recent study by Hirokawa and Keyton of actual organizational groups supports the overall utility of the systems framework, including a focus on the group's context, for examining small groups.[8] These researchers asked several continuing groups what factors helped and hindered their group's progress. The factors fell into three categories: individual (e.g., member motivation and interest), group (e.g., group leadership), and organizational (e.g., assistance from the organization, including continuing informational support as needed). These findings emphasize the complexity of the group process and suggest that outcomes depend on input factors relating to members, on throughput processes such as leadership, and on environmental factors often beyond the group's control.

Most groups are part of a larger organizational structure and must interact with individuals and other groups within that structure. Interestingly, for groups dealing with complex tasks in a very uncertain environment, how often members communicate within the group is not as important to their performance as is how often they interact with others in the surrounding environment.[9] This demonstrates how important it is for groups to match their internal abilities to process information with the external informational demands of the environment they are embedded in. Even nonorganizational groups are

Environment

The context or setting in which a small group system exists; the larger systems of which a small group is a component.

also part of an environment. For instance, the environment of a family may be the neighborhood or the general society in which it lives.

It is critical to remember that groups are affected by their environments. The church board described here was highly influenced by its environment, the congregation and the larger Unity church ministry. As effective as this group's throughput processes were, how successful do you think it would have been without the financial, moral, and informational support of its congregation and the Unity church? Not very successful!

Recognizing the important role of the environment on the group system is an important first step in understanding group processes; however, it is only a first step. Putnam and Stohl remind us that, while the group's environment influences its internal communicative dynamics, that very environment is also shaped by the group.[10] The boundaries between groups and their environments are fluid and permeable. Members of a group are simultaneously members of other groups; they bring the influence of those other groups into the first group. Members also carry into the group their outside role interests or agendas, which can subtly or overtly affect group interaction. Sally brought to the church board a sample of bylaws from the church where her husband had ministered. Fluctuation in group membership also affects the permeability of the group's boundaries, as was shown by the different perspectives Gary and Don brought to the group. Last, fluidity and permeability of group boundaries vary depending on the commitment members demonstrate to the various groups to which they belong. How well one group's identity is constructed in light of multiple memberships influences the group's dynamics and the strength of that group's self-identity. A major strength of the church group was the sense of belonging that members created and acted on.

Several realities of our social world help account for the reciprocal relationship between a group and its environment. First, members of groups, because they belong to other groups, create situations in which they often communicate between groups. Bill, the lawyer on the church board, talked to his office partners about the board and vice versa. These interactions simultaneously influenced both groups—the church board and his office partners. Second, groups often have to coordinate their actions with other groups within the same parent organization. The church group had to coordinate with other church committees, such as the finance committee and the worship committee. Third, there is frequent internal and external communication about how group goals should be interpreted, the extent of the group's authority, and support (or lack of it) for the group's actions. At one point in a board meeting, Norm relayed Reverend Lacy's feedback about the proposed bylaws, which resulted in some changes to the bylaws. Fourth, members all bring their own ways of speaking, their own sense of "group." The church board established a democratic discussion format early in its history with comments such as this one of Bill's: "Why doesn't everybody think of the important things that must be accomplished over the next, say, six months, and next week let's make a tentative schedule and organize how we're going to get everything done. Does that sound all right to you?"

The *bona fide group perspective*'s most recognized contribution is its focus on the embeddedness of smaller groups in larger systems and recognizing that those boundaries are not only permeable but fluid.[11] Identifying a *group* then is not as straightforward as traditional definitions of *group* would lead us to believe. Complicating matters is the reality that many of these smaller groups use computer technology to do their business and interact with their environment. The use of these technologies has prompted even bona fine group theorists to take a second look at this ever complicated relationship between a group and its environment.[12]

Consider This 2.3

Before you read this next section, stop to consider the ways in which virtual groups, or groups in which the members interact not face-to-face but via computer or other technology, are influenced by their environments. Do you think such groups are more, or less, subject to influence from outside the group? Why?

Bona Fide Virtual Groups   Most of the research in small group communication has focused on groups whose members meet face-to-face. We began to speculate in Chapter 1 about how group processes may change in groups whose members do not meet face-to-face. The reality of our global world is that many companies who might not otherwise ever collaborate on tasks are doing so with the help of computer technology that allows the members of multiple groups to interact with each other without being on the same site. For instance, the Boeing 767 airplane is the result of collaboration between Boeing engineers, who designed the fuel and cockpit; Aeritalia SAI engineers, who developed the fins and rudder; and multiple Japanese firms, whose responsibility was the main body of the plane.[13]

Modern day organizations are rapidly changing. More and more they are composed of employees who do not work in the same place or at the same time. Some of these organizations are virtual—that is, they are not an "office" but a network of members connected by computer who may never see each other face-to-face. Members of these work groups may only contact each other via electronic mail (e-mail) or videoconferencing. The **collaborating group** is one in which its members come from different organizations and form a temporary alliance in order to attain a particular purpose.[14] You are likely to find these groups in such industries as telecommunication, aerospace, motor vehicle, electronic, and computer.

Bona fide group theorists have begun to tackle understanding these groups. They posit that collaboration is primarily a communicative phenomenon. Their task then is to understand how participants in these kinds of collaborations manage their roles, multiple contexts, boundaries, and tasks. Traditional small group

Collaborating Group

A group whose members come from different organizations to form a temporary alliance for a specific purpose.

concepts are thrown into new light. For instance, traditional groups internally manage their knowledge and can easily find out where to get needed information, but the tasks of collaborating groups can be so innovative and multidimensional as to be beyond the knowledge of any member. In addition, members may have no clue as to who to contact for the information. Commitment in collaborating groups is complicated by a variety of commitments held by participating members. Formal positions of power are often unrecognizable in these groups so much so that power positions are continually negotiated. Decision-making procedures often created internally in traditional groups are, in collaborating groups, impacted by the norms of parent companies, cultural changes, orders given by external agents and even decisions made outside the group. For example, UNIX is a desktop environment and the result of collaboration between a variety of computer companies. Any decisions made by one or more of those companies on products unrelated to UNIX might possibly have affected the decisions made during the collaboration.

The model in Figure 2.1 illustrates several of the many variables included in each of the main system categories. The hopper at the top of the figure represents inputs flowing into the machinery of the system, where they are processed and changed during the throughput process. The exit channel at the bottom represents the system's outputs. The tube on the right side represents the feedback channel that provides responses to the system's outputs. Surrounding the entire system is its environment that also provides resources that affect the system.

Open System

A system with relatively permeable boundaries, producing a high degree of interchange between the system and its environment.

This particular model represents an **open system**, meaning that the group interacts freely with its environment. The perforations in the system's boundaries illustrate this characteristic that lets resources flow freely between the environment and the group. For example, a classroom group that receives relevant information from the instructor, from other classmates, from friends outside class, and from media or news sources is an open system. The church board had a high degree of interchange between itself and the congregation that was a main part of its environment, which made it an extremely open system. For example, board meetings were open and anyone from the congregation could attend them. In addition, the board frequently held "town meetings," at which congregation members were invited to share their opinions

Closed System

A system, such as a small group, with relatively impermeable boundaries, resulting in little interchange between the system and its environment.

about the running of the church. In contrast, a **closed system** has relatively little interchange between the group and its environment. Its boundaries are more solid and adaptations to the exigencies of the environment are limited. A cloistered monastery, where monks interact with each other but have little contact with outsiders, illustrates a closed system. However, there is no completely closed human system.

Communicating across Boundaries

In our previous discussion, we have stated that a group's environment is important to a group's success noting that effective groups match their information process abilities with that of the informational demands of the environ-

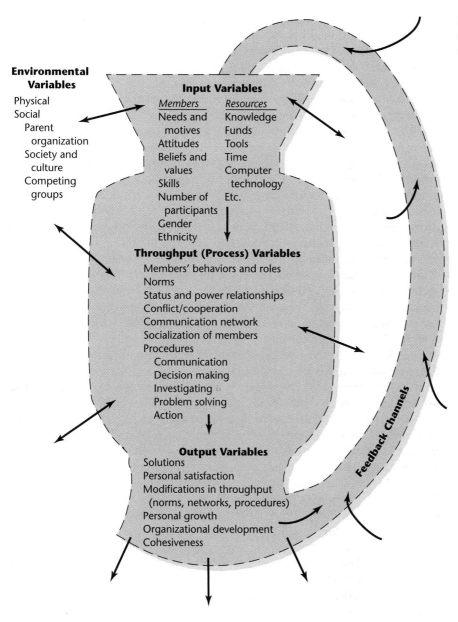

FIGURE 2.1 Model of a group as an open system.

Environmental Variables

Physical
Social
  Parent
    organization
Society and
  culture
Competing
  groups

Input Variables

Members	*Resources*
Needs and	Knowledge
motives	Funds
Attitudes	Tools
Beliefs and	Time
values	Computer
Skills	technology
Number of	Etc.
participants	
Gender	
Ethnicity	

Throughput (Process) Variables

Members' behaviors and roles
Norms
Status and power relationships
Conflict/cooperation
Communication network
Socialization of members
Procedures
  Communication
  Decision making
  Investigating
  Problem solving
  Action

Output Variables

Solutions
Personal satisfaction
Modifications in throughput
  (norms, networks, procedures)
Personal growth
Organizational development
Cohesiveness

Feedback Channels

ment. Ancona and Caldwell suggest that groups need members who serve as **boundary spanners** by constantly monitoring the group's environment to bring in and take out information relevant to the group's success.[15] The first of the three major functions that boundary spanners serve is initiating transactions to import or export needed resources, such as information or support. For instance, in our example of an effective group, Norm contacted Reverend Lacy for advice about organizing the new congregation and help in gaining

Boundary Spanner

A group member who monitors the group's environment to import and export information relevant to the group's success.

approval from the association. Another boundary-spanning function consists of responding to initiatives of outsiders. Someone may ask a group member what the group discussed at a particular meeting; that member must then decide whether and what information to relate. The final function involves changes in the membership of the group—new people may be brought into the group either temporarily or permanently. For example, in an unorthodox move, members decided to invite Gary's wife, Christy, to attend church board meetings in his place as a nonvoting member during a two-month stretch when he was unable to attend meetings. This enabled Gary to keep up with the board information and maintain, through Christy, relationships that he had formed. The management of the group's relationship with the environment is crucial and can spell success or failure for the group. If the church board had decided to be secretive and not share openly with the congregation what was discussed and decided at board meetings, the congregation would have been unlikely to support the church with time, energy, and resources.

Ancona and Caldwell, in a five-year study of product-development teams, further explored the behaviors of boundary spanners.[16] Their research uncovered key strategies these team members use to carry out their functions as boundary spanners. (See Figure 2.2.) When Norm solicited feedback from Reverend Lacy he was acting in an *ambassadorial capacity* for the church group. Ambassadors check out the environment to see who supports the group; bring in information from the environment in summary form; and may also attempt to persuade outsiders to the desires, goals, and importance of the group. Strategies involving *task coordination* occur when members coordinate technical issues and thus tend to talk laterally across all relevant groups. Design problems may be addressed as well as the coordination of schedules and deadlines and securing resources needed by the group. *Scouting* activities involve general scanning of the outside for relevant information and ideas that can be used by the group, including figuring out what the competition is doing. Ambassadorial, task-coordination, and scouting strategies all involve the group engaging its environment proactively. The last strategy, *guarding*, is characterized by actions by the group to close itself off from the environment. These ef-

FIGURE 2.2
Boundary spanner functions and strategies.

> **Boundary Spanner Functions**
>
> 1. Initiate transactions between the group and its environment to import and export resources.
> 2. Respond to the initiatives from outsiders.
> 3. Initiate temporary or permanent group membership.
>
> **Boundary Spanner Strategies**
>
> 1. Ambassador.
> 2. Task coordinator.
> 3. Scout.
> 4. Guard.

forts can be seen as a way the group has of controlling information that may damage its profile.

Ancona and Caldwell argue fervently that a pattern of isolation is not beneficial to productive groups.[17] Successful product teams engaged in consistent communication with their environment. High levels of ambassador activity as well as task coordination are necessary if product teams are to perform well. An entrenched pattern of scouting means a group spends too much time thinking about its task and not enough time getting down to business. Groups that remain cut off from their environments are low performers even if they believe they have the necessary information to complete the task or that their output will be judged independent of their process. Although this research involved production teams, any task group should heed Ancona and Caldwell's call for consistent and extensive communication across group boundaries.

Characteristics of Effective Problem-Solving Groups

A secondary group's effectiveness can be determined only by comparing its accomplishments (outputs) with its stated goals and assessing its impact on its environment. The standards summarized in Figure 2.3, represent the ideal input, throughput, output, and environmental variables toward which discussion groups should strive, even though most will fall short.

Input Variables

1. **Members share basic values and beliefs about the purpose of the group and each other.**

   For instance, if one member of a project group believes deeply that the project is worthwhile and intends to commit substantial time to it but another member thinks the assignment is busywork and decides to "blow it off," the group is not likely to reach consensus or interact smoothly. Ideally, members' attitudes toward each other, the group, and the group's task are positive. Members should be able to count on each other to complete tasks, support the decisions of the group, and act in a trustworthy way toward the other members. In our story about the effective church board, members demonstrated their commitment to the group and to doing a good job with such statements as "It's really important to me to have a church where I feel comfortable" and "I'm willing to give whatever time is necessary to pull this off!"

2. **The number of members is small enough for all to be active participants and to be perceptually aware of each other as individuals, yet large enough to supply the variety of knowledge and competencies needed to achieve high-quality outputs.**

   A divergence of backgrounds and perspectives is needed, but similarity in goals and values will make it possible for all members to support group decisions. Ideal groups achieve a balance between diversity and similarity;

FIGURE 2.3
Characteristics of an effective discussion group.

Input Variables

1. Members share values and beliefs toward the purpose of the group and each other.
2. The number of members is small enough for all to be active participants who are aware of each other, yet large enough to supply knowledge and competencies.
3. The group's purpose is understood and accepted by all members.
4. The group's relationships to other groups and organizations are clear, and members know what resources are available from these groups and organizations.
5. The group has sufficient time to do its work.
6. The group has a meeting place that provides for members' needs and is free of distractions.

Throughput Variables

1. Members can predict each other's behaviors.
2. Roles are stable, mutually understood, and accepted.
3. Members have relatively equal status, so they can exert influence based on knowledge, ideas, and skills.
4. Norms and the values underlying them are understood and adhered to, or discussed openly and changed if counterproductive.
5. Communication flows in an all-channel network.
6. Members are skilled and considerate when expressing themselves.
7. All members understand and share procedures that are efficient and lead to goal achievement.

Output Variables

1. Members perceive that the group purpose has been achieved.
2. Members feel satisfaction with their roles, the group process, and their relationships with other members.
3. Cohesiveness is high.
4. There is consensus on the role and leadership structure.
5. The group creates a culture that reflects its unique qualities and value.
6. The parent organization (if one exists) is strengthened by the group's work.

Environmental Factors

1. The environment (usually an organization) should publicly recognize the accomplishments of the group and reward the group as a group.
2. The environment should supply whatever informational resources a group needs.
3. The environment should supply whatever resources and expertise are needed by the group.
4. The environment should provide a supportive atmosphere for the group.

this balance is more important than size. For example, five people with different perspectives but similar values might agree on a goal, yet supply different sets of information about the problem and possible solutions. Thus, they will perform more effectively than 10 people whose perspectives are exactly the same or three people who can't agree on either basic values or goals. Cultural diversity or heterogeneity within a group has been shown to improve the quality of solutions because of improved decision making and idea generation.[18]

3. **The group's purpose is understood and accepted by all members.**
   All members perceive the goal alike and give it priority over personal goals or needs incompatible with group objectives. Members whose personal values or goals are at odds with a group goal interfere with efficiency. For example, if the purpose of a religious study group is to share and understand a variety of beliefs, but one or two members attempt to convert others, the group will have problems.

4. **The group's relationships to other groups and organizations in its environment are clear, and members know what resources are available from these groups and organizations.**
   Group members perform the appropriate boundary-spanning activities and know how they relate to the organization that created the group, to competing groups, and to the environment. The area of freedom and limitations on the group are understood both by the group and by affected people in the environment. The group knows how to adapt to changing environmental circumstances including the demands and special circumstances of computer technology.

5. **The group has sufficient time in which to do its work.**
   If research is needed to understand the problem, group members should have enough time to do it thoroughly. Groups need time to work through all the phases of the problem-solving process or to digest and process information and ideas. In short, members must have and commit enough time to do their work as a group thoroughly and well. For example, they should not try to find a solution to a city's congested traffic in a 40-minute meeting. Recall that the church board met every week for two years before it considered its main goals met.

6. **The group has a place to meet that provides for members' needs and allows discussions without distractions.**
   A committee that has no adequate room in which to meet regularly will expend much energy just finding and changing meeting places and trying to get members to those places. A quality circle cannot discuss problems well in a noisy assembly room, nor can a personnel committee evaluate job candidates in a room where strangers wandering in and out compromise privacy.

Throughput Variables

1. **Members are dependable and reliable.**

    A member who undertakes an assignment can be counted on to carry it out, whether that involves gathering information, typing and distributing a report, or scheduling a Sunday speaker for the service. Members can be counted on to attend scheduled meetings, notify the group if this is not possible, and perhaps send a knowledgeable substitute in their place if appropriate.

2. **Roles of members are relatively stable, mutually understood, and accepted by all members.**

    There is both sufficient role definition to permit members to predict each other's behavior (for example, on the church board Marina was consistently task oriented and organized and Bill was consistently democratic), as well as sufficient flexibility to permit anyone to make needed contributions to either the task or interpersonal relationships (for instance, other members besides Marina were task oriented and organized, and Marina also contributed to the positive feelings: "I'm overcome with gratitude!"). There is an equitable division of labor. The leadership position has been settled satisfactorily, but all members share leadership functions.

3. **Members have relatively equal status so all can exert influence on the basis of their own knowledge, skill, and ideas rather than status differences internal or external to the group.**

    On the church board, Bill's external status as a lawyer was relatively high, but that didn't stop Norm, the massage therapist, from saying, "Hang on a second, Bill. . . . That will take longer than one week," when he reminded Bill of the need for Reverend Lacy's perspective. That was possible because inside the group, the status of members was relatively equal. Equal status promotes teamwork. Members spend their energies achieving the goals of the group, not competing against each other for power and position. When all members feel equal, they freely contribute ideas, opinions, and suggestions; they don't hold back. This gives the group more information to work with.

4. **Norms (rules) and the values underlying them are understood and adhered to, or are discussed openly and changed when found to be unproductive.**

    A consistently productive problem-solving group has a culture of beliefs, values, and standards that encourages thorough searching for and testing of facts and ideas. For example, diversity of opinion was important to the church board; at one point, Bill suggested putting one or two people on the bylaws committee who felt strongest about limiting the power of the minister; Marina said, "Bill, that's a good idea! We need to make sure their point of view is included." When a member expressed a concern, that member would often conclude by asking, "Does anyone else feel bothered by this or is it just me?" This allowed the others to express their views, to address the problem, and to participate in finding a solution.

5. **The flow of communication reveals an all-channel network.**
   A high proportion of remarks are directed to the group as a whole, not to individual members. There are no sidebar conversations during the group meeting, yet members are free to approach any and all other members when a meeting is not in progress. Members build on each other's ideas.

6. **Members are skilled in expressing themselves interpersonally and are considerate of other members.**
   In the church board, Gary felt insecure about his ability to express ideas, but he was willing to share his opinions, did so clearly, and was encouraged by the other members. Group members should express their ideas with sensitivity so as not to evoke defensiveness in the others. Bill, although he was the designated leader of the group, often followed suggestions he made with, "Sound OK?" or "Is that all right with all of you?" or something similar that affirmed his respect for the others' opinions.

   Gender can complicate the perceptions of member behavior. The gender of the speaker and the listener as well as the perceived relationship between the interactants can influence perceptions of respect and considerateness. For instance, although males and females use controlling behavior in negotiation, men are seen as more controlling.[19]

7. **All members understand and share procedures that are efficient, prevent overlooking important issues and facts, and lead to goal achievement.**
   In a problem-solving group, all members understand and follow a procedure that is based on systematic methods of problem solving, and they share in exercising control over this procedure. The group decides what changes should be made in its procedures. In addition, it is helpful for group members to share specific discussion techniques appropriate to the purpose of the group, and to participate in establishing the agenda. For example, at one point, the church board tried every-other-week meetings for a while, but Norm concluded they weren't working for him. He brought it up to the group, gave the members reasons why they might reconsider ("Things really pile up in two weeks, and sometimes there's a big delay in our response . . ."), and asked the others what they thought. The whole group then had a chance to evaluate and modify their procedures.

Output Variables

1. **Members of the group perceive that its purpose has been achieved.**
   Members support the best decisions and solutions to problems. The church board members talked about several accomplishments they had achieved, including receiving bylaws approval from their congregation and their association, and saving enough money for half a year's salary for a minister. Solutions decided upon by a group should be accepted by most or all of the people affected.

2. **Members experience personal satisfaction with their respective roles in the group, the discussion and group work process, and their relationships with the other members.**

   For example, Bill says, "I think about what we've created and I'm energized again," and Gary says, "I'm grateful for your encouragement and support." The fact that at one point the board decided to meet more frequently, not less, indicates a high degree of satisfaction with the activity.

3. **Cohesiveness is high.**

   Members have a strong sense of identification with the group and give it high priority among competing demands for their time and attention. Cohesiveness among board members was evident ("This has been one of the best experiences of my life . . ."). A high degree of trust exists among members, as when Gary revealed his original insecurity about being a member of the board.

4. **There is consensus on the leadership and role structure of the group.**

   If asked independently, each member would name the same person(s) as designated leader of the group and as choice for leader in the future. For example, Bill emerged as the group's designated leader because he organized well, was democratic, and put in considerable work. He was drafted to coordinate the steering committee, and was later elected board chair. The rest of the members' roles developed as a result of their interests and expertise in relation to the needs of the group. Thus, members shared in leading the group.

5. **The group creates a culture that reflects its unique qualities and values.**

   Each group creates a culture or personality that is different from every other group. In effective groups, that culture is a positive one that supports the values of the members and reflects to the members what is most important in that group. For example, in the church board, members sometimes stopped a discussion for a brief prayer, particularly if a disagreement was under way. The prayer reminded members that disagreeing with ideas was acceptable but being disagreeable to other people was not. These brief prayer breaks were an important part of the group's culture. Clearly, in a different kind of group, prayer breaks would not have been appropriate or welcomed.

6. **The parent organization (if one exists) is strengthened as a result of the small group's work.**

   The organization is better off as a result of the group's work. In the church board's case, this requirement clearly was met. The board helped create a viable church that grew, received its denomination's approval, and eventually hired its first minister. The parent organization as well as the community was well served. An inclusive workplace not only entails a diverse workforce, in this case diversity among church members, but also an organization or even group that is active in the community, may participate at all levels including state and federal, and collaborates across national boundaries.[20] Barak's discussion of social work organizations emphasizes the need to recognize the much larger systems (beyond parent organizations) that groups are embedded in.

Environmental Factors

1. **The environment (usually an organization) should publicly recognize the accomplishments of the group and reward the group as a group.**

   Praise and recognition for one's efforts are highly motivating. In contrast, ignoring someone's efforts is demoralizing. Group members will be motivated to work efficiently and productively when they know there will be praise and other rewards for their efforts. The church board was publicly recognized and thanked by the congregation at several points during the process of creating the new congregation.

2. **The environment should supply whatever informational resources a group needs.**

   Nothing is more frustrating to group members than to be given a charge but not the information or data needed to complete the charge. In addition, as members begin their work, they often find that they need information they had not anticipated. It is especially important that the parent organization continue to give the group access to whatever information members find they need to complete their task in a timely manner.

3. **The environment should supply whatever resources and expertise are needed by the group.**

   Sometimes organizations provide initial training and orientation for group members, especially for brand new groups, but often forget that groups may need continuing training and access to specialized procedures and expertise. For instance, a problem-solving group may benefit from bringing in a consultant to help them develop their creativity as a group. Ideally, the group's environment is supportive of such group needs and continues to supply resources, training, expertise, coaching, or whatever else a group needs to be productive.

4. **The environment should provide a supportive atmosphere for the group.**

   Groups are sometimes demoralized when their efforts are consistently second-guessed or interfered with by the parent organization. In addition, organizations sometimes tend to load a group, particularly one that has been successful in the past, with too many priorities to handle well. Instead, the ideal environment for a group is a nurturing and supportive one that gives the group room to negotiate without stifling or overburdening it.

Few groups you experience may measure up to these standards as well as the church board did. However, you now have a model of an effective small group as a basis for comparison and should be able to spot at least some of the sources of difficulty in any group that is not producing satisfactory outputs.

SUMMARY

1. Systems theory provides a framework for understanding something complex, such as small groups. The small group was described as an open system with input, throughput (process), and output variables, and having the properties of interdependence between components, nonsummativity, and interdependence with its environment.

2. Input variables include such items as members' skills, knowledge, and other resources. The group, as a system, processes these resources through communication among members, thereby transforming them into outputs including tangible products, such as reports or recommendations, and intangible products, such as cohesiveness or changes in members' perceptions.

3. Ideal input, throughput, output variables, and environmental factors were described, with examples provided from the church board introduced at the beginning of the chapter.

KEY TERMS

 Test your knowledge of these key terms by visiting the Online Learning Center website at mhhe.com/galanes11

Boundary spanners	Input variables	Output variables
Closed system	Interdependence	System
Collaborating group	Multiple causation	System-level variables
Environment	Nonsummativity	Throughput variables
Feedback	Open system	Variables
Individual-level variables		

EXERCISES

 Go to self-quizzes on the Online Learning Center at mhhe.com/galanes11 to test your knowledge of the chapter concepts

1. Compare the church board discussed in the chapter to the Mafia. Compare each group in terms of the concepts listed below.
   a. Open versus closed systems.
   b. Interdependence of the parts of the system.
   c. Nonsummativity.
   d. Boundary-spanning activity.
   e. Characteristics of the group's culture.

2. In this chapter, several input, throughput, and output variables of small secondary groups were identified. What others do you think should be included? Why? Your answer should include a modification of Figure 2.1.

3. Think of the best and the worst small secondary groups in which you have participated. Why were they the best and worst? What characteristics of the inputs and the throughputs seem to have made the most difference? As a class, generate your own criteria for effective inputs and throughputs.

BIBLIOGRAPHY

Katz, Daniel, and Robert L. Kahn. *The Social Psychology of Organizations*. 2nd ed. New York: Wiley, 1978. See Chapter 2.

Von Bertalanffy, Ludwig. *General System Theory*. New York: George Braziller, 1969.

Wood, Julia T., Gerald M. Phillips, and Douglas J. Pedersen. "Understanding the Group as a System." In *Small Group Communication: A Reader*. 6th ed. Robert S. Cathcart and Larry A. Samovar, eds. Dubuque, IA: Wm. C. Brown, 1992, 5–17.

NOTES

1. Edward A. Mabry, "The Systems Metaphor in Group Communication," in *The Handbook of Group Communication Theory and Research*, ed. Lawrence Frey (Thousand Oaks, CA: Sage, 1999): 71-91.
2. Stephen W. Littlejohn, *Theories of Human Communication*, 7th ed. (Belmont CA: Wadsworth/Thomson Learning, 2002).
3. George F. Will, "A New Level of Worrying," *Newsweek* (July 22, 1996): 72.
4. Abran J. Salazar, "Understanding the Synergistic Effects of Communication in Small Groups: Making the Most Out of Group Member Abilities," *Small Group Research* 26 (May 1995): 169-99.
5. Randy Y. Hirokawa and Dierdre D. Johnston, "Toward a General Theory of Group Decision Making: Development of an Integrated Model," *Small Group Behavior* 20 (November 1989): 500-23.
6. Benjamin J. Broome and Luann Fulbright, "A Multistage Influence Model of Barriers to Group Problem Solving: A Participant-Generated Agenda for Small Group Research," *Small Group Research* 26 (February 1995): 25-55; Cynthia Stohl and Michael E. Holmes, "A Functional Perspective for Bona Fide Groups," *Communication Yearbook* 16, (1993): 601-14; Jeremy Rose, "Communication Challenges and Role Functions of Performing Groups," *Small Group Research* 25 (August 1994): 411-32.
7. Broome and Fulbright, "A Multistage Influence Model."
8. Randy Y. Hirokawa and Joann Keyton, "Perceived Facilitators and Inhibitors of Effectiveness in Organizational Work Teams," *Management Communication Quarterly* 8 (May 1995): 424-46.
9. Deborah G. Ancona and David F. Caldwell, "Bridging the Boundary: External Activity and Performance in Organizational Teams," *Administrative Science Quarterly* 37 (December 1992): 634-65.
10. Linda L. Putnam and Cynthia Stohl, "Bona Fide Groups: An Alternative Perspective for Communication and Small Group Decision Making," in *Communication and Group Decision Making*, 2nd ed., eds. Randy Y. Hirokawa and M. Scott Poole (Thousand Oaks, CA: Sage, 1996): 147-78.
11. Jennifer H. Waldeck, Carolyn A. Shepard, Jeremy Teitelbaum, W. Jeffrey Farrar, and David Seibold, "New Directions for Functional, Symbolic Convergence, Structuration, and Bona Fide Group Perspectives of Group Communication," in *New Directions in Group Communication*, ed. Lawrence R. Frey (Thousand Oaks, CA: Sage, 2002): 3-24.
12. Cynthia Stohl and Kasey Walker, "A Bona Fide Perspective for the Future of Groups," in *New Directions in Group Communication*, ed. Lawrence R. Frey (Thousand Oaks, CA: Sage, 2002): 237-52.

13. Ibid.

14. Ibid.

15. Deborah G. Ancona and David F. Caldwell, "Beyond Task and Maintenance: Defining External Functions in Groups," *Group & Organization Studies* 13 (December 1988): 468-94.

16. Deborah G. Ancona and David F. Caldwell, "Bridging the Boundary: External Activity and Performance in Organizational Teams."

17. Ibid.

18. Beth Bonniwell Haslett and Jenn Ruebush, "What Differences Do Individual Differences Make?" in *The Handbook of Group Communication Theory and Research*, ed. Lawrence Frey (Thousand Oaks, CA: Sage, 1999): 115-38.

19. N. Burrell, William Donohue, and M. Allen, "Gender-Based Perceptual Biases in Mediation," *Communication Research* 15 (1988): 447-69.

20. Michal E. Mor Barak, "The Inclusive Workplace: An Ecosystems Approach to Diversity Management," *Social Work* 45 (July 2000): 339-43.

© Bob Daemmrich/The Image Works

THE FOUNDATIONS OF COMMUNICATING IN GROUPS

The three chapters in Part II provide theoretical information about communication particularly relevant to communicating in small groups. These chapters are intended to serve as a foundation on which to build your understanding of the throughput processes in a small group, discussed in Chapter 2. This foundation includes information about the communication process itself, how nonverbal and verbal behaviors function together, and how culture impacts the communication dynamics between small group members. Specific guidance is provided to help improve your personal competencies as a group member, especially in speaking, listening, and interpreting during group meetings.

HUMAN COMMUNICATION PROCESSES IN SMALL GROUPS

Central Message

Communication is a complex, symbolic process that group members must both observe and understand so they can coordinate their efforts to achieve the group goal.

STUDY OBJECTIVES

As a result of studying Chapter 3 you should be able to:

1. Explain communication as a symbolic, personal, transactional process that is not always intentional.
2. Differentiate between the content and relationship dimensions of interpersonal communication.
3. Explain the fallacy in each of five communication myths.
4. Describe how signals are encoded, transmitted, received, interpreted, and responded to in a communication transaction.
5. Describe some of the differences between computer-mediated communication and face-to-face communication.
6. Give an example of a complete communication transaction and explain why such transactions are important.
7. Identify and describe the four general listening preferences.
8. Identify and describe each of six pitfalls to effective listening.
9. Explain the process of active listening.

Po and some of his college friends started a small software company in the Silicon Valley. Po, Tony, May, Tamika, and Kevin took computer classes together and over time discovered they had one thing in common—the desire to get rich quick in the computer business and retire early. Po had been working on a software program to benefit utility companies in their billing. He shared his ideas with his friends, who decided to join Po in creating a software company. With the program in its final stages it was time for them to decide how to market their product. They conducted a series of meetings to develop a marketing plan. Their first task would be to assess their finances, and Kevin, their accountant, was assigned to give a report to the group. But lately, Kevin tended to be late to their meetings. During one meeting Tamika remarked, "Man, what time is it already? Kevin—he's 10 minutes late! If he had gotten here on time, we'd have been done by now. I'm tired of this." Po, in frustration, declared, "I'm tired of waiting on the jerk, too, okay?" And May replied, "I don't have time for this." Po, growing impatient, switched directions with, "Let's just go ahead and get started and try to get the ball rolling. Tony, did you find out who our major competition is?" The meeting proceeded without Kevin.

In Chapter 1 we made a case for recognizing small groups as our most important social formation, central to our lives, with communication central to the life of a small group. As this story shows, what and how we communicate with each other as group members creates the nature of the small groups we participate in. *Communication* is like the nerve network of a small group; it is the verbal and nonverbal process by which individuals forge themselves into a group, maintain the group, and coordinate their efforts: "Communication is the lifeblood that flows through the veins of groups. Communication is not just a tool that group members use; groups are best regarded as a phenomenon that emerges from communication."[1] No communication, no group. This chapter provides a foundation for understanding the term *communication*, which is *the* fundamental throughput process of all groups.

If you have previously studied communication, the next two chapters may be a review for you. Nevertheless, because communication scholars sometimes use key terms in different ways, we recommend that you at least survey these chapters to understand how we use key terms.

What Is Communication?

Communication

A process in which signals produced by people are received, interpreted, and responded to by other people.

Many definitions of the term *communication* exist. We define **communication** as the process by which people create and send signals that are received, interpreted, and responded to by other people. The purpose of this process, for the small group, is to develop meaning that is shared sufficiently for the members to accomplish the group task. Meaning is never completely shared between two people, let alone among the four or five who typically constitute a small group. However, for group members to achieve their interdependent goal, at least *some* shared meaning must occur.

Principles of Communication

In this section, we first present five principles of communication before we elaborate on the communication process in greater detail. In addition, we discuss several myths about communication. Different authors subscribe to different communication principles, but the following are the ones that are generally accepted by scholars and to us seem particularly important for understanding communication in small groups. We consider several of these principles in greater detail in Chapter 4.

1. **Human communication is symbolic**.

   This, perhaps, is the most important principle of communication. *Meaning* is not transferred from one person to another; rather, people send messages to each other that must be interpreted. In the movie *Brainstorm*, the main character invented a headphone device that could transfer experiences directly from the brain of one person to another without first having to *encode* the experiences into words. Of course, we can't do this—yet! We must use verbal and nonverbal signals to send our thoughts to another person. In this encoding process, we convert our thoughts, feelings, beliefs, and experiences into the words, sounds, and gestures that we hope others will interpret as we mean them. The receiver then uses the reverse process of *decoding*, attending to what was sent and interpreting it, to try to determine what was meant.

   [handwritten: encoding/decoding]

   The **signals** that humans exchange may be either *signs* or *symbols*. **Signs**, such as tone of voice, face and body characteristics, have an inherent, natural connection with what they represent. For example, if you scowl because you hear something you dislike, there is a natural connection between your feeling of dislike and your scowl. Similarly, your blush of embarrassment is a sign directly connected with your feeling of embarrassment. In contrast, **symbols** are arbitrary signals created by people to represent experiences, objects, or concepts. For example, there is no automatic or inherent reason why we call something we write with a *pen*. We could just as easily have agreed to call it a *dog, tree*, or *la plume*. Similarly, the *okay* gesture, the circle we make with thumb and forefinger, is an arbitrary symbol; it means something different in other cultures, such as in South America, where it means something obscene. This reliance on symbols is an important characteristic of human communication and is a major reason why meaning can never be shared exactly.

2. **Communication is personal.**

   Meaning itself is not conveyed. The symbolic nature of communication is by definition arbitrary. Thus the same word can have different meanings to different people. You may have heard the popular claim, "meanings are in people, not in words." This principle is even more important when we consider that many of the concepts we necessarily use in everyday conversation are abstract: fairness, excellence, effective. For instance, excellence to you may mean striving for an A grade on a project, with no typographical errors

   [handwritten: ambiguity]

Signals

Any stimulus a person can receive and interpret, including both signs and symbols.

Signs

A signal that has an inherent relationship with what it represents, such as a blush or scar.

Symbol

An arbitrary, human-created signal used to represent something with which it has no inherent relationship; all words are symbols.

and all information thorough and complete; for a fellow group member, excellence may mean getting the project completed on time, even if there are mistakes and missing information. Both of you are using the same word or symbol, but you aren't meaning the same thing at all! The greater the abstractness of a symbol the more possible meanings there are for the symbol and thus the more ambiguous the symbol becomes. Your backgrounds, experiences, and the culture from which you came—all of these things affect the meanings you give to the words you and others use. We discuss in detail the effects of culture on the communication process in Chapter 5.

3. **Communication is a transactional process.**

   This principle follows from the previous two. *Transactional* implies that participants in a communication encounter must cooperate and work together to achieve mutual meaning and understanding. From the previous example, if we know that the verbal symbol (i.e., word) *excellent* has different connotations to different people, and we want to make sure we understand each other about our project, then we must work together, communicatively, to determine what we jointly mean by *excellent.* In addition, *transactional* implies that the sender-receiver roles occur simultaneously, not alternately. While I am describing what an excellent project means to me, I simultaneously see your frown, and guess that you don't agree with my description. Thus, communication is *both* a sender *and* receiver phenomenon simultaneously for each person involved in the process. Finally, the concept of *process* implies that communication is an ongoing event with no clear beginning or end. If we argue about how excellent our project will be, then the next time we meet we will carry the memory of that argument with us. Thus, communication is ever changing, not static, but constantly in flux.

anti-static

Consider This 3.1

In our story, Po, Tamika, May, and Tony believe that Kevin has a problem being "on time." Note Tamika's exclamation, "he's 10 minutes late!" But what does it mean to be late? "Being on time" and "late" are interpretations of behavioral events (e.g., we agreed to meet at 2 P.M. and it is 2:30 and Kevin has not shown up). In this case, the group members are sharing with each other their own experiences of time. Can you think of examples that show how time is experienced differently in different cultures, perhaps one in which 30 minutes past a set time for a meeting would not be considered "late"?

4. **Communication is not always intentional.**

   This principle is sometimes stated as "You cannot NOT communicate," and not all communication scholars agree with this position.[2] For example, Infante et al. believe that for an event to "count" as communication, the sender must have intended to communicate with the receiver.[3] "You cannot NOT communicate" was never meant to imply that *all* behavior is communication, only that all communication in a social setting (e.g., a group) is behavior and behavior has no opposite (i.e., you cannot *not* behave). For instance, when two or more humans are in each other's perceptual awareness, they cannot stop sending nonverbal signals to each other, which the receivers pick up, interpret, and respond to. Kevin's absence from his group communicates various things to his group. Thus, in a social setting, one probably cannot avoid communicating.[4] The way symbols are interpreted may not be the way they were intended; remember symbols vary in degree of arbitrariness, abstractness, and ambiguity. Kevin may not at all intend to communicate to his colleagues that he does not care enough for the business to be on time. Moreover, people do not always *know* what they intend, and may have multiple intentions for their words or actions.[5] Nevertheless, in a social setting like a group, you do not have the option of not communicating, because even silence will be interpreted by your fellow group members.

5. **Communication involves content and relationship dimensions**. Any **message**, the set of signals from one person to others, contains both dimensions simultaneously. The *content* or denotative dimension of the message is the subject, idea, or topic of the message—the *what* of the message. The *relationship* dimension of the message refers to what the message reveals about how the speaker views his or her relationship to the other participants—the *how* of the message.

At the content level, Tamika's first remark presents a fact—that Kevin has not arrived at the designated time—and an opinion—that the group could have finished its meeting if members had been able to start on time. Clearly, these colleagues feel angry and frustrated that Kevin has failed them again. Po's calling Kevin "a jerk" indicates that Kevin's behavior pattern is straining the good will of the others. Now notice Po's final remark: "Let's just go ahead and get started . . . Tony, did you . . . ?" This comment clearly illustrates the relationship level of communication, which concerns how the speaker views his or her relationship to the other members. Po takes charge here by suggesting the group begin without Kevin, then asks Tony for a report. At the content level, Po seems to be making a procedural suggestion ("Let's get started") and asking Tony for information. At the relationship level, however, Po is saying, "I have enough authority in this group to suggest how to proceed, and I'm taking charge now." The rest of the members accept Po's relational definition, and the meeting gets under way. Why? Po is the designated leader of the group, and he is behaving appropriately for his position. The actions of the others support this behavior and thus Po's authority is sustained. In this instance, Po does not overstep his relational bounds.

The relationship dimension, which is often conveyed nonverbally through tone of voice and movement, can show that the speaker considers him- or herself to be dominant, subservient, or equal to the other

Message

Either a set of signals from one person to others or interpretation/ response of a listener to a set of signals.

<u>members</u>. Attitudes of arrogance, dominance, submissiveness, distrust, superiority, neutrality, or concern are not often stated; rather, listeners interpret them from nonverbal cues or how a message is expressed. Note that characteristics such as distrust, dominance, and neutrality convey even subtler distinctions of the relationship dimension of messages: responsiveness, liking, and power.[6] We convey *responsiveness* to others when we show them how much or how little we are interested in their communication through eye contact, posture, and facial expressions. Westerners generally express interest with sustained eye contact, whereas in other cultures sustained eye contact could be interpreted as disrespect for authority. In conversation, interactants who synchronize each other's facial expressions and posture may be expressing comfortableness with each other.[7] *Liking*, or for that matter dislike, for others can be expressed with smiles, friendly touching, and frowns. Considering the example above, expressions of anger, frustration, and labeling Kevin a "jerk" are indications of levels of liking or affection in the group. Finally, relationship-level meaning also contains expressions of *power* as we negotiate our status and influence with others. Perhaps both Kevin and Po are in a power struggle over leadership. Kevin's absence can be seen as irresponsible or maybe Kevin is making the group wait for him. Making others wait can be used by people as an expression of status. Remember the last time you went for a doctor's visit or waited on a professor?! In this case, Po responded to Kevin's absence by asserting his dominance and his assertion was accepted by others in the group.

In our experience, these relationship-level meanings cause many of the misunderstandings we observe in small groups. To illustrate, what if May had turned to Tamika and said, in a commanding tone of voice, "Tamika, you take notes for the meeting." Tamika would probably have wanted to say, "Who died and made you queen?" Group members often react strongly to a peer who seems to command and direct because the manner suggests superiority to the other members and perhaps dislike.

Computer-Mediated Communication and Face-to-Face Communication in Small Groups

So far, we have discussed small groups that meet in real time and face-to-face. But since the advent of computers and more recently the explosion of Internet capabilities, groups no longer need to meet face-to-face in real time. We pointed this out when we discussed, in Chapter 2, how collaborating groups can overcome the limitations of space and time with computers. **Computer-mediated communication**, or CMC, is the formal phrase used to refer to the use of computers to interact with others. CMC can take a variety of forms, including e-mail or electronic mail, chat rooms, electronic bulletin boards, listservs, videoconferencing, and decision-making software. More and more

Computer-Mediated Communication (CMC)

Group members' use of computers to communicate with one another.

group members use computer technology to communicate with each other between and during meetings. A question to ask is: "How different is computer-mediated communication from face-to-face communication?" To address this question, let's look at one kind of computer-mediated communication available to groups: the net conference.

Net conference is a general term used to refer to a conference electronically mediated by *networked* computers.[8] The *videoconference* is one of the more popular types of these kinds of conferences. Videoconferencing involves both audio and video net-mediated communication, whereas an audioconference can be as simple as a telephone conference call. Telephone conference calls are a popular way on college campuses of conducting job search interviews and oral defenses of dissertations when committee members attend different universities. In *computer conferences*, group members actually sit in front of their computers and send messages to each other that appear on their computer terminals. Types of net conferences vary in expense and usefulness. However, as the expense of travel for executives to attend face-to-face meetings continues to increase and as more and more organizations are created, even expensive net conferencing techniques will pay off in the long run. In addition, companies are becoming very sophisticated in their abilities to develop specialized computer software designed for their employees, linked to a network, to work simultaneously on any number of tasks.

Although this kind of computer technology has its advantages, the question remains: "Do computer-mediated meetings have disadvantages in comparison to face-to-face group meetings?" Depending on the kind of net conference, participant nonverbal messages like facial expressions and body language are missing or exaggerated.[9] For example, during a videoconference participants can see each other; however, they are only as close to each other as the camera allows. This means that distance between participants is only simulated, *not* duplicated. And although you can see each other in a videoconference, you are not actually in each other's physical presence. Turn taking is easier face-to-face because in net conferencing there is often a delay of half a second. What happens then is that participants often overlap each other. In addition, participants are tied to their computer and this can restrict gestures. The sense of sharing, involvement, and team spirit can be low. Immediate verbal and nonverbal feedback usually does not occur or it is delayed. This could be harmful if the group is trying to build consensus about something, but it may not matter if participants are just trying to generate a list of ideas.[10]

Computer-mediated group communication versus face-to-face group communication brings up the issue of social presence. **Social presence** refers to how much group members perceive the communication medium is like face-to-face interaction socially and emotionally. This perception depends on the degree to which members perceive that other members are actually there during interaction.[11] *Asynchronous* communication, or communication where there is a delay between messages (e.g., e-mail), promotes less social presence

Net Conference

A conference that takes place electronically over networked computers.

Social Presence

The extent to which group members perceive that a particular communication medium is socially and emotionally similar to face-to-face interaction.

TABLE 3.1   Comparison of strengths.

Teleconferences	Face-to-face meetings
• They can be useful for information sharing, routine meetings. • Quantity and quality of ideas are equal to face-to-face meetings. • In negotiations, evidence is more persuasive than personality. • Participants may pay more attention to what is said. • In conflict, more opinion change may occur than in face-to-face meetings. • Audioconferences/computer conferences are cost-effective.	• Face-to-face meetings are better when group cohesiveness and interpersonal relationships are important. • Group organization is easier to maintain. • Participants can exchange more messages more quickly. • Important nonverbal information (facial expressions, uses of space) is available. • People generally prefer face-to-face meetings. • Participants are more confident of their perceptions in face-to-face meetings.

Source: Adapted from Gene D. Fowler and Marilyn E. Wackerbarth, "Audio Teleconferencing versus Face-to-Face Conferencing: A Synthesis of the Literature," *Western Journal of Speech Communication* 44 (Summer 1980): 236–52.

than synchronous, more simultaneous communication. One factor that can influence social presence is the complexity of the group's task. The tougher the task, the less adequate some CMC can become because the medium's channels are not adequate. However, individuals using CMC can become very creative when it comes to creating the social presence of face-to-face communication. Several factors can improve the effectiveness of net conferences.[12] Each of these factors is somehow related to creating social presence. Sandwiching the conference between face-to-face meetings can enhance the sense of groupness between members. Using a trained moderator can improve the process. So will making sure that members are aware of the rules and guidelines for speaking, and they agree to abide by specified time limits. Tasks such as routine meetings and information sharing are more effective via a net conference. For much more complex tasks in which disagreement is likely to occur, face-to-face meetings are still preferable. However, computer conferences have been used effectively to help members in conflict achieve consensus. Table 3.1 compares the strengths of face-to-face and net conferences or what used to be called teleconference meetings.

Although CMC may appear to be a different kind of communication, the communicative processes involved are still symbolic, personal, transactional, not always intentional, and involve content as well as relationship dimensions. We will elaborate on CMC in later chapters.

Myths about Communication

Misunderstandings about communication are perpetuated by a number of communication myths. Here are five of the most pervasive ones:

1. **I understand communication. I've been communicating all my life!**
   What if your 90-year-old Aunt Tilly said, "I know how to drive—I've been driving all my life!" Just because we do something often doesn't mean we do it well. Most people do not think reflectively about their communication behavior so they can improve it.

2. **All human problems are communication problems.**
   This statement trivializes the very real value differences that divide humans. Environmentalists who want to save the Bering Sea ecosystem, one of the world's richest and commercially valuable marine environments, may understand perfectly well the concern of fishermen who fear for their jobs and livelihoods—but they disagree over values and appropriate courses of action. Communicating more and better may do nothing to resolve their disagreements.

3. **If communicators use good communication techniques, they will automatically have good communication.**
   Becoming a good communicator does require practicing techniques of effective encoding and decoding. However, communication involves much more than that. The most important "skill" for improving communication involves having an attitude of wanting to be a good communicator. You can make mistakes with the techniques you use, but if people sense your basic good intentions they will often forgive your communicative lapses and you can be quite effective in coordinating meanings with them. Only if you *want* to be a good communicator can the skills and suggestions in most communication books help you. What promotes good communication? Almost always, group members' understanding of the communication process, their attitudes toward both the process and other people, and their abilities to listen enhance good communication.

4. **I didn't misunderstand him; he misunderstood me.**
   Both sender and receiver must cooperate to create clear, mutually understood messages; remember, communication is not linear but transactional. If a message is misunderstood, the effective communicator will accept a share of the responsibility (not blame!) and work to improve future transactions.

Consider This 3.2

Kevin finally arrives an hour after the scheduled time for the meeting. Tamika confronts him and asks him why he does not care enough to get to their meetings on time. Kevin tells her that he swore he heard Po tell him the meeting was scheduled for 3 P.M. not 2 P.M. If communication is seen as linear, then who is to blame for Kevin's "lateness"? On the other hand, from a transactional perspective, how do they all share in this circumstance? What might they say to each other if they looked at their circumstance transactionally—that is, if they took the point of view that they all created the situation?

5. **Good communication achieves perfect understanding among participants**.
    Perfect understanding is impossible. Moreover, some messages are intended to mislead rather than enlighten. Have you ever answered vaguely to the question, "How do you like my new hairstyle?" In this case, the lack of clear, unambiguous communication purposefully avoids hurting someone's feelings. In addition, because communication is both symbolic and personal, the best we can do is come close enough to understanding that we can complete the work of the group.

A Description of a Communication Transaction

Now that we have looked at main principles and widespread myths about communication in general, let's go back to our definition of communication (*the process by which people create and send signals that are received, interpreted, and responded to by other people*) and use it to analyze a communication transaction, which is modeled in Figure 3.1. **Noise**, or interference with the participants' ability to achieve mutual understanding, can happen at any point in the communication process. Noise is always present to some extent; that doesn't mean that communication has broken down, but that the limitations of human communicating always make perfect understanding an impossibility.

To start the process, something occurs to a group member that he or she wants to share. That member then encodes the thought, feeling, or idea by putting it into words and gestures. This process, of course, happens without a lot of conscious thought. You typically don't stop to think how to arrange your face into a scowl when you are expressing your displeasure—you just *do* it. However, you probably have had the experience of intending to say something, but the words came out wrong, or the thought was not expressed as precisely as you would have liked. This glitch in encoding is a type of noise.

Noise

Interference in the communication process; can occur at any step in the process, from the sender's original encoding of the message to the receiver's decoding of it.

FIGURE 3.1 An interpersonal communication transaction.

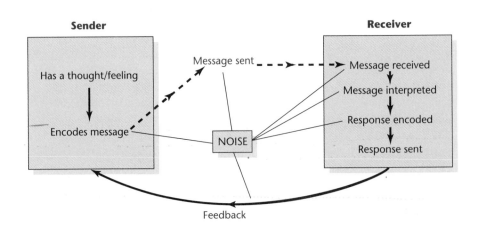

In small group communication, we usually assume the communicators are face-to-face. After the speaker has encoded the thought and sent it (i.e., spoken the words with accompanying nonverbal signals), another person must then receive the communication. This may sound simple, but the receiving process, which we call *listening*, is tricky, an additional source of noise. First, the receiver must *hear* what the speaker has said. Listeners often mishear or hear only part of what a speaker said. One of us attended a group meeting where a member said, "I don't have time to do that," but another member failed to hear the *don't*, and assumed the first member would handle a particular task. Fortunately, a third member, who suspected the misunderstanding and clarified it, quickly straightened out the problem.

Once the receiver has physically heard the message sent, he or she must then *interpret* the message, another stage where noise interference often occurs. Major misunderstandings can occur during this step because of the symbolic and personal nature of communication. We may use the same words or gestures but mean very different things by them. For example, Raul comes to the first meeting of his group early. He greets everyone in a friendly way when they arrive, sits at the head of the rectangular table, and makes numerous suggestions. One member thinks, "Wow, I like his self-confidence. He'll really be an asset to the group." Another member thinks, "What an arrogant jerk. What makes him think he's in charge?" Note the different interpretations on the part of the receivers to the same actions. Later, as the members get to know each other better, they may modify their interpretations. The second member may conclude, "Well, he comes on a little strong to begin with, but actually he's really friendly and hard working."

A vital determinant of how we interpret messages comes from the culture in which we were raised. The culture or cultures we identify with give us the rules for what is appropriate communication behavior. Differing cultural rules can interfere with understanding in a small group. For example, consider our attitudes toward speaking in general. "Being quick on one's feet" in many speech communities of the United States means that people are expected to speak effectively and silence is often viewed negatively.[13] Silence is risky because it could mean a lack of connection with others, lack of information or knowledge, and even a dismissal of one's being (i.e., giving the silent treatment).[14] Other cultural groups such as some Native Americans value silence and place a secondary value on speaking. Leon Rising Wolf, a member of the Blackfeet Nation uses the phrase, "deeply communicative silence," to characterize his nation's communication style.[15] This form of communication is *listener active* and values a nonlinguistic copresence with another higher than the more *speaker active*, linguistic form of communication valued in other speech communities. Talking, for the Blackfeet, can be risky in that it may interfere with the connectedness participants experience or may presume a level of authority the communicator does not have. The effects of culture on small group communication are covered in more detail in Chapter 5.

That's how you will understand it, by asking questions.

P.B, City Administrator

Feedback

In the context of a communication transaction, this is the listener's response to a message from the sender.

The final step in the communication transaction is **feedback**. As with feedback to a system, feedback in the context of a communication transaction is the listener's response to a message (i.e., output) from the sender, and it provides a number of important functions in the communication process. First, it helps reduce the harmful consequences of noise that interfere with mutual understanding. For instance, a member who isn't sure she heard a speaker correctly could say, "I didn't catch that, could you run it by again?" Or, a member who heard the speaker but isn't sure how to interpret the statement can say, "Does that mean that you can help me with that assignment, or not?" In addition, giving feedback to other members implies, "I am listening to you and you are a valued member of this group." Chopra observed, for instance, that when group members did not give each other supportive feedback, retaliation, withdrawal, and defensive behaviors increased.[16]

What you're saying and what you're hearing are two different things. So to adjust, readjust your message, is something I'm learning to do.

L. H., Director, State-Level Strategic Planning

In the groups to which you belong, notice whether there is a difference in how much members typically respond to each other. Are you, like most of us, more comfortable in groups in which members react openly and clearly (even to disagree), or in ones in which reaction is minimal? Do you agree with Jablin, who found that subordinates would rather have a boss disagree openly than ignore them, which is perceived as highly insulting?[17] We suggest you monitor your own feedback and change it if you routinely fail to respond to speakers.

Listening and Responding during Discussions

The level of understanding among group members depends more on how they listen and respond than on how they speak. Earlier, we explained that communication involves encoding, sending, hearing, interpreting, and responding to messages. **Listening** comprises the steps of hearing and interpreting. *Hearing* is a physiological process that involves the reception of sound waves by the ear. It is only the first element of listening, which also includes the *interpretation* of those sound waves (and other signals). A person with acute hearing may be a poor listener who does not interpret others' statements accurately or respond appropriately. In contrast, someone with considerable hearing loss may be a good listener who is motivated to understand others the way they want to be understood.

Listening

Receiving and interpreting oral and other signals from another person or source.

Consider This 3.3

In 1996 someone estimated that every morning in the United States 15 million meetings take place. Consider that in a six-person group, every time 5 minutes of information is repeated because of poor listening, a total of 30 minutes is wasted.[18] Taken together that is a lot of wasted time! Are you a good listener? Why? When you are not as effective a listener as you would like to be, what has happened? Interested in improving your listening? Read on.

Roach and Wyatt suggest four important things good listeners remember.[19] First, good listeners pay attention to the context of what is said. Have you ever been quoted "out of context"? If so, you know that context can change the entire meaning of what is said. Suppose Tiffany says she's not sure the president of your organization will read your group's entire report right away because the president is in the middle of performance reviews with all the committee heads. Saying "Tiffany said the president won't bother to read our report" seriously distorts what Tiffany said and ignores the context of the president's being too busy *at the moment* to give the report full attention.

The art of listening is worth the effort.

T. T., President, Health Care Policy Institute

Second, good listeners pay attention to the feelings of the speaker. Remember the affective component of a message? When Malcolm says, "Yes, that idea is fine," in a resigned, flat tone of voice, he's probably expressing a negative feeling about the idea, without actually saying so. A good listener will verify that interpretation: "Malcolm, you said you like it but you don't sound too enthused. Would you share your concerns with us?"

Third, when the organizational pattern a speaker uses is confusing, good listeners help speakers make themselves clear by asking questions to clarify. For example, Shanda is a statistics whiz who completed all the computer analyses for your group's project. She knows her stats so well that she skips steps in explaining them to the rest of you, who are lost. You can help her communicate more clearly by asking her questions that encourage her to fill in the gaps.

Finally, it is important to interpret silence carefully. Silence may mean that people don't understand what was said, that they don't agree, that they are apathetic, or that they are hoarding information as a power play. Or as we saw in our discussion of the Blackfeet, silence may mean a respect for the interconnectedness of the group members. Group leaders often mistake silence for agreement when it may be something else. Again, a well-timed question will help interpret silence correctly.

Listening is vital.

J. J., CEO and General Manager, Utility Company

Poor listening is easier to detect in a dyad than in a small group where one person can "hide" for long periods of time.[20] Compare a nine-person group to a dyad. In a nine-person group, if all members are participating equally, then each member listens about 90 percent of the time! Thus, the social pressure on members to listen is not as intense in a group as it is in a dyad and bad listening is easier to hide. Because people can fake listening, only when someone speaks do other participants have a basis for judging that person's listening behavior. Making irrelevant comments and asking questions about something that has already been explained are evidence of poor listening.

Most of us think we are good listeners, but evidence suggests otherwise. At times, group members are not even aware of the current topic of discussion. Berg found, for instance, that topics were switched about one time per minute in discussions he observed. Members were hardly listening or responding to what previous speakers had said.[21] This finding was confirmed by other investigators in a variety of cultures and situations.[22] Nichols and Stevens reported that students listening to lectures on which they knew they would be tested retained only about half the new information presented.[23] We have found that when members of small groups (whether college students or corporate personnel in training groups) are required to paraphrase what a previous discussant said to that person's satisfaction, they can do so only about half the time. This is true even when participants know that they will be assessed for accuracy in listening. How much, then, must group members misunderstand when they are *not* on guard?

The cost of poor listening is high. Jobs are completed incorrectly, shipments go awry, and people are hurt or killed because they or someone else didn't listen well. A good listener is, unfortunately, a rare commodity of great value to a group. Bechler and Johnson found that individuals who are perceived by their fellow group members as being skilled listeners (e.g., stayed focused on the discussion, maintained eye contact with the speaker, and so forth) are also perceived as being leaders.[24] In fact, we think good listening is one of the most important skills a leader can exhibit.

Listening Preferences

By now we hope you have gotten the idea that good listening in a group is an invaluable skill and poor listening can produce terrible group outcomes. We have mentioned why some of us are not very good listeners and suggested four things to remember if you want to improve your listening. In addition, you should understand that all of us bring to our group experiences different listening preferences, which if not recognized, can produce problems for the group. Have you ever thought that perhaps your strengths and weaknesses as a listener are tied to your learned listening preference?

Kittie Watson, a specialist in listening and small group communication, has identified four general listening preferences: people-, action-, content-, and time-oriented listeners.[25] No one preference is better than another because each has its advantages and disadvantages. The trick to managing different listening preferences is to be able to identify the listening preferences of all members, including yourself, in group interaction and shifting your preference to fit the needs of the group.

People-oriented listeners are concerned about how their listening behavior affects relationships. Appearing attentive and nonjudgmental, these listeners are the ones people go to when they want someone to listen to them. Behaviors indicative of this preference are the use of "we" more than "I," use of emotional appeals in discussion and debates, and willingness to show vulnerability. These members may be heard telling a personal story to calm down members who may be upset or angry. People-oriented listeners may also become distracted by others' problems, may avoid conflicts to maintain a sense of harmony, and may engage in too many side conversations during meetings.

Action-oriented listeners in your groups are focused on the job at hand. They help the group stay on task by remembering details and providing feedback about the goal. They enjoy listening to well-organized material. On the other hand, these members can appear overly critical, may interrupt too much if they believe the group is getting off track, and may lose interest if the discussion appears to be going nowhere.

Content-oriented listeners are the group members who really enjoy analyzing the things they hear and are drawn to highly credible sources. You may observe these members using graphs, quoting sources, bringing research to the group, and dissecting the information and arguments of others. These listeners can also be seen as overly critical and maybe even intimidating to other members. Their analytical skills, while valuable, may also slow the group down and can even serve to devalue information they do not see as important, such as anecdotes.

Time-oriented listeners can be identified by their attempts to schedule group meeting and activity times, their sensitivity to nonverbal cues that may indicate impatience, and their focus on moving the group along in a timely manner. The creative and spontaneous discussions so necessary to problem solving can pose difficulties for these listeners. They also discourage additional discussion as the group nears the end of its scheduled meeting time.

People-Oriented Listener

A listener who is sensitive to others, nonjudgmental, and concerned about how his/her behavior affects others; can become distracted from task by others' problems.

Action-Oriented Listener

A listener who focuses on the task, remembers details, and prefers an organized presentation.

Content-Oriented Listener

A listener who enjoys analyzing information and dissecting others' arguments; can be seen as overly critical.

Time-Oriented Listener

A listener sensitive to time; may be impatient or try to move group prematurely to closure.

Consider This 3.4

Look back at the story about Po and the others at the beginning of the chapter. Given the information you have, which listening preferences are manifested in the dialogue? How do the preferences help the discussion? How might they hinder the discussion?

No one preference is the best. Preferences are learned, so you are not locked into one of them. Each group member preference is influenced by many factors, including the nature of the relationships between group members and time constraints. Observe the members in your group for behavioral patterns that identify their preferences. Be willing to shift your preference to suit the immediate needs of the group and be willing to encourage the productive use of all the preferences. Let's turn now to a discussion of some of the more common behaviors that stand in the way of our becoming better listeners and of optimizing our listening preferences.

Pitfalls to Listening Effectively

Our listening is impaired when we are tired, preoccupied, or overloaded with information and noise. But even when we are not bothered by such interference or concerns, we still may listen poorly as a result of bad habits we are not aware of. We either do not pay attention carefully to the speaker, or we pay too close attention—to the wrong things! The following are behaviors that interfere with good listening:

1. **Pseudolistening**.
   Pseudolistening refers to faking the real thing. Pseudolisteners nod, smile, murmur polite responses, look the speaker in the eye, and may even give verbal support like "right" or "good idea." But behind the mask, the pseudolistener has "zoned off" on a daydream, a personal problem, sizing up the speaker, or mentally preparing a response. When such behavior is challenged, most pseudolisteners blame the speaker ("That stuff he was saying was boring") when they really hadn't given the speaker a chance.

2. **Sidetracking**.
   Related to pseudolistening is **sidetracking**, when you allow something another member said to send you off into your own private reverie. As a consequence, sometimes you may sidetrack the conversation in a completely inappropriate direction, thereby wasting the group's time.

3. **Focusing on irrelevancies and distractions**.
   Sometimes distractions such as background noises, room furnishings, and the air temperature make it difficult for us to concentrate on the speaker. At other times, undue attention to speaker characteristics such as dialect, appearance, or personal mannerisms causes us to miss important points. As one woman from Georgia said to her group: "Damn it, listen to what I have to say, not to how I speak. It makes me really mad when someone says, 'Oh, how you talk is so cute, I just can't pay attention to what you are saying.'"

4. **Silent arguing**.
   Many people listen selectively for information that confirms views they already hold. When they hear information that contradicts their chosen po-

Pseudolistening

Responding overtly as if listening attentively, but thinking about something other than what the speaker is saying.

Sidetracking

A poor listening habit whereby one group member spins off on a private reverie unrelated to what another group member has said, or whereby one group member moves the conversation in a direction completely different from what was being discussed.

sitions, silent arguers carry on an internal argument that opposes what they think the speaker has said.

You cannot mentally rehearse a reply at the same time you are striving to understand another. If you listen primarily to find flaws and argue them in your mind, you are unlikely to understand the speaker, the context of the remarks, and the meaning the speaker intends. We are not saying, "Don't argue." We are suggesting that you make sure you understand others first, well enough to be able to paraphrase their remarks *to their satisfaction*, before you disagree.

5. **Premature replying**.
    Similar to silent arguing, **premature replying** need not involve disagreement. Most commonly, a person prepares mentally to make a remark before fully understanding the speaker's comment or question. Also, group members who know each other well think they know what others are going to say before they say it—but they aren't always right! Jumping to a conclusion before the other has finished speaking results in a disjointed discussion in which the subject keeps switching.

<table>
<tr><td></td></tr>
</table>

Premature Replying

Responding before you fully understand the comment or question.

> I think you can learn to keep your mouth shut and listen.
>
> *J. T., CEO and General Manager, Utility Company*

6. **Listening defensively.**
    When we feel psychologically threatened, we don't listen well. Feeling vulnerable, we generally quit listening in order to invent ways to defend ourselves and attack the perceived threat. This is called **defensive listening**. For example, later in the meeting of our software colleagues, May verbally attacks Kevin several times. Kevin defends himself by attacking May back: "What's your problem? You've been riding my case all day!" Unfortunately, this won't help solve the group's problem. When we feel attacked is often the very time when we most need to understand the perceptions and values of the other person. Still later, after Tamika politely but directly confronts Kevin's behavior, his honest, nondefensive response to her indicates that he is not feeling attacked. You may have noticed that evaluation or judgment is part of most of these nonlistening behaviors. The sequence is entirely reversed from what it should be. Only *after* we understand each other's ideas are we able to judge appropriately. We need to be empathic listeners who try to understand what the other means *from his or her point of view*, with the motivation to receive information being greater than the motive to evaluate and criticize.[26]

Defensive Listening

Thinking of how to defend some aspect of one's self-image while appearing to listen to what another is saying.

We assume now that you want to improve your listening behavior in groups. With your attitude in the right frame of mind and armed with an understanding of listening preferences and pitfalls, we present some tested techniques to help you take responsibility for your listening habits.

Effective Listening in the Small Group

Small group members must first work at understanding each other if they hope to be effective, and listening is a key component of enhancing under-standing. Effective listening is an *active* process requiring as much effort as speaking. Engaged listeners show signs of physical activity, including an accel-erated heartbeat and postural shifts. In contrast, heart rates of poor listeners frequently slow to the level of sleep! Listening takes an act of will, a decision to listen. No matter how great the speaker is, it is the listener who chooses how to listen, to whom, and when. Thus, Watson reminds us, it is the listener who holds the power in small group interaction and, therefore, it is to our ad-vantage to understand and use effective listening techniques.[27] One of the best techniques for increasing understanding is *active listening*.

Active Listening   A good test of how well you have been listening is a tech-nique called **active listening**. This technique virtually forces the listener to understand a speaker before replying or adding to a discussion. The main rule is that you must state in your own words, or **paraphrase**, what you under-stand the previous speaker meant, then ask for a confirmation or correction of your paraphrase. Active listeners paraphrase; they do not repeat word for word. After all, a parrot can repeat, but that doesn't mean that the parrot has understood! A paraphrase in the listener's own words forces the listener to process the information cognitively, allowing the original speaker to deter-mine whether the message was understood as intended or not. The original speaker can then reply to the paraphrase (i.e., give feedback) by accepting or revising it or asking the listener to try again. Only when the original speaker is fully satisfied that the listener has understood what was intended does an ac-tive listener proceed with agreement, disagreement, elaboration, change of topic, or whatever. The following dialogue illustrates the technique:

Ed: Requiring landowners to farm in such a way that topsoil is not lost is ab-solutely necessary if we really want to protect the Earth for our children. (opinion)

Gail: If I understand you, you think we should require that farming practices prevent possible erosion of the topsoil because erosion destroys the Earth for living things? (paraphrase of Ed's opinion)

Ed: Right, Gail. (confirmation and acceptance of the paraphrase)

Another example:

Consuelo: If every college graduate were required to demonstrate some com-petence in using a computer, that might help right at graduation. But comput-ers are changing so rapidly that grads would be no better off in a few years than if they had no such training, unless they kept up-to-date or had to use a computer all along. (opinion)

Taylor: Do I understand you right? Are you saying that a computer science course should *not* be required to get a degree? (attempted paraphrase of Con-suelo's opinion)

Active Listening

Listening with the intent of understanding a speaker the way the speaker wishes to be understood and paraphrasing your understanding so the speaker can confirm or correct the paraphrase.

Paraphrase

Restatement in one's own words of what one understood a speaker to mean.

Consuelo: No, just that it should be more than just how to use a computer. You ought to understand computers, and what they do and don't do. (rejects the paraphrase and attempts to clarify)

Taylor: So you think there should be a requirement for a graduate to be able to explain what computers can and can't do, as well as be comfortable with a computer. (second attempt at paraphrasing Consuelo's opinion)

Consuelo: Yes, more than a course as such. (confirms Taylor's paraphrase)

Taylor: I agree with that idea, and think we should also have a requirement for ability to investigate, organize, and write a term paper. (His paraphrase confirmed Taylor is now free to add his opinion, on a new topic, to the discussion.)

Every idea proposed in a discussion should be evaluated, but only when you are sure you understand it to the satisfaction of the speaker. Active listeners confirm their understanding *before* they express their positive or negative evaluation. Only at that point is critical listening in order, evaluation by the listener as to whether the statement is relevant, defensible, likely to be effective, was carefully thought through, and so forth.

Sometimes active listeners cannot hear adequately or are not confident of their understandings. If so, they will say so quickly, asking the speaker to repeat or clarify. Only then will they disagree, add more information, or express whatever is their honest reaction.

Active listening slows the pace of interaction. If you are not used to listening actively, you may at first find yourself with nothing to say for a moment after the other finishes speaking. Keep practicing; soon you will find yourself making spontaneous responses instead of preplanned or irrelevant remarks. Above all, don't pseudolisten, which often damages trust and cooperation.

SUMMARY

1. Human communication is a complex transactional process that involves the generation, transmission, receipt, and interpretation of verbal and nonverbal signals. Effective small group communication is about sharing enough meaning that group members can coordinate their efforts to complete the task of the group.

2. Human communication is necessarily an inexact process because it is a complex symbolic, personal, transactional, and often an unintentional process. Messages always include both content and relationship dimensions. Relationship-level meaning involves responsiveness, liking, and power messages. Several myths help perpetuate misunderstandings about its process.

3. Computer-mediated communication poses special issues for group members if social presence is to be created and maintained in net conferencing.

4. During a communication transaction, a sender encodes a message by putting it into words and nonverbal signals; a receiver then decodes the message by hearing it, interpreting it, and responding to it.

Noise, or interference with understanding meaning, can occur at any time. Thus, understanding is facilitated through feedback.

5. Listening is a complex process that involves both hearing and, more important, accurate interpretation.

6. People have four general listening preferences: action-oriented, content-oriented, people-oriented, and time-oriented.

7. Several specific pitfalls to listening include focusing on irrelevancies, pseudolistening, sidetracking, silent arguing, premature replying, and defensive listening.

8. Active listening, when a listener paraphrases what the speaker has just said and asks for confirmation, facilitates mutual understanding.

KEY TERMS

Test your knowledge of these key terms by visiting the Online Learning Center website at mhhe.com/galanes11

Action-oriented listener	Listening	Pseudolistening
Active listening	Message	Sidetracking
Communication	Net conference	Signals
Computer-mediated communica-	Noise	Signs
tion (CMC)	Paraphrase	Social presence
Content-oriented listener	People-oriented listener	Symbols
Defensive listening	Premature replying	Time-oriented listener
Feedback		

EXERCISES

Go to self-quizzes on the Online Learning Center at mhhe.com/galanes11 to test your knowledge of the chapter concepts

1. Discuss the following in small groups, then share your ideas with the class as a whole: "How and where in the small group system can noise interfere with the process of communication?"

2. Select a topic (preferably a controversial one) and then discuss it in small groups while you practice active listening. A discussant may not have the floor or add anything new to the conversation until he or she has paraphrased what the previous speaker meant (both ideas and feelings) to the speaker's complete satisfaction. If the paraphrase is not accepted, the discussant tries again until the speaker accepts the paraphrase. One member of the group should not participate but should keep count of how many times paraphrases are accepted or rejected. Be sure to count every attempt to rephrase. Afterward, discuss the implications of active listening, how to improve communication, and how you felt during this discussion.

3. Prepare a chart for recording observations of listening behaviors and responses of members of a discussion group. This chart should have three columns headed as follows: *active listening, premature replying,* and *sidetracking.* With several classmates, observe either a live or recorded discussion. As you observe, note each instance of these behaviors.

    Now compare your observations with those of your fellow observers. What do you conclude about the listening-responding behavior of discussants? What was the effect of the members' listening behaviors on the group outcomes?

BIBLIOGRAPHY

Mader, Thomas F., and Diane C. Mader. *Understanding One Another: Communicating Interpersonally.* Dubuque, IA: Wm. C. Brown, 1990.

Roach, Carol A., and Nancy J. Wyatt. "Successful Listening." In *Small Group Communication: A Reader.* 6th ed. Robert S. Cathcart and Larry A. Samovar, eds. Dubuque, IA: Wm. C. Brown 1992, 301-25.

Stewart, John. *Bridges Not Walls.* 8th ed. New York: McGraw-Hill, 2002.

NOTES

1. Lawrence R. Frey, "The Call of the Field: Studying Small Groups in the Postmodern Era," in *Group Communication in Context: Studies in Natural Groups*, ed. Lawrence R. Frey (Hillsdale, NJ: Erlbaum, 1994): ix–xiv.

2. See especially Michael T. Motley, "On Whether One Can (Not) Not Communicate: An Examination via Traditional Communication Postulates," *Western Journal of Speech Communication* 54 (1990): 1–20.

3. Dominic A. Infante, Andrew S. Rancer, and Deanna F. Womack, *Building Communication Theory* (Prospect Heights, IL: Waveland Press, 1990): 8–10.

4. Janet B. Bavelas, "Behaving and Communicating: A Reply to Motley," *Western Journal of Speech Communication* 54 (1990): 593–602.

5. Glen H. Stamp and Mark L. Knapp, "The Construct of Intent in Interpersonal Communication," *Quarterly Journal of Speech* 76 (1990): 282–99.

6. Alfred Mehrabian, *Silent Messages: Implicit Communication of Emotions and Attitudes,* 2nd ed. (Belmont, CA: Wadsworth, 1981).

7. Joseph Capella, "The Biological Origins of Automated Patterns of Human Interaction," *Communication Theory* 1 (1991): 4–35.

8. Tyrone Adams and Norman Clark, *The Internet: Effective Online Communication* (Fort Worth, TX: Harcourt, 2001): 112–19.

9. Ibid.

10. S. R. Hiltz and M. Turoff, "Virtual Meetings: Computer Conferencing and Distributed Group Support," in *Computer Augmented Teamwork: A Guided Tour*, eds. R. P. Bostrom, R. T. Watson, and S. T. Kinney (New York: Van Nostrand Reinhold, 1992): 67–85.

11. Everett M. Rogers, *Communication Technology: The New Media in Society* (New York: Free Press, 1986).

12. Compiled from Larry L. Barker, Kathy J. Wahlers, Kittie W. Watson, and Robert J. Kibler, *Groups in Process: An Introduction to Small Group Communication*, 3rd ed. (Englewood Cliffs, NJ: Prentice Hall, 1987): 208 and Robert J. Johansen, J. Vallee, and K. Spangler, *Electronic Meetings: Technical Alternatives and Social Choices* (Reading, MA: Addison-Wesley, 1979): 113–15.

13. Judith N. Martin and Thomas K. Nakayama, *Experiencing Intercultural Communication: An Introduction* (Boston, MA: McGraw-Hill, 2001): 102–103.

14. Donal Carbaugh, "'I Can't Do That!' but I 'Can Actually See Around Corners': American Indian Students and the Study of Public Communication," in *Readings in Intercultural Communication: Experiences and Contexts*, 2nd ed., eds. Judith N. Martin, Thomas K. Nakayama, and Lisa A. Flores (Boston, MA: McGraw-Hill, 2002): 138–148.

15. Ibid.

16. Amarjit Chopra, "Motivation in Task-Oriented Groups," *Journal of Nursing Administration* (1973): 55–60.

17. Fred Jablin, "Message-Response and 'Openness' in Superior-Subordinate Communication," *Communication Yearbook ii*, ed. Brent Ruben (New Brunswick, NJ: Transaction-International Communication Association, 1978): 293–309.

18. Kittie W. Watson, "Listener Preferences: The Paradox of Small-Group Interactions," in *Small Group Communication: Theory and Practice*, 7th ed., eds. Robert S. Cathcart, Larry A.

Samovar, and Linda Henman (Madison, WI: Brown & Benchmark, 1996): 268–82.

19. Carol A. Roach and Nancy J. Wyatt, "Successful Listening," in *Small Group Communication: A Reader*, 6th ed., eds. Robert S. Cathcart and Larry A. Samovar (Dubuque, IA: Wm. C. Brown, 1992): 301–25.

20. Watson, "Listener Preferences," 270.

21. David M. Berg, "A Descriptive Analysis of the Distribution and Duration of Themes Discussed by Task-Oriented Small Groups," *Speech Monographs* 34 (1967): 172–75.

22. Ernest G. Bormann and Nancy C. Bormann, *Effective Small Group Communication*, 4th ed. (Minneapolis: Burgess, 1988): 120.

23. Ralph G. Nichols and Leonard Stevens, "Listening to People," *Harvard Business Review* 35 (1957): 85–92.

24. Curt Bechler and Scott D. Johnson, "Leadership and Listening: A Study of Member Perceptions," *Small Group Research* 26 (February 1995): 77–85.

25. Watson, "Listening Preferences," 271–75.

26. Charles M. Kelley, "Empathic Listening," in *Small Group Communication: A Reader*, 4th ed., eds. Robert S. Cathcart and Larry A. Samovar (Dubuque, IA: Wm. C. Brown, 1984): 296–303.

27. Watson, "Listening Preferences," 269.

VERBAL AND NONVERBAL SIGNALS IN SMALL GROUP COMMUNICATION

Central Message

Effective group members send and interpret verbal signals in harmony with nonverbal signals and realize that all their actions are potential messages to other members.

STUDY OBJECTIVES

As a result of studying Chapter 4 you should be able to:

1. Describe the nature and function of each of the three major components of language.

2. Describe the nature of bypassing, abstract language, and emotive words, including how they disrupt discussions and how to prevent or correct such disruptions.

3. Express your ideas during a discussion so that your statements are organized, clear, and relevant to the preceding remarks.

4. Explain three major principles of nonverbal communication.

5. Explain six major communicative functions performed by nonverbal signals.

6. Name and give examples of eight types of nonverbal signals, and explain how each contributes to communication among small group members.

For some months, a small neighborhood in Fresno, California, had been the site of vandalism resulting in damaged property. Neighbors were upset about what had happened to their quiet neighborhood. Taking the lead, one neighbor, a retired school teacher, contacted her next-door neighbor, a small farmer from Laos. Together neighbors decided to ask three other families to join their efforts to stop these crimes. A meeting was called one weekend evening in the hope that they could all draw up a plan of action. One neighbor entered the room carrying a stack of articles on how homeowners could best arm themselves. He took the chair at the head of the table and boldly asked when they were going to get this meeting going. Another neighbor shyly asked if everyone was present, only to be interrupted by the take-charge neighbor who proclaimed, "We have to stop those Hispanic gang bangers with the only thing they understand—force at the end of a gun barrel." The retired school teacher, thinking, "This guy is going to be trouble," asked him to please refrain from labeling all criminals as "Hispanic gang bangers" and noted that arming themselves was one option they would consider, but first they needed to hear from the rest of the group. At this point, the neighbor slouched down in his chair, threw his papers on the floor, and, pushing back his chair, isolated himself from the rest of the group. The small farmer then clarified that this meeting was not about reaching a decision but to hear the concerns of the neighbors and ask questions of a police officer they had invited to the meeting.

Group communication begins before any member says a word. We begin to form opinions about each other on the basis of what we see and hear. One member slinks into the room without looking at anyone and takes a seat in a corner: "Better not count on much from that one," you think. The next person, dressed in a dark business suit, strides confidently to the head of the table and deposits a briefcase: "Arrogant, will try to boss us around," you think. Members' clothing, looks, manners, where they sit, how much space they claim—all these and other nonverbal signals affect how relationships among members develop. Given the verbal and nonverbal behaviors of the boisterous neighbor in our story, what first impressions might you have drawn?

In a small group, the primary medium for exchange of information and ideas is the words members use. Although discussion is the heart of group interaction, verbal and nonverbal signals operate together to create meaning; they are indivisible. Higginbotham and Yoder state, "It is impossible to study either verbal or nonverbal communication as isolated structures. Rather, these systems should be regarded as a unified communication construct."[1] We artificially separate verbal from nonverbal signals only to help you assess the contribution each makes to *meaning* during discussions. At different times and for various reasons we may attend more to the words or more to the nonverbal signals, but almost *no* group communicating is entirely verbal or nonverbal.

In this chapter, we first present an overview of the nature of language and its relationship to culture, some things that often go wrong when we speak to each other, and how informed word choices and arrangements can facilitate the group process. The latter part of the chapter summarizes research and theory about the characteristics of nonverbal communication.

The Nature of Language

Any language—Spanish, Vietnamese, English—consists of a language (words) and rules about how to use them. In addition, each community of users of a language (i.e., co-culture) develops its own unique language system. Cultures, co-cultures, corporations, families, clubs, and other groups often have their own languages that identify someone as belonging to that group or culture. For example, theater students call the *waiting room* the *green room*. Gloria's stepdaughter Molly and her friends call boys they don't like *corndogs*. "We were slashdotted" is the Internet colloquialism used when customers overwhelm and thus ruin a popular site such as a restaurant after a glowing review.

The appropriate way to use language depends on the situation and we all have learned to adapt our ways of speaking for a variety of situations. For instance, we use a different way of speaking when we meet someone in a church, synagogue, or mosque from the one we use during a tailgate party at a football stadium. Physicians explain a medical procedure to a patient differently from how they discuss the procedure among themselves. We must use the way of speaking shared by group members if we want to be understood and accepted.

Symbolically, he is a chien, hund, cane, perro, and dog; or Wolf to his best human pal.
© Jean-Claude Lejeune

Of all the characteristics of language, the most important to keep in mind is that all *language is symbolic.* You learned in Chapter 3 that words have no inherent meanings. As symbols, *words have no meaning or reality apart from the persons using them and responding to them.* Human communication is symbolic, and only if speakers and listeners have approximately the same **referent** for a word will they have perceptual similarity. *This cannot be taken for granted!* For instance, our neighborhood group at the beginning of the chapter had to decide collectively what *they* meant by "taking action" to restore their neighborhood, not just what *one member* may have meant.

Even if discussants speak the same language, they may use the same word to refer to different things. Consider the word *food*. As illustrated in Figure 4.1, when Joe says, "Let's go get some food," his referent is a cupcake and soft drink from the nearest vending machine. Mary envisions alfalfa sprouts on whole wheat bread, and Herbie pictures a five-course meal at a fine restaurant. Obviously, Joe's words have different meanings to these three people. If this were a group recommending a break for lunch, clarification would be necessary!

Clearly, we communicate effectively with symbols only when we have similar referents for them. Imagine that the designated leader of your group asks you to keep a "detailed" list of what the group discussed. The leader means, "word-for-word account of the entire discussion," and you assume that

Referent

Whatever is denoted by a symbol or statement.

FIGURE 4.1 One statement, different referents.

"a broad description of major decisions" will suffice. Your group will have problems, even though neither of you was wrong. Each of you used the same symbol ("detailed") to refer to something different, which emphasizes the personal nature of communication—meanings are in people, not in words. To complicate matters, language is not static but dynamic; it changes constantly as our world changes.

Consider This 4.1

Our language has changed to reflect and give meaning to the influence of computer technology on our world. A bit of computer humor recently passed along on the Internet pokes fun at this change. Remember when a "window" was something you hated to clean and a "ram" was the cousin of a goat? "Meg" was the name of your girlfriend and "gig" was a job for the night. "Memory" was something that you lost with age, a "CD" was a bank account, "log on" was adding fuel to the fire, "hard drive" was a long trip, "mouse pad" was where a mouse lived, and "backup" happened in your commode. Now they all mean different things and that really "mega bytes"!

Language and Culture

Language and culture are intimately tied to each other in an ever-spiraling, reflexive relationship and together have a profound impact on shared understanding in group discussions. On one hand, language use helps to fashion the complex, multiple cultural realities you navigate daily; on the other hand, those cultural realities help give meaning to what you say and how you say it. We are all deeply immersed in language and as such there is not anything we perceive that is not somehow affected by our language.[2] A tenet of the commonly known Sapir-Whorf hypothesis is "The background linguistic system (in other words, the grammar) of each language is not merely a reproducing instrument for voicing ideas but rather is itself the shaper of ideas, the program and guide for the individual's mental activity, for his [or her] analysis of impressions."[3]

Consider This 4.2

You are an avid snow skier and have learned all sorts of terms to describe the varying snow conditions you might encounter. What might a list of such terms look like? Given all these terms, can you see how you are able to distinguish or perceive different kinds of snow compared to a group member who has never seen snow?

In other words, some researchers believe that language in fact *determines* how we experience our world; although such deterministic views have been softened, it is clear that our language systems help shape what we perceive in several fundamental ways.[4] How you behave verbally and nonverbally helps you identify as a member of any number of cultural groups, probably before you even say a word. In turn, your behavior is given meaning by placing it in any number of cultural contexts. Culture is something that is learned or a set of expectations and behaviors we absorb. *Gender* behavior too can be viewed as largely culturally taught behaviors. With little conscious effort we learn to become *female* or *male* in the same way we learn to become a Hmong or Latina. Let's take a look at how language and culture are interrelated by looking at the language use of females and males.

Language, Culture, and Gender

Gender

Learned and culturally transmitted sex-role behavior of an individual.

Sex

Biologically determined femaleness or maleness.

Learned characteristics and psychological attributes of masculinity and femininity is called **gender**, as opposed to our **sex** or inherent biological characteristics with which we are born. Researchers do not know precisely which differences have biological origins (i.e., sex differences) and which have cultural origins (i.e., gender differences); however, research suggests that many differences are learned, not inborn. Moreover, research findings are often inconsistent. Female and male gender roles have been changing rapidly in the past 40 years, so differences observed many years ago do not necessarily hold true today. In addition, current research findings will almost certainly be out of date years from now because our roles as men and women continue to change.

We caution you that although there appear to be differences in the way men and women communicate, there are far more similarities between the genders than differences. Whether men and women represent two distinct communicative cultures is a highly contentious issue. Burleson argues that to study gender as a culture inaccurately characterizes men and women as more different than similar, promotes harmful stereotypes, and misrepresents differences that actually do exist in the communication between men and women.[5] Thus, to conceptualize communication between men and women as "intercultural communication" is not the same as identifying the cultural variables in male-female communication; in fact, it may obscure them.[6] We cannot resolve the issue here but we want to introduce it to you so you remember that we still have a lot to learn about sex and gender in small group communication.

An extensive review of findings about gender differences has been provided by Stewart et al.[7] In spoken communication gender differences have been observed in verbosity, interrupting, and initiating behaviors. Men talk more and interrupt more, but that may be changing, as recent research with college students did not find these differences. Women initiate more topics but, in part because men provide more minimal responses ("uh huh," or "yeah") without elaboration, more topics introduced by women are dropped in conversation than those introduced by men. Women often ask questions to maintain conversations; however, men usually ask questions to acquire information. Women speak more deferentially and tentatively. In the past, women were reported to ask more *tag* questions ("It's a good idea, *isn't it?*"), but recent research does not confirm those early findings.

Most researchers propose cultural rather than biological or psychological explanations for the differences that have been observed. For instance, Maltz and Borker concluded that men and women seem to have different rules about what constitutes friendly conversation, about how to conduct such conversation, and what certain behaviors mean.[8] For women, backchannel responses (mm-hmms) seem to mean, "I'm paying attention to you, keep talking," but for men they seem to mean, "I agree with you" or "I follow you so far." A male speaker receiving "mm-hmms" from a woman is likely to believe she agrees with him, but a woman speaker receiving only occasional "mm-hmms" from a man is likely to believe he is not listening. Men often complain that women *say* they agree with them but it's impossible to tell what women *really* think; women often complain that men don't listen. Both complaints may stem from misunderstandings caused by two conflicting sets of cultural rules for conducting conversation.

The view that male-female differences in communication are primarily culture based is further supported by a review of recent gender comparison studies.[9] Mulac et al. characterize men's talk as direct, succinct, personal (heavy use of "I"), and instrumental (task-oriented). Women's talk is characterized as indirect, elaborate, contextual, and affective. Note that these differences are tendencies, not inviolable rules. The differences between men's and women's communication are attributed to cultural learning rather than biology. McCroskey et al. report that women display more facial and other signs of emotion than men.[10] In situations where males tend to sit or stand upright with their legs apart and hands on hips, women often clasp their hands together and fold their arms across their bodies. Women sit and stand closer to others, especially other females, than men do. Men sit closer to women than to other men, but require more personal space than females. Stewart et al. suggest that men's normal behavior signifies power and status, whereas women's conveys subordination.[11] Women display more signs of interpersonal liking (immediacy), men more signs of power (potency). Both sexes display responsiveness, although the nature of the responsiveness differs.

In the small group field, gender differences have been investigated more than other intercultural phenomena. In an early summary of such research, Baird reported that women were more expressive (paying attention to the relationships among group members, expressing concern for others, displaying emotions) and men were more instrumental (oriented to the task, factual, analytical).[12] More recent research indicates that male-female behaviors have changed, but some differences still appear. For example, Smith-Lovin and Brody found that men interrupt women more often than other men, but women interrupt men and women equally.[13] Men give more supportive interruption attempts ("I agree. We should . . .") in all-male groups, but the more women in the group, the less likely the men are to interrupt supportively. Men are less likely to yield to negative interruption attempts, women much more likely to yield to them. They concluded that men seem to consider sex to be a status variable, whereas women do not, but the findings are more complex than previously thought. Women do not simply give in to higher-status individuals; instead, an interplay of sex, status, group composition, and gender salience affects the specific interaction.

There are questions as to whether the differences exist. Verdi and Wheelan suggest that differences are exaggerated.[14] They found that all-male and all-female groups behaved the same, but mixed-sex groups behaved differently; group size seemed to be a more important factor than sex. Although early findings showed that men talked more than women, recent studies have produced mixed results. Mabry even found that women dominated group interaction and seemed to prefer interaction with other women more than with men, and that men showed subtle forms of resistance to a dominant presence of women.[15]

Some researchers have found that male leaders of small groups are more effective, but recent findings show that both men and women can behave in similar ways in groups, and neither sex is more effective than the other. Jurma and Wright observed that the leader's sex made no differences in members' perceptions of leaders who lost reward power during group discussions.[16] They concluded that men and women are equally capable of leading task-oriented groups. This conclusion is supported by Andrews, who noted that it is more important to consider the unique character of a group and the skills of the person serving as leader than sex.[17] She suggested that a complex interplay of factors (including how much power the leader has) influences effectiveness. Power was also a factor in Duerst-Lahti's study of successful, high-status businesswomen and men.[18] Contrary to the findings of others, women were not frozen out of conversations. The women talked more often but for shorter periods, gave more indications of verbal support, and freely challenged the men. They had power in the group, and their ideas and proposals were included in the final product. They seemed to have mastered the use of power just as effectively as the men.

Several studies suggest that, despite *actual* behavior, men and women are *perceived* differently. For instance, Carli found that men and women behaved similarly, but that women spoke more tentatively in mixed-sex dyads. However, they were more influential with men, but less so with other women, when they spoke tentatively.[19] Burrell et al. compared trained and untrained mediators of both sexes.[20] No male-female differences were observed in the behavior of trained mediators, but untrained female mediators were more controlling. However, the men, whether trained or not, were *perceived* as more controlling.

Shimanoff and Jenkins lament that an individual's gender alone can change how a person or message is heard and evaluated.[21] They stress that group members need to remember that they constitute a system; members' focus should not be on one person fulfilling the role of leader but on leadership as the responsibility of all group members. Thus, it behooves group members to acknowledge and challenge sex role stereotypes which, if left unchecked, can deprive the group of valuable human resources. After all, group members have been found to be more satisfied and productive when the most qualified members lead, and research has shown repeatedly that such individuals are just as likely to be female as male.

Biological sex often serves as a status characteristic that may affect women's credibility in groups. Propp found that, in mixed-sex groups, information provided by women is evaluated more stringently.[22] Information introduced by males was twice as likely to be used by the group in its decision-making process. This was especially true when that information was new and not known generally by the rest of the members. Propp suggests that biological sex is used as a status cue, and this puts women's expertise at a disadvantage during decision making. In another study by Taps and Martin, how female behaviors were evaluated depended on whether the group was sex balanced or lopsided.[23] In all-female groups, women who gave *internal* accounts for their opinions (e.g., "Based on my previous experience, I think . . .") were more influential and more well liked However, the reverse was true for male groups with only one woman. In that case, women who gave *external* accounts (e.g., "Based on research done by Dr. Smith, I think . . .") were more influential. In sex-balanced groups, the types of accounts didn't seem to matter. These findings have strong implications for how groups are constituted, especially in the workplace.

Other studies indicate that perceptions depend on factors other than gender. Canary and Spitzberg examined how men and women handled conflict episodes.[24] They concluded that the *approach* (i.e., using win-win strategies), not the sex, determined effectiveness, with each sex perceived as being equally effective.

About the only things we can conclude from this brief review are that gender expectations and behaviors are in a state of rapid flux, and that differences are largely a result of culture rather than sex. Remember, whatever is learned can be changed.

This discussion of language and culture has only scratched the surface, and is not intended to be exhaustive. It is intended to encourage you to think about your own behavior with an eye toward sensitizing you to ethnocentric behavior that may cause problems in a group. We will explore further the impact of culture on group communication in Chapter 5 when we discuss, race, class, and age. In the rest of this chapter, we will examine general characteristics of verbal and nonverbal signals in small group communication.

Problems Resulting from Language Choices

The difficulties that face group members from different cultures can seem insurmountable. However, you have also seen how easy it is even for people who speak the same language to misunderstand each other. In addition, we have pointed out that an important ethical principle for group members is to make a sincere effort to comprehend one another. Fortunately, understanding that symbols (including all words) have no absolute or certain referents can help you prevent a variety of misunderstandings and problems common in discussions. Three of the most troublesome problems include bypassing, lack of clarity, and using emotive words.

> My philosophy is, "Let's sit and talk about it. Let's figure it out, are we on the right track, are we not on the right track, what is it we need to do to get on the right track?"
>
> *P. W., Community Volunteer*

Bypassing

A misunderstanding that results from two people not realizing they are referring to different things by the same words, or who have the same referent for different words.

Bypassing   **Bypassing** occurs when two discussants have different referents for the same word or phrase but think they have the same meanings, or when they think they disagree but really do not, because they use different words to indicate the same referent. For example, one of us observed a group arguing about whether *feminism* was good or bad. One young woman, believing feminism meant that men and women should have the same rights, particularly in the workplace, could not understand how another group member could be opposed to it. On the other hand, the man who disagreed with her believed *feminism* meant that women should be preferred over men and should receive higher salaries than men because of past discrimination and underpayment. This group wrangled for 15 minutes before someone, listening carefully, said, "I think you two actually agree," and asked each to explain what *feminism* meant. When they realized they had been using the word to refer to different phenomena, they were then free to discover that they actually *agreed* with each other that men and women performing the same work should receive the same pay.

Bypassing is particularly problematic when discussants become self-righteous, with each believing the other is wrong or stupid. In the earlier example of the word *detailed*, if both you and the designated leader act as if the other's use of the word was wrong, then feelings will be hurt, as will the group's productivity. Our boisterous neighbor in our opening story insisted that "taking action" meant nothing less than using force to fight force. Instead, remember that it is normal for people to use words differently and that effective communication occurs only if discussants use the same code and definitions; they must be in agreement on the referents for their words at any given time. Whenever a symbol is used that could be misunderstood, ask for clarification: "What do you mean by *detailed*? How much detail do you want me to go into?" Taking a bit of extra time initially saves time in the long run.

High-Level Abstraction

A word, phrase, or statement commonly used to refer to a broad category of objects, relationships, or concepts; typically refers to intangibles such as love, democracy, and so forth.

Lack of Clarity   Two factors contribute to lack of clarity in discussions: abstractness and ambiguity. In discussions of ideas, many statements are necessarily **high-level abstractions**, lacking specific referents. Think of such terms as *justice, fairness, democratic, high quality, civil rights*, and so on. As we move away from terms referring to specific and unique items, the degree of abstractness increases, as does the potential for misunderstanding. Consider the following set of terms, each of which is more vague than the ones before:

The 2003–2004 Curriculum Committee of the Department of Communication

Departmental committee

Committee

Problem-solving group

Small group

Group

Living system

When the first term is used among members of the Department of Communication, the picture in the listeners' minds is almost certain to be similar to the picture in the speaker's mind. However, when we talk of a *committee*, any one of many committees could come to mind. Only terms that name unique objects are likely to be completely clear. For example, one member of a group discussing classroom procedures and policies said, "Lecturing is a poor method of teaching." Another responded, "Oh, no it isn't." An argument ensued until a third member asked for **concrete** examples (lower-level abstractions). The speakers were then able to agree on specific instances of effective and ineffective lecturing, and particular contexts in which lecturing was either a good or a poor choice of teaching strategy. The vagueness thus reduced, the group agreed on a less abstract statement: "Lecturing, if well organized, filled with concrete examples, and done by a skilled speaker, can be an effective means of presenting factual information and theoretical concepts. It is usually less effective than discussion for changing attitudes or developing critical thinking skills."

Leathers found that highly abstract statements consistently disrupted subsequent discussion, with the degree of disruption increasing as the statements became more abstract. His groups contained "plant" discussants who were trained to make abstract statements like "Don't you think this is a matter of historical dialecticism?" After such a statement, most of the other discussants became confused and tense; some withdrew from further participation.[25]

Lack of clarity is also produced by **ambiguity**, or communication that could reasonably be interpreted in more than one way. Several factors can cause ambiguity. Sometimes words can be interpreted in more than one way. For example, one of our colleagues once wrote in a letter of recommendation: "You will indeed be fortunate if you can get him to work for you." The writer meant that the person being "recommended" was a lazy employee and "you'll be lucky if you can get him to do any work." However, the recipient of the letter likely took it to mean that the future employer of this job candidate would be fortunate indeed to have such a promising employee.

Concrete

Low-level abstractions that refer to specific objects, experiences, and relationships; they thus help clarify abstract terms.

Ambiguity

Lack of clarity that occurs when a communication can be reasonably understood in more than one way.

A mixed message, one in which the words seem to imply one meaning but the actions indicate something different, can produce ambiguity, too. For example, the group leader might say, "Take as long as you like to consider this item," while at the same time looking at the clock and stuffing things into a briefcase. Such ambiguous messages are difficult to interpret and disrupt effective communication in the group.

Lack of clarity sometimes results when opinions are uttered in sentence fragments or in an evasive manner. Spontaneous participants quite commonly utter sentence fragments; they mention a subject, but never finish making a point about it, at least not in words. Sometimes, a nonverbal signal—a shrug, a facial expression, a gesture—completes the sentence, but anyone not watching will miss the point, and those watching may misunderstand. A fragment like the following can confuse listeners:

> Maybe we should divide . . . there seem to be a lot of issues . . . a lot of confusing bits and pieces . . . will make a lousy solution.

This statement could have easily been uttered directly and clearly, leaving little doubt in listeners' minds about what was intended:

> Maybe we should divide our investigation of how student-athletes are treated academically by dividing the issue into component topics, such as recruitment, advising during orientation, advising after enrollment, and monitoring compliance with NCAA rules. Otherwise, we may get all these topics mixed up, overlook some problems, and produce an incomplete or shoddy report.

People use vague language for several reasons. Occasionally, a group member will try to enhance personal status by using technical jargon the others don't use. Sometimes, this is done to conceal ignorance of the issue. At other times, the speaker may be trying to cover up or evade answering the question directly, such as a politician saying: "Revenue enhancement is very important, and we will have to explore every available avenue for overcoming the economic paralysis caused by the deficit. No one likes new taxes, and I can promise you we'll investigate all options." (We think that means taxes are going up!) When you encounter this, don't be snowed by a show of technical expertise or jargon. Ask the speaker to explain in terms you know.

Members can and should try to prevent the confusion that results from abstractness and ambiguity by asking for clarification. Remember that group members who are ethical strive for mutual understanding; this means they try to be clear and to help others make themselves clear. So, as a speaker, you help produce clarity by using language appropriate to the particular group situation, by providing specific examples to illustrate the abstract terms you use, and by making your actions and words congruent. For example, the statement "I think we can produce an excellent report, one that addresses all three major aspects of the topic, uses references no older than two years, and is grammatically perfect" tells your listeners what you mean by the abstract term "excellent." Encourage others to give you feedback, and welcome questions from other members as opportunities to improve mutual understanding.

When I go into a group, I'm not there so I can tell them what to do. I'm there so we can all figure out what to do and listen to everybody, and put it together as a group.

M.S., Vice President, Financial Service Firm, retired

As a listener, when you aren't sure what a speaker means, ask for clarification or for a specific illustration: "Jamal, you said we could take as long as we liked, but you seem rushed. Would you rather we table this discussion to a later meeting?" or "What do you mean by a 'detailed' report, Maria?" Paraphrase and ask the speaker to confirm or correct your understanding. Work transactionally *with* the speaker to create a baseline of common meaning.

Lack of clarity because of abstractness and ambiguity can also plague groups that choose to use computers to communicate with each other formally and informally. The use, for example, of electronic mail or e-mail can help groups reduce the time they spend in face-to-face meetings.[26] This can be particularly beneficial for groups whose members may not live near each other or are simply very busy people. Although using e-mail may not be beneficial when the group is actually making decisions, it has been shown to help when they are initially tossing around ideas and when they are ready to map out the execution of their project.[27] Composing clear and accurate e-mail messages is just as important online as it is face-to-face. How might you do just that? Table 4.1 lays out some simple rules to follow when using e-mail.[28]

Emotive Words **Emotive words** are words that evoke strong feelings in others; these connotative words recall highly pleasant or unpleasant images and experiences. Some emotive words are the fighting, snarl, or trigger words that produce strong reactions—unthinking, instantaneous responses by a person reacting to the word as if it were the actual thing. For instance, the man mentioned earlier with the strong negative feelings about the word *feminist* had an image of feminists as man-hating, bra-burning, controlling females with

Emotive Words

Words that evoke specific emotions, connote more than they denote, and serve as triggers for recalling pleasant or unpleasant experiences.

- When you want to make a strong point use asterisks (*point*).
- Book titles can be designated with underline marks.
- Avoid the use of special format codes such as color and boldface unless you know your group members can see them on their computers.
- Any acronyms like FtF (face-to-face) should only be used if they have been previously explained or defined—do not assume your group members understand them.
- Dates should be written out because 9/11/02 in one part of the world means September 11 and in other parts of the world November 9.
- Simplicity and conciseness are preferred on e-mail, not lengthy dissertations.
- Judiciously use your subject lines to cue people to the topic of your e-mail. This helps users decide which e-mails to read and which to avoid or save for later.

TABLE 4.1 E-mail rules for clarity.

no sense of humor. Powerful physiological reactions to words with highly negative connotations are normal, but they involve nonthinking responses. Recall that group members are ethically obliged to strengthen, not weaken, one another's identity and self-concept; therefore, intentionally using emotive words to hurt someone or to see if you can get a rise out of someone is not only inappropriate, it is unethical.

When a discussant, or something he or she values, is called one of these negative terms, the response is usually defensive or hostile. Constructive, open-minded discussion ends. But this doesn't need to happen. You can state your opinion, even if it is controversial and others are likely to disagree, in a way that does not deliberately push somebody's "hot button." Most negative emotive words have neutral alternatives you can use instead. For example:

Negative Connotation	Neutral or Positive Connotation
Egghead	Intellectual
Broad	Woman
Manipulative	Persuasive
Jock	Athlete

Why should we pay attention to such language? Groups can get sidetracked from their goals by hurt feelings and lost harmony. Remember, you want your ideas and opinions to get a fair shake in your group's discussions, but someone you have offended with an emotive word will be unable to consider fairly and objectively the merits of what you propose. So, using such language hurts the group's ultimate outcome.

Discussants must be sensitive to current usage and to the feelings of other group members; in other words, remember the *observer* part of being a good participant-observer. Sometimes the use of trigger words is not intentional. We might use a word and only afterward find out a group member was offended. These unintentional trigger words are referred to as **hidden antagonizers.** For example, a Caucasian group member with no prejudicial intention may say *colored* and a black member may respond defensively. Our black students have told us they now prefer the term *African American* or even *American to black*, which was the preferred term for many years. One discussant might say, "Nebraska has socialistic electric power distribution," meaning that such facilities are owned by the public and managed by a voter-elected board. Although *socialistic* is used appropriately to define a company owned by a social body (the citizens of Nebraska), some Nebraskans wouldn't take kindly to that adjective. *Publicly owned* would have been a better choice; it is equally descriptive, but doesn't carry the negative connotations of *socialistic*.

The use of sexist terms is a major problem for many groups. Terms that once were used interchangeably to refer to all people, as well as males specifically, are now rejected as biased against women. For instance, the word *man*

Hidden Antagonizers
Unintentional trigger words, not intended to offend, that do in fact provoke emotional reactions.

[handwritten margin note: ex: christ & the Samaritan & "living water"]

has been used in the past when the person referred to could be either male or female (patrolman, chairman, businessman, postman). Language is dynamic; it changes to fit changing circumstances. What was once acceptable is now inappropriate. Any word that implies a sex criterion for filling a role or performing a task may disrupt many discussions. Ivy and Backlund, experts in gender and communication, propose, "If people would spend more time figuring out how a listener will best hear, accept, understand, and retain a message and less time figuring out how they want to say something to please themselves, then their communication with others would vastly improve."[29] We believe this is a worthwhile golden rule for managing all forms of potentially hurtful word choice.

The worst form of stigmatizing is name-calling. Adrenaline rises as we prepare to fight physiologically and psychologically when called by such names as *pig, chauvinist, feminazi, whitey*, or *nigger*. Name-calling is unethical. It deflects attention from the issues before a group, destroys trust, elicits defensive reactions, and does nothing to promote effective group discussion.

What can you do to prevent or reduce the negative effects of stigmatizing? First, recognize that people have feelings about everything and these feelings are not to be rejected. When people or their beliefs are challenged, their concepts of self are also challenged and must be defended. Monitor your own behavior; be aware that your feelings and evaluations are just that—YOUR feelings and opinions, *not truths*. Take responsibility for your own opinions and express these opinions provisionally: "It seems to me that . . . ," or "I don't like . . . ," for example, makes it clear you know you are expressing your opinion only.

Finally, when you hear someone else express a trigger term, you can reduce the potential harm by restating the emotive statement in neutral form and inviting contrasting feelings or points of view. For example, a statement like "Doctors are money-grubbing pigs at the American feed trough and we can't get health care reform because of their greed!" might be rephrased as follows: "Jamisha believes that health care reform will be difficult because physicians have strong concerns about losing their current incomes. What do the rest of you think?" Replacing the emotive terms with neutral ones and soliciting a variety of opinions and feelings allow the group to examine the idea objectively, in a mood of skeptical inquiry, so the conclusion will be based on more complete information.

Consider This 4.3

Review the story that began the chapter. During the meeting one member asked the loud neighbor not to use the phrase "Hispanic gang bangers." How might the neighbor who used the phrase and called for the neighbors to arm themselves have stated his ideas in a less threatening manner, yet still showed how serious he was about his idea?

As we noted, stigmatizing and name-calling are unethical behaviors because they attempt to undermine other members' self-concepts. They sidetrack the group into arguments that deflect it from its goal and cause the group to reject what may be valuable information because it was poorly stated. As a speaker, you should be sensitive to other group members so as not to stigmatize them, their values, or their beliefs. As a listener, rephrase stigmatizing statements so that they are neutral. That way, if members disagree, it will be on the merits of the idea, not because of the trigger words. If a member persists in stigmatizing others, make it clear—politely, but directly and firmly—that such behavior is not acceptable.

Improving Communication by Organizing Remarks

The ability to speak in a fluent and polished style is not essential to being a valuable group member but, as we have already discussed, clarity is. Organizing your remarks makes it easier for others to interpret them as you intend. The following are guidelines for organizing remarks:

1. **Relate your statements to preceding remarks**.
    Your fellow group members should see clearly how your remark contributes to the discussion. Your statement should not appear to come out of the blue. You should connect it to the topic under discussion and, most of the time, to the immediately previous remark. For example, in a group investigating the loss of widely used library reference materials, Nguyen has just said, "A major problem for the library is replacing magazines with articles that have been cut out." You say, "Yes, that is a major reason why reference materials aren't available, and I *also* found out that every encyclopedia had articles removed. The librarian told me it costs $2,000 per year to replace them." Your remark will make sense to other group members because it relates directly to Nguyen's statement, it is relevant at this particular time in the discussion, and the point is clear.

    ha! that's great!

2. **Speak concisely**.
    When other members' eyes glaze over, shut up; you've talked too long. State your ideas simply, briefly, and clearly—once! We all know participants who restate every point several times or use 200 words for what could be said in 20. This hogs "air time" and causes listeners to tune out.

3. **State one point at a time**.
    Usually, you should not contribute more than one idea in a single speech because a group can discuss effectively only one idea at a time. For instance, if you say, "Many people are injured when bumpers fail. Furthermore, I think cars should be required to have antilock brakes, and there's also a problem of the steering wheel that locks when the ignition shuts off," one person might reply about the bumpers, another about the brakes, and a third about the steering. A confused discussion will result. An exception to this guideline might be if you are submitting a multipoint

report to the group, in which case it will help if you distribute a handout that lists or outlines the main points.

In this section we have described the nature of spoken language and several of the pitfalls to avoid during small group discussion. We now turn to an equally important component of messages, nonverbal signals.

Nonverbal Signals in Small Group Communication

Nonverbal signals include all signals *except* the actual words themselves. They are vital to small group communication. For instance, Ray Birdwhistell, an early pioneer in the study of body-movement signals, believed that only about 35 percent of meaning is communicated verbally when people are face-to-face; the other 65 percent is evoked by nonverbal signals.[30] Nonverbal signals supplement our words and tell listeners how to interpret our words. However, nonverbal codes are culture-bound. Most of what follows is about mainstream American culture and is *not necessarily valid* for people from other countries or from certain subcultures of the United States. We address the effects of culture in Chapter 5; here, we first consider general principles about nonverbal communication, then the specific functions performed by nonverbal signals.

Nonverbal Signals

Messages other than words to which listeners react.

Principles of Nonverbal Communication

There are three major principles necessary for understanding nonverbal communication. These principles concern the flow of nonverbal signals, their lack of specificity, and what happens when nonverbal and verbal signals contradict one another.

1. **You cannot stop sending nonverbal signals to other members of a small group**.
   This is often stated as "you cannot *not* communicate" and means that, in the presence of another person, you cannot help sending signals that others can potentially receive and interpret (although the interpretation may be completely incorrect). One of us taught a small group seminar in which one member, afraid that others would get to know her too well, decided she would not communicate. She refused to look at the other members, made few verbal contributions, and even turned her chair slightly aside so others could not see her face. Of course she communicated—that she did not care about other members and was "too good" for the rest of the group. Although this was not the message she intended, this was the meaning attributed to her by the others. You may not participate verbally, but you cannot be physically present without affecting the mood, climate, cohesiveness, and interpersonal relationships of the group. The question is not "Will I communicate?" but "*What* will I communicate?"

2. **Nonverbal signals are highly ambiguous.**

   Consider what a smile can mean: feelings of friendship, agreement with a proposal, amusement, acknowledgment of another, gloating over someone's misfortune, feelings of superiority, or simple liking. Looking at your watch might be interpreted as boredom, but it could also mean the person has to take medication on a fixed schedule or has another meeting in a few minutes. To prevent misunderstandings, verbal clarification is needed.

   ## Consider This 4.4

   In our neighborhood story, one of the members asked "shyly" if everyone was present. What are the nonverbal behaviors that are often taken to mean *shy*? Can you think of any other ways those very same behaviors may be interpreted?

3. **When nonverbal and verbal signals seem to contradict each other, people will usually trust the nonverbal signals.**

   A fellow group member, fists clenched and brows drawn tight, shouts, "NO, I'M NOT MAD!" Do you believe him? Marriage counselors are taught to look for these discrepancies, such as the wife who says, "I love my husband," while she shakes her head to indicate "no." There is good reason why we tend to believe nonverbal elements when there is an inconsistency: nonverbal signals are less subject to a person's conscious control. Few of us are able consciously to control sweating, blushing, blood pressure, tension levels of internal organs, and so forth. Most of the time in group meetings we are not fully aware of what our feet, hands, faces, and bodies are doing. Some of us have been taught to control our speech rate, vocal tone, or pitch, and most of us exercise considerable control over the words we utter. Thus, nonverbal communication is relatively spontaneous and easier to trust than the more easily manipulated stream of words. This is especially the case when the nonverbal and verbal signals conflict and less so when they are more congruent; then we pay more attention to the verbal signals.

   Just as nonverbal signals can be inconsistent with verbal ones, nonverbal signals are sometimes inconsistent with each other. For example, consider the group member who leans forward, nods at what you say, and seems to be paying rapt attention, but stifles a yawn while sneaking a peek at the clock. What are you to make of that? The pattern of overall nonverbal behavior is more important than any individual signal.

   Sometimes, inconsistent nonverbal signals result from the sender's internal confusion or uncertainty. For example, a group member may both like and dislike different elements of someone's proposal; this genuine confusion may appear as mixed signals in the form of a positive head nod with a frowning face.

Nonverbal signals supplement the words.
© Nita Winter/The Image Works

To avoid sending mixed messages, be honest and clear. If you as a speaker are confused, help other members interpret your remarks by honestly revealing your confusion. If you are confused or puzzled by the mixed messages of another, say so, and help the other person clarify his or her intent.

Functions of Nonverbal Communication

Awareness of the functions of nonverbal communication will enable you to respond appropriately to others and make your own signals more clear to them. Nonverbal signals serve six major functions during group interaction:

1. **Supplementing the verbal**.
   Nonverbal signals may repeat and reinforce the verbal message. For example, a person points to item three on a chart and simultaneously says, "Now look at the third item on our list of ideas." Sometimes, nonverbal signals elaborate what is said. For instance, a discussant may say, "It will be about *this* high when it is finished," and holds his hand 3 feet from the ground.

2. **Substituting for words**.
   Many gestures are substitutes for spoken words. Thumb and forefinger forming an O with the other three fingers held out stands for *okay* in the United States, as does the thumbs-up signal. If a committee chair asks, "Are we ready to vote?" and members shake their heads from side to side, the group will not vote.

"Are you sure*?" Non-verbal signals help us express emotions.*

© Syracuse Newspapers/
The Image Works

3. **Contradicting verbal messages.**

   As we discussed earlier, <u>sometimes nonverbal signals contradict what a</u> <u>person says</u>. For instance, a member might say, "Yes, I'll go along with that," but in such a way that you expect him or her to give no real support to the idea. In such a case, point out the contradiction and ask for clarification: "You said you'd go along with the proposal, but something about the way you said it sounded as if you really don't like it very much. What do you feel?"

4. **Expressing emotions.**

   As the previous example illustrates, <u>our feelings are communicated more</u> <u>often by nonverbal signals than by what we say</u>. Say, "I agree with you," in a variety of ways, and notice how each seems to indicate a very different feeling. A smile or nod can signal, "I like your proposal." Negative feelings are communicated nonverbally as well. For instance, some vocal aspects of anxiety are immediately detectable.[31] Particular voice characteristics are associated with both passive and active feelings.[32] Vocal qualities, posture, and facial expressions can all communicate feelings.

   When group members engage in computer-mediated communication like e-mail or even some forms of net conferences they are faced with the reality that they cannot see each other. We discussed in Chapter 3 how social presence is impacted by the use of computers. CMC lacks the emotional cues group members can normally get when they are face-to-face. **Emoticons** or <u>typographical emotional symbols are used in CMC to convey emotions in plain text</u>.[33] September 19, 2002, actually marks the 20th

Emoticons

Symbols and combinations of characters used in computer-mediated communication to help convey relational messages and social presence.

anniversary of one of the most popular emoticons—the smiley face :-).
Scott Falhman of Carnegie Mellon University created this emoticon as a
way to mark or indicate a joke in plain text. If you want to read about
how his original post was tracked down you can log onto
http://research.microsoft.com/mbj/Smiley/Joke_Thread.html.

Use emoticons in your e-mails to let group members to show the emotional tone of your remarks. For example, ;-) can mean flirtatious or sarcastic, :-D can mean laughing at you; :-* can mean a wry smile, and so on. Remember though that context can help you determine their judicious use.
Their informal use among group members probably will not be a problem;
however, if group members are e-mailing a business for information or to
ask questions they should not be used. Emoticons are generally considered sophomoric and should be avoided in business communications.[34]

5. **Regulating interaction**.
   Certain nonverbal messages, called **regulators**, direct the flow of interaction among group members. For example, such things as leaning forward, taking an audible breath, or relaxing nonverbally communicate
   turn-taking. Turn-taking happens almost automatically, without much
   conscious thought, but discussion leaders also consciously employ head
   nods, eye contact, and hand movements to indicate who should speak
   next. Favorable nods indicate, "keep talking," but lack of response or
   looking away may signal, "Shut up." Students raise their hands in classes
   to show they want to be recognized. Many of these regulatory cues are visual. A group that one of us observed had a blind member who could not
   see visual regulatory cues. He frequently talked out of turn or cut the
   other members' speaking turns short. The others were upset at what they
   perceived to be arrogant and self-centered behavior, but a discussion
   about regulatory cues helped the group discover the extent to which we
   depend on visual regulatory cues to regulate interaction. The discussion
   increased members' sensitivity to the communicative problems some
   blind people experience.

   > **Regulators**
   >
   > Nonverbal signals
   > used to control who
   > speaks during a
   > discussion.

   Turn-taking is problematic during computer-mediated communication.[35] When groups use net conferencing they can be engaged in synchronous interaction. Although they can "talk to each other" so to speak,
   they will be out of sync with each other. There is about a half-second
   delay between speaking and hearing. When you begin to speak during a
   pause the other will probably start speaking before you are done. This
   delay of feedback throws off the ability of those using net conferences to
   respond to each other effectively. This timing problem affects the use of
   humor in net conferences (there is less compared to face-to-face) and
   amount of interaction (monologues are common in net conferences).[36]

6. **Indicating status relationships.**
   Sitting at the end of the table indicates leadership or a desire for high influence in the group. A member who stakes out more than an average
   amount of territory at a table (briefcase, books, coffee cup, etc.) shows

dominance or superiority, as does suddenly getting very close to another, a penetrating stare, loud voice, or a patronizing pat or other touch.[37] High-status members tend to have more relaxed postures than lower-status members. On the other hand, uncrossing arms and legs, unbuttoning a coat, and a general relaxation of the body often signals openness and a feeling of equality.[38] Emergence as a perceived leader has been related to shoulder, head, and arm gestures.[39] Body orientation, the angle at which a participant's shoulders and legs are turned in relation to the group as a whole or another person, indicate how much one feels a part of the group and often that one is more committed to a subgroup than to the group as a whole.[40]

Consider This 4.5

Identify as many functions as you can of the nonverbal behavior displayed by the boisterous neighbor in our opening story.

Effective group members understand the principles and functions of non-verbal communication we have just discussed and use their understanding to be sensitive to nonverbal behavior. For example, one of us observed a normally quiet group member fold his arms in a closed gesture in response to a statement made by the group's chair. The chair, recognizing that this gesture could be interpreted in a number of different ways, asked the member to share his opinions directly with the group. It turned out that the member strongly disagreed with the emerging group consensus for several excellent reasons the others had not considered. The chair's alertness and sensitivity helped make this member's information available to the entire group.

Types of Nonverbal Signals

Interpreting nonverbal signals appropriately requires that we look at the *pattern* of signals rather than at just a single cue. At the same time, we need to be aware of the various types of nonverbal signals so as to avoid overlooking any. Those listed below are especially relevant to communication among group members. Proceed with caution in your study of nonverbal signals. There is considerable cross-cultural variation in the types of nonverbal behavior exhibited by people from different cultures.

Physical Appearance   Members of a new group react to each other's appearances long before they begin to judge each other's expertise and competencies. The judgments may or may not be correct, but they are formed initially from nonverbal signals that cannot be concealed, such as race, sex, physique, and mode of dress. We attribute factors such as intelligence and likability to people on the basis of what we initially observe of them. Of course, we may change our judgments later, but they are formed initially from a variety of nonverbal signals.

Cultural factors influence our responses to physical appearance as well. Americans apparently have a clear picture of what a leader should look like. We tend to be prejudiced against endomorphs (heavy bodies), whom we often perceive as lazy, sloppy, stupid, and undependable, but also as jolly and easy to get along with. Ectomorphs (tall and skinny) are perceived as frail, studious, and intelligent. Mesomorphs (muscular types) are more likely than others to be perceived as leaders. Height is particularly important. The taller a person is, the more likely she or he is to be looked up to, literally, as a leader; short people have to try harder to be seen as potential group leaders.[41] We often are not aware we have these prejudices, so it is especially important that we teach ourselves to react to what a person does rather than to physical appearance.

Space and Seating There have been many studies of how we use **proxemics**, or personal space and territory, to communicate. We signal our need to be included by how we orient our bodies to the group. The neighbor who wants to arm the neighborhood pushes his chair away from the group when another member of the group challenges him. A person who sits close to other members, directly in the circle in a flexible seating space, close to a circular table, or at a central point at a square or rectangular table signals a need to belong or a sense of belonging; a member who sits outside the circumference, pushed back from a table, or at a corner may be signaling a desire to withdraw. Sitting within range of touch indicates that we feel intimately or personally involved, whereas sitting from just outside touch distance to several feet away signals a more formal, businesslike relationship.[42] Patterson found that group members making collective (group) decisions sit closer together and in more of a circle than when making individual judgments.[43] Stacks and Burgoon discovered that closer distances (18 inches) make group members more persuasive and credible than distances of 36 or 54 inches.[44]

Proxemics
The study of uses of space and territory between and among people.

What is a comfortable distance varies from one individual or one culture to another. In South America, southern and eastern Europe, and Arab countries, people prefer to stand close, whereas in northern Europe, North America, and Japan, people prefer more space.[45] In fact, members of Arabic cultures feel reassured when they stand close enough to be able to smell their conversational partners. Westerners, however, are usually uncomfortable with such close contact and tend to back away, causing Arabs to mistrust their intentions.

In small groups, individuals usually try to place themselves at a comfortable conversational distance according to the norms of their own cultures. Naturally, this can cause problems if the participants are members of cultures with divergent norms about appropriate distance; they may interpret unexpected behavior of others as rudeness or aggressiveness. We know a New England native who becomes extremely uncomfortable in crowded spaces and

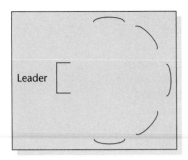

FIGURE 4.2
Typical spacing
between designated
leader and other
members of a small
group.

perceives as pushy those who try to close the space. On the other hand, one of us once had a friend from Alabama who kept moving closer to her co-workers in Ohio, who kept backing away. Finally, they began to joke about her "invasion of their personal space," and both she and her co-workers learned something about their own co-cultural rules.

Females tend to sit closer than males and tolerate crowding better. People of the same age and the same social status sit closer together than people of different ages and statuses. The better acquainted people are, the closer they tend to sit. Thus, members of a long-standing group characterized by high interpersonal trust would be comfortable sitting close together in a small room, but people just beginning to form into a group would need more space. Even so, humans are highly adaptable, so when a room or other constraint violates our preferred distances, we adjust, at least for a short time.

A member's status affects how others react to violations of space norms. Burgoon et al. found, for instance, that if low-status group members violated the group's norm regarding space, other members saw them as less persuasive, sociable, and attractive. In contrast, high-status members enhanced their status by moving closer than the group norm specified, and even more if they moved farther away.[46] Thus, it is generally advisable for you to follow group space norms rather than violate them, but if you are a high-status group member, you may have some leeway.

Leadership emergence in a group is related to space. Dominant people and designated leaders usually choose central positions in the group, such as at the head of a rectangular table or across from as many others as possible. Other members frequently avoid sitting next to a designated leader, so the circle ends up looking like the diagram in Figure 4.2.[47] This reinforces the leader's position, allows the leader a comprehensive view of the group, and facilitates the leader's coordination and control.

People sitting across from each other speak more often to each other than people sitting side by side.[48] However, when a group has a dominating leader, "sidebar" conversations tend to break out between people sitting next to each other. Thus, we can conclude that conversation normally flows across the circle, and leaders should sit where they can maintain eye contact with as many group members as possible.

Seating preferences have been found to vary across cultures. Summarizing research in this area, Ramsey explains that Americans show liking with close interpersonal seating, a forward lean, direct orientation toward the other, and eye contact. Leaders seem to gravitate to head positions, with high-status individuals sitting nearby. Similar behaviors occur in Japan, where the leader sits at one end of a rectangular table, and, the lower the rank, the farther away the seat. In some cultures, teachers and others need to be careful in assigning seats for fear of inadvertently violating cultural taboos about who may sit next to whom. In a few cultures, people sit opposite each other when they have differences to settle, but sit side by side in rows when eating or enjoying one another's company.[49] Most of what we know about seating patterns comes from research on Westerners; it may not hold true for people of other cultures.

Seating and spatial features of the group's environment, such as fixed-space permanent features like walls and doors, and movable features like furniture, influence the group's interactions.[50] In a large room, group members may choose to sit closer together than normal. If a group is meeting in a space normally used for another activity, the normal use of that space may change the group's interaction; for example, meeting in a member's living room may encourage informality. Meeting around a formal conference table encourages somewhat formal interaction, whereas meeting in a lounge with comfortable sofas does not. Sometimes, simply rearranging a group's meeting place can turn a chaotic group into a productive one. One of us advised a student committee whose meetings were characterized by general disorganization, repetition, and sidebar conversations. The room used by the group was normally set up for large assemblies, with a head table on a raised platform at the front, which the members used for their discussions. The president sat at the center of the long table, with the rest of the members sitting on either side of her along one side of the table. Only the members directly next to the president could both see and hear her without great difficulty. The group was advised to stop using the table and instead to rearrange the chairs in a circle. After just one meeting, members reported substantial improvement.

Issues of proxemics and group interaction take on a different meaning when group members are using different forms of net conferences like the ones we discussed in Chapter 3. *Paraproxemics* refers to the illusion of proximity individuals may have when they are using videoconferences for group business.[51] If the camera zooms in on a person, that may create intimacy; however, if that camera gets too close members may become threatened. Remember too that being tied to your computer can limit the space you have to gesture or move. Keep in mind that while proximity can be simulated in net conferencing it cannot be duplicated.

Eye Signals   Eye movements can signal disgust, dislike, superiority, or inferiority, as well as liking; the rules for eye contact are highly culturally dependent. For most middle-class white Americans, establishing eye contact is the first step to conversing. Americans use eye contact when they seek feedback, when they want to be spoken to, and when they want to participate more actively.[52] For many middle-class Americans, lack of eye contact is perceived as dishonesty, rudeness, apathy, or nervousness.[53] Burgoon reported that students given free choice of seating arrangements in small classes chose to sit in a circular or U-shaped pattern for their meetings so they could maintain eye contact with as many other members as possible.[54] Although a stare may indicate competitiveness, in a cooperative group it shows friendship and cohesiveness.[55] Eye contact is important, but must be interpreted carefully in context with other verbal and nonverbal signals.

[margin handwriting: Oculesics (eye contact)]

Americans prefer direct eye contact with their conversational partners, but in some cultures (e.g., most Native American cultures) this is perceived as rude, and in still others (e.g., Arabic cultures) intense staring is the norm.[56] Hispanic children are taught to lower their gaze to indicate respect, but this can backfire in cases where Hispanic children interact with members of the dominant American culture.[57] For example, white American teachers and police officers sometimes misinterpret a lowered gaze as sullenness. Many African Americans, too, tend to avoid eye contact, especially with someone of higher status.[58]

Facial Expressions   Facial expressions indicate feelings and moods. Without a word being spoken, you can perceive anger, support, disagreement, and other sentiments. Eckman et al. found that at least six types of emotion could be detected accurately from facial expressions.[59] People with poker faces, who change facial expression very little, tend to be trusted less than people whose expressive faces signal their feelings more openly. But even poker-faced people leak their feelings by physiological changes they can't readily control, such as sweating or blushing.[60] If group members show few facial expressions, watch for other revealing physiological signs.

Consider This 4.6
Computer-Mediated Microexpressions

The face is quick! Some expressions last a mere 200 milliseconds and your eye blinks are over in less time. A net conference camera connected to a good Internet connection can transmit 24 frames every second. This can drop to 1 second or less during a bad connection. The consequence to group discussion is that many facial microexpressions are lost.[61] What difference do you think this might make in a virtual group?

Be careful assuming that facial expressions, such as smiling, mean the same in all cultures. For example, a smile in Japan may be a spontaneous expression of pleasure, but it may also represent the desire not to cause pain for someone else.[62] A smiling Japanese may say to you, "I just came from my mother's funeral." According to Japanese rules of etiquette, it is extremely bad form to inflict unpleasantness on someone else; thus, no matter how bad someone feels inside, a cheerful face must be presented to the world.

Movements   The study of how we communicate by movement is called **kinesics.** We reveal our feelings with bodily movements and gestures. We show tension by shifting around in a chair, drumming fingers, swinging a foot, or twitching an eye. Such behavior may signal frustration, impatience with the group's progress, or annoyance. Alert group members will attempt to track down the source of tension by pointing out the kinesic signs and asking what may be producing them.

Kinesics

Study of communication through movements.

According to Scheflen, body orientation indicates how open to and accepting of others a group member feels.[63] Members turn directly to those they like and away from those they do not like. Leaning toward others indicates a sense of belonging, whereas leaning away signals a sense of rejection. Members who sit at angles tangential to the rest of the group may not feel included or want to belong.

When members are tuned in to each other, they tend to imitate each other's posture and movements. This behavior is called *body synchrony*. Scheflen observed many instances of parallel arm positions, self-touching behavior, and leg positions indicating congruity.[64] Several studies found that group members are more likely to imitate the movements and gestures of members with high status and power than those with low status.[65] We can infer who has power and status in a group by observing which members are mimicked by others.

In discussion groups, body movements often regulate the flow of discussion. For example, speakers often signal that they are finished speaking by relaxing and stopping hand gestures.[66] Scheflen reported that a speaker who is concluding a point makes a noticeable postural shift.[67] A listener can bid for the floor by leaning forward, waving a hand, and simultaneously opening the mouth.

Vocal Cues   Vocal cues, or **paralanguage**, are any characteristics of voice and utterance other than the words themselves. Included are variables such as pitch, rate, fluency, pronunciation variations, force, tonal quality, and pauses. Extensive research since the 1930s indicates that listeners attribute certain characteristics to speakers based on these vocal cues,[68] including such things as attitudes, interests, personality traits, adjustment, ethnic group, education, and anxiety level and other emotional states.[69] Tone of voice is an excellent indicator of a person's self-concept and mood. For instance, frightened people tend to speak in tense, metallic tones; anxious people have nonfluencies such as interjections, repetitions, hesitations, sentence correction, and even stuttering in their speech. Pierce relates the story of a woman from New York City who offended many guests by her bossiness at a party.[70] She appeared to be ordering everyone around, but Pierce observed that her words seemed perfectly polite and appropriate for the situation. It was her *intonation pattern* that was offensive. Her particular pattern, appropriate and customary for New York City dwellers, was perceived as domineering by persons from other areas.

How we react to statements such as "I agree" or "Okay" depends much more on the pitch patterns and tone of voice than on the words themselves. For example, sarcasm and irony are indicated primarily by a tone of voice that suggests the words should be taken *opposite* to what they seem to mean. Children generally do not understand sarcasm, and even one-third of high school seniors take sarcastic statements literally.[71] Sarcasm in a group is easily misunderstood.

In both movement and voice, animation tends to increase status within the group. People who speak quietly in a low key have little persuasive impact. They seem to lack much personal involvement with what they say.

Paralanguage

Nonverbal characteristics of voice and utterance, such as pitch, rate, tone of voice, fluency, pauses, and variations in dialect.

Vocalics

However, members whose vocal qualities change too extensively may be seen irrational, not to be trusted as leaders or credible sources. Taylor found, however, that excessive vocal stress was judged more credible than a monotonous vocal pattern.[72] You are advised to vary your vocal tone and use vocal cues to emphasize the verbal content of your remarks.

Cultural differences have been observed in the use of the **backchannel**, which refers to vocalizations such as *mm-hmmm, uh-huh*, and *yeah-yeah-yeah* that are uttered while another is speaking to indicate interest and active listening. We showed this earlier in our discussion of language, culture, and gender. In addition, Caucasian Americans do not give such backchannel responses as frequently as African Americans, Hispanics, and people of southern European origins.[73] This can lead to friction if members who use the backchannel frequently think those who do not are not really attuned and listening well, whereas the less active backchannel responders perceive their fellow members as being rude for interrupting so often.

Dialect may also cause misunderstandings. **Dialect** entails regional and social variations in pronunciation, vocabulary, and grammar of a language. Because dialect influences perceptions of a speaker's intelligence and competence, it can seriously affect employability and performance,[74] as well as credibility. Most countries including the United States, Canada, Great Britain, and Japan, have regional and social class language deviations to the "standard" dialect. We tend to stereotype individuals with nonstandard dialects. People who use *dees* and *dose* instead of *these* and *those* are identified as lower-status speakers and accorded lower credibility ratings. Speakers of the general American dialect are rated higher than Appalachians and Bostonians on sociointellectual status, dynamism, and being pleasant to listen to. Those who speak a French-Canadian dialect are rated as poor and ignorant in comparison with those who speak an English-Canadian dialect. Teachers tend to rate students who use dialects other than general American as less confident and more ignorant.

It is important to be aware of judgment errors that result from such perceptions. However, as intercultural communication becomes more widespread, cultures become increasingly similar in some respects.[75] Surprisingly, William Labov, a renowned professor of sociolinguistics, has not found this to be the case with respect to dialect.[76] He predicted that, because of the homogenization of the American marketplace, he would find a standardization of dialect in the United States. In a three-year attempt to create a "phonological atlas" of the United States, he found that our dialects are stronger and more distinct than ever before. Even areas of the country, such as the West Coast, that have not had strong accents show regional dialects. For instance, "bed" in California is pronounced "bad"; in the Great Lakes region, it is pronounced "bud," and in the south, "bayed." Communities show their distinctiveness by how they speak; individuals show their uniqueness by consciously varying their accents.

Backchannel

Nonverbal vocalizations such as mm-hmm and uh-huh that are uttered while another is speaking; partly determined by one's culture, can indicate interest and active listening.

Dialect

A regional variation in the pronunciation, vocabulary, and/or grammar of a language.

Time Cues   Few of us think of time as a nonverbal dimension of communica- *Chronemics*
tion. Perceptions of time are highly culturally dependent. Americans think of
time as a commodity to be spent or saved. People in Western cultures tend to
regulate their activities by the clock, but people in many other cultures act according to inner biological needs or natural events.

In the fast-paced culture of the American business world, being considerate of group members' time is important; Americans usually will allow only
about a five-minute leeway before they expect an apology.[77] People who
come late to meetings (except because of absolutely unavoidable circumstances) are judged to be inconsiderate, undisciplined, and selfish. Likewise, it
is considered improper to leave a meeting before the announced ending time,
unless some prior arrangement or explanation has been made. Forcing others
to keep to your time schedule is the prerogative of high-status individuals.[78] It
implies that your time is more important than that of the other members, and
marks you as inconsiderate and arrogant.

Let's take a closer look at time and culture to understand better why individuals from different cultures may treat time differently. Hall describes the
Spanish culture of New Mexico as *polychronic*, whereas the Anglo culture is
monochronic.[79] The Spanish do several things at a time; the Anglos tend to do
one thing at a time. The Spanish are casual about clocks and schedules; they
are frequently late for appointments and meetings. Anglos are offended by
such behavior. The cultures of Latin America, the Middle East, Japan, and
France are polychronic, whereas the cultures of northern Europe, North America, and Germany are monochronic.[80] In these cultures, time is treated as a
tangible *thing* that can be spent, killed, and wasted; time is perceived as more
relational in communal cultures, which integrate task and social needs and
hold more fluid attitudes about time.

Time also is a commodity in the group's interaction (i.e., "air time"). People can abuse this resource by talking too much or too little. Harper et al.
found that persons who talked somewhat more than average were viewed favorably on leadership characteristics. Those who talked an average amount
were the most liked. Extremely talkative members were regarded as rude and
selfish, members the group could do without.[81] Derber refers to excessive
talking as *conversational narcissism*.[82]

Touch   Touch is an important nonverbal dimension in interpersonal communi- *Haptics*
cation. It is vital to group maintenance in most primary groups and athletic
teams, but may be nonexistent in many American work groups and committees.
The kind of touching people expect and enjoy depends on their acculturation
and the type of relationship they share with others. For instance, touch between
strangers, other than a handshake, tends to threaten most Americans.

Touch between individuals may occur to show play, positive feelings, or
control, to get a job done, as part of a greeting or farewell, and of course we
touch each other accidentally. Jones and Yarbrough found that *control*

touches occur most often followed by positive affect touches.[83] *Control touches* are efforts to gain attention or request compliance and are most often accompanied by some sort of verbalization such as "Move over." Positive affect touches are most often signs of affection and associated with our primary groups but can occur in business settings. They found that some work teams may engage in spontaneous and brief touches to show support.

Touch among group members can strengthen unity and teamwork. Families join hands to say grace before a meal; football players pile on hands in a huddle; actors hug each other after a successful performance. The type of touch, as well as the setting, determines the reaction. Pats are usually perceived as signs of affection and inclusion. Strokes are generally perceived as sensual, inappropriate in a small group meeting. A firm grip on an arm or about the shoulders is usually a control gesture, interpreted as a "one-up" maneuver; among a group of equals, this may be resented. A gentle touch may be a means of getting someone to hold back and not overstate an issue. Many a group member has been restrained from saying something hostile by a gentle touch on the arm during a heated argument.

As with other nonverbal cues, people vary widely in the extent to which they accept and give touches. Andersen and Leibowitz found that people range from those who enjoy touch to those who react negatively to being touched.[84] For example, the handshake, a standard American greeting, is by no means universal. The willingness to touch hands suggests a belief in the equality of people.[85] This typically Western notion contrasts with the Hindu belief in a hierarchical society. Hindus greet each other by bringing their own palms together at the chest. Muslims, who according to the *Koran* are all brothers, hug each other shoulder to shoulder. The Japanese bow in greeting, but prefer to avoid physical contact. You can see how a culture's power distance (such as a belief in equality versus a belief in hierarchy) influences such things as the appropriate nonverbal form for a greeting, and also how easy it is for misunderstandings to occur in small groups with members of different cultures.

It is crucial that you touch others in a group only when you sense they accept both you and the touch. Although touching can strengthen team bonds, you must respect the rights of those who prefer not to be touched, and never touch unless it is comfortable for you. A forced touch is detectable and seems phony or manipulative.

On the other hand, it is appropriate to give a gentle pat as a sign of solidarity to those who like being touched, even in work-related committee and task force meetings. You should go easy on touching in secondary groups, but you need less diligence in primary groups, many of which have norms of showing warmth and affection physically.

Often the unconscious nonverbal signals we have discussed determine how much we like or trust someone. We all have a tendency to like people we perceive as similar to us, but we are unaware that our feelings are often based on *nonverbal* similarity.[86] It is important for us to recognize this normal tendency and consciously suspend judgments of others in intercultural settings where the same nonverbal behaviors have different meanings.

SUMMARY

1. Effective discussion requires appropriate use of language. If coordination is to be achieved, people must work to ensure that the same words refer to the same referents.

2. Language and culture are related in often complex ways. Our languages help shape how we encounter and give meaning to our worlds and our cultures help give meaning to our language behaviors.

3. Troublesome language problems and misunderstandings include bypassing, lack of clarity, and emotive words that stigmatize others, all of which should be recognized and avoided.

4. Because you cannot stop sending nonverbal signals, you cannot *not* communicate in the presence of other group members. By their nature, nonverbal signals are ambiguous. When verbal and nonverbal signals contradict each other, most perceivers trust their interpretations of the nonverbal rather than the verbal signals.

5. Language and nonverbal signals function jointly. Nonverbal signals communicate emotion, establish relationships among members, supplement and clarify verbal expressions, substitute for words, and regulate the flow of talk.

6. Interpretation of nonverbal signals is highly culturally dependent. Major categories of nonverbal signals particularly relevant to small groups include appearance; spatial relations, seating arrangements, and distances; eye contact; facial expressions; body movements and gestures; vocal cues; time; and touch.

KEY TERMS

 Test your knowledge of these key terms by visiting the Online Learning Center website at mhhe.com/galanes11

Ambiguity
Backchannel
Bypass
Concrete
Dialect
Emoticons

Emotive words
Gender
Hidden antagonizers
High-level abstractions
Kinesics
Nonverbal signals

Paralanguage
Proxemics
Referent
Regulators
Sex

EXERCISES

 Go to self-quizzes on the Online Learning Center at mhhe.com/galanes11 to test your knowledge of the chapter concepts

1. Listen to a recorded discussion or to a discussion among several classmates. Each time someone utters a cliché you recognize, write it down. Record your impression of any effect the cliché had on subsequent discussion. What did you discover? Share your findings with fellow observers.

2. Describe an instance of misunderstanding resulting from each of the following types of verbalization. You may do this from memory, direct observation, or recorded discussion. Describe specifically what was said and what happened in response.
   a. High-level abstraction or ambiguity.
   b. Sexist language.
   c. Ethnic or racial epithet.

3. In a practice group discussion session, all members should refrain from giving any bodily or vocal responses to the comments of others (i.e., no head nods, leaning forward, hand gestures, "uh huh" comments, facial expressions, etc.) for about 10 minutes. Each person should make at least one major comment. Then, for the next 10 minutes, everyone should react nonverbally (physically and vocally) as fully and completely as possible. Finally, talk about what you felt during each nonverbal response pattern and what this shows about group communication.

4. Watch a videotape of a small group meeting, but turn off the sound so the words cannot be heard. What do you think the members are talking about? What does each member's individual behavior seem to indicate? Watch the group again, this time with the sound, and see how accurate you were. Discuss what specific nonverbal behaviors contributed to your judgments.

5. Secure a play script. Choose a scene at random, and practice changing the meaning of the scene by varying the vocal qualities: pitch, rate, expression, tonal quality, and so forth. Next, practice reading the scene several times, this time keeping the vocal qualities constant but changing the gestures, distances between characters, facial expressions, and so forth. What did you discover?

BIBLIOGRAPHY

Andersen, Peter A. "Nonverbal Communication in the Small Group." In *Small Group Communication: A Reader*. 6th ed. Robert S. Cathcart and Larry A. Samovar, eds. Dubuque, IA: Wm. C. Brown, 1992, 272–86.

Andersen, Peter A. *Beside Language: Nonverbal Communication in Interpersonal Interaction*. Palo Alto, CA: Mayfield, 1995.

Burgoon, Judee K. "Spatial Relationships in Small Groups." In *Small Group Communication: A Reader*. 7th ed. Robert S. Cathcart, Larry A. Samovar, and Linda D. Henman, eds. Dubuque, IA: Brown & Benchmark, 1996, 241–53.

Burgoon, Judee K., David Buller, and W. Gill Woodall. *Nonverbal Communication: The Unspoken Dialogue*. New York: Harper & Row, 1989.

Condon, John C. *Semantics and Communication*. 3rd ed. New York: Macmillan, 1985.

Leathers, Dale G. *Successful Nonverbal Communication: Principles and Applications*. 2nd ed. New York: Macmillan, 1992.

NOTES

1. D. J. Higginbotham and D. E. Yoder, "Communication within Natural Conversational Interaction: Implications for Severe Communicatively Impaired Persons," *Topics in Language Disorders* 2 (1982): 4.

2. See John Stewart and Carol Logan, *Together: Communicating Interpersonally*, 5th ed. (New York: McGraw-Hill, 1998): 80–86.

3. John B. Carrol, ed., *Language; Thought and Reality: Selected Writings of Benjamin Lee Whorf* (New York: Wiley, 1956): 212–13.

4. Myron W. Lusting and Jolene Koester, *Intercultural Competence: Interpersonal Communication across Cultures* (New York: HarperCollins, 1993).

5. Brant R. Burleson, "Proponents of 'Alien Cultures View' Need to Come Down to Earth," *Chicago Tribune* (November 23, 1997).

6. Aki Uchida, "Bring the 'Culture' Back In: A Culture-Building Approach to Gender and Communication," *Women & Language* XX (Fall 1997): 15–24.

7. Lea P. Stewart, Alan D. Stewart, Sheryl A. Friedley, and Pamela J. Cooper, *Communication between the Sexes: Sex Differences and Sex-Role Stereotypes*, 2nd ed. (Scottsdale, AZ: Gorsuch Scarisbrick, 1990): 43–114.

8. Daniel N. Maltz and Ruth A. Borker, "A Cultural Approach to Male-Female Miscommunication," in *Language and Social Identity*, ed. John J. Gumperz (Cambridge: Cambridge University Press, 1982): 195–216.

9. Anthony Mulac, Pamela Gibbons, and Stuart Fujiyama, "Male/Female Language Differences Viewed from an Inter-Cultural Perspective: Gender as Culture," paper presented at the Speech Communication Association Annual Convention (November 1990), Chicago.

10. James C. McCroskey, Virginia P. Richmond, and Robert A. Stewart, *One on One: The Foundations of Interpersonal Communication* (Englewood Cliffs, NJ: Prentice Hall, 1986): 244–47.

11. Stewart, Stewart, Friedley, and Cooper, *Communication between the Sexes*, 92–106.

12. John E. Baird, "Sex Differences in Group Communication: A Review of Relevant Research," *Quarterly Journal of Speech* 62 (1976): 179–92.

13. Lynn Smith-Lovin and Charles Brody, "Interruptions in Group Discussions: The Effects of Gender and Group Composition," *American Sociological Review* 54 (June 1989): 424–35.

14. Anthony F. Verdi and Susan A. Wheelan, "Developmental Patterns in Same-Sex and Mixed-Sex Groups," *Small Group Research* 23 (August 1992): 356–78.

15. Edward A. Mabry, "Some Theoretical Implications of Female and Male Interaction in Unstructured Small Groups," *Small Group Behavior* 20 (1989): 536–50.

16. William E. Jurma and Beverly C. Wright, "Follower Reactions to Male and Female Leaders Who Maintain or Lose Reward Power," *Small Group Research* 21 (1990): 97–12.

17. Patricia H. Andrews, "Sex and Gender Differences in Group Communication: Impact on the Facilitation Process," *Small Group Research* 23 (February 1992): 74–92.

18. Georgia Duerst-Lahti, "But Women Play the Game Too: Communication Control and Influence in Administrative Decision Making," *Administration and Society* 22 (August 1990): 182–205.

19. Linda L. Carli, "Gender, Language, and Influence," *Journal of Personality and Social Psychology* 59 (1990): 941–51.

20. Nancy A. Burrell, William A. Donahue, and Mike Allen, "Gender-Based Perceptual Biases in Mediating," *Communication Research* 15 (1988): 447–69.

21. Susan B. Shimanoff and Mercilee M. Jenkins, "Leadership and Gender: Challenging Assumptions and Recognizing Resources," in *Small Group Communication: Theory and Practice*, 7th ed., eds. Robert S. Cathcart, Larry A. Samovar, and Linda D. Henman (Madison, WI: Brown & Benchmark, 1996): 327–44.

22. Kathleen M. Propp, "An Experimental Examination of Biological Sex as a Status Cue in Decision-Making Groups and Its Influence on Information Use," *Small Group Research* 26 (November 1995): 451–74.

23. Judith Taps and Patricia Yancey Martin, "Gender Composition, Attributional Accounts, and Women's Influence and Likability in Task Groups," *Small Group Research* 21 (November 1990): 471–91.

24. Daniel J. Canary and Brian H. Spitzberg, "Appropriateness and Effectiveness Perceptions of Conflict Strategies," *Human Communication Research* 14 (1987): 93–118.

25. Dale G. Leathers, "Process Disruption and Measurement in Small Group Communication," *Quarterly Journal of Speech* 55 (1969): 288–98.

26. Tyrone Adams and Norman Clark, *The Internet: Effective Online Communication* (Fort Worth TX: Harcourt, 2001).

27. Jacob Palme, *Electronic Mail* (Norwood, MA: Artech House, 1995).

28. Adams and Clark, *The Internet*.

29. Diana K. Ivy and Phil Backlund, *Exploring Genderspeak: Personal Effectiveness in Gender Communication* (New York: McGraw-Hill, 1994): 17.

30. Ray L. Birdwhistell, lecture at Nebraska Psychiatric Institute, Omaha, NE, May 11, 1972.

31. J. Starkweather, "Vocal Communication of Personality and Human Feeling," *Journal of Communication* 11 (1961): 63–72.

32. Joel R. Davitz and Lois J. Davitz, "Nonverbal Vocal Communication of Feeling," *Journal of Communication* 11 (1961): 81–86.

33. Adams and Clark, *The Internet*.

34. Ibid.

35. Ibid.

36. J. Tang and E. Isaacs, "Studies of Multimedia-Supported Collaboration," in *Information Superhighways: Multimedia Users and Futures*,

ed. S. Emmott (San Diego, CA: Academic Press, 1995): 123-60.

37. Erving Goffman, *Relations in Public* (New York: Harper & Row, 1971): 32-48.

38. Gerald E. Nierenberg and H. H. Calero, *How to Read a Person like a Book* (New York: Pocket Books, 1973): 46.

39. Edward A. Mabry, "Developmental Aspects of Nonverbal Behavior in Small Group Settings," *Small Group Behavior* 20 (1989): 192-203.

40. Stewart L. Tubbs, *A Systems Approach to Small Group Interaction* (Reading, MA: Addison-Wesley, 1978): 185.

41. J. B. Cortes and F. M. Gatti, "Physique and Propensity," in *With Words Unspoken*, eds. L. B. Rosenfeld and J. M. Civikly (New York: Holt, Rinehart and Winston, 1976): 50-56.

42. Edward T. Hall, *The Silent Language* (Garden City, NY: Doubleday, 1959).

43. M. L. Patterson, "The Role of Space in Social Interaction," in *Nonverbal Behavior and Communication*, eds. A. W. Siegman and S. Feldstein (Hillsdale, NJ: Erlbaum, 1978): 277.

44. Don W. Stacks and Judee K. Burgoon, "The Persuasive Effects of Violating Spatial Distance Expectations in Small Groups." Paper presented at the Southern Speech Communication Association Convention, Biloxi, MS (April 1979).

45. William B. Gudykunst and Stella Ting-Toomey, *Culture and Interpersonal Communication* (Newbury Park, CA: Sage, 1975): 124-28.

46. J. K. Burgoon, D. W. Stacks, and S. A. Burch, "The Role of Interpersonal Rewards and Violations of Distancing Expectations in Achieving Influence in Small Groups," *Communication* 11 (1982): 114-28.

47. R. F. Bales and A. P. Hare, "Seating Patterns and Small Group Interaction," *Sociometry* 26 (1963): 480-86; G. Hearn, "Leadership and the Spatial Factor in Small Groups," *Journal of Abnormal and Social Psychology* 54 (1957): 269-72.

48. B. Steinzor, "The Spatial Factor in Face to Face Discussion Groups," *Journal of Abnormal and Social Psychology* 45 (1950): 552-55.

49. Sheila J. Ramsey, "Nonverbal Behavior: An Intercultural Perspective," in *Handbook of Intercultural Communication*, eds. Molefi K. Asante, Eileen Newmark, and Cecil A. Blake (Beverly Hills, CA: Sage, 1979): 129-31.

50. Judee K. Burgoon, "Spatial Relationships in Small Groups," in *Small Group Communication: A Reader*, 6th ed., eds. Robert S. Cathcart and Larry A. Samovar (Dubuque, IA: Wm. C. Brown, 1992): 289-90.

51. Adams and Clark, *The Internet*.

52. James McCroskey, C. Larson, and Mark Knapp, *An Introduction to Interpersonal Communication* (Englewood Cliffs, NJ: Prentice Hall, 1971): 110-14.

53. Peter A. Andersen, "Nonverbal Communication in the Small Group," in *Small Group Communication: A Reader*, 6th ed., eds. Robert S. Cathcart and Larry A. Samovar (Dubuque, IA: Wm. C. Brown, 1992): 274.

54. Burgoon, "Spatial Relationships in Small Groups," 295.

55. R. V. Exline, "Exploration in the Process of Person Perception: Visual Interaction in Relation to Competition, Sex, and the Need for Affiliation," *Journal of Personality* 31 (1963): 1-20.

56. Donald Klopf, *Intercultural Encounters: The Fundamentals of Intercultural Communication* (Englewood, CO: Morton 1987): 177.

57. Stewart Tubbs and Sylvia Moss, *Human Communication*, 5th ed. (New York: Random House, 1997): 414.

58. Dorothy L. Pennington, "Black-White Communication: An Assessment of Research," in *Handbook of Intercultural Communication*, eds. Molefi K. Asante, Eileen Newmark, and Cecil A. Blake (Beverly Hills, CA: Sage, 1979): 387.

59. P. Eckman, P. Ellsworth, and W. V. Friesen, *Emotion in the Human Face: Guidelines for Research and an Integration of Findings* (New York: Pergamon Press, 1971).

60. R. W. Buck, R. E. Miller, and W. F. Caul, "Sex, Personality, and Physiological Variables in the Communication of Affect via Facial Expression," *Journal of Personality and Social Psychology* 30 (1974): 587-96.

61. Adams and Clark, *The Internet*, 119.

62. Branch Lotspiech, personal conversation, June, 1990.

63. Albert. E. Scheflen, "Quasi-Courtship Behavior in Psychotherapy," *Psychiatry* 28 (1965): 245-56.

64. Albert. E. Scheflen, *Body Language and the Social Order: Communication as Behavioral*

Control (Englewood Cliffs, NJ: Prentice Hall, 1972): 54–73.

65. Judee K. Burgoon and T. Saine, *The Unknown Dialogue: An Introduction to Nonverbal Communication* (Boston: Houghton Mifflin, 1978).

66. S. Duncan, Jr., "Some Signals and Rules for Taking Speaking Turns in Conversations," *Journal of Personality and Social Psychology* 23 (1972): 283–92.

67. Scheflen, *Body Language and the Social Order*.

68. N. D. Addington, "The Relationship of Selected Vocal Characteristics to Personality and Perception," *Speech Monographs* 35 (1968): 492; Ernest Kramer, "Judgment of Personal Characteristics and Emotions from Nonverbal Properties of Speech," *Psychological Bulletin* 60 (1963): 408–20.

69. Davitz and Davitz, "Nonverbal Vocal Communication of Feeling."

70. Joe E. Pierce, "Life Histories of Individuals and Their Impact on International Communication," in *Intercultural and International Communication*, ed. Fred L. Casmir (Washington, DC: University Press of America, 1978): 525.

71. P. A. Andersen, J. F. Andersen, N. J. Wendt, and M. A. Murphy, "The Development of Nonverbal Communication Behavior in School Children Grades K–12" (Paper presented at the International Communication Association Annual Convention, Minneapolis, May, 1981).

72. K. D. Taylor, "Ratings of Source Credibility in Relation to Level of Vocal Variety, Sex of the Source and Sex of the Receiver" (M.A. thesis, University of Nebraska at Omaha, 1984).

73. Peter A. Anderson, "Nonverbal Communication in the Small Group," in *Small Group Communication: A Reader*, 6th ed., eds. Robert S. Cathcart and Larry A. Samovar (Dubuque, IA: Wm. C. Brown, 1992): 278.

74. Klopf, *Intercultural Encounters*, 178.

75. Tubbs and Moss, *Human Communication*, 414.

76. William Labov, "Acute Inflection: Speech Patterns Buck National Homogeneity," *Civilization* (June/July 1999): 30.

77. Hall, *The Silent Language*.

78. Martin Remland, "Developing Leadership Skills in Nonverbal Communication: A Situational Perspective," *Journal of Business Communication* 3 (1981): 17–29.

79. Edward T. Hall, "The Hidden Dimensions of Time and Space in Today's World," in Cross-Cultural Perspectives in Nonverbal Communication, ed. Fernando Poyatos (Toronto: C. J. Hogrefe, 1988): 145–52.

80. Edward T. Hall, *The Dance of Life*, summarized in Gudykunst and Ting-Toomey, *Culture and Interpersonal Communication*, 128–30.

81. R. G. Harper, A. N. Weins, and J. D. Natarazzo, *Nonverbal Communication: The State of the Art* (New York: Wiley, 1978).

82. C. Derber, *The Pursuit of Attention* (New York: Oxford University Press, 1979).

83. Stanley E. Jones and A. Elaine Yarbrough, "A Naturalistic Study of the Meanings of Touch," *Communication Monographs* 52 (1985): 19–56.

84. P. A. Andersen and K. Leibowitz, "The Development and Nature of the Construct 'Touch Avoidance,'" *Environmental Psychology and Nonverbal Behavior* 3 (1978): 89–106.

85. Klopf, *Intercultural Encounters*, 178.

86. Walburga von Raffler-Engle, "The Impact of Covert Factors in Cross-Cultural Communication," in *Cross-Cultural Perspectives in Nonverbal Communication,* ed. Fernando Poyatos (Toronto: C. J. Hogrefe, 1988): 96.

THE EFFECTS OF CULTURE ON SMALL GROUP COMMUNICATION

Central Message

The United States is a pluralistic culture comprising many different co-cultures. This, and the fact that American business is becoming increasingly transnational, means that members of small groups must recognize, accept, adjust to, and welcome cultural differences in communication.

STUDY OBJECTIVES

As a result of studying Chapter 5 you should be able to:

1. Define culture and explain why knowledge of cultural differences in communication is important for effective group discussion.
2. Explain the advantages that can come from diversity in groups and organizations.
3. Describe six major dimensions on which cultures differ.
4. Describe specific ways in which cultures differ in language use and nonverbal behavior.
5. Explain why race, socioeconomic class, and generational differences may be viewed as cultural differences, and describe the differences that have been observed.
6. Describe the ethical principles group members should use to address and embrace cultural differences.

Martha, who grew up and attended college in New York City, had always wanted to work in California. During spring semester of her senior year, with her degree in computer science almost in hand, Martha landed a job interview with a software development firm in Silicon Valley. The firm's software development team, a self-managed work group, was responsible for its own interviewing and hiring. Members wanted to have a strong sense of any person they were considering for a position—Would that person be a good "fit" with the rest of the team?—and they had a good track record. Martha would spend an entire day with the team, attending their meetings, shadowing various members, eating lunch with them, and so forth. The team wanted to see how she handled herself in the kinds of work situations that were everyday occurrences for them.

Martha prepared carefully for her interview. She read up on the company, knew the kinds of software it was known for, updated her portfolio of college projects, and selected her clothes for the interview very carefully—new navy blue suit, matching pumps, white shell, discreet jewelry. She was ready!

Martha's first inkling that something might go wrong occurred when team representative Jorge met her at her hotel. Jorge was wearing jeans, a San Francisco 49ers' cap, and a T-shirt with a fish tie handpainted on the front. When they got to the company's building, she noticed that all the workers were similarly dressed—casually, with a certain irreverent style. Team members asked her to talk a bit about her background before they started their meeting, and she relaxed a bit. After all, she had prepared for how to sell herself. About five minutes into her presentation, Jorge interrupted to suggest that he take her on a tour of the building before the next meeting. They left, and the other team members began to talk. "Thinks a lot of herself, doesn't she," said Akimi. "She talks so fast I couldn't follow half of what she said," complained Scott. "She's wired pretty tight," agreed Montana. The group concluded that Martha would probably not be a good fit with the culture of this particular team, in part because she didn't seem like a team player. Within a half hour of first meeting her, they decided not to extend her a job offer.

This story underscores three important points we make in this chapter. The first is that cultural diversity presents a tremendous challenge to small groups because it forces members to pay more careful attention to their communicative behavior and to give up preconceived stereotypes if the group is to succeed. The second point is that cultural differences can exist even among individuals from the same country, who speak the same language, and have similar educations, as Martha's failed job interview demonstrated. Finally, cultural diversity represents a potentially valuable resource and should be embraced, not eliminated.

Information about culture fills textbooks! We present cultural information, where relevant, throughout this text. In this chapter, our goal is to present you with a framework for understanding cultural differences, but we do not pretend to cover culture in depth. Instead, we hope this framework helps you appreciate the difficulty cultural and co-cultural differences create in small groups. We also believe this offers you a tool for diagnosing what has gone wrong and how it can be repaired.

In this century, Americans of Asian, Hispanic, African, Middle-Eastern, and eastern European ancestry will outnumber Caucasians of western European ancestry. Called the "browning of America" by *Time* magazine,[1] this phenomenon will have a profound effect on *all* forms of communication. Transactions between people of different ethnic and racial groups require patience and attention to the communication process. You don't have to leave the U.S. for this phenomenon to affect you. The change, already well under way, will come to you; you will soon participate in groups with people whose backgrounds are markedly different from your own, if you haven't already.

> If you really believe in teamwork, then you're going to have to respect different viewpoints, because otherwise it's just going to be hollow.
>
> *J. T., CEO, Public Utility*

You may have heard discussions recently about the value of diversity in the workplace. The term *diversity* is often used in workplace contexts to refer primarily to gender and race, but we use the term to encompass a wide variety of differences, including ethnicity, race, age, social class, education, and sexual preference, among others.[2] Contemporary approaches to diversity go beyond tolerance of differences; they celebrate and capitalize on differences without necessarily trying to force assimilation into the dominant culture of the U.S.[3] These approaches demand sensitive and effective communication. Haslett and Ruebush, in their review of how individual and cultural differences can affect a group, conclude that without awareness and sensitivity, groups can experience highly differential rates of participation, poor management of conflict, and factionalism between in-groups and out-groups.[4] Good communication can reduce this so the potential benefits can be realized. Table 5.1 summarizes the potential competitive advantages that effective diversity management offers an organization.

Recent studies suggest that cultural diversity can be a real plus. Diversity can enhance a group's performance, assuming that the group's communication process allows members to integrate their diverse perspectives.[5] McLeod and her associates explicitly studied the effects of ethnic diversity on a brainstorming task.[6] They compared ethnically homogeneous (all-Anglo American) groups with ethnically diverse (Anglo, Asian, African, and Hispanic American) groups and found that the diverse groups came up with more creative solutions. However, they also found that the diverse groups had more negative feelings about their groups than the homogeneous groups. To us, these findings highlight the importance of studying the effects of culture; diversity can be an important source of energy and creativity in all areas of American work, but we must somehow learn to appreciate our differences so we can work together productively.

TABLE 5.1
Competitive
advantages of
effective diversity
management.

Resource acquisition	Companies known for effective diversity management develop reputations as desirable places to work, and thus can recruit a highly skilled labor pool.
Marketing advantage	As markets become diverse, a diverse workforce provides increased awareness and competitive advantage.
System flexibility	Appreciation of varying viewpoints produces greater openness to ideas and helps a company handle challenges and changes.
Creativity	Diverse viewpoints enhance creativity, decision making, and performance.
Problem solving	Diverse viewpoints lead to better decisions because a wider range of perspectives is considered and issues are analyzed more thoroughly and critically.
Cost reduction	Failure to integrate all workers leads to higher turnover, absenteeism, and so forth; effective diversity management saves money.

Source: Information taken from T. H. Cox and S. Blake, "Managing Cultural Diversity: Implications for Organizational Competitiveness," *Academy of Management Executive* 5 (1991): 45–56; cited in Susan Kirby and Orlando C. Richard, "Impact of Marketing Work-Place Diversity on Employee Job Involvement and Organizational Commitment," *Journal of Social Psychology* 140 (June 2000).

The culture in which a person is raised profoundly affects every aspect of that person's communication behavior, starting with the interpretation process we discussed in Chapter 3. Communication among people of diverse backgrounds (hence with diverse communication patterns) is challenging. Unfortunately, most people are **ethnocentric**: they believe their personal native culture is superior and judge everyone else's behavior by the norms of their own culture. But successful communication among culturally diverse individuals requires them to give up their ethnocentricity.[7] The software development team members who interviewed Martha couldn't get past her New York style, with its fast-paced talk and aggressive verbal pattern. In relaxed California, that style says "She thinks she's all that," but in New York, people are taught to promote their accomplishments and talents when given an opportunity. The team concluded, ethnocentrically, that Martha was not a team player because she promoted her accomplishments and spoke fast without pausing for others to jump in. They interpreted her actions through their own cultural filter.

The software development team isn't unusual. Many of us stereotype the behavior of cultural groups different from our own, then negatively evaluate that behavior. Speicher's analysis of a conflict between an African American male and a white female concluded that the participants' failures to recognize cultural differences contributed to the conflict and to the negative evaluation of the other person.[8] Leonard and Locke examined stereotypes held by African

Ethnocentric

The belief that one's own culture is inherently superior to all others; tendency to view other cultures through the viewpoint of one's own culture.

Effective groups, more and more, require sensitivity to cultural differences.
© Gary Conner/PhotoEdit

Americans about whites, and vice versa.[9] Each group evaluated the other negatively on the basis of the group's stereotypical communication behavior. African Americans had worse impressions of the whites than the other way around, but neither group's evaluations suggested a supportive climate for communication. Perhaps enhanced cultural understanding can begin to undo such negative assessments.

I love to have people of all stripes [on a team].

A. B., College Dean

In this chapter we try to sensitize you to ways in which other cultures and co-cultures differ from the "dominant culture" of the United States, thereby improving your sensitivity and your communication in groups. Instead of presenting a laundry list of cultures and the characteristics associated with each (a lengthy catalog!), we focus primarily on several broad dimensions on which cultures differ. We offer three important caveats. First, from the vast and growing field of intercultural communication, we present only information we believe to be most relevant to small group communication. Second, in many instances we are overgeneralizing. For example, when we say that "white, middle-class Americans prefer direct eye contact," we know there is a lot of variation in the preferences of white, middle-class Americans. We urge you to remember that sometimes there will be as much within-group as between-group variation, especially for pluralistic cultures such as the United States. Third, there has been relatively little research on intercultural communication *within small groups*. Although much is known about how Mexicans and Arabs behave within their own cultures, almost nothing is known about how Mexicans and Arabs behave when they work *together* in the same small group.

In many instances, we are making logical, best guesses about what happens when individuals of different cultures must interact within the same setting. We rely heavily on findings from studies of interpersonal intercultural communication, applying them to small group settings. We turn now to a definition of terms important to your understanding of the effects of culture on small group communication.

We have already used several terms in common usage, but now we define them according to our usage in this book. These terms are *culture, cultural identity, co-culture, intracultural*, and *intercultural communication*.

What Is Culture?

Culture refers to the pattern of values, beliefs, symbols (including language), norms, and behaviors shared by an identifiable group of individuals. During enculturation, or becoming part of a culture, you are taught how to perceive the world, to think, to communicate, and to behave. The teaching is done both formally and informally as you learn the lifestyle of the family and community. Small primary groups, starting with the family, are vital to this process and are the chief way individuals become enculturated. This process happens so gradually and automatically that, unless something happens to make us question our behavior, we rarely are aware of how culture affects us; our own culture's effect on us is invisible, unless we make a point of looking for it. **Cultural identity** refers to the degree to which a person learns, accepts, and identifies with the symbols, meanings, and standards of behavior common to a particular group.[10] Individuals are *taught* such things as language, how and when to speak, how to perceive the world, what is and is not appropriate behavior, and so forth. As with most of us, members of Martha's interview team were oblivious to how their cultural identities affected both their own communication behavior and their interpretation of Martha's behavior.

Our definition of *culture* is intentionally broad. *Culture* as we define it refers to *any* group of people with a shared identity. For example, a *cultural grouping* can refer to ethnicity (black, white, Hispanic, Greek), a professional grouping (college students, communication professors, nurses, accountants), an interest grouping (hunters, duplicate bridge players), or even socioeconomic class (working class, middle class). In short, any symbol system that is "bounded and salient" to individuals may be termed a culture.[11]

Sometimes a grouping that sees itself as distinct, but is part of a larger culture, is termed a **co-culture**. We use the term *co-culture* rather than the more common *subculture* because we agree with Orbe's argument that *subculture*, which simply refers to size—a smaller grouping within a larger culture—can also imply inferiority.[12] Co-culture, on the other hand, reminds us that the "United States is a country of many cultures, each of which exists simultaneously within, as well as apart from, other cultures . . . [and] no one culture is inherently superior over co-existing cultures,"[13] although one culture may dominate. Co-cultural groupings can form on the basis of any shared identity.

Culture

The patterns of values, beliefs, symbols, norms, procedures, and behaviors that have been historically transmitted to and are shared by a given group of persons.

Cultural Identity

The identification with and acceptance of a particular group's shared symbols, meanings, norms, and rules for conduct.

Co-culture

A grouping that sees itself as distinct but is also part of a larger grouping.

For example, your coauthors consider themselves to be part of the co-culture *professional educators*. We share certain values and beliefs with other professional educators that are very important to us: a belief in the value of education, similar ideas about what does and does not constitute a good education, a desire to place education high on a list of funding priorities, and so forth. When we interact with professional educators (at our universities, at professional conferences, during chance encounters on airplanes, etc.), we take these beliefs for granted—we accept them as "givens." Other examples of co-cultural groupings include rural and urban; white collar and blue collar; eastern, southern, western, and midwestern United States; Roman Catholic and Jewish; and many more.

Each of us belongs to several different co-cultures simultaneously. For example, Gloria is white, middle-class, Greek American; Kathy is white, middle-class, a military brat; Jack is white, middle-class, a shepherd. Whether a particular co-cultural identification is important in a given circumstance depends on the specific features of that circumstance. Gloria's identification as a Greek American is more salient when she attends festivals where there is Greek food and dancing than when she attends professional conferences. Kathy thinks of herself as a military brat when she talks about how much she has moved or when she attends high school reunions with those who went to Wagner High School on Clark Air Force Base in the Philippines.

It is important to understand your culture because it affects *everything* you do, particularly your communication behavior.[14] The behaviors and attitudes we adopt from our culture are learned, not innate, but they are lasting. Cultures do change, but slowly. During **intracultural communication** (among individuals from the same culture or co-culture), much of the communication behavior can be taken for granted. But during **intercultural communication** (among individuals from different cultures or co-cultures), participants must be alert to the added potential for misunderstanding.

> Know yourself more than anything else.
>
> *P. B., City Administrator*

Our opening story of Martha was chosen to emphasize that intercultural communication is not limited to encounters between people from different countries. An Anglo American manager talking to an Arabic counterpart certainly represents an instance of intercultural communication, but so does a native of Cupertino, California, talking to someone from New York City. In fact, a conversation between people from different countries can be more *intra-* than *inter*cultural (e.g., as between an Anglo American and an Anglo Canadian).

In a sense, *every* act of communication has intercultural elements because each individual is a *unique* blend of learned behaviors.[15] Intercultural communication is a continuum with *intercultural* communication at one end and *intracultural* communication at the other.[16] As is shown in Figure 5.1, all encounters are more or less intercultural, but none is purely one or the other. Thus, communication among members of an Inuit family living in a remote

Intracultural Communication

Interaction between and among individuals from the same culture or subculture.

Intercultural Communication

Interaction between and among individuals from different cultures or co-cultures.

FIGURE 5.1
Degrees of
intercultural
communication.

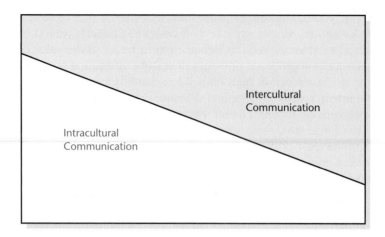

Intercultural
Communication

Intracultural
Communication

area of Alaska will be almost purely *intra*cultural, whereas a conference of Japanese and American legislators who do not speak each other's languages would be extremely *inter*cultural. The more intercultural communication becomes, the greater the potential for communication malfunctions.

Now that we have introduced you to these important terms, we turn to a discussion of six broad characteristics that differ from culture to culture and significantly influence group members' communication behaviors. As mentioned earlier, this information is not a list of characteristics and the cultures associated with them, although we provide cultural examples to illustrate. It is a framework to help you understand where communication differences originate, diagnose misunderstandings, and decide how you will act.

Cultural Characteristics That Affect Communication

A number of researchers have investigated particular characteristics that differ across cultures.[17] We focus on six that are especially relevant for communication in small groups. These are *worldview; individualism versus collectivism; power distance; uncertainty avoidance; masculinity versus femininity;* and *high- versus low-context communication.* As with intra- and intercultural communication, each dimension will be thought of as a continuum. We describe each end of the continuum, but recognize that cultures do not fall exclusively at one end or the other. Cultures are complex; they exhibit the following characteristics in varying degrees. These characteristics are summarized in Table 5.2.

Worldview

One's beliefs about
the nature of life, the
purpose of life, and
one's relation to the
cosmos.

Worldview

Worldview encompasses how we perceive the nature of the world around us, our relationship to it, and the purpose of life. Every culture has a worldview that serves to explain why things are the way they are and where humans fit into the grand scheme of life; this cultural characteristic is highly resistant to change. For example, people from cultures that believe fate controls all human events are more likely to "go with the flow" because they believe their destinies are predetermined. They are not likely suddenly to become "movers and shakers" of events. In contrast, people from cultures that believe people control events will respond quite differently. Some Asian and many Native American cultures are much more likely to conceive of life as a river that flows, making it more appropriate for individuals to flow with the river than to try to navigate against it. North Americans and some western Europeans have the opposite conception. They say things like, "If at first you don't succeed, try, try again," indicating a worldview that hard work, with or against the river, is valued. In terms of communication behavior in small groups, developing *patience* and allowing discussion to proceed at its own pace without forcing it to a conclusion may be more natural in a go-with-the-flow culture, but difficult for many Americans who want to get to the point in a hurry so they can get things done. A culture's worldview is an all-emcompassing dimension, like an umbrella, that affects that culture's activity orientation, values, customs, and beliefs.

Consider This 5.1

There is value to being patient and "going with the flow," *and* there is value to "making things happen." How do you think a group could potentially benefit from each worldview? How might a group's decisions be affected positively from having both worldviews represented in the group?

Activity Orientation **Activity orientation** refers to whether a culture emphasizes *being* or *doing*.[18] Some cultures (e.g., the Hopi) emphasize spontaneity, being "in the moment," and being in harmony with nature. In contrast, the majority culture of the United States represents a *doing* orientation, where activities that produce tangible accomplishments are highly valued. For instance, Americans usually ask, "What do you do for a living?" when they first meet someone. We tend to define people more by what they *do* or what they have achieved than by what they *are*. When members from both *doing* and *being* cultures meet in a group, communication may be difficult and consensus decisions may be impossible.

Activity Orientation

The extent to which a culture emphasizes doing or being, taking charge or going with the flow.

Values Worldview also affects values. The horrible events of September 11, 2001, brought to the forefront value differences between Americans and some Middle Easterners, and aroused the curiosity of many Americans about Arabic culture. The following story, highlighting differences between American and Arab values, exemplifies the types of value differences that can create communication challenges in a small group. Imagine that a man is in a small boat with his mother, wife, and child when it capsizes. Only he can swim, and he can save only one of the other three people. Whom should he save? Rubenstein found that *all* the Arabs he asked would save the mother because a man can always get another wife and child, but he has only one mother. Of 100 American college freshmen, 60 said they would save the wife and 40 the child. They laughed at the idea of saving the mother.[19] Such fundamental differences in values may be impossible to resolve.

Customs and Beliefs   The customs, habits, and beliefs of a culture are also affected by that culture's worldview and values. Thus, in a culture where one's purpose in life is associated with bringing honor and good fortune to one's family, communication is likely to center on one's family. A Nigerian student told us how unfriendly he thought Americans were when he first came to the United States. His friends on campus said "Hello" to him and kept walking. In Nigeria, the friends would have stopped, inquired about his mother, father, brothers and sisters, aunts and uncles, and so forth. They would have had a long conversation about their respective families. Imagine that Nigerian student in a group of focused, "get down to business" American students!

Individualism versus Collectivism

Individualistic Culture

Culture in which the needs and wishes of the individual predominate over the needs of the group.

Collectivist Culture

A culture in which the needs and wishes of the group predominate over the needs of any one individual.

Some cultures place higher value on individual goals, but others value group goals more. Gudykunst and Ting-Toomey note that in **individualistic cultures** the development of the individual is foremost, even when this is at the expense of the group, whereas in **collectivist cultures** the needs of the group are more important, with individuals expected to conform to the group.[20] As is suggested by the terms, conformity is valued in collectivist cultures, but diversity and dissent are more esteemed in individualistic cultures. People in the United States admire the person who "marches to a different drummer." The identity of *I* takes precedence over *we*, so we give high priority to *self*-development, *self*-actualization, and individual initiative and achievement. We go so far as to encourage group members to leave a group if they feel their individual values, beliefs, and preferences are being compromised. In contrast to this are most Asian and Native American cultures. For example, a Chinese proverb states, "The nail that sticks up is pounded down." This means that if a member is standing out from the group, the group has the right—even the obligation—to force the individual to conform. In collectivist cultures, the goals, wishes, and opinions of the in-group (the dominant group) always prevail; such cultures value cooperation within the group and slow consensus building rather than direct confrontation in which individual opinions are debated.

This distinction between collectivist and individualistic cultures is important in mixed-culture small groups, primarily because of the effect on communication behaviors. For example, members of individualistic cultures, who see themselves as relatively more independent than interdependent, value verbal clarity more than members of collectivist cultures.[21] Recent research has found, in bargaining situations, the more collectivist the buyer and seller were, the higher the joint profits they earned.[22] The seller's collectivism was the key factor. You may have noted that much of the advice we give in this text about speaking clearly, concisely, and to the point reflects our own enculturation into the mainstream, individualistic culture of the United States.

Consider This 5.2

Brislin et al. provide an example of the collectivist versus individualistic cross-cultural theme.[23] Native Hawaiian children come from a collective culture. A Caucasian teacher from the individualistic mainland found that her attempts to motivate the children by having them compete against each other for prizes were not working. How do you analyze this situation? What could you do to remedy it?

Power Distance

Cultures differ with respect to their preferred **power distance**, which is the degree to which power or status differences are minimized or maximized.[24] In low power-distance cultures, such as Austria, Israel, and New Zealand, people believe that power should be distributed equally. The United States is a relatively low power-distance culture. We prize equality under the law; our Declaration of Independence asserts that "all men are created equal." We regard it as unfair for some to receive privileges accorded to them only by accident of birth instead of being earned by hard work or merit. In contrast, high power-distance cultures, such as the Philippines, Mexico, Iraq, and India, generally have a rigid, hierarchical status system and prefer large power distances. In high power-distance cultures, people believe that each person has his or her rightful place, that leaders or others with power should have special privileges, and that the authority of those with power should not be questioned.

Hofstede noted that larger cultures usually develop higher power distances. Larger groups need more formalized leadership and communication structures to maintain themselves than smaller groups do. Power tends to be concentrated in the hands of a few people, with others accepting the fairly rigid hierarchy as normal and desirable.[25]

Lustig and Cassotta have summarized research that examines how power distance might affect small group communication.[26] They found that power distance is related to leadership styles and preferences, conformity, and discussion procedures. High power-distance cultures value authoritarian, directive leadership, whereas low power-distance cultures value participative, democratic leadership. We Americans tend to assume, ethnocentrically, that everyone wants a chance to participate in decisions that affect them. That reflects our deeply held cultural values stemming from our relatively low power-distance culture. However, an American group leader trying to use a participative leadership style in a group of Mexicans or Filipinos is likely to be seen as inept or incompetent. Power distance is also related to the discussion procedures members

Power Distance

The degree to which a culture emphasizes status and power differences among members of the culture; status differences are minimized in low power distance cultures and emphasized in high power-distance cultures.

prefer. Participation in group discussions and decisions is preferred by persons who believe their individual opinions should be valued regardless of status (i.e., low power-distance cultures), but decision making by the leader, with minimal participation from the group, is the norm in high power-distance cultures. People from high power-distance cultures believe it is appropriate for low-status group members to conform to the desires of high-status members; however, in low power-distance cultures, members will be less likely to conform.

Uncertainty Avoidance

Uncertainty Avoidance

The degree to which members of a culture avoid or embrace uncertainty and ambiguity; cultures high in uncertainty avoidance prefer clear rules for interaction, whereas cultures low in uncertainty avoidance are comfortable without guidelines.

Uncertainty avoidance refers to how well people in a particular culture tolerate ambiguity and uncertainty.[27] Does unpredictability make us anxious or eager? Low uncertainty avoidance cultures have a high tolerance for ambiguity, are more willing to take risks, have less rigid rules, and accept a certain amount of deviance and dissent. Great Britain, Sweden, and Hong Kong are such countries. At the other end of the continuum are countries such as Greece, Japan, and Belgium, where people prefer to avoid ambiguous situations. These cultures establish rules and clear-cut norms of behavior that help individuals feel secure. All members of the culture are expected to behave in accordance with the standards of behavior, and dissent is not appreciated. People from such cultures often have a strong internalized work ethic. The United States is a fairly low uncertainty avoidance culture.

When low and high uncertainty avoidance individuals come together, they may threaten or frighten each other.[28] Low uncertainty avoidance people, such as most Americans, are perceived as too unconventional by their high uncertainty avoidance counterparts. On the other hand, high uncertainty avoidance people are seen as too structured or uncompromising by the low uncertainty avoiders.

Uncertainty avoidance affects preferences for leadership styles, conformity, and discussion processes.[29] Cultures high in uncertainty avoidance rely on clear rules, consistently enforced, with the leader expected to structure the work of the group and behave autocratically. They prefer structure and clear procedures. In contrast, low uncertainty avoidance cultures prefer democratic leadership approaches. High uncertainty avoidance cultures value predictability and security; nonconformist behavior threatens this predictability. Conformity to the leader and group opinion is the norm for high avoidance cultures, whereas dissent and disagreement are tolerated, even encouraged, in low avoidance cultures. Lustig and Cassotta postulate that this should produce groups that are more task-oriented in high uncertainty avoidance cultures and more relationship-oriented in low uncertainty avoidance cultures.

Masculinity (as applied to culture)

The quality of cultures that value assertiveness and dominance.

Femininity (as applied to culture)

The quality of cultures that value nurturing and caring for others.

Masculinity versus Femininity

Masculinity refers to cultures that value stereotypical masculine behaviors such as assertiveness and dominance.[30] This is contrasted with **femininity**, referring to cultures that value behaviors such as nurturing and caring for others.

Masculine cultures, which include Japan, Austria, Mexico, and Venezuela, prize achievement, accumulation of wealth, aggressiveness, and what we would call "macho" behavior. Feminine cultures, which include the Scandinavian countries, The Netherlands, and Thailand, value interpersonal relationships, nurturing, service to and caring for others, particularly the poor and unfortunate. The United States is a moderately masculine culture.

Lustig and Cassotta observe that masculinity and femininity manifest in a number of preferences related to small groups.[31] With respect to leadership, masculine cultures are more comfortable with a controlling, directive style. Such cultures value objectivity and control, qualities exhibited by authoritarian leaders. Feminine cultures, which value relationships and subjectivity, prefer a more participative, democratic leadership style. Conformity is also likely related to the masculinity-femininity dimension. Stereotypical masculinity , with its emphasis on assertiveness and ambition, does not value conformity highly. In contrast, femininity, which stereotypically values cooperation and group-based decision making, expects and values conformity. Finally, social roles between men and women are more clearly differentiated in high masculine cultures. Males are more likely to undertake task-related roles and females socioemotional ones. This affects the roles performed in small groups. It also affects who will compete for the leadership role and whether women will be accepted in leadership and other high-status positions.

Low- versus High-Context Communication

The final cultural characteristic we will consider is what Hall termed low-versus high-context communication.[32] A culture with **low-context communication** is one where the primary meaning of a message is carried by the verbal, or explicit, part of the message, whereas in **high-context communication** the primary meaning is conveyed by certain features of the situation. In other words, in a high-context culture, what is *not* said may be more important in determining meaning than what *is* said. Typically, there is such a high degree of consensus that words aren't needed; members of the culture share the same understandings and can take much for granted. In low-context cultures, such as those of Germany, Switzerland, the Scandinavian countries, and the United States, direct, clear, and unambiguous statements are valued. The suggestions we provided in Chapter 4 for conducting organized and effective group discussions are appropriate for low-context cultures such as ours. We expect people to state precisely what they mean so there can be little room for doubt, no matter what the situation (i.e., context) happens to be. The same verbal message given in different contexts means about the same thing. For example, "No, I don't agree with that idea" means much the same thing whether you are in a meeting of co-workers, at the family dinner table, or meeting with your church board. In contrast, high-context cultures such as China, Japan, and South Korea prefer ambiguity, with several shades of meaning possible, because this helps preserve harmony and allows people to save

Low-Context Communication

Communication wherein the primary meaning of a message is carried by the verbal or explicit part of the message.

High-Context Communication

Communication wherein the primary meaning of a message is conveyed by features of the situation or context instead of the verbal, explicit part of the message.

face. In China, instead of "No, I don't agree with that idea," you are more likely to hear, "Perhaps we could explore that option." You would have to be well versed in Chinese communication patterns to know whether that statement means "No, we don't like it" or "We like it very much, but we must build consensus slowly" or "We don't know whether we like it or not until we explore it more fully." Moreover, you would also have to be astute at reading clues in the situation—for instance, is this in reaction to the boss's suggestion, or to a younger co-worker's? Complicated, isn't it? To us, with our low-context bias, it seems as though the Chinese are beating around the bush.[33]

Low-context cultures also tend to be individualistic, and high-context cultures tend to be collectivist.[34] Collectivist cultures operate by consensus of the group; individuals try not to risk offending another member of the group as this might upset a delicate balance of agreement and harmony. Apparently, ambiguity allows individuals to express opinions tentatively rather than directly without the risk of affronting others and upsetting the balance. Because low-context cultures such as the United States display cultural diversity where little can be taken for granted, verbal skills are probably more necessary, and thus more valued.[35] In a high-context culture such as Japan, the high degree of cultural homogeneity means that more can be taken for granted (and thus remain unspoken) during the communication process. In fact, most Japanese value silence more than we do and are suspicious of displays of verbal skills.[36]

> Sometimes the best contribution is from the person you wouldn't have expected.
>
> *B. H., Director, State Award Program*

You can imagine how difficult group communication can be when members from a high-context culture try to interact with members from a low-context culture. Your author, Gloria, once observed a student group that included Qing-yu, who was from Taiwan. The American students were used to lively debate and accustomed to speaking out in favor of or in opposition to one another's ideas, but in Qing-yu's culture, disagreement is indicated very subtly. Qing-yu's quiet, subdued behavior in the group irritated the American students, who kept trying to get her to behave more like them. The harder the Americans tried to force her to take a stand, get to the point, and be direct, the more she retreated into her familiar orientation of ambiguity and indirectness. The misunderstanding was severe.

The six characteristics we have just discussed determine what is considered appropriate verbal and nonverbal communicative behavior in a particular culture. (See also Table 5.2.) In the previous chapter, we discussed several effects of cultural differences on nonverbal communication. Here, we focus on language issues related to cultural or co-cultural differences. Nonverbal signals are inherently ambiguous and readily subject to misinterpretation,

TABLE 5.2 Dimensions of culture and associated characteristics.

Worldview	"Being" Orientation	"Doing" Orientation
	Go with the flow. Fate controls human events. Patience is valued.	Make things happen. People control events and are in charge of their own fates. Prefer getting to the point quickly.
Collectivism/Individualism	Collectivism	Individualism
	Group is standard of reference; group is valued over individual. Value harmony and conformity. Value slow consensus building.	Individual is standard of reference; individual is valued over group. Value dissent and diversity. Value debate and disagreement.
Power Distance	High-Power Distance	Low-Power Distance
	Status differences maximized. Status hierarchy based on birth/position in society is normal; people are not created equal. Prefer authoritarian, directive leadership.	Status differences minimized. Status hierarchy based on birth/position in society is unfair; people are created equal. Prefer democratic, participative leadership.
Uncertainty Avoidance	High Uncertainty Avoidance	Low Uncertainty Avoidance
	Uncomfortable with ambiguity. Prefer clear rules and norms, high structure. Prefer structured leadership.	High tolerance for ambiguity. Comfortable with loose, flexible rules. Prefer democratic leadership.
Masculinity/Femininity	Masculinity	Femininity
	Value assertive behaviors. Value achievement. Emphasize objectivity, control. Prefer autocratic leadership.	Value caring, nurturing behaviors. Value relationships with others. Emphasize subjectivity. Prefer participative leadership.
High/Low Context	High Context	Low Context
	Message carried by the context, nonverbal content. Culturally homogeneous; much meaning can be safely assumed. Prefer indirect communication.	Meaning carried by the words, verbal content. Culturally diverse; meaning cannot be taken for granted. Prefer clear, direct communication.

whether cultural differences exist or not. But language seems more precise. We may be tempted to assume that verbal language is less susceptible to cultural misunderstanding—but we would be wrong! The following section describes language issues related to cultural and co-cultural differences.

Language Issues Related to Cultural Differences

Our most important symbol system is our language, including both vocabulary and rules of usage. As we explained in Chapter 4, the fact that we use different symbol codes (i.e., languages) is not the only factor that makes communication difficult. Some researchers also believe that language in fact *determines* how we experience our world; although such deterministic views have been softened, it is clear that our language code helps shape what we perceive in several fundamental ways.[37] For example, several languages, including German and Spanish, have more than one form of the pronoun *you*. A formal or polite version is used to address people the speaker doesn't know very well; an informal or familiar form is used to address family members and friends. What does this say about the relative formality, display of respect, and egalitarianism in such cultures? Some Native American languages, such as that of the Hopi, have no past, present, or future verb tenses. These cultures are spontaneous and experience *time* as what happens in the present moment. Thus, language barriers are not limited to different word usages; they are also caused by *perceptual* differences that can be equally troublesome.

Not only are symbol systems and usages different, but preferred organizational patterns differ as well.[38] Consider what many of you have been taught by your English teachers, who suggest starting an essay with a main thesis, developing the thesis and supporting it with evidence, and presenting a clear conclusion that summarizes the main points. That linear presentation is the preferred organizational pattern for U.S. English. However, other cultures or co-cultures prefer different patterns. Many Eastern cultures, for instance, prefer a narrative approach to the topic and use a more inductive than deductive pattern. Sometimes students who complain about experiencing difficulty in courses taught by non-native teaching assistants or professors are reacting more negatively to organizational patterns than to the mispronunciation of some words. Individuals in the United States who live in generational poverty, where family members have lived in poverty for at least two generations, use a nonlinear narrative style as well.[39] Stories are not told sequentially, from beginning to end, but in a circular way, with the most emotional content provided first.

Inability to use the same language code (i.e., to speak the same language) presents significant obstacles to understanding. Consider how stressful it must be for the many international students in colleges and universities throughout the United States who must expend considerable energy listening and trying to decipher the content of messages; little energy is available for the nuances and subtleties of the interaction. Even something as simple as the word *yes* can cause problems. Koreans sometimes use *yes* when an American might say *no.* "Didn't you go to school yesterday?" elicits the following Korean response: "Yes, I didn't."[40] Although *yes* sometimes means agreement, it can also acknowledge that the Korean listener has heard a question, or that the Korean fully understands what the speaker is saying and is encouraging him or her to continue. Koreans use *yes* to maintain harmony and the appearance of harmony by avoiding appearing negative.

Communication difficulties can occur even between native speakers of the same language. For example, one of our colleagues, a native-born Canadian, circulated a memo asking us to provide our yearly activity reports in "point form." Faculty members were confused until someone noted that *point form* to a Canadian means *outline form* to someone from the United States. Misunderstandings between native language speakers can be humorous and are usually cleared up quickly, but misunderstandings between non-native speakers can sometimes be deadly. Many air traffic controllers around the world issue their instructions in English. When a controller in Madagascar said, "Clipper 1736 report clear of runway" the American pilot interpreted that as clearance to take off. The controller had meant, "Report that you have cleared the runway." The result of this linguistic mistake was a crash where 600 people died.[41]

One final example illustrates pitfalls that can occur with the verbal aspects of intercultural communication. In graduate school, Gloria worked on a committee to analyze data by computer. Two Arab students were members of this committee. Responsible for writing the instructions for the computer analysis, Gloria named the file "BEGIN" to indicate "here's where to start." The Arab students, believing she had named the file *BEGIN* after Menachem Begin, prime minister of Israel, felt they had been deliberately insulted and protested vehemently to the course professor. They were focusing on cues most salient to them. Gloria was oblivious to the possible double meaning. It took a long time to unravel the source of the friction, but even though the mistake was innocent, trust among the group members was permanently impaired.

Communication Challenges Posed by Co-Cultures

Earlier we described cultural and co-cultural communication rules and patterns as things that are learned, expectations and behaviors that we absorb. The United States contains many co-cultures that exist, some of them more visible than others. In this next section, we examine differences in the characteristics, values, and communication based on race, age, and socioeconomic class.

Co-Cultural Differences Based on Race: African American Communication Patterns

In this section we discuss several of the communication differences observed between African Americans and Caucasian Americans. We do not intend to imply that relationships between Hispanics and European Americans, or

Asians and African Americans, are not equally important. In fact, in the near future, Hispanics will be the largest minority group in the United States, with profound implications for communication. However, we elected to discuss black-white communication because misunderstandings here appear to be among the most serious and volatile at this time. African Americans and Caucasian Americans perceive each other as threatening and have generally negative evaluations of each other,[42] so it seems especially important to help each group understand the other. We remind you again that even though we discuss African American communication patterns as though African Americans were a uniform group, this is not the case. We agree with Orbe, who notes that the considerable diversity *within* the African American community has been largely ignored by researchers.[43]

Foeman and Pressley have summarized research that describes "typical" (although we caution you again that there is no such thing as "typical") black communication, particularly in organizational settings.[44] Black culture in the United States is an oral culture, so verbal inventiveness and virtuosity of expression are highly valued. What many whites perceive as boastfulness Foeman and Pressley call *assertiveness*, which takes both verbal and nonverbal forms (for instance, trying to top someone else's boast, strutting across the street). Black managers are perceived as forthright or overly reactive. In a conflict, for instance, a black is more likely to confront an individual directly, whereas a white manager is more likely to approach the problem indirectly. Consequently, some blacks perceive whites as underreactive, but some whites see blacks as overreactive. Degree of responsiveness (expressiveness) differs; blacks are more likely to respond both verbally and physically (e.g., gesturing often with their hands), whereas whites tend to focus on verbal responses. Blacks make less direct eye contact, but they compensate by standing closer to their conversational partner than most whites. These differences in cultural communication patterns can create serious misunderstandings. For instance, a white expecting more eye contact may be likely to repeat or rephrase statements in order to get the expected signs of understanding (such as eye contact), whereas the black person feels the white person is being condescending.

The black culture is more collective than the more dominant white culture of the United States. According to Foeman and Pressley, this may lead to such strong black identification with blacks *as a group* that a black person may be unwilling or unable to work with people of different ethnic groups. However, the communal structure of the black culture helps offset the discrimination and prejudice blacks still receive in this culture.

African Americans and European Americans express themselves verbally in different ways. Blacks are more playful than most whites in their use of language and relish playing verbal games. Foeman and Pressley explain that blacks *signify* (or hint) at questions rather than asking them directly because they perceive disclosure of personal information to be voluntary; thus, questions are implied so that the person being asked will not feel vulnerable or obliged to answer. In addition, blacks use the backchannel (or *call-response*) to indicate interest and involvement in the discussion. For example, in black churches the services resemble a dialogue, with congregation members freely calling *Amen, Go ahead, Preach* to the minister; such responses would be less frequent in most white churches. Differences in black-white uses of the backchannel, as we discussed earlier, can create misunderstandings and cause hurt feelings.

One of us noticed an illustration of these verbal differences. The week after John Kennedy, Jr., was killed in an airplane crash, Rev. Jesse Jackson was being interviewed by Cokie Roberts in a television tribute to Kennedy. In response to a question about Kennedy's work with the disadvantaged, Rev. Jackson began to speak movingly and at length about the young man. He was using the cadences and extended style of many black preachers and it was clear that he was just getting started when Cokie interrupted him to say, "So in other words, there was substance to [Kennedy]." In one short sentence, Cokie, who seemed a little frustrated at how long it was taking Rev. Jackson to answer her question, summarized concisely what he had been saying and went on to her next question. The "typical" white, to-the-point style bumped up against the "typical" flowery, elaborated style of black preachers in an interesting way.

Consider This 5.3

Assume you are the only African American (or Caucasian American) in a group of white (or black) students. How do you think you would feel? What thoughts would run through your mind? How, if at all, do you think your behavior would change?

In the United States, it is often difficult for someone from one co-culture to participate fully in a group dominated by members of a different co-culture. Many African Americans, including some of the most successful, say they must behave cautiously and carefully in groups of white Americans; they can never fully relax.[45] In many ways they have developed bicultural competencies—one set of behaviors for African American groups, another for primarily white groups. This balancing act can be exhausting, but many African Americans believe that if they do not conform to the communication rules of the dominant, European American culture, they will pay a high price.

Co-Cultural Differences Based on Age

Over our many years of teaching, we have noticed more "nontraditional" (i.e., older) students in our classes than was true 20 or 25 years ago. We have also noticed that events that have helped shape us as teachers, such as the assassination of President John F. Kennedy and Watergate, are things our students know only from their history books. Age and generational differences have produced interesting challenges for us and for our students, who increasingly participate in multigenerational groups.

Orbe notes that co-cultural patterns come from the lived experiences of members of the co-culture.[46] The significant events people live through together contribute to formation of the worldview, values, and communication preferences co-cultural group members exhibit. Hicks and Hicks have examined such events with respect to the four generations that currently predominate in the United States, and have identified a number of key differences that make it difficult for members of different age groups to communicate effectively.[47] The following generational descriptions are, of course, overgeneralizations; however, significant happenings—political assassinations, the explosion of the Internet—have significantly influenced each generation's values and approach to life.

The **builder generation**, born from 1901 to 1945, lived through the Great Depression and World War II. They experienced the four-term presidency of Franklin Roosevelt, the polio epidemic, the Japanese attack on Pearl Harbor, the U.S. drop of atomic bombs on Hiroshima and Nagasaki, and the Red Scare fear of communism. Most were adults during the 1950s economic boom, when ordinary people could buy houses, appliances, cars. This generation tends to be cautious about money, defers gratification, and believes in discipline, self-sacrifice, and working toward the common good. Members tend to value conformity and traditional role relationships between the sexes; they can lack spontaneity.

The **boomer generation**, about which much has been written, grew up when television became widely available. Born from 1946 to 1964, boomers experienced the divisiveness of the Vietnam War, political assassinations in the United States, the civil rights movement, the advent of the birth control pill, and the massive mistrust of government precipitated by Watergate. This is a confident generation, willing to challenge authority and tackle big causes. Their sheer size—for a long time this was the largest generation—means that they have been catered to by marketers and producers. Thus, boomers believe they are right all the time, are self-absorbed, and feel free to break rules when they think that's best for them. They also are willing to work hard and expect to be fulfilled in their work.

The **X generation**, born from 1965 to 1976, are sandwiched between two very large generations. They were the first to experience divorce on a massive scale and many became latchkey children. They feel abandoned or emotionally neglected, and have a higher suicide rate than the other generations. They believe they are entitled to the good life, and they don't want to wait for it. They want to prove themselves, but feel the boomers aren't giving them a chance to do so. They are flexible, are comfortable with pluralistic points of view, and are used to change. X-ers display commitment to diversity, which they value more than conformity.

The final generation, the **net generation**, was born between 1977 and 1997. This is the largest generation in terms of numbers, but they are too young yet to have made their influence fully felt. Net-geners are the first fully wired generation—they grew up with computers, e-mail, answering machines, cell phones, voice mail, CDs, and DVDs. They have never known a world without AIDS. Major influences include the Internet and the death of Princess Diana. Members of this generation are in touch with their friends constantly through electronics, even though their friends may be widely scattered. Net-geners have been doing collaborative work ever since their elementary school days; they are comfortable in group settings, are open minded and tolerant, and are nonlinear thinkers. But they also don't like to conform to bureaucracy and organizational rules.

Net Generation

Individuals born from 1977 to 1997; the first truly "wired" generation, comfortable with technology in all forms.

> I think differently about the world than someone who is a grandparent. And then the person straight out of college thinks differently. So I really like to have those people with sort of differing life stages [on a team].
>
> *B. H., Director, State Program*

Generational differences can severely tax the resources of a group if members aren't sensitive to them. When e-mail was just becoming widely used at her university, Gloria chaired a university committee that included builders, boomers, and a Net-gen student representative. The boomers had become used to using computers and e-mail; the student had grown up with computers. One builder refused to use e-mail for communication; he preferred written memos. Because he was a valuable group member in every other way, Gloria chose to accommodate him by printing out hard copies of all e-mail messages and sending them to him via campus mail. Today, years later, everyone uses e-mail, although some builders and boomers have not learned to navigate the net with the ease of the X-ers and Net-geners.

One of us observed a classroom group with difficulties caused in part by generational value differences. The boomer member, who was the age of the Net-geners' mothers, attempted to organize the work of the group, to establish regular meeting times, and to coordinate the library research of the group. In her journal, one of the Net-gen students lamented that she felt "ordered around" by her mother and was having a hard time accepting this boomer student as a peer. She wanted to disagree and to suggest alternative ways of finding information—such as using the Internet for research—but felt uncomfortable about contradicting somebody who reminded her of her mother. Eventually, partly because of the sensitivity of the boomer member, this group was able to talk and joke about their generational differences and to learn from one another. One particularly interesting difference in this group was that the Net-gen students thought of the Internet *first* as a way to research a topic, whereas the boomer thought first of print sources.

Age or generational differences in small groups have not been investigated much. Two recent studies of media use found generational differences. Kuo found that X-ers in Taiwan used electronic media significantly more than others.[48] Shah, et al. found different patterns of media usage for informational purposes, with builders using newspapers, boomers using television, and X-ers using the Internet.[49] Timmerman, in his study of age and racial diversity of baseball and basketball teams, found both age and racial diversity related to impaired performance on basketball teams.[50] This negative relationship between diversity and performance seems to be a relatively recent phenomenon of the last 20 years. Timmerman speculates that diversity is likely to be more challenging for teams where task interdependence is high, as in basketball. These results support further study into the effects of generation-related co-cultural differences.

Co-Cultural Differences Based on Socioeconomic Class

As with generational differences, the effects of socioeconomic class differences in small groups likewise have not been widely investigated. However, numerous studies attest to differences in communication patterns based on socioeconomic class. We like to think we belong to a classless society, but we don't. Socioeconomic class is not based solely on income. Jackman found that class distinctions are also determined by education, job authority, and skill.[51] In addition, people are readily able to classify others by socioeconomic class. Jackman's research participants showed a high degree of consensus when they were asked about the social class into which particular occupations fit. Furthermore, class differences produce differences in values and communication patterns. Ellis and Armstrong examined television depictions of middle-class and non-middle-class (lower-class and poor) families and found implicit messages about how people of difference classes communicate.[52] For instance, middle-class males used longer sentences and generally more complex speaking patterns than non-middle-class males. Middle-class people of both sexes used more adverbs. The word *ain't*, never used by middle-class speakers, served to mark someone as non-middle class.

Communication within the family exhibits class-based communication patterns. Ritchie discovered that families of parents whose jobs entailed a high degree of openness and autonomy in the workplace—in other words, parents of higher socioeconomic class—demonstrated greater conversational orientation within the family, and less conformity.[53] The families that Jordan observed showed relationships among social class, perceptions of time, and media usage.[54] Parents in middle- and upper-class families socialized their children to observe deadlines and structure their time. They used a linear, sequential structure for activities in the home by encouraging their children to do one thing at a time and to complete one task before going on to another. They planned their schedules in advance and adhered to them. The working-class families used looser organizational patterns and tended to do several things at once, such as watch television, eat dinner, and talk to each other at the same time. Schedules were not planned in advance or were changed spontaneously. Jordan speculates that a family's use of time may be related to the perception of time as a resource, which itself may be class based. For instance, middle- and upper-class families perceived time as a scarce commodity that should be managed well and not wasted, and taught their children to perceive time in the same way. In such families, media usage, particularly watching television, was not seen as a particularly good use of time. Working-class parents did not perceive media use as either a good or bad use of time. Interestingly, working-class parents were more concerned about the content of media usage than upper- or middle-class parents. These preferences can produce subtle differences in what individuals from different socioeconomic classes accept as normal or appropriate in a group.

We could find no studies that looked at the effect of class differences within small groups. However, in our own teaching, we have observed the effects (usually bad ones) of communication differences that are class based. A recent book by Payne describes several of the key communication patterns, related to the co-cultures of class, that can cause problems.[55] Payne, a teacher and principal, has been successful in working with both children and adults from backgrounds of what she calls *generational poverty*, in which a family has experienced socioeconomic poverty for at least two generations. Payne notes that the communicative and daily living rules differ greatly for people from poor, middle, and wealthy classes. Each class experiences its own ethnocentricity, assuming that its rules are both known and appropriate. Middle-class individuals, who include many of the teachers, managers, and professionals in the United States, assume that "everyone knows the rules" for how to do things. But the poor and the wealthy have different values and communicative rules! What are some of those differences?

Middle-classes value achievement and believe they can affect the future with the choices they make in the present. Individuals in generational poverty focus on the present. They believe the future is controlled by fate and they cannot do much to change it. Wealthy classes respect the past; they make decisions based on tradition and history. They prize social connections.

Payne notes that different classes use discourse in different ways. Individuals from backgrounds of generational poverty use discourse as a form of entertainment. For all discourse, they use the casual register—an informal meandering conversational style the middle class uses between friends. It is characterized by vague word choice, incomplete sentences, reliance on nonverbal signals to complete thoughts, and a limited vocabulary of 400 to 800 words. The narrative pattern is circular, where the speaker talks around an issue before getting to the point. This contrasts significantly with the formal register style middle-class and wealthy speakers use for most conversations. Formal register uses complete sentences, standard sentence construction and syntax, a more extensive vocabulary, specific words, and the speaker gets right to the point. In Table 5.3, the story of Cinderella, told in both casual and formal discourse, illustrates some of these differences.

The formal register version is told in chronological order, from beginning to end, and demonstrates cause, effect, and conclusion. It follows the typical problem-solving pattern of sequential logic—first one thing happens, then the next, then the next. The casual register version it more entertaining and relies on audience participation. The narrator expects others to jump in and help tell the story. For middle-class readers, the story will appear disorganized. However, and this is an important point to remember, the story has its own logic, an emotionally based one, where the most important emotional elements are highlighted first.

These differences are interesting, but their point here is to highlight the potential challenges of diverse groups. Imagine how frustrating it can be if you think it's important for a speaker to get right to the point, and you encounter someone in your group with a wandering narrative style. Similarly, can you envision how rude and boring it must seem to someone with a colorful, spiraling narrative style to be paired with a sequential, get to-the-point partner? That is why we think it is important for group members to understand each other's rules and assumptions.

Challenges for Co-Cultural Group Members

This discussion of race, age, and social class has only scratched the surface, and is not intended to be exhaustive. It is intended to encourage you to think about your own behavior with an eye toward sensitizing you to ethnocentric behavior that may cause problems in a group. Orbe suggests that members of co-cultures that are not part of the dominant culture can become marginalized in groups and organizations.[56] If they want their views represented, they must expend energy thinking about how their communication affects and is received by members of the dominant culture. There are a number of strategies they use, but they may or may not be successful in being heard.

Consider This 5.4

Would you like to know how well a group you belong to is managing its diversity? Linda Larkey has developed a brief scale to assess individuals' perception of their interactions in a culturally diverse environment. In Chapter 15, Figure 15.9, we will present the four dimensions of this scale that specifically assess aspects of diversity: inclusion (whether everyone feels included), ideation (whether diverse ideas are welcomed), understanding (how well diverse members understand one another), and treatment (are members of co-cultural groupings treated the same as majority members). Have the members of your group answer the questions on this instrument and discuss the results.[57]

Formal Register Version (abbreviated because of familiarity)

Once upon a time, there was a girl named Cinderella. She was very happy, and she lived with her father. Her father remarried a woman who had three daughters. When Cinderella's father died, her stepmother treated Cinderella very badly and, in fact, made her the maid for herself and her three daughters. At the same time in this land, the King decided that it was time for the Prince to get married. So, he sent a summons to all the people in the kingdom to come to a ball. Cinderella was not allowed to go, but she was forced to help her stepsisters and stepmother get ready for the ball. After they left for the ball, and as Cinderella was crying on the hearth, her fairy godmother came and, with her magic wand, gave Cinderella a beautiful dress, glass slippers, and a stagecoach made from pumpkins and mice. She then sent Cinderella to the ball in style. There was one stipulation. She had to be home by midnight.

At the ball, the Prince was completely taken with Cinderella and danced with her all evening. As the clock began striking midnight, Cinderella remembered what the fairy godmother had said and fled from the dance. All she left was one of her glass slippers.

The Prince held a big search, using the glass slipper as a way to identify the missing woman. He finally found Cinderella; she could wear the glass slipper. He married her, and they lived happily ever after.

Casual Register Version (bold type indicates the narrator; plain type indicates audience participation)

Well, you know Cinderella married the Prince, in spite of that nasty old stepmother. Pointy eyes, that one. Old hag! **Good thing she had a fairy godmother or she never would've made it to the ball.** Lucky thing! God bless her ragged tail! Wish I had me a fairy godmother. **And to think she nearly messed up big time by staying 'til the clock was striking 12. After all the fairy godmother had done for her.** Um, um. She shoulda known better. Eyes too full of the Prince, they were. They didn't call him the Prince for no reason. **When she got to the ball, her stepsisters and stepmother didn't even recognize her she was so beautiful without those rags.** Served 'em right, no-good jealous hags. **The Prince just couldn't quit dancing with her, just couldn't take his eyes off her. He had finally found his woman.** Lucky her! Lucky him! Sure wish life was a fairy tale. Kind like the way I met Charlie. Ha ha. **The way she arrived was something else—a coach and horseman—really fancy. Too bad that when she ran out of there as the clock struck 12 all that was left was a pumpkin rolling away and four mice!** What a surprise for the mice! **Well, he has to find her because his heart is broken. So he takes the glass slipper and hunts for her—and her old wicked stepmother, of course, is hiding her.** What a prize! Aren't they all? **But he finds her and marries her. Somebody as good as Cinderella deserved that.** Sure hope she never invited that stepmother to her castle. Should make her the maid!!

TABLE 5.3
Cinderella, in formal and casual register.

Source: Ruby K. Payne, *A Framework for Understanding Poverty* (Highlands, TX: aha! Process, Inc., 2001, 47–48 (Reprinted by permission).

Two recent studies by Kirchmeyer indicate that minority members of groups are often the lowest contributors.[58] Two plausible explanations for this are that minorities may lack a sense of belonging to the group and that, although they may be skilled in communication within their own culture, they may lack the skills to communicate effectively in groups composed primarily of whites. Kirchmeyer found that minority status affected contribution levels, and she cautions that multicultural groups may not be encompassing the multiple perspectives of all their members in the final products. This view is supported by Teboul's study of minority hires in organizations.[59] He notes that minority new hires encounter more setbacks in becoming truly part of their organizations, experience more relational isolation, and learn that certain relational doors are closed to them. This represents a significant loss to all of us. Whether we are black or white, young or old, middle class or poor, Protestant or Jewish, urban or rural, we must begin to recognize that differences are just that—differences!

> Things work or don't work based on whether the relationship you establish . . . works. So I need people who are able to get along with other people, but in a way to get the work done, not just get along.
>
> *P. T., University Director of Planning and Development*

In the film *The Color of Fear*, eight men of different races discuss their pesonal experiences with racism. Communication scholar Tadasu Imahori, who is Japanese American, discusses his reaction to watching the European American in the film deny that racism is a problem in this country.[60] He observes that he can easily relate with the other men who had experienced racism, but were unable to convince the white man of the validity of their experiences. This illustrates a main point we want to convey in this chapter: it is imperative in small groups to invite and acknowledge the experiences, perceptions, and viewpoints of all members. Someone's perspective may be different, but does not make it invalid, wrong, uneducated, or stupid. We must learn to manage diversity effectively. Failure to do so has hurt members' feelings, demonized individuals who represent the dominant culture of the United States, fostered reverse discrimination, pinpointed certain groups or individuals as being responsible for all diversity-based problems, reinforced stereotypes, and demoralized everyone.[61] When we don't embrace and encourage group diversity, we deprive groups of the ideas, creativity, and problem-solving efforts of *all* members.

Behaving Ethically in Intercultural Interactions

By now, you know that what is considered rhetorically sensitive and appropriate communication depends on the culture. If communication rules differ in each individual culture, are there any universal or overarching principles that preserve the integrity of individual cultures, yet let members of those cultures work together? Kale suggests two broad principles that should govern inter-cultural interactions: we should protect the worth and dignity of all human be-ings, and we should act in such a way as to promote peace among all peo-ple.[62] The following ethical guidelines follow from these broad principles:

1. **Communicate in a way that extends empathy and respect to all members of the group**.
   Similar to the ethical principle described in Chapter 1, this principle re-quires that you work to understand others as they want to be understood. This is more challenging between group members of different cultures be-cause there are fewer "givens," but there are things you can do. First, re-member that all discussions are to some extent intercultural; be aware of and sensitive to cultural differences and view them as potential strengths for a group, not liabilities. Resist making judgments about the intelligence or motives of others. Encourage all members to get to know each other beyond the task demands of the group. Finally, initiate discussion of the differences. You will help group members move toward greater under-standing and empathy if you explicitly acknowledge differences and will-ingly discuss them, not in a judgmental way but as an opportunity to learn more about your fellow group members and yourself.

2. **Work to incorporate the key cultural values of all members into the group's procedures and outputs.**
   Of course this is easier said than done, but failure to do this denigrates the cultural values of those members who are ignored. This also means that all members must adjust their normal ways of interacting to accommodate differences. Bantz's work with an intercultural research team provides sev-eral specific suggestions for managing cultural diversity.[63] In that team, ex-plicitly establishing common goals and deadlines addressed the needs of members high in uncertainty avoidance, and differences in power dis-tance norms were handled by segregating tasks and varying the leadership styles accordingly. Differing needs for cohesion were addressed by alter-nating task and social aspects of the work. Notice that these ways of han-dling the diversity recognized the legitimacy of the differing cultural norms, showed the members' ability to adapt, and demonstrated respect for all concerned—all ethical goals.

   Specific suggestions to help you put these ethical principles into effect in your small groups are summarized in Figure 5.2.

FIGURE 5.2
Guidelines for
ethical intercultural
interaction.

> **In intercultural small group communication,**
>
> **Remember that every discussion is intercultural to some extent**. Because we each have unique backgrounds, we do not use verbal and nonverbal signals to mean exactly the same things.
>
> **Recognize and accept differences; view them as strengths of the group, not liabilities**. Instead of judging others as wrong for behaving in ways different from yours, recognize that each of us is the product of our culture. Resolve to learn from each other, not to try change each other.
>
> **Resist making attributions of stupidity or ill intent; ask yourself whether the other member's behavior could have cultural origin**. When another member's behavior seems rude, inconsiderate, our unusual, ask yourself whether you could be observing a cultural difference in what is considered appropriate behavior before you decide the other member is worthless to the group.
>
> **Be willing to discuss intercultural differences openly and initiate discussion of differences you observe**. Instead of being uncomfortable or pretending that differences do not exist, be willing to ask for and share information about cultural norms and rules. When you observe differences, you can enrich everyone's understanding by pointing them out and initiating a discussion about how cultures vary.
>
> **Be willing to adapt to differences**. Instead of insisting that others follow the prescriptions of your culture, be willing to adapt your behavior to different cultural practices when appropriate. Try to incorporate the key values and needs of each culture into the group's procedures and outputs.

SUMMARY

1. All interactions are to some extent intercultural, but some much more than others. Being able to work effectively in intercultural small groups will be increasingly necessary in the next decades. Everyone must abandon ethnocentricity and learn to appreciate, rather than denigrate, diversity.

2. Cultures vary along several key dimensions, including worldview, or beliefs about the nature and purpose of life, which help determine our values, activity orientation, customs, and beliefs; the degree of individualism; the degree of power distance; the extent to which people avoid uncertainty; whether a culture values stereotypically masculine or feminine behavior; and the extent to which people rely more on the words or the context to determine the meaning of something.

3. Language differences between cultures or co-cultures can also cause major misunderstandings.

4. Race, age, and social class differences can be viewed as cultural differences. Different races, generational groupings, and social classes have different rules for behaving.

5. Two ethical principles should guide intercultural interactions in groups: the worth and dignity of humans should be protected, and peace among all people should be promoted.

KEY TERMS

 Test your knowledge of these key terms by visiting the Online Learning Center website at mhhe.com/galanes11

Activity orientation	Ethnocentric	Masculinity (as applied to culture)
Boomer generation	Femininity (as applied to culture)	Net generation
Builder generation	High-context communication	Power distance
Co-culture	Individualistic cultures	Uncertainty avoidance
Collectivist cultures	Intercultural communication	Worldview
Cultural identity	Intracultural communication	X generation
Culture	Low-context communication	

EXERCISES

 Go to self-quizzes on the Online Learning Center at mhhe.com/galanes11 to test your knowledge of the chapter concepts

1. List all the cultures and co-cultures with which you feel a strong identification. Form groups of five or six; share and discuss your lists. What do you think are the most salient characteristics of the cultures or co-cultures on your list? How do the members of each one expect you to behave? Do the features of any of the cultures contradict each other? If so, how? How do you handle it when you experience conflict between the expectations of two co-cultures to which you belong?

2. One important co-cultural grouping is your family. Form groups of five or six and have each person discuss what the communication norms are in his/her family. (You may want to narrow this to focus on only one kind of situation, such as having dinner with your family.) Are there norms that might surprise family members? Are there norms your family follows that differ from the norms of your classmates' families? Are there norms governing what you should *not* talk about?

3. As a class, look at movies that depict intercultural encounters of various kinds, including male-female encounters. For example, *Witness, My Big Fat Greek Wedding, The Four Seasons, When Harry Met Sally, The Joy Luck Club, Gandhi, The Color of Fear*, and *A Stranger Among Us* depict international or intercultural encounters. As a class, address the following questions:

   How did the two cultures in the movie differ? (Be sure to discuss the characteristics of worldview, collectivism versus individualism, low versus high power distance, low versus high uncertainty avoidance, and low versus high context.)

   What communication problems did the differences create?

   Were the communication difficulties resolved? If so, how?

   How were the people from the two cultures changed by the encounters?

   How realistic were the portrayals of the two cultures?

4. Ask several international students to visit your class and describe communication customs and behaviors in their home countries. Ask them what they found most different or hardest to adjust to in conversations in the United States. How do they think their communicative behaviors have changed as a result of encounters with Americans?

5. Ask native-born American students who have either traveled extensively or lived for long periods of time in other places to talk about their experiences adjusting to other cultures. What did they find most different or hardest to adjust to about the communication behavior of the people in the other cultures? How has their behavior changed as a result of their travels?

6. Use one or more of the intercultural "critical incidents" described in *Intercultural Interactions: A Practical Guide* (listed in the Bibliography below) to create a role-play or skit for the class. Discuss what each individual in the role-play or skit might do to repair the interpersonal damage that may have occurred and to prevent such "mistakes" in the future.

7. Go to a public place (e.g., airport, restaurant, or museum) and observe the differences between how men and women behave. Take note of such things as how they sit and stand, how they seem to use personal space, their facial expressions and gestures, and so forth. What generalizations are you comfortable making from your observations? Share your findings with the class.

BIBLIOGRAPHY

Brislin, Richard W., Kenneth Cushner, Craig Cherrie, and Mahealani Yong. *Intercultural Interactions: A Practical Guide*. Beverly Hills, CA: Sage, 1986. Provides 100 realistic intercultural case studies and asks the reader to speculate upon the sources of misunderstanding.

Hicks, Rick, and Kathy Hicks. *Boomers, X-ers, and Other Strangers: Understanding the Generational Differences that Divide Us*. Wheaton, IL: Tyndale, 1999.

Lustig, Myron W., and Laura L. Cassotta, "Comparing Group Communication across Cultures: Leadership, Conformity, and Discussion Processes." In *Small Group Communication: A Reader*. 6th ed. Robert S. Cathcart and Larry A. Samovar, eds. Dubuque, IA: Wm. C. Brown, 1992, 393–404.

Lustig, Myron W., and Jolene Koester, eds. *Among Us: Essays on Identity, Belonging, and Intercultural Competence*. New York: Longman, 2000.

Martin, Judith N., and Thomas K. Nakayama, *Experiencing Intercultural Communication: An Introduction*. Mountain View, CA: Mayfield, 2001.

Payne, Ruby K. *A Framework for Understanding Poverty*, new revised edition. Highlands, TX: aha! Process, Inc., 2001, especially Chapters 1 through 4.

Porter, Richard E., and Larry A. Samovar. "Communication in the Multicultural Group." In *Small Group Communication: A Reader*. 6th ed. Robert S. Cathcart and Larry A. Samovar, eds. Dubuque, IA: Wm. C. Brown, 1992, 382–92.

NOTES

1. William A. Henry, "Beyond the Melting Pot," *Time* (April 9, 1990): 29–35.

2. C. W. Von Bergen, Barlow Soper, and Teresa Foster, "Unintended Negative Effects of Diversity Management," *Public Personnel Management* 31 (Summer 2002). Accessed on Internet, July 20, 2002.

3. John M. Ivancevich and Jacqueline A. Gilbert, "Diversity Management," *Public Personnel Management* 29 (Spring, 2000). Accessed on Internet July 20, 2002

4. Beth Bonniwell Haslett and Jenn Ruebush, "What Differences Do Individual Differences in Groups Make?" in *The Handbook of Group Communication Theory and Research*, ed. Lawrence R. Frey (Thousand Oaks, CA: Sage, 1999): 115–138.

5. Martha L. Maznevski, "Understanding Our Differences: Performance in Decision-Making Groups with Diverse Members," *Human Relations* 47 (May 1994): 531–52; Haslett aand Ruebush, "What Differences Do Individual Differences in Groups Make?"

6. Poppy Lauretta McLeod, Sharon Alisa Lobel, and Taylor H. Cox, Jr., "Ethnic Diversity and Creativity in Small Groups," *Small Groups Research* 27 (May 1996): 248–64.

7. Young Yun Kim and Brent D. Ruben, "Intercultural Transformation: A Systems Theory," in *Theories in Intercultural Communication: Inter-*

national and Intercultural Communication Annual, Vol. 12, eds. Young Yun Kim and William B. Gudykunst (Newbury Park, CA: Sage, 1988): 299–321.

8. Barbara L. Speicher, "Interethnic Conflict: Attribution and Cultural Ignorance," *Howard Journal of Communication* 5 (Spring 1995): 195–213.

9. Rebecca Leonard and Don C. Locke, "Communication Stereotypes: Is Interracial Communication Possible?" *Journal of Black Studies* 23 (March 1993): 332–43.

10. Mary Jane Collier and Milt Thomas, "Cultural Identity: An Interpretive Perspective," in *Theories in Intercultural Communication: International and Intercultural Communication Annual*, Vol. 12, eds. Young Yun Kim and William B. Gudykunst (Newbury Park, CA: Sage, 1988): 113.

11. Ibid., 103.

12. Mark P. Orbe, "From the Standpoint(s) of Traditionally Muted Groups: Explicating a Co-cultural Communication Theoretical Model," *Communication Theory* 8 (February, 1998): 1–26.

13. Ibid., 2

14. Donald W. Klopf, *Intercultural Encounters: The Fundamentals of Intercultural Communication* (Englewood, CO: Morton, 1987): 27–30.

15. Larry E. Sarbaugh, "A Taxonomic Approach to Intercultural Communication," in *Theories in Intercultural Communication: International and Intercultural Communication Annual*, Vol. 12, eds. Young Yun Kim and William B. Gudykunst (Newbury Park, CA: Sage, 1988): 22–38.

16. Young Yun Kim, "On Theorizing Intercultural Communication," in *Theories in Intercultural Communication: International and Intercultural Communication Annual*, Vol. 12, eds. Young Yun Kim and William B. Gudykunst (Newbury Park, CA: Sage, 1988): 12–13.

17. E. Glenn (with C. G. Glenn), *Man and Mankind: Conflict and Communication Between Cultures* (Norwood, NJ: Ablex, 1981); Edward T. Hall, *Beyond Culture* (New York: Anchor Press, 1977); Geert Hofstede, *Culture's Consequences: International Differences in Work-Related Values* (Beverly Hills, CA: Sage, 1980); F. Kluckhohn and F. Strodtbeck, *Variations in Value Orientations* (New York: Row, Peterson, 1961); Charles H. Kraft, "Worldview in Intercultural Communication," in *Intercultural and International Communication*, ed. Fred L. Casmir (Washington, DC: University Press of America, 1978): 407–28; Larry E. Sarbaugh, "A Taxonomic Approach to Intercultural Communication."

18. Kluckhohn and Strodtbeck, *Variations in Value Orientations*.

19. Moshe F. Rubenstein, *Patterns of Problem Solving* (Englewood Cliffs, NJ: Prentice Hall, 1975): 1–2.

20. William B. Gudykunst and Stella Ting-Toomey, *Culture and Interpersonal Communication* (Newbury Park, CA: Sage, 1988): 40–43.

21. Min-Sun Kim and William F. Sharkey, "Independent and Interdependent Construals of Self: Explaining Cultural Patterns of Interpersonal Communication in Multi-Cultural Organizational Settings," *Communication Quarterly* 43 (Winter 1995): 20–38.

22. Deborah A. Cai, Steven R. Wilson, and Laura E. Drake, "Culture in the Context of Intercultural Negotiation: Individualism-Collectivism and Paths to Integrative Agreements," *Human Communication Research* 26 (October 2000): 591–617.

23. Richard W. Brislin, Kenneth Cushner, Craig Cherrie, and Mahealani Yong, *Intercultural Interactions: A Practical Guide* (Beverly Hills, CA: Sage, 1986): 207–8, 219.

24. Hofstede, *Culture's Consequences*.

25. Ibid.

26. Myron W. Lustig and Laura L. Cassotta, "Comparing Group Communication across Cultures: Leadership, Conformity, and Discussion Procedures," in *Small Group Communication: A Reader*, 6th ed., eds. Robert S. Cathcart and Larry A. Samovar (Dubuque, IA: Wm. C. Brown, 1992): 393–404.

27. Hofstede, *Culture's Consequences*.

28. Myron W. Lustig and Jolene Koester, *Intercultural Competence: Interpersonal Communication across Cultures* (New York: HarperCollins, 1993).

29. Lustig and Cassotta, "Comparing Group Communication across Cultures."

30. Hofstede, *Culture's Consequences*.

31. Lustig and Cassotta, "Comparing Group Communication across Cultures."

32. Hall, *Beyond Culture*.

33. Linda Wai Ling Young, "Inscrutability Revisited," in *Language and Social Identity*, ed. John J. Gumperz (Cambridge: Cambridge University Press, 1982): 79.

34. Gudykunst and Ting-Toomey, *Culture and Interpersonal Communication*, 45.

35. Roichi Okabe, "Cultural Assumptions of East and West," in *Intercultural Communication Theory: International & Intercultural Communication Annual*, Vol. 7, ed. William B. Gudykunst (Beverly Hills, CA: Sage, 1983): 21–44.

36. Donald W. Klopf, "Japanese Communication Practices: Recent Comparative Research," *Communication Quarterly* 39 (Spring 1991): 130–43.

37. Lustig and Koester, *Intercultural Competence*.

38. Ibid.

39. Ruby K. Payne, *A Framework for Understanding Poverty* (Highlands, TX: aha! Process, Inc., 2001).

40. Myung-seok Park and Moon-soo Kim, "Communication Practices in Korea," *Communication Quarterly* 40 (Fall 1992): 398–404.

41. "Englishes Are the International Language," *Michigan Today* (June 1995): 17.

42. Leonard and Locke, "Communication Stereotypes."

43. Mark P. Orbe, "Remember, It's Always Whites' Ball: Descriptions of African American Male Communication," *Communication Quarterly* 42 (Summer 1994): 287–300.

44. Anita K. Foeman and Gary Pressley, "Ethnic Culture and Corporate Culture: Using Black Styles in Organizations," *Communication Quarterly* 35 (Fall 1987): 293–307.

45. Mark P. Orbe, "Remember, It's Always Whites' Ball."

46. Mark P. Orbe, "From the Standpoint(s) of Traditionally Muted Groups."

47. Rick Hicks and Kathy Hicks, *Boomers, X-ers, and Other Strangers: Understanding the Generational Differences that Divide Us* (Wheaton, IL: Tyndale, 1999).

48. Cheng Kuo, "Consumer Styles and Media Uses of Generation X-ers in Taiwan," *Asian Journal of Communication* 9, no. 1, (1999): 21–49.

49. Dhavan V. Shah, Nojin Kwak, and R. Lance Holbert, " 'Connecting' and 'Disconnecting' with Civic Life: Patterns of Internet Use and the Production of Social Capital," *Political Communication* 18 (April 2001): 141–162.

50. Thomas A. Timmerman, "Racial Diversity, Age Diversity, Interdependence, and Team Performance," *Small Group Research* 31 (October 2000): 592–606.

51. Mary R. Jackman, "The Subjective Meaning of Social Class Identification in the United States," *Public Opinion Quarterly* 43 (Winter 1979): 443–62.

52. Donald G. Ellis and Blake Armstrong, "Class, Gender, and Code on Prime-Time Television," *Communication Quarterly* 37 (Summer 1989): 157–169.

53. David L. Ritchie, "Parents' Workplace Experiences and Family Communication Patterns," *Communication Research* 24 (April 1997): 175–87.

54. Amy B. Jordan, "Social Class, Temporal Orientation, and Mass Media Use within the Family System," *Critical Studies in Mass Communication* 9 (December 1992): 374–86.

55. Ruby K. Payne, *A Framework for Understanding Poverty*.

56. Mark P. Orbe, "From the Standpoint(s) of Traditionally Muted Groups."

57. Linda K. Larkey, "The Development and Validation of the Workforce Diversity Questionnaire: An Instrument to Assess Interactions in Diverse Workgroups," *Management Communication Quarterly* 9 (February 1996): 296–337.

58. C. Kirchmeyer and A. Cohen, "Multicultural Groups: Their Performance and Reactions with Constructive Conflict," *Group & Organization Management* 17 (1992): 153–70; C. Kirchmeyer, "Multicultural Task Groups: An Account of the Low Contribution Level of Minorities," *Small Group Research* 24 (February 1993): 127–48.

59. J. C. Bruno Teboul, "Racial/Ethnic 'Encounter' in the Workplace: Uncertainty, Information-Seeking, and Learning Patterns among Racial/Ethnic Majority and Minority New Hires," *The Howard Journal of Communication* 10 (April–June 1999): 97–121.

60. Tadasu Todd Imahori, "On Becoming 'American,'" in *Among Us: Essays on Identity, Belonging, and Intercultural Competence*, eds.

Myron W. Lustig and Jolene Koester (New York: Longman, 2000): 68–77.

61. Stella Ting-Toomey, "Rhetorical Sensitivity Style in Three Cultures: France, Japan, and the United States," *Central States Speech Journal* 39 (Spring 1991): 28–36; Mary Jane Collier, "A Comparison of Conversations among and between Domestic Culture Groups: How Intra- and Intercultural Competencies Vary," *Communication Quarterly* 36 (Spring 1988): 122–44.

62. David W. Kale, "Ethics in Intercultural Communication," in *Intercultural Communication: A Reader*, 6th ed., eds. Larry A. Samovar and Richard E. Porter (Belmont, CA: Wadsworth, 1991).

63. Charles R. Bantz, "Cultural Diversity and Group Cross-Cultural Team Research," *Journal of Applied Communication Research* 21 (February 1993): 1–20.

Larry Dale Gordon/Getty Images

DEVELOPING THE SMALL GROUP

For a collection of individuals with diverse backgrounds and personalities to coalesce into a small group, members must develop such group variables as roles, norms, communication patterns, a status hierarchy, effective procedures, cohesiveness, and a stable leadership structure. This section examines key characteristics of the individuals who compose a group and explains how members develop these important throughput processes. In addition to theoretical perspectives, practical information to help you function as a group leader is also provided.

THE MEMBERS

Central Message

The number of members and their personal characteristics are input variables that seriously affect group communication and productivity.

STUDY OBJECTIVES

As a result of studying Chapter 6 you should be able to:

1. Know how many members should compose a specific small group.

2. Describe traits such as preference for procedural order, cognitive complexity, and self-monitoring and explain how each can affect problem-solving discussions.

3. Describe each dimension of the Myers-Briggs Type Indicator® and explain the positive contribution each type can make to group discussion.

4. Describe behaviors that indicate an attitude of responsibility for the success of a small group, and the ethical standards supportive of such an attitude.

5. Explain how a high level of communication apprehension can affect group outcomes.

6. Describe attitudes such as authoritarianism, egalitarianism, and open-mindedness; behaviors associated with each; and their effects on a group.

Advertising agencies typically accomplish much of their work in teams. A client—a car manufacturer, a restaurant, a line of cosmetics—is assigned a team of individuals. One particular agency we know about had an exceptionally productive and successful team of five people. Ben, the team's leader, was the head of the retailing division and handled the meetings. Candi, the account executive, served as liaison between the agency and the client. The others described her as "buttoned down." Marija was the media buyer, Vinnie was the art director, and Toni was the copywriter. The team members took it as a matter of personal pride that they were often given the most demanding clients and toughest assignments. The team also represented a variety of perspectives and work styles. Such a combination often derails a team if members don't know how to work with others whose styles, perspectives, and approaches are different. But members of this team worked well together. Ben and especially Candi were highly task focused and able to keep everyone on track. Both took seriously their responsibilities for keeping the project within budget. But they both truly appreciated Vinnie and Toni who, although sometimes taking the group's discussion on a tangent, often came up with just the right theme, just the right visual image, or just the right slogan for a particular ad campaign. Marija, the number cruncher, had an excellent command of figures about how much exposure per dollar various media would provide. Toni, though usually fulfilling a creative role, consistently helped the team focus on the project by asking lots of questions about the client, the target market, the product, and the main images the client wanted to project. In other circumstances, it would be easy to imagine this group self-destructing over differences in work styles, but these open-minded, committed, and competent members had learned both to appreciate and to work with their differences, and they were highly successful.

Both the individual characteristics of members and their mix affect how a small group functions and how productive it is. LaFasto and Larson, in their study of outstanding teams of all sorts, discovered that excellent team members possessed two overall competencies, a working knowledge of the problem and the ability to work in a team.[1] They found six specific factors that mattered the most: experience, problem-solving ability, communication that was both open and supportive, a desire to act rather than be passive, and a personal style that was positive and optimistic. Members of the advertising team mentioned in our story demonstrated all of these characteristics. Productive group members are, or become, skilled and knowledgeable regarding the group's task, really want the group to succeed, and are communicatively competent collaborators. The right people can make group work rewarding, even joyous. Whether we like it or not, group members evaluate each other on such things as their perceived interaction skills and, more often than not, dislike is often based on *lack* of interaction skills. In Chapter 5 we discussed cultural influences that affect member behaviors. Here, we describe how the number of members and their individual characteristics can help produce a winning team.

Group Size

Theoretically, each member brings some different knowledge, perspectives, and skills relevant to the group's purpose. For complex, nonroutine problems, groups of individuals with diverse skills, information, and perspectives are more effective than homogeneous groups.[2] But that does not mean the more, the better. At some point the increasing cost and difficulty of coordinating the work of more people outweighs the gain. Thelen's principle of **least-sized groups** says we should strive for a group as small as possible, but that has all the expertise and diverse points of view necessary to complete the task well.[3]

> That's a real key thing—how big, how small do you make the group, who needs to be in on the discussion, who doesn't.
>
> *A. B., University Dean*

As group size increases, the complexity of interpersonal relationships increases geometrically. In a three-person group, only three two-person relationships can exist, but in a group of 10 members there can be 45. As numbers increase, so does the discrepancy in the amount of talking done by different members, with a tendency for one person to do relatively more talking.[4] Leadership becomes more centralized and formal, with increasing demands on designated leaders to regulate and keep order. Increased size produces lower

Least-Sized Group

The principle that the ideal group contains as few members as possible so long as all necessary perspectives and skills are represented.

As groups get larger, they are harder to coordinate, have less equal participation rates, and are less satisfying than smaller groups.
elektraVision/Index Stock Imagery, Inc.

member satisfaction and cohesiveness, higher competitiveness, increased aggressiveness, increased withdrawal, and fragmentation of work,[5] although some of the negative effects of group size can be offset by a teambuilding program,[6] which we discuss in Chapter 8. On the other hand, groups of fewer than four members can produce tension and may feel constrained.[7]

Consider This 6.1

Many groups are larger than the ideal, sometimes reaching 15 or 20 members. Organizers often believe, for political reasons, that they must include certain people or ask representatives of particular departments. Can you think of other reasons why some groups end up being large? Do you think these reasons are legitimate? Why or why not? What can you do if you find yourself in a group that is larger than ideal?

Other factors being equal, five to seven members is an optimal size for participant satisfaction and cohesiveness. This size is small enough to permit informality, allow everyone a chance to speak up, keep down social loafing (nonparticipation), and facilitate consensus decisions, yet provide the diverse information and points of view needed for quality decisions. In practice, many groups are larger for reasons that have little to do with efficiency or effectiveness.

Personal Behavior: Characteristics, Attitudes, and Competencies

Trait

A relatively enduring, consistent pattern of behavior or other observable characteristic.

Attitude

A network of beliefs and values, not directly measurable, that a person holds toward an object, person, or concept; produces a tendency to react in specific ways toward that object, person, or concept.

A small group's most important resource is its members. A group cannot be productive if members are lazy, uncooperative, or incompetent. Your personal traits, personality characteristics, attitudes, and competencies are a major factor that helps determine whether a group succeeds or fails. Hirokawa and his colleagues recently analyzed stories group members offered to explain why groups succeed or fail.[8] Members who were knowledgeable and skillful, had high motivation for the group task, were willing to listen and to share information, and expressed pleasure, excitement—as well as fear—about the task were perceived to help a group succeed. On the other hand, group failure was attributed to members who were selfish and resentful, were either overconfident and cocky or demonstrated no enthusiasm for the task, failed to share information, and were poor listeners. We hope this isn't you! We encourage you to use this chapter as a tool for self-evaluation and personal goal setting.

A **trait** is a consistent pattern of behavior or other observable characteristic. Traits are influenced by both genetics and environment, and our behavior is also determined by our attitudes. An **attitude** is a cluster of values and beliefs held by a person toward an object, person or type of persons, or concept. We infer attitudes from what people say and do. Recent research has confirmed that some personal traits and attitudes produce behaviors that are better for groups than others.[9] For instance, an extremely individualistic attitude makes it hard for someone to operate well as a member of a team.

Personal Traits

A number of personal traits have been shown to influence behavior in groups, including psychological sex type[10] and verbal argumentativeness.[11] We will now discuss three general traits that have a significant bearing on the type of group member someone can be. These traits are thinking patterns (cognitive complexity), self-monitoring, and preference for procedural order.

Cognitive Complexity   How members act in discussions of complex problems, especially when there are wide differences among members' perspectives and preexisting beliefs, is seriously affected by a trait psychologists call *cognitive complexity*. Related to but different from general intelligence, **cognitive complexity** refers to an individual's ability to interpret multiple signals simultaneously: how differentiated, abstract, and organized someone's ability to process information is. In common terms, this is a measure of complex-to-simplistic thinking—Do you think in only either/or terms, or can you perceive shades of gray? People high in cognitive complexity employ more differentiated arguments in speaking, are better able to integrate their goals with those of listeners in these arguments, and can better accept and build on others' feelings and beliefs during discussions than people lower in cognitive complexity.[12] Cognitively complex discussants ask more questions and provide more objective information during discussions of class policies than do their less developed classmates; complex people do not assume to know the other's viewpoint. Less developed discussants use their own frames of reference as if these are also the viewpoints of others. During group decision making, high complexity persons can arrive at consensus much better than less complex persons, who speak as if they already know the experience and viewpoints of fellow group members.[13] We suggest you seek out and listen closely to feedback about your own speaking. If you seem to be low in cognitive complexity, you can begin to assume less, ask more questions, and check out what you think others want, feel, and think.

Cognitive Complexity
How well developed a group member's construct system for interpreting signals is; cognitively complex individuals are able to synthesize more information and think in more abstract and organized terms than are cognitively simple individuals.

Self-Monitoring   A second cognitive variable important to how we interact with others in problem solving is called *self-monitoring*. **Self-monitoring** refers to the degree to which a person monitors and controls self-presentation in social situations: "*High self-monitors* attend closely to cues from other participants regarding situationally appropriate behavior and use these cues to guide their social actions. *Low self-monitors* rely on their own attitudes in determining what social behavior to exhibit. . . ."[14] High self-monitors, then, are keenly aware of whether others' responses to their behavior suggest approval or disapproval of that behavior. They can adjust their behavior to achieve desired responses better than low self-monitors by displaying

Self-Monitoring
The extent to which someone pays attention to and controls his or her self-presentation in social situations; high self-monitors are able to assess how others perceive them and adapt their behavior to elicit a desired response.

behaviors and role functions appropriate to the group. Modifying behavior instead of following initial inclinations ". . . is the primary mechanism by which high self-monitors emerge as leaders."[15] In other words, sensitivity to cues from others is not sufficient; flexibility and skill in *adjusting one's behavior* as a small group member is also necessary. We discuss how self-monitoring is related to leadership emergence in Chapter 9.

> I'd rather not have individuals in the team that have big egos, because we're going to have to right-size their egos before they can go forward.
>
> *M. K. S., Vice President, Investor Services Firm, retired*

Rhetorical Sensitivity

Speaking and phrasing statements in such a way that the feelings and beliefs of the listener are considered; phrasing statements so as not to offend others or trigger emotional overreactions.

Overlapping the trait of self-monitoring is the characteristic called **rhetorical sensitivity**. Rhetorically sensitive persons monitor what they say, adapting their statements to how they think other members of the group may react.[16] You might have doubts about the ethical standards of self-monitors who are rhetorically sensitive, but we do not. The rhetorically sensitive person is not a *reflector* who says what she thinks others want her to say, or a *noble self* who says whatever comes to mind. Rather, before speaking out, rhetorically sensitive people search consciously for the most effective way to express their point in order to help ensure that other members give their points the fairest possible hearing. They are careful not to insult or inflame other members.

Preference for Procedural Order   A third cognitive trait desirable in members of problem-solving groups is the ability to think critically and systematically. Gouran reported a tendency for most discussion participants to accept inferences without challenging them, even when patently flawed reasoning was involved.[17] For thorough evaluation of proposed solutions, individuals skilled in all aspects of critical thinking along with group procedures that encourage thorough critical evaluation of all solutions are needed. Critical thinking and systematic thinking may be linked in a personality trait referred to as **preference for procedural order** (PPO), which is characterized by a need or desire to follow a clear, linear structure during problem solving. Putnam described the rationale for such a personality measure, development of a questionnaire for measuring it, and its importance to how groups function as problem solvers.[18] Later research by Hirokawa and associates suggests that high PPO persons do much better in choosing among alternatives when a highly structured problem-solving procedure (such as is presented in Chapter 11) is followed by the group. High PPO persons did not seem to think as clearly as possible during loosely structured discussions. However, groups of low PPO persons who are comfortable with less structured discussion did equally well whether following a procedure of high or low structure. No mixed-PPO groups were considered, but this research suggests that systematic procedures would improve (or at least not reduce) the output quality of most decision-making groups.[19]

Preference for Procedural Order

A trait characterized by need or desire to follow a clear, linear structure during problem solving and decision making.

Most groups are likely to be composed of members with varying preferences for order and structure. Half the students Pavitt surveyed preferred a loose "reach testing" decision-making process and the other half preferred a more linear structure, perhaps combined with reach testing.[20] Groups whose members' preferences are similar will have an easier time working together.

Personality Characteristics

In our experience, personality differences and differences in how members approach work create the most frustration in groups. The differences themselves are not the problem; the problem occurs because group members do not know how to work with (much less appreciate) people who are very different from themselves. Of the hundreds of personality characteristics we could have selected to discuss here, we have chosen to talk about the Myers-Briggs Type Indicator® because it is one of the most widely known and researched classification systems. In addition, we think you will have a relatively easy time recognizing yourself within this classification system.

The **Myers-Briggs Type Indicator**®(MBTI) is a personality measure, based on the work of psychologist Carl Jung, that categorizes individuals along four dimensions on the basis of how they relate to the world around them.[21] A mother and daughter psychologist team, Isabel Briggs Myers and Katherine Briggs, extended Jung's work and developed the personality measure currently in widespread use. Each of the MBTI dimensions assesses a particular aspect of how we interact with the world. Each dimension represents a continuum, with a descriptor anchoring each end of the continuum (e.g., extravert and introvert). We each have a preference, sometimes strong but sometimes mild, for one end or the other of the continuum. The MBTI measures our preferences along each of the four dimensions and describes our personality types on the basis of what combination of dimensions we exhibit. No one is a "pure" type—each of us displays some characteristics of all the dimensions. However, the anchor points for each dimension display markedly different communication and behavior preferences from each other.

Consider This 6.2

If you want to know what your own Myers-Briggs classification is, you can take a version of the MBTI®, called the Jung Typology Test, for free at the following website: www.humanmetrics.com/cgi-win/JTypes2.asp. After you answer all the questions, click "Score It" and your four-letter code will display. After reading the following descriptions, how accurate is your code? How well does the MBTI® help explain the way you like to work? What types of people are most difficult for you to work with?

The **extraversion-introversion dimension** assesses whether you focus on the outer world or your own inner world. Extraverts focus outwardly. They

Myers-Briggs Type Indicator®

A personality measure based on the work of Carl Jung that categorizes individuals based on how they relate to the world around them.

Extraversion-Introversion Dimension

The Myers-Briggs Type Indicator® dimension concerned with whether one's focus is the external world (extraversion) or one's internal, subjective landscape (introversion).

are sociable, like people, often talk to figure out what they think, and generally enjoy working with others in a group. Not so introverts, who much prefer to work alone. Introverts think things through and don't share ideas unless they've figured out first what their positions are. Extraverts don't mind being interrupted, but introverts hate it. Extraverts happily collaborate with others to make decisions, whereas introverts are comfortable making decisions independently. It may seem that extraverts are ideally suited for group work and introverts are not, but introverts can be very thoughtful and careful in evaluating information and can contribute a great deal to group interaction. These two types operate so differently within a group that they may easily misunderstand one another or fail to appreciate each other's contributions to the group. The MBTI code letter for extraversion is E and the letter for introversion is I.

> [You might have to say], "During this meeting, the introverts are going to need time to talk, so you extroverts, there's nothing wrong with a 10-second pause. You don't have to pick up on everybody's phrases."
>
> *P. T., Director, University Planning and Development*

Sensing-Intuiting Dimension

The Myers-Briggs Type Indicator® dimension concerned with the type of information individuals use; sensers prefer facts and figures whereas intuiters prefer to dream about possibilities.

The **sensing-intuiting dimension** assesses the type of information group members prefer to use. Its code letters are S (sensing) and N (intuiting). Sensing individuals prefer and trust facts and figures. They operate in the here and now and are very much rooted in what they can actually apprehend through their physical senses. Intuiting individuals, in contrast, prefer to dream about possibilities and to make connections between seemingly unconnected ideas and thoughts. They easily make intuitive leaps, which sensing individuals mistrust because they prefer concrete information. Intuitives see the big picture whereas sensing individuals tune in to the details, which bore the intuitives. Imagination, invention, and creativity are important to intuitives. In a group, these are the idea people who comfortably leap from idea to idea, but may be short on follow-through. Sensing individuals, however, are careful, able to provide specific facts and illustrations to support the big ideas, and can provide the grounding that intuitives sometimes lack. Both types provide skills groups need.

Thinking-Feeling Dimension

The Myers-Briggs Type Indicator® dimension concerned with how individuals prefer to make decisions; thinkers are objective and fact-based whereas feelers are subjective and emotion-based.

The **thinking-feeling dimension,** coded T and F, refers to how individuals prefer to make decisions, whether through careful analysis of objective evidence (thinkers) or empathy and subjective connection with others (feelers). Thinkers are comfortable with a systematic, critical thinking process. They like to analyze data and arrive at verifiable conclusions. They are task-oriented and like holding everyone to a single standard. In contrast, feelers tune in readily to the interpersonal relationships among group members and prefer to adjust the standards to meet individual circumstances. Feelers worry about group harmony and will make sure a group takes individual feelings into account in making a decision. Thinkers may forget to take others' feelings into account, but will evaluate evidence critically and come to a logical conclusion. Clearly, thinkers and feelers operate by different internal logic systems in making decisions, yet each system is an important one for a group to consider.

The last dimension, the **perceiving-judging dimension,** concerns how people organize the world around them. Perceivers, coded P, are spontaneous and flexible and react well to change. They like to gather as much information as they can prior to making a decision. At their worst, they are easily distracted and will postpone making a decision until they've collected every piece of information possible—usually an impossible accomplishment. Judgers, coded J, are decisive and sure in making decisions. They make a plan and can stick to it. However, they don't like to change plans once they are made and can become stubborn and rigid. Perceivers constantly second-guess decisions they have made, worrying that they may have forgotten something important. Judgers are never truly comfortable until the group's work is completed and are excellent at keeping the group focused on the task; however, perceivers can roll with the punches if the group's plan falls through. Perceivers are more excited by starting new projects, whereas judgers are more excited by completing them. You can probably see how perceivers and judgers frustrate each other, yet how each one's strengths balance the weaknesses of the other.

> Everybody's different. They all have different talents, they all have different strengths and weaknesses, and they all do their jobs in very different ways.
>
> *P. B., City Administrator*

These dimensions combine to form 16 different personality types. For instance, someone assessed as ESTJ is extroverted, relies on facts and figures, likes to think things through objectively, and is decisive. A person with an INFP configuration is likely to be shy and quiet, dreamy, empathetic with the other group members, and spontaneous. The most important point to remember about the Myers-Briggs Type Indicator® classifications is that each dimension provides a potential benefit to the group—but only if members recognize the potential strengths in having diverse personalities in the group. If members do not recognize this, they may let frustrations, natural when different personality types try to work together, escalate into unproductive conflict. The chart in Table 6.1 summarizes the MBTI dimensions.

Consider This 6.3

Which people on the advertising team introduced earlier would be likely to have the most difficult time working together? Why do you think some people are able to work with others whose personalities and styles are very different, and others are not?

Communicative Attitudes

Attitudes about personal responsibility, other people, and ways of expressing thoughts are vital to how much a member contributes to group goal achievement. The kind of member others most appreciate is someone who will work

Perceiving-Judging Dimension

The Myers-Briggs Type Indicator® dimension concerning how people organize the world; perceivers are spontaneous and flexible whereas judgers are decisive and sure.

TABLE 6.1
Characteristics of
the Myers-Briggs®
Dimensions.[22]

Extraversion-Introversion (Where Is Your Focus?)	
Extraversion (E)	**Introversion (I)**
Focus on external world.	Focus on inner world.
Sociable.	Shy, reserved.
Use talk to clarify your own thinking.	Think things through before sharing verbally.
Enjoy working in a group.	Enjoy working alone.
Don't mind being interrupted.	Hate being interrupted.
Comfortable making decisions collaboratively.	Comfortable making decisions independently.

Sensing-Intuiting (What Type of Information You Prefer to Use)	
Sensing (S)	**Intuiting (N)**
Trust facts and figures, what can be perceived through the senses.	Trust imagination and intuition, what can be imagined.
Prefer concrete information and ideas.	Prefer to dream about possibilities.
Detail-oriented.	"Big picture"–oriented.
Stay in "here and now."	Future-oriented.
Can find specific facts/evidence to illustrate an idea.	Dream about possibilities and make intuitive leaps among seemingly unconnected ideas.
Grounded.	Inventive.

Thinking-Feeling (How You Make Decisions)	
Thinking (T)	**Feeling (F)**
Carefully analyze objective information to make decisions.	Use empathy and subjective feelings to make decisions.
Systematic, critical thinker; like to analyze data to arrive at conclusion.	Tune in to feelings of others and take them into account.
Task-oriented.	Relationship-oriented.
Hold all to a single standard.	Adjust standards to meet individual circumstances.
Use evidence to come to logical conclusion, regardless of individual feelings.	Take others' feelings into account in group decision.

Perceiving-Judging (How You Organize Your World)	
Perceiving (P)	**Judging (J)**
Gather as much information as possible before deciding.	Decisive; can make quick decisions.
Spontaneous and flexible; react well to change.	Stick to a plan once made; dislike change.
Excited by starting new projects.	Excited by finishing projects.
Second-guess decisions you've made yourselves.	Certain; don't second guess.
Make sure group considers all relevant information.	Keep group focused on task.

hard on behalf of the group; others least appreciate someone who is there in name only, or someone whose attitude is negative or cynical.[23] Pay particular attention to your attitudes about your group and your fellow group members, and give yourself an attitude adjustment if you need to!

A Sense of Responsibility for the Group's Success   Perhaps the most important attitude of ideal small group members is summarized by the phrase *a sense of responsibility for the success of the group*. Constructive members feel a personal responsibility to do whatever they can to help the group achieve its goals. They are *dependable*. Responsible members put accomplishment of group goals ahead of selfish wants. They are guided by a number of ethical standards, such as:

1. No member has a right to act in a way that would be disastrous if done by all members.

2. No one has a right to expect more effort from other members than he or she makes for the group.

3. Every member should be faithful in carrying out assignments for the group, and if prevented from doing so, should immediately notify the group and explain what went wrong.

4. A member should share any relevant information and ideas for the group to use in solving problems.

The extent to which group members naturally feel a collective responsibility for the group may in part be culturally based. In extremely collectivist cultures, there is no "self" separate from the group. Members of collectivist cultures, by definition, naturally put the good of the group ahead of their own individual good, and do not perceive this as the sacrifice that someone from an individualistic culture would perceive it. Perhaps the ultimate in feeling responsibility for and to a group was exemplified in the 1980s film *Black Rain*, where the Japanese detective said he would willingly commit ritual suicide if he failed to meet his obligation to the group.

The kinds of pronouns used by members indicate commitment to the group: *we, us*, and *our* rather than *you* and *your*. Commitment is also demonstrated by members who volunteer to do a fair share of the work and can be counted on to get it done. In our student project groups, social loafers cause the greatest friction among members. In sum, the valuable group member is fully responsible and trustworthy. If you refuse to act that way, other members are better off without you; maybe they can replace you with a useful member.

Willingness to Communicate   To be a productive member, your *willingness to communicate* must be greater than your need to protect yourself from disagreement or embarrassment. People who have relevant information or see flaws in proposals but do not speak up actually harm the group by taking up a member slot that a more outspoken person with needed resources might have

Communication Apprehension (CA)

Anxiety or fear of speaking in a variety of social situations, including in group settings; reticence; shyness.

occupied. They could be called *excess baggage* of the group. These people manifest the trait of **communication apprehension** (CA, sometimes called *shyness* or *reticence*), which manifests itself with varying degrees of self-concern, self-doubt, fear, anxiety about speaking, and defensiveness toward others. In this book we are concerned only about communication apprehension experienced by participants in a group's discussion, not in public speaking, family relations, and so on. Communication apprehension has far greater negative repercussions in group settings than in those other settings.[24] For example, McCroskey and Richmond say that high CA group members speak much less than members low in CA, choose seats where leaders can overlook them, make more irrelevant comments, are less likely to become a group's leader, and are likely to express strong agreement, even when inwardly they disagree. High CAs are perceived as making little contribution to the group. Others see them as less desirable members than low CAs. High CAs even have a lower opinion of *themselves* than other members have of them.[25]

A reticence about speaking may have a cultural origin. Porter and Samovar explain that in certain cultures, particularly high-context ones, people do not speak as much as people in low-context cultures such as that of the United States.[26] They do not rely on verbal communication to the same extent and are sometimes suspicious of people who talk a lot. A member of this type of culture may have a very difficult time adapting to the noisy, verbal, direct communication style of Americans. It is particularly important for others in the group to recognize this possible source of reticence to communicate and to demonstrate patience.

If you are relatively high in CA as a group member, what can you do? Your college or university may have a center where you can learn such helpful techniques as *systematic desensitization* or *cognitive restructuring*. Although fearful of group settings, if high CAs are willing to engage in small group activities, this exposure can help lessen their anxieties.[27] McCroskey and Richmond add that an in-depth understanding of the communication process and of specific skills can help. To that end, we next consider the attitudes and skills of communicating assertively as opposed to communicating either aggressively or passively.

Assertiveness

Behavior that shows respect both for your own and others' rights, in contrast to passive and aggressive behavior.

Passiveness

Nonassertive behavior that allows one's own rights and beliefs to be ignored or dominated, often to avoid conflict, even at the expense of good decision making.

Aggressiveness

Behavior designed to win or dominate that fails to respect the rights or beliefs of others.

I also love to have people who are highly motivated, and who really want to learn, and are not afraid.

B. H., Director, State Program

Assertiveness refers to communicative behavior reflecting respect both for oneself and for other group members. Assertive people communicate openly to other members as equals. Assertiveness lies on a continuum, illustrated in Figure 6.1, between **passiveness** (nonassertiveness) and **aggressiveness** in communicating. Aggressive people are highly dominant and often authoritarian; they try to force ideas and practices on others. They call names, demand, insult, threaten, command, shout, pound the table, and frequently drown out others who are speaking. Rather than challenging informa-

Aggressive	Assertive	Nonassertive (passive)	

FIGURE 6.1
Assertiveness lies between aggressiveness and nonassertiveness.

tion or reasoning as such, they often attack other people. Emotional bullies, their motto might be, "Do it my way or fight!" Aggressive behavior may stem from psychopathology, from cultural practices, inability to handle frustration, or just a lack of verbal skills for dealing constructively with conflict.[28] No matter what the cause, this behavior is destructive to productive discussion, cohesiveness, and teamwork. We think that both aggressive and passive behavior violate the ethical principles described in Chapter 1 and earlier in this chapter. If you want to know how assertive your communication or that of your fellow group members is, you may want to complete the assertiveness rating scale shown in Figure 15.13 in Chapter 15.

Passive discussants, like high CAs, go along with a majority rather than argue, even when they disagree. In going along despite doubts, they are unethical, untrue to themselves, and therefore untrue to the group. Passive members tend to make little eye contact, speak so softly they are hard to hear, and won't resist aggressors. The stereotyped "yessers" shown in Figure 6.2 epitomize passive behavior. Their motto might be, "We'll do it your way; nothing is worth fighting over." The most harmful type of passive member engages in **passive-aggressive behavior,** which is highly destructive to teamwork. Passive-aggressives attempt to get their way subtly; they sabotage rather than

Passive-Aggressive Behavior

Behavior that appears on the surface to be cooperative but subtly sabotages group work, such as when members "forget" to carry out an assignment.

"Aye." "Aye." "Aye."   "All those in favor say 'Aye.'"   "Aye." "Aye." "Aye."

FIGURE 6.2
Passive "yessers" do not express genuine agreement.

confront in the way an assertive person does. Instead of saying, "I don't like that policy" or "I disagree," they may be late with an assigned report, "forget" to carry out an assignment, fail to attend a meeting, or neglect to do their share of the group work.

In contrast to both aggressors and passives, assertive members disagree openly and explain why. They explain what they think as clearly as possible and state what they want. Even more important, they try hard to understand the information, ideas, perspectives, and wants of other members, and to co-orient so a mutually satisfactory decision may be found.

Egalitarianism

Belief in the equality of all people; results in the preference for including all group members in problem solving, not just a few high-status members.

Authoritarianism

Tendency to accept uncritically the information, ideas, and proposals of authority figures such as a high-status group member or leader; results in preference for strong leaders and follower subservience.

Egalitarianism-Authoritarianism   *Egalitarianism* and *authoritarianism* are contrasting ways of seeing human relationships. **Egalitarianism** is the belief in the equal importance of all persons; this is a tenet of the U.S. Declaration of Independence. Egalitarian people encourage full participation by all group members; they tend to be free of bigotry and stereotypes. They abhor bossiness and dictatorial behavior in self and others. In contrast, members high in **authoritarianism** prefer a controlling leader and will dominate a group when placed in a position of leadership. High authoritarians accept uncritically information and ideas expressed by or attributed to authorities (i.e., experts). They ask opinions of others less often, act less friendly, and make more directive comments ("Do this!") than egalitarians.[29]

Egalitarianism and authoritarianism are, in part, culturally based. Lustig and Cassotta note that members of high power distance cultures, which include the Philippines, Mexico, India, and Venezuela, have been socialized to accept clear distinctions between leaders and followers, and thus should be more comfortable with authoritarian group leadership.[30] Similarly, cultures high on masculinity, which value control, objectivity, and assertiveness are also likely to prefer authoritarian leadership. In contrast, cultures high in femininity or low in power distance, such as the Scandinavian countries, should favor democratic leadership. Individualism may be related to egalitarianism as well. In individualistic cultures, where self-initiative is rewarded, democratic leadership is likely to be preferred.

In the dominant culture of the United States, we value egalitarian behavior and expect our group leaders to involve us in decision making. As we have noted, other cultures do not assume that everyone has an equal right to participate; they expect the leader to assume strict, authoritarian control. However, for most of the groups in which you will find yourself in the United States, you are safest to adopt an egalitarian attitude.

Open-Mindedness   The preceding description of cognitive traits and attitudes toward other persons and communicating has implied the ideal attitude of productive team members toward new information and ideas—*open-minded*, or curious and low in prejudices. Hirokawa et al.'s research credited member openness, effective listening, and information as factors in a group's success,[31] and LaFasto and Larson observed that effective members are open to the ideas and opinions of the other members.[32] <u>Open-minded members are low in the trait called **dogmatism.** The more dogmatic people are, the less willing they are to try to understand new ideas, to listen to or accept evidence that contradicts their present beliefs, and to base conclusions on the total pool of information available to the group.</u>[33] Arguments based on evidence and sound reasoning can change the positions of open-minded persons, but will not influence dogmatic persons, whose decisions are based more on prior beliefs, internal needs, and emotions than a desire to know the truth and be logically consistent.

Dogmatism

A tendency to hold rigidly to personal beliefs; closed-mindedness to evidence and reasoning contrary to one's beliefs.

Dogmatic people see things in either-or, black-or-white terms. One of us, while discussing the relative merits of collective bargaining with several highly educated individuals, was dismayed to hear such dogmatic utterances as, "I'm just against unions in principle. They're wrong. I wouldn't even consider joining one." Others said, "Unionism is good. Management just doesn't care about us who do the real work." Neither statement demonstrates open-minded use of evidence or reasoning, and neither makes allowance for exceptions. People who talk like this, without qualification, question, or evidence, can block group consensus.

Consider This 6.4

The advertising team described at the beginning of this chapter succeeded in part because members were willing to hear each other out. What effect do you think a dogmatic team member would have had? What are the biggest problems a dogmatic member creates for a group? How could the members have handled a dogmatic member?

Ideally, group members would all be open-minded. We are sure you do not want to behave dogmatically and so create roadblocks to group co-orientation and unity. A little self-monitoring can help a lot. *Ask* for points of view that differ from yours, and be sure you listen actively to them. If you observe dogmatism to be a problem in a continuing group, tackle the problem head-on by describing it. Keep reminding the group that mutual respect is essential for group cooperation and for effective performance.

SUMMARY

1. Groups need diversity of information, perspectives, and skills, but too many members complicate the discussion process. Groups should be *least-sized*: as small as possible with the requisite diversity and variety needed to do the job.

2. Ideally, group members facing a typical discussion task should be high in cognitive complexity so they can deal with complex multifaceted problems. Members who are high self-monitors, and thus rhetorically sensitive, think carefully before speaking.

3. Groups, particularly those with members high in preference for procedural order, generally perform better when they follow some systematic process for solving problems.

4. The Myers-Briggs Type Indicator® helps members understand basic personality differences rooted in how people perceive the world; ideally, members appreciate the diverse strengths these differences bring to the group.

5. Members should have a sense of responsibility for the success of the group, exhibited by their dependability, commitment to group goals, and follow-through in completing their fair share of the group's work.

6. Members who are high in communication apprehension, are passive, passive-aggressive, or aggressive, create problems for a group. Ideal members are assertive.

7. Group members should strive to develop egalitarian rather than authoritarian attitudes, which inhibit optimum group functioning.

8. Successful group members are willing to communicate openly, without dogmatism about their own opinions, which is the point of small group discussion.

KEY TERMS

 Test your knowledge of these key terms by visiting the Online Learning Center website at mhhe.com/galanes11

Aggressiveness
Assertiveness
Attitude
Authoritarianism
Cognitive complexity
Communication apprehension
Dogmatism

Egalitarianism
Extraversion-introversion dimension
Least-sized groups
Myers-Briggs Type Indicator®
Passive-aggressive behavior
Passiveness

Perceiving-judging dimension
Preference for procedural order
Rhetorical sensitivity
Self-monitoring
Sensing-intuiting dimension
Thinking-feeling dimension
Trait

EXERCISES

 Go to self-quizzes on the Online Learning Center at mhhe.com/galanes11 to test your knowledge of the chapter concepts

1. Discuss the following question with your classmates, first in small groups, then as an entire class: How much can we trust each other to be truthful and to carry a fair share of work in the small groups we form in this class?

2. For one week keep a journal in which you write daily reports of examples of self-monitoring and rhetorical sensitivity. These may be your own efforts or those of others. At the end of the week, share your examples with your classmates.

3. Are you low or high in preference for procedural order? Have all the lows meet in one corner of the room and all the highs in the other. Each group should make two lists:
    a. In what ways is a member like me (high or low PPO) an asset to a group?
    b. In what ways is a member like me (high or low PPO) a detriment to a group?

    After the class reconvenes, the highs should read their list to the class as a whole. The lows should feel free to contribute assets or detriments the highs forgot. Next, the lows should share their list, with the highs contributing. What did you learn from this exercise?

4. Look again at the descriptions of the Myers-Briggs Type Indicator® dimensions and determine your own classifications by taking the Web-based scale mentioned in the chapter. In a small group of fellow students, share your types with each other and make two lists:
   a. For the pole position of each dimension (e.g., extraversion as one pole, introversion as the other pole), what are the advantages of having a member like that in the group?
   b. For the pole position of each dimension (e.g., extraversion as one pole, introversion as the other pole), what are the disadvantages of having a member like that in the group?

5. In a small group of fellow students discuss each of the following questions. One person should report your conclusions to the class.

   a. What kinds of behaviors suggest that a discussant was open-minded? Dogmatic?
   b. What effects have dogmatic persons had in groups to which you have belonged?
   c. How do you feel when a fellow group member speaks dogmatically? When a member speaks with an open-minded attitude?

6. After a topical discussion of some issue on which class members are widely divided in opinions (such as abortion, gun control, smokers' rights, or responsible sex), have every participant rate each of the others on the degree to which his or her behavior manifested open-mindedness versus dogmatism.

BIBLIOGRAPHY

Kroeger, Otto, and Janet A. Thuesen. *Type Talk: The 16 Personality Types That Determine How We Live, Love, and Work*. New York: Dell, 1988.

LaFasto, Frank, and Carl Larson. *When Teams Work Best: 6,000 Team Members and Leaders Tell What It Takes to Succeed*. Thousand Oaks, CA: Sage, 2001, 1–32.

McCroskey, James C., and Virginia P. Richmond. "Communication Apprehension and Small Group Communication." In *Small Group Communication: A Reader*. 5th ed. Robert S. Cathcart and Larry A. Samovar, eds. Dubuque, IA: Wm. C. Brown, 1988, 405–19.

NOTES

1. Frank LaFasto and Carl E. Larson, *When Teams Work Best: 6,000 Team Members and Leaders Tell What It Takes to Succeed* (Thousand Oaks, CA: Sage, 2001): 1–32.

2. Susan E. Jackson, "Team Composition in Organizational Settings: Issues in Managing a Diverse Work Force," in *Group Process and Productivity*, eds. Stephen Worchel, Wendy Wood, and Jeffry A. Simpson (Newbury Park, CA: Sage, 1992): 138–73.

3. Herbert A. Thelen, *Dynamics of Groups at Work* (Chicago: University of Chicago Press, 1954): 187.

4. Robert F. Bales et al., "Channels of Communication in Small Groups," *American Sociological Review* 16 (1952): 461–68.

5. J. A. Schellenberg, "Group Size as a Factor in Success of Academic Discussion Groups," *Journal of Educational Psychology* 33 (1959): 73–79; E. B. Smith, "Some Psychological Aspects of Committee Work," *Journal of Abnormal and Social Psychology* 11 (1927): 73–79; Richard B. Powers and William Boyle, "Common Dilemma Choices in Small vs. Large Groups" (Paper presented at American Psychological Association, Anaheim, CA, August 1983).

6. Albert V. Carron and Kevin S. Spink, "The Group Size–Cohesion Relationship in Minimal Groups," *Small Group Research* 26 (February 1995): 86–105.

7. Phillip E. Slater, "Contrasting Correlates of Group Size," *Sociometry* 21 (1958): 129–39.

8. Randy Y. Hirokawa, Daniel DeGooyer, and Kathleen Valde, "Using Narratives to Study Task Group Effectiveness," *Small Group Research* 31 (October 2000): 573-91.

9. Brian H. Spitzberg, "Interpersonal Competence in Groups," in *Small Group Communication: A Reader*, 6th ed., eds. Robert S. Cathcart and Larry A. Samovar (Dubuque, IA: Wm. C. Brown, 1992): 431.

10. James Joseph A. Diliberto, "A Communication Study of Possible Relationships between Psychological Sex Type and Decision-Making Effectiveness," *Small Group Research* 23 (August 1992): 379-407.

11. Dean Kazoleas and Bonnie Kay, "Are Argumentatives Really More Argumentative? The Behavior of Argumentatives in Group Deliberations over Controversial Issues" (Paper presented at the Speech Communication Association Conference, New Orleans, LA, November 1994).

12. Susan L. Kline, Cathy L. Hennen-Floyd, and Kathleen M. Farrell, "Cognitive Complexity and Verbal Response Mode Use in Discussion," *Communication Quarterly* 38 (1990): 350.

13. Ibid., 357-58.

14. Robert J. Ellis and Steven F. Cronshaw, "Self-Monitoring and Leader Emergence: A Test of Moderator Effects," *Small Group Research* 23 (1992): 114-15; see also Robert J. Ellis, Raymond S. Adamson, Gene Deszca, and Thomas F. Cawsey, "Self-Monitoring and Leadership Emergence," *Small Group Behavior* 19 (1988): 312-24.

15. Ellis and Cronshaw, "Self-Monitoring and Leader Emergence," 123.

16. Roderick P. Hart, Robert E. Carlson, and William F. Eadie, "Attitudes toward Communication and the Assessment of Rhetorical Sensitivity," *Communication Monographs* 47 (1980): 2-22.

17. Dennis S. Gouran, "Inferential Errors, Interaction, and Group Decision-Making," in *Communication and Group Decision Making*, eds. Randy Y. Hirokawa and Marshall Scott Poole (Beverly Hills, CA: Sage, 1986): 93-111.

18. Linda L. Putnam, "Preference for Procedural Order in Task-Oriented Small Groups," *Communication Monographs* 46 (1979): 193-218.

19. Randy Y. Hirokawa, Richard Ice, and Jeanmarie Cook, "Preference for Procedural Order, Discussion Structure, and Group Decision Performance," *Communication Quarterly* 36 (1988): 217-26.

20. Charles Pavitt, "Describing Know-How about Group Discussion Procedure: Must the Representation be Recursive?" *Communication Studies* 43 (Fall 1992): 150-70.

21. Synthesized from the following sources: Isabel Briggs Myers, *Introduction to Type: A Description of the Myers-Briggs Type Indicator* (Palo Alto, CA: Consulting Psychologists Press, 1987); Otto Kroeger and Janet Thuesen, *Type Talk: The 16 Personality Types That Determine How We Live, Love, and Work* (New York: Dell, 1988); Otto Kroeger with Janet A. Thuesen, *Type Talk at Work: How the 16 Personality Types Determine Your Success on the Job* (New York: Dell, 1992); and Paul D. Tieger and Barbara Barron-Tieger, *Nurture and Nature: Understand Your Child's Personality Type—And Become a Better Parent* (Boston: Little, Brown, 1977): 5-62.

22. Ibid.

23. Gloria J. Galanes (Unpublished research based on interviews with individuals identified by peers as excellent group leaders, 2002).

24. James C. McCroskey and Virginia P. Richmond, "Communication Apprehension and Small Group Communication," in *Small Group Communication: A Reader*, 5th ed., eds. Robert S. Cathcart and Larry A. Samovar (Dubuque, IA: Wm. C. Brown, 1988): 405-19.

25. K. W. Hawkins and R. A. Stewart, "Effects of Communication Apprehension on Perceptions of Leadership and Intragroup Attraction in Small Task-Oriented Groups," *Southern Communication Journal* 57 (1991): 1-10.

26. Richard E. Porter and Larry A. Samovar, "Communication in the Multicultural Group," in *Small Group Communication: Theory and Practice*, 7th ed., eds. Robert S. Cathcart, Larry A. Samovar, and Linda D. Henman (Boston, MA: McGraw-Hill, 1996): 306-15.

27. Rebecca B. Rubin and F. F. Jordan, "Effects of Instruction on Communication Apprehension and Communication Competence," *Communication Education* 46 (1997): 104-14.

28. Dominic A. Infante and Charles J. Wigley III, "Verbal Aggressiveness: An Interpersonal Model

and Measure," *Communication Monographs* 53 (1986): 61–67.

29. William A. Haythorn, Arthur Couch, D. Haefner, P. Langham, and L. F. Carter, "The Behavior of Authoritarian and Equalitative Personalities in Groups," *Human Relations* 3 (1956): 54–74; Stanley Milgram, "Some Conditions of Obedience and Disobedience to Authority," *Human Relations* 9 (1965): 57–76.

30. Myron W. Lustig and Laura L. Cassotta, "Comparing Group Communication Across Cultures: Leadership, Conformity, and Discussion Processes," in *Small Group Communication: Theory and Practice*, 7th ed., eds. Robert S. Cathcart, Larry A. Samovar, and Linda D. Henman (Boston, MA: McGraw-Hill, 1996): 316–26.

31. Randy Y. Hirokawa, Daniel DeGooyer, and Kathleen Valde, "Using Narratives to Study Task Group Effectiveness."

32. LaFasto and Larson, *When Teams Work Best*.

33. Milton Rokeach, *The Open and Closed Mind* (New York: Basic Books, 1960).

FROM INDIVIDUALS TO GROUP: NORMS AND ROLES

Central Message

When individuals collaborating on an interdependent goal begin to interact, their communication shapes them into a group with its own unique culture. The norms and roles that are developed are the building blocks of that culture.

STUDY OBJECTIVES

As a result of studying Chapter 7 you should be able to:

1. Describe the structuration process whereby member communication creates and maintains the group.

2. Explain the sources, characteristics, and remedies for both primary and secondary interpersonal tensions among group members.

3. Describe the two major phases through which most small groups pass and the kinds of group behavior prevalent during each.

4. Define group socialization and describe the phases of socialization.

5. Explain how group rules and norms develop; be able to recognize, state, and describe their effect on the group.

6. Explain the relationship between member behaviors, the functions of those behaviors, and the development of roles in a group.

7. Describe task, maintenance, and self-centered behavioral functions.

8. Explain how group members can manage the role conflicts that arise when membership in one group competes with membership in another group.

Six medical school faculty members, three psychiatrists with M.D.s, a psychologist, and two social workers, were selected by their deans to develop an instructional program to teach new methods for identifying psychological disorders.[1] All six members were outstanding teachers and competent in their respective areas. They were given the freedom to develop any program they wished as long as it could be funded by outside grants.

During their first meeting, the members decided to base all group decisions on sound reasoning. Julian was selected leader, perhaps because of his "take charge" nature. The members insisted that he was expected to encourage input by all members and equalize member influence. Julian made strong efforts to meet their expectations because he strongly believed that their best decisions would be those based on input from all members. He even went so far as to consult books on small group communication for ideas about how best to equalize participation and influence.

However, the group ran into problems over time. First, group members, strongly entrenched in the medical culture, afforded the M.D.s greater clout. As a result, those without medical degrees found their comments lacked influence. They talked less and less, did not push for their ideas, and after meetings would complain to each other. Second, the group was under pressure to continue to seek funding or their project would end. This pressure led to Julian's increased influence because his contacts enabled him to secure funds for two years.

Soon the group formed into a small clique with Julian as its authoritarian leader. He talked more than any other member. When he rephrased others' remarks, he did so in a way that mirrored his own ideas. Those without M.D.s came to rely on his interpretations and lost influence in the group. Conflicts were not dealt with in a constructive manner and meetings were tense. Despite all their best intentions, Julian found himself the leader of an autocratic clique. How did this group's initial democratic spirit get away from the members? We will look for answers in this chapter and the one that follows.

We have described verbal and nonverbal communication in a small group as the most important throughput variable by which a group's work is accomplished. In this chapter, we begin our focus on how communication helps a group develop from a collection of individuals into a group; later chapters will extend this discussion. The system perspective serves as our framework. Small group systems are created in *and* through the communicative behavior of members, producing outcomes like cohesiveness, a status hierarchy, and decisions. Likewise, small groups can change themselves by revising their interaction and, as we saw with our medical group, can go astray from their original intentions. Note that these group characteristics can be discussed as *both* throughput and output variables because the development of group processes (throughput) is also one of the accomplishments (outputs) of small group interaction. The "pecking order" of the medical group emerged out of their interaction (as output) and simultaneously served to guide and give sense to their discussion (as throughput). Rather than focus on individual characteristics per se, as in Chapter 6, we look at the impact of member behavior on system-level variables as a whole.

Development of Group Culture

We discussed *culture* in Chapter 5 as a group of individuals that can be identified by its shared patterns of values, beliefs, symbols, language, rules, and so forth. We discussed different ethnicities, international groupings, and race, gender, class, and age as culture. In this chapter we see that small groups develop unique cultures, just as societies and other large groupings do. So when we talk about culture and small groups, we mean three things: members bring their own cultural experiences into the group as input variables, each group has its own unique small group culture (output), and the members' communicative processes create and maintain the group's culture (throughput and output).

Group culture is the pattern of values, beliefs, norms, and behaviors that are shared by group members and that shape a group's individual "personality" (sometimes called *syntality*). Many factors weave together to create a group's culture, including the content and pattern of interactions, the roles members enact and their interrelationships, and the norms and rules guiding the group's interactions. Each group has a unique mix of members, purposes, rules, and behaviors that cannot be duplicated exactly in other groups. For instance, some groups behave informally, with lots of joking and low power distance. Other groups display hostility, aggressive verbal behavior, and divisive conflict. Still others adhere to strict, formal interaction rules with polite, controlled communication. How do these differences come about? We examine some of the processes most important to the development of a group's culture in this and the next chapter. We remind you that a group's culture is never static; rather, it continually evolves, adapting to the changing circumstances of the group and its environment. In a sense, a group's culture is always developing, and never completed.

> **Group Culture**
>
> The pattern of values, beliefs, and norms shared by group members, developed through interaction and incorporating members' shared experiences in the group, patterns of interaction, and status relationships.

Communication and the Structuring of Small Groups

We have consistently noted the role communication plays in the creation and maintenance of a small group. This is explained by the theory of *structuration*, authored by the sociologist Anthony Giddens. **Structuration** attempts to explain how social systems become produced and reproduced over time and space. Fundamental to his theory is the idea that social systems are produced by how members of the social system use the system's rules and resources (e.g., money). A system is also reproduced by using those same rules and resources or by creating new rules and resources, which then create a different social system. The stability observed in the social system occurs because its members use previously established rules and resources consistently.

Structuration theory was applied to the dynamics of the small group in 1980.[2] Structuration refers to how individuals form a small group by exchanging verbal and nonverbal signals that ultimately establish the norms and rules shaping members' behaviors. The group's structure is comprised of rules and resources. Rules are guidelines for how actions are to be done. In our opening

> **Structuration**
>
> The concept that a group creates and continuously re-creates itself through members' communicative behaviors; the group's communication both establishes and limits how the group develops.

case, an example of a rule is that all decisions will be based on sound reasoning. Resources are those aspects (e.g., materials and possessions) of a group that are used by members to control the behavior of other members. In our opening case an example of a resource is the higher status afforded the M.D.s. Rules and resources are the tools group members use to interact with each other as well as the tools they use to help them interpret member actions. These structures are created and recreated *along with* the group system.

The theory of structuration, developed by Poole and associates, thus embraces three important assumptions.[3] First, the behavior of group members is constrained by such things as the general rules of the society in which they live, the structures of the particular group in which they find themselves, and the behavior of the other members. For example, the rules of corporate America frown on executives settling their differences with a fistfight. Members of a group that has developed a formal, polite atmosphere would be embarrassed by a member who slaps another on the back and says, "Hey, babe, how's your sex life?" The other members would disapprove of the offending member's behavior, and if the behavior continued, might try to remove that person from the group. The medical group in our opening story was constrained by the presence of the M.D.s and the need to secure external funding.

The second important assumption is that people have free will—they can choose to follow the rules of the group or not. Although there may be unpleasant consequences for a member who doesn't follow a group's rules, there is no *law*, like the law of gravity, that forces conformity. In our medical group, despite all attempts by Julian and members' original wishes, a majority of them did not follow the "spirit" of democracy.

The third important assumption of structuration is that group creation is a process; the group not only creates itself initially but also continuously *re-creates* itself, changing in incremental ways, always in a state of *becoming*, with communication as the instrument for this creation and constant re-creation. This incrementalism is often the reason groups like our medical group can find themselves "off track" long after the initial changes started happening; the patterns sneak up on you and become entrenched.

Structuration theory places our focus on how group members, using available rules and re-sources, create and re-create their groups over time. With every act, group members are always in the process of structuring their groups. If the group dynamics remain the same it is because members are continuously using the same rules and resources, and if the dynamics change it means the members have acted in a way to change the structure.

The theory of structuration is quite complex. However, the main point is this: the *communication among members* is what creates group rules in the first place, and once rules and structures are in place, communication is what keeps them there, or changes them, as the case may be. Suppose a company appoints a group of several managers to develop long-range strategy. Two members, Mauricio and Cary, have worked together before and naturally call each other by first names. Mauricio introduces Cary to Carol, an acquaintance of hers, by his first name, and pretty soon the rest of the group members are calling each other by first name instead of Mr., Ms., or Dr. As they wait for the meeting to begin, members talk about mutual interests such as sports and jazz music, and several find common outside interests with other members. Norms of informality and friendliness have begun to develop among these members, and these norms will begin to affect other aspects of the communication among members, such as how they deal with disagreement. For instance, assume that at a later group meeting, Cary says, in a formal and accusing tone of voice, "I respectfully disagree with the proposal offered by my esteemed colleague Ms. Hernandez," and continues to make a formal speech relating his objections. The rest of the members will probably say something like: "When did we get so formal, Cary? What's the big deal here? Why are you sounding like a prosecutor?" What they are saying, in another way, is: "We've developed norms of informality and friendliness, which you are violating. Your behavior seems inappropriate to us." Of course, Cary has free choice about his behavior. He can choose to continue in his formal, prosecutorial way, but if he does, that may either change the informality and friendliness norms to ones more formal and adversarial, or it may cause the other members to ignore Cary and ostracize him from the group.

Consider This 7.1

You are no doubt currently a member of at least one group. Think about one way your group does something. For instance, how do you work, play, greet each other, and so forth? Now consider how your group created that practice and currently maintains it.

A variety of internal and external factors influences the types of structures groups create, including member characteristics and preferences, the nature of the group's task, and such structural dynamics as the interplay between important (but perhaps conflicting) values. The members of the medical group valued democratic principles, but the pressure to get the job done and the deference given to a medical degree led members to encourage controlling leadership.[4] This contradiction caused tension within the group and an eventual split. Sunwolf and Seibold found several conflicting values in their study of jury decision making resulting from numerous contradictions between internal and external factors.[5] For instance, although the jury was told to use judicial resources should any confusion occur, the jury developed the norm that no jury member could send a note outside the group asking for help before first securing permission from the group. In addition, several members of the jury struggled with reporting inappropriate behavior to the court. The expectations that the law should be followed clashed with the social rule of not telling on your friends. Sunwolf and Seibold concluded: "One of the inherent contradictions of group life in jury deliberations occurs in situations in which the attempt to obey the directive to maintain their group's existence simultaneously requires them to collaborate in a reluctant cover-up of member misconduct."[6] These examples also illustrate the point we made in Chapter 2 regarding the fluid nature of boundaries between groups and their multiple environments. Often these boundaries are constructed in group interaction while simultaneously serving to connect the group to *and* separate it from its environment.

Adaptive Structuration Theory

Structuration theory has been used to explore four areas of concern for small group scholars: mapping the development of small group decisions; showing how input variables are actually used in group interaction and such use affects group outputs; describing how arguments between group members are used to structure the group's decision-making process; and showing how group decision making is impacted by the use of computer technology.[7] We now examine this last area.

Adaptive structuration theory is a particular version of structuration theory introduced by Poole and DeSanctis.[8] This version of structuration theory is used to show how the structures (i.e., the rules and resources) of computer technology get used during small group decision making when group decision support systems (GDSS) are used. GDSS are computer-based hardware and software systems designed to improve the quality and speed of group problem solving, especially idea generation, information organization, evaluation of options, and decision making. For example, several GDSSs help groups brainstorm.

Poole and DeSanctis look at which rules and features of GDSSs are actually used by the group, how they are used, and how such use influences group outcomes.[9] They conclude that the technology itself becomes an integral part of producing and reproducing the group system. A GDSS has two important characteristics: its spirit, or intention, and the features built into the technology. The spirit refers to the goals the technology is designed to achieve. The features are the rules of how the GDSS is supposed to be used. Both elements work together. A particular GDSS's rules may promote or detract from its spirit, or intent, depending on how the group members actually adapt the GDSS. For instance, a particular GDSS may intend to generate discussion by all group members. Its rules are designed to support this goal because the facilitator is supposed to paraphrase each remark before a new one is entered on the computer screen. However, a particular group may decide to skip this step, thus violating the rule for how the GDSS is supposed to be used. This may undermine the GDSS's spirit. Poole and DeSanctis hypothesized that if groups use the GDSS faithfully, following both the rules and the spirit, if members are comfortable with the GDSS, and if they agree about how the GDSS should be used, then the group will produce more predictable outcomes than groups that act contrary to the spirit of the GDSS, are not comfortable with it, and do not agree about how it is to be used. Research has found that the more restrictive the design of a particular GDSS, the less the group tries to control the

Adaptive Structuration Theory

A version of structuration theory that focuses on how the rules and resources of computer technology are used in the structuration process.

GDSS and the more the group tries to work *with* it. In addition, using the GDSS the way it was designed to be used produces greater group consensus than adapting it contrary to its intent. We will discuss GDSS use in group decision making in Chapter 14.

We agree with Poole that structuration offers advantages over other social scientific theories.[10] Structuration captures the complexity of human behavior by recognizing that, although human beings are free agents, certain limitations and constraints keep their behaviors in small group systems within certain boundaries while recognizing that change is possible. Yet at the same time it offers a "way out" for members with little power who, by enacting changes in behavior that over time, can change the group's structure. It also explains why unintended consequences can occur in group interaction. We especially like the communicative focus of structuration theory, for it reminds us to look at the *communicative behavior* of members to learn about a group. We now turn to a discussion of how this communication behavior affects tension in the group and serves to develop the group's norms and roles.

Tension Among Group Members

Somehow, what starts as a collection of individuals with an interdependent purpose must become a group that functions as a unit to complete that purpose. One of the first issues a group must address is how it will manage the interpersonal tensions that are a normal part of its development. Just as individuals experience varying levels of tension, so do entire groups. In fact, a certain amount of tension is desirable. Can you imagine taking an exam when you felt so relaxed you could barely motivate yourself to read the questions? An optimum amount of tension can help us perform at peak capacity, but too much or too little impairs our ability to function well. The same is true of groups, which must learn to manage tensions productively for the ultimate good of the group.

Primary Tension

Bormann described two types of group tension, primary and secondary. **Primary tension** results from primary sources, or the interpersonal relationships among members, whereas secondary tension is directly task related. Bormann describes primary tension as being ". . . the social unease and stiffness that accompanies getting acquainted."[11] He describes the symptoms of primary tension as extreme politeness, apparent boredom, yawning and sighing, a lot of long pauses, and tentative statements uttered in soft tones. At this point, members are asking themselves, "Will they like me? Will this be a group I enjoy working with?" The politeness and apparent boredom are only a facade covering the tensions we all feel when we are with people we don't know well. However, if this primary tension is not overcome, group members will get stuck in a mode of overpoliteness, formality, and hesitancy to disagree, which will hurt their ability to think critically.

Primary Tension

Tension and discomfort in members that stems from interpersonal (i.e., primary) sources, including the social unease that occurs when members of a new group first meet or during competition for power among members.

A second form of primary tension, also resulting from relationships among members, can arise abruptly when there is self-centered competition for power and status within the group. Although the issue may appear to be a matter of who will perform certain jobs for the group, the real issue is the desire and struggle for personal power, which underlies much human behavior. Thus, what appears to be secondary tension is really primary tension disguised as disagreement over ideas.

Consider This 7.2

How did all the group members, including Julian and the non-M.D.s, contribute to the emergence of their "pecking order" which turned out to be a source of this form of primary tension?

Several things can be done to reduce a group's primary tension. For example, taking time to get acquainted is worthwhile. Members can talk about themselves, their backgrounds, interests, and hobbies, experiences relevant to the group's purpose, feelings about being in the group, and so on. In fact, this movement toward intimacy via self-disclosure is a characteristic of cohesive groups.[12] It may pay to have a social hour or party, with no formal agenda. Joking, laughing together, and finding common interests can help diminish primary tensions. Even members of a group that will meet only once can profitably spend a few minutes introducing themselves so they can orient themselves to each other as parts of a group. Indeed, members who have worked together in many meetings often spend the first few moments of their meeting chitchatting and confirming their relationships before getting down to work.

Primary tensions over power are more difficult to resolve. Rules and procedures for making decisions and assigning work can help prevent or alleviate these tensions. Other times, direct confrontation may be needed. We develop these ideas in several subsequent chapters.

Secondary Tension

Secondary Tension

Tension and discomfort experienced by group members that stem from task-related (i.e., secondary) sources, including conflicts over values, points of view, or alternative solutions.

Secondary tension is work-related tension resulting from the differences of opinion among members as they seek to accomplish their task. It is inevitable, because members perceive problems differently and disagree about goals, means for achieving them, and criteria by which to evaluate ideas. Secondary tensions are a direct result of the need to make decisions *as a group*. Sometimes these tensions become uncomfortably high.

Secondary tension looks and sounds different from primary tension. Voices become loud and strained. There may be long pauses followed by two or more members trying to talk at once. Members twist and fidget in their seats, bang fists on the table, wave their arms, interrupt each other, and may even get up and pace around the room. They may try to shout each other down, call each other names, or aggressively question each other's intelligence or motives. While a couple of members verbally attack each other, the rest of the group may sit stiffly and awkwardly, not knowing what to do.

Although it may seem easier to ignore secondary tensions because dealing with them can be uncomfortable or even painful, groups that deal with these tensions directly will experience several advantages. First, attempts to duck the tension-producing issue don't work. As Bormann says, "The problem . . . if ignored or dodged will continue to . . . impede their progress. Facing up to secondary tensions realistically is the best way to release them."[13] If secondary tension is not managed, it will continue to disrupt the group. Second, groups that find integrative ways to manage their secondary tension experience greater cohesiveness as a result of having worked through the tension. The members know they can disagree with each other yet still experience a sense of trust and commitment. Finally, the group may find that the tensions have caused the members to look more carefully at task-related issues, which usually produces a better final product.

What can group members do to manage secondary tension? Bales found that three categories of behaviors reduced tension among members: agreeing, showing solidarity, and tension release.[14] Showing agreement is socially rewarding to the person agreed with, as if to say to that person, "I value you and your opinion." The more often people are agreed with openly, the more they relax and communicate positively with each other, and the less defensive they become.

A member can show solidarity by indicating commitment to the group. Using *we* to refer to the group, speaking well of other members, offering to help, expressing confidence in the group, and talking about the importance of the group and its task are all ways to show solidarity and encourage members to move away from self-centeredness and antagonism.

Humor, too, can help release secondary tension, so long as the humor does not ridicule another member or is used to ignore the disagreement. Enjoying a joke together makes it easier to listen better and find agreement. In *Pattern for Industrial Peace*, Whyte described how a union staff representative did this repeatedly by using fishing photos whenever discussion among representatives of the steel company and union got overheated with secondary tension.[15]

Phases in the Development of Small Groups

Just as the occurrence of primary and secondary tension is predictable and normal in groups, other developments are relatively predictable, too. The more you know about these typical group processes, the more you will be able to identify what is usual, what is helpful, and what should be changed for the group to function more effectively. A number of researchers have studied how groups develop and change over time; they have found that groups progress through identifiable phases. This is an evolutionary process that happens gradually, without clear demarcations to separate the phases.[16] Each phase can be identified by the types of interactions and behaviors the members exhibit.

Bales was one of the first researchers to investigate a group's progression through predictable phases.[17] He identified two concerns with which a group must deal. First, the group must develop the kinds of interpersonal relationships that provide stability and harmony, allowing the group to function cooperatively. These are the *socioemotional concerns*: Second, the *task concerns* involve the group's attention to its job, to completion of whatever its task is. Groups tend to cycle between these two concerns, focusing first on one, then the other. Early in the group's **formation phase,** the socioemotional dimension predominates as members attempt to work out the kinds of relationships they will have with each other. Note the connection here to primary tension. Initial reduction of primary tension, by working through interpersonal concerns, allows a group eventually to become fully efficient in completing its task. Groups that resolve their early socioemotional issues become increasingly able to take relationships among group members for granted, and thus can shift their attention and energy to the task. As socioemotional remarks and behaviors in a group decrease, task-related remarks and behaviors increase and eventually surpass them. In the **production phase** of a group's life cycle, when the group has reached socioemotional maturity, task behaviors will predominate. The group will achieve its peak in task efficiency. This progression can be seen over the life of an effective group, as well as over the course of a single group meeting.

It is important to recognize that groups must handle process (formation) and production (task) concerns *simultaneously*: At the very first meeting, a group must begin the process of forming into a functioning unit by establishing the interpersonal relationships, leadership structures, and status hierarchies that enable it to work efficiently—the formation function. The group *also* must deal with its task: what its charge is, how the task should be approached, who is to do what, and so forth. Thus, the group must contend with both kinds of functions throughout its life span. Although the interpersonal concerns predominate at first, task concerns are still present. If everything proceeds smoothly for the group, gradually more and more of its time can be spent directly on task concerns and less on interpersonal concerns as it moves to its production stage. However, at no point can group members disregard socioemotional concerns. Thus, we envision a group following essentially two broad developmental stages, a formation phase where process norms unfold and a production phase where group members focus on the task, as depicted in Figure 7.1. These phases are not distinct. Instead, a group's attention shifts gradually, but never completely, from process to production concerns.

Any group's communication evolves in identifiable patterns that change over the course of a group's life. Our previous description was designed to

Formation Phase

The stage in the development of a group during which relationship issues predominate as members work out their relationships with each other.

Production Phase

The stage in the development of a group during which task concerns predominate after a group has reached some socioemotional maturity.

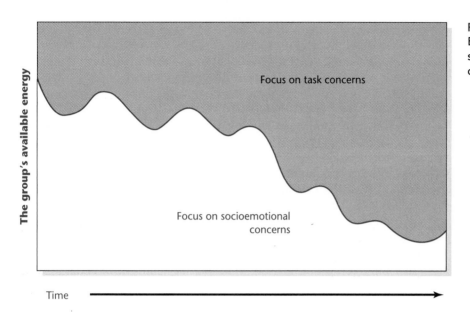

FIGURE 7.1
Balancing task and
socioemotional
concerns.

give you a broad overview of the typical patterns found in a group's formation and production phases. It highlights only the most obvious characteristics of each phase. It may seem that groups move cleanly through these phases, but be aware that we have oversimplified the descriptions. Group development is often messy, with no clear distinctions between phases.

One thing we have not mentioned is the effect that new members have on a group's development, both in newly formed and existing groups. How do individuals and groups socialize new members and become changed themselves in the process? We turn our attention now to this question.

Group Socialization of Members

When we hear the word *socialization* we generally think about someone who is learning to become part of a group or even society at large. Just as children are socialized into families and society, people are socialized into newly formed and established groups. Typically, socialization processes have been studied in organizational research focusing on how the organization molds the newcomer to its culture.[18] Recent research in communication has begun to take seriously not only the socialization process in small groups but it also recognizes the active role the new member plays in affecting the existing small group.

Carolyn Anderson, Bruce Riddle, and Matthew Martin define **group socialization** as a reciprocal process of social influence and change in which both newcomers and/or established members and the group adjust to one another. It is the process using verbal and nonverbal communication to create

Group Socialization

The social influence and change process during which both newcomers and established members adjust to one another.

and re-create a group's unique culture and group structures, engage in relevant processes and activities, and pursue individual and group goals.[19] This definition supports our belief in the central role of communication in all group processes, including the socialization of members.[20] This definition is lengthy, so let's take it apart and apply it to an example. Consider what happened to the following theater group. Actors had been practicing for weeks, but one week before opening night, leading man Richard was told he needed emergency surgery—immediately! The cast was devastated. Of course, cast members were worried about Richard, but they also were concerned about losing six weeks of rehearsals, during which the troupe had developed into a cohesive group. The director thought about canceling the show, but she asked an experienced actor friend of hers to assume Richard's role. Opening night was delayed a week to give Ted time to learn the lines and the troupe time to integrate a new member.

First, the adapting and adjusting that happens when a new group forms or when new members join an established group occurs through communication among group members. Communication is instrumental in reducing the anxiety that is often felt during this time of high uncertainty. Riddle et al. use uncertainty reduction theory to explain why new and old members communicate. Uncertainty reduction theorists argue that people are driven to make sense of their worlds and will seek information to reduce the anxiety produced by high levels of uncertainty. New and established members of groups communicate to reduce the uncertainty surrounding how decisions are made, how conflict should be handled, how to behave, and their role in the group.[21]

Effective group socialization is facilitated when everyone involved practices open communication, accepts the new member, and exhibits a desire to recognize the positive change new members can bring. If the community theater members do not talk to each other about the new cast member, welcome him into the troupe, and see his presence as a way to move in new directions, then his willingness to replace Richard will probably be wasted.

Second, the definition highlights the importance of recognizing that effective socialization requires a balance between individual member and group goals as well as comparable positive satisfaction levels between the member and the group. Generally, socialization processes in a group are more likely to succeed when the new members report satisfaction with communication.[22] The new cast member, the director, and the rest of the troupe must have similar goals and levels of comfort if his stepping in for Richard is to be a positive experience.

Third, the definition emphasizes that socialization is an ongoing process involving not only the new member, but also the rest of the group. If you are a member of this troupe, what might you do to help the new member feel at ease? If you are the director how might you help the cast and the new member get through a new formation phase to get focused on the play? If you are the new member, what could you do to help the other cast members be comfortable with you? These questions involve how the cast, the director and the new member could manage this kind of change. Understanding the phases of group socialization may help you further consider how the community theater group and the new member can effectively manage his entrance into the cast.

Phases of Group Socialization

Anderson and colleagues describe five phases of group socialization: antecedent, anticipatory, encounter, assimilation, and exit.[23] These are presented in Table 7.1. Each phase has unique communication needs. As you study the phases, remember the following things: this model assumes that group members are typically also members of other groups, that socialization involves both newly forming groups and established groups dealing with new members, that groups may move through these phases at different speeds and may revisit one or more of these phases as they accept or reject new members, and finally that behaviors in one phase have a ripple effect through the other phases.

In the **antecedent phase,** group inputs, including individual characteristics, listening styles, and cultural differences, affect a group's throughput and output variables. All members, including Ted in our above example, bring to a group their own attitudes, motives, and communication traits, which profoundly influence how ready and able they are to be socialized into a group and to engage in group work and relationship building. For instance, consider *grouphate*, described in Chapter 1.[24] Many of the ideas and attitudes people bring to new or existing groups are based on previous experiences in groups. A member whose previous groups have struggled to get anything done may very well internalize this experience and show a negative bias toward groups

Antecedent Phase

Prior to group socialization, the phase in which group members' individual characteristics affect their readiness and willingness to socialize members effectively.

Antecedent Phase

Individual member characteristics (listening styles, culture, attitudes) that influence member readiness and ability to engage in effective socialization of member(s).

Anticipatory Phase

Members' initial expectations about each other and the socialization process.

Encounter Phase

Member expectations meet with the actual behaviors as they negotiate member and group goals.

Assimilation Phase

Members and group have worked out a comfortable fit with each other.

Exit Phase

Group disbands or a member leaves the group and group adapts to the loss.

TABLE 7.1 Phases of group socialization.

and group work. In our classes, we repeatedly hear students verbalize their dislike for anything resembling group work because of horrific experiences in the past. If you feel this way, you may be pessimistic about joining a group and accepting a new member.

Another antecedent factor that affects group socialization is our motive for communicating in groups. Recall our discussion of listening styles. Some of us listen in order to sustain the relationships in the group and others to make sure the work gets done. Others focus their listening on meeting a time schedule and others on only information from trusted sources. These listening preferences, linked to our motives for communicating, influence the effective socialization of members. For instance, those members who communicate in order to build relationships rather than control others or distance themselves from others report more satisfaction with the group. Those who communicate in order to accomplish the work talk more in the group. Members highly motivated for both reasons are likely to be more willing to engage the socialization process.[25]

Communication apprehension and verbal aggressiveness are two other antecedent factors influencing group socialization. Individuals or group members who are not comfortable talking in groups (communication apprehension) would make it hard to participate actively in socialization. Remember that if socialization in groups is to be effective members have to communicate with each other to reduce the uncertainty inherent in the socialization experience. On the other hand, verbally aggressive group members may be quite comfortable talking but attack others when they express disagreement. This communication alienates others and does not promote positive socialization experiences.[26]

Anticipatory Phase

During group socialization, the phase where members' expectations of each other and the group set the stage for what will occur during socialization.

The **anticipatory phase** of group socialization involves all the initial expectations members have of each other and the group. These expectations are the grounds for what the individual anticipates will happen over the course of the group's life. Have you ever expected really to like someone and anticipated a successful meeting with him or her, only to have your expectations crushed afterward? Suppose the director had enthusiastically talked about Ted's talents, thereby leading the cast to anticipate a master actor and great opening night. In turn, Ted had been told about the great cast he was joining. Both parties would anticipate a successful experience. However, if their expectations were not accurate, socialization could be a disaster. In both examples, the more the expectations differ from the actual experience, the more the members will experience anxiety and perhaps even anger.

Socialization involves *both* individual expectations (Ted) and group expectations (cast). Individuals enter new or existing groups with all sorts of expectations, including estimating how well they will be received and how much they will be respected as an individual. Ted may predict that he will be well received and although he is stepping in for Richard, the cast will understand he brings his own interpretation to the role. If he is wrong, this can produce a negative experience and stressful entry into the group—even perhaps an unsuccessful adjustment. For the cast (in this case an existing group) their anticipatory phase begins when Ted decides to take over for Richard. If cast members are open to the adjustment ahead of them, they are more likely to socialize Ted into the group successfully.

We asked you earlier to think abut what each party could do to help welcome Ted. Group socialization is enhanced when groups systematically have in place ways to welcome new members.[27] In the case of our community theater cast, this could include a meeting with Ted in which members introduce each other and talk about their expectations, an informal dinner with Ted, and a tour of the theater, stage, and dressing rooms. Stewart Sigman calls these kind of activities *audition practices* and they help both the new member and the group draw more realistic expectations and experience less primary tension during socialization.[28]

The third phase of group socialization is the **encounter phase:** The learning that takes place in all forms of socialization begins in earnest in this phase when the expectations of the anticipatory phase meet the realities of the group and lasts for an indefinite period.[29] During this time the individual and the group create or adjust the group's norms, culture, climate, goals, roles, and leadership structure—topics that follow our discussion of socialization.

Earlier in our discussion of group socialization we alluded to how important it is to negotiate a balance between individual and group goals. During this phase, members also negotiate their roles in the group. The addition of a new member can disrupt the roles already established in a newly forming or existing group. Communication about individual role expectations and careful assessment of what the group needs are necessary if socialization is to be a positive experience. For instance, newcomers who proactively seek information about role expectations are socialized more effectively than those who do not seek this kind of information.[30] We talk more about roles and norms later in the chapter.

The **assimilation phase** is characterized by a member's full integration into the group and its structures.[31] New members are comfortable with the group culture, show an active interest in both the group's task and relationships. In turn the existing members accept the new member. Members blend productively and supportively, enacting the kind of communication necessary to sustain the group's culture. If this integration does not occur smoothly, as is often the case, secondary tension can throw the group back into the anticipatory and encounter phases. Do not let these regressions surprise you because, over a group's life span, members will often have to negotiate the good fit between themselves and the group.

The fifth phase of group socialization is the **exit phase:** Earlier we remarked that group socialization is a process that continues over the course of a group's life. This process is experienced at both the individual and the group level and actually ends when the new member leaves or when the group ceases to exist. Exiting a group can be a difficult transition to make and is one group members often minimize.[32] If a member leaves, such as Richard

Encounter Phase

During group socialization, the phase where member expectations meet the realities and members begin to adjust to each other in actuality.

Assimilation Phase

During group socialization, the phase where members are fully integrated into the group and its structures.

Exit Phase

During socialization, the phase that encompasses the process members experience when a member leaves the group or the group disbands.

in our community theater example, the group must deal with why he left, how he left, how his departure changes their communication, and what comes next. When an entire group disbands, members deal with variations of the same issues.

Sometimes individuals leave a group psychologically before they actually leave physically. Kathy, one of your authors, watched as one of her colleagues and a good friend retired. Almost a year before he actually left the department, he mentally pulled out. Kathy observed his interest in department issues fade, which affected what issues he fought for and how he voted in faculty meetings. If you or anyone else leaves a group voluntarily, let others know you are leaving, help the group adjust to your leaving, and try to remain in some sort of contact after you leave. This kind of behavior can help avert such things as grouphate.

Group turnover is common. How many times have you watched as a member left, and then found yourself dealing with the loss and the adjustment to a new member? This process can be filled with uncertainty and resentment or it can be managed quite well. One way a group can effectively manage turnover is to develop a positive group attitude toward turnover—see it as a way to redefine who you are. When an entire group ends, do not treat it lightly—how you disband can and does impact the kind of experiences you take into the next group. Keyton recommends that groups give themselves an opportunity to say good-bye and process their experience.[33]

> Have confidence that the members of your group have a lot to contribute, and that one of your roles is to try to encourage that support, that contribution, to draw those people out.
>
> *B. A., Educational Administrator, retired*

Group socialization is a complex process spanning the entire cultural life of a group. Recognizing its characteristics deepens our understanding of group phases and reminds us that groups usually must adapt to losing and gaining members. Socialization involves important input, throughput, and output variables. Looking at socialization through the lens of structuration theory reminds us that how members socialize newcomers into the group can reinforce existing rules or be a powerful change agent to promote better processes of socialization. For instance, groups must learn how to avoid in- and out-group communication so as not to alienate new members.[34]

Our discussions of socialization and structuration of group culture has consistently mentioned the importance of the group's rules and the members' roles in the socialization process. In the following sections we take a closer look at both rules and roles of group interaction.

Development of Group Norms

When individuals begin to interact as members of a group, the full range of human behaviors is potentially available to them. Perhaps they will listen politely to each other, or maybe they will interrupt and insult one another. Somehow, the members must develop a set of rules and operating procedures to co-ordinate their individual behaviors into a system. Some **rules** are formalized guidelines for behavior that may be written down and taken into the group as an input variable. For example, *Robert's Rules of Order*, Newly Revised, is used by many organizations as a guide for governing face-to-face interaction.[35] Robert includes an entire section of rules that apply to any committee of an organization using his parliamentary manual.

However, most of the normal operating procedures for a group are developed gradually, with tacit rather than explicit consent of the group members. For instance, if Kara comes late to a meeting and other members make a point of chastising her, Kara will likely arrive on time for subsequent meetings and the group has "decided" on a rule that members should arrive on time. Such an informal rule, or **norm,** is seldom written down; instead, it is ". . . an idea in the minds of the members of a group, an idea that can be put in the form of a statement specifying what the members . . . should do, ought to do, are expected to do, under given circumstances."[36] This section focuses on these informal rules, or norms: prescriptions from group behavior that emerge out of group communication and are an important process variable of group interaction.

Norms reflect cultural beliefs about what is appropriate or inappropriate behavior, as we discussed in Chapter 5. Although the norms of an individual group may be specific to that group, chances are they will mirror general cultural norms. For instance, if physical violence is prohibited by the general culture, with disagreements handled through discussion, then a group established in the context of this larger culture will also be likely to use discussion instead of physical violence to settle disputes. As Shimanoff stated,

> When group members come together for the first time, they bring with them past experiences and expectations regarding cultural and social rules and rules for specific groups they assume may be similar to this new group. It is out of these experiences and expectations as well as its unique interaction . . . that a particular group formulates its rules.[37]

Norms are not imposed by an authority outside the group but are imposed by members on themselves and each other. Various types of peer pressure, ranging from slight frowns to ostracism, enforce them. It is important for group members, particularly new members, to be aware of these norms because to violate them may mean punishment, loss of influence, and perhaps exclusion from the group.

Norms guide and regulate the behavior of group members. They govern how and to whom members speak, how they dress, what they talk about and when, what language may be used, and so on. The whole process of communication among group members is rule-governed.[38] Rarely do norms specify absolutes; rather, they indicate ranges of acceptable and unacceptable behavior. For instance, a particular group may endorse a prompt starting time for its meetings. However, being 4 minutes late may be tolerated without comment, but coming 15 minutes late would not.

Rules

Statements prescribing how members of a small group may, should, or must behave, which may be stated formally in writing, or informally as in the case of norms.

Norm

An unstated informal rule, enforced by peer pressure, that governs the behavior of members of a small group.

The development of group norms may be obvious in groups where members meet face-to-face. However, our earlier discussion of adaptive structuration theory showed that group members can and do appropriate into their group interaction the particular rules of computer technology, making those rules their own. Students using e-mail as part of a course have been shown to develop their own way of using this kind of computer-mediated communication.[39] Some groups used it to chat, others to coordinate schedules, and others to talk to those who were not present. Further, conformity to the emergent norms increased over time.

Consider This 7.3

Review the opening story of our medical group. Besides the norm related to rational decision making, what other norms developed in this group. Think for a moment of all the groups to which you have belonged. Your role probably changed considerably through time as you changed, as new people were added to or left a group, or as the problem facing the group changed. Do you see any patterns to your role behavior?

During the formation stage of a new small group, norms are developed rapidly via the structuration process described earlier, often without members realizing what is occurring. The group's first meeting is particularly critical in establishing that group's norms. At that time, behaviors typical of primary tension in the formation phase—speaking quietly, suppressing disagreement, making tentative and ambiguous statements—can become norms if not challenged. Although members may openly discuss and state rules at their first meeting, norms usually evolve over time and seem to exist below the level of conscious awareness of most members. Often, a norm is brought to a group's awareness only after a member violates it, a new member questions it, or an observer points it out.

Conformity

Following groups norms and not deviating from them.

Conformity, or following group norms over time, helps reinforce those norms.[40] Conformity to group norms helps the group function as a whole and work in an environment with less ambiguity. In addition, group members can show each other acceptance and loyalty to the group through their conformity. Conformity to group norms, although contrary to the individualism valued by some cultures, remains an important way group members have of measuring the reasonableness of their own behaviors, ideas, and opinions. Are we acting consistently or inconsistently with the prevailing group expectations?

How quickly do group members conform to norms? Five conditions seem to influence conformity to group norms.[41] The first are individual characteristics. For example, older people are less likely to conform. Second, members follow well-articulated and well-enforced norms more. Third, the more members who conform to the norm, the more likely it is that others will follow.

Fourth, highly cohesive groups tend to generate more conformity to their norms. Finally, members who support the goals of their group are more likely to follow that group's norms.

> Certain groups have the dysfunction of having a norm that only happy talk is allowed.
>
> *A. B., University Dean*

General norms direct the behavior of the group as a whole, whereas *role-specific norms* concern individual members with particular roles, such as the designated leader. The medical group discussed in our chapter opening developed a general norm related to rational decision making. Role-specific norms for Julian included his rephrasing and redefining of the others' ideas. He also developed the norm of talking more than the others. Notice that these norms are stated as rules, even though they are not imposed on the group by an external authority or parent organization. Examples of each type of norm follow:

General Norms (Applicable to Every Member)	Role-Specific Norms (Applicable to Specific Members)
Members should sit in the same position at each meeting.	The leader should prepare and distribute an agenda in advance of each meeting.
Members should address each other by first names.	The leader should summarize from time to time, but other members may do so if a summary is needed.
Other members should not disagree with the chair's ideas.	The secretary should distribute minutes of the previous meeting at least three days before the next meeting.
No one may smoke during meetings.	Gulshan may play critical tester of all ideas by asking for evidence.
Members may leave the meeting to get something to drink, but should return to their seats promptly.	Terrell should tell a joke when the climate gets tense during an argument.
Members should arrive on time for meetings.	Julian should restate other members' remarks in his own words.

If norms generally exist below the level of conscious awareness, how can group members discover what their norms are? Norms can be inferred and confirmed by observation. New members, especially, should be sensitive to the group's norms so they do not inadvertently violate important ones. There are two types of behavior to watch for especially:

1. **<u>Behaviors that occur repeatedly and with regularity, by one or all members:</u>**
   <u>Repetitions of a behavior are evidence that a norm exists regulating it.</u>
   Thus group members should look for answers to questions such as: "Who talks to whom?" "How do members speak?" "What kind of language do they use?" "What do they talk about and for how long?" "Where do they sit?" "When do they move about and for what reasons?" and "How is the group brought to order?"

2. **<u>Punishment of a member for infraction of a rule:</u>**
   <u>The strongest evidence of a norm is a negative reaction or punishment directed at a member who does not conform to the norm.</u> Deviance from a group norm may take several forms: nonconformity to a general norm (e.g., avoiding sound reasoning); specific role deviance (e.g., secretary not distributing the minutes); deviance from gender, class, age, ethnic social role expectations (e.g., nurse questioning the M.D.'s opinion); and breaking from past patterns (Julian begins to defer to the faculty members on the committee).[42]

   Observers looking for norms should pay attention to behaviors that elicit negative reactions, ranging from a bit of head shaking, to surreptitious and disapproving glances passing between members, to forceful negative comments or even threats. Notice behaviors to which members react with gestures of rejection, such as frowns, head shaking, and tongue clucking. What acts do members studiously ignore, as if out of embarrassment? Listen for negative comments: "It's about time you got here," "Let's stick to issues and not go blaming each other," and "Maybe you'll have your report ready for our next meeting." Note, particularly, those actions that elicit negative responses from more than one person, a sure bet that a norm important to the group has been infringed. Weaker support for the existence of a norm is provided when violators correct themselves and the other members visibly approve the correction.

> You've either got common purpose for something or you don't, and if you've got somebody rowing against you while you're trying to row in the other direction, it's very disruptive.
>
> *J. J., CEO and General Manager, Utility Company*

Changing a Norm

Norms have a tremendous effect on the processes and outcomes of the group. Group members should not only be aware of them, but also act to change them if they appear to be detrimental. Just because members conform to a norm does not mean the norm is good for the group overall. For instance, a norm implying that low-status members may not disagree with high-status members interferes with the critical evaluation of ideas, as we saw in our medical group. Or, groups that permit members to criticize ideas as soon as they have been proposed may find that members are reluctant to make innovative suggestions, so creativity is stifled. In such cases, individuals should not "sit back and take it" but work to change the rules. Small persistent changes can be effective because they are not as noticeable to those who may resist the change.[43] A social worker in our medical group was successful in temporarily moving the group into a more democratic climate. She decided to refuse Julian's attempts to rephrase her comments, which in turn helped him be more aware of his pattern of changing other's ideas to reflect his own. The group managed this new pattern for a while, but when a crisis arose, members, including Julian, fell back into old ways. Had the social worker persisted in her attempts, she might have been successful in changing the autocratic norm. As long as the resources and rules upholding the norm persist, then that norm of discussion will continue.

Using a full frontal assault, particularly one that may be perceived as a personal attack, will not be successful either and will make the person demanding the change seem like a deviant. Instead, following a few simple guidelines can help you change norms without unnecessary trauma. First, the member desiring the change must establish an identity as a loyal member of the group and speak not as an outsider but as a member committed to the group's well-being. Second, the member should carefully observe the offending behavior and keep a record of how often it occurs and what the consequences are to the group. Armed with specific information and obvious concern for the good of the group, the member is ready for the next step, constructive confrontation.

The member should pick an appropriate time, indicate his or her concern with something that appears to be causing trouble for the group, state the specifics calmly and clearly, then ask whether other members share the concern. For instance, rather than saying, "We never get started on time and I'm sick and tired of it," the member should say instead: "For the past 4 meetings, we have started our work anywhere from 15 minutes to half an hour late. We seem to have a rule that we don't have to observe our announced starting time, which makes our meetings run late. Two of us have another committee meeting directly following this one, and for each of these late meetings we have missed the conclusion of our business. This means that we need to spend additional time at the next meeting bringing everyone up-to-date. Does anyone else share my concern?" If the norm was subconscious, it now has been brought to the attention of the group and becomes part of the surface agenda of the group where it can be discussed openly. If the member is wrong about the norm, the group can correct the perception without disparaging the concern. However, if the individual is right, the group will appreciate the concern and likely decide to change the norm. Even if the other members agree to a new norm, they may still need gentle reminders until the new behavior becomes habituated, part of "our way of doing things."

An example will clarify how one or more members can invoke change in a group's culture. A study group meeting in a small town library held weekly learning discussions to compare modern Protestant, Catholic, and Jewish theology. The study group had tried to be clear from the beginning that participants were there to come to an understanding of these three religious traditions. However, at times members forgot and attempted to convert one another. Discussion during these times would erupt into an uproar with several people talking or shouting at once. One particular evening one of us was present tape-recording the group for a research project. Just after the meeting had formally adjourned, a member said to the study group, "You know, I'm really bothered by our tendency to all talk at once sometimes, and not listen to each other." He then turned to your author, Jack, and said, "Jack, could some of us hear the recording you just made to see how we must sound to you?" When they heard themselves, there were groans: "Did we really sound as bad as that?" Members left the meeting in clusters of two and three, talking about what they had just realized. At the next meeting, the game of "uproar" again exploded, but this time a member said, "Remember the tape recording!" and order was resumed. There was no more interrupting for nearly an hour, and when it did occur, it lasted only several seconds before participants sheepishly shut up and offered apologies. The group had developed a new norm. Thus, although norms are usually developed generally without conscious intent, they are not fixed in stone and can be changed, with persistence, as the group's situation warrants. But always keep in mind a valuable lesson from structuration theory—any change in group interaction may have unforeseen consequences.

Development of Role Structure

When they hear the term *role*, most people think of parts in a play or movie. Play scripts contain interlocking roles, each of which is a different character in the cast. A member's **role** represents the cluster of behaviors performed by that member and the overall functions those behaviors perform for the group, just as an actor's role consists of all the lines and actions of the character in the play. Like Brad Pitt, whose various film roles have included a spy in *Spy Games*, a tragic alter ego in *Fight Club*, and a tormented brother in *Legends of the Fall*, individuals enact many diverse roles in the numerous groups to which they belong. In one group the role might be *daughter* or *son*, in another *lead carpenter*, and in yet another *church treasurer*. A given individual might be a leader in one group and play a supporting role in another. The role a person enacts in any particular group is a function of that person's personality, abilities, and communication skills, the talents of the other members, and the needs of the group as a whole.

A particular role embraces a set of behaviors that perform some function for the group. There is a difference between a *behavior* and a *behavioral*

Role

A pattern of behavior displayed by and expected of a member of a small group; a composite of a group member's frequently performed behavioral functions.

function. At the individual level, every verbal or nonverbal act by a group member is a **behavior,** but at the group level, the function that behavior performs in the group system is called its **behavioral function.** For example, the joke Yukiko tells in a group is the *behavior*. However, Yukiko's joke can serve a variety of *functions*, depending on how she tells it, what else is happening in the group at the time, and so forth. Perhaps her joke relieves tension during an argument (a positive behavioral function), but perhaps it gets the group off track or makes fun of another member (negative behavioral functions). A behavioral function, then, is the *effect* of member behavior on the social structure (throughput) and task accomplishment (output) of the group. Some functions are shared widely among group members (such as providing information or providing opinions); others may become the exclusive domain of one member (such as keeping group records or joking to relieve tension).

Role Emergence

Most small groups have certain *formal* roles, usually appointed or elected positions. A *chair* has the responsibility for calling meetings, planning agendas, and coordinating the work of the other members. A *secretary* is responsible for taking notes and distributing minutes of meetings. In these cases, the duties associated with a particular role are specified in advance, sometimes in writing. However, in most small groups members create and modify their own *informal* roles as the group progresses. Informal roles, also called *behavioral roles*, reflect the personalities, behaviors, and habits of the members in a particular group; they are not specified in advance but develop through the interaction among members.

The informal role a particular individual plays in a small group is worked out in concert with the other members and is determined largely by the relative performance skills of the rest of the group members. This is accomplished primarily through trial and error. For example, Ty-isha may have a clear idea of how the group can accomplish its tasks; she will make attempts to structure the group's work: "I suggest we first make a list of all the things we need to do to finish our project." If no one else competes to supply that structuring function, and if the other members see that structuring behavior as helpful to the group, they will reinforce and reward Ty-isha's statements and actions: "Okay, Ty-isha that sounds like a good idea." This reinforcement, in turn, is likely to elicit more of those structuring behaviors from Ty-isha. On the other hand, if several members are also competent to structure the group's work, the group members collectively will reinforce the actions of the member they perceive to be the most skilled in this performance area. If Ty-isha is not reinforced as the group's "structurer," she will search for some other way to be valuable to, and valued by, the group. For instance, she may help clarify the proposals of the other members ("In other words, are you saying that . . . ?") or become the group's critical evaluator ("I think there are two major flaws with that proposal."). *Every member needs a role that makes a meaningful contribution to the group.*

Behavior

Any observable action by a group member.

Behavioral Function

The effect or function a member's behavior has on the group as a whole.

Consider This 7.4

Think for a moment of all the groups to which you have belonged. Your role probably changed considerably through time as you changed, as new people were added to or left a group, or as the problem facing the group changed. Do you see any patterns to your role behavior?

Because an individual's role depends on the particular mix of people in the group, that person's role will vary from group to group. A major principle of small group theory is this: *The role of each group member is worked out in the interaction between the member and the rest of the group* and continues to evolve as the group evolves. Thus, a well-organized person may end up leading one group and playing a supporting role in another, depending on the characteristics and competencies of all members relative to one another.

Classifying Group Roles

Group researchers have developed a variety of systems for classifying group roles. Hare, in a 1994 historical review of research about group roles, recommends that group researchers begin to describe roles in terms that would be understood by the group members themselves.[44] One such system is the functional role classification system described by Benne and Sheats.[45] These researchers classified members' roles on the basis of the functions those roles performed for the group. They defined three main categories of behavior: task, maintenance (socioemotional), and individual. Task behaviors directly affect the group's task. Maintenance or socioemotional behaviors affect the relationships among members, thus indirectly affecting the task. Individual behaviors are self-centered behaviors that help neither the task nor the relationships, but function to satisfy the individual at the expense of the group.

Although Benne and Sheats's system was first described many years ago, recent research verifies its current usefulness as a classification system. Mudrack and Farrell, noting that there has been little direct empirical investigation into this system, conducted a study to determine how well this three-category system describes typical member behaviors from the perspective of the members themselves.[46] They found that the task, maintenance, and individual distinctions Benne and Sheats described hold up. Although their study suggested a five-category model as being most precise, the addition of the two factors (one was a task subcategory, the other a maintenance subcategory) actually did not measurably improve the usefulness of the model. Mudrack and Farrell concluded that the three-category system—task, maintenance, and individual—is fairly accurate.

To some extent, all classification systems oversimplify the situation by suggesting that a remark or nonverbal behavior performs only one function in a group; in fact, remarks are fluid and affect both dimensions. For example, assume Teresa says to Mona and Melvin, "I think you guys are bypassing each

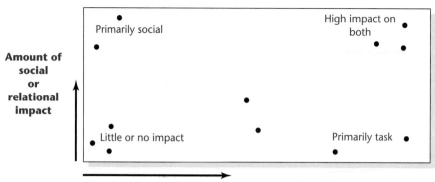

FIGURE 7.2   Task and social/relational impact of member behaviors.

• Specific act or behavior

other, and you should listen more carefully." That statement, even though it focuses on the ways members are relating to each other (a socioemotional concern), also has a bearing on the task accomplishment of the group, especially if Melvin and Mona start paying better attention to each other. Moreover, Teresa's statement implies that she has the right to intervene with expert information about the group's process, which says something about her relationship to the group. Thus, although many researchers consider actions to be *either* task- *or* relationship-oriented, it is more accurate to say that an act may have considerable impact on *both* dimensions.[47] In fact, Mudrack and Farrell found that the gatekeeper role, a maintenance role we describe later, and the information-seeker role, a task role, straddled both categories.[48] Figure 7.2 depicts these two major dimensions and illustrates how individual acts can affect each dimension to a greater or lesser degree.

Most researchers agree that both task and socioemotional needs must be met for a group to be effective. What follows is a list of behavioral functions, based on Benne and Sheats's classification that groups need to achieve their goals. Figure 7.3 illustrates the roles three group members might enact using various combinations of the following behaviors.

Task Functions   **Task functions** affect primarily the task output of the group. Some of the most helpful, with statements that exemplify those functions, are:

Initiating and orienting: proposing goals, plans of action, or activities; prodding the group to greater activity; defining position of group in relation to external structure or goal. ("Let's assign ourselves tasks to finish before the next meeting.")

Information giving: offering facts and information, evidence, or personal experience relevant to the group's task. ("Last year, the library spent $12,000 replacing lost materials.")

Task Functions

Task-oriented member behaviors that contribute primarily to accomplishing the goals of a group.

FIGURE 7.3 Roles
of three members
of a small group.

IDEA LEADER

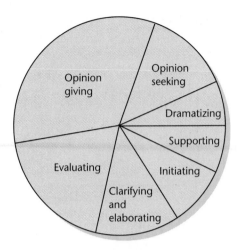

DEVIL'S ADVOCATE

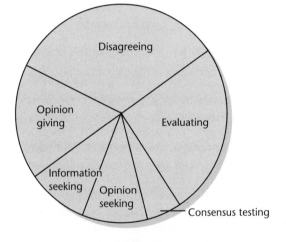

SOCIOEMOTIONAL LEADER

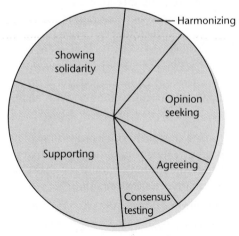

Information seeking: asking others for facts and information, evidence, or relevant personal experience. ("Juan, how many campus burglaries were reported last year?")

Opinion giving: stating beliefs, values, interpretations, judgments; drawing conclusions from evidence. ("I don't think theft of materials is the worst problem facing the library.")

Clarifying: making ambiguous statements clearer; interpreting issues. ("So does 'excellent' to you mean that the report should be perfect grammatically?")

Elaborating: developing an idea previously expressed by giving examples, illustrations, and explanations. ("Another thing that Toby's proposal would let us do is. . . .")

Evaluating: expressing judgments about the relative worth of information or ideas; proposing or applying criteria. ("Here are three problems I see with that idea.")

Summarizing: reviewing what has been said previously; reminding the group of a number of items previously mentioned or discussed. ("So, by next week, Angie will have the research finished and Carl will have the charts done on the computer.")

Coordinating: organizing the group's work; promoting teamwork and cooperation. ("If Meagan interviews the mayor by Monday, then Joyce and I can prepare a response by Tuesday's meeting.")

Consensus testing: asking if the group has reached a decision acceptable to all; suggesting that agreement may have been reached. ("We seem to be agreed that we'll accept the counteroffer.")

Recording: keeping group records, preparing reports and minutes; serving as group secretary and memory. ("I think we decided that two weeks ago. Let me look it up in the minutes to be sure.")

Suggesting procedure: suggesting an agenda of issues, or special technique; proposing some procedure or sequence to follow. ("Why don't we try brainstorming to help us come up with something new and different!")

I think about it constantly. . . . On a daily basis, 40 percent of my time is spent working with people issues.

> *J. M., Executive Coach and President, Marketing Agency*

Maintenance (Relationship-Oriented) Functions   **Maintenance functions** influence primarily the interpersonal relationships of members. We think the following seven functions, with sample statements, are especially vital to task groups:

Establishing norms: suggesting rules of behavior for members; challenging unproductive ways of behaving as a member; giving negative response

Maintenance Functions

Relationship-oriented member behaviors that reduce tensions, increase solidarity, and facilitate teamwork.

when another violates a rule or norm. ("I think it's unproductive to call each other names. Let's stick to the issues.")

Gatekeeping: helping some member get the floor; suggesting or controlling speaking order; asking if someone has a different opinion. ("Ruben, you look like you want to make a comment. Do you want to say something about the proposal?")

Supporting: agreeing or otherwise expressing support for another's belief or proposal; following the lead of another member. ("I think Joi's right; we should examine this more closely.")

Harmonizing: reducing secondary tension by reconciling disagreement; suggesting a compromise or new alternative acceptable to all; conciliating or placating an angry member. ("Jared and Sally, I think there are areas where you are in agreement, and I would like to suggest a compromise that might work for you both.")

Tension relieving: making strangers feel at ease; reducing status differences; encouraging informality; joking and otherwise relieving tension; stressing common interests and experiences. ("We're getting tired and cranky. Let's take a 10-minute break.")

Dramatizing: evoking fantasies about people and places other than the present group and time, including storytelling and fantasizing in a vivid way; testing a tentative value or norm through fantasy or story. ("That reminds me of a story about last year's committee. . . .")

Showing solidarity: indicating positive feeling toward other group members; reinforcing a sense of group unity and cohesiveness. ("Wow, we've done a great job on this!" or "We're all in this together!")

Whereas the preceding functions are necessary to effective small group functioning, there is another category of functions detrimental to the group. They represent an individual member's hidden agenda.

Self-Centered Functions

Actions of a small group member, motivated by personal needs, that serve the individual at the expense of the group.

Self-Centered Functions   **Self-centered functions** refer to those member behaviors that serve the performers' unmet needs at the expense of the group. We think the following three are especially harmful:

Withdrawing: avoiding important differences; refusing to cope with conflicts; refusing to take a stand; covering up feelings; giving no response to the comments of others. ("Do whatever you want, I don't care," or not speaking at all.)

Blocking: preventing progress toward group goals by constantly raising objections, repeatedly bringing up the same topic or issue after the group has considered and rejected it. ("I know we already voted, but I want to discuss it again!") It is *not* blocking to keep raising an issue the group has not really listened to or considered.

Status and recognition seeking: stage hogging, boasting, and calling attention to one's expertise or experience when this is not necessary to establishing credibility or relevant to the group's task; game playing to elicit sympathy; switching subject to area of personal expertise. ("I think we should do it the way I did it when I won the 'Committee Member of the Year' award.")

This list is by no means exhaustive; it could be expanded considerably with such categories as *special interest pleading, advocating, confessing*, and similar harmful functions. Self-centered functions manipulate and use other members for selfish goals that compete with what the group needs.

Although researchers believe that both task and maintenance roles are essential to effective group functioning, task roles seem overly important to group members themselves, according to Mudrack and Farrell.[49] Members clearly recognize the contributions task roles make to the group effort, but they do not seem to value the contributions of the maintenance roles, nor did they devalue the individualistic roles. Mudrack and Farrell recommend researchers continue to study how members evaluate these categories of roles.

We cannot emphasize enough how important it is for you to understand the types of roles a small group needs and how you, as a group member, can perform appropriate roles for the group. Plas, writing about the importance of participatory management approaches in American industry, says:

> One of the keys to working well within teams is learning how to differentiate roles—process roles as well as task roles. Successful teams—no matter where you find them—are made up of individuals who know how to define roles for themselves and how to work with the roles that other team members have adopted.[50]

Role Management across Groups

Equally important to understanding the role structure your group needs to function effectively is the recognition that effective management of group roles also recognizes those that members bring into the group from other groups. The bona fide group perspective discussed in Chapter 2 has been instrumental in reminding us that group members are often simultaneously members of other groups. One implication of this fact is that our roles in one group may or may not be in conflict with the time and commitment expectations of our roles in other groups. The important implication of this to our discussion of group roles is that roles in other groups can and do impact our negotiation and management of roles in other groups. How do we manage the roles in our church or community groups with our roles in work and family groups? Michael Kramer studied a community theater group in order to answer such a question.[51]

Most of us desire and seek membership in what Kramer calls "life enrichment groups" such as church and community volunteer groups. We can also experience difficulty in managing our time and commitment in those groups as they clash with the time and commitment demands of our family and work groups. The trick is not only creating but also maintaining and then negotiating the roles in these life enrichment groups so that we can maintain a balance between those groups and other relevant ones.

Kramer discovered that members of the theater group expressed to others the importance of home and work commitments *and* showed how important the theater group was to them. Part of the negotiation of conflicting intergroup roles was to talk about the importance of both sets of roles while also showing the sacrifice some made to the theater group. People who could not balance their home or work role commitments with the theater group simply did not try out for the production. Those who did join the group would talk to co-workers and family members about their participation in the theater group as part of negotiating the role commitments in both.

When people experience conflicts between multiple group membership commitments they can either segment or integrate them.[52] These theater members segmented their theater roles by time of day and by limiting the amount of time they committed to the theater roles. During the day their work or family roles took precedence, whereas at night their theater roles were more important. They also made it clear early in production that they would commit to this group for six weeks. Committing to some life enrichment groups for a limited amount of time is possible given their finite life span compared to work and family membership. However, Kramer warns that as more and more of us work at home this kind of segmentation may not be possible and it may make negotiation of multiple interpgroup roles more difficult for people.

SUMMARY

1. A group's culture, including its norms and patterns of behavior, is formed through the process of structuration or how the verbal and nonverbal interaction among members both creates and maintains the group. Structuration processes apply to face-to-face as well as to groups appropriating computer technology.

2. All groups must find ways to deal with their primary (interpersonal) and secondary (task-related) tensions.

3. Groups develop in stages, typically moving from the formation stage to the production stage, but members always need to deal simultaneously with socioemotional and task concerns, at all stages.

4. Group socialization of new and/or established members and the group is a complex process of learning how to fit together. Effective communication is important to socialization, and effective socialization influences other group processes such as norms and roles. Socialization involves antecedent, anticipatory, encounter, assimilation, and exit phases.

5. Whereas formal rules may exist to govern some of the group's interaction, informal rules (norms) that guide members' behaviors evolve—sometimes unconsciously—with the tacit approval of the members themselves. This holds true with some

modification in groups using computer-mediated communication.

6. With their personal behaviors and skills, group members carve out roles in conjunction with other group members.

7. All groups need both task and maintenance functions to be performed; self-oriented roles detract from the group's purpose.

8. Effective management of role structure is relevant to within-group processes as well as intergroup processes.

KEY TERMS

 Test your knowledge of these key terms by visiting the Online Learning Center website at mhhe.com/galanes11

Adaptive structuration theory	Exit phase	Production phase
Antecedent phase	Formation phase	Role
Anticipatory phase	Group culture	Rules
Assimilation phase	Group socialization	Secondary tension
Behavior	Maintenance functions	Self-centered functions
Behavioral function	Norm	Structuration
Conformity	Primary tension	Task functions
Encounter phase		

EXERCISES

 Go to self-quizzes on the Online Learning Center at mhhe.com/galanes11 to test your knowledge of the chapter concepts

1. Observe a small group during at least one discussion; take notes on what behaviors you observe and what norms these behaviors imply. Then, using the format that follows, record all the norms you infer from your observations by stating each as a rule of conduct for members. Try to identify at least 15 or 20 norms. Briefly describe the observed behaviors on which each norm is based. Finally, indicate whether you think the norm helped the group increase its output (+), had no effect on output (0), or reduced the group's output (–).

Specific Behavior That Provides Evidence of the Norm

Norm		Effect

2. Select a small group to which you have belonged since it was first formed and which has met at least several times. Describe the phases in that group's development as best you recall them. What phases did you see? How did you know when the group left one phase and entered another? Did the phases overlap? Do your fellow group members recall the phases as you do, or differently?

3. Using the list of behavioral functions as a guide (pages 187–191), several observers should classify each remark made by each of several members of a group according to the functions. This gives you a tally of how often each person performs each function. How would you describe each member's role? Draw a role profile, similar to Figure 7.3, for each person, and label the informal role each performed.

BIBLIOGRAPHY

Ellis, Donald G., and B. Aubrey Fisher. *Small Group Decision Making: Communication and the Group Process*. 4th ed. New York: McGraw-Hill, 1990, Chapter 5.

Feldman, Daniel. "Development and Enforcement of Group Norms." *Academy of Management Review* 9 (1984): 47–53.

Poole, Marshall S. "Group Communication and the Structuring Process." In *Small Group Communication: A Reader*. 7th ed. Robert S. Cathcart, Larry A. Samovar, and Linda D. Henman, eds. Dubuque, IA: Brown & Benchmark, 1996, 85–95.

NOTES

1. This story is a modified version of a case found in Marshall S. Poole, "Group Communication and the Structuring Process," in *Small Group Communication: A Reader*, 7th ed., eds. Robert S. Cathcart, Larry A. Samovar, and Linda D. Henman (Dubuque, IA: Brown & Benchmark, 1996): 89–91.

2. Bryan Seyfarth, "Structuration Theory in Small Group Communication: A Review and Agenda for Future Research," in *Communication Yearbook 23*, ed. Michael Roloff (Thousand Oaks, CA: Sage, 2000): 341–79.

3. Marshall S. Poole, David R. Siebold, and Robert D. McPhee, "Group Decision Making and the Structurational Process," *Quarterly Journal of Speech* 71 (1985): 74–102; Marshall S. Poole, David R. Seibold, and Robert D. McPhee, "A Structurational Approach to Theory-Building in Decision-Making Research," in *Communication and Group Decision Making*, eds. Randy Y. Hirokawa and Marshall S. Poole (Beverly Hills, CA: Sage, 1986): 237–64; and Poole, "Group Communication and the Structuring Process," 85–95.

4. Poole, "Group Communication and the Structuring Process."

5. Sunwolf and David R. Seibold, "Jurors' Intuitive Rules for Deliberation: A Structurational Approach to Communication in Jury Decision Making," *Communication Monographs* 65 (1998): 282–307.

6. Ibid., 303.

7. Seyfarth, "Structuration Theory in Small Group Communication."

8. Craig Scott, "Communication Technology and Group Communication," in *The Handbook of Group Communication Theory and Research*, ed. Lawrence Frey (Thousand Oaks, CA: Sage, 1999): 432–72.

9. Seyfarth, "Structuration Theory in Small Group Communication."

10. Poole, "Group Communication and the Structuring Process."

11. Ernest G. Bormann, *Discussion and Group Methods: Theory and Practice*, 3d ed. (New York: Harper & Row, 1990): 132–39.

12. David B. Barker, "The Behavioral Analysis of Interpersonal Intimacy in Group Development," *Small Group Research* 22 (February 1991): 76–91.

13. Bormann, *Discussion and Group Methods*, 139.

14. Robert F. Bales, *Interaction Process Analysis* (Reading, MA: Addison-Wesley, 1950).

15. William F. Whyte, *Pattern for Industrial Peace* (New York: Harper, 1951).
16. B. Aubrey Fisher and Randall K. Stutman, "An Assessment of Group Trajectories: Analyzing Developmental Breakpoints," *Communication Quarterly* 35 (Spring 1987): 105-24.
17. Bales, *Interaction Process Analysis*.
18. Bruce Riddle, Carolyn Anderson, and Matthew Martin, "Small Group Socialization Scale: Development and Validity," *Small Group Research* 31 (October 2000): 554-72.
19. Carolyn Anderson, Bruce Riddle, and Matthew Martin, "Socialization Processes in Groups," in *Handbook of Group Communication Theory and Research*, ed. Lawrence Frey (Thousand Oaks, CA: Sage, 1999): 139-63.
20. Ibid.
21. Riddle et al., "Small Group Socialization Scale."
22. Ibid.
23. Anderson et al., "Socialization Processes in Groups."
24. Joann Keyton, *Group Communication* (Mountain View, CA: Mayfield, 1999): 115.
25. Anderson et al., "Socialization Processes in Groups," 147.
26. Ibid., 148.
27. Ibid., 149.
28. Stewart Sigman, "The Applicability of the Concept of Recruitment to the Communication Study of a Nursing Home: An Ethnographic Case Study," *International Journal of Aging and Human Development* 22 (1985-86): 215-33. See also Melanie Booth-Butterfield, Stephen Booth-Butterfield, and Jolene Koester, "The Function of Uncertainty Reduction in Alleviating Primary Tension in Small Groups," *Communication Research Reports* 5 (1988): 146-53.
29. Anderson et al., "Socialization Processes in Groups," 151.
30. K. E. W. Morrison, "Information Usefulness and Acquisition During Organizational Encounter," *Management Communication Quarterly* 9 (1995): 131-55.
31. Anderson et al., "Socialization Processes in Groups," 152.
32. Ibid., 164.
33. Joann Keyton, "Group Termination: Completing the Study of Group Development," *Small Group Research* 24 (1993): 84-100.
34. Riddle et al., "Small Group Socialization Scale," 567.
35. Henry M. Robert, *Robert's Rules of Order*, Newly Revised (Glenview, IL: Scott, Foresman, 1990): 471-521.
36. George C. Homans, *The Human Group* (New York: Harcourt Brace Jovanovich, 1950): 123.
37. Susan B. Shimanoff, "Coordinating Group Interaction via Communication Rules," in *Small Group Communication: A Reader*, 6th ed., eds. Robert S. Cathcart and Larry A. Samovar (Dubuque, IA: Wm. C. Brown, 1992): 255.
38. Shimanoff, "Coordinating Group Interaction."
39. Tom Postmes, Russell Spears, and Lea Martin, "The Formation of Group Norms in Computer-Mediated Communication," *Human Communication Research* 26 (July 3): 341-71.
40. J. Dan Rothwell, *In Mixed Company*, 4th ed. (Fort Worth, TX: Harcourt, 2001): 63.
41. Steven Beebe and John Masterson, *Communicating in Small Groups*, 6th ed. (New York: Addison-Wesley): 82-83.
42. Gay Lumsden and Donald Lumsden, *Communicating in Groups and Teams*, 3d ed. (Belmont, CA: Wadsworth/Thomson Learning, 2000): 281.
43. Poole, "Group Communication and the Structuring Process."
44. A. Paul Hare, "Types of Roles in Small Groups: A Bit of History and a Current Perspective," *Small Group Research* 25 (August 1994): 433-48.
45. Kenneth D. Benne and Paul Sheats, "Functional Roles of Group Members," *Journal of Social Issues* 4 (1948): 41-49.
46. Peter E. Mudrack and Genevieve M. Farrell, "An Examination of Functional Role Behavior and Its Consequences for Individuals in Group Settings," *Small Group Research* 26 (November 1995): 542-71.
47. A. J. Salazar, "An Analysis of the Development and Evolution of Roles in the Small Group," *Small Group Research* 27 (1996): 475-503.
48. Mudrack and Farrell, "An Examination of Functional Role Behavior."
49. Ibid.
50. Jeanne M. Plas, *Person-Centered Leadership: An American Approach to Participatory Management* (Thousand Oaks, CA: Sage, 1996): 88.
51. Michael W. Kramer, "Communication in a Community Theater Group: Managing Multiple Group Roles," *Communication Studies* 53 (2002): 151-70.
52. Ibid., 162-65.

FROM INDIVIDUALS TO GROUP: FANTASY AND COHESIVENESS

Central Message

In addition to norms and roles, a group's culture also comprises the communication network, status hierarchy, fantasy life, and degree of cohesiveness of the group, all of which are created by communication.

STUDY OBJECTIVES

As a result of studying Chapter 8 you should be able to:

1. Explain how the group's communication pattern creates its communication network and describe several common communication networks, including the effect each has on group outputs.

2. Explain how a status hierarchy forms and how status differences affect group process and output.

3. Describe how fantasy chains contribute to the formation of a small group's culture.

4. Explain cohesiveness and describe nine techniques for enhancing it in a small group.

5. Differentiate supportive from defensive communication behaviors and explain how they contribute to a group's climate.

6. Explain what teambuilding involves and illustrate how it can be used to increase group cohesiveness, including in virtual teams.

7. Explain the theory of SYMLOG and illustrate how the SYMLOG method can provide insights about a small group's culture.

When the U.S. women's soccer team won the World Cup championship in 1999, star player Mia Hamm said, "Everything I am I owe to this team."[1] By all objective measures, this team represented a stellar example of unity, trust, and teamwork. The cohesiveness and commitment of the members drove them to achieve outstanding individual effort. For example, starter Michelle Akers battled chronic fatigue syndrome and bad knees for a long time, yet she was one of the mainstays of the team. Shannon MacMillan, a starter on the 1995 women's team, came off the bench to score a goal against North Korea. But she didn't use her performance to lobby for a starting position. Instead, she said, "I'm going to do anything I'm asked for this team. My heart and soul is with it." Briana Scurry's save and Brandi Chastain's final kick past the Chinese goalie in the sudden death kickoff won the game for the United States; Chastain said about the kick, "I felt very confident. My team trusted me." According to assistant coach Lauren Gregg, after the 1995 1-0 loss to Norway, the humiliated women vowed never to let that happen again and talked constantly about what they could do, both individually and collectively, to win again. Clearly, this was a cohesive, productive team. What creates the kind of cohesiveness and teamwork that would cause a Mia Hamm, a sports star admired by many, to credit the team rather than herself for her performance?

Tony DiCicco, coach of the women's team, was largely responsible for molding the members, ranging from the quiet, intense Scurry to the gregarious, funny Julie Foudy, into the unified, high-performance team it became. DiCicco, who had previously coached men, took over the women's team in 1994. He learned quickly that the women responded well to challenges but poorly to chastisement, so he decided to employ a positive style. The postgame videos the women were shown did not include replays of their mistakes but included only their "best moves and winning decisions," a strategy DiCicco calls "catching them being good." Most of the women had been together for a long time, some since before the World Cup game in 1991, so they knew each other well. To increase trust, the motivational psychologist DiCicco hired had the team participate in a "trust walk," where blindfolded team members were led down a dangerous cliff by their teammates. She also created an individualized videotape for each player of her best moves and plays, set to music selected by the player herself. Although the tapes were designed to be viewed individually, team members eventually ended up sharing them and watching them together. The women performed exercises such as standing in a line while holding balloons between their bodies and trying to move in symmetry. DiCicco also had the women switch roommates at every stop to prevent cliques from forming. He was pleased when, upon giving the women a night off, they all chose to go out to dinner together.

There's no question that talent, ability, and individual initiative played a part in the team's success, but individual talent doesn't always translate into team performance, as we learned in Chapter 2. The women, with DiCicco's guidance, were able to create a culture of trust, unity, and support so the team could put all their talents together to win.

> The ones that have been most exciting for me are when you see the group gel.
>
> *M. I., Human Resources Manager, Manufacturing Company*

In this chapter we continue our study of group culture, focusing on how individuals come together to form a successful group with its own unique personality. There are two important points we want to emphasize again. First, all the elements of culture we discuss in this and the previous chapter are part of the throughput processes of the group. They are developed as members exchange verbal and nonverbal signals with one another, in other words, as members communicate. Second, these processes develop simultaneously. We talk about them one by one simply for clarity and convenience. Now we turn our attention to a group's communication networks, status hierarchy, fantasy life, and cohesiveness.

Communication Networks

A group's **communication network** is the pattern of message flow, or who speaks to whom during discussions. If Miguel calls on others one by one, they may develop the habit of not speaking until he calls on them. If Andrea speaks frequently, she may find others looking (literally) to her for some comment on each new issue. Infrequent interactants will find themselves increasingly ignored. A network of who speaks to whom emerges as a function of individual behaviors. The network may change as new problems arise that bring different members' specific knowledge or skills to the forefront, or as socioemotional concerns develop in the group. However, every small group is generally typified by one of the major network types described here and pictured in Figure 8.1.

Communication Network

Who talks to whom in a group; which interpersonal channels are used.

Each type of network has strengths and weaknesses; none is universally better than any other. Whether a network facilitates problem solving depends on the task. For instance, usually a group of peers develops an all-channel network in which all participants are free to comment on a one-to-one basis with all others and to the group as a whole. A wheel network is one in which all

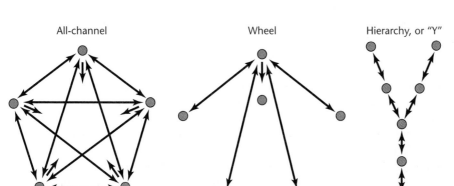

All-channel   Wheel   Hierarchy, or "Y"

FIGURE 8.1
Communication networks.

comments are directed toward one central person (usually the designated leader) who alone has authority to speak to the other members. A "Y," or hierarchical network, occurs when an autocratic leader speaks to lieutenants who in turn talk to subordinates. People at the ends of the Y rarely talk to the leader directly. Both the Y and wheel networks are more efficient for simple tasks, but in each, the central person is generally more satisifed with the communication and participation in the group than the more peripheral members. Another danger in these types of networks is that the central member may suffer from stressful information overload or may create a bottleneck hampering information flow. In addition, communication in restricted networks may break down into two or more private conversations during a group meeting.

> The success of this group depends on the involvement, the excitement, and the sharing amongst the group that's there, not the facilitator.
>
> *M. I., Human Resources Manager, Manufacturing Company*

On the other hand, the all-channel network, although slower when tackling complex problems, permits rapid communication among all members without having to get clearance from a central gatekeeping authority. Members are free to say what they want while ideas are still fresh in mind and pertinent. Communication flows freely; at least half the remarks are made to group members as a whole and all members can hear and tune in to one-to-one or one-to-few comments. The all-channel network pays off in several ways. Morale is highest, and such groups tend to perform better on complex tasks when compared with restricted network groups. Even in all-channel groups, the flow of verbal messages may at times resemble a wheel or a hierarchy, such as during an emergency or under extreme time pressure.

Status Hierarchy

Status

The position of a member in the hierarchy of power, influence, and prestige within a small group.

Status refers to the relative importance, prestige, and power of a member in a small group. As roles emerge, each person is placed in a sort of pecking order, like the one you saw emerge in the medical group in Chapter 7. Several advantages accrue to members of high status. High status is socially rewarding, so such members feel important and worthwhile. Other group members defer to them, grant them a disproportionate share of the group's attention, agree with their proposals, and seek their advice and opinions. People occupying formal, high-status roles (e.g., manager or CEO) may be given such tangible signs of status as large offices, private secretaries, and powers not granted to other members. Moreover, designated leaders, even of work teams and committees, are often given deference, support, and more eye contact.

Effects of status are numerous. High-status members talk more than low-status members and address each other more often than do low-status members, who address their remarks more often to high-status members than to each other.[2] Low-status members also send more positive messages to high-status members than to other low-status members, another reward of high status.[3] Low-status members are interrupted more and their comments are ignored more often than the comments of those with higher status. High-status members tend to talk more to the group as a whole, whereas low-status members express most of their comments to individuals (the classic Y network).

> I don't like to go to meetings where, in order to be part of the team, you just nod and tell the leader he's a genius.
>
> *B. H., Director, State-Level Program*

In addition to being granted a number of psychological or material rewards, high-status members are expected to meet certain responsibilities within the group. They are expected to work especially hard to accomplish the group's goals, and to uphold the group's norms. They may lose status by failing to fulfill the group's expectations, although they may be given additional leeway to bend the rules, called **idiosyncracy credit,** that other members do not receive.[4] This means that, for members who have made an exceptionally valuable contribution to the group, certain rules can be bent. Recent research confirms this view. Estrada et al. found a high correlation between idiosyncracy credit and leadership—the group members to whom others were willing to award idiosyncracy credit also were perceived as leaders.[5] When this was the case, the group's performance was enhanced. However, they also found some low-performing groups in which idiosyncracy credit was not related to group leadership. Estrada et al. speculate that in such groups the members' attention is diverted from the task.

Status within a small group may be *ascribed* or it may be *earned*. At first, before members know each other well and are sure what their respective contributions will be to the group, status is **ascribed** on the basis of each member's position outside the small group. It is based on such things as wealth, education, occupation, personal fame, or position in the group's parent organization. For example, a committee composed of a company CEO, the vice president of manufacturing, a senior accountant, two employees from the marketing division, and a college student intern in marketing will initially have that order of ascribed status. However, status can also be **earned** or achieved on the basis of a member's individual contributions to the group. The intern who conducts considerable research on behalf of the group and is a key contributor will have higher earned status than the senior accountant who completes no assignments. In some instances, the importance of variables that contribute to ascribed status, such as sex, appears to be shifting, as we noted in Chapter 5.

One of the supposed benefits of computer-mediated communication (CMC) in a group is that status differences are minimized because in many CMC groups, members remain anonymous, thus status cues aren't visible. However, Scott's recent review of communication technology and its effects questions this assumption.[6] For one thing, anonymity is largely irrelevant in organizational groups—members are identified and know with whom they work. Influence from the face-to-face context carries over to the CMC context.

Idiosyncracy Credit

Additional leeway in adhering to group norms, given to a member for valuable contributions to the group.

Ascribed Status

Status due to characteristics external to the group, such as wealth, level of education, position, physical attractiveness, and so forth.

Earned Status

Status earned by a member's valued contributions to the group, such as working hard for the group, providing needed expertise, being especially communicatively competent, and so forth.

True anonymity, however, can minimize ascribed status social cues. Flanagin et al. found that men in CMC situations tried to make the CMC interaction more like a face-to-face (FTF) interaction, but women in CMC situations tried to preserve reduced social cues of CMC interaction. These authors speculate that reducing the status-lowering social cues gives women greater influence in the group, whereas maintaining the status cues of FTF interaction enhances the influence of men.[7]

Ideally, a group's relationships and relative status differences are somewhat flexible so that different members can become more influential as their particular knowledge and skills are pertinent to the issues or problems facing the group at any point in time. Wood found that paying undue attention to ascribed status differences negatively affected a group's ability to accomplish its task.[8] It is important to note that lower status does not mean *of little value*. Lower-status members are not necessarily unhappy in the group; cohesive groups value the contributions of each member, and each member knows it. Only when members say things like, "We could have done just as well without Morgan and Jolene on this committee," can we infer that lower status definitely means "inferior." More typically, everyone in the group might follow the lead of a normally quiet, low-status person who seems to have just the information or ability the group most needs at a given moment. That person might later slip back into a more usual low-profile position, but the contribution will have been noted and appreciated.

Recent research by Bonito suggests that members take into account both external status characteristics and member behaviors in the group when they make judgments about the value of their own and others' participation in a group.[9] External status characteristics—age, gender, appearance—contribute to expectations about how and how much someone will participate in a group. Although status differences have been found to be related to differential rates of participation, they are not reliable predictors. Members' behavior in the group and contribution to the task also influence others' perceptions of their participation. People differ with regard to which factors they pay more attention to. In any case, rigid status hierarchies based on external status characteristics can diminish the participation of all members.

Consider This 8.1

Sometimes a member's culture can affect that member's ascribed status in a group. Cultural variables such as ethnicity, sex, area of the country someone is from, and so forth, influence how others perceive you. What specific cultural variables can affect a member's status in the group and how might they affect other members' perceptions? Does that variable increase or decrease the member's status? What could you do if a cultural characteristic of yours is negatively affecting your group status? What could you do if you perceive that another member's group status is being affected by a particular cultural characteristic?

Fantasy Themes

We have said before that a group's culture is produced by the interaction among group members. We discussed how roles and norms emerge as elements of a group's culture, but one of the most powerful ways in which group culture is created is through *fantasy*. Technically, **fantasy** refers to "the creative and imaginative shared interpretation of events that fulfill a group's psychological or rhetorical need to make sense of their experience and to anticipate their future."[10] Fantasy, in this sense, does not mean fictitious or unreal. It means that during certain periods of the group's interaction, rather than discussing events happening in the here and now of the group, the members are telling stories, relating past events, and sharing anecdotes that have a bearing *at the unconscious level* on the group's process. In other words, group members rarely set out consciously to establish the group's culture. Instead, they just talk. Some of that talk appears to be tangential to the group's real task, but in fact it meets psychological and rhetorical needs of the members.

When a group member says something not directly related to the present task of the group, that member has introduced a fantasy. This happens often during a discussion, with many fantasies going no further. However, sometimes group members pick up on the fantasy introduced by one group member and elaborate on it. Several members join the fantasy by adding their pieces to the story, in a kind of group storytelling. A fantasy that members elaborate on is called a **fantasy chain,** first described by Bales.[11] During a fantasy chain the speed of the interaction typically picks up, voices become louder, and a sense of excitement can be detected. The mood is electric. A fantasy chain may last from as little as half a minute to as much as half an hour. Eventually the chain peters out, often when one member pulls the group back on task. Fantasy chaining is a rhetorical tool for creating shared images of the group and its environment. In Chapter 3 we noted that communication is transactional; during fantasy chaining, group members transact, without preplanned intent, to create meaning for the group. This storytelling activity plays a crucial role in structuration of a group's culture.[12]

Fantasy

A statement not pertaining to the here-and-now of the group that offers a creative and meaningful interpretation of events and meets a group's psychological or rhetorical need.

Fantasy Chain

A series of statements by several or all group members in which a story is dramatized to help create a group's view of reality.

Consider This 8.2

Fantasy is one way groups create a common vision. In what other ways do you think groups create a common vision? What differences might there be between visions created through fantasy and visions created in other ways?

Fantasy chains develop in a fairly predictable way.[13] First, some form of ambiguity or uncertainty exists in the group. One member begins the fantasy by introducing a core image that somehow relates to the uncertainty. Other members spread that core image by adding their own elements to the fantasy, creating a group metaphor, rather than just an individual one. Finally, when the fantasy chain has ended, the group members have converged on a particular picture of the group's reality.

Fantasies are *about* something; the content of the fantasy is called the **fantasy theme.** There is an obvious or *manifest* theme to the fantasy chain, and a *latent*, or below-the-surface theme that, when examined, reveals the culture, values, and norms of the group. Often, fantasies have heroes and villains, plot lines, and a well-developed ethical structure that gives moral or psychological guidance to a group. To interpret the latent meaning of a fantasy, Bales suggests looking for a sudden insight rather than trying to analyze the fantasy systematically.

Fantasy is rooted in the theory of **symbolic convergence,** which was articulated and developed by Bormann. Symbolic convergence theory acknowledges that humans are storytelling creatures who create and share meaning through talk.[14] *Convergence* refers to the fact that during interaction the private symbolic worlds of individuals often overlap, or converge. When that occurs, as it must to some extent in a group or there would be no group, meaning is shared; the symbolic, personal communication of two or more individuals constructs a shared reality that bonds the individuals, helps them discover how they feel about certain events, reveals shared values, and guides them to action. In other words, symbolic communication theory "accounts for the creation and maintenance of a group consciousness through shared motives, common emotional activity, and consensual meanings for events."[15] We will now turn from this fairly abstract discussion to several specific examples of how fantasy helps shape a group's reality.

In the short and simple fantasy chain below, members of a student group are planning publicity for their annual Career Day seminar.[16] Chris asks Kevin what the previous year's group did for publicity:

Fantasy Theme

What the actual content of a fantasy or fantasy chain is about.

Symbolic Convergence

The theory that humans create and share meaning through talk and storytelling, producing an overlapping (convergence) of private symbolic worlds of individuals during interaction.

Discussion	Commentary
Chris: Kevin, do you know what they did last time?	Chris asks a direct, task-relevant question.
Kevin: Yeah, somewhere I've got a list here. All they really did was put an ad in the school paper and then sent around this tacky memo to the faculty about a week ahead of time asking them to announce it in classes. It was embarrassing!	Kevin answers Chris, but introduces the fantasy about the "embarrassing" performance of last year's group.
Deirdre: I can't believe that's all they did!	Deirdre, animated, picks up on Kevin's criticism of the previous group.
Lori:: It was John's fault—he didn't want to do *anything*, and the group didn't do anything!	Lori adds her part.

Discussion	Commentary
Tony: What a bunch of lazy wimps!	Tony contributes.
Chris: We've already done more than they ever did, and we've just gotten started.	Chris contributes, and adds the idea that *this* group has already done better than the last one.
Kevin: I know! We're going to look a lot better than they did!	Kevin adds to Chris's idea.
Lori: Okay, I like trashing those guys as much as you do, but we're really getting off track.	Lori stops the fantasy by getting the group back on track.

In this segment, the group starts out addressing its task directly, but quickly gets off task as members enjoy trashing the previous year's group. Kevin introduces the fantasy, with all group members participating in the fantasy chain until Lori, the group's designated leader, stops the chain and returns the group to its task.

What function has this fantasy served? The manifest theme of the fantasy is, "Last year's group did a rotten job of publicity." Remember, though, that fantasies help create shared meanings for the *present* group. In this sequence, trashing the previous group builds up the performance of the present group by comparison, as hinted at in Chris's comment, "We've already done more than they ever did." By saying what a lousy group the previous year's group was, this group is not so subtly saying, "We're so much better." The group is setting standards of excellence, establishing norms of professionalism missing in the previous group that motivate the members to do better. The following is an example from the church board introduced in Chapter 2. The group has been discussing routine matters when Marina initiates the fantasy:

Discussion	Commentary
Marina: I just noticed that spider plant in the corner. It's doing great! In fact, better than when it was in our living room!	Marina introduces the fantasy about the plant, apparently irrelevant to the group's task.
Sally: It really is healthy. Look at all the spider babies it's produced.	Sally picks up the fantasy and adds to it.
Norm: It seems to be happier here than when we had it at home. That peace lily in the corner looks pretty good, too.	Norm adds to the chain.
Sunni: You should see the plants in the sanctuary. They look so happy and healthy.	Sunni extends the fantasy to include the sanctuary plants as well.
Bill: Maybe we should bring in that half-dead shamrock in our kitchen. Do you think this environment would revive it?	Bill extends; his statement about the beneficial effects of the church environment hints at the meaning of the fantasy for this particular group.

Gary: It's all that tender, loving care!

Gary contributes.

Dick: They do look good, but we've got a lot to cover yet. Can we get back to the agenda?

Dick acknowledges, but brings the group back to its task.

The ostensible, or manifest, theme of this fantasy is how good the plants in the church look. The latent theme, which is not terribly disguised, is members' belief that they have helped create a positive, supportive atmosphere that is healthy for plants and, by extension, other living things (especially people). Thus, this particular fantasy chain reinforces the church board members' desire to do something important, life giving, and good for the congregation. It also solidifies their commitment to the task.

Fantasies perform several functions for small groups. First, they help the members create the group's unique identity.[17] The two examples just discussed demonstrate that function. The student group helped define itself as an excellent, hard-working, professional team by comparing itself favorably with the previous group. Church board members intensified their commitment to the job of establishing a new congregation and patted themselves on the back for creating a nurturing atmosphere.

Second, fantasies help a group deal with threatening or difficult information that members might feel reluctant to address directly. To illustrate, Morocco related the story of the first meeting of a research group whose student members believed their leaders were not providing them with enough direction.[18] One student recalled seeing a film about an experiment in which baby monkeys were deprived of maternal nurturing. The other members, who had seen the movie in school, began to contribute by adding details and developing a plot and dramatic images associated with the movie. The social and sexual development of the monkeys in the movie had been impaired by the lack of parental care, and this image served to symbolize the reality that these group members were *currently* experiencing. In essence, the group said, "The lack of attention and help on the part of the leaders will ultimately harm us."

Third, fantasies help direct a group's actions by subtly endorsing or condemning particular courses of action. For example, Putnam and her associates describe a contract bargaining situation between two committees, one of teachers and the other of administrators.[19] The administrators constructed a fantasy chain about one of the teachers, whose constant head nodding reminded them of a woodpecker or a toy bird bobbing up and down on a cup. Their fantasy theme created a shared image of the teachers as well meaning but inexperienced. Later during the bargaining situation, the teachers appeared to renege on a proposal they had earlier accepted. The administrators could have made a big deal of this by escalating the conflict, but the image of the teachers as inexperienced rather than unscrupulous led them to perceive the teachers' actions as an innocent mistake. This benevolent interpretation by the administrators gave the teachers latitude to err without derailing the bargaining process. The effect was to maintain good feelings all around. The fantasy, in part, inspired this outcome by molding the administrators' perceptions of the teachers' shortcomings.

Finally, fantasies can be entertaining and fun for the group. In the previous example, the administrators' committee kept itself happily entertained by imagining the teacher who nodded constantly as a woodpecker and a whirligig bird. Fantasies help groups exercise their imaginations and creativity. They are powerful shapers of a group's culture.

Development of a Group's Climate

Communication scholars have generally focused their efforts on understanding group tasks and the factors that influence them. However, group relationships are equally important, even though they have received relatively less attention.[20] **Group climate** refers to a group's emotional and relational atmosphere. How well do members work together? Do they seem to like each other? Are members' identity and relational needs being met? Is the atmosphere tense or relaxed? In this section, we discuss two elements that contribute to group climate: cohesiveness and supportiveness.

Group Climate

A group's emotional and relational atmosphere.

Cohesiveness

Cohesiveness refers to the common bonds and sentiments that hold a group together. When a group is high in cohesiveness, the relationships among members are, on the whole, attractive to them; they have a high degree of "stick togetherness" and unity. Highly cohesive groups behave differently from less cohesive groups. They display more characteristics of primary groups than less cohesive groups.[21] They have higher rates of interaction. Members express more positive feelings for each other and report more satisfaction with the group, such as was demonstrated by the women soccer players choosing to go out to dinner together. Members are willing to cooperate and collaborate with each other.[22] In addition, cohesive groups exert greater control over member behaviors.[23] High cohesiveness is associated with increased ability to cope effectively with unusual problems and to work as a team in meeting emergencies. Production groups, if highly cohesive, can produce more than less cohesive groups, but may not do so if members are being influenced by intragroup norms for less production. Although results of individual studies have been mixed, two recent meta-analyses of cohesiveness research have found that, in general, highly cohesive groups are more productive.[24] The nature of the task influences the cohesiveness-productivity relationship.[25] If the task is one that requires a high degree of coordination and interdependence among members, with communication an essential factor in the group's task completion, then cohesiveness enhances productivity, such as was demonstrated by the women's soccer team.

Cohesiveness

The degree of attraction members feel for the group; unity.

> If you're going to have a team that works really well, has a good time, and meets objectives, you've got to get their heart in it.
>
> *M. S., Vice President, Financial Service Firm, retired*

Cohesiveness is often discussed as if it were a single construct, but in fact there are several dimensions to cohesiveness. Two studies support the idea that cohesiveness can involve both personal relationships and commitment to the group's goal. Johnson and Fortman found that cohesiveness entails both task and interpersonal dimensions.[26] Cohesiveness that is due to interpersonal attraction and liking produces different results than cohesiveness that is based on commitment to the task or goal. Chin et al. also found two factors that contribute to cohesion: belonging and morale.[27] Belonging refers to whether a member feels a part of the group—without this, that member won't want to associate with the other members. Without high morale, group members won't be motivated to work on the task. These authors adapted the Perceived Cohesion Scale, previously used with large groups, for use in small groups, with acceptable results. This brief scale is contained in Consider This 8.3.

Consider This 8.3

How cohesive is a particular group you belong to? To assess your own feelings, take the brief Perceived Cohesion Scale below, using the following scale: strongly agree, 7 points; quite agree, 6; slightly agree, 5; neither agree nor disagree, 4; slightly disagree, 3; quite disagree, 2; strongly disagree, 1.

1. I feel that I belong to this group.
2. I am happy to be part of this group.
3. I see myself as part of this group.
4. This group is one of the best anywhere.
5. I feel that I am a member of this group.
6. I am content to be part of this group.

Add up your points. The higher the number, the more cohesiveness you feel. You may want to ask your fellow group members to take the scale and discuss results within the group. To what extent do you believe this scale captures what you think of as cohesiveness?

There is an optimum level of cohesiveness beyond which performance decreases.[28] Whether or not a cohesive group is productive also depends on the degree to which members accept their task. Cohesive groups are productive only when the members have both high acceptance of organizational goals implicit in the group's task *and* a strong drive (motivation and enthusiasm) to complete the task.[29] This was certainly the case with the excellent teams studied by Larson and LaFasto.[30] However, groups that are highly cohesive but socially oriented rather than task-oriented may end up accomplishing nothing.[31]

Highly successful and cohesive groups tend first to get acquainted and interested in each other as people. This type of self-disclosure increases cohesiveness, commitment to the task, and productivity.[32] Members can be heard saying, "I'm proud of our group, we really thrash out ideas until we arrive at the best, then we team up." However, high cohesiveness can also pressure members to conform to the majority or to high-status members' desires, which can result in a less-than-thorough critical evaluation of ideas, leading to what is called *groupthink*, which we discuss in Chapter 12.

Although high cohesiveness can be associated with pitfalls such as groupthink, cohesiveness can produce great results. A group that accomplishes its objectives, provides members with satisfaction in their participation, offers prestige in belonging, and is successful in competing with other groups is very attractive to its members. This can help produce highly committed and enthusiastic members who stay the course when problems arise and win world championships.

Cohesiveness is fostered to the extent that members know and like each other as individuals, by their frequency of interaction, and by the amount of influence each exerts on the group. In addition, some evidence suggests that cohesive groups cooperate in creating a dominant sensory metaphor as a group, and that cohesiveness can be monitored through metaphor.[33] For example, when a group is first established, various members indicate their understanding by saying, "I see," "I hear you," or "I grasp that." Each of these metaphors for "I understand" concentrates on a different sense—sight, sound, or touch. In cohesive groups, members tend to converge on a particular sensory metaphor. If the visual metaphor is "chosen," for example, members will all start saying, "I see," "I've got the picture," and "I've spotted a flaw." This happens below the level of conscious awareness and indicates that the members have influenced each other in subtle but significant ways.

Interestingly, open disagreement is more frequent in highly cohesive groups, probably because a climate of trust gives each member the security needed to openly disagree on issues, facts, and ideas.[34] On the other hand, if high-status members indicate that they perceive disagreement to be a personal affront and demand compliance, then cohesiveness may become groupthink and be maintained at the expense of high-quality decision making.

Cohesiveness, then, is generally desirable. Here are our suggestions to enhance cohesiveness:[35]

1. **Allow time for members to get to know each other.**
   Members do not have to become best friends, but it helps if they feel comfortable with one another. You can foster this with an unstructured period of chitchat, perhaps before a meeting begins or after it has ended—maybe at happy hour. The performance of even short-term teams benefits if members spend time getting to know one another.[36]

Spending some time doing that [engaging in small talk] and laughing about that, that's part of the payoff for being in the group, that's part of what satisfies them about their group membership.

A. B., University Dean

2. **Set clear, attainable group goals.**
   A long-term goal is easier to achieve if it is broken down into several short-term goals. In addition, goals should be challenging but not impossible to reach because failure is demotivating. One of the most important characteristics that differentiates high-performing, cohesive teams from mediocre ones is having a compelling goal that is clear.[37]

3. **Treat members like people, not machines.**
   The efficient, highly oiled machine is *not* the best metaphor for the kinds of groups we have been discussing. People have human needs for warmth, affection, and esteem that should be recognized. As we have said before, group work is not just about meeting control needs and task accomplishment, but meeting needs for inclusion and affection as well.[38]

4. **Develop a group identity, with group traditions and rituals.**
   Talk about the group as *we*, not *you*. Develop nicknames for the group, insignia indicating membership, or mascots for the group. Encourage traditions and rituals, which give added meaning to the group's culture. Refer to past events with pride, and encourage the group to develop a rich fantasy life.

5. **Stress teamwork.**
   Members, especially designated leaders or high-performance members, should avoid talking about "my accomplishments." The team performance should come before individual glory. A friend of ours, who has since become an effective group leader, told us she failed in her first leadership assignment because she kept taking credit for work the group had completed. She demoralized the team.

6. **Get the group to recognize good work.**
   Encourage members to compliment and praise one another. Coach DiCicco talked about how one of his players, Michelle Akers, inspired him.[39] Low-status members, especially, need attention and recognition. Look for ways to support other members with their group work assignments, but also with non-group-related activities. Another friend says he praises publicly, but chastises privately. When group members and the team do good work, he lets everyone, within the team and outside, know about it.

7. **Reward and celebrate group accomplishments.**
   Although many organizations reward individual performance, groups should be rewarded *as groups*. These can be tangible or intangible rewards, including recognition dinners, public praise, letters of commendation, and so forth. Outstanding leaders look for things to celebrate and do

so in a variety of ways.[40] One such leader, a manager at a major corporation, put signs up all over her building about her team's outstanding performance, then bought drinks and snacks for the entire team at a restaurant after work. Another leader sends handwritten, personalized thank-yous.

8. **Support both disagreement and agreement.**
   A norm of freedom of expression and openness should be maintained. Highly cohesive groups show more disagreement, with conflict encouraged, not repressed. Often, when conflicts are resolved, group members feel closer than ever and are more cohesive.

9. **Have fun!**
   Teamwork isn't only about completing work—it's about enjoying and appreciating your fellow group members. Having fun, laughing together, enjoying a non-task-related activity, can help unify a group. The most satisfying teams have members who give the group not only their best thinking but their hearts as well.

Building Cohesiveness and Productivity in Virtual Teams

A **virtual team** is one in which the members' interactions take place primarily through some combination of electronic systems, such as telephone, computer, fax, videoconferencing, instead of face-to-face.[41] Virtual teams must do what face-to-face teams do—accomplish work and promote good team relationships—but because members typically do not work in the same location or meet in person regularly, they face additional challenges. Jarvenpas has identified nine behaviors that help build trust in virtual teams, including social communication, communication that conveys enthusiasm, methods to deal with technological and task uncertainty, individual initiative, predictable communication, substantive and timely feedback, positive leadership, transitions from procedure to task focus, and calm reactions to crisis.[42] Virtual teams are relatively new, but they are becoming more common throughout corporate America. The following suggestions will help you form a cohesive, productive virtual team.[43]

Virtual Team

A group that meets primarily or exclusively through some combination of electronic means (computers, telephones, videoconferences, and so forth).

1. **Establish an identity for the team.** Make sure that all members know who is on the team, where they are located, and how they can be reached via e-mail, telephone, and so forth. Creating a name for the team is helpful also. Some team leaders ask members to post a picture with brief biographical information on a team website, so all members can see and know a bit more about their fellow team members. If members are widely dispersed geographically, it may help to post a map showing where each member is located.

2. **Manage the team's uncertainty: clarify the team's purpose, specific outcomes to be achieved, and time line.** Face-to-face teams have the luxury of allowing the team's goals and chronology to evolve, at least to

some extent, but virtual team members need this spelled out specifically when the team is formed. The time frame may change later, but having it outlined keeps everyone on the same page.

3. **Manage technology issues: make sure members agree on the technology to be used, have been trained in it, and are reasonably comfortable with it.** Satisfaction with technology comes in large measure from comfort with it. A team member who can't use the technology appropriately will shy away from virtual teamwork—no one wants to look dumb in front of his or her peers. In addition, members should standardize what they will use. If the team will be preparing a document to which everyone contributes, agree in advance which word processing program will be used, and so forth. Hold whatever training sessions are necessary to help people get over the hump of using something new.

4. **If possible, have the members meet face-to-face, particularly at the beginning of their work as a virtual team.** Although this isn't always practical or possible, it helps build a team feeling. This may be the single most important thing a manager can do to promote trust and teamwork. Ideally, members can meet periodically throughout the team's work, but at least an initial meeting will help.

5. **Make sure members know the communication rules to be used for the team's business.** Sometimes, virtual communication can seem abrupt or even rude because many of the nonverbal cues that provide context or can soften a negative message are missing. Members, particularly if they are new to the technology, must be encouraged to be more precise with their language, because the primary messages, at least on computers, are conveyed through text. In addition, it may be helpful for the group's leader, with the input of the group, to establish expectations, such as for how often members will be expected to check into the virtual meeting site, and so forth. Members should, of course, observe common courtesies with each other.

6. **Have a virtual location—chat room, bulletin board, folder—where the team's documents and records are kept.** Face-to-face teams have minutes and memos to help them keep track of the task. Virtual teams can also have access to such organizing information, which helps them keep on task and captures the group's collective memory.

7. **Encourage regular communication, including informal social communication among members.** Regular, predictable, and frequent interaction, using whatever electronic forms the team has agreed to, helps keep members connected to each other and aware of each other. In addition, as with face-to-face teams, encouraging informal, nontask communication helps build trust and a satisfying team experience.

Supportiveness

LaFasto and Larson's work with numerous kinds of teams over many years has revealed that there are significant differences in climate between high-performing teams and ones that are merely OK (or worse):

> With rare exceptions, members of effective teams describe the atmosphere of the team in positive terms. The team is relaxed, comfortable, informal, fun, warm. Teams that are good at problem solving have a way of making their members feel accepted, valued, and competent. Members of poor teams, on the other hand, tend to describe the climate as tense, overly critical, political, cynical, inhibiting, cold, or too stiff and formal.[44]

The members of excellent teams are consistently described as supportive, interested, and willing to help the rest of the members succeed.[45] For instance, they bolster other members' confidence, pitch in to help each other, and listen well to each other. Nonsupportive members, in contrast, are "me" oriented, disinterested in the others, and do only the jobs they are assigned. They may be social loafers. LaFasto and Larson make a point that supportive members aren't just "get-along" members who don't rock the boat or don't actively disagree with others' ideas. Caring deeply about the work of the group, they freely challenge ideas and opinions. They also work hard on behalf of the group, and display warmth and affection to the other members.

What LaFasto and Larson observed is consistent with what Gibb observed many years ago.[46] Gibb observed members of many teams and asked them what behaviors were helpful and not helpful within the team. The two opposite communication climates he defined, a supportive climate and a defensive one, are created by the communication among members. It is what members do and say, how they treat each other, that creates the group's climate.

A **supportive climate** is one that values each member. Members know they are wanted and appreciated, that their ideas and opinions are important to the group. Members behave toward one another in the most ethical of ways, confirming and supporting each other. Members build each other up. However, in a **defensive climate,** members tear each other down and violate the ethical principle, mentioned in Chapter 1, that states members should not belittle or ridicule one another. Defensive climates carry an element of judgment, which makes members feel as if they are being evaluated and found wanting. If you have ever worked in a defensive climate, you know that only a portion of your energy is being directed to the group's task. Much of it is going to protect yourself from psychological attack. Members feel as if they have to walk on eggshells around their fellow group members. You can't do your best work that way, so ultimately the group's work suffers.

> There's nothing worse than negative mouth. It hurts the people in the meeting.
>
> *D. W., Director, Volunteer Organization*

Supportive Climate

A group climate in which each member is valued and appreciated.

Defensive Climate

A group climate in which members attack and belittle each other, and where members feel they have to defend themselves from possible attack.

Gibb described six dimensions of group climate, which we discuss here and summarize in Figure 8.2. It is very important to note that defensiveness and supportiveness are conveyed as much—or more—through nonverbal signals as through verbal ones. In particular, defensiveness is often conveyed through paralanguage. When you read the defensive statements we provide as examples, imagine they are being said in a snotty or sarcastic tone of voice. We present first the supportive then the defensive behaviors.

FIGURE 8.2
Supportive and defensive communication.

Supportive Communication	Defensive Communication
Description: Tries to understand other points of view; takes responsibility for one's own opinions and beliefs. "I've noticed that, for the last few meetings, we've started 15 minutes after the announced starting time."	**Evaluation:** Judges and criticizes; blames other people. "What's the MATTER with you people? Is there some REASON why we can't get started on time?"
Problem orientation: Tries to solve the problem; enlists others' help; invites others' ideas. "What do you all think we should do?"	**Control:** Tries to be in charge; dominates; insists on having one's own way. "Here's what I've decided we're going to do."
Spontaneity: Open, honest, genuine communication. "That's a great idea! One problem I see with it is. . . ."	**Strategy:** Manipulative communication that tries to steer the group in a particular direction. "Don't you think it would be better if . . .?"
Empathy: Demonstrates caring and understanding; shows members they are valued. "Congratulations! That's a great job, but we're really going to miss you."	**Neutrality:** Demonstrates lack of understanding and lack of concern; indifference. "You're leaving? Can I have your office?"
Equality: Minimizes status differences and power distance; encourages members to contribute equally. "Nice to meet you, Suzie. Go ahead and call me Gloria, not Dr. Galanes."	**Superiority:** Makes status differences clear; maximizes power distance; pulls rank. "Nice to meet you, Suzie. I'm Dr. Galanes."
Provisionalism: Expresses opinions tentatively; open to others' ideas and opinions. "Right now I'm leaning toward Option A, but I'd like to know what you all think."	**Certainty:** Expresses opinions dogmatically and with no room for others' opinions; know-it-all attitude. "Option A is the ONLY thing that will work!"

Description versus Evaluation   When members describe something, they use "I" messages, take responsibility for their observations, and attempt to understand the others' points of view. Above all, they do not blame the other members. They may ask, for instance, "I've noticed that, for the last few meetings, we've started 15 minutes after the announced starting time," said in a neutral, interested but nonjudging tone. When members evaluate something, they judge it, find it lacking, and imply that the others are at fault. They may say, for instance, "What's the MATTER with you people? Is there some REASON why we can't get started on time?" Can you hear the difference?

Problem Orientation versus Control   When members show a problem orientation, they are focused on solving the problem and inviting others to help solve it. They do not have a predetermined idea of what must happen. Instead, they honestly engage in a search, with the others, for a solution to the group's problem. With a control orientation, however, members have a predetermined solution they know is right, and they want to control the group so their solution is accepted. They insist on having things their own way—nothing else will do. A control orientation does not necessarily come across as nasty. A member can be very nice, but stubborn, unwilling to bend or yield to someone else. In one group we observed, where members were charged with planning a workshop, one member politely but firmly refused to consider any of the other members' suggestions—the only format she was willing to consider was her own. Members became frustrated, demoralized, and ultimately disinterested.

Spontaneity versus Strategy   Spontaneous communication is free, honest, and genuine. Members don't have to guard their words and tiptoe around issues to say what they mean. They are respectful and open in their communication. When members are communicating strategically, they try to bend the group to their way of thinking, but in a way that seems manipulative and perhaps deceitful. Instead of honestly disagreeing, which is spontaneous communication, strategic communication may sound like this: "Don't you think it would work better if . . .?" Note the phrasing of that question—it isn't an honest question or statement, because the way it is stated ("Don't you think . . .") presupposes the answer. If this were a genuine statement, the member would say, "I think it would work better if. . . ." or "What do you think would work better?"

Empathy versus Neutrality   Empathy is the ability to place yourself in someone else's shoes. Empathetic words and actions convey to others that members understand and care about them. For instance, a member may ask another, "How is your mother after her surgery?" or say, "I know you're swamped with that crisis project. Call me Tuesday and I'll help with your section of the report." One of us knew an elementary teacher undergoing chemotherapy for cancer. Her classroom was furthest away from the women's rest room. The weekend before she was to return to teaching, her principal, without fanfare and demonstrating heartwarming empathy, moved her classroom next to the rest room. This kind gesture told her she was valued. Neutral communication, in contrast, conveys lack of caring. The neutral speaker does not necessarily have to be mean, but his or her words and actions show disinterest. For instance, one faculty member announced she was leaving for another university, and several faculty at the meeting congratulated her and said they would miss her. One faculty member said, "When you go, can I have your office?" It sounded like he couldn't wait until she left!

Equality versus Superiority   Communication that demonstrates equality minimizes the status differences among members. It serves to reduce the power distance that may exist. For instance, a faculty committee chair may say to the student committee member, "Just call me Gloria, not Dr. Galanes." This makes it easier and less inhibiting for the student to contribute to the group's discussion. In contrast, superior messages increase the power distance and let everybody know what the pecking order is. Members communicating with superiority pull rank, emphasize their higher status, and act better than the others: "This is my area of expertise, and I know I'm right." If this is the team leader, this approach is directive and authoritarian, whereas equality demonstrates egalitarian attitudes.

Provisionalism versus Certainty   This final dimension concerns tentative as opposed to certain communication. Provisional statements leave some room for doubt and they invite discussion. The speaker may have a point of view, but doesn't state his or her case dogmatically. For instance, someone who says, "Right now I prefer Option A, but there may be a better solution, and I'd like to see us discuss the issue" is speaking provisionally. Here's a similar statement, conveyed with certainty: "Option A is the only thing that will work!" That shuts down discussion and constrains others from sharing their views, particularly if their views conflict! Provisional communication acknowledges the point about small group discussion—several heads are better than one, but that won't be realized if members are prevented from sharing their viewpoints.

In much the same way that face-to-face groups create supportive and defensive climates, virtual groups that meet only online create such climates as well. In describing her participation in an e-mail discussion list devoted to the television series *Dr. Quinn, Medicine Woman*, Bird notes that the communication among members contributed to creating a nurturing community.[47] Bird observes that the list is generally free of flaming and insults, largely because the list owner is "overwhelmingly" supported by members in taking disciplinary action when members step out of line. Members receive a code of conduct from the list owner when they first subscribe, which participants themselves actively enforce. People are removed from the list for using profanity, racist comments, and personal invective, although members will give those who inadvertently violate the rules, particularly new members, a second chance. Participants, who are almost all women, freely disagree with each other—sometimes vehemently—but they generally disagree respectfully. Members express that they feel listened to, and believe that they belonged to a virtual family or community. Bird describes a high level of trust and openness in this community, and although she does not use the word "supportive," what she describes is just that, a supportive, virtual group.

Teambuilding

Sometimes a group needs something out of the ordinary to help it develop or improve its cohesiveness. *Teambuilding* is the current term for special programs designed to accomplish such goals. **Teambuilding** refers to any planned program of activities designed to enhance teamwork or improve a group's performance. In addition to enhancing group climate and cohesiveness, teambuilding activities can be used to improve group decision making, help members learn more effective ways of handling conflict, increase creativity, and improve communication skills and many other group throughput processes. Often, teambuilding activities occur during retreats that take groups out of their normal settings and encourage them to focus on the teambuilding topic.

> **Teambuilding**
>
> A set of planned activities designed to increase teamwork, cohesiveness, or other aspects of group performance.

The best teambuilding programs are tailored to meet the unique needs of each specific group. For instance, the trust-building activity designed for the women's soccer team and the videotapes created for each individual player are examples of how good teambuilding is particularized for each individual team. This text provides a foundation for you to determine where to focus teambuilding activities for a particular group. The information provided in Parts 3 through 5, which deal with throughput processes and observation techniques, can be especially helpful as you decide where to focus your teambuilding activities.

Teambuilding activities can be effective and lasting. For instance, Carron and Spink found that a teambuilding program helped a very large group increase its cohesiveness.[48] Glaser described a three-day teambuilding retreat designed for department leaders of a fire management unit.[49] The teambuilding topics included communication skills, consensus building, and problem solving. Glaser found that, even three years later, members continued to report substantially improved teamwork.

> You're still trying to build an esprit de corps among those people, and a great part of that is they begin to feel friendly toward their neighbor or the person across the table from them or the person leading.
>
> *P. W., Community Volunteer*

A teambuilding session may be planned by a group's leader, one of the members, a subgroup within the group, or an outside consultant or facilitator. We have designed and facilitated many teambuilding sessions in our consulting work with a variety of groups, including union personnel, a large dental practice, departments within our respective universities, a construction company, and a church board, to name just a few. Some day you may be asked to plan a teambuilding session for one of the groups to which you belong. The following are suggestions for teambuilding planners.[50]

1. **Define the purpose of the teambuilding activity.**
   Teambuilding can potentially address dozens of topics. As a planner, be sure you know what the group's most pressing needs are and what you want the teambuilding to accomplish so you will select the appropriate activities to meet your goals. The observation and evaluation tools in Chapter 15 can help you pinpoint key areas to address.

2. **Take the group out of its usual setting.**
   Members can become distracted if they can be reached by the telephone, secretaries, co-workers, family members, and so forth. Taking the group away from its normal setting encourages members to concentrate on what the teambuilding is designed to cover.

3. **Have a plan, but be willing to let go of it.**
   As a teambuilding facilitator, it is especially important for you to have a clear picture of how you will start the process because that sets the tone for the entire teambuilding session. However, you may find that one activity is working particularly well at accomplishing the goals of the session, and that the group isn't ready to move on to the next planned activity. When that is the case, you must be flexible enough to let go of the larger plan and go with what is working. For instance, members of a group with whom one of us consulted seemed to be gaining a lot from their discussion of personality characteristics and learning styles. Your author quickly decided to eliminate one planned activity so the discussion could continue. Conversely, an activity you planned may be a bust or may not take as long as you had thought, so you must be ready with an alternative to keep the session moving.

4. **Help members recognize the strength in their own diversity.**
   Often, when team members work together day in and day out, they lose sight of the fact that diversity of skills and working styles can be a strength for any team. Instead, members get bogged down with the frustration and irritation of dealing with others whose styles are very different from their own. An important goal of many teambuilding activities is to remind members of the strengths they have. In a session one of us facilitated, members had been sniping at each other. The laid-back members thought others were too picky, and the perfectionist members called the others sloppy. An activity designed to illustrate both the strengths and weaknesses of

each work style generated lively discussion and vocal appreciation on the part of both subgroups.

5. **Find ways to incorporate meaningful rituals and celebrations in the teambuilding activity.**

   A group's culture is formed not only by members' attention to the group's work. Rituals and celebrations, similar to the fantasies we discussed earlier, help create a rich culture, a shared sense of identity, and high cohesiveness. For example, the church board described in Chapter 2 held a teambuilding retreat after new board members had been elected for the coming year. The board president, facilitator for this teambuilding activity, incorporated religious rituals into the retreat, including a symbolic communion service. Although this type of activity might not be appropriate for a business organization, as a facilitator you should look for ways to weave rituals meaningful to the members into the teambuilding. For instance, some organizations conduct "roasts" of their top officials; these help build solidarity and cohesiveness among organization members.

Consider This 8.4

If you had been Coach DiCicco and your team had lost the 1995 World Cup, what would you have done to build the team back up? Why do you think DiCicco's methods worked? Think of a group that you belong to or that you know. What would you want teambuilding activities to accomplish for this group, and why?

SYMLOG: Depicting Cohesiveness

Several of the processes we have discussed so far, especially group cohesiveness, can be depicted using **SYMLOG,** which is an acronym for the SYstem for the Multiple Level Observation of Groups. Developed by Bales, SYMLOG is both a theory and a methodology that permits a three-dimensional diagram to be constructed of a group.[51] Examples of such diagrams are provided in Figures 8.3 and 8.4. (Instructions for producing a simplified, SYMLOG-like diagram are included in the *Instructor's Manual.*) You can see, even without detailed information about SYMLOG theory, that the first group (Figure 8.3) is fragmented and polarized, but the second (Figure 8.4) is unified and cohesive.

SYMLOG theory rests on the assumption that behavior of each group member in a group can be classified along each of three independent dimensions: dominant versus submissive; friendly versus unfriendly; and task-oriented versus emotionally expressive.[52] SYMLOG may be used in one of two ways. With the scoring method, external observers score the verbal and non-verbal behaviors of members as they interact in real time. The rating method is

SYMLOG

SYstem for the Multiple Level Observation of Groups, both a theory about member characteristics and effects on group interaction, and a methodology that produces a three-dimensional "snapshot" of a group at a given point in time.

easier, requiring no special training; external observers or group members themselves complete a 26-question rating scale evaluating each member's behavior. The results are tallied in a particular way so each member can be placed on the SYMLOG diagram.

Each of the three dimensions is represented by a pair of letters that anchor the pole positions. For example, *P* (positive) stands for *friendly* and *N* (negative) stands for *unfriendly* behavior. On the diagram, the more friendly a member is toward the other members of the group, the farther the circle is placed to the right. The more unfriendly members are located farther to the left. (In Figure 8.3, Ed is the most friendly and Ann the most unfriendly.) Task orienta-

FIGURE 8.3   SYMLOG diagram of a noncohesive group.

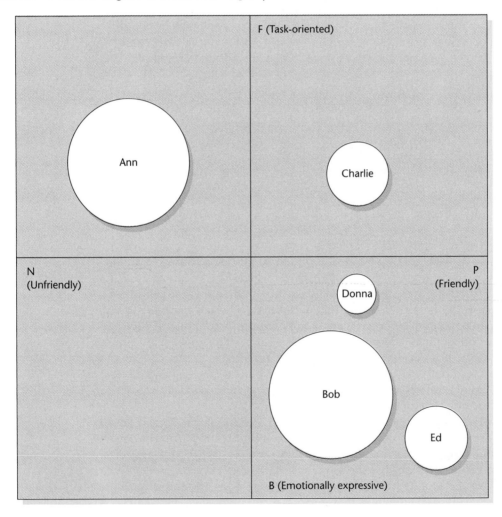

tion is represented by *F* (forward); the more task-oriented a member is, the closer he or she is to the top of the diagram. Emotional expressiveness is represented by *B* (backward); these members are closer to the bottom of the diagram. (In Figure 8.3, Ann is the most task-oriented, and Ed the most emotionally expressive.) The third dimension is depicted by the size of a member's circle; dominant members have larger circles than submissive ones. (In Figure 8.3, Ann and Bob are the most dominant, Donna the most submissive.)

You can readily see that the group shown in Figure 8.3 is not cohesive. Ann is dominant, task-oriented, and negative toward her fellow members. She tries to dictate what happens in the group. Bob is dominant, but friendly and emotionally expressive, which gets the group off track frequently; almost certainly, Bob's behavior clashes with Ann's desire to stick to the task. Charlie, who is moderately dominant, task-oriented, and friendly, is in the ideal position for a democratic, group-centered leader, but he's all by himself. Just by looking at the diagram you can tell that these people do not work well as a team. Members are dissimilar, they clash, there appears to be little cohesiveness, and there are wide variations in the degree of participation members exhibit.

> We expect team-type behaviors out of our employees. . . . You could not work here very long without teamwork-type skills.
>
> *M. I., Human Resources Manager, Manufacturing Company*

The diagram in Figure 8.4 tells a different story. This group seems unified, with all members in the upper-right-hand quadrant (which Bales calls the *decision-making quadrant*). Members are sufficiently task-oriented to complete the group's assignment, but friendly enough toward each other that their interaction is probably harmonious. This is a picture of a productive and efficient group. As you can see, a SYMLOG analysis provides a "snapshot" of a group as a whole system whose component parts (the members) operate interdependently. SYMLOG is a particularly helpful tool to use during teambuilding activities because it so clearly displays the degree of cohesiveness.

Group work is not just about getting the task done. It is also about forming satisfying relationships with the other members. The most memorable teams you will experience are those that have group members who do good work and enjoy one another in the process. Relational satisfaction has not been studied as extensively as task accomplishment, but communication scholars are recognizing its importance. Members are more satisfied when they feel involved, know they belong to the group, and are satisfied with their group relationships.[53] The factors we have discussed in this chapter—cohesiveness and supportiveness—contribute to relational satisfaction. The assessment rating scale, Figure 15.10 in Chapter 15, will help you assess how satisfied you and your team members are with relationships in the group.

FIGURE 8.4   SYMLOG diagram of a unified, productive group.

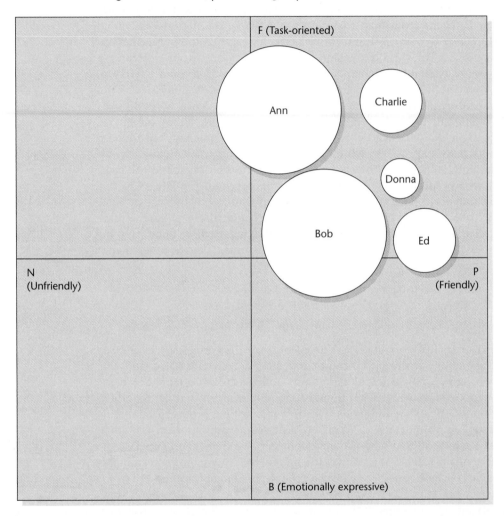

1. Communication shapes a group's communication network, which can be the wheel, the Y, or the all-channel network, which is ideal for a small discussion group.

2. A member's placement within the communication network and his or her role influences that member's status within a group. Ideally, members rely on earned rather than ascribed status within a group.

3. Fantasy is important to how groups create their culture. Fantasy chains, which are based on the principle of symbolic convergence that humans create meaning through their talk, help members create a shared reality, deal with uncomfortable information, and decide what actions to take.

4. Each group establishes a group climate. Cohesiveness, the bonding between mem-

bers, is a big contributor to group climate and generally helps increase a group's productivity; cohesiveness can be fostered in a virtual group as well as face-to-face.

5. Effective groups develop a supportive group climate, but ineffective ones often create a defensive climate.

6. Teambuilding, or planned activities to enhance group performance, can increase group cohesiveness or address dozens of other group concerns.

7. SYMLOG, which is both a theory and a methodology, is a tool members can use to gain insight into how a group functions and to assess its level of cohesiveness.

KEY TERMS

 Test your knowledge of these key terms by visiting the Online Learning Center website at mhhe.com/galanes11

Cohesiveness	Defensive climate	Symbolic convergence
Communication network	Supportive climate	SYMLOG
Fantasy	Idiosyncracy credit	Teambuilding
Fantasy chain	Status	Virtual team
Fantasy theme	Ascribed status	
Group climate	Earned status	

EXERCISES

 Go to self-quizzes on the Online Learning Center at mhhe.com/galanes11 to test your knowledge of the chapter concepts

1. Observe a group (live or video) and, by yourself, rank the members according to the status you believe each has in the group. How much relative power and influence do you think each one has? Do you observe ascribed or earned status differences? If so, to what are they due? Then share your ranking with others in your class. How close were your rankings? What specific behaviors led you to rank the members as you did?

2. Tape record a group's interaction and listen to the tape later to identify fantasy themes. (Listen especially for periods when the group seems excited and the energy level seems to pick up.) What function do you think the fantasy theme is serving for the group? What does it say about the group's shared reality?

3. Think of a group to which you belong or with which you are familiar. With a group of classmates, design a teambuilding activity for this group. First, decide what aspects of group discussion would be most beneficial for the group, then create activities you think would highlight these aspects.

BIBLIOGRAPHY

Bales, Robert F. *SYMLOG Case Study Kit*. New York: Free Press, 1980.

Bormann, Ernest G. *Small Group Communication: Theory and Practice*. 3rd ed. New York: Harper & Row, 1990, Chapters 5, 7, and 8.

Clark, Neil. *Teambuilding: A Practical Guide for Trainers*. New York: McGraw-Hill, 1994.

Lipnack, Jessica, and Jeffrey Stamps. *Virtual Teams: Reaching across Space, Time, and Organizations with Technology*. New York: Wiley, 1997.

NOTES

1. Information for this story was compiled from several sources. Most information came from Mark Starr and Martha Brant, "It Went Down to the Wire . . . and Thrilled Us All," *Newsweek*, (July 19, 1999): 45–54; with additional information from Bill Saporito, "The New Dream Team," *Time* (July 19, 1999): 60–67; and David Leon Moore, "Goalkeepers: Don't Expect Any Handouts," *USA Today* (Friday, July 9 1999): 1C–2C.

2. J. I. Hurwitz, A. F. Zander, and B. Hymovitch, "Some Effects of Power on the Relations among Group Members," in *Group Dynamics: Research and Theory*, 3rd ed., eds. D. Cartwright and A. Zander (New York: Harper & Row, 1968): 291–97.

3. Dean C. Barnlund and C. Harland, "Propinquity and Prestige as Determinants of Communication Networks," *Sociometry* 26 (1963): 467–79.

4. E. Hollander, "Conformity, Status, and Idiosyncrasy Credit," *Psychological Review* 65 (1958): 117–27.

5. Michelle Estrada, Justin Brown, and Fiona Lee, "Who Gets the Credit? Perceptions of Idiosyncrasy Credit in Work Groups," *Small Group Research* 26 (February 1995): 56–76.

6. Craig R. Scott, "Communication Technology and Group Communication," in *Handbook of Group Communication Theory and Research*, ed. Lawrence R. Frey, (Thousand Oaks, CA: Sage, 1999): 432–72.

7. Andrew J. Flanagin, Vanessa Tiyaamornwong, Joan O'Connor, and David R. Siebold, "Computer-Mediated Group Work: The Interaction of Member Sex and Anonymity," *Communication Research* 29 (February 2002): 66–93.

8. Carolyn J. Wood, "Challenging the Assumptions Underlying the Use of Participatory Decision Making Strategies: A Longitudinal Case Study," *Small Group Behavior* 20 (1989): 428–48.

9. Joseph A. Bonito, "The Effect of Contributing Substantively on Perceptions of Participation," *Small Group Research* 31 (October 2000): 528–53.

10. Ernest G. Bormann, "Symbolic Convergence Theory and Communication in Group Decision Making," in *Communication and Group Deci-sion Making*, eds. Randy Y. Hirokawa and Marshall S. Poole (Newbury Park, CA: Sage, 1986): 221. For a thorough review of the development and use of symbolic convergence theory, see Ernest G. Bormann, John F. Cragan, and Donald C. Shields, "Three Decades of Developing, Grounding, and Using Symbolic Convergence Theory," in *Communication Yearbook* 25, ed. Willam B. Gudykunst (Thousand Oaks, CA: Sage, 2001): 271–313.

11. Robert F. Bales, *Personality and Interpersonal Behavior* (New York: Holt Rinehart and Winston, 1970): 105–8, 136–55.

12. Eric E. Peterson, "The Stories of Pregnancy: On Interpretation of Small-Group Cultures," *Communication Quarterly* 35 (1987): 39–47.

13. Catherine C. Morocco, "Development and Function of Group Metaphor," *Journal for the Theory of Social Behavior* 9 (1979): 15–27.

14. Bormann, "Symbolic Convergence Theory."

15. Linda L. Putnam, Shirley A. Van Hoeven, and Connie A. Bullis, "The Role of Rituals and Fantasy Themes in Teachers' Bargaining," *Western Journal of Speech Communication* (Winter 1991): 87.

16. This fantasy chain is a slightly expanded version of the one that occurs near the beginning of the leadership segment, part 1, of the videotape ancillary to this text, *Communicating Effectively in Small Groups*.

17. Morocco, "Development and Function of Group Metaphor," 15–27.

18. Morocco, "Development and Function of Group Metaphor."

19. Putnam, Van Hoeven, and Bullis, "The Role of Rituals and Fantasy Themes in Teachers' Bargaining."

20. Joann Keyton, "Relational Communication in Groups," in *Handbook of Group Communication Theory and Research*, ed. Lawrence R. Frey (Thousand Oaks, CA: Sage, 1999): 192–222.

21. David B. Barker, "The Behavioral Analysis of Interpersonal Intimacy in Group Development," *Small Group Research* 22 (February 1991): 76–91.

22. Carolyn M. Anderson, Bruce L. Riddle, and Dominic A. Infante, ""Decision-Making Collaboration Scale: Tests of Validity," *Communication Research Reports* 15 (1999): 245-55.

23. Harold L. Nixon II, *The Small Group* (Englewood Cliffs, NJ: Prentice Hall, 1979): 74-76.

24. Charles R. Evans and Kenneth L. Dion, "Group Cohesion and Performance," *Small Group Behavior* 22 (1991): 175-86; Stanley M. Gully, Dennis J. Devine, and David J. Whitney, "A Meta-Analysis of Cohesion and Performance: Effects of Level of Analysis and Task Interdependence," *Small Group Research* 26 (November 1995): 497-520.

25. Gully et al., "A Meta-Analysis of Cohesion and Performance."

26. M. E. Johnson and J. G. Fortman, "Internal Structure of the Gross Cohesiveness Scale," *Small Group Behavior* 19 (February 1988): 187-96.

27. Wynne W. Chin, Wm. David Salisbury, Allison W. Pearson, and Matthew J. Stollak, "Perceived Cohesion in Small Groups: Adapting and Testing the Perceived Cohesion Scale in a Small-Group Setting," *Small Group Research* 30 (December 1999): 751-66.

28. Lynne Kelly and Robert L. Duran, "Interaction and Performance in Small Groups: A Descriptive Report," *International Journal of Small Group Research* 1 (1985): 182-92.

29. Charles N. Greene, "Cohesion and Productivity in Work Groups," *Small Group Behavior* 20 (1989): 70-86.

30. Carl E. Larson and Frank M. J. LaFasto, *TeamWork: What Must Go Right/What Can Go Wrong* (Newbury Park, CA: Sage, 1989).

31. Wood, "Challenging the Assumptions."

32. Frederick G. Elias, Mark E. Johnson, and Jay B. Fortman, "Task-Focused Self-Disclosure: Effects on Group Cohesiveness, Commitment to the Task, and Productivity," *Small Group Behavior* 20 (1989): 87-96.

33. William F. Owen, "Metaphor Analysis of Cohesiveness in Small Discussion Groups," *Small Group Behavior* 16 (1985): 415-26.

34. Barker, "The Behavioral Analysis of Interpersonal Intimacy."

35. Synthesized from Ernest G. Bormann & Nancy C. Bormann, *Effective Small Group Communication*, 2nd ed. (Minneapolis: Burgess, 1976): 70-76; and Gloria J. Galanes (unpublished research based on interviews with peer-nominated excellent leaders, 2002).

36. Vanessa Urch Druskat and D. Christopher Kayes, "Learning versus Performance in Short-Term Project Teams," *Small Group Research* 31 (June 2000): 328-53.

37. Larson and LaFasto, *TeamWork*; Frank LaFasto and Carl Larson, *When Teams Work Best: 6,000 Team Members and Leaders Tell What it Takes to Succeed* (Thousand Oaks, CA: Sage, 2001): 65-83.

38. Ernest G. Bormann and Nancy C. Bormann, *Effective Small Group Communication*, 4th ed. (Edina, MN: Burgess, 1988): 74-76.

39. Bill Saporito, "The New Dream Team," *Time* (July 19, 1999): 60.

40. Gloria J. Galanes (unpublished research).

41. Anthony M. Townsend and Samuel M. DeMarie, "Are You Ready for Virtual Teams?" *HR Magazine* 41 (September 1996): np; accessed via EBSCOhost on World Wide Web, August 2, 2002.

42. Sirkka Jarvenpas, quoted in Carla Joinson, "Managing Virtual Teams," *HR Magazine* 47 (June 2002): np; accessed via EBSCOhost on World Wide Web, August 2, 2002.

43. Synthesized from the following sources: Joinson, "Managing Virtual Teams;" Jessica Lipnack and Jeffrey Stamps, *Virtual Teams: Reaching Across Space, Time, and Organizations with Technology* (New York: Wiley 1997); Townsend and DeMarie, "Are You Ready for Virtual Teams?"

44. LaFasto and Larson, *When Teams Work Best*; 68.

45. LaFasto and Larson, *When Teams Work Best*, 14-15.

46. Jack R. Gibb, "Defensive Communication," *Journal of Communication* 11 (1961): 141-48.

47. S. Elizabeth Bird, "Chatting on Cynthia's Porch: Creating Community in an E-mail Fan Group," *Southern Communication Journal* 65 (Fall 1999): 49-65.

48. Albert V. Carron and Kevin S. Spink, "The Group Size–Cohesion Relationship in Minimal Groups," *Small Group Research* 26 (February 1995): 86-105.

49. Susan R. Glaser, "Teamwork and Communication: A Three-Year Case Study of Change," *Management Communication Quarterly* 7 (February 1994): 282-96.

50. Suggestions synthesized from Neil Clark, *Team-building: A Practical Guide for Trainers* (New York: McGraw-Hill, 1994); Glenn M. Parker, *Team Players and Teamwork* (San Francisco: Jossey-Bass, 1991); Glenn H. Varney, *Building Productive Teams: An Action Guide and Resource Book* (San Francisco: Jossey-Bass, 1989); and our own experiences.

51. Robert F. Bales and Stephen P. Cohen, *SYMLOG: A System for the Multiple Level Observation of Groups* (New York: Free Press, 1979). Space constraints prevent including a complete description of SYMLOG theory and methodology here; we refer readers who are interested in learning to construct a complete SYMLOG diagram for their groups to a workbook, R.F. Bales, *SYMLOG Case Study Kit*, (New York: Free Press, 1980). The *Instructor's Manual* for this text includes instructions and necessary forms for completing a simplified, SYMLOG-like diagram so students can have a better idea of what SYMLOG can do.

52. Lynne Kelly and Robert L. Duran note that in some recent writings, Bales refers to the third dimension as acceptance versus nonacceptance of authority, which designation seems more appropriate when assessing group member values as opposed to behaviors; in "SYMLOG: Theory and Measurement of Small Group Interaction," in *Small Group Communication: A Reader*, 6th ed., eds. Robert S. Cathcart and Larry A. Samovar (Dubuque, IA: Wm. C. Brown, 1992): 39–52.

53. Carolyn M. Anderson, Matthew M. Martin, and Bruce L. Riddle, "Small Group Relational Satisfaction Scale: Development, Reliability, and Validity," *Communication Studies* 52 (Fall, 2001): 220–33.

PERSPECTIVES ON LEADERSHIP IN SMALL GROUPS

Central Message

Small group leadership is an interactive phenomenon; it results from communicative behaviors appropriate to group task and relational goals, other members' behaviors, the context, and other contingencies.

STUDY OBJECTIVES

As a result of studying Chapter 9 you should be able to:

1. Define the concepts of *leadership, leader, leadership emergence,* and *designated leader.*
2. Explain the five sources of interpersonal influence (power) in a group and how they are involved in small group leadership.
3. Describe the process of leadership emergence.
4. Explain the three major approaches to small group leadership (traits, styles, and contingency approaches) and describe specific models included under each approach.
5. Name and describe nine communicative competencies important for small group leaders.
6. Explain how leaders and members are interdependent, and describe the LMX model.
7. Explain *distributed leadership* and why it is an appropriate model for small, task-oriented groups.

Jennifer, Robyn, Jiang, and Andreas comprise the broadcast advertising team in the corporate offices of a California-based retail company. Jennifer is the team's designated leader and their broadcast media buyer. Jiang, their promotions coordinator, is responsible for planning and directing promotional events, such as the back-to-school campaign, which coincide with the television and radio advertisements. He also makes sure that all of Jennifer's business records are kept up-to-date. Andreas, their production coordinator, assists Jennifer in writing, producing, and directing all television and radio commercials. Robyn, their broadcast advertising coordinator and Jennifer's administrative assistant, is primarily responsible for creating and maintaining working relationships with television and radio sales representatives. The company's quarterly profits are directly tied to successful media campaigns, which themselves are directly tied to how well this team works together.

Jennifer has been associated with the company for well over 20 years and is highly regarded in the advertising community. But everything does not always run smoothly for this broadcast advertising team. Although highly respected by her peers, Jennifer is a leader who must be in control of all tasks and the team's socioemotional environment. She tends not to let other members of the team make mistakes or create their own successes.

This leadership style poses problems for team members in a couple of areas. High turnover is common in this division. New employees are regularly being trained, often inadequately. New employees are never fully informed about their job responsibilities because Jennifer tightly controls the flow of information to them, but she is often too busy to work with them. Too often, they learn how and what they are supposed to do when they have been reprimanded by Jennifer for making a mistake. This creates resentment among the team and costs the company money for wasted time. Further resentment is created by her desire to control their socioemotional environment. For instance, if Andreas writes a poor advertising script, she expects one of his coworkers to tell him rather than convey the bad news herself. Yet this retail company is successful in part because the broadcast advertising group produces effective advertising. At what point is ineffective leadership considered a problem? Who is responsible for change? Is the character of a group solely determined by one person's behaviors? If you were an outside consultant what would you say to this division? These and other issues will be touched on in this chapter.

> Leaders inspire other people to do great things and to do their best. . . . Great leaders do get the best out of people.
>
> *P. B., City Administrator*

According to Larson and LaFasto, the final ingredient for effective group performance is team leadership, with the right person serving in the leadership role.[1] Because small groups are everywhere, you will certainly have your turn serving as a small group leader. This can be a source of self-esteem, recognition, and appreciation; it can also be a nightmare.

Much of the conventional wisdom about what makes a good leader is simply wrong. Many people hold oversimplified beliefs about effective leadership that interfere with their learning to function well as small group leaders. We hope this and the next chapter will dispel those beliefs, as well as help you discover the communication competencies you must develop to perform well as a leader.

In Chapter 9 we examine the concepts of *leader* and *leadership*, describe the process of leadership emergence, review historical and contemporary perspectives about leadership, examine the relationship between leaders and members, and develop an argument in favor of *distributed leadership* for most small task-oriented groups. In Chapter 10 we focus on the duties commonly expected of designated small group leaders in our culture and provide specific suggestions on how to perform them.

Leadership and Leaders

The terms *leadership* and *leader* are related, but one refers to a process, the other to a person.

Leadership

Most social scientists define **leadership** as interpersonal influence. The following definition by Hackman and Johnson reveals the importance of communication in the leadership process:

> Leadership is human (symbolic) communication which modifies the attitudes and behaviors of others in order to meet group goals and needs.[2]

This definition incorporates two important implications. First, the term *modifies* suggests that influence via communication, as opposed to physical coercion or other forms of force, is the heart of the process we term leadership. We aren't talking about an "attitude adjustment" through force, but through interaction and persuasion, human symbolic activity. Second, this definition implies that only influence directed toward accomplishment of a *group* goal can truly be termed *small group leadership*. Too many people equate leadership with power, but they are not the same. True, leadership involves power; however, other members of a group also control group interaction with their power resources.[3] What power resources might the members of the broadcast-advertising team have to pull off successful advertising campaigns while working for a superior with strong control issues?

Sources of Influence (Power) The ability to influence others stems from **power** that is derived from a particular source, or base. Leaders and followers transact to create a relationship based on perceived power. Leaders can influence the conduct of others to the extent that their power is perceived and acknowledged by followers. The sources of power identified by French and Raven include reward, punishment, legitimate, referent, and expert.[4]

Leadership

Influence exerted through communication that helps a group achieve goals; performance of a leadership function by any member.

Power

The potential to influence behavior of others, derived from such bases as the ability to reward and punish, expertise, legitimate title or position, and personal attraction.

Leaders can *reward* followers by giving them both tangible and intangible items such as special attention, acknowledgment, compliments, personal favors, special titles, money, and material goods. For instance, Lucas found that telling members they were high performers within their work teams (whether they were or not) and giving them a high-status job title actually increased their satisfaction, performance, commitment to the organization, and turnover.[5] Jennifer may come down hard on her broadcast-advertising team but she lets them leave early and gives the team free tickets to social events like concerts and baseball games. Leaders can also *punish* by withholding these same items. For example, the frown a leader may give a latecomer is a form of punishment. *Coercion* is a special form of punishment power that uses threats or force to "influence" others. Although good leaders may effectively use punishment (especially the fear of losing something important, such as belonging to the group or the respect of the others), they do not use hardball tactics to coerce or force compliance. Coercion breeds resentment, sabotage, and rebellion, which are not desirable small group outcomes. We do not consider coercion to be genuine leadership as we define it.

> Any time you have more power than the other human being, and authority, you have to be very careful about how you use that power and authority.
>
> *M. S., Vice President, Financial Service Firm, retired*

Legitimate power stems from a special position or role acknowledged by the followers. For instance, in a police task force, lieutenants are accepted as having the right to give orders to sergeants, who themselves may give orders to patrol officers. However, legitimate power includes only influence that is accepted as appropriate by followers. Thus, a committee chair does not have the right to tell members how to dress or wear their hair, although a supervisor might have such power.

Referent power is based on attraction or identification with another person. Some referent leaders have charisma that causes others to want to associate with them and imitate their behavior. For example, one of us skipped a class in high school because the referent leader of our small group of friends suggested it. Ideally, however, discussion leaders model positive behaviors for the other members to admire and emulate, such as listening, considering all sides of an issue, and keeping remarks orderly. The more leaders are admired and respected, the more members copy their behavior, and thus the greater their power to influence the group.

Expert power comes from what others believe a member knows or can do. The person with expert power is influential because he or she is perceived as having knowledge or skills vital to the group. For instance, if your group is responsible for producing a panel discussion for the rest of your class and you happen to be the only member who has ever participated in a panel discussion, you have expertise the others value, which gives you power in that particular group.

Usually a leader's power stems from more than one source. The more sources on which a person's power rests, the more that person has the potential to dominate a group. Conversely, the more these bases of power are distributed among members, the more likely verbal participation is to be shared, decision making to be collaborative, and satisfaction high. In other words, leadership can be provided by all members exercising their influence in service to the group goal. We expand on this idea later.

Leaders

The term *leader* refers to a person, or sometimes to a special position occupied by a person.[6] A **leader** in a small group is a person who influences the behavior of others through communication. We use the term *leader* to refer to three related types of individuals: a person who exerts influence toward achievement of a group's goal, a person who is perceived by the others as being a leader (influencer), and a person who has been appointed or elected to a leadership position (e.g., chair, team leader, coordinator, or facilitator). A person elected or appointed to a leadership position is called a **designated leader.**

Having a designated leader usually helps provide stability to a group. Numerous studies have shown that small groups with stable leadership are more effective in goal achievement than small groups that fail to settle issues about who is responsible for what. A group whose energy is siphoned off in a leadership struggle produces poor outcomes, dissatisfied members, and low cohesion.[7] In contrast, groups with designated leaders *accepted by the members* have fewer interpersonal problems and often produce better outcomes than groups without designated leaders.[8] The implication is clear: even in a group in which influence (and thus leadership) is widely shared, someone must coordinate the flow of communication and the work of the members.

Having the title *designated leader* gives someone legitimate power, but that person must still earn the respect and support of other members. A designated leader's behavior will be evaluated and may frequently be challenged by the members. If the designated leader's power rests solely on the legitimacy of the title, someone else with more broadly based power will likely emerge as a more influential informal leader.

Even though all members of a small group bear responsibility for the success or failure of the group, the designated leader shoulders special responsibility for the group's work. As Stech and Ratliffe put it, both "group members and outsiders tend to hold the leader accountable for group beliefs, proposals, actions, and products."[9] This confers tremendous obligation on the designated leader to attend to how the group is functioning as a system and ensure that needed leadership services are provided. Not all leaders in a group are designated, however; many emerge over time. We now turn your attention to leadership emergence.

Leader

A person who uses communication to influence others to meet group goals and needs; any person identified by members of a group as leader; a person designated as leader by election or appointment.

Designated Leader

A person appointed or elected to a position as leader of a small group.

[handwritten margin note:] A leader is a person who... ① exerts influence toward achievement of a group's goal. ② is perceived by the others as being a leader (influencer). ③ has been appointed or elected to a leadership position.

Designated leaders
greatly affect small
groups.
© Michael Newman/
PhotoEdit

**Leadership
Emergence**

The process by
which someone
emerges as the
leader of an initially
leaderless group in
which all members
start out as equals.

Leadership Emergence The process of **leadership emergence,** whereby
one individual who starts out on an equal footing with other members but
emerges to be perceived as the group's leader, has been charted by Aubrey
Fisher, known for his focus on the communicative dynamics of small group
decision making.[10] He developed his model (refer to Figure 9.1) from his own
conclusions after listening to numerous hours of audiotaped small group interaction. The model is a description of member contention for leadership after
one or more members make a move toward leadership.

The three-stage model presumes that all members are potential candidates
for leadership. Stage 1 is characterized by one or more members (see, for example, member E) falling from consideration almost immediately. Such members may perceive themselves as unable to lead or uninterested in leading for a
number of reasons (e.g., too busy). Also, if some members exhibit behaviors
others see as nonleaderlike (e.g., quiet, uninformed, or dogmatic) they will be
eliminated.[11]

Stage 2 is characterized by the remaining members' bids for leadership
being supported by other members. A and C are still in contention and enlist
the help of B and D, who back out of contention but serve as lieutenants to A
and C, respectively. Notice that two cliques or coalitions form around both A
and C. Fisher noted that stage 2 can be lengthy, with verbal sparring typical.
Eventually, one contender fails at her or his bid and drops out. The candidate
that falls out of contention usually is too directive and communicatively offensive to others (e.g., talks too much, is manipulative).[12]

In stage 3, C falls out completely and A is left as leader. Member E's support may or may not be important. If E's activity stays low, his or her support

FIGURE 9.1   A model of emergent leadership.

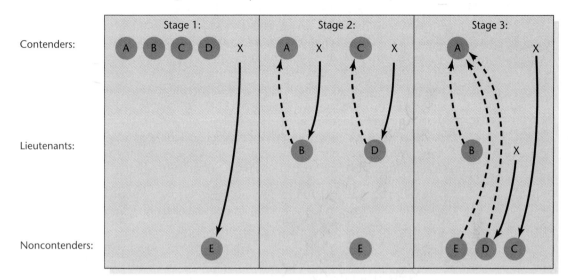

is not significant. However, if E becomes active, both A and C might vie for E's support because alliance with E could be extremely important to either one. Member D could also shift support to A during C's failed attempt to emerge as leader.

Fisher's model as depicted in Figure 9.1 is basic and can involve several variations. For instance, leadership emergence may involve only two stages. It can occur painlessly and quickly when only one member secures a lieutenant and the rest of the group follows along. Sometimes an early leader emerges who is later deposed, which causes the leadership emergence process to recycle back to stage 2. Finally, the leadership emergence process may not involve a stage 3 if the two contenders cooperate as coleaders.

You will note that while Fisher's model describes general processes based on the quantity and quality of communication, there is a sense that some personal characteristics (e.g., skills in verbalizing) are associated with who emerges as leader. In fact, it has been popular to explain leadership emergence by searching for the personal characteristics of the emergent leader.

Personal Characteristics of Emergent Leaders   Several recent studies of leadership have found a number of traits associated with leadership emergence. One of these is **self-monitoring**, discussed briefly in Chapter 6, which refers to individuals' abilities to monitor, in a given situation, both social cues and their own actions.[13] High self-monitors are sensitive to contextual cues, socially perceptive, and able to respond flexibly according to what seems needed at any given time. Zaccaro et al. found that more than half the variance of leadership emergence was explained by self-monitoring.[14] This was confirmed by

Self-Monitoring

An individual's ability to monitor other people's reactions to his/her behavior, and adjust in response.

a double standard exists between the sexes; men are encouraged, while women are looked down upon

Ellis and Cronshaw, who found that males who were high self-monitors emerged as leaders because they were better able to adapt their behaviors to fit the needs of the group.[15] However, this was not true for women, probably because female high self-monitors, who are sensitive to subtle clues, sometimes sense that their leadership behavior is perceived as inappropriate. They may then modify their actions to tone down that leadership behavior. These authors discovered that high self-monitors do in fact monitor social cues and are able to modify their responses; they are more likely to emerge as leaders across situations. However, low self-monitors, whose actions are motivated more by internal than external cues, can also emerge as leaders in situations in which they have favorable attitudes toward expressing leadership; they will not emerge as leaders if they hold unfavorable attitudes about leadership.[16]

> There's a little bit, too, of finding out what's your natural style. . . .
> Like what might work for me is not necessarily going to work for somebody else.
>
> *L. H., Director, State-Level Strategic Planning*

Verbal style, together with the content of communication, also is associated with leadership emergence.[17] Consistent with earlier studies, Baker found that members whose communication style was quiet, tentative, or vague were perceived as uncommitted to the group and not knowledgeable about the group's task. These members were quickly eliminated as potential leaders because others did not believe they contributed ideas or helped organize the group. Those who did emerge as leaders made more attempts to suggest procedures for the group and thus helped get the group organized. The emergent leader's participation profiles were high in procedure giving, moderate in idea giving, and low in stating opinions. Leaders' and members' styles were consistent in what Baker describes as mundane style: informal, unimaginative, ordinary. High-status members who were not leaders had a dramatic style that, though unusual, was tolerated because of their perceived helpfulness to the group.

A recent study by Pescosolido found that informal, or emergent, leaders of groups strongly influence the other group members' perceptions about their ability to get the job done, particularly early in the group's life.[18] Such leaders seemed to be able to help members make sense of information and events in a positive way. Early on, they are able to shape the group's perceptions about what its capabilities are, and to set expectations for group success.

Years ago, biological sex was associated with group leadership in that males were more likely to emerge than females (for more about gender and sex and small group communication see Chapters 3 and 4). However, biological sex has not been a useful predictor of who will emerge as a leader in a group. Psychological gender, on the other hand, may be more useful. Regardless of sex, those individuals enacting a masculine communication style (i.e., independent, self-reliant, willing to take a stand) emerged more often as leader than those enacting feminine and nonandrogynous communication styles.[19] Generally, groups appear to choose leaders on the basis of performance, most especially task performance. Hawkins observed mixed-sex groups and analyzed transcripts of their communication.[20] She found that task-relevant communication, not gender, was the factor that explained who emerged as leader. Furthermore, she found no significant differences in the amount of task-relevant remarks contributed by men and women. Sex, gender, and leader emergence are difficult processes to unravel. Shimanoff and Jenkins remind us that research, time and again, provides evidence that men and women lead equally well and group members are equally satisfied with both male and female leaders.[21]

This finding about the importance of task-focused communication is consistent with the findings of De Souza and Klein.[22] They hypothesized that the nature of the task would affect leadership emergence. They found that the type of task did not influence emergence, but that members' individual abilities to contribute to the task and their commitment to the group goal were associated with their emergence as leaders. They also discovered that groups with emerged leaders outperformed those without them. This latter finding is supported by Kurth, who found that group members themselves considered groups with emerged leaders more successful.[23]

Sometimes a group member will emerge as a leader even though the group already has a designated leader. Wheelan and Johnston followed four individuals identified by their peers as informal leaders in groups with formal leaders.[24] They found that the behavior of such leaders did not completely follow the behavior either of traditional emergent or designated leaders. Such individuals did talk more than most of their fellow members, but their talk was not more task-oriented, as is true with emergent leaders. Member leaders contributed more to the socioemotional aspect of the group, but not always in a positive way. They were more likely to challenge the designated leaders. They built coalitions with other members and generally displayed antiauthority positions. Wheelan and Johnston note that the presence of such members can have a substantial effect on the group's interaction but that too little is known about such members; they call for more research into informal member-leaders.

Consider This 9.1

What does the process of leadership emergence tell you about how to *not* become a leader? The following rules, if followed, will probably result in low status and if followed well will get you out of being a leader.[25] Miss as many group meetings as possible. Say very little. Jump to be the group's secretary. Do what you are told. When you do contribute be dogmatic, verbally aggressive, and act like you know it all—do so early in the group's history. When you can, play the role of the joker. Finally, show a disdain for leadership. What other things can you do to make sure you are *not* a group's leader?

Theoretical Approaches to Leadership

As with other social scientific phenomena, the study of leadership has moved from simplicity to complexity. In this next section, we present several of the most important approaches to the study of leadership. The most useful contemporary theories are based on models of communication. We urge you not to become rigidly attached to any one theory because all of them contain useful insights; moreover, new discoveries may simplify the complexity that currently exists.

Traits Approaches

Our discussion of leadership emergence has focused on communication characteristics, broadly, and specific personal characteristics often referred to as traits. A *trait* is a characteristic of a person. Some traits, such as eye color or height, are unchangeable; others, such as self-monitoring, are subject to some control. The **traits approach** to leadership examines how traits are related to leadership and assumes that leaders are more likely to have certain traits than other group members are. You just read how several traitlike characteristics have been associated with leadership emergence.

The earliest studies of leadership (from before the Christian epoch through the 1930s) assumed that people were collections of relatively fixed traits, with one leadership situation being much like another. Researchers who investigated leadership from this perspective looked for the trait or traits that distinguished leaders from followers. They believed that leaders were a special class of people who were born, not made. Social scientists used a number of personality measures in an effort to discover the traits of leaders. Some studies found that leaders tended to have higher IQs, and were taller, more attractive, and larger than nonleaders.[26] However, inconsistent results led scientists to reject the theory that leadership can be explained solely or even primarily on the basis of traits.

> I honestly believe that good leaders are born, not made.
>
> *P. B., City Administrator*

Traits Approach

The approach to leadership that assumes leaders have certain traits that distinguish them from followers or members of a group.

Consider This 9.2

Despite our unsuccessful efforts to identify those traits that distinguish leaders from nonleaders, we still have fun playing with the physical characteristics associated with leaders, especially when we try to predict presidential elections. Consider the 2000 election, for instance. Did you know that male leaders brush their hair from the left (Al Gore brushed from the right)? Only 5 of 41 presidents have been left-handed (all front runners in the 2000 race were right-handed). The taller presidential candidate enjoys a 3–1 advantage over other contenders (Bill Bradley was 6 feet 5 inches tall). And finally, some say "royal" blood is the best predictor in a presidential election; George W. Bush is the most "royal" of any president.[27] What traits do you associate with leaders?

Modern trait approaches examine a variety of complex personality characteristics such as enthusiasm, verbal facility, creativity, critical-thinking ability, self-confidence. Although they are labeled traits, they seem to represent behaviors that leaders perform rather than invariable, unchangeable characteristics. In short this approach, although intuitively appealing, has been less than helpful to us in our attempts to understand complex leadership processes. Personality characteristics are not easily measured and, most important, this approach does not help distinguish between good and bad leaders nor does it explain why leadership changes in a group.[28] Stogdill noted that "leadership is a relation that exists between persons in a social situation, and that persons who are leaders in one situation may not necessarily be leaders in other situations."[29]

We believe his conclusion that leadership is not a universal set of traits is valid; however, it seems equally clear that people with the ability to adapt their behaviors and who possess communication skills that help clarify the group's task and motivate other members will be influential in groups.[30] Foreshadowing our discussion of contingency approaches, we may say appropriate leader behaviors in a group are shaped by the needs of the group. A person with the ability to respond flexibly, whether that is a trait or behavior, will likely be influential in a group.

Styles Approaches

Styles approaches focus on the pattern of behaviors a leader exhibits in a group. Early style theorists attempted to discover whether there was one ideal style for small group leaders. More recent style theorists have looked at styles in relationship to member and task characteristics, suggestive of contingency approaches to leadership discussed later.

Considerable research has examined the behaviors of designated leaders classified as *democratic, autocratic,* and *laissez-faire,* which are summarized in Figure 9.2. **Democratic leaders** encourage members to participate in group decisions, including policy-making decisions ("What ideas do you have for organizing our task?"). **Laissez-faire leaders** take almost no initiative for structuring a group, but they may respond to inquiries from members ("I don't care; whatever you want to do is fine with me."). **Autocratic leaders** tightly control their groups, making assignments, directing all verbal interaction, and giving orders ("Here's how I've structured your task. First, you will. . . ."). They ask fewer questions but answer more than democratic leaders, and make more attempts to coerce but fewer attempts to get others to participate.[31]

> Sometimes you need to lead like a Spartan [autocratically] and sometimes it's better to lead it like an Athenian [democratically].
>
> *P. B., City Adminstrator*

The autocratic and democratic styles of leadership described here correspond closely with the Theory X and Theory Y assumptions described by management theorist Douglas McGregor.[32] Theory X assumes that people don't

---

Styles Approach

The leadership approach that studies the interrelationship between leader style and member behaviors.

Democratic Leaders

Egalitarian leaders who coordinate and facilitate discussion in small groups, encouraging participation of all members.

Laissez-Faire Leaders

Do-nothing designated leaders who provide minimal services to the group.

Autocratic Leaders

Leader who try to dominate and control a group.

FIGURE 9.2 Comparison of autocratic, democratic, and laissez-faire leadership styles.

	Autocratic	Democratic	Laissez-faire
Characteristics	Theory X assumptions. Directive; controlling. Speaks with certainty. Gives orders; makes assignments. Makes decisions for group.	Theory Y assumptions. Participative; invites input. Speaks provisionally. Makes suggestions; helps structure group time. Involves group in decisions.	Asks group to take charge. Doesn't necessarily voice opinion. Expects group to decide everything.
Typical statements	"I've decided that this is what you're going to do . . ."	"What ideas would you suggest for getting this done?"	"Whatever you decide is okay with me."
Useful when	Group members are unmotivated, uninterested, or unfamiliar with task. Emergency situations occur.	Group members are knowledgeable, interested. Group has time to discuss and deliberate.	Group members are experts, have worked together before, can assume group leadership.

like to work and must therefore be compelled by a strong, controlling leader ("boss") who supervises their work closely. In contrast, Theory Y assumes that people work as naturally as they play, and are creative problem solvers who like to take charge of their own work. Leaders who accept the assumptions of Theory Y behave democratically by providing only as much structure as a group needs, allowing members to participate fully in decision making and other aspects of the group's work.

Research findings have been consistent about the effects of leadership style on group output.[33] Democratically led groups are generally more satisfied than autocratically led groups; most people in our culture prefer democratic groups. Autocratic groups often work harder in the presence of the leader, but they also experience more incidents of aggressiveness and apathy. Democratic groups whose leaders provide some structure and coordination are better problem solvers and their members are more satisfied than those in laissez-faire groups without structure. Research continues into the complex relationship among leadership style, satisfaction, and productivity. A recent meta-analysis found a correlation between style and productivity only when the type of task was taken into account.[34] Democratic leadership is more productive in natural settings and, in laboratory settings, seems to produce higher productivity on moderately or highly complex tasks.

The link between democratic leadership and satisfaction is not strong. A recent meta-analysis of this relationship by Foels et al. found that members' satisfaction depends on a number of moderating factors.[35] The relationship is stronger in artificial laboratory groups than bona fide groups. It is also stronger in larger groups. These authors speculate that, because larger groups are less cohesive than smaller groups, instituting a democratic style may affect member satisfaction because it softens the reduced, size-based cohesiveness. Finally, the democratic leadership-satisfaction relationship was stronger the more males there are in the group, but only in artificial groups. In both real and artificial groups, women are less satisfied with autocratic leadership and more satisfied with democratic leadership. Men in real groups prefer autocratic leadership; their satisfaction fell with democratic leadership. In contrast, in artificial groups, the more male the group, the greater the satisfaction with democratic leadership. Foels et al. think this may occur in part because artificial groups are composed of college students, with more liberal views of what is appropriate leadership, whereas in the work world, men are accustomed to a more task-oriented, directive style.

Satisfaction with leadership style is highly culture-dependent. Lustig and Cassotta note that an autocratic style will be preferred in cultures with high power distance, such as Mexico, the Philippines, and India.[36] Similarly, cultures that demonstrate a stereotypically masculine orientation, including Japan, Austria, and Venezuela, would likewise prefer autocratic leadership.

Although a leadership style that provides some degree of structure appears to be the most desirable for both productivity and satisfaction in the United States, several contingent factors (including cultural values) affect how much structure and control a particular group seems to need; that is, you cannot separate any one style from the situation leaders and followers find themselves in.[37] Even Jennifer, designated leader of the advertising team in our opening story, who typically engages in a controlling leadership style, finds herself adjusting to the situation and to the peculiarities she discovers in each new employee. We next consider contingency approaches.

Contingency Approaches

All **contingency approaches** assume that group situations vary, with different situations requiring different leadership styles. These approaches explicitly acknowledge that factors such as members' skills and experience, cultural values, the type of task, and the time available affect the type of leadership likely to be effective. Contingency approaches acknowledge the complexity of small group systems, with all factors such as task, members, and environment affecting each other interdependently.

> What will work for one group won't work for another.
>
> *P. W., Community Volunteer*

Not only do most current researchers accept contingency assumptions, but so do group members. Wood asked members of continuing small groups with task, social, and dual task-social objectives what they expected of designated leaders. Members expected different behaviors of the leaders

Contingency Approaches

The study of leadership that assumes the appropriate leadership style in a given situation depends on factors such as members' skills and knowledge, time available, the type of task, and so forth.

depending on the group's focus, although a moderate degree of team spirit was expected by leaders of all types of groups.[38] Griffin found that the amount of structuring and directive behavior expected from supervisors depended on the level of growth needs of subordinates. People with high growth needs (i.e., who enjoy challenging jobs) most preferred participative, considerate supervisors, whereas employees with lower growth needs preferred more autocratic leadership.[39] A complex relationship was found among member needs, leadership style, and member satisfaction, giving credence to the general contingency hypothesis of leadership in small discussion groups.

Downs and Pickett also examined contingencies of leader style and member needs.[40] Groups of participants with high social needs were most productive with task-oriented procedural leaders and least productive with no designated leader. Groups of people low on interpersonal needs did equally well with designated leaders who provided task structuring only, with leaders who provided both task structuring and socioemotional leadership, and with no designated leader. Groups with some members high and some low in interpersonal needs performed somewhat better without a designated leader.

The contingency approach is also supported by Skaret and Bruning, who noted that satisfaction involves a complex interaction between leader behavior and work group attitudes.[41] The following traits of followers influence the type of leadership they preferred: degree of authoritarianism and dogmatism, need for achievement, and locus of control (whether one feels in control of one's own life or governed by fate).[42] From the research and theory surveyed, we can safely conclude that a discussion leader needs to be flexible, adapting to situational contingencies, but that in almost all situations in the United States, a democratic structuring approach will be productive, or will at least not be counterproductive.

Functions Approach

The study of functions performed by leaders; the theory that leadership is defined by the functions a group needs and can be supplied by any member.

The Functions Approach   The **functions approach** is a subtype of contingency theory that assumes groups are most productive when specific functions are performed by leaders as needed. The two major categories of functions are those that focus on interpersonal relationships (various writers call this *maintenance, socioemotional, social leadership,* or *initiating consideration*) and those concerned with the group's task (also called *instrumental leadership* or *initiating structure*). Examples of these kinds of functions were described in Chapter 7.

Several researchers have attempted to identify specific task and maintenance functions needed for effective leadership. One of the earliest category systems for studying behavioral functions was the Interaction Process Analysis developed by Bales.[43] Benne and Sheats identified a variety of task and maintenance functions they claim are productive for the group, along with a set of functions that are counterproductive.[44] Several of the Benne and Sheats functions are included in the lists in Chapter 7. Fisher identified four functions performed by leaders, whom he saw as providing a mediating function between group events and activities and the final outcome:

1. Leaders provide sufficient information, as well as the ability to process and handle considerable information.

2. Leaders enact a variety of functions needed within the group.

3. Leaders help group members make sense of decisions made and actions performed within the group by doing such things as supplying good reasons for those actions.

4. Leaders focus on the here and now, stopping the group from jumping to unwarranted conclusions or adopting stock answers too quickly.[45]

Another major function of leadership is captured in Weick's metaphor of *leader as medium*.[46] Task groups usually confront a variety of interpersonal and task obstacles that must be overcome. One of the most difficult is the need to reduce a vast amount of complex and often equivocal information to an understandable level. Goal achievement requires group members to devise a set of rules and procedures for narrowing the number of plausible interpretations so they can devise an appropriate course of action. Weick says the basic function of leadership is to assist the group in creating an organizing scheme of rules and procedures for problem solving. The leader is the medium, or mechanism, through which this is accomplished. As you saw from our story of the broadcast advertising team, their leader, Jennifer, does not do a very good job of helping her employees narrow down plausible interpretations for any number of work tasks, especially their job responsibilities. She is a poor *medium*.

We view the functions approach as a contingency approach because two assumptions are implicit in the model. First, at different points in the group, different functions will be needed. For instance, *initiation* is needed to get the group started; *gatekeeping* is needed to facilitate participation, and so forth. Because of each group's unique combination of member skills, attitudes, behaviors, and so on, a different mix of functions is required. Second, the model suggests that any member of the group, not just the designated leader, can perform any of the functions. It assumes that the necessary functions must be performed by *someone* for the group to be effective, but not necessarily by the designated leader. This approach sets the stage for viewing group leadership behavior as a property of the *group*, and a function of the interaction between the person whose title is *leader* and the other members.

> Have you seen people lead meetings who are not members? I have. And you can see people do that in subtle and direct ways who are very, very skilled.
>
> *J. J., CEO and General Manager, Utility Company*

Fiedler's Contingency Model   Some contingency approaches assume that there are limits to leaders' abilities to adapt; in other words, people are relatively inflexible. Leadership behaviors are traitlike in that leaders have styles they prefer and use more effectively than other styles. Fiedler's contingency model of leadership reflects this view. He concluded that there are three factors upon which appropriate leader behaviors are contingent: leader-member relations, task structure, and strength of leader position (or legitimate) power.[47] The central thesis of Fiedler's work is that individuals' personal needs and characteristics make them suited for leadership only in certain types of contingencies, so it is more productive to match prospective leaders to situations than to try to change the individual's style. This also implies that a group's leadership situation will remain relatively stable. Extensive application has been made of this theory in placing supervisory personnel. According to Fiedler, problem-solving groups are generally best served by democratic structuring leaders with concerns for people, rather than by autocratic or nonstructuring leaders. However, in other types of situations (for instance, during emergencies or in leading primary groups), either a more autocratic or a more relationship-oriented style would be more productive.

Hersey and Blanchard's Situational Model   Other contingency approaches assume that people are flexible enough to adapt their behavior to meet the needs of many groups. Representative of this approach is the model of leadership adaptability and style developed by Hersey and Blanchard.[48] These authors postulate that leadership behaviors can be located along two dimensions, relationship orientation (giving socioemotional support) and task orientation (coordination efforts, instructions, advice and so forth). A leader can be high on one, both, or neither dimension. (Figure 9.3 illustrates these dimensions.) However, whether a leader is effective depends on his or her ability to adapt to the needs of the members at all points during the life of the group. For instance, a new group of inexperienced members needs more task but less relationship behavior from the leader until members understand their charge and objectives. As members become familiar with the task, the leader should begin to increase relationship behavior. Eventually task behavior can be reduced and, at full member readiness, socioemotional support can be withdrawn, because the group's dependence on the leader is minimal. This model, which has not been widely tested empirically, implies that the leader must be able to analyze a group's situation and the readiness level of the members in order to provide the right amount of task instruction and socioemotional support. It also implies that a group's situation is not static, but changes throughout the life of the group.

> Structure is necessary for lack of [task] maturity. . . . As the groups mature, you reduce the structure.
>
> *J. H., Regional Director, Social Service Agency, retired*

Hersey and Blanchard's model places great faith in the leader's ability to adapt to the needs of the group. There is support for believing that many leaders are flexible, as the self-monitoring studies reported earlier suggested. Wood found, for example, that the discussion leaders she observed demonstrated behavioral flexibility. The comments of the designated leader varied depending on the stated purpose of the discussion and the previous success

Effective Style of Leader

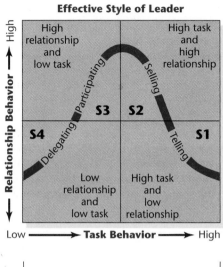

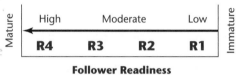

Follower Readiness

FIGURE 9.3 Task and relationship needs of maturing groups.

Source: Adapted from P. Hersey and K. Blanchard, *Management of Organizational Behavior: Utilizing Human Resources,* 7th ed. Englewood Cliffs, NJ: Prentice Hall, 1996. (Reprinted by permission.)

or failure of the committee. Leaders tended to compensate as needed, depending on what had occurred at previous meetings, by providing more or less structure. Wood noted, "The most important and obvious conclusion is that leaders of purposive discussions do engage in adaptive behavior."[49] Her results have been confirmed. Sorenson and Savage observed greater variety in the effective leaders' communicative styles than in those of ineffective leaders. In particular, leaders should attend to the degrees of dominance and supportiveness they exhibit.[50] Drecksell, too, found that leaders covered a wide range of functions, and their interaction was more complex than the interaction of other members.[51]

Communicative Competencies Approach In an attempt to provide a model that acknowledges contingencies without overwhelming us with complexity, Barge and Hirokawa recently proposed a Communication Competency Model of Group Leadership.[52] The **communicative competencies model** is based on the assumptions that leadership involves behaviors that help a group overcome obstacles to goal achievement, that leadership occurs through the process of communication, and that communication skills (competencies) are the means used by individuals to lead small groups. This model maintains the task and relationship distinctions noted by many researchers, but provides an organizing scheme for the overwhelming array of facts and conjectures relating to group leadership. We consider it a contingency approach because it assumes that the actual context facing the leader and group is constantly shifting, so the task and relational communicative competencies

Communicative Competencies Model

The model that assumes that the communication-related skills and abilities of members are what help groups overcome obstacles and achieve their goals.

needed vary from moment to moment. Group leaders must be highly flexible to draw from a personal repertoire of such competencies. We next direct your attention to the competencies we believe to be the most important to leadership and which we urge you to cultivate as personal skills.

Communicative Competencies of Effective Discussion Leaders

Knowing the behaviors and competencies that distinguish effective task group leaders can help you select a group's leader wisely and learn to be a better leader yourself. The following are specific communicative competencies exhibited by effective discussion leaders. Both task and relational competencies are needed.

> The leader usually sets the tone and each leader has his own style. I've seen lots of different styles be successful.
>
> *L. O., CEO, Health Care Collaborative*

1. **Effective small group leaders communicate actively, clearly, and concisely.**

   Numerous studies have found emergent leaders to be high in verbal participation, although not necessarily the highest in a group.[53] Reynolds found that leaders maintained their influence by staying involved in group discussion and decision making.[54] But amount of talk alone is only a small part of verbal competency; Russell found that group leaders had higher levels of communicative skills than other members.[55]

   What are these skills? Lashbrook found that leaders were perceived as speaking more clearly and fluently than other members.[56] Facility in verbalizing problems, goals, values, ideals, and solutions characterizes effective discussion leaders. Barge and Hirokawa theorized that the more complex the group's task, the more ambiguous the member roles, and the more negative the climate, the more important are the leader's communication skills.[57]

2. **Effective group leaders communicate a good grasp of the group's task.**

   Above all else, their communication behaviors reveal extensive knowledge about the task, skills for organizing and interpreting that knowledge, and an understanding of procedures that facilitate task accomplishment. They have technical know-how, are credible to the members, and know when to ask others for help.[58]

3. **Effective group leaders inspire team members' confidence in themselves.**

   Effective leaders set clear expectations and let their members know they have confidence in members' abilities. The leaders Jung and Sosik studied empowered their members, which affected both the members' collective confidence and their performance.[59] LaFasto and Larson found that effective leaders bolster members' self-assurance by providing clarity about performance goals, by assigning members responsibilities that demonstrate the leader's trust in them, and by accentuating the positive.[60] These authors note that we like to be around positive people who make us feel competent. Showing confidence in team members increases their desire to achieve while it decreases their fear of failure. This can produce extraordinary successes.

4. Effective group leaders skillfully mediate information and ideas supplied by all members.

Such leaders are especially competent in analysis of statements and in the kinds of critical thinking that lead to thorough evaluation and integration of information. They are good at providing structure to unorganized information, at asking probing questions to bring out pertinent information, and at evaluating inferences and conclusions drawn from information. They help all members focus on activities relevant to the group's goal.[61]

5. Effective group leaders express their opinions provisionally.

Most Americans prefer their leaders not to express ideas dogmatically. Maier and Solem demonstrated that groups whose leaders suspended judgment and encouraged full consideration of minority viewpoints produced better solutions than did other groups.[62] Moreover, groups whose leaders withheld their opinions about solutions until later in a discussion produced more and better alternatives to a solution than groups whose leaders expressed their opinions early.[63] Groups prefer open-minded leaders.[64]

6. Effective group leaders express group-centered concern.

From interviews with 90 successful leaders in various professions, Bennis and Nanus reported "there was no trace of self-worship or cockiness in our leaders."[65] Larson and LaFasto found that outstanding team leaders "articulate the team's goal in such a way as to inspire a desire for and eventual commitment to the accomplishment of the goal" and exhibit personal commitment to that goal in both words and deeds.[66] Furthermore, such leaders readily confront members who are more self- than group-centered.[67]

7. Effective group leaders model a collaborative climate by respecting and supporting others.

LaFasto and Larson's excellent leaders worked to establish a collaborative climate and to make it safe for group members to communicate.[68] Building on his studies of democratic leaders, Rosenfeld claimed that when ". . . people are equals with whom they work, the rewards and punishments are to be shared."[69] Such leaders are sensitive to nonverbal signals and the feelings these signify. Kenny and Zaccaro reported that leadership depends heavily on competencies in perceiving the needs and goals of members, then adjusting behaviors to these needs.[70] Effective discussion leaders are courteous.

This may be particularly important in a virtual environment, where members don't normally (or ever) interact face-to-face. Oakley suggests that defensive communication may find a "natural home" in the impersonal atmosphere of a virtual team because members are typically chosen on the basis of their expertise, and thus may be tempted to present opinions and information as "certain and unchallengeable."[71] She recommends that team leaders make a special effort to promote the social aspects of team work and to help align members' priorities with organizational priorities in a way that will interest and excite them.

8. **Effective group leaders promote celebration of diversity and sensitive diversity management.**
   Effective group leaders make sure to include *all* members in the team's work and play. Team members perceive them as impartial, not showing favoritism to particular members.[72] Leaders also make time for group members to get to know one another and learn to appreciate one another as individuals. Watson et al. found that the performance of ethnically diverse teams especially benefited from leadership that focused on relational aspects of the team.[73] In contrast, focus on the task was more effective for teams that were not diverse.

9. **Effective group leaders share rewards and credit with the group.**
   As Fiedler and Chemers pointed out, "Leadership is an amazing ego-involving activity."[74] Leaders are often tempted to take credit for the accomplishments of the group and to consolidate their personal power. But effective leaders share as equals both within the group and when dealing with outsiders. They give credit to the group for accomplishments, and work to develop the leadership competencies of all members.[75] In short, effective leaders are skilled in communicating appreciation for efforts of members.

   I think who gets the credit, who gets the accolades, really makes a big difference, and I think if you're in charge and you always try to corner that, you make a big mistake. . . . Don't be full of yourself.

   J. R., Lobbyist and Former State Representative

Consider This 9.3

How does Jennifer, the leader of the broadcast advertising group, violate these guidelines? How would you advise her, specifically?

The Relationship Between Leaders and Followers

All contingency approaches assume an interdependent relationship between the communication behavior of the leader and the behavior, skills, preferences, and expectations of the members. In fact, although we discuss leaders and members separately, we do so only for convenience; leader-member behaviors form a unit, an interdependent system. Whether a leader's behaviors are effective depends in large part on both the perceptions and behaviors of the other members.

Most people in our culture want their leaders to perform structuring behaviors, but to be considerate as well. Pavitt and Sackaroff found that experienced group members expected leaders to be enthusiastic and organized, and to encourage participation from all members as well as suggest procedures for the group.[76] This was confirmed by Ketrow, who found that a person who served as a procedural specialist was identified most often as a group's leader, and the task specialist was perceived as being most influential.[77] Infante and Gordon discovered that subordinates preferred a communication style they described as *affirming* (relaxed, friendly, and attentive) and low in verbal aggressiveness (attacks on others' self-concepts).[78]

One characteristic that may affect what members perceive and prefer is sex. Several studies suggest that women enact leadership differently than men, perhaps because members perceive different behavior as appropriate for men and women. Andrews found that although men and women had equal potential as leaders, women were uncomfortable calling themselves *leader* and preferred the designations *organizer* or *coordinator,* apparently because they perceived a stigma attached to the leader label.[79] This finding is supported by Owen, who noted that women distance themselves from the label of *leader.*[80] He also observed that women became leaders by outworking men in a group, and that they used more themes of cohesion. It is likely that women's leadership behavior is constrained by expectations of members. Watson found, for instance, that women who enacted a dominant approach were less influential than women who enacted a considerate approach to leadership, especially with males.[81] However, women gave dominant female leaders higher ratings of effectiveness, but, regardless of style, women liked female bosses less than men did. Watson suggests a problem-solving approach for female leaders that takes into account the difficulties women sometimes have in dealing with perceptions of others.

Leader-Member Exchange (LMX) Model

One model that has looked systematically at the nature of the interdependent relationship of leader-member behaviors and perceptions is the **Leader-Member Exchange (LMX) model,** which suggests that supervisory leaders develop different kinds of leadership relationships with different members, depending on leader and member characteristics. Members differ in the amount of *negotiating latitude* they are allowed by leaders; a member with a high negotiating latitude is given a great deal of leeway to design and perform his or her job, whereas a member with low negotiating latitude is not accorded such freedom by the leader. Generally, members with higher negotiating latitude are more satisfied and more committed to the organization or group. The members' degree of negotiating latitude is transacted through a reciprocal

Leader-Member Exchange (LMX) Model

The leadership model based on the finding that supervisors develop different kinds of leadership relationships with their subordinates, depending on characteristics of both the leader and members.

interaction process with the leader, whose impression of the member's capabilities helps determine in large part what degree of negotiating latitude will be permitted.[82]

> I think that's the challenge and the responsibility of a leader, to maximize the contribution that the group can make by tapping in to the best that each of the group members has to offer.
>
> *S. P., Vice President, Human Resources, Manufacturing Company*

McClane found support for an interaction between leader and member characteristics, with the best leader-member fit determined by congruence on the need for power.[83] Leaders with high power needs gave greater negotiating latitude to members with high power needs; likewise, leaders with low power needs gave greater negotiating latitude to members with low power needs. Characteristics such as sex, locus of control, and need for achievement were not related. Clearly, leaders with high power needs take a different approach to forming groups than leaders with low power needs; both types of leaders appear to be more comfortable with members who share their assumptions about the appropriate use of power. By extension, members are more likely to be satisfied with leaders who share their assumptions by rewarding them with higher negotiating latitude.

In a different study, McClane compared groups with wide variations in the amount of negotiating latitude and groups with little variation.[84] His results suggest that high differentiation (having some members with high negotiating latitude and some with little latitude in the same group) may have an undesirable effect on a group, particularly if the members accorded high negotiating latitude are seen as an elite core group with the rest feeling like hired hands. These results have been confirmed by Lee, who found that members with little negotiating latitude perceived less fairness than members with high latitude.[85] Those members who thought things were fair also perceived the work group's communication to be more cooperative. Although it is normal for leaders to interact differently with different members, clearly, they must tread carefully in doing so.

The foregoing discussion is designed to remind us that neither the leader nor the members operate in a vacuum; instead, their interactions are shaped by each other. Models such as the LMX remind us that, even though we isolate leadership and treat it as an individual variable for study purposes, in fact it is a *system-level* variable that is a property of the group as a whole, not of the individual called the group's leader.

The Case for Distributed Leadership

We have said several times that small group leadership is the property of the group, not the individual who happens to hold the title of leader. We believe strongly that although a group's designated leader bears a lot of responsibility for coordinating and structuring the group's activities, all members can and should be equally responsible for the leadership of the group. The idea of **distributed leadership** explicitly acknowledges that the leadership of a group is spread among members, with each member expected to perform the communication behaviors needed to move the group toward its goal. A group that distributes leaderships is, in Hersey and Blanchard's terms, mature; the designated leader can largely withdraw from both task and relationship activity because the group members themselves are able to supply these for the group. Remember, a group may be able to function without a leader, but it cannot function without leadership. For example, Counselman described a group that had been active for 17 years without a designated leader.[86] Various leadership functions had been picked up by members of the group. The most important of these were providing structure, gatekeeping, setting group norms, and adhering to the group's task. We know this is unusual; most groups can and should use the services of a designated leader. However, this case verifies the important point we made earlier about locus of leadership in a group: it belongs to the group.

> The best sign of the leader is, when the work is done, the team says, "We did it ourselves."
>
> *J. M., Executive Coach and President, Marketing Firm*

Barge provided support for the distributed leadership concept when he compared two models of group leadership—one where the leader was an active, directive influence in the group; and a leaderless model, where all members engaged in the leadership process.[87] He discovered that the better predictor of group productivity was overall leadership activity, as opposed to the activity of the designated leader alone. In contrast to what we might expect, the more productive groups were not more controlling or directing. Instead of demonstrating a sender mode, the productive groups enacted a listener mode, reflecting a more contemplative approach with increased sensitivity to the environment and the other members. Barge concluded that while an individual leader's behavior may not necessarily help a group achieve its goals, the overall group leadership behavior does.

> If you're just sitting back there and thinking, "Well, this meeting is not going anywhere," well, you have some tools, you have some ability to take that in your hands.
>
> *J. J ., CEO and General Manager, Utility Company*

Gastil's studies of small group democracy also provide support for distributed leadership. Gastil says that democratic leadership distributes responsibility among members, empowers them by improving their general abilities and leadership skills, and helps the group in its decision-making process.[88] In examining factors that interfere with small group democracy, he notes that all the obstacles he identified were negatively related to comprehension and

Distributed Leadership

The concept that group leadership is the responsibility of the group as a whole, not just the designated leader; assumes all members can and should provide needed leadership services to the group.

showing consideration for other members.[89] Listening, in other words, is potentially an important communication skill for members of groups with distributed, democratic leadership.

These findings affirm for us the concept we have of an ideal group. Most of your groups will have a designated leader, and we are not suggesting doing away with designated leaders. Instead, we invite you to consider what an ideal, responsible, mature group looks like, one in which all members of the group accept responsibility for its leadership. Members understand enough about the group process to know what functions are needed at what times, and they can supply those functions skillfully. Each member has, and acts on, a personal commitment to the group. Each member can step in to the leadership position and function effectively, with the support and contribution of the other members. Leadership is distributed throughout.

SUMMARY

1. Leadership is a process of using human communication skills to help the group achieve its goal. Leadership is the process by which influence is exercised and the leader is a person who has been appointed, elected, or has emerged to fill the group leader position (or role).

2. Someone's power to influence may stem from reward, punishment, legitimate, referent, or expert sources. Coercion is not considered an appropriate source of power in a group.

3. Leadership emergence can be captured in a three-stage model depicting how some members fall out of contention for leadership and others garner support.

4. Several approaches to the study of leadership were examined. Early traits approaches, which assumed that leaders were born rather than made, have been discredited. Styles approaches examine the effect of democratic, autocratic, and laissez-faire styles on such outcomes as productivity and satisfaction. Current contingency approaches assume that the style needed depends on the group and its situation.

5. Most contemporary researchers accept the contingency view of leadership. Important contingency theories include Fiedler's, Hersey and Blanchard's, the functions approach, and the communicative competencies approach.

6. Nine essential communicative competencies of effective group leaders were described.

7. Leadership is the property of the *group* because the behavior of leader and members constrains and shapes the behavior of the other. The Leader-Member Exchange model was presented as an example of how leaders and members affect each other.

8. A distributed leadership model suggests that in an ideal and mature group members are as responsible for the productivity and effectiveness of the group as is the designated leader.

KEY TERMS

 Test your knowledge of these key terms by visiting the Online Learning Center website at mhhe.com/galanes11

Autocratic leaders	Distributed leadership	Leadership
Communicative competencies model	Functions approach	Leadership emergence
	Laissez-faire leaders	Power
Contingency approaches	Leader	Self-monitoring
Democratic leaders	Leader-Member Exchange (LMX) model	Styles approaches
Designated leader		Traits approach

EXERCISES

 Go to self-quizzes on the Online Learning Center at mhhe.com/galanes11 to test your knowledge of the chapter concepts

1. In groups of four to six, discuss the following question for 15 minutes; then your group's spokesperson should report your conclusions to the rest of the class:

   "In addition to the communicative competencies listed in this chapter, what others do you think leaders of small task-oriented groups need, and why?"

2. Working alone, make a list of examples of small group leaders influencing followers through each of the five types of power. Share your examples with several classmates. Can you draw any tentative conclusions from your shared examples?

3. Think of an initially leaderless classroom group to which you have belonged. Did that group have an emergent leader? If so, describe the process you observed of how that individual emerged as a leader. What traits and communication behaviors seemed related to this instance of leadership emergence?

4. Discuss the notion that different types of groups need different types of leaders. What contingencies can you identify that may have a bearing? From your experience, can you give examples of when a leader should have modified his or her behavior to fit the group needs? Do you think there is a best style of leadership to fit all situations?

5. In groups of four to six, discuss the strengths and potential drawbacks of using distributed leadership in a group. Assume you are a designated leader who wants all your group members to be responsible for the group. How would you go about introducing and implementing distributed leadership?

BIBLIOGRAPHY

Barge, J. Kevin, and Randy Y. Hirokawa. "Toward a Communication Competence Model of Group Leadership." *Small Group Behavior* 20 (1989): 167–89.

Bennis, Warren, and B. Nanus. *Leaders: The Strategies for Taking Charge*. New York: Harper & Row, 1985.

Cathcart, Robert S., Larry A. Samovar, and Linda D. Henman. *Small Group Communication: Theory and Practice*. 7th ed. Madison, WI: Brown & Benchmark, 1996, Section 7.

Hackman, Michael Z., and Craig E. Johnson. *Leadership: A Communication Perspective*. Prospect Heights, IL: Waveland Press, 1991.

Larson, Carl E., and Frank M. J. LaFasto. *TeamWork: What Must Go Right/What Can Go Wrong*. Newbury Park, CA: Sage, 1989.

NOTES

1. Carl E. Larson and Frank M. J. LaFasto, *Team-Work: What Must Go Right/What Can Go Wrong* (Newbury Park, CA: Sage, 1989): 118.

2. Michael Z. Hackman and Craig E. Johnson, *Leadership: A Communication Perspective* (Prospect Heights, IL: Waveland Press, 1991): 11.

3. E. Hollander, "Leadership and Power," in *The Handbook of Social Psychology* 3, vol. II, eds. G. Lindzey and Elliot Aronson (New York: Random House, 1985): 485–537.

4. John R. P. French and Bertram Raven, "The Bases of Social Power," in *Group Dynamics: Research and Theory*, 3rd ed., eds. Dorwin Cartwright and Alvin Zander (New York: McGraw-Hill, 1981): 317.

5. Jeffrey W. Lucas, "Behavioral and Emotional Outcomes of Leadership in Task Groups," *Social Forces* 78 (December 1999): 747–78.

6. Marvin E. Shaw, *Group Dynamics: Research and Theory*, 3rd ed. (New York: McGraw-Hill, 1981): 317.

7. Ernest G. Bormann, *Discussion and Group Methods*, 2nd ed. (New York: Harper & Row, 1975): 253–69; Nancy L. Harper and Lawrence R. Askling, "Group Communication and Quality of Task Solution in a Media Production Organization," *Communication Monographs* 47 (1980): 77–100.

8. E. P. Hollander, *Leadership Dynamics* (New York: Free Press, 1978): 13–16.

9. Ernest Stech and Sharon A. Ratliffe, *Working in Groups* (Skokie, IL: National Textbook Company, 1976): 201.

10. Donald Ellis and B. Aubrey Fisher, *Small Group Decision Making: Communication and the Group Process* (New York: McGraw-Hill, 1994): 203–6.

11. Ernest G. Bormann, *Small Group Communication: Theory and Practice*, 3rd ed. (New York: Harper & Row, 1990) 205-14, 291–92; John C. Geier, "A Trait Approach to the Study of Leadership in Small Groups," *Journal of Communication* 17 (1967): 316–23.

12. John C. Geier, "A Trait Approach to the Study of Leadership in Small Groups," 316–23.

13. M. Snyder, "Self-Monitoring Processes," in *Advances in Experimental Social Psychology*, vol. 12, ed. L. Berkowitz (New York: Academic Press, 1979).

14. Stephen J. Zaccaro, Roseanne J. Foti, and David A. Kenny, "Self-Monitoring and Trait-Based Variance in Leadership: An Investigation of Leader Flexibility across Multiple Group Situations," *Journal of Applied Psychology* 76 (1991): 308–15.

15. Robert J. Ellis and Steven F. Cronshaw, "Self-Monitoring and Leader Emergence: A Test of Moderator Effects," *Small Group Research* 23 (February 1992): 113–29.

16. Steven F. Cronshaw and Robert J. Ellis, "A Process Investigation of Self-Monitoring and Leader Emergence," *Small Group Research* 22 (November 1991): 403–20.

17. Deborah C. Baker, "A Qualitative and Quantitative Analysis of Verbal Style and the Elimination of Potential Leaders in Small Groups," *Communication Quarterly* 38 (Winter 1990): 13–26.

18. Anthony T. Pescosolido, "Informal Leaders and the Development of Group Efficacy," *Small Group Research* 32 (February 2001): 74–94.

19. Judith A. Kolb, "Are We Still Stereotyping Leadership? A Look at Gender and Other Predictors of Leader Emergence," *Small Group Research* 28 (1997): 370–93.

20. Katherine W. Hawkins, "Effects of Gender and Communication Content on Leadership Emergence in Small Task-Oriented Groups," *Small Group Research* 26 (May 1995): 234–49.

21. Susan Shimanoff and Mercilee M. Jenkins, "Leadership and Gender: Challenging Assumptions and Recognizing Resources," in *Small Group Communication: Theory and Practice*, 7th ed., eds. Robert S. Cathcart, Larry A. Samovar, and Linda Henman (Madison: WI: Brown & Benchmark, 1996): 327–44.

22. Gita De Souza and Howard J. Klein, "Emergent Leadership in the Group Goal-Setting Process," *Small Group Research* 26 (November 1995): 475–96.

23. Lita Kurth, "Democracy and Leadership in Basic Writing Small Groups" (Paper presented at the

Annual Meeting of the Conference on College Composition and Communication, March 1995).

24. Susan A. Wheelan and Frances Johnston, "The Role of Informal Member Leaders in a System Containing Formal Leaders," *Small Group Research* 27 (February 1996): 33-55.

25. Ellis and Fisher, *Small Group Decision Making*, 210-12.

26. Ralph M. Stogdill, *Handbook of Leadership: A Survey of Theory and Research* (New York: Free Press, 1974): 63-82; Marvin E. Shaw, *Group Dynamics*, 2d ed. (New York: McGraw-Hill, 1976): 274-75 and Chapter 6.

27. "Predictions: If the Crown Fits . . . ," *Newsweek*, August 23, 1999 p.8.

28. Ellis and Fisher, *Small Group Decision Making*, 182.

29. Ralph M. Stogdill, "Personal Factors Associated with Leadership: A Survey of Literature," *Journal of Psychology* 25 (1948): 64.

30. Charles Pavitt and Pamela Sakaroff, "Implicit Theories of Leadership and Judgments of Leadership among Group Members," *Small Group Research* 21 (1990): 374-92.

31. Lawrence B. Rosenfeld and Timothy B. Plax, "Personality Determinants of Autocratic and Democratic Leadership," *Speech Monographs* 42 (1975): 203-8.

32. Douglas McGregor, *The Human Side of Enterprise* (New York: McGraw-Hill, 1960).

33. Ralph K. White and Ronald Lippett, "Leader Behavior and Member Reaction in Three 'Social Climates,'" in *Group Dynamics: Research and Theory*, 2nd ed., eds. Dorwin Cartwright and Alvin Zander (Evanston, IL: Row, Peterson, 1960): 527-53; William E. Jurma, "Effects of Leader Structuring Style and Task-Orientation Characteristics of Group Members," *Communication Monographs* 46 (1979): 282; Malcom G. Preston and Roy K. Heintz, "Effectiveness of Participatory versus Supervisory Leadership in Group Judgment," *Journal of Abnormal and Social Psychology* 44 (1949): 344-45; George Graen, Fred Dansereau, and Takau Minami, "Dysfunctional Leadership Styles," *Organizational Behavior and Human Performance* 7 (1972): 216-36; Norman R. F. Maier and Ronald A. Maier, "An Experimental Test of the Effects of 'Developmental' vs. 'Free' Discussions on the Quality of Group Decisions," *Journal of Applied Psychology* 41 (1957): 320-23; William E. Jurma, "Leadership Structuring Style, Task Ambiguity and Group Members' Satisfaction," *Small Group Behavior* 9 (1978): 124-34.

34. John Gastil, "A Meta-Analytic Review of the Productivity and Satisfaction of Democratic and Autocratic Leadership," *Small Group Research* 25 (August 1995): 384-410.

35. Rob Foels, James E. Driskell, Brian Mullen, and Eduardo Salas, "The Effects of Leadership on Group Member Satisfaction," *Small Group Research* 31 (December 2000): 676-701.

36. Myron W. Lustig and Laura L. Cassotta, "Comparing Group Communication across Cultures: Leadership, Conformity, and Discussion Processes," in *Small Group Communication: Theory and Practice*, 7th ed., eds. Robert S. Cathcart, Larry A. Samovar, and Linda D. Henman (Boston: McGraw-Hill, 1997): 316-26.

37. Ellis and Fisher, *Small Group Decision Making*, 184.

38. Julia T. Wood, "Alternative Portraits of Leaders: A Contingency Approach to Perceptions of Leadership," *Western Journal of Speech Communication* 43 (1979): 260-70.

39. R. N. Griffin, "Relationships among Individual, Task Design, and Leader Behavior Variables," *Academy of Management Journal* 23 (1980): 665-83.

40. Cal W. Downs and Terry Pickett, "An Analysis of the Effects of Nine Leadership–Group Compatibility Contingencies upon Productivity and Member Satisfaction," *Communication Monographs* 44 (1977): 220-30.

41. David J. Skaret and Nealia S. Bruning, "Attitudes about the Work Group: An Added Moderator of the Relationship between Leader Behavior and Job Satisfaction," *Group & Organization Studies* 11 (1986): 254-79.

42. M. L. Chemers, "Leadership Theory and Research: A Systems-Process Integration," in *Basic Group Processes*, ed. P. B. Paulus (New York: Springer-Verlag, 1983): 9-39.

43. R. F. Bales, *Interaction Process Analysis* (Cambridge, MA: Addison-Wesley, 1950).

44. Kenneth D. Benne and Paul Sheats, "Functional Roles of Group Members," *Journal of Social Issues* 4 (1948): 41–49.

45. B. Aubrey Fisher, "Leadership as Medium: Treating Complexity in Group Communication Research," *Small Group Behavior* 16 (1985): 167–96.

46. Karl Weick, "The Spines of Leaders," in *Leadership: Where Else Can We Go?* eds. M. McCall and M. Lombardo (Durham, NC: Duke University Press, 1978): 37–61.

47. Fred E. Fiedler, *A Theory of Leadership Effectiveness* (New York: McGraw-Hill, 1967).

48. Paul Hersey and Kenneth Blanchard, *Management of Organizational Behavior: Utilizing Human Resources*, 7th ed. (New York: Prentice-Hall, 1996).

49. Julia T. Wood, "Leading in Purposive Discussions: A Study of Adaptive Behaviors," *Communication Monographs* 44 (1977): 152–65.

50. Ritch L. Sorenson and Grant T. Savage, "Signaling Participation through Relational Communication: A Test of the Leader Interpersonal Influence Model," *Group & Organization Studies* 14 (September 1989): 325–54.

51. Gay L. Drecksell, "Interaction Characteristics of Emergent Leadership" (Unpublished doctoral dissertation, University of Utah, 1984).

52. J. Kevin Barge and Randy Y. Hirokawa, "Toward a Communication Competency Model of Group Leadership," *Small Group Behavior* 20 (1989): 167–89.

53. Charles G. Morris and J. R. Hackman, "Behavioral Correlates of Perceived Leadership," *Journal of Personality and Social Psychology* 13 (1969): 350–61.

54. Paul D. Reynolds, "Leaders Never Quit: Talking, Silence, and Influence in Interpersonal Groups," *Small Group Behavior* 15 (1984): 411.

55. Hugh C. Russell, "Dimensions of Communicative Behavior of Discussion Leaders" (Paper presented to Central States Speech Convention, Chicago, April 1970).

56. Velma J. Lashbrook, "Gibb's Interaction Theory: The Use of Perceptions in the Discrimination of Leaders from Nonleaders" (Paper presented at the Speech Communication Association, Houston, December 1975).

57. Barge and Hirokawa, "Toward a Communication Competency Model."

58. Frank LaFasto and Carl Larson, *When Teams Work Best: 6,000 Team Members and Leaders Tell What It Takes to Succeed* (Thousand Oaks, CA: Sage, 2001): 130–35.

59. Dong L. Jung and John J. Sosik, "Transformational Leadership in Work Groups: The Role of Empowerment, Cohesiveness, and Collective-Efficacy on Perceived Group Performance," *Small Group Research* 33 (June 2002): 313–36.

60. LaFasto and Larson, *When Teams Work Best*, 121–30.

61. Fisher, "Leadership as Medium," 205–7.

62. Norman R. G. Maier and A. R. Solem, "The Contributions of a Discussion Leader to the Quality of Group Thinking: The Effective Use of Minority Opinions," *Human Relations* 5 (1952): 277–88.

63. Lance E. Anderson and William K. Balzer, "The Effects of Timing of Leaders' Opinions on Problem-Solving Groups: A Field Experiment," *Group & Organization Studies* 16 (March 1991): 86–101.

64. Franklyn S. Haiman (From a paper given at the Speech Communication Association Annual Conference, Chicago, December 1984).

65. Warren Bennis and Burt Nanus, *Leaders: The Strategies for Taking Charge* (New York: Harper & Row, 1985): 57.

66. Larson and LaFasto, *TeamWork*, 121–23.

67. Ibid., 135.

68. LaFasto and Larson, *When Teams Work Best*, 108–20.

69. Lawrence B. Rosenfeld, *Now That We're All Here . . . . Relations in Small Groups* (Columbus, OH: Charles E. Merrill, 1976): 76.

70. D. A. Kenny and S. J. Zaccaro, "An Estimate of Variance Due to Traits in Leadership," *Journal of Applied Psychology* 68 (1983): 678–85.

71. Judith G. Oakley, "Leadership Processes in Virtual Teams and Organizations," *Journal of Leadership Studies* 5 (Summer 1998): 3–17.

72. LaFasto and Larson, *When Teams Work Best*, 121–28.

73. Warren E. Watson, Lynn Johnson, and George D. Zgourides, "The Influence of Ethnic Diversity on Leadership, Group Process, and Performance," *International Journal of Intercultural Relations* 26 (February 2002): 1–16.

74. Fred E. Fiedler and Martin M. Chemers, *Leadership and Effective Management* (Glenview, IL: Scott, Foresman, 1974): 5.

75. Larson and LaFasto, *TeamWork*, 126-27.

76. Pavitt and Sackaroff, "Implicit Theories of Leadership and Judgments of Leadership among Group Members," 374-92.

77. Sandra M. Ketrow, "Communication Role Specializations and Perceptions of Leadership," *Small Group Research* 22 (November 1991): 492-514.

78. Dominic A. Infante and William I. Gordon, "How Employees See the Boss: Test of Argumentative and Affirming Model of Supervisors' Communicative Behavior," *Western Journal of Speech Communication* 55 (Summer 1991): 294-304.

79. Patricia Hayes Andrews, "Sex and Gender Differences in Group Communication: Impact on the Facilitation Process," *Small Group Research* 23 (February 1992): 74-94.

80. William Foster Owen, "Rhetorical Themes of Emergent Female Leaders," *Small Group Behavior* 17 (November 1986): 475-86.

81. Carol Watson, "When a Woman Is the Boss: Dilemmas in Taking Charge," *Group & Organization Studies* 13 (June 1988): 163-81.

82. G. B. Graen and T. A. Scandura, "Toward a Psychology of Dyadic Organizing," in *Research in Organizational Behavior* 9, eds. L. L. Cummings and B. Shaw (Greenwich, CT: JAI, 1987): 175-208.

83. William E. McClane, "The Interaction of Leader and Member Characteristics in the Leader-Member Exchange (LMX) Model of Leadership," *Small Group Research* 22 (August 1991): 283-300.

84. William E. McClane, "Implications of Member Role Differentiation: An Analysis of a Key Concept in the LMX Model of Leadership," *Group & Organization Studies* 16 (March 1991): 102-13.

85. Jaesub Lee, "Leader-Member Exchange, Perceived Organizational Justice, and Cooperative Communication," *Management Communication Quarterly* 14 (May 2001): 574-589.

86. Eleanor F. Counselman, "Leadership in a Long Term Leaderless Group," *Small Group Research* 22 (May 1991): 240-57.

87. J. Kevin Barge, "Leadership as Medium: A Leaderless Group Discussion Model," *Communication Quarterly* 37 (Fall 1989): 237-47.

88. John Gastil, "A Definition and Illustration of Democratic Leadership," *Human Relations* 47 (August 1994): 953-75.

89. John Gastil, "Identifying Obstacles to Small Group Democracy," *Small Group Research* 24 (February 1993): 5-27.

SERVING AS DESIGNATED LEADER

Central Message

A designated leader is expected to perform a variety of administrative, structuring, and developmental activities on behalf of the group. A democratic designated leader encourages members to enact a variety of leadership functions while serving as a completer for functions not being supplied by other members.

STUDY OBJECTIVES

As a result of studying Chapter 10 you should be able to:

1. Articulate a personal philosophy of small group leadership that supports distributed leadership enacted by a group-centered, democratic leader.

2. Name the three major types of services expected of designated small group leaders and describe specific ways of providing them.

3. Produce written messages essential to the work of small secondary groups, including meeting notices and agendas, minutes, and reports to other groups and organizations.

4. Describe the ethical principles that guide group leaders.

The executive committee of a regional home health agency faced a critical task. The agency had decided to pursue Joint Review Commission accreditation. The application itself was lengthy and had to include an in-depth self-study, which was due in about a year. The problem, however, was that the executive committee had been meeting weekly for over six months without making any progress on the self-study. Celinda, the agency's director of operations and designated chair of the executive committee, was frustrated. She wanted the committee, all registered nurses who were department heads at the agency, to take ownership of the project, decide what would be contained in the various sections of the report, collaborate on gathering the data and information needed, and take responsibility for writing the report. Although the department heads *said* they wanted to work together on the report, they seemed listless at meetings and did only what Celinda specifically assigned them to do. They didn't seem to talk freely with one another or to exhibit the kind of open exchange of information necessary for completing such a massive task.

This health agency executive committee was in trouble. If things did not turn around, they would not meet the deadline for submitting the accreditation application. Celinda faced several obstacles, not the least of which was to get the executive committee members involved and committed to their task. One of the hardest jobs of a designated leader is to recognize there is a problem, diagnose the problem, figure out what actions to take, and implement change.

> When I started my administrative career, these are not skills that I had . . . I had to learn a lot of this by watching other leaders.
>
> *B. A., Educational Administrator, retired*

In Chapter 9 we explained that current theories of leadership focus on the leader's communication competencies, including the ability to perceive what a group needs and to adjust behavior accordingly. We supported the idea that leadership be appropriately distributed among members, who also benefit from improving their communicative competencies. However, developing these competencies can be a challenge; just because someone is designated as a group's leader does not automatically mean the group will receive the leadership services it needs. Thus, we cannot exaggerate how important it is for you to develop leadership competencies if you are to be effective either as a member or especially as a group leader:

> [T]he right person in a leadership role can add tremendous value to any collective effort, even to the point of sparking the outcome with an intangible kind of magic.[1]

Larson and LaFasto concluded that outstanding leaders begin by articulating a clear goal for the group in such a way that every member feels a desire for and commitment to that goal, and then developing a plan for achieving the goal that will ". . . unleash the energy and talents of contributing members."[2] This was the task facing Celinda. In this chapter we present specific suggestions to guide your performance as a designated leader, a kind of "leader's manual." We note again that it is appropriate for *all* members, not just the leader, to perform these duties as well. We first discuss general principles guiding the leader's relationship to the group as a whole, then describe the three major types of duties leaders are expected to perform for small groups in the United States, and finally present ethical principles important for small group leaders.

Group-Centered, Democratic Leadership

To reiterate a major theme from Chapter 9, we believe that leadership should be tailored to fit the specific situation facing the group. In some situations, such as with members who are inexperienced or unwilling, more controlling forms of leadership are appropriate, at least initially. In other situations, with highly experienced and capable members, a designated leader may not even be necessary. However, most situations will fall between those two extremes.

At the same time, however, democratic leadership is the ideal form according to the standards and values of American culture. It recognizes the equality of all members by encouraging member participation in all group decisions. As Donald Petersen, the CEO whose leadership during the 1980s pulled Ford Motor Company from near-bankruptcy to profitability, said: "Employee involvement requires participative management. Anyone who has a legitimate reason, who will be affected by a decision, ought to have the feeling that people want to know how he or she feels."[3] This belief is a cornerstone of our political foundation. We stress that this is the *ideal*. In group situations that do not seem to call for democratic leadership, we believe the leader should exert the *least* amount of control necessary to help the group achieve its goal.

It may appear that we are contradicting ourselves when we say, "Be the type of leader a group needs, but be democratic." What we mean is that a leader should first recognize the group's current reality and serve the group as needed, but work toward achieving the ultimate goal of the ideal group. In an ideal group, members are committed, responsible, and mature, and leadership services are distributed among all members so any person could serve well as the designated leader.

Leader as Completer

If group members are capable enough to serve as the group's leader, what does that leave for the designated leader to do? The metaphor we suggest is that the members are the bricks and the leader is the mortar that binds them together, as shown in Figure 10.1. The bricks provide the support and substance of the group, but the mortar allows the whole group to hold its

FIGURE 10.1
The leader as "completer" of the group.

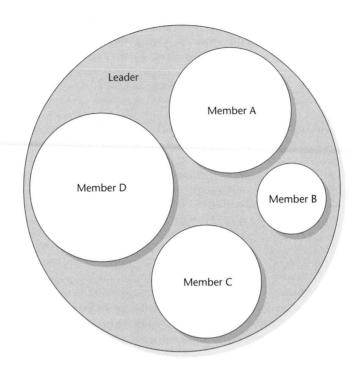

Leader

Member A

Member D

Member B

Member C

shape—completes the structure, so to speak. This concept of the **leader as completer,** as articulated by Schutz, suggests that ". . . the best a leader can do is to observe what functions are not being performed by a segment of the group and enable this part to accomplish them" or, if necessary, perform them.[4] Ellis's study of leadership patterns confirmed this notion of stewardship.[5] His work suggests that leaders are not distinguished from other members by their performance of a set of specific behaviors. Instead, leaders vary their communication to each member, whereas the other members' communication behavior is consistent no matter whom they address.

Being a leader, you've got to be a jack-of-all-trades.

P. B., City Administrator

The model we propose promotes *distributed leadership*, where every member of the group is ultimately responsible for the group. This model makes several demands on *both* the leader and the members. Members should be competent enough both to know what the group needs at any given time and to meet that need by saying and doing the right thing. For example, if the group has digressed too long, a member can, and *should*, jump in with something like: "I think we've gotten off track. Can we get back to the topic?" The leader, too, should be competent enough to recognize the need and be able to jump in *if someone else in the group has not already provided the needed leadership behavior*. This means that the leader is primarily a monitor or medium of the group's *process*, with the principal responsibility for maintaining a long-range perspective on the group's progress.

Responsibilities and Techniques of Discussion Leaders and Chairs

Being leader of a group can be time consuming, but if the group has developed along the democratic lines suggested, the tasks will be shared. For example, a group one of us belonged to discussed explicitly how leadership functions were to be distributed; one person was made responsible for calling meetings, a second for taking notes and having them distributed, and a third for soliciting items for the agenda from other members. During the discussion periods, the position of discussion leader rotated among members, as did the position of social chair. Ideally, every member can assume responsibility to supply whatever leadership services appear to be needed at any given time—the essence of distributed leadership. This process somehow broke down in Celinda's executive committee.

In Chapter 9 we presented information about contingencies that may affect the degree of control appropriately assumed by the designated leader. Contingency theory, which we support, requires leaders to be astute in their analyses of the group's situation and members' needs. Designated leaders, to function well as completers, must be flexible so they can adjust their behavior to the needs of the group. How does the leader know how to adjust? Attending to the following contingencies can help you optimize your leadership style:

1. **Group purpose and goals.**
   Learning, personal growth, and value-sharing groups need far less structure and control than secondary groups charged with recommending solutions to complex problems. In addition, specific procedures (brainstorming, buzz group procedures, problem census, nominal group technique, etc.) require considerable procedural control.

2. **Member expectations.**
   A designated leader will initially need to conform to what members expect of the role, but this can later be changed through explicit discussion of the leader's job and through development of the members' own leadership skills. As mentioned in Chapter 5, expectations are largely determined by culture.

3. **Member skills and maturity.**
   As Hersey and Blanchard reported, members who are used to working together, who understand the task, and who are effective communicators need less leader control than inexperienced members or newly formed groups.[6]

4.   Member involvement in the group's task.

When members perceive that the task is important to them personally, they may resist tight procedural control by a leader. The members of the health agency's executive committee, although publicly declaring they wanted to work together, were not doing so and Celinda had to figure out why if she was to get them involved again.

Consider This 10.1

You know a couple of things about the health agency's executive committee. The committee was composed of all registered nurses who were all department heads at the agency. In addition, they were struggling with an accreditation application which involves a self-study. They all believed their task to be an important step for the agency. It didn't seem as if there should have been a problem. What do you think their underlying problems might have been?

5.   The leader's skill and experience.

Democratic leadership calls for skills in listening, organizing, summarizing, and timing that take a long time to develop. Don't forget that the other group members can—and should—be invited to serve as resources.

6.   The time factor.

If a decision must be made in a hurry, a group will welcome strict control of its procedures. When time is not limited, less leader control is needed.

What should leaders actually do? LaFasto and Larson, using data about teams that they have collected for over 20 years, identified six things that excellent team leaders do.[7] First, they define the group's goal clearly and keep it alive. Second, they work to foster a collaborative climate where members feel safe to share and to disagree. Third, good leaders build confidence in their team members by assigning important responsibilities to the team and making sure the team is well educated regarding the issues. Fourth, they demonstrate credibility by being knowledgeable about the team's issues, experienced, and have the ability to secure help for the team as needed. Fifth, they don't allow the team to get bogged down with too many priorities or competing priorities. Finally, good leaders manage the team's performance so that expectations are clear and members receive constructive feedback in meeting them.

These functions fall into three broad categories of service that you'll be expected to perform as designated leader: administrative duties, discussion coordination, and group development. The advice we give about how to supply these services is based on research findings and the democratic philosophy we espouse. Ideally, each organization has a leader's manual describing the specific duties and responsibilities, so leaders don't have to guess what they are supposed to do.

Administrative Duties

Leaders handle numerous administrative duties; the most important ones are assembling the team, planning for meetings, following up on meetings, maintaining liaison with other groups, and managing the group's written communication.

Assembling the Group   Even before the group has its first meeting, the leader (or organizational member to whom the group reports) has spent time thinking about who will be in the group and what the group will do.[8]

1. **Select group members carefully.**
   Group leaders don't always have the luxury of picking the group members, but when they do, effective leaders carefully consider who should be part of the group. Think through what skills, expertise, and personal characteristics are needed for the group's particular task, then select just the people you need and no more! You want motivated, positive people who will contribute. If others need to know what's happening with the group, you can place them on the routing list to receive information from the group, but they don't necessarily need to be part of the group itself.

2. **Develop a group charter.**
   A **group charter** is a written document that describes the purpose of the group, its specific charge, its area of freedom, its membership, what output the group must produce, and other key information such as deadlines. This may be a formal document approved by the parent organization or an informal memo circulated at the first meeting, but having a group charter helps keep all members on the same page.

3. **Make sure members commit to the group's goals.**
   You may have to recruit group members by personally explaining the purpose of the group and why you want them to be part of it. It's all right to have members who are skeptical and may need to be convinced, but you are better off without a potential member who cannot commit to the group's goals.

Group Charter

A written document that describes a group's purpose, composition, goals, and all other key information.

Planning for Meetings   Once you've selected the group, you will start to hold meetings. To use everyone's time well, make sure you have your pre-work finished prior to each meeting. The following checklist can guide your planning:

> It takes a great deal of time to prepare for meetings and to keep people informed.
>
> *L. H., Director, State-Level Strategic Planning*

1. **Define the purpose of the meeting.**

   First, decide whether you need a meeting. Do *not* call a meeting if you can get the job done using other communication avenues (telephone, fax, e-mail, memo), when there isn't time for participants to prepare adequately, when one or more essential people cannot participate, or when the issues are personal and better handled privately.[9]

   Define the purpose of the meeting clearly. "To talk over our coming year as a committee" is *not* adequately defined as an objective, but "To establish an agenda of problems for committee actions during the coming six months" is clear. Be sure to formulate *specific* outcomes, such as a written report, list of recommendations, and so forth, to be produced from the meeting.

2. **Establish starting and ending times for the meeting.**

   People are busy; respect their time by starting and ending a meeting on time. Running overtime will kill member involvement and attendance and is a barrier to operating democratically.[10] Setting an ending time encourages the group to use its time well. If the work cannot be finished, plan additional meetings.

3. **If special resource people are needed for the meeting, advise and prepare them.**

   Small groups frequently need to question specialists with unique knowledge and skills or experience. Such invited resource persons need to know in advance what information to prepare and what to expect. For instance, Celinda and her boss had to brief the two consultants about the group's history and their current perceptions of the group's problems. In this particular case, the consultants did not come to only one meeting but worked with the committee for six weeks.

4. **Think through the tools you may need for the meeting.**

   There are countless tools you can use to help you accomplish what you want to do in a particular group meeting. We describe several of these in Chapter 14. For instance, if you need creative solutions, there are several brainstorming variations that are designed just for that purpose. If you need to plan implementation of a complex project, a PERT chart can help you. Or, you may want to select or design some sort of ice breaker to get the team started. There are numerous resources to help you, such as *The Memory Jogger*™, a pocket-sized book briefly describing several tools.[11]

5. **Make all necessary physical arrangements.**

   Has the meeting room been reserved? Are handouts, notepads, chalk, charts, and possibly beverages ready? Leaders should *think about* the selection and use of their meeting space. Among other things, members need to be able to see and hear other members, be able to view any audiovisual materials, and the room should comfortably fit the size of the group. It should not be too large or else you run the risk of creating psychological distance between participants.[12]

6. **Have all the appropriate technology you need and make sure it works.**

   How many times have you waited for someone to fix a computer so a PowerPoint presentation can proceed? Make sure you have the equipment you need and that it works. If you are leading a virtual team, make sure members not only have the technology necessary, but also have been trained in how to use it.

7. **Prepare a procedure for evaluating the meeting.**

   Groups should regularly evaluate their meetings, even if the evaluation is brief. This may take the form of an oral postmortem at the end of the meeting or a written evaluation. Appropriate postmeeting reaction forms, described in Chapter 15, can be prepared to help you do this.

8. **Notify members of the purpose or agenda, necessary preparation, and time and place of the meeting.**

   The chair is responsible for seeing that members are notified and given ample opportunity to prepare for a meeting. In large organizations, this duty may be delegated to a staff person, such as professional secretary, but it is still the *responsibility* of the leader.

   > We put [the agenda] up on an overhead and say, "These are our goals for the meeting. Does everyone agree with these?"
   >
   > *L. O., CEO, Health Care Collaborative*

Following Up on Meetings Two kinds of follow-up are needed: touching base with group members and making sure the group's reports are getting to the right groups or individuals. Leaders often call or e-mail group members between meetings for a variety of reasons. One important reason is to make sure members are working on their assignments and have all the information and resources they need to complete their individual tasks. For instance, the leader can make a brief phone call before the next meeting to ask tactfully whether the member encountered any trouble in completing the assignment; this serves as a gentle reminder and helps keep the group on track. But leaders also help maintain good social relationships by interacting with members between meetings. You may want to know what a quiet member really felt about a meeting, or whether a member involved in a disagreement needs to vent to someone. Don't underestimate the value of keeping in regular touch with your group.

In addition, a chair often prepares and sends letters, memoranda, formal reports, notices of group decisions, advice prepared by the committee, and so forth, to appropriate people. This includes getting copies of minutes prepared and distributed, but also involves writing formal resolutions, sending updates to key outside groups, or carrying out whatever decisions for action the group has made. Although the group decides *what* to do, *who* does it is often the group's designated leader.

Liaison

Communication between or among groups; interfacing; a person who performs the liaison function.

Liaison   A **liaison** serves as spokesperson for the group to other groups or to the parent organization; usually this is the designated leader's job. In most organizations, the chairs of standing committees in an organization coordinate with each other. For instance, many organizations have regular meetings of division managers. Whenever you act as liaison, keep in mind that you represent *your group* rather than yourself.

Occasionally committee chairs will be interviewed by public media. Try to anticipate this happening, so you can be prepared to answer reporters' questions. The chair's statements should accurately reflect the group's work, findings, and beliefs. If internal controversies arIse during discussion, the chair normally does not share these outside the group. As one of our friends put it, "Family business is family business, and the group is a family."

Managing Written Communication for a Group   Group discussion involves mostly oral communicating, but a group needs written messages and records. These provide continuity from meeting to meeting; remind members of their assignments; confirm agreements and accomplishments; provide legal documentation of attendance, decisions, and actions; bring absentees up to date; and inform the parent organization and others about what the group is doing. Most committees are required to keep minutes of all meetings and to submit written reports to specified personnel. Even a single-meeting conference group needs a written record. For example, one of us belonged to a community theater for which the written record of an *ad hoc* personnel review committee provided evidence used in a lawsuit to defend the theater from a former employee's assertion that he was fired arbitrarily. Lacking this record, the theater probably would have lost the suit.

Four categories of written messages that contribute to small group leadership are personal notes, meeting records, meeting notices and agendas, and reports and resolutions. All these written messages (except personal notes) can be circulated to members electronically and made available to the group via the e-mail or the World Wide Web. In fact, the Web provides an easy, convenient way to make up-to-date documents available instantly to all group members. It is up to the leader to set aside the virtual space where such documents can be stored (or to recruit a techno-savvy volunteer).

Personal Notes.   The typical conference room is pictured with notepads and pencils at each seat because taking notes focuses group members' listening so they aren't likely to lose sight of the group goal or switch subjects. When you take notes, don't try to record a transcript of the whole discussion. Instead, keep track of the thrust of the discussion by jotting down just a key word or two. Personal notes help you, as leader, summarize discussion when needed, double-check the minutes, and follow up between meetings to ensure that assignments are being completed. Examples of personal notes are provided in Figure 10.2.

FIGURE 10.2   A discussion leader's personal notes.

October 8, 2003 --- Everyone present

Discussion topic: what topics should we include in our class presentation on group polarization?

Main criteria:

   Judy & Bill --- to get an "A" info must be accurate
   Bart --- has to have practical application
   Bev --- Dr. Brilhart wants innovative presentation
   Everybody should have a part in presenting the topic to the class.

Topics

 * Definition of group polarization (all agreed)
   Risky shift (Hal says can become a cautious shift w/ cautious members --- this term is outdated)
 * Exercises to demonstrate when group takes risks & when it becomes cautious --- Judy says there's a bunch of these in a book she has
 * Need to show how this applies in _real_ life.

 * _Decisions Made_
Assignments: Me (applications); Judy & Bill (library research); Hal & Bev (exercises -- w/ Judy's book)

Next meeting --- Wed., October 15

Group Records.   All ongoing committees should maintain accurate and comprehensive **minutes** that serve as official summary records of the important content of meetings, especially of decisions made. The designated leader is responsible for seeing that minutes are recorded, that they are accurate, and for distributing them to members before the next meeting. That task is often delegated to a secretary or a volunteer from the group. An original copy of all minutes should be kept in a safe place as a permanent record of the group's work.

Minutes help a group function efficiently because they prevent wasted time and unnecessary tension. Without such a written record, members often forget important information, fail to complete assignments, or argue about what was decided. For instance, the church board mentioned in Chapter 2 frequently referred to the minutes to recall what decisions members had made about various policies such as the rental charge for facilities, procedures for becoming a member, and so forth. The minutes prevented wasted time and unnecessary tension.

Minutes

A written record of every relevant item dealt with during a group meeting, including a record of all decisions.

Minutes focus on the content, not the process of discussion. They record all task-oriented information shared during the meeting, all ideas proposed as solutions, all decisions and how they were made (majority, consensus, consent), all assignments, and any plans or procedures for future action. Any handouts distributed at a meeting are attached to the official set of minutes.

The format of minutes may vary depending on the nature of the group and bylaws of the parent organization. Minutes of a task force or other *ad hoc* committee may take the form of a summary report, whereas minutes of standing committees (which typically consider more than one topic or problem per meeting) list items of business in the order they were discussed. Minutes should be signed by the writer, with a copy sent to each member as soon as possible before the next meeting, often as an e-mail attachment. This gives members a chance to check them for accuracy and correct them at the beginning of the next meeting. Figure 10.3 is an example of minutes from a student project group that dealt with only one major topic during its entire life.

The next example of minutes, shown in Figure 10.4, comes from the church board of Chapter 2. The format, suggested by Sally, the secretary, allows members to see immediately what items were considered and what actions were taken without having to comb through a lot of narrative.

Meeting Notices and Agendas.   A notice of each meeting should be sent to all members in time to allow them to prepare for the meeting. A **meeting notice** is a memorandum that normally includes the who, what, when, where, and why of a meeting prior to the meeting. The notice should include the purpose of the meeting, with specific outcomes to be achieved, and the agenda listing all items of business to be taken up. It also should include any relevant facts, reading sources, or other preparation members should make prior to meeting. For the first meeting of any group, the notice should have a list of all group members.

An **agenda** is a list of the items of business, topics, and other matters in the sequence they will be considered in the meeting. For a continuing group, approval or correction of the previous meeting's minutes is usually the first item of business. For a standing committee or board, the agenda might include a number of problems on which the group is working. For a task force, the agenda might be two or three questions about facts and findings on the problem to which the task force was assigned. Figure 10.5 is an example of a combined meeting notice and agenda.

Ideally, reports to be distributed to members should be meeting notice and agenda. The report might include tables, graphs, duplicated copies of text, lists, and drawings. Likewise, prior to the meeting the report maker needs to prepare visual aids such as charts, diagrams, and graphs. Such a report is mentioned in the minutes by citing it ("see attached") and a copy stapled to the official set of minutes.

Meeting Notice

A written message providing the time, place, purpose, and other information relevant to an upcoming meeting.

Agenda

A list of items to be discussed at a group meeting.

FIGURE 10.3 **An example of minutes.**

Report of Third Meeting of Polarization Instruction Group

Date of Meeting: Wednesday, March 12, 2003
Time and Place: 7:30-9:00 P.M. in Room 8, Craig Hall
Attendance: Bev Halliday, Inez Salinas, Terrell Washington, Bill Miklas, Judy Hartlieb

Report of Second Meeting
   Judy distributed copies of the report of the second meeting to all members. It was approved. It was decided that Judy would be responsible for recording and distributing reports of each group meeting.

Goals
   A suggested outline for problem solving presented by Terrell was followed. This led to a discussion of group polarization and to determining the actions to be taken involving the group's "problem."
   The group goals were identified as 1) understanding group polarization, 2) conducting a presentation with a class exercise on polarization for the class, and 3) each member being able to write a personal essay about the group experience.

Exercise Portion of Presentation
   After some discussion of the type of exercise to be used in the presentation, it was decided that Inez would be responsible for trying to locate a book with sample exercises that could be considered by the group at the next meeting. Bill will also have primary responsibility for this portion of the presentation and will see that copies of the test are produced and ready for the class. The other group members will individually brainstorm for exercise ideas, and further discussion of these will take place during our class meeting of Tuesday, March 18.
   Criteria for class exercises were discussed. It was concluded that the purpose of the exercise would be to demonstrate the phenomenon of group polarization at work. The exercise would be divided in such a way that each individual in the class would first take it alone and then with a small group, and see what shifts occurred.

Leader and Role
   The group determined that the leader would be responsible for developing agendas and outlines for future meetings and should serve as an overall controller and fill-in or backup person for other group members. Bev was selected by unanimous vote to fill this role as group leader.

Structure of Presentation
   A structure and time schedule of the presentation was decided on:
   5 minutes—Each member of the class takes the exercise individually.
   10 minutes—The class is divided into four groups, with four of our small group members serving as observers. Each group will determine how to solve the exercise problem.
   5 minutes—One member of our group will present a short report on group polarization research to the class. At the same time, the four observers will be finishing their notes regarding what happened in their respective groups.
   5 minutes—The four groups will each discuss what occurred in the group. The observer may start the discussion or serve as a guide/reference person, answering questions and giving insight into what happened with polarization in the group.
   5 minutes—The class as a whole will have the opportunity to share what was observed and experienced within the groups. The observers may again start the discussion and open the floor to any class member's contribution.

Additional Member Roles
   Bill agreed to present the five-minute oral report on polarization to the class.
   Terrell will be responsible for arranging meeting places and will serve as a backup to any member who might be absent.

Adjournment and Next Meeting
   The meeting adjourned at approximately 9:00 P.M. Further planning will take place on Tuesday, March 18, during class time.

FIGURE 10.4   Another example of minutes.

Board of Directors Meeting Minutes
April 16, 2003

Present: Bill Prior, Norm Kerris, Gary Sloane, Don Bowles, Sally Schultz (directors): Sunni Prior, Marina Kerris, (invited guests); Jane Simmons, church secretary.

Call to order: Opening prayer was given by Sally. Minutes of the April 9 meeting were approved as presented.

Topic	Discussion	Actions/Recommendations
Attendance/ offering	120—Sunday, April 13 Total deposit—$1552.52 Building fund—$5858.00	
Founders Sun., May 18	Marina will attempt to get the SMSU Gospel Choir to sing for a 30-minute program. Covered dish supper to follow service. Jody (Hospitality Committee) in charge of setup.	
Adult Sun. School	Roy Hackman will be teaching from "Spiritual Economics" starting April 29.	
Rental of facilities	Ada Cole asked cost of renting sanctuary for a workshop. Discussion centered on cost of utilities/wear and tear.	Norm moved, Don seconded, that we establish a policy of charging $30 per half day for all rentals. Passed.
Circle Suppers	Bill shared information about Circle Supper program; it has been very successful at the Columbia church. Discussion followed, and several names suggested to organize.	Sally moved, Gary seconded, that we ask Jean Ames to coordinate; that we hold them monthly on second Saturday. Passed.
Search Committee	Marina reported we have 10 applications; search committee will telephone interview and ask 3 to come for a full interview.	

Meeting adjourned at 8:30 P.M. Don gave the closing prayer.

Respectfully submitted,

Sally Schultz

Formal Reports and Resolutions.   Many small groups must submit written reports of their work to a parent organization or administrator. Such reports are often the end product of a committe's work, and may include findings, criteria, and recommendations. Usually, the liason person submitting the written report also gives a brief oral summary.

Date: February 14, 2003
To: Curriculum Committee (Berquist, Bourhis, Galanes, Stovall, Sisco)
From: Kelly McNeilis, chair
Re: Next meeting of the Curriculum Committee

The next meeting of the Curriculum Committee will be on Friday, February 21, from 1:00 to 3:00 P.M. in Craig 320.

AGENDA (by the end of the meeting we must have an answer for each of the following questions):

1. What will be the focus of our departmental assessment (student outcomes, student perceptions, alumni perceptions, or something else)?
2. What areas of the department should be assessed?
3. Whom will we recommend as members of subcommittees to plan assessment procedures for each area decided under #2?

FIGURE 10.5
An example of combined meeting notice and agenda.

The designated leader is responsible for submitting the report, but the actual writing may be done by one or two members. A draft of the proposed report is circulated to all members, inviting their suggestions for revisions and additions. The group then meets to discuss, amend, and eventually approve the draft report. The final version is signed by all members, copied, and submitted.

If the final written report involves a resolution or main motion for the parent organization to consider, the committee chair presents copies to all members of the organization and formally moves its adoption during the section of the assembly's agenda called *Reports of Committees*. The chair makes a brief persuasive speech and answers questions about the motion. Other members of the committee help in answering questions, and may make further supportive speeches. Formats for such motions can be found in any comprehensive manual of parliamentary procedure, such as *Robert's Rules of Order*, Newly Revised, or the organization may have its own special format for motions.

Administrative Duties for Virtual Groups   Leaders of virtual teams are responsible for the same administrative functions as leaders of face-to-face (FTF) teams, but the duties are carried out electronically. Whereas members of FTF teams use technology to enhance their FTF work, the technology is the only way a team exists. All the administrative duties described here can be accomplished electronically, including "discussion" among members and joint work. For instance, most word processing programs provide for document sharing, where several individuals can work on a single document. Virtual meeting programs have a whiteboard where group members can simultaneously or at different times sketch out their ideas graphically. Even voting can be handled via e-mail.

The leader of a virtual team will likely set up a website for the team and virtual chat space for members to interact. Members can interact in real time or whenever it is convenient for them individually. The leader should ensure that all documents relevant to the group—minutes, reports, information—are stored electronically, to be accessed by team members whenever necessary. Because virtual teams lack the full complement of nonverbal signals and text can easily be misinterpreted, leaders of virtual teams will need to be explicit about the rules for communicating, the expectations regarding the team, the goals and time frame, and so forth.

Leading Discussions

Administrative duties of designated leaders precede and follow small group meetings. Now we consider what leaders are expected to do *during* actual meetings. In general, leaders must tend to both relational and task goals. The following guidelines will help you balance these broad goals.

Opening Remarks   Opening remarks set the stage for the meeting by creating a positive atmosphere and helping focus the group on its task. They should be brief. Here are several guidelines:

1. **Make sure members and guests have been introduced.**
    This may seem obvious, but sometimes leaders can become so task focused that they forget this step. Getting acquainted helps members feel comfortable with each other, which makes it easier for them to contribute. Sometimes, you may want to provide name tags. If you are in a group whose leader forgets introductions, you should jump in with something like: "I'm not sure I know everyone. Could we take a moment to get introduced?" The leader will likely thank you for fixing the oversight.

Consider This 10.2

Think of a problem you have dealt with in a group. Pretend that it is your responsibility to deliver the opening remarks for initiating a discussion of the problem. Write the introduction you would use.

2. **Review the group charter at a group's first meeting, and review or explain the specific purpose of the present meeting including what outcomes should be accomplished.**
    Basically, you are like a band director getting everyone to start on the same page. You may need to allow for discussion of the charter and the meeting agenda, and it's better to do that early rather than late, to prevent misunderstandings.

3. **See that any special roles are established.**
    Will the group need a recorder in addition to the designated leader? Will the group have a member acting as a special observer? The group may

choose to rotate such jobs so various members receive practice performing them.

4. **Distribute any handouts.**

   Handouts may include written materials from the parent organization or administrator, copies of findings, case problems, outlines to structure the problem-solving procedure of the group, and an explanation of a special discussion technique.

5. **Establish initial ground rules.**

   Make sure everyone knows the rules for the group! For instance, you may want to affirm that confidentiality regarding the group's discussions must be maintained. Or, if your meeting involves discussion about a controversial issue, you may want to remind members of the principles for effective listening and respectful disagreement. The leader of a virtual group may want to reinforce the rules for effective online communication, including refraining from flaming others.

6. **Suggest procedures to follow.**

   If you think the group will benefit from using a particular procedure or technique, such as the problem-solving procedure in Chapter 11 or one of the techniques mentioned in Chapter 14, present it to the group as a suggestion. Explain the procedure, give members a copy of the procedure, and make sure the group agrees before you proceed. Members should know in advance whether decisions will be by consensus or majority vote.

7. **Focus initial discussion on the first substantive agenda issue with a clear question.**

   Your focus question may require a simple answer: "Tyrone, will you give us last week's sales figures?" Or, it may need considerable discussion: "What do we think are the reasons for the drop-off in attendance?" In either case, the right question helps launch the group into the substantive portion of the agenda. Questions are discussed in more detail in Chapter 11.

Structuring Discussions   Once the group members are oriented toward both each other and the task, the leader can help the group function efficiently by adding structure to the group's deliberations. The following suggestions will assist you.

Consider This 10.3

Stop and do not read further yet. Think back to the group discussions you have been involved in. What were the most significant problems in these discussions? What were the best qualities of these discussions? Now, read on and see if the following suggestions touch what you believe to be the best and worst aspects of group discussions.

1. **Keep the discussion goal-oriented.**
   You have already focused the group with presentation of the team charter or the meeting agenda. This helps the group stay on track. Some digression, such as fantasy, helps establish a group's culture, but if a digression lasts too long, bring the discussion back on track with statements such as: "How will this help us achieve our goal?" or "What does that have to do with what we were discussing?" Topic switching is common, so you'll need to be on constant guard against it.

2. **Temporarily "park" off-topic items in the "parking lot," to be taken up later.**
   When a member brings up something he or she thinks is worth discussing, but is off the current topic, place that new topic or item on a separate flip chart, board, or piece of notepaper (sometimes referred to as the "parking lot") for consideration later. This accomplishes several things. It acknowledges the member's idea, which is supportive. It helps ensure that potentially important topics are actually considered by the group and aren't dismissed just because they are off the current topic. Finally, it helps keep the group on track by encouraging members to complete one topic before embarking on a new one. After the group works its way through the agenda, it can then discuss the items in the parking lot.

   [Early on] I presumed that it wasn't important for me to say too much or to try to structure too much, because I thought other people know these things. And finally, you're at an age where you realize, "My goodness, they really don't know these things!"

   T. T., President, Health Care Policy Institute

3. **Use summaries to make clear transitions between items.**
   Help the group make a smooth transition from one topic or agenda item to the next by achieving closure on the current issue. You can do this by summarizing what the group has decided or concluded, asking whether the summary is adequate, and then checking to see whether the group is ready to move on: "So, we've decided that building a tunnel under National Avenue will be too costly and probably will not solve the jaywalking problem, right? [Pause to verify understanding.] Now, are we ready to go on to the next item, the overhead bridge? [Pause again to give people time to respond.]" Smooth transitions help keep the group on track.

4. **Help the group manage its time.**
   Ideally, the group will address all or most items on the agenda, but members can get so involved in the discussion that they lose track of time. Nothing is more frustrating that running out of time before you have a chance to discuss an issue important to you! It's up to the designated leader to keep track of time and monitor progress on the agenda: "We are only on our third agenda item, with 15 minutes left. Are we ready to wrap this topic up,

or would you rather deal with the remaining agenda items at a special meeting next week?" (But also remember the pitfalls of being a time-oriented listener, which we discussed in Chapter 3; balance is the key.)

5. Bring the discussion to a definite close.

This should be done no later than the scheduled ending time for the meeting, unless all members consent to extending the time. The conclusion includes a summary of the progress the group has made and the assignments given to members. Many leaders thank the group, ask for a brief evaluation of the meeting ("How well did this meeting accomplish what you wanted to accomplish today?"), and remind members of the next meeting.

Equalizing Opportunity to Participate   Each member needs a fair share of "air time" in the group. It's up to you to ensure that everyone has an equal opportunity to speak, with no one stage hogging or withdrawing. There are several things you can do to produce such equality:

1. Address your comments and questions to the group rather than to individuals.

Unless you want to elicit a specific item of information or respond directly to what a member has said, speak to the group as a whole. Make regular eye contact with everyone when you ask questions, especially with less talkative members.

2. Make sure all members have an equal opportunity to speak.

You may have to act as **gatekeeper,** regulating who will speak next so that everyone has a fair, equal chance. Eye contact with less talkative members shows them you expect them to speak, whereas looking at talkative members encourages them to talk more. We suggest you make a visual survey of the entire group every minute or so. If you see a nonverbal sign that a silent member has something to say, you can help that person get the floor: "Pieta, did you want to comment on John's proposal?" or "Pieta, you seem concerned about John's proposal. Would you share your concerns with us?" That opens the gate to Pieta without putting her on the spot if she has nothing to say. Sometimes reticent members can be assigned roles that *require* their participation. For instance, someone might be asked to investigate an issue and report to the group, or be asked to serve as *devil's advocate,* which forces participation. If you know a member is well informed but has not spoken out, try encouraging participation without forcing: "Selim, I think you studied that issue. Could you give us any information about it?"

> **Gatekeeper**
>
> Any member of a small group controlling the flow of messages among members, particularly someone who enables other members to speak and participate.

The chair needs to make sure that you don't just call on those people who are jumping in to monopolize the conversation, but to make sure all opinions are heard.

L. O., CEO, Health Care Collaborative

Controlling long-winded members is often harder than encouraging quiet members, but verbal monopolizing *must* be controlled for the sake of the group. The following techniques range from the most subtle to the most direct:

a. When feasible, seat talkative members where you can seem to overlook them naturally, and try not to make eye contact when you ask a question of the group.

b. When a windbag has finished one point, cut in with a tactful comment, such as, "How do the *rest* of you feel about that issue?" to suggest that someone else speak.

c. Suggest a group rule that each person make one point only, then give up the floor to others, or that each person's comments be held to one minute. You can be lighthearted about this—some groups have used squirt guns, timers, or nerf balls to remind members when it's time to yield the floor.

d. In private, tactfully ask the excessive talker to help you encourage quiet members to speak: "Your ideas have been very helpful to the group, but because you are so articulate, I'm concerned that others feel intimidated about participating. How can you help me get Susan and Juan to contribute to the discussions more often?"

e. Have an observer keep a count of how often or how long each member speaks, and report the findings to the group. If a serious imbalance is apparent, the group can decide what to do.

f. As a last resort, ask the person to control talking or leave the group: "While your ideas are excellent, your constant talking prevents other members, whose ideas are equally good, from contributing. This hurts both group morale and decision making. For the sake of the group, if you will not control your talking, I think you should leave the group."

3. **Listen with real interest to what an infrequent speaker says, and encourage others to do the same.**
Nothing discourages a speaker more than a lack of listening. Yet the evidence is clear that most people ignore comments from a member who previously has said little. Leader intervention can help an infrequent speaker get a fair hearing.

4. **Avoid commenting after each member's remark.**
Some designated leaders fall into this pattern unaware, producing a wheel network of verbal interaction. Other leaders do this to overcontrol the group. Listen, speak when you are really needed, but don't become the constant interpreter or repeater of what others say.

5. **Bounce requests for your opinions on substantive issues back to the group.**
Some people have a tendency to accept uncritically what a leader says. Under most circumstances, you encourage independent thinking by members if you withhold your opinions until others have expressed theirs. You

might reply "Let's see what other members think first. What do the rest of you think about . . . ?" When you do offer an opinion, give it as only one point of view to be considered, not as the *right* interpretation.

6. **Remain neutral during arguments.**

When you get heavily involved in an argument, you lose the perspective needed to be a completer and mediator, to summarize, and to perform all the other communicative behaviors of a good leader. If you realize evaluation is needed, point that out and ask others to provide it. At most, act as a devil's advocate for a point of view that otherwise would not be considered, and tell the group that you're playing the devil's advocate role. Of course, you are always free to support decisions as they emerge.

Stimulating Creative Thinking   Groups are potentially more creative than individuals, but often group outputs are mediocre or worse. Sometimes creativity must be stimulated deliberately. Leaders can do several things to encourage creativity:

1. **Defer evaluation and ask group members to do the same.**

The main idea behind brainstorming, described in Chapter 14, is to defer evaluation of ideas until members have no more ideas to suggest. Evaluation stifles creativity; who wants to suggest an idea that will get shot down? To stimulate creativity, the group must establish a safe climate where people feel safe to propose innovative suggestions. When a group member criticizes a suggestion, gently remind that person of the "defer evaluation" rule.

2. **Try brainstorming and other creativity-enhancing techniques.**

Brainstorming not only requires deferred judgment, it also encourages members to be playful with ideas. Chapter 14 contains several techniques that temporarily disable the logical part of the mind so the creative mind can emerge

3. **Encourage the group to search for more alternatives.**

When no one seems to be able to think of any more ideas, you can ask an idea-spurring question: "What *else* can we think of to . . . ?" or "I wonder if we can think of five more ways to . . . ?" Often, the most creative ideas are ones that pop up after the group thinks it has exhausted its possibilities.

4. **One at a time, ask how each component of a solution or item might be improved.**

For instance, you might ask "How could we improve the appearance of . . . ?" or "How could we add to the strength of . . . ?"

5. **Be alert to suggestions that open up new areas of thinking, then pose a general question about the new area.**

For example, if someone suggests putting up posters in the library that show users how much theft costs them, you might ask "How *else* could we publicize the costs of theft to the library?"

Stimulating Critical Thinking   After a group has done its creative thinking, it must then subject the various options to rigorous evaluation before it reaches a final position. Sometimes groups develop norms of politeness that makes this impossible. Here are ways to encourage good critical evaluation:

1. **If the group gets solution-minded too quickly, suggest more analysis of the problem.**
   This is a common problem and a major source of faulty decision making. Chapter 11 presents a systematic method for helping a group focus on problem analysis.

2. **Encourage members to evaluate information.**
   For example:

   a. To check the relevance of evidence, ask: "How does this apply to our problem?" or "How is that like the situation we are discussing?"

   b. To evaluate the source of evidence, ask: "What is the source of that information?" "How well is Dr.So-and-so recognized in the field?" or "Is this consistent with other information on the subject?"

   c. To check on the credibility of information, ask: "Do we have any information that is contradictory?"

   d. To encourage thorough assessment of a group member's suggestion, ask: "How will implementing that solve our problem?" or "How will the students (union members, secretaries, neighborhood residents, etc.) react to that suggestion?"

   e. To test a statistic, ask how it was derived, who conducted the study, or how an average was computed.

   f. Bring in outside experts to challenge the views of the group.

3. **Make sure all group members understand and accept the standards, criteria, or assumptions used in making judgments.**
   For example, you might ask: "Is that criterion clear to us all?" "Does everyone agree that using our professional association's guidelines is a good idea?" or "Do we all accept that as an assumption?"

   I think, as a team leader, you have to model the behaviors that you want the team to practice.

   L. H., Director, State-Level Strategic Planning

4. **See that all proposed solutions are thoroughly tested before they are accepted as final group decisions.**
   Encourage the group to apply the available facts and all criteria. Be especially careful to consider possible harmful effects of all proposed solutions.

   a. Ask questions such as the following to encourage thorough evaluation:

      ■ Do we have any evidence to indicate that this solution would be satisfactory? Unsatisfactory?

- Are there any facts to support this proposal?
- How well would that idea meet our criteria?
- Would that proposal solve the basic problem?
- Is there any way we can test this idea before we decide whether or not to adopt it?
- What negative consequences might this proposal produce?

  b. Ask members to discuss tentative solutions or policies with trusted people outside the group.

  c. One or more members can be asked to take the role of critical evaluator or devil's advocate so that all ideas are challenged and everyone has a chance to air doubts.

  d. Divide the group into two subgroups under different leaders to evaluate all alternatives, then rejoin to iron out differences.

  e. Before reaching a binding solution with far-reaching consequences, hold a "second chance" meeting at which all doubts, ethical concerns, or untested assumptions can be explored.

5. Help prevent groupthink.

Groupthink, described in detail in Chapter 12, is a dysfunctional process that occurs when the group values agreement and team spirit more than disagreement and thorough evaluation of issues. Here are suggestions for helping a leader prevent groupthink:

  a. Model the behavior you want by encouraging people to disagree with you and listening actively and respectfully when they do.

  b. Assign the role of critical evaluator to each member or establish a subgroup to serve in that capacity.

  c. Don't state your own preferences at the beginning of a decision-making or problem-solving session; members may want to please you and blindly follow your lead.

  d. Establish two or more independent subgroups to work on the same problem, thereby setting up a useful competition.

  e. Don't allow the group to become insulated from outside ideas, thoughts, opinions. Encourage members to get feedback from knowledgeable or interested outsiders.

  f. Use available computer technology to encourage systematic problem solving, such as the computerized support systems we describe in Chapter 14. Such systems can force more thorough evaluation.

Fostering Meeting-to-Meeting Improvement   A group doesn't achieve its ultimate goal by chance. After each meeting, the designated leader should assess how well the meeting's goals were accomplished and how the meeting could have been improved. That, then, suggests a road map for improving future meetings:

1. **Determine how the meeting could have been improved.**

   After a meeting, take a few minutes to reflect on it. You want to consider whether the group received the leadership services it needed at the right time. Were the meeting's purposes clearly communicated? Did members agree on the goals? Was the entire agenda covered in timely fashion? Was the meeting well structured? Did members stay on the topic, for the most part? Take a few moments to consider the members. Did everyone participate? Did anyone talk too much? Not enough? Did you talk too much? Too little? Were the members allowed to digress too often? Not enough? Did the members seem to enjoy the discussion? After answering these and other questions, you can plan your strategy for the next meeting.

   You can reflect afterward for five minutes, what were the things that went well in that meeting, what were some things that you might have done differently.

   B. A., Educational Administrator, retired

2. **Determine the most important changes to be made at the next meeting and adjust behavior accordingly.**

   After examining all the areas where you could improve the group meeting, concentrate on improving the two or three that are most potentially harmful to the group. If one or two members monopolized the floor, plan ways to curtail their participation. If someone seemed upset, you may want to touch base by calling or e-mailing that member. If the agenda was half completed, keep better track of time and allow fewer digressions at the next meeting. Feel free to share the plan with the members: "Last week, we got through only half the items on our agenda. This week, I'm going to pay more attention to our time, and I'll be stepping in more often to help us stick to one issue at a time. I'd appreciate your help with this, too."

Structuring Discussions in Virtual Groups Virtual groups often "meet" asynchronously, or not all at the same time. Although the same suggestions apply, the leader doesn't usually try to structure an actual meeting or conversation. However, because of the increased potential for misunderstanding when members don't interact face to face, it is particularly important that expectations be made clear at the beginning. First, once you have made the task demands and the rules for interacting known, monitor the conversation to make sure people aren't flaming or insulting one another. Step in quickly if they are. Second, encourage regular task meetings and electronic "check-ins." Depending on the nature of the task, you may ask members to check in daily or weekly. If someone isn't checking as often as required, call or e-mail to find out why. Third, encourage nontask communication so members can develop a sense of team connection. That may mean setting aside a chat room just for social interaction. Finally, be familiar with the technological tools that work well for virtual groups and don't hesitate to use them. For instance, some online meeting programs use structured procedures to help ensure systematic problem solving. In addition, several programs help guide electronic brainstorming to enhance creativity.

Developing the Group

Developing the group involves two fundamental processes: helping the group evolve into an effective team, and helping the individual members grow to their potentials so distributed leadership can work effectively. Few people start out knowing how to be effective team members or leaders. Developing the communication skills needed takes practice. As leader, you can help develop the talent on your team.

> What I *love* is the leadership piece and the talent development piece, and it's something that I study, and that I have worked on for years and years.
>
> *J. M., Executive Coach and President, Marketing Agency*

Helping Individuals Grow   An important job for the leader is to develop the members' leadership skills, including the members' abilities to assess the group's throughput processes and suggest appropriate changes. Here are several suggestions:

1. **Encourage members to assess the group's processes and make suggestions.**

    Sometimes the impetus for group growth can be supplied just by asking the group to examine itself and ask "How are we doing?" Periodic self-assessment is a characteristic of outstanding teams.[13] You can build self-assessment into the group's processes. For instance, a short period of evaluation can end each meeting: "How well do you think our meeting went today?" and "How might we make our next meeting more productive?" The answer to the second question led the church board in Chapter 2 to rearrange its agenda so that "new business" would be discussed early in the meeting, before group members became tired and uncreative.

    Another suggestion might be to designate someone as a process observer to watch the interactions and share observations with the group as a whole. The job of process observer may rotate among members so everyone gets practice observing and assessing. The group may also bring outside consultants in to evaluate the group and offer suggestions for improvement, as Celinda did for the health agency executive committee. Suggestions for what to observe and how to provide feedback are in Chapter 15.

2. **Model the behavior you want others to adopt.**

    As designated leader, you can model group-centered, thoughtful, responsible behavior. Your own behavior does a lot to promote teamwork and develop the trust needed for collaboration. Encourage others to evaluate your suggestions, and react open-mindedly and nondefensively to others' criticisms.

3. **Give members practice at performing needed group duties.**

Suggest ways in which group members can serve the needs of the group. For instance, rotate the job of recorder so several members get practice. Give members the chance to report on their areas of expertise to the group and to perform special tasks for the group. Let members substitute for you as discussion leader or liaison to other groups. Don't jump in right away when you see that the group needs something; give the other members a chance to respond before you do.

Establishing and Maintaining Trust   True collaboration (literally, "working together") is possible only when members trust each other. Larson and LaFasto found that interviewees from outstanding teams almost always mentioned trust when asked about their group's climate: "Trust is one of those mainstay virtues in the commerce of mankind. It is the bond that allows any kind of significant relationship to exist between people. Once broken, it is not easily—if ever—recovered."[14] Analysis of their data shows four components of trust: honesty (no lies, no exaggerations); openness (a combination of open-mindedness and willingness to share); consistency (predictability, dependability); and respect (treating others with fairness and dignity). After six weeks of observation and interviews with all the executive committee members, the consultants concluded that lack of trust in Celinda and each other was their *key* problem. Part of their reluctance to work on the self-study stemmed from fear of problems the self-study might expose. Did you guess their problem correctly?

The following suggestions can help you establish and retain a climate of trust:

1. **Establish norms, based on ethical principles, that build trust.**

Communication that builds trust is based on three important ethical principles: working to understand others, communicating to enhance others' identities and self-concepts, and behaving like a responsible group member. Specific behaviors that promote trust are listening actively, encouraging others to explain themselves, helping others with assignments or tasks, maintaining confidentiality, getting assignments done when promised, making sure you understand someone's position before disagreeing, and making others feel free to disagree without being treated as weird or politically incorrect.

2. **Confront trust violators and other problem members.**

Two of the most common complaints are that groups tolerate members who put self over group and that designated leaders fail "to confront and resolve issues associated with inadequate performance by team members."[15] If repeated efforts by you and other members to improve things are unsuccessful, it is far better to remove offenders from the group than to allow trust to erode and group energy to be deflected into destructive avenues.

3. **Encourage members to understand and embrace their diversity.**
   As we have said, diversity can be a group's greatest strength, but not if members can't capitalize on that diversity. The leader can help the team recognize one another's differences and the unique strengths provided by those differences. Whether the group's diversity is based on personality characteristics, differences in stage of life, or varying cultural or co-cultural backgrounds, encouraging members to get to know each other at more than a superficial level can help produce understanding and appreciation. A first step can be not making negative judgments about people just because they are different from you!

   It may help to invite an outside trainer in to conduct a workshop about differences and their value. A library staff we know participated in a trainer-led workshop on personality differences revealed by color preference. The staff had fun learning about how different people preferred to approach work. That helped them see that others weren't being contrary, they were just trying to work in the way they felt most comfortable. The staff began to use color vocabulary in a teasing, but friendly, way: "Oh, you're being so green! We blues will never understand you!" The workshop helped improve staff relationships and work efficiency.

4. **Be a principled leader.**
   Larson and LaFasto suggest that effective team leaders exemplify the kind of group-centered leadership we have described.[16] Principled leaders put the needs of the group ahead of their individual needs and behave in ethical ways consistent with the group's norms. For instance, they do not say they want group participation, then squash members' attempts to participate. Good group leaders have a vision of the group's future, which they convey clearly; they inspire members to work toward that vision. They show personal commitment to the team's goals. Moreover, they work to expose the talents of the other members. Leaders create leaders by giving members the experience and latitude they need to act with self-confidence. Although Celinda was pained to learn that committee members did not trust either each other *or* her, she did not respond defensively. Instead, she supported the committee members in their efforts to identify their fears, establish a time line, and assign responsibilities to each member.

Promoting Teamwork and Cooperation Establishing a climate of trust will do more than anything else to develop cooperation and teamwork among members. Chapter 8 provided several suggestions for promoting cohesiveness and teamwork in a group, which we won't repeat here. Instead, we provide suggestions a designated leader is in the best position to do:

1. **Plan some fun for the group.**
   Fun could be a party, snacks before a meeting, a celebration when a major task is completed, happy hour after work, and so forth. Good task leaders sometimes have trouble with humor. Lee observed, for instance, that

many of the most efficient leaders lacked human warmth, but groups need *both* efficiency *and* satisfying interactions.[17] He suggested that taskmasters relax and allow digressions, which can relieve secondary tension. Let the group chain out fantasies that enrich its life and contribute to establishing shared beliefs and values. If this is hard for you, enlist the help of members who are good at it. This builds relationships and ultimately helps work go more smoothly.

2. **Promote the group.**

As one of our friends said, if the team leader isn't the team's biggest fan, who is? It's the leader's unique responsibility to make sure that the group is known within the organization for its good work. Let people in the organization, particularly higher-ups, know when the team has accomplished something valuable for the organization, make team members' accomplishments visible to others, and talk about the successes of the group. Members will know you support them with your loyalty and backing, and will work hard for the team.

3. **Share all rewards with the group.**

Designated leaders often receive praise from authority figures for work the group has done. Wise leaders give credit to the group.

4. **Get group input and buy-in about promoting teamwork.**

Ask team members to recall the best group they've ever been part of, and to identify the behaviors that contributed to that team feeling. Ask them to suggest how that can be recreated in the present group. Their suggestions will provide the guidelines and norms for the group, with the added advantage that they came from the members themselves.

5. **Confront members whose behavior is hurting the team.**

One of the worst things you can do is ignore individualistic, selfish behavior that hurts the team. It will not go away on its own, and you must address it, constructively. Talk to the member privately first, focusing on the behavior you believe is problematic. Say, "Roger, when you type on your laptop while others are talking, we interpret your behavior as lack of interest in the team," not "You jerk! What do you think you're doing ignoring what people are saying?" If you suspect a hidden agenda item is interfering with group functioning or goal achievement, you may want to bring this up in the group: "Alicia, you have rejected every suggestion the group has proposed without examining it fully. We're all becoming frustrated and angry. Is there something going on that we should know about?"

Sometimes, two members just don't like each other and let their personal feelings erupt in team meetings. In such cases, you may have to have what a friend of ours calls a "Come to Jesus" meeting with them. This friend told two warring women on her team that she wanted them to act with respect and friendliness toward each other in the team meetings, even if they had to fake it. She thought they ended up becoming good friends, but found out years later that they had, indeed, faked it because they wanted to stay on her team. Nevertheless, they stopped the offending, harmful behavior.

6. **Keep arguments focused on facts and issues, not personalities.**
   Step in at once if any member starts an attack on another's personality, ethnicity, or character. However, recognize also that members may have strong feelings about some issues, so don't squelch expressions of feeling, as long as those expressions do not denigrate others.

   Groups have to celebrate the completion of their tasks. . . . Groups need to enjoy their accomplishments and feel good about their accomplishments.

   B. A., Educational Administrator, retired

7. **When a group seems to be deadlocked, look for a basis on which to compromise.**
   Perhaps you can synthesize parts of several ideas into a consensus solution or suggest a mediation procedure, such as the *principled negotiation procedure* described in Chapter 13.

Developing Virtual Groups   Virtual group leaders face particular challenges in developing the group, but creating an online community is possible. As we have said previously, insist on netiquette among members and enforce the rules. Encourage nontask communication. Support members in taking specialized training pertinent to the group's task. More and more, such training may be available online through a university or corporate distance learning program. But perhaps the most valuable thing you can do, if at all possible, is get the group together for a face-to-face meeting at the beginning of their work together. This really helps solidify the connections. And if you can provide for additional face-to-face meetings throughout the team's life, so much the better.

Ethical Principles for Group Leaders

As we have suggested, the leader's behavior should serve as a model for members to follow. As Hackman and Johnson said, "Responsible leaders maintain the highest possible standards of ethics."[18] These authors suggest several principles for leaders that we believe are relevant for small groups:

1. **Do not intentionally send deceptive or harmful messages.**
   Not only should leaders tell members the truth, they should hold *truth* to be an appropriate standard for the group's decision making. To us, this means ensuring that *all* relevant information, whether it supports the leader's position or not, is presented to the group and that the group evaluates all information in an unbiased, fair way.

2. **Place concern for others above concern for personal gain.**
    A leader should not take advantage of the power of the leader position for personal gain or advantage. Hidden agendas, whether belonging to the leader or members, should not be allowed to interfere with the needs of the group. Moreover, as we have mentioned previously, leaders should refrain from actions that might harm the self-esteem of members.

3. **Establish clear policies that all group members are expected to follow.**
    Group procedures and rules are clearly understood, and ethical leaders follow the same rules and norms that members are expected to follow.

4. **Respect the opinions and attitudes of members and allow members the freedom to consider the consequences of their actions.**
    This principle supports democratic, group-centered leadership that encourages equal opportunity for all to participate. It also supports our preference for distributed leadership and acknowledges how important it is for leaders to develop the capabilities of members.

Consider This 10.4

You have tried to create a group culture which promotes distributed leadership. However, one member consistently refuses to carry out his responsibilities; he always has a reason why something is not done. You very much want to create a group culture in which all members can consider the consequences of their own actions. You have even, purposely, *not* done the work for this member to show what happens when work is not completed on time. The problem is that you face a deadline and the project report must be turned in soon. What do you do? When is enough, enough? Where do you draw the line?

5. **Stand behind members when they carry out policies and actions approved by the group.**
    Ethical leaders support members who carry out the plans of the group. They do not save their own skins by leaving group members hanging.

6. **Treat members consistently, regardless of sex, ethnicity, or social background.**
    Members are valued for their contributions to the group. Ethical leaders minimize external status differences to encourage participation by all.

As with other desirable behaviors, the leader should model ethical behavior that will serve as a standard for members to follow. By doing so, the leader will help create a climate of trust and a spirit of cohesiveness.

SUMMARY

1. Good leaders provide the degree of coordination and structure appropriate to the group's situation, yet encourage group members to mature so they can assume distributed leadership of the group. The leader acts as a completer, providing essential group services not provided by other group members.

2. Outstanding designated leaders, including leaders of virtual teams, articulate group goals clearly, adhere to high standards of performance, and promote equality among group members.

3. In the United States, group leaders are expected to provide administrative services, facilitate discussions, and help the group develop.

4. Designated group leaders should establish a climate of trust by modeling for the other group members the ethical principles presented.

KEY TERMS

Test your knowledge of these key terms by visiting the Online Learning Center website at mhhe.com/galanes11

Agenda	Leader as completer	Meeting notice
Gatekeeper	Liaison	Minutes
Group charter		

EXERCISES

Go to self-quizzes on the Online Learning Center at mhhe.com/galanes11 to test your knowledge of the chapter concepts

1. Based on your most recent experiences in group discussions, make three lists: (a) your most important strengths as a discussion leader; (b) your most serious weaknesses; and (c) the steps you plan to take to add to your strengths and to reduce your weaknesses.

2. Think of leaders of small groups to which you have belonged and discuss the following with class members:
   a. Who was the worst leader? List the specific characteristics and behaviors that led to your judgment.
   b. Who was the best leader? List the specific characteristics and behaviors that led to your judgment.
   c. Which of these behaviors were most important in distinguishing between the two?

3. Split the class in half. One-half will serve as observers and the other as discussants; later, they will switch roles. The discussants should form groups of four or five, with approximately equal numbers of observers per group. Each group should select a designated discussion leader and a case problem or question of interest (for instance, how to improve the quality of undergraduate education at your college, how to reduce cheating, etc.). The observers should be prepared to observe the leader's behavior and answer the following questions:
   a. What functions did the leader perform? How effective was each? How appropriate was each?

b. At what points during the discussion did the leader fail to supply some needed leadership service? Did someone else step in to provide it? What was the effect on the group?

c. Overall, how effective was the leader?

4. After a meeting of five or six members of your class or of your project group, each member should write the minutes for the meeting. Exchange your minutes with those written by all other members of the group; compare, then see if you can agree as a group on an official report of the meeting.

5. In groups of four to six, discuss the ethical principles suggested for group leaders. Make a list of other principles by which you think group leaders should abide. Share your lists with the class.

BIBLIOGRAPHY

Cathcart, Robert S., and Larry A. Samovar, eds. *Small Group Communication: A Reader.* 6th ed. Dubuque, IA: Wm. C. Brown, 1992, especially Section 8.

Fisher, B. Aubrey. "Leadership: When Does the Difference Make a Difference?" In *Communication and Group Decision-Making.* Randy Y. Hirokawa and Marshall S. Poole, eds. Beverly Hills, CA: Sage, 1986, 197–215.

LaFasto, Frank, and Carl. Larson, *When Teams Work Best: 6,000 Team Members and Leaders Tell What It Takes to Succeed.* Thousand Oaks, CA: Sage, 2001, especially Chapter 4.

Schwarz, Roger M. *The Skilled Facilitator: Practical Wisdom for Developing Effective Groups.* San Francisco: Jossey-Bass, 1994.

Tropman, John E. *Making Meetings Work: Achieving High Quality Group Decisions.* Thousand Oaks, CA: Sage, 1996, part 2.

NOTES

1. Carl E. Larson and Frank M. J. LaFasto, *Team-Work: What Must Go Right/What Can Go Wrong* (Newbury Park, CA: Sage, 1989): 118.

2. Larson and LaFasto, *TeamWork,* 121–23.

3. Donald E. Petersen, cited in "Management Digest," a special advertising section of *Newsweek* (March 5, 1990): 19.

4. William C. Schutz, "The Leader as Completer," in *Small Group Communication: A Reader,* 3rd ed., eds. Robert S. Cathcart and Larry A. Samovar (Dubuque, IA: Wm. C. Brown, 1979): 400.

5. Donald G. Ellis, "Relational Control in Two Group Systems," *Communication Monographs* 36 (1979): 153–66.

6. Paul Hersey and Kenneth Blanchard, *Management of Organizational Behavior,* 7th ed (New York: PrenticeHall, 1996).

7. Frank LaFasto and Carl Larson, *When Teams Work Best: 6,000 Team Members and Leaders Tell What It Takes to Succeed* (Thousand Oaks, CA: Sage, 2001): 97–156.

8. Gloria J. Galanes, (Unpublished research based on interviews with excellent group leaders, 2002).

9. Michael Z. Hackman and Craig E. Johnson, *Leadership: A Communication Perspective* (Prospect Heights, IL: Waveland Press, 1991): 129.

10. John Gastil, "Identifying Obstacles to Small Group Democracy," *Small Group Research* 24 (February 1993): 5–27.

11. Francine Oddo, ed., *The Memory Jogger*™ (Salem, NH: GOAL/QPC, 1994).

12. Roger M. Schwarz, *The Skilled Facilitator: Practical Wisdom for Developing Effective Groups* (San Francisco: Jossey-Bass, 1994).

13. Larson and LaFasto, *TeamWork,* 130–31.

14. Ibid., 85.

15. Ibid., 136.

16. Ibid., 118–29.

17. Irving J. Lee, *How to Talk with People* (New York: Harper & Row, 1952): 158–60.

18. Hackman and Johnson, *Leadership:* 205.

© Michael Pole/Corbis

EFFECTIVE PROBLEM SOLVING IN THE SMALL GROUP

Problem solving is the reason most secondary groups exist. Because problems solved by groups affect us all, we need to understand how to make the problem-solving process in groups the best it can be. Part IV describes the nature of problem solving, provides vital information to improve group decision-making processes, and explains how you can use conflict to enhance group problem solving and decision making.

CHAPTER
11

PROBLEM-SOLVING DISCUSSION

Central Message

Problem solving is most effective when a group explores the problem thoroughly and generates a variety of possible solutions, which members then evaluate on the basis of their possible consequences. Following an appropriate adaptation of the general Procedural Model of Problem Solving helps a group do this.

STUDY OBJECTIVES

As a result of studying Chapter 11 you should be able to:

1. Analyze the undesirable present situation, the obstacles, and the goal of any problem.

2. List the characteristics any problem has and explain their importance when developing a procedural outline for group problem solving.

3. Plan procedural outlines for the group's problem-solving process to ensure that no step crucial to the quality of the solution is overlooked.

4. Understand the importance of being clear about the criteria or standards by which the group will judge possible solutions.

5. List the five components of the general Procedural Model of Problem Solving (P-MOPS), explain the importance and nature of each step, and be able to adapt the model for discussing any sort of problem.

6. Use the Single Question format to help a group engage in the vigilant interaction necessary to arrive at the best possible solution to a problem.

7. Understand the ways computer technology can help and hinder group problem solving.

In a tragic accident on his honeymoon, Tyrell Washington, a 24-year-old African American man, dived into a swimming pool and broke his neck at C4, paralyzing him from the neck down, with minimal movement in his right hand. After surgery, Tyrell was transferred to a rehabilitation hospital in a large city two hours from his home, where several experts collaborated to help with his care. Weekly "plan of care" meetings were held to confer about Tyrell's care. The meetings were run by a medical doctor with a specialty in spinal cord injuries, and attended by two nurses assigned to this wing, a psychologist, a medical social worker, an occupational therapist, and a physical therapist. Each provided a unique perspective on each patient.

At one particular meeting, when Tyrell had been at the rehabilitation hospital for five months, his primary care nurse noted that he had lost two pounds during the previous week; although this weight loss was not immediate cause for alarm, the nurse asked the others if they had observed anything unusual going on with Tyrell. The psychologist supported her, saying that the patient seemed depressed and had made statements such as, "It would have been better for everybody if I'd drowned," which indicated that he did not accept his physical condition. The physical therapist noted that Tyrell's physical range of motion in his arms and legs had improved, but at their last session, he had seemed to be fatigued and asked to end the session early. The social worker added that Tyrell's family was worried about finances; Tyrell's disability insurance would not pay for all the modifications he would need to the house he and his wife had bought before their wedding and his mother was particularly concerned about what he'd be able to do when he left the hospital. His job with a regional trucking company provided excellent benefits but depended on his physical ability and strength to do the job. He wasn't trained to do anything else.

Because the family lived two hours away, after the initial crisis of his injury, family members, including his wife, came to see him only on weekends, so he was alone most of the day. The occupational therapist said Tyrell had not shown interest in using any of the assistive devices, such as a toothbrush holder designed for quadriplegics. After further discussion about Tyrell's physical and emotional condition, the doctor decided that providing him with a mild antidepressant would be warranted, and the psychologist and social worker decided to work together to identify resources to help improve Tyrell's ability to cope with his situation and his future. The group went on to discuss the next patient.

Although groups usually surpass individuals in solving complex problems, the adage "To fail to plan is to plan to fail" is even truer for group problem solving than for individuals' complex endeavors. All too often, authorities assume that if they assemble a group of intelligent, knowledgeable individuals, effective problem solving will result automatically. Not so! Not only do problem-solving group members need to have expertise about the problem, as did the group in our opening story, they also need to know how to proceed *as a group* to be sure all aspects of the problem have been examined. For high-quality solutions, groups must attend to *both* information and the process of problem solving; indeed, without the latter they may not even be able to complete their assignments. For example, a group of principals and teachers Wood observed for more than a year were unable to complete their task. Their expertise was sufficient, but the group members lacked essential group problem-solving skills.[1] If the doctor in Tyrell's hospital hadn't made it possible for other medical specialists to provide relevant information, and if he hadn't listened to that information, Tyrell's problem might easily not have been addressed.

Consider This 11.1

The group charged with overseeing Tyrell's care represented diverse experts in health care. What contribution to the whole did each person make? Were all the relevant parties represented at the meeting? Is there anyone else you think should have been represented at the meeting?

When asked how they solve problems, most people will say something like "get the facts, weigh the alternatives, and make a decision." That's not a bad procedure, though incomplete, but extensive observation reveals that both individual and group problem solving is usually more haphazard.[2] The problem-solving groups Berg observed changed themes on average every 58 seconds, often without completing discussion of the issues or themes raised.[3] In the typical problem-solving discussion, someone mentions a problem, someone else suggests a way to solve it, the group briefly discusses the idea, and then it is adopted or something else is proposed, perhaps with brief periods of discussing the problem itself. Groups often flit from idea to idea, until time begins to run out and a decision is made quickly with no plans to implement it.

As you might imagine, this haphazard procedure is unlikely to produce an adequate solution to a complicated problem, such as how to reduce the cost of health care or increase the literacy of the adult population of the United States. Vital elements of the problem may be neglected, innovative thinking is unlikely, and evaluation is not thorough. Organizing problem-solving discussions helps groups balance participation, improve reflectiveness, coordinate group members' thinking, and establish important ground rules for proceeding.[4] A systematic procedure is needed to solve complex problems effectively.

This chapter will help you understand the importance of *procedures* information in problem solving. We differentiate problem solving from decision making, analyze the major dimensions that problems have, and present two general but flexible models for efficient and effective group problem-solving discussions.

Problem Solving and Decision Making

Many writers use the terms *problem solving* and *decision making* synonymously, but we want you to distinguish clearly between them, for there is a major difference. **Decision making** refers to the act of *choosing* among options that already exist. **Problem solving** is a more comprehensive, multistep procedure through which a group develops a plan to move from an unsatisfactory state to a desired goal. Problem solving usually requires a group to make numerous decisions; it also involves *creating* or *discovering* alternatives, not just choosing among them. Thus, decision making is one part of problem solving. An example may clarify this difference. A task force in Springfield, Missouri, was charged with solving the problem of what to do with solid waste. The group needed to make a number of decisions in the course of identifying the city's various options and developing a plan for the handling of solid waste. In contrast, a committee charged with selecting from three possible sites the best location for a solid waste materials recovery facility is strictly a decision-making group. We discuss decision making in detail in Chapter 12.

> A meeting ought to solve a problem or move ahead.
>
> *P. T., Director, University Planning and Development*

Decision Making

Choosing from among a set of alternatives.

Problem Solving

A multistage procedure for moving from some unsatisfactory state to a more satisfactory one, and developing a plan for doing so.

Effective Problem Solving

The present chapter will show how you can make group problem solving effective. First, we define the concept of "problem" and the components common to all problems. Then we explain the conditions that must exist for group problem solving to be effective.

Problem

Problem

The discrepancy between what should be happening and what actually is happening.

A **problem** is a discrepancy between what actually *is* happening and what *should* be going on. All problems have three major components: an existing situation that is undesirable, a goal or desired state, and obstacles to reaching the goal, as shown in Figure 11.1. Understanding the general character of these three components is essential to planning problem-solving procedures.

1. **Undesirable present situation.**
   Unless someone is dissatisfied with the way things are, no problem exists; a problem, then, is in part a matter of human awareness and feelings. For example, imagine that a club to which you belong has gradually been losing members, but no one has felt anything was wrong. But at your next regular meeting the secretary points out that you do not have a quorum needed to conduct business. Someone else says your continued existence as an organization is threatened. *Now* you feel concerned that the situation is unsatisfactory. Recognition of this undesirable present situation is the beginning of a problem for you.

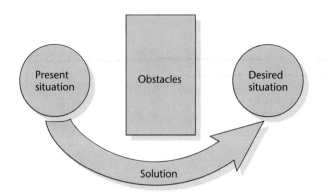

FIGURE 11.1
Components of a problem.

2. **Goal.**

The perception of an unsatisfactory situation usually suggests a **goal** (a desired situation), even if it's at first vague. In our example, you can already say that you want to increase your membership and attendance at meetings so your organization can survive. You might soon be able to state the goal precisely: "To increase membership by 50 percent and double attendance at meetings."

> Goal
>
> The desired outcome a group works to achieve.

The enjoyment that I get out of that is the fact that I helped them through that discussion and overcame the obstacles . . . to get some kind of end result.

M. I., Human Resource Manager, Manufacturing Company

3. **Obstacles.**

An **obstacle** is anything that interferes with reaching the goal. Lack of information, inadequate funds or equipment, and a lack of needed skills would be obstacles, as would anything that must be changed, removed, or overcome. In our example, one immediately obvious obstacle is the lack of information about why membership and attendance have been dropping.

> Obstacle
>
> Something that interferes or stands in the way of solving a problem.

Problem solving is the procedure undertaken to arrive at a solution, including both a plan for arriving at the goal and the actual execution of the plan. Then, if the solution does not achieve the goal, further problem solving will be needed.

Problem Characteristics

Obviously, a problem-solving plan must suit the specific characteristics of the actual problem. What are these characteristics? In his classic synthesis of group dynamics, Shaw described five characteristics of problems that small groups tackle: *task difficulty, solution multiplicity, intrinsic interest, cooperative requirements*, and *population familiarity*.[5] To these we add *acceptance requirements, technical requirements*, and the group's *area of freedom*. Only the most general steps in the problem-solving procedures will be the same for all problems.

Task Difficulty

Degree of problem complexity and effort required to solve a problem.

Task difficulty refers to the problem's complexity, hence the effort, knowledge, and skill needed to achieve the goal. Groups generally are asked to tackle complex problems, those for which a number of different perspectives must be considered, not simply to choose among equivalent alternatives. For instance, consider recent government task forces assigned to recommend improvements in the American health care system, reduction of the budget deficit, or improvement of learning levels of high school graduates—problems beyond the capacity of any single person. Solving these problems is more complex than recommending an acceptable theme for a junior–senior prom.

Solution Multiplicity

Extent to which there are many different possible alternatives for solving a particular problem.

Solution multiplicity refers to the number of conceivable or feasible alternatives for solving the problem. To illustrate, there are usually only a few useful ways to get from your residence to your classroom, but there are innumerable ways to decorate your living room. Structured procedures like *brainstorming* have long been available to help us think of more possible alternatives when solution multiplicity is even moderately high.[6]

Intrinsic Interest

Extent to which the task itself is attractive and interesting to the participants.

Intrinsic interest was defined by Shaw as "the degree to which the task in and of itself is interesting, motivating, and attractive to the group members,"[7] reminding us of Larson and LaFasto's finding that outstanding teams had clear, elevating goals. Berkowitz found that, when group members were highly interested in their task, they preferred sharing in control of the group's procedures, but they preferred strong procedural control by a discussion leader when interest was low.[8] Our experience verifies this finding: if interest is high, members at first want to express opinions and feelings and will resist strict procedural control. After they have vented their feelings, procedural control of the problem-solving procedure is more likely to be accepted.

Ideally, groups would discuss only intrinsically interesting problems. In actuality, people are assigned to committees that deal with a variety of problems, some of little interest to them. If this is the case, members should discuss it openly and either change their attitudes or request that some other group tackle the problem.

Cooperative Requirements

The degree to which members must coordinate their efforts for a group to complete its task successfully.

The phrase **cooperative requirements** means the degree to which coordinated efforts are essential to satisfactory completion of a task. Increased complexity requires members to talk to each other, share information, and cooperate, in short, to be competent communicators.

Population Familiarity

The degree to which members of a group are familiar with the nature of a problem and experienced in solving similar problems.

The **population familiarity** dimension is the level of members' knowledge about and previous experience with the task. It is no surprise that groups with experienced members tend to perform better than groups with inexperienced ones.[9] When population familiarity is low to start, the problem-solving procedure should concentrate on analysis of the problem. But sometimes very knowledgeable people become smug and unwilling to think of new approaches. Then procedures to increase innovation may be essential.

The **acceptance requirements** dimension refers to the extent to which a proposed solution must be acceptable to people whom it will affect. Legislation enacted to solve public problems has often backfired when acceptance requirements were overlooked. A task force recently created a planning and zoning ordinance for a county near where Jack, one of the authors, lives, but citizen groups, although acknowledging a need for some such law, refused to accept it. The United States has experienced epic struggles over laws controlling alcohol, marijuana, and driving. Sometimes a group must give heavy consideration to the acceptability of a solution, other times little or none.

The **technical requirements** characteristic of a solution refers to whether it must be technically feasible or match some standard of technical excellence. For instance, U.S. automakers have had to rethink their procedures for quality control of their products, and some have done so with great success. The Food and Drug Administration has technical standards of both safety and effectiveness that all proposed new drugs must pass.

A group's **area of freedom** refers to the amount of authority given the group, which is either implied or stated in a *charge* to a group. A **charge** is an assignment given to a subordinate group by a parent organization or person with authority to do so. A charge specifies what a group is to do, including an area of freedom that defines the extent and limits of the group's authority. Group members need to be clear about and accept both the charge and the area of freedom. For example, an advertising team charged with creating an ad campaign for a sports car and with recommending the television stations for the advertising spots is exceeding its area of freedom if it actually purchases the spots without permission.

Considering each of the problem characteristics just described will help you determine the appropriate procedure for solving a problem. Discussing all these variables should be done by members very early, especially if the problem is a complex one requiring numerous meetings, so that an appropriate plan or outline can be devised that takes all aspects of the problem into account. The plan will then include research inputs needed, the discussion process for the group, and implementation of the final result, as suggested by Figure 11.2.

Organizing Problem-Solving Discussions

Procedures and communication for group problem solving have been investigated by social scientists in many fields, especially during the last half of the 20th century. From their findings we present a group of guiding principles for any discussion of complex problems by small groups, a general procedural format that can be adapted to virtually any problem, and an alternative procedure that allows a group preferring a looser structure to generate its own unique procedure without serious danger of lapses in critical thinking.

Acceptance Requirements

The degree to which the solution for a given problem must be accepted by the people it will affect.

Technical Requirements

The degree to which the solution for a given problem is technically feasible or must meet standards of technical excellence.

Area of Freedom

The scope of authority and responsibility of a group, including limits on the group's authority.

Charge

The assignment or goal given to a group, usually by a parent organization or administrator.

FIGURE 11.2
How problem
characteristics affect
the procedure for
group problem
solving.

Problem Characteristic	Adaptation of Problem-Solving Procedure
1. Intrinsic interest is high.	A period of ventilation before systematic problem solving.
2. Task difficulty is high.	Detailed problem mapping; many subquestions.
3. Solution multiplicity is high.	Brainstorming.
4. Cooperative requirements are high.	A criterion step, creating and ranking explicit criteria.
5. High level of acceptance is required.	Focus on concern of people affected when evaluating options.
6. High level of technical quality is required.	Focus on evaluating ideas, critical thinking; perhaps invite outside experts to address group.
7. Population familiarity is high.	Focus on criteria and creation of multiple options.
8. Need only one or a few stages of the problem-solving process.	Shorten procedure to only steps required.

You're there to help them make the best use of their thought processes, not to give them and espouse what you think.

N. T., Senior Communication Associate,
State Social Service Agency

Vigilant Interaction Theory

Vigilant Interaction
Theory

The theory that
suggests effective
group decision
making depends on
group members
careful analysis of all
aspects of the
problem and
thorough
assessment of pros
and cons of all
alternatives.

Vigilant Interaction Theory (also called *Functional Theory*) states that the quality of a group's performance depends directly on the quality of the group's interaction.[10] If members are thorough and careful (i.e., vigilant) in how they think and talk about the problem, then the outcome is likely to be of higher quality than if they are not. Based on earlier work by Gouran that linked critical thinking and communication to high-quality inferences,[11] Vigilant Interaction Theory suggests a group address four general issues before making the final decision about how to solve a problem. These four issues are the core of Vigilant Interaction Theory:

1. Is there something about the current state of affairs that requires improvement or change?

2. What do we want to achieve or accomplish in deciding what to do about the problem?

3. What are the choices available to us?

4. What are the positive and negative aspects of those choices?[12]

These four issues are also the heart of the general Procedural Model (P-MOPS) we present in the next section of this chapter. Productive groups usually take up these issues in a more or less organized sequence, though the sequences may vary from discussion to discussion.[13] The single biggest error by groups that reach faulty solutions is *omission* of one or more of these steps, or failure to be thorough in discussing them. Both laboratory studies of group problem solving using college students and a field study of committees in a large utility company support Vigilant Interaction Theory. The study of the committees in the utility corporation found empirical support for the hypotheses relating all four major steps in vigilant problem-solving interaction to the quality of the groups' final recommendations for improving the health of employees.[14] In a study of a Midwestern manufacturing firm, Propp and Nelson discovered continued support for the importance of groups addressing these four issues.[15] They found that the most consistent predictor of group performance was vigilant attention to assessing the nature of the problem or task facing the group. In addition they found that this particular group addressed a fifth issue: *What procedures should we use to address how we want to solve our problem?* The effective handling of this concern appears to be most important when a group faces several different, difficult decisions. Vigilant Interaction Theory, because it focuses on how competent *communication* is related to the quality of group decisions and solutions, continues to be a fruitful area for future research.[16]

In summarizing research on the relationship between the quality of group interaction during problem-solving discussion and the quality of the final solutions reached, Hirokawa said:

> It should be clear at this point that effective group decision-making usually does not happen by accident. In most cases, a group is able to make a high-quality choice because the system of reasoning that it employed in arriving at a final choice was characterized by: (1) proper understanding of the problematic situation, (2) appropriate choice-making objectives, (3) accurate evaluation of the positive and negative qualities of available choices, and (4) warranted utilization of high-quality information in arriving at a final decision. [17]

Even when groups have the needed resources of valid information and member thinking skills, they may still do poorly if knowledgeable members lack persuasive skills (communicative competence) or hold back on information and arguments because of personal likes and dislikes of other members. Communicative competence and focus on the group task are essential to high-quality outcomes. Focus on both the task and vigilant interaction can be facilitated by effective discussion structure.

The Need for Structure

Using some systematic procedure for problem solving is generally a good idea, as we have argued. Some people tend to be **intuitive problem solvers** who size up a situation, then arrive at a solution without consciously following any

Intuitive Problem Solvers

People who size up a situation, then arrive at a solution without consciously following any perceptible procedure.

perceptible procedure. They jump to a solution instinctively, often with an "Ah-ha!" reaction. We all experience intuition, and intuitive insights can be valuable. For example, a scientist struggling with a problem may have a sudden insight that points to the solution or a feeling about the way to proceed. However, as valuable as intuition is, we should not rely on it alone to solve problems. Those scientists who experience intuitive flashes still must test and critically evaluate those insights to determine whether they will work or to refine them so they can be used. So it is with groups; using intuitive solutions is fine—so long as group members have thoroughly evaluated those solutions before adopting them.

Systematic Problem Solvers

Organized problem solvers who follow a definite series of steps or sequence, such as those provided by P-MOPS.

Systematic problem solvers, on the other hand, think their way through a set of logical steps, a structure of problem solving like the Vigilant Interaction issues investigated by Hirokawa. There are many different types of structured processes groups can use, and many are based on philosopher John Dewey's *reflective thinking* model of how individuals make decisions. Some versions of this are sometimes given the title *standard agendas*. All are designed to help groups organize their problem solving so that no important steps are neglected.

> We do not veer from the agenda. If you have something that is not on the agenda, we're going to put it in the parking lot.
>
> *D. W., Executive Director, Volunteer Organization*

Some of the advantages of structuring group problem solving have been presented earlier in this chapter. There are others. For instance, Scheidel and Crowell found that uninstructed groups tended to spiral considerably from discussing problem issues to problem solutions, a sequence called "reach-testing."[18] Observers rate the quality of such discussions lower than discussions organized with the structure of reflective thinking or Vigilant Interaction.[19] Even low task-oriented participants rate structured discussions higher than those in which the designated leader fails to help organize the problem-solving procedure.[20] In a study by Brilhart, participants following a highly structured problem-solving procedure made a greater proportion of statements relevant to the issue of problem solving than when the leader did not clearly guide the group through such a structure.[21] Poole concluded that following a structured procedure often provides logical priorities and reminds discussants of something they forgot to do (such as analyze the problem thoroughly) in an earlier stage of problem solving.[22] So long as the logical priorities are incorporated into a sequence (e.g., problem analysis before proposing solutions), no one structure appears consistently to surpass others. In a study by Brilhart and Jochem, the quality of final decisions reached by groups following three different problem-solving structural outlines was not significantly different (though a significant proportion of the participants preferred one of these structures).[23] That no one structure produced superior final decisions was confirmed in experiments reported by Bayless and Larson, but Larson did find that using *no* structural pattern for problem solving produced definitely inferior solutions.[24]

Some theorists have argued that following a systematic linear procedure is not normal for small groups; however, the groups they observed had not been trained either in problem solving or in group procedures. Trainers in business and industry invariably have recommended teaching corporate personnel such procedures as a necessity before instituting participative management techniques such as quality circles or self-managed work teams. In a recent article, three researchers associated with a corporation in which numerous scientists conduct research and development in small teams argued forcefully for a highly systematic, structured format of problem solving by trained scientists to prevent the kinds of mistakes often attributed to "random error." These writers say that the epitome of discovery is to "methodically gather and analyze all the available data about an observable phenomenon. Contrary to what many are teaching, systematic problem solving is *not* a rigid set of specific techniques or a single prescribed discussion format. . . . [but] a matter of effective group *communication* and data *handling*."[25] The high degree of structuring helps keep the attention of the group focused by using pointed questions to which specific answers are sought, though the group may need to start discussion less rigidly. In fact, group participants themselves seem to want methods and procedures to help groups function more effectively, according to Broome and Fulbright.[26] They found that experienced group participants who were more representative in terms of age and professional status than typical college students identified methodological deficiencies as significant barriers to effective group problem solving. These participants wanted tested procedures to help them deal with complex problems more productively.

> That whole first kick-off meeting, you have to have it all organized and structured for them. And once they know what is going to happen, they breathe a sigh of relief and then they start figuring out how they're going to do it.
>
> *J. M., Executive Coach and President, Marketing Agency*

Recent research by Hirokawa supports the importance of using systematic procedures. In one study, the groups with the highest-quality decisions used a vigilant decision-making procedure and engaged in second guessing, or retrospective questioning of previous choices.[27] In another study, Hirokawa found that it was not so much the particular procedure groups used that determined the quality, but whether certain important functions were performed.[28] That is, for effective group problem solving, groups must thoroughly and accurately understand the problem, must have a variety of acceptable alternatives, and must evaluate each alternative carefully, especially assessing the negative consequences that might result from each alternative. Groups that do this, regardless of the particular decision-making technique used, perform better than those that don't. However, consistent with Larson's findings, using *any* procedure is more effective than using none because systematic procedures help ensure that the critical functions are attended to.

Hirokawa found that differences in decision quality are linked directly to how well groups satisfy these and other decision functions such as understanding the requirements for an acceptable choice.[29] He also found that assessment of positive and negative qualities is important at different stages of a group's deliberation. For instance, effective groups first seem to spot the serious defects when they initially screen alternatives. Once they find an alternative that appears to be free of fatal flaws, they switch strategies and begin to detail the positive aspects of the alternative. Moreover, research that tests functional theory in natural settings has shown that groups may adapt differently to the decision functions.[30] For instance, the establishment of criteria may not be as explicitly obvious in the group discussion between members who have worked together for awhile. Over time their criteria for the best solutions get established early on and are used again in future problem-solving discussions. Thus, Hirokawa argues that "instruction needs to move away from discussion procedures and formats (e.g., 'standard agendas') and more toward the effects or consequences of those procedures and formats" in a variety of groups facing a multitude of different kinds of problems.[31]

Hirokawa views group problem solving as a complex interplay among a variety of individual-level and group-level variables that include members' cognitive and psychological characteristics, their personal motives and communication skills, decision rules under which the group operates, the relationships among the members, and the communication patterns of the group.[32]

Included in these considerations is the impact of culture on individual problem-solving preferences. We all have the cognitive components necessary for problem solving, but those components get used differently across cultures. Our dominant culture teaches and trains us to use a variety of problem-solving modes that have been alluded to in this section on structure. Culture helps shape how we process information from the environment, classify it into relevant categories, and the *logic* or approach we take to using the information to solve problems.[33]

We discussed low-context/individualistic cultures in contrast to high-context/collectivist cultures in Chapter 5. The low-context/individualistic cultures like the United States and Britain tend to shape a preference for more impulsive decision making, lower tolerance for ambiguity and *field independent* logic for problem solving. Field independence values isolating the details, looking for causes and effects, downplaying the emotional aspect of the problem, and using either/or thinking. In contrast, in high-context/collectivist cultures such as Hispanic cultures and Japan, there is a demonstrated preference for attending to all the factors involved in the problem, or *field dependence*, thinking long and hard about those factors so a correct decision can be made, and greater tolerance for ambiguity. To make a guess about how to solve a problem is to admit one did not take the time to think about it.[34] In North America, for example, decisions made by an individual or majority vote are more acceptable than they are in Japan. The Japanese value consensus after lengthy consideration of a problem. In North America decisions are made quicker than in Japan but implemented more slowly, whereas in Japan, after lengthy problem solving, solutions are implemented quickly.[35]

Consider This 11.2

In 1999, Japan experienced its worst nuclear emergency. This crisis was noteworthy not just because of the lives lost and people harmed from radiation exposure, but also because critics noted how slow the Japanese government was to act. Critics pointed out that the Japanese mode of problem solving values long deliberation and consensus building as opposed to quick and decisive decisions by an expert; this contributed to the slow response.[36] For what types of decisions do you think quick decision making should be used? For what types of decisions should decision making be slow and deliberate?

Recognizing the multitude of individual-level and group-level variables that can come into play when a group attempts to solve a problem can feel overwhelming and make the process seem daunting. However, the question remains whether individuals who rate low in critical thinking tests and low in preference for procedural order can be taught to accept and follow different systematic problem-solving procedures and use them to their advantage. The evidence indicates they can. Further, none of us appears to be purely intuitive or systematic as problem solvers; in terms of a currently popular theory, we have *both* left and right brain hemispheres that can function in problem solving. How much of our approach to problem solving is genetically determined and how much is learned from parents, teachers, and colleagues is open to question. But Nisbett and Ross successfully taught subjects to replace simplistic intuitive strategies (which led to many errors in problem solving) with formal structural and statistical procedures used by scientists.[37] Sternberg demonstrated that impulsive people, who did poorly in solving problems on IQ tests, could be taught to proceed more systematically and successfully.[38]

Discussing Criteria

Systematic problem-solving procedures help groups clarify *criteria* for an effective solution. **Criteria** are the standards against which available options must be judged, and group members must agree on criteria before a solution is adopted. Theorists have long argued about whether and when a problem-solving discussion should include a step during which the group talks about, proposes, and decides on specific explicit criteria. Some textbooks have argued that reflective thinking requires deciding on criteria as part of the problem analysis, or at least before talking about solutions. Other theorists have argued that criteria should be discussed explicitly, but only after having accumulated all the possible solutions first. Still others say little about criteria. Evidence provides no simple, single answer to the questions of whether and

Criteria
Standards for judging among alternatives; may be absolute (must) or relative.

when to discuss criteria during group problem solving. In the first study to address this question, Brilhart and Jochem found that the quality of final decisions was not affected by *when* criteria were discussed or by whether discussion of criteria was a separate step in the problem-solving outline the group used. However, significantly more of the participants preferred to discuss criteria *after* brainstorming rather than discussing them before brainstorming or not explicitly discussing them at all.[39]

Both Poole and Hirokawa have suggested that the actual sequence may not matter so much as the intellectual content of problem discussion (i.e., Vigilant Interaction Theory). Criteria may not need to be discussed explicitly if they are well known. Hirokawa et al. explored the importance of *evaluation clarity* in applying criteria. Evaluation clarity is high when criteria are clearly presented to the group as part of the charge or the presentation of the problem and are understood by all members. Evaluation clarity is low when standards are not presented to the group, are fuzzy, or are not understood alike by all members. In their experiment, Hirokawa et al. asked students to select one of several alternative punishments for a student guilty of plagiarism. Some groups were given explicit criteria; others were not told on what basis to evaluate the possible punishments. These authors concluded, "when evaluation clarity is high, group decision performance is only weakly related to the establishment and utilization of evaluation criteria. However, when evaluation clarity is low, group decision performance is strongly correlated with a group's efforts to establish and utilize appropriate evaluation criteria."[40]

The previous studies suggest that when criteria are already well known and shared in advance of a group's problem-solving discussion, it is not necessary to discuss them. However, when there is no advance convergence among members on criteria for an effective solution (i.e., evaluation clarity is low), explicit discussion about criteria will probably improve solution quality. We think that it is a real leadership service to determine whether criteria are explicitly understood and agreed upon and, if not, to get the group to state criteria as clearly as possible before extensively evaluating alternatives. Further, if the problem is high in solution multiplicity, we recommend delaying discussion of criteria until *after* listing possible solutions. When options are few or technical demands are high, it may be wise to discuss criteria as part of the problem analysis unless they have been presented unequivocally as part of the charge or problem statement to the group.

Consider This 11.3

Do you think the criteria for Tyrell's care (in our opening story) are likely to have been clear to all the medical professionals collaborating on his care? Is it likely that each professional might have perceived the problem differently? If you had been the doctor in charge of the meeting, what could you have done to clarify criteria and make sure the medical professionals were using the same criteria? Is it likely that Tyrell's wife or his minister would use the same criteria?

The research reported and analyzed earlier suggests that systematic procedures can help groups use members' critical thinking skills and knowledge to advantage, thus arriving at better solutions to complex problems. We are now ready to consider a structural model that helps members incorporate Vigilant Interaction Theory into their problem-solving discussion.

P-MOPS: A General Procedural Model of Problem Solving for Structuring Problem-Solving Discussions

As we have repeatedly pointed out, the effectiveness of a specific problem-solving procedure is affected by contingencies of problem characteristics, member experiences, member traits and preferences, corporate culture, and so forth. Effective problem solving requires that such key issues be dealt with thoroughly. Trying to find a way to offset the human tendency to be guided by internal states more than by what others say and do in problem-solving discussions has led us to the development of a general **Procedural Model of Problem Solving (P-MOPS).**

The acronym P-MOPS has a double purpose: It helps us remember the full name of the model, and in punlike fashion indicates that the purpose of the model is to help groups "mop up" all the details or logical necessities for high-quality problem solving. We say that this is a *general* procedural model because, although it provides a systematic structure based on both scientific method and Vigilant Interaction Theory, it can be adjusted to all the contingencies faced by groups solving all kinds of problems.

The following are the major basic steps in P-MOPS:

I. Problem description and analysis: *What is the nature of the problem facing the group?*

II. Generation and elaboration of possible solutions: *What might be done to solve the problem we've described?*

III. Evaluation of possible solutions: *What are the probable benefits and possible negative consequences of each proposed solution?*

IV. Consensus decision: *What seems to be the best possible solution we can all support?*

V. Implementation of the solution chosen: *How will we put our decision into effect?*

This model assumes that the leader, perhaps with the help of all members, has formulated a written outline containing specific questions about all sub-issues the group must consider to be sure that no important contingency will be overlooked. P-MOPS, then, is not a rigid recipe or mathematical formula, but a guide that can be tailored to help you consider logically the vital issues involved in complex problem solving. After we present an explanation of each step in P-MOPS, we will show you two adaptations of the P-MOPS procedure and give you tips for its use.

Procedural Model of Problem Solving (P-MOPS)

An adaptable five-step general procedure, based on the scientific method, for structuring problem-solving discussions.

I. What is the nature of the problem facing us?

Early in the discussion the group needs to focus most talk on the details of what is unsatisfactory, what led to the undesirable situation, what is ultimately desired, and what the obstacles to that goal might be. First, if the group has been given a charge, members need to be sure they understand and agree on their charge. For instance, instructors frequently assign group projects in small group communication courses. That assignment is a charge. If you have such an assignment, make sure all members of your project group understand the charge as intended by the instructor. Second, be sure you are clear about the form your output is to take: a panel discussion presented to the class? a video or film presentation? a written recommendation designed to solve a campus or local problem? Can you explain how you will be graded: as a group, as individuals, or by some combination of both? Will each member be required to write a case study analyzing your group? If so, what format must the paper follow? Will you need to keep a journal of group activities, or some other record?

Important principles for guiding the investigation and discussion of the nature of your problem/goal include:

A. Focus on the problem before thinking about how to solve it. What would you think if you drove your rough-running car into a garage and the service manager immediately said, "You need new valves in your engine," without so much as looking under the hood? Most of us would drive away as quickly as possible. A competent technician, after questioning you about how the car was acting, might attach an engine analysis computer before making a tentative diagnosis. Just so, one of the most common failings in group problem solving is getting solution-centered before thoroughly diagnosing the problem. Writers concerned with business groups have noted this tendency and the potential harm it can cause.[41] Time spent in this step often saves headaches later, whereas fudging on problem analysis leads to such outcomes as unnecessary conflict, wasted time, and solutions that don't work.

B. State the problem in the form of a single, unambiguous *problem question*, not a *solution question*. **Problem questions** focus on the undesired state of affairs and the goal, whereas **solution questions** suggest a solution, a means of arriving at the goal, and thus tend to short-circuit the thinking of discussants to that one solution. Examples of both types of questions can be seen in Figure 11.3.

C. Map the problem thoroughly. Think of the problem as an uncharted area with only vague boundaries. To map the problem, the group must gather key information about the problem such as *who, what, why, when, how long, where, how, how serious, what limitations*, and *what feelings*. Participants must *share* all they know about the situation: facts, complaints, conditions, circumstances, factors, happenings, relationships, effects, and so forth. They may discover that they need to

---

Problem Question

A question that does not suggest any particular type of solution in the question itself.

Solution Question

A question in which the solution to a problem is suggested or implied by the question itself.

FIGURE 11.3
Solution versus
problem questions.

Solution Questions	Problem Questions
How can I transfer a man who is popular in his work group but slows down the work of other employees in the group?	How can I increase the work output of the group?
How can we increase the publicity for our club's activities so attendance will be increased?	What can we do to increase attendance at our club's activities?

FIGURE 11.4
Maps of a problem
before and after
discussion.

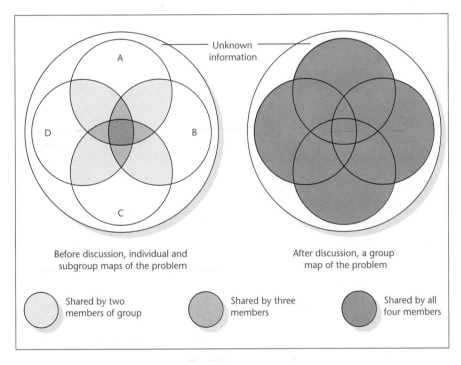

Before discussion, individual and subgroup maps of the problem

After discussion, a group map of the problem

Shared by two members of group

Shared by three members

Shared by all four members

learn a lot more before proceeding with a plan of action, so then they must answer such questions as, "How will we get the information we need?" and "Who will look up what?"

Figure 11.4 illustrates the mapping of the problem, before and after information is gathered, shared, and interpreted. The large circle represents all that could be known and understood about the problem. Each of the members—A, B, C, and D—comes to the initial meeting with some information and opinions about it, a unique personal map represented by the four inner circles. Some information is shared by two members, some by three, and a small amount by all four. And some

FIGURE 11.5
Absolute versus
relative criteria to
guide plans for a
club's annual picnic.

Absolute (*Must* Be Met)	Relative (*Should* Be Met)
Entertainment must not cost over $400.	Location should be convenient, that is, within 30 minutes' driving time for all members.
Must be enjoyable to members and their families. (*Enjoyable* means: provide a variety of activities designed to appeal to people ranging in age from 3 to 80.)	Facilities should be comfortable, for example, shelter in case of rain, electrical outlets, hot and cold running water, restroom facilities and so on.

useful information is not yet known to *any* member. Once the members have discussed the problem freely and shared all the information they have, the group map looks like the second large circle, much closer to the "real" problem.

One of the greatest obstacles to such problem-centered thinking is a member (especially if this is a designated leader) who comes to the group with the problem already solved in his or her own mind. The presenter of a problem must set preconceived solutions aside; mutual influence is a hallmark of teamwork in group problem solving.

D. Be sure the group members agree on criteria, as we discussed earlier. In addition to establishing standards that the group must use to judge solutions, criteria also express the values shared by group members. Two people with different values will use different criteria to evaluate options, and therefore can arrive at very different solutions.[42] Recall the Rubenstein study (see Chapter 5) of Arab and American students who were asked whom they would save; *all* Arabs chose the mother, but *none* of the Americans did. In this case, Arab and American values supported widely divergent criteria for evaluating the decision (i.e., whom to save). Unless agreement exists about criteria, consensus on a solution is unlikely.

Criteria must be ranked or prioritized. Be sure to give highest priority to criteria that *must* be met. Ideas can then be rejected if they do not meet *absolute* criteria, and those that remain can be ranked on how well they meet *relative* criteria (see Figure 11.5). Moreover, criteria should be stated as quantitatively as possible; criteria like "efficient" are too abstract to be measurable, but may help a group arrive at standards of "efficiency" that can be measured.

E. Be sure all members understand the group's area of freedom alike. Any policy solution must be evaluated from the standpoint of the charge.

During the first step of the P-MOPS model, an outlined series of questions can guide the group's description and analysis of a complex problem. The questions in Figure 11.6 are suggestive; such questions must be tailored to the specific problem and asked in the explicit language of that problem. Everyone

What does this problem question mean to us?
What is our charge and area of freedom?
What is unsatisfactory at present?
  Who (or what) is affected?
  When, where, and how?
  How serious do we judge the problem to be?
  How long has the problem existed?
  Do we need to gather any additional information to assess the nature and
    extent of the problem adequately?
What conditions have contributed to the problem?
  What appear to be causative conditions?
  What precipitated the crisis leading to our discussion?
What exactly do we hope to accomplish (the goal, desired situation)?
  What obstacles to achieving the desired goal exist?
What information do we need before we can find a satisfactory solution?
  What additional subquestions must we answer?
  How might we find answers to these subquestions?
  What are the answers to these subquestions?
How can we summarize our understanding of the problem to include the present
  and desired situation and causal conditions?

FIGURE 11.6
Questions to guide
problem analysis.

should be encouraged to ask any and every question he or she thinks needs an answer before planning a strategy to overcome all obstacles between the group and its goal.

II. What might be done to solve the problem?

If you try panning for gold in an Ohio stream, you probably won't make any money. You *might* succeed in finding gold in a stream in Arizona, Colorado, or California. As this analogy suggests, if there are no good ideas in the list being considered by a group, the solution recommended or adopted will fail to achieve the goal or may even make the situation worse. It is crucial in step II that a group have as many ideas as it can find and invent so it can choose the best or, if necessary, redefine the goal and problem. Also, you would not want to have nuggets wash out of your gold pan or lose track of a briefly mentioned idea that could turn out to be part of the best solution to a complex problem. Good technique prevents losing nuggets; *writing down each idea proposed as a solution* (preferably where everyone can see it and not forget it) will prevent losing ideas. A couple of principles can improve the group's success at finding and inventing solutions:

A. Defer judgment during discussion while collecting and inventing proposals. This is the heart of the technique called "brainstorming" presented in Chapter 14. Judgment stifles creative thinking and increases apprehension about others' responses to ideas. When solution multiplicity is low, or when thorough exploration of the problem leads to a sudden insight into a solution, group members should still make an effort to think of other possible solutions, perhaps by asking "What else *might* we do?" If nothing else is uncovered, the solution should still be evaluated thoroughly against all available criteria, and especially for possible negative consequences. The proposed solution may be refined and improved considerably through such critical thinking/discussion.

B. Often during this part of the problem-solving procedure, a participant will think of some detail of the problem that ought to be explored more fully, a sort of "Let's examine that rock again—it might have gold in it." The group will then need to cycle back to further mapping of the problem, and *should* do so instead of doggedly pursuing still further solutions at the moment just for the sake of following procedure. The group can pick up where it left off after it has backtracked to investigate and clarify the problem further, and will be better informed for making an intelligent choice among solutions. Such second-guessing is characteristic of effective problem-solving groups.[43]

Consider This 11.4

Using the first two steps of the P-MOPS procedure, how would you analyze Tyrell's problem in our opening case? What are the possible options the team might consider for dealing with the problem? Can you see the connection between how you define the problem and how you think about handling it?

III. What are the probable benefits and possible negative consequences of each proposed solution?

Once the problem has been thoroughly analyzed, with alternatives accumulated and criteria clearly understood by all members, the group is ready to evaluate the alternatives. For group problem solving to work optimally, pros and cons of each solution must be explored. Members must all have achieved convergence on explicit criteria if evaluation clarity is to occur. If not done previously, the first substep in this stage of group problem solving is to establish criteria. Every member must feel free to express opinions openly and honestly, without being attacked personally or attacking anyone else, for the group to achieve the best possible outcome.

Norms that promote critical examination of issues are desirable:

A. Evaluation should be viewed as a cooperative venture, a team effort to prevent mistakes.

B. Feelings, ideas, opinions, and even hunches should be shared openly and evaluated without any reflection on the person who expresses them. Anonymous computer messages may be a way to support this norm in groups experiencing power struggles.

C. Members should insist on exploring assumptions and implications of every idea, especially the potential negative consequences. Ideally, the person who proposed an idea will *invite* such critical evaluation.

D. Personal attacks and *ad hominem* remarks are unacceptable as substitutes for evidence and argument. Sensitivity to others' feelings and insensitivity to criticism of one's own ideas are called for. Ascribed status differences based on corporate positions, wealth, education, race, or any criterion other than relevant knowledge should play no part in evaluation discussion.

E. Members should often paraphrase what they think are the positions, feelings, and values of those with whom they disagree, always in a mood of inquiry—"Am I right about what you have just said?"

F. New issues should be raised or a challenge offered to an idea only when there is enough time to discuss the question thoroughly, not just before time to adjourn. If this happens, schedule another meeting to delay the final decision.

G. Trickery, bargaining, manipulation, deception, pressure to concur, and other breaches of communicative ethics are unacceptable. If noticed by any member, such unethical conduct should be pointed out at once and rebuked.

> I want to come away with the number one, the best solution possible to that issue or problem, and. . . . I get excited when that solution is so far off of what anyone expected.
>
> *M. I., Human Resource Manager, Manufacturing Company*

IV. What is the best possible solution we can all support?

If a decision seems to have emerged during evaluation of alternatives, the discussion leader should test for consensus. If everyone now agrees with one solution, the group is ready for the final stage of a complete problem-solving cycle. If two or more alternatives are still under consideration, the group should discuss such consensus-building questions as:

- Which solution seems most likely to be accepted and supported by all persons affected by it?

- Is there some compromise solution we can all accept as being likely to achieve our objectives without creating new problems?

- Could we combine parts of our remaining ideas to create a solution we can all accept?

Once the group has decided which solution to recommend or adopt, the stage has been set for the final phase of this problem-solving discussion: implementation.

> I think part of a team leader, the last step, is bringing the group to some sort of action, and then implementation.
>
> *L. H., Director, State-Level Strategic Planning*

V. What will we do to put our solution into effect?

Unfortunately, many groups arrive at policy decisions or solutions with no plans for putting them into effect. For example, a committee charged with making a recommendation to a parent organization needs to decide who will make the report, in what form, and with what support from the entire group, and perhaps plan a campaign to prepare the general membership to accept the suggestion. A construction crew may need to acquire raw materials and schedule construction time. Competent leaders see that a group has worked out all necessary details of implementation, or that doing so has been assigned to someone. At this point the group should decide on answers to such questions as:

- Who will do what, when, and how?

- Do we need any follow-up evaluation of how well our solution is working? If so, how will we do that?

PERT, described in Chapter 14, is a helpful procedure for planning implementation of a multistep solution.

You can see that the general Procedural Model of Problem Solving is flexible by design and can be adapted to fit almost any problem. In many cases the charge to a group will involve only some phases of the total problem-solving procedure: The group is to recommend several options, but not choose one; the group is to prepare an extensive investigation and analysis of the problem, but make no recommendations; the group is to implement a policy previously decided by another group. In such instances, only the relevant stage of P-MOPS would be used.

> The obligation of the chair or leader is to fill in the blanks between point A and point Z.
>
> *T. T., President, Health Care Policy Institute*

However you tailor P-MOPS to fit your problem, help group members remember the P-MOPS issues by putting the P-MOPS outline in plain view of all members (through a visual display or a handout) and charting the group's progress. For instance, as members complete their description and analysis of the problem, their findings can be posted on newsprint, wallboards, or on a computer display. This helps keep members focused on the *group* goal instead of diverting to personal agenda or social items. In one study on an early version of P-MOPS, students preferred to have the procedure in front of them on a chart rather than just having the leader explain the procedure or announce each new question or step as the group came to it.[44] Kelly and associates insist that the progression of a discussion be made visual to a group, perhaps with flipcharts, as it moves through steps.[45] In a recent article about how computers can be used to help groups solve complex problems, Broome and Chen note that two of the best uses of computer technology are for displaying ideas graphically and recording them as the group proceeds.[46] Whatever procedural outline you use, P-MOPS or something else, we recommend visual display of the steps in the procedure and of the group's progress.

We have made the point several times that providing some structure to decision making generally improves decision-making quality. However, rigidly adhering to any system or structure can be counterproductive, so whatever structure or procedure you use, be careful not to use it in such a lock-step way that you harm the decision-making process. Pacanowsky notes that certain kinds of complex problems, called "wicked" problems, are particularly difficult to solve using overly structured procedures.[47] Wicked problems are those with no known format for finding a solution. The group may be at the point of generating solutions when someone realizes that the problem has been defined wrongly and suggests recycling to an earlier step in the problem-solving process. Your procedures, whatever they are, should be flexible enough to allow for this, especially for complex problems.

The following two figures show you how P-MOPS can be tailored to address complex or simple problems. Examples of two leaders' outlines modifying P-MOPS are presented in Figures 11.7 and 11.8. In Figure 11.7, the outline deals with all the complexities of parking on an urban campus.[48] From the outline, you can see how major criteria were arrived at and used to evaluate proposals. Figure 11.8 is a leader's simple outline for structuring discussion of a problem for which few solutions were possible and discussion time was limited.

The Single Question Format: A Less Highly Structured Format

> You don't know sometimes what's going to come at you. The winds are going to change. And so you adjust, but you still know where you're going to go.
>
> *L. H., Director, State-Level Strategic Planning*

In the event a group chooses not to use some adaptation of P-MOPS, perhaps because members are low in preference for procedural order, it is still essential for discussion to be vigilant to be sure of arriving at the best solution possible. As designated leader, you could ask the group to apply a procedure created by Larson, which was based on a series of studies by another researcher of how successful problem solvers reasoned.[49] When using this **Single Question format,** early in the discussion the group must decide on the issues that need to be dealt with, how to answer these questions, and then proceed to do so. The list of questions provides structure to the discussion

Single Question Format

A special procedure for structuring problem-solving discussions that is more suitable for members low in preference for procedural order than more highly structured linear procedures.

FIGURE 11.7
Leader's procedural outline for improving parking on a college campus.

PROBLEM QUESTION: What should be done to improve student parking at Southwest Missouri State University?

I. What is the nature of the problem students encounter with parking at SMSU?
   A. What is the scope of our concern with student parking?
      1. Do any terms in the question need to be clarified?
      2. What authority do we have?
      3. Do we need to determine the authority and duties of departments involved with campus parking?
   B. What is now unsatisfactory about student parking?
      1. What have we found to be unsatisfactory?
         a. Have any studies been done?
         b. What complaints have students been making?
      2. Does any other information exist about student parking that we need to consider?
   C. What goals does the committee hope to achieve by changes in parking that we need to consider?
   D. What obstacles may stand in the way of improving parking for students?
      1. What do we know about what is causing the problem(s) we've described?
      2. How much interest do involved persons have in this problem?
      3. What limits are there on resources that might be needed?
         a. Funds?
         b. Space?
         c. Personnel?
         d. Other?
      4. Are there any other obstacles to changing student parking?
   E. How shall we summarize the problem(s) with student parking at SMSU?
      1. Do we all perceive the problem the same?
      2. Should we subdivide the problem?
         a. If so, what are the major subproblems?
         b. In what order shall we take them up?
II. What solutions to the student parking problem(s) we've described are possible?
III. What are the relative advantages and disadvantages of each proposed solution?
   A. Do we need to further clarify our criteria?
   B. What are the advantages and disadvantages of each proposal?
      1. Might any have unacceptable negative consequences?
      2. How effective might each be?
      3. How well does each meet our other criteria?
IV. What do we agree to recommend to the proper authorities as a solution to the student parking problem?
V. How will we make our recommendations for improving student parking?
   A. To whom will our recommendations be given?
   B. In what format will we make them?
      1. Written?
      2. In person?
      3. Other, or a combination?
   C. Do we need to plan any follow-up?
   D. Who will do what, when, and how?

I. What sort of written final exam should we have for our class?
  A. How much authority (area of freedom) do we have?
  B. What facts and feelings should we take into account as we seek an answer to this question?
II. What are our objectives (criteria) in deciding on the type of exam?
  A. Learning objectives?
  B. Grades?
  C. Type of preparation and study?
  D. Fairness to all?
III. What types of written final exam might we have?
IV. What are the advantages and disadvantages of each?
V. What will we recommend as the form of our written exam?

FIGURE 11.8
Leader's procedural outline for a brief problem-solving discussion.

and should ensure that the major concerns of Vigilant Interaction Theory are met. Here is the format developed by Larson:

  I. What is the single question that, when answered, means the group knows how to accomplish its purpose?

  II. What subquestions must we answer before we can answer the single question we have formulated?

  III. Do we have sufficient information to answer the subquestions with confidence?

  A. If "yes," what are our answers? (Then go to V.)

  B. If "no," the group continues to IV or adjourns to look for answers.

  IV. What are the most reasonable answers to the subquestions?

  V. If our answers to the subquestions are adequate, what is the best solution to the problem?

The church board to which you were introduced in Chapter 2 used a version of the Single Question format to develop the church's first annual budget. Because the church was new, it had no past financial history on which to rely for budgetary information. The *single question* was, "What will be our annual budget for fiscal year 2000?" Board members knew that if they could estimate the costs of fixed expenses and the money needed by each committee, they would have a good idea of the annual budget. Thus, the subquestions asked: "What will be the individual budgets for all the subcommittees?" and "What will be our fixed expenses?" Because members did not have the information available at the initial budget meeting, they adjourned so the treasurer could meet with the committee heads to get the needed information. When all the individual subquestions were answered, the broad single question was answered as well.

FIGURE 11.9 An
example of the
Single Question
problem-solving
procedure.

I. What is the single question . . . ?
What is the most environmentally benign, politically acceptable, and
economically feasible way to dispose of solid waste from Springfield and
surrounding counties?
II. Subquestions
In what ways could the solid waste of the Springfield area be disposed of?
How much will each feasible method of waste disposal cost the citizens of
Springfield and surrounding counties?
What will facilities and start-up cost?
What will continuing operation cost?
Will the method generate enough revenue to pay its costs?
What might be harmful effects of each method of disposal?
What effects will each method have on water, air, land, and components of
the environment?
What health hazards might each method create?
What problem might we have in getting voters to accept each method?
What group or groups are likely to oppose each method?
How well has this method been accepted elsewhere?
How workable is the method?
What personnel or training would be required?
What has its dependability been elsewhere?
How long will this method serve Springfield?
III. The task force engaged in extensive research efforts, including paying
consultants, hiring an engineering consulting firm, and making several trips
to observe facilities used by other cities.
IV. The task force recommended that a MRF (Material Recovery Facility) with
composting and limited landfill usage be recommended to voters. After an
extensive information campaign involving newspapers, public forums, and
broadcast media, voters approved the MRF concept. City council passed an
ordinance requiring that residents not be allowed to send waste materials to
private facilities to ensure generation of a sufficient amount of revenue to
operate the MRF. A coordinator of the project has been hired, and a firm has
been contracted with to build and operate the MRF.

You will notice that this format calls for a thorough analysis of the problem, then a search for any missing information, followed by construction of a
solution based on findings and interpretations of the group. A final step, not
mentioned by Larson in his original article, would be, of course:

VI. How will we put our decision into effect?

An example of an initial outline that might have been created by a group
following the Single Question format is shown in Figure 11.9. Such an outline
is a product of the first part of the discussion, and it keeps being refined and
added to as the group's investigations and discussions proceed toward their

goal. Every member must have a copy of the questions as they are generated, answers as they are provided, and an agenda for each meeting. Using this format calls for close teamwork and decision making by consensus.

Computer Technology and Group Problem Solving

Group support systems (GSS) are computer-based systems designed to improve the quality and speed of group problem solving. Specifically, they exist to help groups with such tasks as generating ideas, evaluating options, and making decisions. Many systems are designed to allow group members to work collaboratively on a problem even if they are in different locations at different times. Some GSS are highly specialized. For example, several are designed to improve the idea-generation step of brainstorming. Others are more general and are designed to improve the entire problem-solving and decision-making process. Examples of less sophisticated GSS include e-mail, voice messaging, and computer conferencing. Two of the better-known support systems for problem solving are GroupSystems and Software Assisted Meeting Management (SAMM). Both include modules designed to help groups in every area of problem solving.[50] They are especially helpful when group members want to evaluate solutions because they offer ways to structure group interaction so that members can honestly react to each other's suggestions and ideas.

GSS are rapidly increasing in number, ease of use, and effectiveness, especially as more and more organizations use local area networks that allow several computers to be connected to each other. People can employ GSS for either long-term use or for one problem-solving task. For example, workers in geographically dispersed areas can connect via computer to perform group work, even though they may be far apart. Often, however, people meet electronically in the same room, each at his or her own computer terminal. This allows several members to "talk" to each other in real time or synchronously by entering their messages into the computer, which compiles them quickly. It also permits anonymity; *who* submitted a particular comment, idea, criticism, and so forth is not identified. Computer-mediated communication with GSS can lessen productivity loss because member identity is hidden. When members are anonymous, they are less inhibited; status is equalized, quality of participation is improved, and dominance by some members is reduced.[51]

Although anonymity provides important benefits to a group involved in problem solving, it can pose problems as well. Anonymity can prevent productivity loss, but members who do not see each other may not identify with each other or with the group. This lack of identification can lead to hollow or empty decisions. Scott warns that groups should not favor anonymity at the expense of face-to-face meetings—groups should work to combine both modes of communication.[52]

Group Support Systems (GDSS)

Computer-based software and hardware systems designed to help groups improve a variety of group outcomes, such as creativity, problem solving, and decision making.

Consider This 11.5

Group support systems can range from e-mail between members to specialized systems such as SAMM. Do not panic if your group does not have the resources to adapt the more specialized systems for problem solving. Chat rooms are available to anyone with access to a computer. Chat rooms do not cost anything to use and they can be more anonymous than e-mail. Chat rooms are special web sites that allow for synchronous communication and you can use anonymous nicknames. Several online services offer free private chat rooms for your group discussions; yahoo.com and lycos.com are two online services you can use. These kinds of sites include the directions on how chat rooms can be created and used. Have you ever visited a chat room? What do you think its strengths and weaknesses are?

Group decision making via computers seems to be at least as good as traditional, face-to-face group decision making.[53] Members are often more satisfied and like the fact that the computers permit synchronous communication. Studies conducted in organizations using GSS suggest that bigger groups are even more satisfied than smaller ones. GSS in larger groups seem to help members sustain their task focus better, and less time seems to be spent in meetings. In addition, as we mentioned earlier, the anonymity these systems provide can be particularly beneficial in groups comprised of widely variant status as compared to groups of peers. Group support systems also help groups improve their organizational record keeping and memory. These systems track group business proceedings because they are capable of saving them for later. Preservation of group proceedings allows the group to keep track of its accomplishments, avoids any harm to the group because of forgetfulness, and guards against members claiming memory loss for personal gain.[54]

Group members should recognize both the advantages and disadvantages of using GSS. Three specific disadvantages have been explored in research.[55] First, don't assume that all group members are comfortable using computers or that all members even want to use computer technology as a part of their problem-solving activities. At Kathy's university the administration has mandated that all course grades will be submitted online. Some faculty are resisting the mandate because they either do not feel competent using computers or they resist technological advances being forced on them. Second, GSS procedures may actually structure group interaction too tightly. In Chapter 7 you learned about adaptive structuration theory. Groups adapting a GSS must find an effective balance between the spirit of the GSS and the group's own way of using the system in order to avoid any ironic use of the system which could be detrimental to the group. Third, the use of GSS can become problematic if managers or group leaders do not want employees or other group members to have full access to information easily obtained via computers.

Drawing any conclusion about GSS and group problem solving can be premature because the systems are changing daily. To summarize, they seem to be beneficial for certain tasks like idea generation and decision making.[56] However, face-to-face groups do appear to have the advantage when negotiation of complex, cognitive tasks is undertaken by members. The nature of the task is only one factor that influences the benefits of GSS as compared to face-to-face interaction; others come into play as well.[57] Groups that use GSS to enhance problem-solving procedures can benefit from the generation of more alternatives and more even participation among members compared to traditional groups. On the other hand, their use adds time to the decision-making process and consensus may be difficult when GSS is used. Reaching consensus has been found problematic in groups utilizing GSS.[58] However, the problem may not be the use of GSS itself but that using GSS takes more time. If groups allow themselves the time to reach consensus they may be better able to reach a truer consensus because anonymity fosters bolder member participation.[59]

Group member satisfaction levels are lower when GSS is used as compared to face-to-face groups. An important factor influencing the amount of satisfaction in groups using GSS is group member familiarity with computers. Initially, members may respond rather negatively to GSS use. Several reviews of GSS use in groups have found that group members need to be given time to become familiar with the spirit or intention of the system. As long as a GSS is used consistently with its spirit, it can be very effective; however, merely adapting a GSS program without considering its intention may fail. GSS do not do the work for the group, nor do they work if group members fail to use good communication skills. The same communication skills crucial to traditional face-to-face problem solving are still needed when groups use GSS as tools. The most we can say definitively is that GSS are generally good for groups, although they are not useful in every circumstance and must be adapted with care.[60]

SUMMARY

1. Decision making involves choosing among alternatives. Problem solving entails creating or discovering the alternatives. Every problem includes an unsatisfactory situation, a desired goal, and obstacles that must be surmounted in order to reach the goal.

2. The problem-solving process should be tailored to fit the problem's specific characteristics: task complexity, degree of solution multiplicity, intrinsic interest, cooperative requirements, population familiarity, level of technical requirements, acceptance requirements, and the area of freedom.

3. Groups need some structure in the problem-solving process to ensure that no important step is overlooked. No single sequence is better than all others; any structure is better than none at all. All sequences should conform to Vigilant Interaction Theory.

4. Whether and when the group should ex-
    plicitly discuss criteria for evaluating pro-
    posed solutions depends on whether evalu-
    ation clarity is high or low.

5. The Procedural Model of Problem Solving
    (P-MOPS) is a general procedure that in-
    cludes problem description and analysis, a
    search for and evaluation of alternatives, a
    decision, and an implementation plan. It
    can be modified to suit any problem, from
    simple to complex.

6. The Single Question format is a less struc-
    tured alternative that simply asks members
    to agree on key subissues before reaching
    the overall solution.

7. Computer technology can be highly benefi-
    cial for generating ideas, evaluating alterna-
    tives, and helping a group make decisions.
    To maximize the value of group support
    systems (GSS), they should be used in a
    way faithful to their intent and members
    should be well trained in how to use them.

KEY TERMS

 *Test your knowledge of these key terms by visiting the Online Learning
Center website at mhhe.com/galanes11*

Acceptance requirements	Intuitive problem solvers	Single Question format
Area of freedom	Obstacle	Solution multiplicity
Charge	Population familiarity	Solution questions
Cooperative requirements	Problem	Systematic problem solvers
Criteria	Problem questions	Task difficulty
Decision making	Problem solving	Technical requirements
Goal	Procedural Model of Problem	Vigilant Interaction Theory
Group support systems (GSS)	Solving (P-MOPS)	
Intrinsic interest		

EXERCISES

 *Go to self-quizzes on the Online Learning
Center at mhhe.com/galanes11 to test your
knowledge of the chapter concepts*

1. Select a problem you are concerned about,
    write it as a problem question, then analyze it
    into the three major components described in
    this chapter. Use the following format:

    > Problem question—
    >
    > What is unsatisfactory about the current situation—
    >
    > Goal (desired situation)—
    >
    > Obstacles to achieving the goal—

2. Select a problem affecting all members of the
    class, such as the type of final exam or some
    campus or community issue in which all class
    members have a high level of interest. Write a
    paper in which you analyze this problem on
    each of the variables below. Give a rating
    number and a brief explanation of why you
    gave this rating for each variable.

    > Task difficulty—(Use the following scale:
    >   high = 10 to low = 1)
    >
    > Solution multiplicity—(scale of 10 to 1)
    >
    > Intrinsic interest—
    >
    > Cooperative requirements—
    >
    > Population familiarity—
    >
    > Acceptance requirements—

Technical requirements—

Area of freedom—

3. As a class, select two problems for study: one should have a high level of solution multiplicity, one a low level. Each class member will write a leader's outline for structuring a group discussion of each problem, adapting P-MOPS to the characteristics of the problem. Compare outlines in small groups of four or five students each; then as a group write one outline for organizing discussion of each problem.

4. Choose a problem now faced by your school or community, then use the Single Question format to create a sequence of questions and subquestions for guiding a vigilant problem-solving discussion of the problem. Compare outlines or sets of questions in small groups, then combine into one outline that contains all issues group members agree should be explored before deciding on a solution.

5. View a videotape of a problem-solving discussion (for instance, one of the groups in the previous discussion might have been recorded with a camcorder). Either as an entire class or in small groups evaluate the vigilance, structure, omissions, and productivity of the discussion. Point out specific instances when the discussion might have been improved and when member behaviors clearly contributed to the quality of the group product.

BIBLIOGRAPHY

Cathcart, Robert S., Larry A. Samovar, and Linda D. Henman, eds. *Small Group Communication: Theory and Practice*. 7th ed. Dubuque, IA: Brown & Benchmark, 1996, Section 3.

Hirokawa, Randy Y., and Marshall S. Poole, eds. *Communication and Group Decision Making*. Beverly Hills, CA: Sage, 1986, 81–111.

Larson, Carl E., and Frank M. J. LaFasto. *TeamWork: What Must Go Right/What Can Go Wrong*. Newbury Park, CA: Sage, 1989.

Shaw, Marvin E. *Group Dynamics*. 3rd ed. New York: McGraw-Hill, 1981, Chapter 10.

Worchel, Stephen, Wendy Wood, and Jeffry A. Simpson, eds. *Group Process and Productivity*. Newbury Park, CA: Sage, 1992.

NOTES

1. Carolyn J. Wood, "Challenging the Assumptions Underlying the Use of Participatory Decision-Making Strategies: A Longitudinal Case Study," *Small Group Behavior* 20 (1989): 428–48.

2. Irving L. Janis and L. Mann, *Decision Making: A Psychological Analysis of Conflict, Choice and Commitment* (New York: Free Press, 1977); Irving L. Janis, *Groupthink: Psychological Studies of Foreign-Policy Decisions and Fiascoes*, 2nd ed. (Boston: Houghton Mifflin, 1983).

3. David M. Berg, "A Descriptive Analysis of the Distribution and Duration of Themes Discussed by Task-Oriented Small Groups," *Speech Monographs* 34 (1967): 172–75.

4. Susan Jarboe, "Procedures for Enhancing Group Decision Making," in *Communication and Group Decision Making*, 2nd ed., eds. Randy Y. Hirokawa and Marshall Scott Poole (Thousand Oaks, CA: Sage, 1996): 345–83.

5. Marvin E. Shaw, *Group Dynamics*, 3rd ed. (New York: McGraw-Hill, 1981): 364.

6. See, for example, John K. Brilhart and Lurene M. Jochem, "Effects of Different Patterns on Outcomes of Problem-Solving Discussions," *Journal of Applied Psychology* 48 (1964): 175–79; Ovid L. Bayless, "An Alternative Model for Problem-Solving Discussion," *Journal of Communication* 17 (1967): 188–97; and Sidney J. Parnes

and Arnold Meadow, "Effects of 'Brainstorming' Instruction on Creative Problem-Solving by Trained and Untrained Subjects," *Journal of Educational Psychology* 50 (1959): 171–76.

7. Shaw, *Group Dynamics*, 364.

8. Leonard Berkowitz, "Sharing Leadership in Small Decision-Making Groups," *Journal of Abnormal and Social Psychology* 48 (1953): 231–38.

9. James H. Davis, *Group Performance* (Reading, MA: Addison-Wesley, 1969).

10. Randy Y. Hirokawa, "Communication and Group Decision-Making Efficacy," in *Small Group Communication: A Reader*, 6th ed., eds. Robert S. Cathcart and Larry A. Samovar (Dubuque, IA: Wm. C. Brown, 1992): 165–77; Randy Y. Hirokawa and Kathryn M. Rost, "Effective Group Decision Making in Organizations: Field Test of the Vigilant Interaction Theory," *Management Communication Quarterly* 5 (February 1992): 267–88.

11. Dennis S. Gouran, "Inferential Errors, Interaction, and Group Decision-Making," in *Communication and Group Decision Making*, eds. R. Y. Hirokawa and M. S. Poole (Beverly Hills, CA: Sage, 1986): 93–111.

12. Hirokawa and Rost, "Effective Group Decision Making," 4.

13. Randy Y. Hirokawa, "Group Communication and Problem-Solving Effectiveness II: An Investigation of Procedural Functions," *Western Journal of Speech Communication* 47 (1983): 59–74; Marshall S. Poole and Joel A. Doelger, "Developmental Processes in Group Decision-Making," in *Communication and Group Decision Making*, eds. Hirokawa and Poole (Newbury Park, CA: Sage, 1986): 35–61.

14. Hirokawa and Rost, "Effective Group Decision Making," 20–22.

15. Kathleen M. Propp and Daniel Nelson, "Problem-Solving Performance in Naturalistic Groups: A Test of the Ecological Validity of the Functional Perspective," *Communication Studies* 47 (1996): 35–45.

16. John F. Cragan and David W. Wright, "The Functional Theory of Small Group Decision Making: A Replication," *Journal of Social Behavior and Personality* 8 (1993): 165–74.

17. Hirokawa, "Communication and Group Decision-Making Efficacy," 165–77.

18. Thomas M. Scheidel and Laura Crowell, "Developmental Sequences in Small Groups," *Quarterly Journal of Speech* 50 (1964): 140–45.

19. Dennis S. Gouran, Candace Brown, and David R. Henry, "Behavioral Correlates of Perceptions of Quality in Decision-Making Discussions," *Communication Monographs* 45 (1978): 62; William E. Jurma, "Effects of Leader Structuring Style and Task Orientation Characteristics of Group Members," *Communication Monographs* 46 (1979): 282–95.

20. Jurma, "Effects of Leader Structuring Style," 282–95.

21. John K. Brilhart, "An Experimental Comparison of Three Techniques for Communicating a Problem-Solving Pattern to Members of a Discussion Group," *Speech Monographs* 33 (1966): 168–77.

22. Marshall S. Poole, "Decision Development in Small Groups II: A Study of Multiple Sequences in Decision Making," *Communication Monographs* 50 (1983): 224–25; "Decision Development in Small Groups III: A Multiple Sequence Model of Group Decision Development," *Communication Monographs* 50 (1983): 321–41.

23. Brilhart and Jochem, "Effects of Different Patterns," 177–78.

24. Bayless, "An Alternative Model for Problem-Solving Discussion," 188–97; Carl E. Larson, "Forms of Analysis and Small Group Problem Solving," *Speech Monographs* 36 (1969): 452–55.

25. Charles M. Kelly, Michael Jaffe, and Gregory V. Nelson, "Solving Problems," *Research Management* 30 (1987): 20–23.

26. Benjamin J. Broome and Luann Fulbright, "A Multi-Stage Influence Model of Barriers to Group Problem Solving: A Participant-Generated Agenda for Small Group Research," *Small Group Research* 26 (February 1995): 25–55.

27. Randy Y. Hirokawa, "Why Informed Groups Make Faulty Decisions," *Small Group Behavior* 18 (1987): 3–29.

28. Randy Y. Hirokawa, "Discussion Procedures and Decision-Making Performance," *Human Communication Research* 12 (1985): 203–24.

29. Randy Y. Hirokawa, "Group Decision-Making Performance: A Continued Test of the Functional Perspective," *Human Communication Research* 14 (1988): 487–515.

30. Propp and Nelson, "Problem-Solving Performance in Naturalistic Groups," 35–45.

31. Hirokawa, "Discussion Procedures and Decision-Making Performance," 221.

32. Randy Y. Hirokawa and Dierdre D. Johnston, "Toward a General Theory of Group Decision Making: Development of an Integrated Model," *Small Group Behavior* 20 (1989): 500–23.

33. Devorah Lieberman, "Ethnocognitivism, Problem Solving, and Hemisphericity," in *Intercultural Communication: A Reader*, 7th ed., eds. Larry Samovar and Richard Porter (Belmont, CA: Wadsworth, 1994): 178–93.

34. Ibid.

35. Kume Teruyuki, "Managerial Attitudes toward Decision-Making: North America and Japan," in *Communication, Culture and Organizational Processes*, eds. William Gudykunst, Lea Stewart, and Stella Ting-Toomey (Newbury Park, CA: Sage, 1985).

36. J. Dan Rothwell, *In Mixed Company*, 4th ed. (Fort Worth, TX: Harcourt, 2001): 202–3.

37. Richard Nisbett and Lee Ross, *Human Inference: Strategies and Shortcomings of Social Judgment* (Englewood Cliffs, NJ: Prentice Hall, 1980).

38. Robert J. Sternberg, "Stalking the IQ Quark," *Psychology Today* 13 (September 1979): 42–45.

39. Brilhart and Jochem, "Effects of Different Patterns," 179.

40. Randy Y. Hirokawa, John G. Oetzel, Carlos G. Aleman, and Scott E. Elston, "The Effects of Evaluation Clarity and Bias on the Relationship between Vigilant Interaction and Group Decision-Making Efficacy" (Paper presented at the Speech Communication Association Convention, Atlanta, November 1991).

41. For example, see Kelly, Jaffe, and Nelson, "Solving Problems"; Norman R. F. Maier and R. A. Maier, "An Experimental Test of the Effects of 'Developmental' vs. 'Free' Discussions on the Quality of Group Decisions," *Journal of Applied Psychology* 41 (1957): 320–23; and Randy Y. Hirokawa, "Group Communication and Problem-Solving Effectiveness: An Investigation of Group Phases," *Human Communication Research* 9 (1983): 291–305.

42. Moshe F. Rubenstein, *Patterns of Problem Solving* (Englewood Cliffs, NJ: Prentice Hall, 1975): 1–2.

43. Hirokawa, "Why Informed Groups Make Faulty Decisions," 3–29.

44. Brilhart, "An Experimental Comparison of Three Techniques," 168–77.

45. Kelly, et al. "Solving Problems," 22.

46. Benjamin J. Broome and Minder Chen, "Guidelines for Computer-Assisted Group Problem Solving: Meeting the Challenges of Complex Issues," *Small Group Research* 23 (1992): 216–36, especially 228.

47. Michael Pacanowksy, "Team Tools for Wicked Problems," *Organizational Dynamics* 23 (Winter 1995): 36–51.

48. Used with permission of Greg Gravenmeier, student in Jack Brilhart's class.

49. Carl E. Larson, "Forms of Analysis and Small Group Problem-Solving," *Speech Monographs* 36 (1969): 452–55; this format has also been presented in several small group texts.

50. For a more detailed description of these support systems see Joseph E. McGrath and Andrea B. Hollingshead, *Groups Interacting with Technology* (Thousand Oaks, CA: Sage, 1994).

51. Bolanle A. Olaniran, "Group Process Satisfaction and Decision Quality in Computer-Mediated Communication: An Examination of Contingent Relations," in *Small Group Communication: Theory and Practice*, 7th ed., eds. Robert Cathcart, Larry Samovar, and Linda Henman (Madison, WI: Brown & Benchmark, 1996): 134–46.

52. Craig R. Scott, "The Impact of Physical and Discursive Anonymity on Group Members' Multiple Identifications During Computer-Supported Decision Making," *Western Journal of Communication* 63 (Fall 1999): 456–87.

53. Leonard M. Jessup and Joseph S. Valacich, eds., *Group Support Systems: New Perspectives* (New York: Macmillan, 1993).

54. Olaniran, "Group Process Satisfaction and Decision Quality in Computer-Mediated Communication."

55. S. Opper and H. Fresko-Weiss, *Technology for Teams: Enhancing Productivity in Networked Organizations* (New York: Van Nostrand Reinhold, 1992).

56. Andrea Hollingshead, Josheph E. McGrath, and Kathleen M. O'Connor, "Group Task Performance and Communication Technology: A

Longitudinal Study of Computer-Mediated versus Face-to-Face Work Groups," *Small Group Research* 24 (August 1993): 307–33.

57. Izak Benbasat and Lai-Huat Lim, "The Effects of Group, Task Context, and Technology Variables on the Usefulness of Group Support Systems: A Meta-Analysis of Experimental Studies," *Small Group Research* 24 (November 1991): 430–62.

58. Bolanle Olaniran, "Group Performance and Computer-Mediated and Face-to-Face Communication," *Management Communication Quarterly* 7 (February 1994) 256–81.

59. Olaniran, "Group Process Satisfaction and Decision Quality in Computer-Mediated Communication," 256–81.

60. Poppy McLeod, "New Communication Technologies for Group Decision Making: Toward an Integrative Framework," in *Communication and Group Decision Making*, 2nd ed., eds. Randy Y. Hirokawa and Marshall Scott Poole (Thousand Oaks, CA: Sage, 1996): 426–61.

DECISION MAKING IN SMALL GROUPS

Central Message

The extent to which a group employs critical thinking considerably influences its decision-making processes and ultimate decision quality.

STUDY OBJECTIVES

As a result of studying Chapter 12 you should be able to:

1. Describe the relative advantages and disadvantages of group and individual decision making.

2. Explain the group polarization effect.

3. Understand the differences among decisions made by a leader, by majority vote, and by consensus, including the advantages and disadvantages of each procedure.

4. Explain five procedural guidelines for making group decisions by consensus and the reasons for these guidelines.

5. Describe the phases groups often experience during decision making and explain several factors that may influence these phases.

6. Describe the factors that contribute to effective decision making.

7. Define critical thinking and describe how to evaluate information and reasoning to enhance a group's ability to think critically.

8. Describe five common fallacies that inhibit critical thinking and how they impair a group's decision making.

9. Explain what groupthink is and how it interferes with a group's critical thinking.

everal years ago, city officials in O'Fallon, Missouri, knew they would have to find a long-range solution to the city's water treatment problems.[1] O'Fallon was on a deep well system, and the dropping water table signaled that the city couldn't stay on that system forever. Officials sought a long-term solution that would be both cost-effective and efficient—the solution had to provide high-quality water to the citizens of O'Fallon and had to give the city long-term control over costs. Officials had three options to choose from. They could interconnect with other water districts and purchase water that way; they could build a traditional-style water treatment plant; or they could build a membrane treatment plant. These options were evaluated in a series of small group meetings.

Purchasing water from surrounding districts would be easy, but left the city at the mercy of other districts in terms of both quality and cost. The traditional water treatment plant would be cheaper to build, initially, but required more chemicals to treat and was likely to need future upgrades as the Environmental Protection Agency continues to tighten water quality standards. The membrane treatment system, which would be more expensive initially, needed fewer chemicals to provide high-quality water and provided the best long-term control over costs. Officials concluded that the membrane treatment system best met all criteria. It was the first membrane treatment system to be built in Missouri.

Decision making is one of the central activities of small groups. The O'Fallon situation represents a classic example of small group decision making, where a group must choose from among several alternatives. As we shall see later in this chapter, decision making involves both cognitive and psychological information processing, both of which are affected by participation with others.

In the course of solving a problem, groups must make a number of decisions, both trivial and important. Every group task—from choosing a water treatment system to deciding whether or not a defendant is guilty—requires at least one and probably several decisions. Because such decisions are made in concert with others, we must understand how to optimize the group decision-making process. Otherwise, we'll produce disasters, such as the poor decision in 1986 to launch the shuttle *Challenger*, which exploded shortly after takeoff.[2]

We are competing with societies—Japanese, Chinese, South Korean—that are more skilled than we at collective decision making. We dare not remain complacent. Furthermore, we cannot work effectively in small groups without understanding their processes and dynamics.[3]

In the last chapter we described the comprehensive group problem-solving process. Here, we narrow the focus to decision making, with the goal of improving group decision making.

Group versus Individual Decision Making

Group decisions made through discussion are usually superior to individual decisions or to averaging individual decisions.[4] They are usually better than decisions made by members who are especially knowledgeable about a problem.[5]

This is because group members can compensate for each other's weaknesses, with each member's unique information complementing the others' information.[6] Group members can spot each other's errors, recognize truth, and process more information than individuals can.[7] The higher the quality a group's inputs and throughput processes are, the better the group's decisions.

> [Have] the confidence that people can transcend their own self-interest to make a good collective decision.
>
> *A. B., University Dean*

Groups frequently achieve an **assembly effect** in which the decision is qualitatively and quantitatively superior either to the best individual judgment of any member or to the average of the judgments of all the members. This is a kind of decision-making synergy, where the whole becomes greater than the sum of its parts. Two recent studies found evidence of the assembly effect.[8] However, synergy is achieved only when group members interact and work *interdependently* on the task; groups whose members work independently do not achieve this result.[9] For example, if group members complete individual assignments on their own and later compile their individual products into the final group product without discussing each member's individual work *as a group*, then that group will probably not achieve an assembly effect. It is the communication among members that allows this synergy to occur.[10]

Assembly Effect

The decision of group members collectively is superior to adding together the wisdom, knowledge, experience, and skills of the members individually.

Factors Affecting Decision Quality

Several input and throughput factors affect group decision quality, especially the type of task, the abilities of the members, and the type of communication among members. For example, groups have been found superior on **conjunctive tasks,** where each member possesses information needed to solve a problem but no one member has all the needed information. However, groups are not superior at **disjunctive tasks,** which require little or no coordination, often enabling the most expert member working alone to produce a correct answer.[11] Often, groups do both—they cycle between conjunctive and disjunctive tasks and must know when to switch from individual to group decision making. Pacanowsky, for instance, notes that teams can be more efficient when members work individually, then pool their insights to create a team-designed solution.[12] Ideally, members recognize which type of task they are working on and which type of decision making is most suitable.

The abilities of the members is another input factor that affects decision quality. Salazar et al. found that group potential, as defined by individual member abilities, is a "powerful determinant of group decision performance."[13] Gruenfeld and Hollingshead determined that members with high *integrative complexity*—the ability to engage in highly complex reasoning processes—produced group interaction that was more complex and better able to incorporate diverse viewpoints into the ultimate decision, particularly on conjunctive tasks.[14] Similarly, Scudder et al. discovered that when members are

Conjunctive Task

A task where each member possesses information relevant to the decision, but no one member alone has all the needed information; thus, a high level of coordination among members is necessary.

Disjunctive Task

A task in which members work on parts of the group problem independently, with little or no coordination of effort through discussion needed.

predisposed to process information cognitively—that is, they have a high *need for cognition*—decision quality is affected positively.[15] Laughlin et al. ascertained that overall decision-making performance was hurt by weaker members, whose impaired abilities to reason and hypothesize correctly affected the entire group.[16] All these authors recommend further investigation into the relationship of member abilities and group potential to decision quality.

Communication among members, a group's essential throughput process, is an important factor affecting decision quality. Verbal interaction itself, not just a summing of individual members' perceptions or opinions, contributes to the increased decision quality that groups usually exhibit.[17] Salazar et al. suggest that task-relevant communication is perhaps even more important than originally thought.[18] Communication that was goal directed, with issues handled systematically, and where assertions were documented were associated with increased decision quality. Effective groups do a better job of sharing and providing information,[19] focus more of their talk on understanding and establishing criteria for evaluating decisions,[20] and spend more time analyzing the problem, establishing group procedures, and evaluating alternatives.[21] These findings offer strong support for Functional Theory (i.e., Vigilant Interaction Theory) described in the previous chapter. Their findings are consistent with those of Scudder et al., who discovered that groups whose members carefully assessed their options produced better decisions.[22]

Mayer asked participants in bona fide groups in organizations to identify those behaviors they have experienced as either helping or hurting small group decision making.[23] Three factors emerged as being important. By far the most influential factor is the full participation of all group members, and includes such behaviors as encouraging members to contribute, to disagree, and to elaborate on their suggestions. The second two factors pertain to how group members establish the group's climate. Negative socioemotional behaviors—being sarcastic, expressing dislike, personal attacks—hurt decision making, but positive socioemotional behaviors—respecting and supporting others' ideas—improved it.

> A healthy, successful group has that room for all ideas to come forward and then see how they can be made to fit or enhance the mission or the project.
>
> *P. W., Community Volunteer*

It is clear from these and other studies that *both* input *and* throughput factors affect decision-making quality. Hirokawa proposes that input and throughput factors interact, each assuming greater importance in certain circumstances.[24] He suggests that when task "unfavorableness" exists (i.e., when the task is complex, there are multiple acceptable choices, the criteria are not obvious, and the information processing necessary to complete the task is high), then the throughput process of communication will have a greater effect on decision quality.

In addition to affecting decision quality, group involvement in decision making increases the acceptance of a decision.[25] Coch and French demonstrated that when workers have a voice in changing a work procedure, they are more productive and loyal than when the change is imposed on them.[26] As Block and Hoffman wrote, "the effectiveness of gaining members' commitment to change through use of group decision is unquestioned."[27]

However, group decision making is not automatically superior to individual decision making. It takes more time, sometimes one or two members can dominate a discussion, and occasionally the fact that other people are present can push an otherwise well-informed discussant further in a particular direction than he or she would normally go. Burleson et al. found that, although 8 of 10 groups that produced consensus decisions had better decisions than the individual members acting alone, 2 of the 10 produced worse decisions.[28]

Several factors interfere with effective decision making. One of those is whether group members actually exchange the information they have. Dennis discovered that group members didn't share most of the information they had as individuals and didn't use well the information they did share.[29] Their decisions suffered as a result. In addition, the groups using electronic Group Decision Support Systems (discussed in Chapter 14) did a worse job of sharing information, possibly because of anonymity or the difficulty of integrating the information that was shared. Cruz et al. also found that decision making was hurt when members failed to share information fully.[30] Decision making improved when the groups were smaller and when members had little common information. Apparently, this recognition forced members to share what they did have.

Wood observed several factors that impede effective decision making, including members who do not possess needed skills and information or make conscientious efforts to acquire them from outside sources, and members whose social needs prevent them from attending to the task.[31] Poor operating procedures, especially failure to provide the kind of structure and coordination needed to accomplish the task and failure to test for consensus, hurt decision quality. Finally, adherence to ascribed status differences impaired open and honest communication, which prevented critical thinking. As we discussed in Chapter 8, cohesiveness *and* performance norms influence decision quality. Miesing and Preble discovered that groups that were very cohesive and had high performance expectations performed better.[32] Hirokawa found that groups that approached decision making systematically made better decisions than groups that did not.[33] On the other hand, Gouran found that group interaction sometimes promoted collective inferential error if members accepted unusual cases as representative, passively accepted specialized knowledge, and created hypothetical stories that had no basis in fact.[34]

We can sum up the meaning of all this research comparing the quality of individual versus group decision making this way: Groups are usually superior in making decisions about how to solve discussion-type problems, depending on the members' abilities, the type of task, how high their norms are for quality (performance), whether they have sufficient cohesiveness to enforce such norms, how systematic and organized their problem-solving procedures are, how involved the members are, and how skilled and determined they are at coming to valid conclusions on the basis of sound evidence.

Group Polarization

Group Polarization

The tendency for group members to make decisions that are more extreme (more risky or cautious) than they would make individually.

An obvious point about group decision making is that members influence each other. Such influence can produce the **group polarization** tendency, sometimes called the risky or cautious shift, which refers to the finding that group members often make decisions that are more extreme (either more risky or more cautious) than the individual group members' initial preferences.[35] In other words, group members push themselves *further* in a particular direction than where they initially started. Two explanations have been proposed for this.[36]

Social Comparison Theory (SCT) suggests that as members get to know each other's values, they want to appear "correct" and may exaggerate opinions in the direction they believe the group values positively. For example, if you are mildly liberal politically and you are in a group that seems to value liberal thought, then you might be tempted to exaggerate how liberal you are. Thus, if the group or cultural norm favors risk (as with many business decisions in our culture), the group will shift toward risk; if caution is the cultural norm (as with a decision affecting a child's life), the group shifts toward caution.

The second explanation for group polarization is *Persuasive Arguments Theory* (PAT), which says that the number, salience, and novelty of arguments in a particular direction persuade members to move in that direction. Thus, if members favor risk (or caution), there will be more and stronger arguments presented in favor of risk (or caution); the persuasive power of these arguments shifts the group in that direction.

Studies have found some support for both SCT and PAT. Whether SCT or PAT better explains choice shift in a specific group may depend on conditions within the group. For example, Hale and Boster found that as the task became more ambiguous, SCT seemed to explain shifts better, but as task ambiguity decreased, PAT made more sense.[37] Kaplan and Miller learned that the type of task mattered; SCT explanations prevailed for tasks requiring judgment, but PAT explained the choice shifts better for intellective tasks that had correct answers.[38]

An intriguing study of burglar behavior by Cromwell et al. supports the concept of group polarization and confirms that both cognitive and emotional factors come into play during group decision making.[39] Burglars themselves believe they take more risks when working with others, but the evidence suggests otherwise. Burglars normally rate potential targets on the basis of the risks associated with those targets. When burglars work in groups, one burglar may point out risks the others miss, so they collectively take into account risk cues they may not have noticed working alone. For example, in one group of three burglars, two rated a particular house a 6 (with 10 the lowest risk), but the third burglar, a woman, pointed out that the time was nearly 3 P.M., school would soon be out, and many children were likely to be playing nearby. The burglars collectively reassessed the risk as 2.

At the same time, burglars working together apparently increase each other's excitement and egg each other on. In the same study, Cromwell et al. found that burglars in groups were more likely to go on multiple burglary sprees, hitting multiple targets, something that individual burglars did not and would not do. These findings about burglar risk and caution, which seem incompatible, can be reconciled as follows. Burglars deciding to commit a crime experience high rates of arousal, which is influenced by the presence of others. This social facilitation effect can lead to increased risk taking. However, assessing a particular site for degree of risk is actually a low-arousal state and requires information-processing skill, which seems to be helped by the presence of others. Thus, both cognitive and psychological factors appear to be involved in decision making and both are affected by the participation of others. It is interesting to note that one of the major advantages for group decision making—that several heads are better than one—is distinctly helpful during the information-processing phase of decision making, even for burglars.

Thus, decision making can be impaired or improved by the particular norms and arguments that prevail in a group, a lesson learned from structuration theory in Chapter 7. Being aware of these normal group tendencies can help group members guard against bias in decision making.

Consider This 12.1

Have you ever made a decision in a group that was worse than a decision you would have made alone? What were the factors operating on you that inhibited you from helping the group make a better decision? Similarly, have you ever made a decision in a group that was better than a decision you'd have made alone? Why was the group decision superior? What factors seemed to contribute most to the better decision?

Methods of Decision Making in Groups

Groups may use a number of different methods to make decisions. The three most common are by the designated leader, by majority vote, and by consensus. Each can be appropriate, depending on the situation. These advantages and disadvantages are outlined in Figure 12.1.

FIGURE 12.1   Advantages and disadvantages of decision-making methods.

Decision-Making Method	Advantages	Disadvantages
By the Leader	Can be high-quality decision if leader is an expert. Is fast. Group avoids anxiety/ responsibility of decision making.	Lacks others' input, so may not be high quality. Members may not support decision. May cause resentment, reduced cohesiveness, lack of motivation for future.
By Majority Vote	Familiar procedure for Americans. Each vote counts equally. Decision reached fairly quickly	Minority side may stay silent out of fear. Minority may resent outcome; may not support or feel committed to decision. Majority is not always right; decision may be flawed.
By Consensus	All members support decision. Members more satisfied and committed to decision. Decision can be high quality, because all viewpoints are taken into account.	Usually takes more time. Members may feel pressured to conform. May be hard or impossible to achieve

Decision Making by the Leader

Sometimes a designated or emergent leader will think the problem through alone and announce a decision, or will consult with the group and then announce the decision. Group members are then given instructions for executing the decision. The resulting solution may or may not be a high-quality one, but other outcomes of such control by the leader may be resentment, lowered cohesiveness, half-hearted support for the decision, and unwillingness to contribute to subsequent decisions. Members may even sabotage the decision. We once observed a group of faculty members who became furious that their designated leader had made an important decision without consulting them. They called a special meeting to overturn his decision. After discussing their options, they proceeded to make *exactly the same* decision he had made. Clearly their distress was not about the *content* of the decision—it was about the *process* and their belief that the leader had disenfranchised them.

> I don't come in and think, "Here's the answer." I don't give it to them. I try to work with the team to come up with an answer.
>
> *L. T., Senior Policy Associate, State Social Service Agency*

Decision Making by Majority Vote

Making a **majority decision** through voting by a show of hands, saying *aye*, or with written ballot is probably the procedure used most often to settle a difference of opinion in democratic groups. On the plus side, everyone has an equal opportunity to influence the decision by speaking, each vote counts equally, and the decision is reached more quickly than if the group's norms require a consensus decision. The numerical power of the majority wins—no problem if the vote is unanimous. But usually the vote is split, with minority members (losers) sometimes doubting that their ideas have been understood fully and treated fairly. People in a minority may even remain silent for fear of being ridiculed for opinions that deviate from the majority opinion. Not only does the quality of the decision sometimes suffer, but the group may also experience lowered cohesiveness and commitment to the decision. When a group's bylaws *require* that a vote be taken, the group may want to discuss an issue until consensus has been reached, then vote to confirm it "legally."

Majority Decision

Decision made by vote, with the winning alternative receiving more than half the members' votes.

Decision Making by Consensus

A **consensus decision** is one that all members agree is the best that everyone can support. It may be, but is not necessarily, the alternative most preferred by all members. When a true consensus has been reached, the output is usually a superior-quality decision, a high level of member satisfaction, and acceptance of the result. However, reaching consensus may take much more time than other procedures. Furthermore, unanimity—the state of perfect consensus in which every group member believes that the decision achieved is the best that could be made—is not at all common. Sometimes a true consensus cannot be achieved, no matter how much time is spent in discussion.

Consensus Decision

A choice that all group members agree is the best one that they all can accept.

More than just the merit of the decision is involved when a group strives for consensus. Certain personality traits, values, and other characteristics of the members affect a group's ability to achieve consensus, as we mentioned in Chapter 6. For example, Beatty found that groups with members similar in decision-rule orientation were more likely to achieve consensus.[40] Three common decision-rule orientations are attempts to minimize losses (a conservative, pessimistic approach), attempts to maximize gains (a risk-taking, optimistic approach), and the maximum expected utility approach (an attempt to derive the highest average payoffs no matter whether a pessimistic or optimistic future is envisioned). Beatty noted that the degree of comfort members felt with the decision was more important in achieving consensus than the quality of the decision itself. Groups with members whose decision-rule orientations were similar had an easier time achieving consensus. Thus, more than just the merit of the decision is involved when a group strives for consensus.

Consider This 12.2

Imagine two different groups of burglars, one with members whose decision rules attempt to minimize losses and another whose rules attempt to maximize gains. Can you envision how these two different orientations could affect their joint decision making? To the burglars, what might be the advantages and disadvantages of each approach?

Consensus may be superficial when some members accommodate to other higher-status members, including "experts" who express their opinions with exceptional force, a designated leader, or a large majority. Gloria, one of the authors, once completed "Lost on the Moon," a group decision-making exercise in which the group is asked to rank the usefulness of several items to astronauts lost on the moon. Her group included several electrical and mechanical engineers with considerable scientific and technical expertise. She readily conceded to these experts. Interestingly, her individual ranking of the items was better than the group's ranking, but she was swayed by the engineers' confidence in their knowledge. Even though it may be uncomfortable to be the group's opinion deviate, do not suppress your opinions.

> You'd be better off not asking for a team's input than asking for a team's input and getting it and then not taking it.
>
> *J. T., CEO and General Manager, Utility Company*

Conflict is likely in the course of arriving at consensual decisions. Expect it and welcome it, particularly the type of constructive argument that enhances critical thinking and counteracts groupthink, which we discuss later. In the next chapter we present specific suggestions to help you manage conflict.

Consider This 12.3

Each type of decision making is appropriate under certain circumstances. Which types of decisions do you think a leader should make, or under what kinds of circumstances do you think it is all right for a leader to make a decision for a group? Which decisions are necessary to reach by consensus? Which by majority vote?

Suggestions for Achieving Consensus   The process of reaching consensus gives all members an opportunity to express how they feel and think about the alternatives, and an equitable chance to influence the outcome. For important decisions, it is worth the time. Here are some discussion guidelines outlined by Hall for making consensus decisions:

1. Don't argue stubbornly for your own position. Present it clearly and logically, being sure you listen actively to others and consider all reactions carefully.

2. Avoid looking at a stalemate as a win–lose situation. Rather, see whether you can find a next best alternative acceptable to all.

3. When agreement is reached too easily and too quickly, be on guard against groupthink. Don't change your position just to avoid conflict. Through discussion, be sure that everyone accepts the decision for similar or complementary reasons and really agrees that it is the best that can be reached.

4. Avoid conflict-suppressing techniques, such as majority vote, averaging, coin tossing, and so forth, except as a last resort. Although they prevent destructive interpersonal conflicts, they also suppress constructive substantive arguments.

5. Seek out differences of opinion, which are helpful in testing alternatives and evaluating reasoning. Get every member involved in the decision-making process. The group has a better chance of selecting the best alternative if it has a wider range of information and ideas.[41]

Phasic Progression during Decision Making

In Chapter 7 we described how groups experience a formation phase and a production phase as they develop from a collection of individuals into a group. Several people have observed that groups also cycle through relatively predictable phases or stages during the process of decision making and problem solving. Bales and Strodtbeck were among the first to identify this **phasic progression.**[42] During the *orientation* phase, members orient themselves to the task and to one another, if they do not already know each other. In the *evaluation* phase, they decide what they collectively think about the problem or decision. Finally, during the *control* phase, the group has reached enough socioemotional maturity for members to concentrate on completing their task. For each new problem they confront, groups will tend to cycle through all three of these stages, returning to an orientation stage for a new problem once a decision has been reached about a previous problem.

Phasic Progression

The movement of a group through fairly predictable phases or stages, each of which is characterized by specific kinds of statements.

More recently, Fisher observed that experienced decision-making groups pass through four phases as they work toward deciding among a group of alternatives.[43] These phases are orientation, conflict, decision emergence, and reinforcement. They can be identified by the kinds of interactions that occur in each.

Orientation   During the orientation phase, members develop a shared understanding of their task, the facts about available options, and how to interpret them. Signs of disagreement are minimal; ambiguous and favorable remarks are common. This makes sense because, when group members are uncertain about the facts or concerned about how others will perceive them, they will be wary of making strong statements of disagreement that might offend another member. In this early stage, a member is more likely to say, "Well, that idea sounds like it might work, but maybe we should take time to think about it some more," than to say, "That's not going to work at all—we're going to have to try a lot harder if we are to come up with a decent solution." The first remark is ambiguous and tentative, the second is unambiguous and definite.

Conflict   During the conflict phase, members offer initiatives, take stands, disagree, offer compromises, argue for and against proposals, and generally discuss ideas in a more open manner than during orientation. Ambiguous remarks fall to a low level in this phase, but disagreeing and agreeing remarks are common. For instance, Selena says, "I think we should get more information about the impact this might have before we proceed much further." Andrew replies, "Naw, we have all the information we need right now to decide." Then Tina supports Selena: "I agree with Selena. We need to know a lot more or we might really mess things up." Members argue for and against proposals, with most people taking sides. Wishy-washy behavior disappears as opinions are expressed clearly and forcefully.

Decision Emergence   For a group to achieve its goal, it must move, somehow, from a position where each member argues a particular point of view to a position where members are willing to be influenced by one another. This movement is signaled by the reappearance of ambiguity in the group. Whereas the earlier ambiguity served as a way of managing primary tension, now it helps resolve secondary tension by allowing the members to back off from staunchly held positions and save face at the same time. It would be hard on a member's self-image to switch suddenly from "I think we should accept the first proposal" to "I think we should reject the first proposal." A transition is needed; the ambiguity provides this transition, which allows the member to move from "I think we should accept the first proposal" to "*Maybe* you are right. There might be some problems with the first proposal that I hadn't considered. Let's look at it more closely before we decide." Members move gradually toward a common group position. Near the end of this phase a consensus decision will emerge, sometimes suddenly. The members will usually know when this point is reached, and they will all indicate support for the decision. (If this does not occur, then it is appropriate for the group to resolve its disagreement by majority vote.)

Reinforcement   After a group has accomplished its primary objective, it doesn't just immediately move on to a different problem or disband. Members will reinforce each other and themselves for a job well done. They will say such things as, "Wow, it took a long time but we got some really important things done," or "I really like the proposal. It's going to work beautifully," or

"I'm proud of us for coming up with this. You guys are super, and this has been a rewarding experience." Members pat each other on the back and reinforce the positive feelings they have toward the decision and toward each other. This good feeling will carry over to the next meeting.

Fisher believed that unless some outside factor (like severe time pressure) interferes with the group's natural decision-making process, these phases will follow each other in a predictable way, although the proportion of time spent in each phase may vary from decision to decision. It is important to recall, however, that he studied interaction in previously developed groups that had already passed through their formation stage.

As we noted in Chapter 11, Poole and his associates found that groups take a variety of paths to problem solving. Poole's investigations have called into question the idea that most groups experience exactly the same phases, in the same order.[44] Group decision making is more complex than unitary sequences suggest. A number of factors influence not only what phases groups experience, but also in what order the phases occur.[45] For example, some groups experience long, drawn-out conflict phases with little socioemotional integration after the conflict. Others experience lengthy periods of idea development with no overt conflict.

Poole's contingency model of group decision making describes three types of factors that affect phasic progression: objective task characteristics, group task characteristics, and group structural characteristics.[46] *Objective task characteristics* include such factors as goal clarity and potential impact of the decision. For example, if the group's goal is clear at the beginning of the process, members may be able to shorten the orientation phase. *Group task characteristics* include such factors as time and population familiarity. Members are more likely to spend extra time orienting themselves to the task and arguing the merits of various options for a novel task that is unfamiliar to them than they are for a familiar one. Finally, *group structural characteristics* refer to how members of the group work together and include such factors as cohesiveness, conflict, and history. Members who have experienced divisive conflict may either run away from potential arguments in the group or may approach group meetings with their defenses up and boxing gloves on. As you can see, group decision making is complicated, with numerous factors potentially influencing phasic progression.

Note that there is a distinction between the phases that occur during a decision-making cycle and those that occur during the development of a group. These two processes operate in conjunction with each other and can readily be synthesized. In Chapter 7 we described the two developmental phases, formation and production, that groups typically experience. Throughout its entire life, a group must deal simultaneously with process (formation) and production concerns. Within each of these broad phases, a group makes a variety of decisions and may solve more than one problem.

Fisher's work provides the link between a group's development stages with its decision-making stages. For each new major decision a group faces,

FIGURE 12.2
Decision making within the development of a small group.

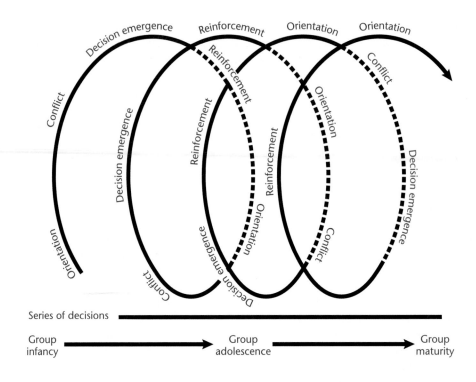

members must orient themselves to each other and to the group's new task, argue for and against the various options available, *decide* something, and achieve some sort of closure through reinforcement of the decision. Thus, from our review of work on phasic progression and from our own experience, we envision a group cycling repeatedly through phases like those Fisher described while moving gradually forward from early formation to full and efficient production. This movement is captured in the spirals of Figure 12.2.

This back-and-forth spiral movement is typical of many continuing groups. Scheidel and Crowell observed the spiral-like progression of a group's problem-solving process and noted that a group does not move in a clear, straight line toward a decision.[47] This spiral-like effect has been observed by others. Sabourin and Geist described the collaborative nature of group decision making as a process in which group members build on each other's proposals.[48] Fisher and Stutman also observed the messy, but ultimately progressive, nature of the spiral model.[49] However, a recent investigation by Pavitt and Johnson suggests that this spiraling movement is not universal.[50] There was great variation in the spiraling exhibited by the groups these authors analyzed, ranging from little or no spiraling to much more than the spiral model indicates. Even so, it may be especially helpful for members high in preference for procedural order to know that such messy cycling between problem analysis to a decision and solution discussion is normal; they can better endure the frustration they feel when groups do not move in an orderly linear sequence from problem analysis to solution implementation. After all, only when they are *not* engaged do troops march in steady, straight lines!

Effective Group Decision Making

There are certain steps a group can take to help ensure that it has made the best possible decision. In the following guidelines, we have synthesized, from many different studies, the key elements of the problem-solving process that directly relate to decision-making effectiveness:

1. **Make sure members understand the problem clearly.**
   If members do not see the problem clearly, they may choose a decision that attacks symptoms instead of causes or that will not work as well as another option. Groups that clearly understand the choice-making situation consistently make better choices.

2. **If members do not already understand the criteria for evaluating the decision, they should be discussed openly.**
   Criteria, as we explained in Chapter 11, are standards that must be met when choosing any option, such as O'Fallon's criteria that its water treatment plant be both efficient and cost-effective. Group members must understand and agree on criteria.

3. **Make sure all members get involved in the process.**
   Group decision making works only if members work to share their knowledge, clear thinking, and effective reasoning. Only in that way can several heads be more effective than one.

4. **Evaluate all the options, using your established criteria, on the basis of both positive and negative consequences.**
   The most effective groups are able to anticipate possible negative consequences and thereby eliminate the worst options right off the bat. Think of all the things that can go wrong with each option, assess how serious each consequence could be, then thoroughly examine the positive aspects of each alternative. Make your final selection based on *both* evaluations.

5. **Select one option, tentatively, and "second-guess" your choice.**
   Don't simply choose to get things over with. Effective groups continue to cycle back over issues previously covered as they encounter new information or think of other things that are pertinent. Even after you have made a tentative choice, go back over your choice as a group, reevaluating your information, reasoning, and assessment, before finally deciding.

When you make a decision, stand behind it, and . . . if you've empowered other people to make decisions, stand behind them.

P. B., City Administrator

Consider This 12.4

It is easy to shortchange the decision-making process, and that may be perfectly acceptable under certain circumstances. Under what circumstances, or for which types of decisions, do you think it is all right to shortchange the decision-making process? For which decisions should you *never* shortchange the process? Can you give specific examples?

The final recommendation for improving the quality of group decisions is so important that we have chosen to devote a separate section to discussing it. *Group members who want to ensure that their decisions are the best that can be made must employ critical thinking skills at each step in the decision-making process.*

Critical Thinking and the Quality of Group Decision Making

Critical Thinking

The systematic examination of information and ideas on the basis of evidence and logic rather than intuition, hunch, or prejudgment.

Critical thinking is the systematic examination of information and ideas on the basis of evidence and logical or probable reasoning, rather than intuition or hunch. Unfortunately, many groups do not encourage critical thinking skills. For instance, Meyers et al. found that group arguments in undergraduate groups consisted of simple assertions almost half the time and that members seldom cited rules of logic or used criteria as standards.[51] In this section we focus on how you can evaluate the evidence and reasoning that link information and ideas.

Evaluating Information

Information—facts, ideas, opinions, data—is the raw material from which a group's decision is made. A group's final decision can be only as good as the information inputs used by the group. Members must evaluate information for accuracy, credibility, and relevance to the group's decisions.

Fact

A verifiable observed event; a descriptive statement that is true.

Distinguishing between Facts and Inferences   It is especially important to distinguish between facts and inferences, opinions, and preferences. Often, group members state opinions as though they were facts, thus leading other group members to accept what may be erroneous conclusions.

A **fact** can be verified as *true* or *false*. If it is false or cannot be verified, it is not a fact. Facts either exist or do not exist; they are not open to argument. A *statement of fact* is a declarative statement that describes an observation of some event. "It is raining outside" is a statement of fact if it really is raining and someone could verify that fact (e.g., by looking out the window). Present events are relatively easy to verify. If the statement of fact refers to a past event, that past event must have actually been observed by somebody. However, because the past event is not presently available to the group for verification, only statements about it can be verified. For example, we cannot verify that George III occupied the throne of England in 1773, but we can verify that records indicate he was king. If several independent sources report the same information as fact, you can be more confident than if it comes from only one source.

An **inference** is an opinion that goes beyond what was actually observed; it makes a leap from a fact to a conclusion based on that fact. A *statement of inference* is a declarative statement that contains an opinion, preference, or conclusion. For example, "The Springfield metropolitan area is growing rapidly" is a statement of inference that goes beyond the *fact* that the area's population was 228,118 in the 1980 census and 325,721 in the 2000 census. *Rapidly* is a relative term; whether we choose to accept this inference as valid depends on what we compare the growth rate to: average growth rate for metropolitan areas in the United States, average growth rate for Missouri metropolitan areas, recent growth rate for areas of similar size, and so on. An inference *is arguable*. The following benchmarks and examples will help you distinguish statements of fact from statements of inference or opinion:

Inference

A statement that goes beyond fact, involves some degree of uncertainty or probability, and cannot be checked for accuracy by direct observation.

Statements of Fact	Examples
Are limited to description.	The population of the Springfield metropolitan area recorded in the 2000 census was 325,721.
Can be made only *after* observation.	On August 9, 2002, Gloria Galanes lived with two cats.
Are as close to certain as humans can get.	The university library's catalog contained 2,437,532 volumes on July 8, 1996.
Only a limited number of facts exist.	After instituting lotteries, three states reduced their tax rates.

Statements of Inference and Opinion	Examples
Go beyond what was observed directly.	Springfield is growing rapidly.
Can be made at any time without regard to observation.	Gloria Galanes likes cats.
Can be made by anyone, observer or not.	The heart of a good university is its library.
Entail some degree of probability, inferential risk, or uncertainty.	We should legalize gambling to reduce the state tax.
An unlimited number can be made about anything.	

Evaluating Survey and Statistical Data   Factual-type statements, including statistics or the results of surveys, need to be evaluated carefully for dependability. Surveying is a sophisticated operation and must be done correctly or the results can be misleading, especially if surveys are based on other than random or scientific sampling. The questions and who asks them can make a big difference in the results.

Ask the following questions when evaluating statistics: Who commissioned the study? How were the data gathered and analyzed? How were questions phrased? You may need the help of an expert to evaluate and interpret statistical data properly, especially if you are basing an important conclusion on those data.

Evaluating the Sources and Implications of Opinions   When first introduced to the differences between facts and opinions, some students act as if statements of opinion are less valuable in a discussion. Hardly so! Facts themselves are not arguable but provide the basis for discussion and debate. Groups must deal not only with what has been verified but also determine priorities of values, ethics, goals, and procedures acceptable to all. Members make inferences about what will probably happen *if* they adopt each possible alternative. For example, facts regarding AIDS and how it is spread are fairly well known, but what a particular board of education will *do* about it depends on the values, opinions, and judgments about policies that will be acceptable to the community.

> If you convey to those people that you are working hard to get good information, then the people that remain [after the committee's recommended budget cuts] will feel like . . . they'll still be treated fairly.
>
> *M. H., former University Department Chair*

Opinions are not all equal, although all people have an equal right to express their opinions. Opinions *can* be evaluated for their validity and appropriate use of fact. First, consider the source of the opinion.

1.   Is this person (or other source) a recognized expert on the subject? How do other experts in the field regard this person? If their opinions are different, how might this be explained?

2.   Does the source have a vested interest that might have influenced the opinion? For example, a flood victim, insurance agent, politician, and taxpayer will have different opinions about whether government should reimburse victims of natural disasters for all their losses.

3.   How well does the source support the opinion with documented evidence? Is the evidence well organized, with supporting statistics and tables and clear reasoning?

4.   How consistent is this opinion with others expressed by the source? If not consistent, is there an acceptable explanation for the person's inconsistency?

Second, consider the implications of the opinion. To what further conclusions does it lead, and are these acceptable to the group? For example, a writer may argue that outlawing private ownership of handguns would protect us from accidents and murderers. What are the implications of this statement? That dangerous devices should not be allowed in the hands of citizens at large? That only nonessential dangerous tools that could potentially be used as murder weapons should be restricted? That eventually all potential murder weapons should be restricted? Another writer may argue that anyone with no felony record should be allowed to use a handgun after demonstrating competence in handling it safely and correctly. What are the implications of that opinion? That only convicted felons use handguns to kill another person? That most accidents would be prevented if people knew how to handle guns safely? That handguns are useful to many people? The point is that when a group decision depends on opinions, it is most important to test these opinions, especially for what they assume and imply.

Consider This 12.5

After the school shootings in Littleton, Colorado, many people said that watching violent television was the cause of the violence in schools, such as at Littleton, or that lack of gun control was the cause of the violence. Arguments were made for censoring television or for enacting stricter gun control laws. How valid do you think these arguments are?

Evaluating the information available to the group is only the first element of critical thinking. It is equally important to evaluate how both information sources and group members reason from this information.

Evaluating Reasoning

Critical thinking requires that conclusions (including decisions) be based on both sound evidence and clear, valid reasoning that connects information with conclusions in an appropriate and defensible way. Once you have evaluated the information (raw data), you must also look at how speakers and writers reason from that information. Are their conclusions logical and plausible, based on appropriate reasoning from information that is offered in support? Here is where *group* decision making can be clearly superior to individual decision making, because one member is usually able to spot a flaw or a reasoning error, called a **fallacy,** that another member missed. Several common fallacies observed in group discussions include overgeneralizing, making *ad hominem* attacks, suggesting inappropriate causal relationships, posing a false dilemma, and making faulty analogies.[52]

Overgeneralizing
An **overgeneralization** is a conclusion that is not supported by enough data. Because something is true about one or a few instances, it is said to be true of all or most instances of the same type. For

Fallacy

A reasoning error.

Overgeneralizing

Assuming that because something is true about one or a few items, it is true of all or most items of the same type.

example, when a person concludes that because *some* college students have defaulted on their government-guaranteed loans, *most or all* college students are irresponsible, that person has overgeneralized. Generalizations are not automatically wrong. After all, that is what statistics do—help us generalize appropriately from a relatively small sample to a large population. The problem occurs when we *over*generalize. To test generalizations, ask whether evidence other than personal testimony is being offered to support the generalization. Ask how many cases the generalization is based on and whether the cases are typical of the phenomenon they are supposed to represent. Try to determine whether the sample offered is biased in any way.

Ad Hominem Attack

An attack on a person rather than his or her argument.

Ad Hominem *Attacks*   An *ad hominem* attack is a statement that attacks a person instead of pointing out a flaw in the person's argument. The attack diverts the group's attention so members debate the merits of the person rather than his or her position on the issue. *Ad hominem* attacks may be explicit ("You can't trust women or minorities to evaluate affirmative action laws fairly!") or veiled ("Why do you think someone like that could help our group?"). In any case, they are a subtle form of name-calling. Determining the credibility of the person supplying information is important, but *ad hominem* attacks do not help evaluate credibility—they condemn individuals on the basis of characteristics irrelevant to the validity of opinions or accuracy of information they provide. And they do *not* help evaluate the arguments advanced by the person for or against some proposal.

Suggesting Inappropriate Causal Relationships   Sometimes people assume that because two events are related or occurred close to each other in time, one must have caused the other. Establishing accurate causal connections is complex and difficult, even using statistical procedures. Common sense suggests that events usually have multiple and complex causes. To suggest that one single event causes another almost always oversimplifies a relationship among numerous variables. For example, we recently overheard a newscaster say that, because female graduates of women-only colleges were more likely to serve on the boards of Fortune 500 companies than graduates of coeducational schools, attendance at women's colleges probably "caused" greater career achievement. This is a preposterous statement! Numerous factors influence career achievement. Many women's colleges are both highly selective and expensive; their students are often bright, grew up in families who own or are connected to Fortune 500 companies, and can afford to attend expensive schools. Attendance at women-only colleges may indeed provide women with greater opportunities for engaging in leadership activities. More likely, native ability, economic resources, and family connections "cause" both attendance at women-only colleges and career achievement. Whenever you see causal connections being posited, look for other reasons why the events might be linked. Only when alternative explanations have been eliminated should a causal connection be accepted as probably true, and then only tentatively.

False Dilemmas   A **false dilemma** poses an either-or choice that implies, wrongly, that only two courses of action are possible. For example, either the university builds a new parking lot *or* students have to walk miles to get to class. Either sex education is taught by the parents *or* by the schools. Each of these statements ignores the fact that other options exist to accomplish both goals—in other words, the dilemma is false. The university could provide a shuttle bus service to transport students from faraway parking lots, schedule classes early or late to alleviate parking crunches at certain times, or set up a car-pooling service to improve the parking situation. Children can be taught sex education by their parents; their teachers; their ministers, priests, or rabbis; committees composed of teachers and parents working together; teams of clergy and parents; and so forth. Just because a writer or speaker does not offer you alternatives should not blind you to their existence. Whenever you are offered an either-or choice, we encourage you to look for additional options or to think in terms of *degree* rather than *good or bad, effective or ineffective*, and so forth.

Faulty Analogies   A **faulty analogy** is a comparison that asks us to stretch a similarity too far. Comparisons help us understand issues more vividly, but all comparisons have limitations. Author Gloria's orange tabby cat may look and act like a tiger, but he does not eat 10 pounds of meat per day and cannot hurt you if he jumps on your lap. We have heard many students complain (we have even complained ourselves!), "You can't really learn how to be a public relations professional in college. It would be like trying to learn to swim from a book, but never getting in the water." At first glance, this remark hits home because there indeed are limitations to what you can learn in school. Examining the analogy more closely, however, reveals that many classroom activities and assignments prepare students for professional practice. Public relations majors practice writing for a variety of audiences, learn principles of graphic design and use them to design materials for a variety of clients, put together dynamic oral presentations, write up job specifications and budgets for proposed projects, and so on. All these are activities that public relations professionals carry out in professional practice. Whenever you hear an analogy being offered as an argument, ask yourself three things: (1) What two things are being compared? (2) How are they similar? and, more important, (3) How are they different or where does the comparison break down? Always ask, "Is the conclusion warranted by *this* analogy?"

The fallacies we have just presented are among the most common, but by no means are they the only ones you will encounter. The important thing is for you and your fellow group members to be alert to mistakes in reasoning so you will not be led by faulty reasoning to make poor decisions.

False Dilemma

Either-or thinking that assumes, incorrectly, that only two choices or courses of action are possible.

Faulty Analogy

An incomplete comparison that stretches a similarity too far; assuming that because two things are similar in some respects, they are alike in others.

Evaluating Information and Reasoning from the World Wide Web

The foregoing information pertains to all sources of information, regardless of the method you used to acquire the information. But because anyone can post virtually anything on the World Wide Web, evaluating Web-based sources poses unique problems. Adams and Clark suggest using six evaluation criteria that look at accuracy, authority, audience, purpose, recency, and coverage.[53]

Accuracy.   How do you know information from the Web is accurate? You can't know beyond any doubt, but three factors can help you. First, be suspicious of information that has not passed through any editorial checks. With traditional print sources, material usually has to be screened by numerous people, including lawyers. That is also true of some Web-based sources, such as those maintained by credible news organizations such as CNN. Accept with caution information that seems to bypass editorial checks. Second, determine whether multiple sources verify the same information. Finally, use your common sense. If something seems too good or too incredible to be true, don't accept it automatically. We found a website that advertised manbeef—human meat for food consumption. It was a spoof, but some people accepted it as true.

Authority.   As with print sources, ask what the source of the information is, and determine whether you would trust that source. Collective or corporate authority, such as CNN or the American Medical Association, adhere to stricter standards for information than most individuals do. Find the information's home page to determine who is providing it. What do you think the American Lung Association says about smoking on its website?

Audience.   For whom is the information being offered? Web designers have particular audiences in mind. Information is tailored to reach particular audiences. It may be too technical, too jargon-filled, or too simplistic for your purposes. It may also be slanted to appeal to a particular audience.

Purpose.   Why is this information being offered? It may be intended to inform, persuade, or entertain you, or advocate for something. You can gain some clue to this by paying attention to what comes after the dot. A .gov ending is sponsored by the government, for instance, and is probably intended to inform. A .com signifies a commercial enterprise and is probably trying to sell you something. Organizational sites are probably advocating a cause or course of action.

Recency.   How current is the site? The Internet allows information to be placed instantly, but some sites are not monitored or updated frequently. A site's date may be the date it was created or the date it was last modified—it isn't always clear. Many sites have an e-mail address that allows you to ask questions or give feedback to the site owners. Use this to find out more.

Coverage.   Is your topic covered in enough depth? The Internet's speed can work against depth of coverage, but often, you can link to additional sites that touch on your topic. Use a variety of sources to get sufficient information.

These suggestions aren't foolproof, but they will help you gauge the value and usefulness of Web-based information. Don't just accept something because it's on the Web. Remember, on the Internet, no one knows if you're a dog!

Critical Thinking and Groupthink   One factor that can significantly impair critical thinking in a small group is groupthink. Coined by Irving Janis, **groupthink** occurs when a highly cohesive group wants to maintain consensus so much that it suppresses confrontation and disagreement, so the group's decisions are not carefully thought through.[54] The group's balance tilts toward maintaining cohesiveness and harmony rather than toward thinking critically. Janis compared two decisions by President John F. Kennedy's National Security Council. The first, a disastrous one, occurred when the United States decided to invade Cuba at the Bay of Pigs shortly after Fidel Castro had established a communist government there. The second is considered a model of effective group decision making; it was the 1963 decision to blockade Cuba when missile sites were discovered there and ships with nuclear warheads to arm them were photographed on their way from the Soviet Union. Janis was intrigued by the fact that essentially the same group of people made decisions of such divergent quality. He found the reason *not* in the individual decision makers' personalities or intentions, but in the *throughput processes* they used. Groups making effective decisions and proposing high-quality alternatives are willing to engage in open conflict, challenge one another's reasoning, and test all information and ideas for soundness. Janis found that Kennedy's advisers did not thoroughly test information before making the Bay of Pigs decision, which explains how such well-educated, intelligent individuals, in the face of evidence to the contrary, *as a group* allowed such a stupid decision to be made.

Please note that just because a group decision turns out badly does not automatically mean the processes used to formulate the decision were influenced by groupthink. Sometimes decisions go awry because of factors over which the group has no control or can't have known about. What makes a decision faulty because of groupthink is the failure to consider all the information available at the time of the decision in a thorough and unbiased way. Highly cohesive groups are particularly vulnerable to the groupthink trap because that very cohesion creates a general desire to keep the members together on a decision. This then leads to pressure for consensus and touches off a fear of anything that seems to threaten the cohesion, particularly conflict. The pressure to achieve consensus is particularly acute in groups experiencing time pressures and with leaders who have a preferred alternative that they attempt to promote.[55]

Groupthink

The tendency of some cohesive groups *not* to subject information, reasoning, and proposals to thorough critical analysis.

Groupthink is revealed in the type of communication members exhibit. Cline compared the conversations of groupthink and non-groupthink groups and found several surprising differences.[56] Although levels of disagreement were similar in both sets of groups, the groupthink groups exhibited significantly higher levels of *agreement*, and these agreements were simple, unsubstantiated ones. Group members ended up making statements and agreeing with themselves. In contrast, the agreements exhibited in the non-groupthink groups were substantive in nature, with different speakers providing different evidence and lines of reasoning to support their assertions. Cline concluded that in groupthink, concern for positive relationships and cohesiveness overrides critical thinking.

Groupthink is a common phenomenon in government, business, and educational groups. It has been implicated in a number of disastrous policy decisions, including NASA's 1986 decision to launch the space shuttle *Challenger*, which exploded just after takeoff.[57] It has also been linked to a number of clearly unethical decisions made in American business, including Beech-Nut's decision to market phony apple juice, E. F. Hutton's decision to kite checks, and Salomon Brothers' illegal bidding in Treasury auctions.[58] In all these decisions, group members had information that should have forewarned them of impending failure, but biases affected how they processed the information, and desire for harmony and cohesiveness sabotaged the decision-making process. It seems that when informational and normative pressures compete, the influence of norms supporting agreement outweigh the pressure to share and evaluate information.[59]

Groupthink is not inevitable in a cohesive group. Aldag and Fuller remind us that such antecedents of groupthink as high cohesiveness and directive leadership do not inherently produce dysfunctions in a group.[60] Bernthal and Insko discovered that high socioemotional cohesiveness was most likely to produce groupthink symptoms, especially when it was paired with low task-oriented cohesiveness.[61] This was confirmed by the meta-analysis of cohesiveness by Mullen et al., who found that cohesiveness based on interpersonal attraction among members can produce the kinds of problems associated with groupthink, but cohesiveness based on commitment to the task has the opposite effect.[62] The effects of cohesiveness are magnified when a group must decide unanimously instead of by majority rule.[63]

A revised model of groupthink that takes these and other factors into account has been proposed by Neck and Moorhead, who add the conditions of time pressures and the importance of the decision to the factors leading to groupthink.[64] These authors believe that two moderating factors, the role of the leader and how methodical the group's decision-making processes are, determine whether the antecedent conditions of cohesiveness, time, and importance will actually produce groupthink. The leader's behavior is particularly important. A leader with a closed communication style discourages member participation in decisions, discourages diverse opinions, states his or her opinions at the outset of a discussion, and does not emphasize the importance of making a wise decision. When groupthink conditions are present, this style is more likely to produce groupthink than an open style that encourages participation.

Symptoms of Groupthink

How can you recognize groupthink? The symptoms of groupthink identified by Janis and others fall into three main categories:

1. **The group overestimates its power and morality.**
   A group may be so optimistic that it overestimates the chances for its programs to succeed. For example, the group of men behind the burglary of the Democratic National Headquarters, which eventually led to the Watergate hearings and President Nixon's resignation in disgrace, believed that they had a morally determined duty to protect the American public by gathering intelligence, no matter by what means, to help the president.

2. **The group becomes closed-minded.**
   Either a high-status leader or the group has a preferred solution, and the group closes itself off to any information contrary to this preferred course of action. A group may also stereotype outside figures who disagree so it doesn't have to pay attention to what they might have to say. NASA officials were so biased in favor of launching that they ignored or devalued information provided by engineers who opposed the *Challenger* launch.

3. **Group members experience pressures to conform.**
   Pressure to conform manifests itself in a variety of ways. First, members censor their own remarks, exemplified in Figure 12.3. If you think

FIGURE 12.3   Groupthink in action.

Reprinted with permission of King Features Syndicate.

everyone else in the group favors a proposal, you will tend to suppress your own doubts and fears. Second, the group members have a shared illusion of unanimity, manifested by the amount of simple agreement discovered by Cline.[65] Because individuals do not express doubts openly, the members think they all agree. Consensus is assumed rather than obtained.[66] Third, a member who does venture a contradictory opinion will experience direct pressure from the rest of the group to conform: "Why are you being so negative, Jim? The rest of us think it's a good idea." The group may also have a number of self-appointed *mindguards* who "protect" the group by deliberately preventing dissonant information from reaching the group—by stopping outsiders from addressing the group, failing to mention contrasting points of view contained in research materials, and so forth. Finally, in groups with rigid status hierarchies, lower-status members are less likely to contradict higher-status members and will avoid issues they think may produce conflict.[67] These conformity pressures are especially dangerous when a group *must* achieve consensus. The need for consensus can lead to an "agreement norm," which curtails disagreement, ultimately causing the decision to suffer.[68]

We offered specific suggestions for preventing groupthink in Chapter 10, but the best suggestion is for every group member to take seriously his or her role as a critical thinker during the decision-making process. Critical thinking is the responsibility of *all* group members, but occasionally a group may appoint a particular member as its *critical adviser*.[69] Also called a *devil's advocate* or *reminder*, a member so designated is responsible for critically evaluating the ideas brought before the group. Criticism is constructive and encourages other members to participate in the critical thinking process. Ideally, groups rotate this role among members so that the criticism is associated with the role and not the particular member. Groups that use this role are less likely to do such things as allow one member to dominate the discussion or make faulty assumptions, thus improving the quality of their decisions.[70] Effective critical thinking can help a group realize its potential for decisions that are superior to individual decisions.

SUMMARY

1. Group decisions are usually better than individual ones, but this depends on several factors, including the type of task, the abilities of the members, whether group norms support high or low production, and the decision-making procedures used. Ideally, groups achieve an assembly effect, that is, the group's decision is superior to the sum-mative effect of all the individual members' decisions.

2. Group decision making entails not only rational but other psychological processes which can lead to a group polarization effect, or the tendency of people in groups to adopt more extreme solutions.

3. Group decisions can be made by the designated leader, by majority vote, or by consensus. Consensus takes more time.

4. To help achieve valuable consensus, envision the process as a cooperative rather than competitive one. Don't be stubborn, avoid win–lose thinking, be on guard against groupthink, don't use conflict-suppressing techniques, but use differences of opinion to improve group outcomes.

5. Groups often pass through predictable phases during decision making, such as the four Fisher identified (orientation, conflict, decision emergence, and reinforcement). Recent researchers, such as Poole, suggest that the types, lengths, and sequence of phases, depend on several group and individual factors.

6. Several factors can improve group decision making: defining the problem carefully, agreeing on criteria, thoroughly evaluating the positive and negative characteristics of all the options, second-guessing the tentative choice and, most important, thinking critically.

7. Both the information available to the group and also the reasoning that links that information to conclusions must be carefully evaluated. Members should be especially watchful for common fallacies that impair reasoning, such as overgeneralizing, *ad hominem* attacks, making inappropriate causal links, posing a false dilemma, and making faulty analogies.

8. Cohesive groups need to guard against groupthink, characterized by failure to evaluate information and reasoning thoroughly. Overestimating a group's morality, close-mindedness, and pressure to conform indicate groupthink. Establishing a devil's advocate role can help counteract this tendency.

KEY TERMS

 Test your knowledge of these key terms by visiting the Online Learning Center website at mhhe.com/galanes11

Ad hominem attack	Fact	Groupthink
Assembly effect	Fallacy	Inference
Conjunctive tasks	False dilemma	Majority decision
Consensus decision	Faulty analogy	Overgeneralization
Critical thinking	Group polarization	Phasic progression
Disjunctive tasks		

EXERCISE

 Go to self-quizzes on the Online Learning Center at mhhe.com/galanes11 to test your knowledge of the chapter concepts

Read the following case problem, then break into groups of five or six and come to a consensus decision. Use the following questions to guide your post-decision evaluation:

1. What problems in choosing did your group have?
2. What seemed to cause these problems?
3. Do you think you made the best choice? Why or why not?
4. What guidelines can you write to apply what you learned?
5. What did you learn from this exercise?

Scholarship Awards Committee

You comprise a Scholarship Awards Committee at State University. A special trust fund was established by an anonymous donor to award one full-tuition scholarship per year, renewable for three years, to a person with demonstrated need for financial assistance, a reasonable expectation of success as a student, and who is unlikely to attend college if not granted some form of aid. There are no other conditions attached to the award except that a student committee must select the winner from a list of applicants supplied by the admissions office. Admissions has given you a list of five eligible applicants and said no other information can be given to you. Who will receive the scholarship? You can award only one scholarship.

Duane, age 16, a white student from a middle-class family, finished high school in three years. He says he rushed through because he could not have tolerated another year of the bull. His mother, a widow with two younger children to support, can work only part-time in her field as a registered nurse. Duane's high school grade average was 3.0. University tests predict a 2.6 college grade-point average in a science curriculum and 3.1 in nonscience. His mother is determined that Duane should be a physician. Duane says he is not sure of what job or profession he wants. He has some emotional problems; a psychiatrist he has seen recommends college because he thinks Duane needs "an intellectual challenge."

Carla, age 17, is a Hispanic student with very high recommendations from the small town high school where she earned a 3.8 grade average. In her senior year she became engaged to Luis, a long-distance truck driver, who wants her to get married at once and forget college. She is known to have spent a few nights with him on a cross-country trip to haul grain. Your university predicts she will earn 2.6 in science and 3.3 in a nonscience program. She says she wants to become a social worker "to help work with migrant children in California." The priest where she attends church says she has a fine mind, but he predicts she will marry and drop out even if she starts college. Her parents are uneducated (less than high school), hard working, law abiding, and very poor.

Melissa, age 26, is an African American divorcee with a seven-year-old son. She had a 2.8 grade average in high school "because I goofed around," but tests predict a 2.9 in science and a 3.6 in nonscience at your university. She says she wants to become an English instructor "in college if I get lucky, or at least in high school." She was a beauty contest winner at 18, but says she is bitter toward men and will never remarry. She gets no child support or other family assistance. Her present boss, a dress shop owner, gives her a good character reference but predicts she will marry rather than finish college.

Sam, age 19, is an African American student who was offered several football scholarships, but they were withdrawn when an auto accident injured his legs. He can get around well but cannot compete in athletics. His high school grade average was barely passing, but entrance test scores predict a 2.5 average in science and 3.0 in a nonscience curriculum. His father, a day laborer, says he can contribute nothing toward a college education for Sam. Sam says he is determined to become a football coach, although he has been advised that may be difficult without a college playing record.

Chou (Joe), age 27, escaped from China after he lost his right hand during the Tiananmen Square massacre. Orphaned as a youngster, he was brought to this country by a local church organization from Hong Kong. He spoke no English when he arrived in the United States, but now is competent. He earned his GED while he lived with the church's minister and wants to become a computer programmer. The university predicts a 3.0 average in science and a 2.8 in a nonscience program. He is limited in his ability to support himself through manual labor; because he cannot work his way through school, he needs financial assistance.

arrested for shoplifting 5 yrs. ago

BIBLIOGRAPHY

Adams, Tyrone, and Norman Clark. *The Internet: Effective Online Communication*. Fort Worth, TX: Harcourt, 2001, 166–75.

Browne, M. Neil, and Stuart M. Keeley. *Asking the Right Questions: A Guide to Critical Thinking*. 3rd ed. Englewood Cliffs, NJ: Prentice Hall, 1990.

Hirokawa, Randy Y. "Discussion Procedures and Decision-Making Performance: A Test of a Functional Perspective." *Human Communication Research* 12 (1985): 203-24.

Isenberg, Daniel J. "Group Polarization: A Critical Review and Meta-Analysis." *Journal of Personality and Social Psychology* 50 (1986): 1141-51.

Mennecke, Brian E., Jeffrey A. Hoffer, and Bayard E. Wynne. "The Implications of Group Development and History for Group Support System Theory and Practice." *Small Group Research* 23 (1992): 524-72. Provides a thorough, current review of group development literature.

NOTES

1. Patrick S. Banger, personal interview, March 18, 2002.
2. Dennis S. Gouran, Randy Y. Hirokawa, and Amy E. Martz, "A Critical Analysis of Factors Related to Decision Processes Involved in the *Challenger* Disaster," *Central States Speech Journal* 37 (1986): 119-35.
3. Joseph D. Anderson, "Working with Groups: Little-Known Facts That Challenge Well-Known Myths," *Small Group Behavior* 16 (1985): 267-83.
4. Jay Hall, "Decisions, Decisions, Decisions," *Psychology Today* 5 (November 1971): 51-54, 86-87; Jay Hall and W. H. Watson, "The Effects of a Normative Intervention on Group Decision-Making Performance," *Human Relations* 23 (1970): 299-317.
5. Irving L. Janis, *Groupthink: Psychological Studies of Policy Decisions and Fiascoes*, 2nd ed. (Boston: Houghton Mifflin, 1983).
6. Mark F. Stasson and Scott D. Bradshaw, "Explanations of Individual-Group Performance Differences: What Sort of 'Bonus' Can Be Gained through Group Interaction?" *Small Group Research* 26 (May 1995): 296-308.
7. Patrick R. Laughlin, Scot W. VanderSteep, and Andrea B. Hollingshead, "Collective versus Individual Induction: Recognition of Truth, Rejection of Error, and Collective Information Processing," *Journal of Personality and Social Psychology* 61, no. 1 (1994): 50-67.
8. Brant R. Burleson, Barbara J. Levine, and Wendy Samter, "Decision-Making Procedure and Decision Quality," *Human Communication Research* 10 (1984), 557-74; Herm W. Smith, "Group versus Individual Problem Solving and Type of Problem Solved," *Small Group Behavior* 20 (1989): 357-66.
9. Patricia M. Fandt, "The Relationship of Accountability and Interdependent Behavior to Enhancing Team Consequences," *Group & Organization Studies* 16 (1991): 300-12.
10. Charles Pavitt and Kelly Kline Johnson, "An Examination of the Coherence of Group Discussions," *Communication Research* 26 (June 1999): 303-21.
11. Herm W. Smith, "Group versus Individual Problem Solving and Type of Problem Solved," *Small Group Behavior* 20 (1989): 357-66.
12. Michael Pacanowsky, "Team Tools for Wicked Problems," *Organizational Dynamics* 23 (Winter 1995): 36-51.
13. Abran J. Salazar, Randy Y. Hirokawa, Kathleen M. Propp, Kelly M. Julian, and Geoff B. Leatham, "In Search of True Causes: Examination of the Effect of Group Potential and Group Interaction on Decision Performance," *Human Communication Research* 20 (June 1994): 529-59.
14. Deborah H. Gruenfeld and Andrea B. Hollingshead, "Sociocognition in Work Groups: The Evolution of Group Integrative Complexity and Its Relation to Task Performance," *Small Group Research* 24 (August 1993): 383-405.
15. Joseph N. Scudder, Richard T. Herschel, and Martin D. Crossland, "Test of a Model Linking Cognitive Motivation, Assessment of Alternatives, Decision Quality, and Group Process Satisfaction," *Small Group Research* 25 (February 1994): 57-82.
16. Laughlin et al., "Collective versus Individual Induction."
17. Burleson et al., "Decision-Making Procedure and Decision Quality."
18. Salazar et al., "In Search of True Causes."
19. Michael E. Mayer, Kevin T. Sonoda, and William B. Gudykunst, "The Effect of Time Pressure and

Type of Information on Decision Quality," *Southern Communication Journal* 62 (Summer 1997): 280–92.

20. Elizabeth E. Graham, Michael J. Papa, and Mary B. McPherson, "An Applied Test of the Functional Communication Perspective of Small Group Decision-Making," *Southern Communication Journal* 62 (Summer 1997): 269–79.

21. Kathleen M. Propp and Daniel Nelson, "Problem-Solving Performance in Naturalistic Groups: A Test of the Ecological Validity of the Functional Perspective," *Communication Studies* 47 (Spring/Summer 1996): 35–45.

22. Scudder et al., "Test of a Model."

23. Michael E. Mayer, "Behaviors Leading to More Effective Decisions in Small Groups Embedded in Organizations," *Communication Reports* 11 (Summer 1998): 123–32.

24. Randy Y. Hirokawa, "The Role of Communication in Group Decision-Making Efficacy: A Task-Contingency Perspective," *Small Group Research* 21 (May 1990): 190–204.

25. M. L. Chemers, "Leadership Theory and Research: A Systems-Process Integration," in *Basic Group Processes*, ed. P. B. Paulus (New York: Springer-Verlag, 1983): 19–20; Randy Y. Hirokawa, "Consensus Group Decision-Making, Quality of Decision and Group Satisfaction: An Attempt to Sort Fact from Fiction," *Central States Speech Journal* 33 (1982): 407–15.

26. Lester Coch and John R. P. French, Jr., "Overcoming Resistance to Change," *Human Relations* 1 (1948): 512–32.

27. Myron W. Block and L. R. Hoffman, "The Effects of Valence of Solutions and Group Cohesiveness on Members' Commitment to Group Decision," in *The Group Problem Solving Process*, ed. L. Richard Hoffman (New York: Prager, 1979): 121.

28. Burleson et al., "Decision-Making Procedure and Decision Quality," 557–74.

29. Alan R. Dennis, "Information Exchange and Use in Small Group Decision Making," *Small Group Research* 27 (November 1996): 532–50.

30. Michael G. Cruz, Franklin J. Boster, and Jose I. Rodriquez, "The Impact of Group Size and Proportion of Shared Information on the Exchange and Integration of Information in Groups," *Communication Research* 24 (June 1997): 291–313.

31. Carolyn J. Wood, "Challenging the Assumptions Underlying the Use of Participatory Decision-Making Strategies: A Longitudinal Case Study," *Small Group Behavior* 20 (1989): 428–48.

32. Paul Miesing and John F. Preble, "Group Processes and Performance in Complex Business Simulation," *Small Group Behavior* 16 (1985): 325–38.

33. Hirokawa, "Consensus Group Decision-Making," 407–14; Randy Y. Hirokawa, "Why Informed Groups Make Faulty Decisions: An Investigation of Possible Interaction-Based Explanations," *Small Group Behavior* 18 (1987): 3–29.

34. Dennis S. Gouran, "Inferential Errors, Interaction, and Group Decision-Making," in *Communication and Group Decision-Making*, eds. R. Y. Hirokawa and M. S. Poole (Beverly Hills, CA: Sage, 1986): 93–111.

35. Marvin E. Shaw, *Group Dynamics*, 2nd ed. (New York: McGraw-Hill, 1976): 70–77.

36. Daniel J. Isenberg, "Group Polarization: A Critical Review and Meta-Analysis," *Journal of Personality and Social Psychology* 10 (1986): 1141–51.

37. Jerold L. Hale and Franklin J. Boster, "Comparing Effects-Coded Models of Choice Shifts," *Communication Research Reports* 5 (1988): 180–86.

38. Martin F. Kaplan and Charles E. Miller, "Group Decision Making and Normative versus Informational Influence: Effects of Type of Issue and Assigned Decision Rule," *Journal of Personality and Social Psychology* 53 (1987): 306–13.

39. Paul F. Cromwell, Alan Marks, James N. Olson, and D'Aunn W. Avary. "Group Effects on Decision-Making by Burglars," *Psychological Reports* 69 (1991): 579–88.

40. Michael J. Beatty, "Group Members' Decision Rule Orientations and Consensus," *Human Communication Research* 16 (1989): 79–96.

41. Hall, "Decisions, Decision, Decisions."

42. Robert F. Bales and Fred L. Strodtbeck, "Phases in Group Problem-Solving," *Journal of Abnormal and Social Psychology* 46 (1951): 485–95.

43. For a complete summary of Fisher's work on decision-making phases, see B. Aubrey Fisher and Donald G. Ellis, *Small Group Decision Making: Communication and the Group*

Process, 3rd ed. (New York: McGraw-Hill, 1990), especially Chapter 6.

44. Marshall Scott Poole, "Decision Development in Small Groups I: A Comparison of Two Models," *Communication Monographs* 48 (1981): 1–24; "Decision Development in Small Groups II: A Study of Multiple Sequences in Decision Making," *Communication Monographs* 50 (1983): 206–32; and "Decision Development in Small Groups III: A Multiple Sequence Model of Group Decision Development," *Communication Monographs* 50 (1983): 321–41; M. S. Poole and Jonelle Roth, "Decision Development in Small Groups IV: A Typology of Group Decision Paths," *Human Communication Research* 15 (1989): 322–56; and "Decision Development in Small Groups V: Test of a Contingency Model," *Human Communication Research* 15 (1989): 549–89.

45. Poole, "Decision Development II" and "Decision Development III."

46. Poole and Roth, "Decision Development V."

47. Thomas M. Scheidel and Laura Crowell, "Idea Development in Small Discussion Groups," *Quarterly Journal of Speech* 50 (1964): 140–45.

48. Teresa C. Sabourin and Patricia Geist, "Collaborative Production of Proposals in Group Decision Making," *Small Group Research* 21 (1990): 404–27.

49. B. Aubrey Fisher and Randall K. Stutman, "An Assessment of Group Trajectories: Analyzing Developmental Breakpoints," *Communication Quarterly* 35 (1987): 105–24.

50. Charles Pavitt and Kelly Kline Johnson, "Scheidel and Crowell Revisited: A Descriptive Study of Group Proposals Sequencing," *Communication Monographs* 69 (March 2002): 19–32.

51. Renee A. Meyers, David R. Siebold, and Dale Brashers, "Argument in Initial Group Decision-Making Discussions: Refinement of a Coding Scheme and a Descriptive Quantitative Analysis," *Western Journal of Speech Communication* 55 (Winter 1991): 47–68.

52. Much of the following information is distilled from M. Neil Browne and Stuart M. Keeley, *Asking the Right Questions: A Guide to Critical Thinking*, 2nd ed. (Englewood Cliffs, NJ: Prentice Hall, 1986).

53. The following information is taken from Tyrone Adams and Norman Clark, *The Internet: Effective Online Communication* (Fort Worth, TX: Harcourt, 2001): 166–75.

54. Irving L. Janis, *Groupthink: Psychological Studies of Policy Decisions and Fiascoes*, 2nd ed. rev. (Boston: Houghton Mifflin, 1983).

55. Gregory Moorhead, Richard Ference, and Chris P. Neck, "Group Decision Fiascoes Continue: Space Shuttle *Challenger* and a Revised Groupthink Framework," *Human Relations* 44 (1991): 539–50.

56. Rebecca J. Welsh Cline, "Detecting Groupthink: Methods for Observing the Illusion of Unanimity," *Communication Quarterly* 38 (1990): 112–26.

57. Dennis S. Gouran, Randy Y. Hirokawa, and Amy E. Martz, "A Critical Analysis of Factors Related to Decisional Processes Involved in the *Challenger* Disaster," *Central States Speech Journal* 37 (1986): 119–35.

58. Ronald R. Sims, "Linking Groupthink to Unethical Behavior in Organizations," *Journal of Business Ethics* 11 (1992): 651–62.

59. Michael G. Cruz, David Dryden Henningsen, and Mary Lynn Miller Williams, "The Presence of Norms in the Absence of Groups? The Impact of Normative Influence under Hidden-Profile Conditions," *Human Communication Research* 26 (January 2000): 104–24.

60. Ramon J. Aldag and Sally Riggs Fuller, "Beyond Fiasco: A Reappraisal of the Groupthink Phenomenon and a New Model of Group Decision Processes," *Psychological Bulletin* 113, no. 3 (1993): 533–52.

61. Paul R. Bernthal and Chester A. Insko, "Cohesiveness without Groupthink: The Interactive Effects of Social and Task Cohesion," *Group and Organization Management* 18 (March 1993): 66–87.

62. Brian Mullen, Tara Anthony, Eduardo Salas, and James E. Driskell, "Group Cohesiveness and Quality of Decision Making: An Integration of the Groupthink Hypothesis," *Small Group Research* 25 (May 1994): 189–204.

63. Tatsuya Kameda and Shinkichi Sugimori, "Psychological Entrapment in Group Decision Making: An Assigned Decision Rule and a Groupthink

Phenomenon," *Journal of Personality and Social Psychology* 65 (August 1993): 282-92.

64. Christopher P. Neck and Gregory Moorhead, "Groupthink Remodeled: The Importance of Leadership, Time Pressure, and Methodical Decision-Making Procedures," *Human Relations* 48 (May 1995): 537-57.

65. Cline, "Detecting Groupthink." (FN 28)

66. Wood, "Challenging the Assumptions" 428-48.

67. Ibid.

68. Anne Gero, "Conflict Avoidance in Consensual Decision Processes," *Small Group Behavior* 16 (1985): 487-99

69. Joann Keyton, *Group Communication: Process and Analysis* (Mountain View, CA: Mayfield, 1999): 63.

70. Beatrice Schultz, Sandra M. Ketrow, and D. M. Urban, "Improving Decision Quality in the Small Group," *Small Group Behavior* 17 (1995): 521-41.

MANAGING CONFLICT IN THE SMALL GROUP

Central Message

If properly managed, the inevitable conflict during a small group's deliberations can improve problem solving and decision making by providing a variety of perspectives that promote critical thinking.

STUDY OBJECTIVES

As a result of studying Chapter 13 you should be able to:

1. Define conflict, and explain both the positive and negative effects it can have on a group.

2. Describe a member who is an *innovative* or *opinion deviate* and explain how such a person can help a group improve its decision making.

3. Describe the four types of conflict that typically occur in small group interactions.

4. Describe the distributive (win–lose) and integrative (win–win) orientations and five specific conflict management styles and their tactics typically used to manage small group conflict.

5. Describe the ethical standards needed for dealing with conflict.

6. Explain the *principled negotiation procedure* for helping a group resolve conflict.

7. Explain three alternative methods for breaking a deadlock when negotiation fails, and describe a mediation procedure a group can use if it is deadlocked.

8. Explain the goals of the Common Ground approach to managing conflict and describe its basic rules for dialogue.

One of the most enduring and intractable conflicts in American society in the past 30 years has been the conflict over abortion between pro-life and pro-choice proponents. This conflict has generated intense, often vicious debate and even violence because the two sides are so far apart on this issue. Or are they? In recent years, the grassroots organization Common Ground Network for Life and Choice has been sponsoring small group discussions, community forums, and seminars designed for joint participation by pro-life and pro-choice individuals.[1] Common Ground started when B. J. Isaacson-Jones, a pro-choice advocate in St. Louis and administrator for an abortion clinic, read a newspaper article by one of her archenemies, pro-life lawyer Andrew Puzder. The article said that even if it was unlikely the two sides would give up their positions, surely they could work together to help impoverished women and their children. Isaacson-Jones and Puzder started meeting and found that they did, in fact, share common concerns. Their initial conversations have spawned discussions throughout the country at which pro-choice and pro-life individuals work together to discover their areas of agreement. Groups have been active in Buffalo, Davenport, Minneapolis, St. Louis, Washington, D.C., Cleveland, and elsewhere.

Common Ground organizers note that they are not trying to force the two sides to compromise. Instead, they visualize the discussions as the intersection of two overlapping circles; each of the circles remains whole, but each fully supports the ideas contained in the overlapping part—the common ground. In one typical format, participants meet in small groups of two pro-lifers, two pro-choicers, and one facilitator, who establishes the ground rules. Common Ground groups are learning groups, not debating societies. Participants are to speak honestly, respectfully, and personally rather than as a representative of a group; they should not try to get the other side to give up its position. Sometimes, before discussion begins, the participants complete questionnaires the way they think people from the opposite side would complete them. Each side holds misconceptions about the other: Pro-choice individuals learn that pro-lifers prefer collaborative instead of authoritarian decision making and pro-life individuals learn that pro-choicers believe that abortion is violent and is not appropriate as a birth control method.

In their small groups, facilitators ask participants to talk about who their heroes are and to share why they hold their respective positions about abortion. Active listening is a hallmark of the Common Ground process; whenever a pro-lifer speaks, a pro-choicer is asked to paraphrase until the original speaker is satisfied, and vice versa. Surprisingly, the two sides agree on and support a number of goals they are willing to work on together, including encouraging men and women to be sexually responsible, fostering equality for women, reducing teen pregnancies, supporting and funding adoption as a choice, and working to remove the conditions that lead women to seek abortions. The two sides have realized that they can work together without abandoning any of their own individual values or beliefs. The organizers hope that finding common ground can encourage discovery of nonviolent and positive solutions to difficult societal problems.

Pick up any popular general interest magazine and you will probably see an article about how to get along at work, at home, with friends. Sometimes, what you read may give you the impression that conflict should be avoided at all costs! The truth is that whenever individuals come together in any sort of social context, disagreement and conflict are inevitable. Trying to avoid conflict is futile and unwise.

Consider This 13.1

Think about times when you thought you had nothing in common with someone you perceived as an adversary. Sometimes you may have had heated conversations and at other times you did what you could to avoid *any* conversation. What were some of the things participants in Common Ground found they could agree on and thus act on together? Imagine a group of pro- and antiaffirmative action individuals participating in a Common Ground project. What might they find they have in common?

Your cultural lens contributes to how you value, approach, and manage conflict.[2] Americans are ambivalent about conflict. Along with values that stress agreement and getting along, we say, "Stick to your guns." We have trouble reconciling the benefits of *both* harmony and conflict. Our more individualistic approach to conflict tends to emphasize the productive value of conflict and directly confronting the issue at hand. Individuals are encouraged to work it out in an open climate while sustaining individual dignity. Other cultures do not experience this tension to the same degree. For example, the same Chinese word means both *crisis* and *opportunity*. Eastern cultures, in particular, see such apparently opposing concepts as harmony and conflict as yin and yang, sides of the same coin. Yet more collectivist cultures like Japan and the Amish tend to see conflict as a threat to relational and community dignity; thus, they lean more toward pacifist responses to conflict, such as avoidance and silence. As you will see, different factors come into play and influence how group members choose to reconcile the tension between harmony and conflict so that agreement *and* disagreement can contribute positively to a group's interaction.

In small groups, conflict is an integral part of problem solving and decision making. It is a natural by-product of trying to come to some agreement about an issue or problem. Each member will perceive the situation in a slightly different way and have different values, priorities, and preferences. These variations in perceptions and beliefs are brought out into the open during discussion. If a group's goal is simply for members to understand each other, these differences can remain unresolved. But if a group's goal is to solve a problem or make a choice, divergent opinions must somehow be reconciled.

Conflict is necessary to effective decision making and problem solving. Why bother to ask a group to solve a problem if you don't think that several heads are better than one? By involving a group, you tacitly acknowledge the value of diversity, the same diversity that guarantees conflict. Conflict *should* occur during group problem solving; if it doesn't, the group members aren't taking advantage of their diversity. Failure to express disagreement and avoiding discussion of conflict-producing issues leads directly to ineffective problem solving and poor decision making.[3] For the group to receive the full benefit of the collective judgment of its members, the members must be willing to disagree, point out errors, and even argue.

Although too much conflict can hurt a group or even destroy it, our experience has been that groups of students err in the direction of too little rather than too much conflict. Most of our students are afraid of disagreement and prefer groups with little or no conflict.[4] The more conflict members experience, the more negatively they view the group experience.[5] For that reason, this chapter stresses the benefits of conflict. We explain how to distinguish beneficial from detrimental conflict and how to manage conflicts to produce the best possible decision or solution.

A Definition of Conflict

Conflict

The expressed struggle that occurs when interdependent parties, such as group members, perceive incompatible goals or scarce resources and interference in achieving their goals.

A variety of definitions exists for **conflict,** ranging from something that occurs when individuals have reached an impasse[6] to a state of genuine difference.[7] We choose Hocker and Wilmot's definition:

> *Conflict* is an expressed struggle between at least two interdependent parties who perceive incompatible goals, scarce resources, and interference from the other party in achieving their goals.[8]

This definition embodies several implications that are consistent with a *communicative* focus on conflict in small groups.

First, the notion of conflict as an *expressed struggle* indicates that conflict involves communicating. While a group member may *feel* internal distress, this distress becomes interpersonal conflict *only when it is expressed*, whether verbally or in such subtle ways as not making eye contact or shifting nervously in one's chair.

Second, parties to a conflict must have an interdependent goal such that it is impossible for one person to attain the goal and not the others. Some groups have understanding of diverse points of view as their goal. In such groups, members do not have to coordinate their beliefs and efforts to agree on a solution. However, many secondary groups must produce something—a report, a proposal, a set of recommendations—that *all* group members must agree to. Such group members are interdependent; one cannot achieve the goal without the others. Therefore, they must find ways of reconciling diverse perspectives and beliefs affecting the decision. For example, Edd may detest Desha's views about what is appropriate treatment of laboratory animals, but that won't matter much unless both are in a group that is charged with recommending a university policy regarding treatment of laboratory animals; for the group to succeed fully, Edd and Desha must reconcile their views enough to collaborate on a policy each can support. Thus, the interdependence group members experience is accompanied by interference. Edd's disagreement with Desha interferes with Desha's having her way, and vice versa. This interference may take the form of Desha trying to persuade the other group members to accept her view, Edd trying to undercut Desha's credibility within the group, or Desha sabotaging Edd's car so he misses an important meeting.

Third, this definition suggests a number of things over which people conflict, such as goals and scarce resources, to which we add values, beliefs, and ways of achieving goals. We have observed numerous student groups whose members disagree on group goals. Maria's goal is to earn an A for a group presentation to the class, but Garry's goal is to do just enough to earn a C. Their divergent goals will cause a problem for the group. In contrast, assume that both Maria and Garry want to receive an A for the presentation, but Maria prefers to involve the class in an exercise followed by discussion, whereas Garry prefers to show and discuss a movie. In this instance, they agree on the goal but differ on the best course of action to reach the goal. Suppose, instead, that Edd believes humans are superior to all other forms of life, which makes it appropriate for laboratory animals to serve human needs, but Desha values all animal life forms equally. This fundamental difference in values may make it impossible for their group to reach consensus on a policy regarding laboratory animals.

You can tell from these examples that some conflicts, such as those over values and goals, are harder to resolve than others. In a group, the more alike members are with respect to basic values and beliefs, the easier it will be for the group to achieve consensus, yet that very similarity may also reduce their creativity.

Fourth, parties to a conflict must *perceive* that they are in conflict. This perceptual dimension is a very important one. There is nothing that automatically labels a situation as *conflict*; instead, conflict depends on how people perceive the situation. For instance, if Thomas disagrees with a proposal you have made, you have a *choice* about how to perceive Thomas's disagreement. You can say, "What a jerk! What makes him think he can do any better!" In this case, you have framed his disagreement as a conflict. However, you could also have said, "I wonder why Thomas disagrees? Maybe there's something in my proposal that I forgot to consider." In this latter case, you have framed his statement of disagreement as a possible attempt on Thomas's part to improve and strengthen your proposal. Thus, perception defines a situation as a conflict.

Perception of a situation is closely associated with emotions and behavior. To illustrate, your feelings can range from mild distress to out-of-control rage, depending on how you perceive the situation. If you think Thomas is a jerk for disagreeing with you or believe he disagreed just to make you look bad in some way, you will feel furious. Furthermore, you may be tempted to seek revenge or escalate the intensity of the conflict. On the other hand, if you perceive Thomas's disagreement to be motivated by a desire to strengthen your idea, then you may be only mildly hurt at his criticism, or even pleased that he cared enough to give your idea such a careful reading. In this latter case, you will behave cooperatively toward Thomas and collaborate to improve the proposal, not try to escalate the conflict. Thus, no perception of conflict, no conflict.

Your perceptions, emotions, and behavior merge with the other person's perceptions, emotions, and behavior to form an interactive system. Remember, you can't be in a conflict situation alone; your behaviors affect other people, as theirs affect you. Suppose you decide Thomas is a jerk, so you rip his criticism of your proposal to shreds. That will certainly affect Thomas, who may now conclude that *you* are a jerk who just can't take constructive criticism. Thomas may now decide to escalate the conflict or try to destroy your credibility within the group. On the other hand, if you indicate to Thomas that you genuinely want to know more about his criticism and the reasons for it, he may decide you are an enlightened, cooperative group member whom he can trust and on whose good judgment he can rely. This may lead him to seek your opinions, support, and ideas in the future.

The fact that members in a group need each other to accomplish group goals is enough to produce stress among group members. Students have reported a variety of sources for group stress such as lack of teamwork, problems coordinating the task, problematic work distribution, dissent among the members, and power struggles.[9] This stress in turn impacts group dynamics because stress undermines a group member's sense of control and when we feel out of control we will engage in behaviors to regain that control. Groups can help reduce member stress by reversing the causes of the stress, perhaps by equalizing the work, being sensitive to each other, completing tasks and rewarding each other, and preparing thoughtfully the work to be completed.

Thus, your perceptions, emotions, and behavior form a feedback loop with the other person's perceptions, emotions, and behavior; each element affects each other element, and none operates independently, as is shown in Figure 13.1. Changing one of the elements will automatically change the others.

Positive and Negative Outcomes of Conflict

Communication scholars concur that conflict has both beneficial and harmful outcomes.[10] We mentioned earlier that without the kind of conflict that comes from a critical examination of an issue, a group is unlikely to make a good decision, but we also have pointed out that conflict can be harmful. We will now examine some of these positive and negative effects.

I like a lot of positive conflict. I don't like 'yes people' at all.

P. B., City Administrator

Benefits of Conflict   Conflict can affect group decision making, teamwork, and satisfaction. Here are several potential benefits of conflict:

1. **Conflict can produce better understanding of both issues and people.**
   We often assume that most people see things as we do and feel as we do, and are often surprised to discover otherwise. When students discover

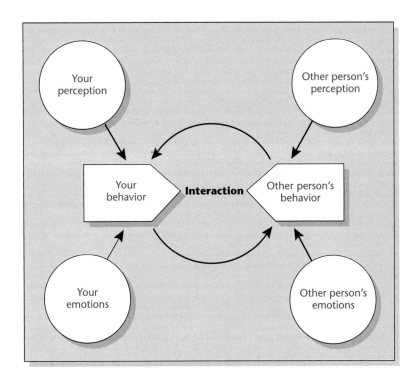

FIGURE 13.1
Perceptions, emotions, behavior, and interaction in a conflict.

others holding differing opinions on an issue, Smith et al. found that they become uncertain about their own positions, seek actively to get more information about the issue, are able to take the perspective of the other students, and are better able to retain information, both about their own position and those of other people.[11] Franz and Jin discovered that, during the first half of a meeting, disagreement fosters learning about the issues.[12] Without this disagreement and kicking issues around, creativity and problem analysis and understanding are shortchanged.

2. **Conflict can increase member motivation.**
   People who do not care will not expend any energy disagreeing about an issue. However, when group members participate in a conflict episode they are actively involved with the issue. They are interested, excited, and pay close attention, so they learn more about the issue. A student in one of our classes could not accept a statement by a fellow group member that nonverbal signals were more potent than words in conveying meaning. Unable to resolve the issue to his own satisfaction, he investigated the issue by using library and personal resources, and discovered the validity of the statement. His search provided some excellent examples the group was able to use in its class presentation—all because he got into an intellectual argument.

As a college debator, I really learned to appreciate the notion of exploring things from all sides and not getting so attached to a particular perspective.

M. H., former University Department Chair

3. **Conflict can produce better decisions.**

This outcome is the goal of good *group* problem solving. Through conflict, you discover first that others disagree, then *why* they disagree. You find flaws in reasoning, holes in arguments, factors that other members failed to consider, or implications that were ignored. Thus you help the group prevent mistakes. One of us belonged to a campus staff charged with developing a plan for cutting costs at a commuter campus. The developer of the plan recommended closing the snack bar at 5 PM. Another member of the staff pointed out that closing at 5 PM would leave many evening students who came to the campus directly from work without food service and might eventually lead to a drop in enrollment. After considerable debate, the committee decided to provide expanded vending machine service, which would accomplish the goal of cutting personnel and utility costs, but not leave the evening students without food.

4. **Conflict can produce greater cohesiveness among group members.**

When a group experiences and resolves conflict successfully, the members learn that the ties holding the group together are strong enough to withstand disagreement. Most of us who have had serious arguments with significant others can recall the closeness we feel after we have "made up." Instead of driving us apart, the conflict serves as a catalyst to strengthen the bonds between us. So it is with groups. The early disagreement Franz and Jin observed produced eventual understanding and consensus later.[13] The twin outcomes of task success and interpersonal tolerance can increase group cohesiveness. For example, in the food service example, staff members felt so good about the final outcome and so positive about each other's willingness to listen to opposing arguments that they adjourned for lunch together in a spirit of camaraderie.

Negative Effects of Conflict Although conflict can be beneficial, we all have seen how harmful it can be. If you have ever said to yourself after a group meeting, "I'll be glad when this project is finished; I hope I never have to work with these people again," you have experienced some of the harmful effects of conflict. These include hurt feelings, lowered cohesiveness, and even group dissolution. One of us had a recent group discussion course end with one group very disappointed in their group experience and each other. Group members were so upset that some of them told friends not to take a group discussion class because people will just end up hating each other.

1. **Conflict can cause bad feelings among group members.**

Most of us do not like to have others disagree with us. This is particularly true when others not only disagree with an idea or proposal we give, but appear to devalue us as people. Their remarks appear caustic, even hostile. This type of perceived attack causes hard feelings. Members may be silent for fear of an attack, thereby depriving the group of valuable information and opinions. (We discuss later how you can deal with such an attack.) Moreover, even a conflict over issues and ideas can be carried on so long that it increases tension and wears group members down to the point where they dread coming to meetings.

2. **Conflict, especially if it involves personal attacks or is carried on too long, can lower group cohesiveness.**
   If you believe that others in a group do not value your contributions, you will not be eager to spend time with that group. If you have a choice, you will spend your time with other groups that seem to value you more. Prolonged conflict and attacks on one's self-concept loosen the bonds of attraction and cohesiveness, which can cause members to reduce the effort they put forth to achieve the group's objectives.

3. **Conflict can split a group apart.**
   A member, who believes a group dislikes his or her ideas, but finds support in other groups, will usually leave the group in which the conflict occurs. Conflict that goes on too long and too intensely tears members apart. One of us once observed a friendship group split up over a political issue. One side believed that busing was an appropriate way to achieve racial equality; the other side disagreed. The two sides did not simply have an intellectual disagreement; they began to impugn each other's goodwill, ability to reason, and commitment to democratic values. Unkind things were said, a rift occurred, and the group died.

Consider This 13.2

How do you know when a conflict has become personal? What specific behaviors in conflict episodes do you perceive as personal? What happens to you when you perceive the conflict has gotten personal? What do you do to escalate a conflict? Are conflicts about certain topics or with certain people more prone to "meanness?" Why?

Expressing Disagreement in a Group

Many people are reluctant to express opinions that differ from a group's majority opinion because expressing such disagreement may cause such a person to be seen as a deviant member by the rest of the group. (This is especially true in other cultures, such as in Asian ones.) A **deviate** is a member who is viewed by the other members as substantially different in some *important* way from the others. Two common types of group deviates are members who do not participate and members who express incompatible views about the issues and test opinions of the group.[14] The second type is more likely to be in-

Deviate

A group member who differs in some important way from the rest of the group members; opinion or innovative deviates can help groups examine alternatives more thoroughly by forcing the group to take a closer look at something.

volved in overt disagreement or conflict in a group. Although the deviate's role may be uncomfortable, it is a potentially valuable one for a group. Reluctant as you may be to express a deviant opinion, ethically you should do it for the good of the group. However, you do not want to rebelliously block or withdraw. Instead, you want to be an *innovative* or *opinion deviate*, someone who disagrees with a proposed action or decision of the group but who is strongly committed to the group and its goals.

> Sometimes you need those difficult people in the group, that person you've got to convince. Once when that happened, we went out to the larger group and it was like there was no question that hadn't already been asked.
>
> *L. T., Senior Policy Associate, State Social Service Agency*

Sometimes it is very hard for an opinion deviate to influence a group. Lindskold and Han found that it was nearly impossible for a single conciliatory member to influence a nonconciliatory group.[15] Thameling and Andrews also found that opinion deviates exerted little influence.[16] Other group members responded more emotionally to deviates than to conforming group members. A sex bias has been observed: members responded more cooperatively to male than to female deviates. Group members appeared to *perceive* male deviates as bright and well informed, and showed a willingness to work with them by asking for evidence, questions, additional information, and so forth; however, they were more likely to *perceive* female deviates as arrogant or overly confident. These researchers suggest that an individual who wants to express a deviant opinion do so cautiously and carefully. If you first develop solid group credentials of loyalty and commitment, other members will trust your motives when you deviate from a majority opinion.

However, even with all these caveats about the difficulty of being an opinion deviate, this kind of disagreement is valuable to the group, particularly for groups in the United States and other Western cultures. Valentine and Fisher found that innovative deviance accounted for one-fourth of group interaction, serving a critical thinking function.[17] What task roles from Chapter 7 might be associated with opinion deviance? Innovative deviance in the form of contradiction, challenging statements by other members, continuing a disagreement started by others, or agreeing with an assertion someone else had attacked was particularly helpful in the group's conflict and decision emergence phases. Furthermore, most innovative deviance occurred immediately prior to consensus, supporting the notion that conflicts can contribute to consensus. Social skill is important, too. Covey found a high correlation between social skill and the use of verbal reasoning in conflict resolution, as well as a negative correlation of social skill with verbal aggression and physical violence.[18] As we noted in Chapter 6, aggressive members are dominant and try to force ideas and practices on others compared to assertive communication reflected in behavior that attempts to respect self as well as others. It is easy to see how assertive innovative deviance is more beneficial to a group compared to aggressive innovative deviance.

The quality of the argument matters, also. Garlick and Mongeau discovered that argument quality was the only factor that allowed a minority subgroup to influence majority attitudes.[19] Argument quality during group disagreement, not the number of members who support a position, seems to be a better predictor of group influence.[20] To elaborate, successful majority subgroups tend to have critical arguers who use challenges and objections that either provide a context for the argument or put off refutations to the argument. Compared to all other subgroups, losing or not, successful minority subgroups are the most consistent in their arguments. This consistency allows them to maintain their initial stance and resist the arguments from the majority, especially if the majority presents an inconsistent line of reasoning. Deviant opinions, skillfully and sensitively expressed, *can* help a group make better decisions.

Types of Conflict

As we have already shown, conflict in and of itself is neither necessarily helpful nor harmful to a group. What matters is what the conflict is about, how it is initiated, and how it is managed. Before we examine several types of conflict that can occur within a group and discuss the potential effects of each, we present a description of conflict in a group of students charged with selecting speakers for their university's Speaker Series.[21] Every major type of conflict occurred in this group.

The Speaker Committee—Kevin, Lori, Chris, Deidre, and Tony—had met several times, but made little progress. Kevin either missed meetings or came late; the others were angry with him. The committee couldn't agree on anything. They argued about whether they should select entertaining or educational speakers, whether they should book one major speaker or several lesser-known ones, whether they should decide by consensus or majority vote, and, most of all, what they should do about Kevin. Occasionally, one of the members would ask a question that encouraged the others to examine their decision and the criteria by which to make their decision, and occasionally a member would make a suggestion that received widespread support. In general, though, they exhibited many problems in managing their conflicts. The conflicts in this group of students illustrate the four types of conflict described as follows.

Substantive Conflict **Substantive conflict,** also called *intrinsic* conflict, is task-related conflict such as disagreement over ideas, meanings, issues, and other matters pertinent (intrinsic) to the task of the group.[22] It involves *what the group should do.* Substantive conflict is the basis for effective decision making and problem solving in a discussion group. It is the vehicle by which ideas, proposals, evidence, and reasoning are challenged and critically examined, doubts are brought into the open, and the group works together to find the best solution. Opinion and innovative deviance described earlier are usually substantive in nature. In our example, the Speaker Committee debated whether an entertaining or educational speaker would be a better choice. The

Substantive Conflict

Conflict resulting from disagreements over ideas, information, reasoning, or evidence.

ensuing argument helped members clarify the purpose of the Speaker Series and presented good reasons for considering each type of speaker.

Affective Conflict

Conflict resulting from personality clashes, likes, dislikes, and competition for power.

Affective Conflict   **Affective conflict,** also called *extrinsic* conflict, is conflict that originates from interpersonal power clashes, likes and dislikes unrelated to the group's task.[23] It represents the *who* in small group conflict and is generally detrimental to the efficient functioning of any group. For example, Speaker Series committee members Lori and Kevin did not like each other and missed no opportunity to disagree or belittle each other. When Kevin said he preferred to schedule an entertaining rather than an educational speaker, Lori said, "I could have expected that from you. Let's not learn—let's party!" This statement revealed that Lori personalized the conflict with Kevin. Her dislike compounded the effects of disagreement over work procedures and ideas. She rarely failed to make sarcastic comments to Kevin throughout the meeting. Such conflict is both difficult to resolve and exceedingly harmful to the group.

Although the origin of this type of conflict is difficult to pin down, our observations of numerous groups suggest that much of it is rooted in one person's acting as if he or she is superior, and another member's refusal to accept this difference in status or power. Most of this "I am superior, more important, more knowledgeable" signaling is nonverbal, projected by subtle patterns of vocal tones, postures, and head/body angles. Much of what is called interpersonal conflict emerges from a struggle for position and power. Recent research has indicated that group members are able to differentiate between personalized (affective) and depersonalized (substantive) conflict, and that the type of conflict affects group consensus.[24] Because affective conflict can impede resolution of substantive issues, Fisher and Brown recommend disentangling relationship and substantive goals and pursuing them independently.[25] Doing so gives the parties a chance to resolve their substantive differences, even though they may never change their feelings about each other. We talk later about how you might do that.

Procedural Conflict

Conflict resulting from disagreement about how to do something.

Procedural Conflict   **Procedural conflict** is a type of substantive conflict over the procedures a group should follow in working toward its goals. Disagreement is about the *how* of group interaction. For instance, members of a group may disagree about whether they should make decisions by consensus or whether majority rule will suffice. In our Speaker Series Committee, Lori proposed splitting up the money available to the committee and letting each person select whatever speaker he or she wanted with his/her share of the money as the most efficient way of deciding the issue. But Deidre pointed out that if every person chose the same type of speaker, the series would be boring. The group then realized the value of consensus decision making. This disagreement over *how* the group made its major decisions is a clear example of procedural conflict. The difference of opinion expressed by Deidre and Lori helped clarify the issue.

Procedural conflict is sometimes used to mask affective or substantive conflict. Putnam notes that it can occur because members genuinely disagree over procedures, but it also can be used to withdraw from another substantive conflict by forcing a vote or otherwise regulating the group's work.[26] Although procedural conflict may seem to be a straightforward difference over how the group should accomplish something, it may be rooted in differing member needs for structure versus freedom. Members high in needs for procedural order are more comfortable with linear procedures than members who prefer less structured procedural order.

Consider This 13.3

Reflect back on our discussion of listening preferences in Chapter 3 and learning styles in Chapter 6. Using your understanding of these preferences and styles, describe how might they produce different kinds of substantive, affective, and procedural conflict in a group?

Our discussion of conflict thus far has focused on issues of conflict in face-to-face (FTF) groups, not computer-mediated communication (CMC) in groups. As you recall, groups can use computers to e-mail members, talk to each other online, and some may use group support systems to help them problem-solve. Early research comparing CMC to FTF groups and conflict expression produced inconsistent results.[27] CMC groups engaged in more inflammatory, profane, and negative interactions compared to FTF groups. However, research into the use of group support systems or GSS, discussed in Chapter 11, were found to exhibit less substantive and affective conflict if they effectively adapted the GSS. Inconsistency in the results suggest that if computer groups were given the time to become familiar with each other and if they adapted effectively to the GSS, then CMC groups may exhibit less damaging conflict expression than FTF groups. However, previous research had not considered the types of conflict.

In a rare study comparing three types of conflict (affective, substantive, and procedural) in both CMC groups and FTF groups, differences were found.[28] Hobman et al. recently found that CMC groups displayed initially more affective and procedural conflict than FTF groups.[29] However, these differences disappeared over time. Both CMC and FTF groups displayed similar amounts of substantive conflict. CMC groups initially, because of the anonymity of CMC, exhibit fewer of the social norms people use to support and maintain positive self-images. Given time, however, substantive conflict in CMC groups declines as members are given the time to get to know each other. The early procedural conflict in CMC groups can be explained by members' initial focus on how to use the computer medium.

Essentially, CMC groups do not follow the same conflict patterns as FTF groups, but they do go on to reach comparable levels over time. Groups that use any type of computer technology need to give themselves the time for social development. They should even consider meeting face-to-face, initially, giving themselves the opportunity to establish social and procedural norms acceptable to their group.[30]

Inequity Conflict

Conflict about perceived unequal workloads or contributions to the group effort.

Conflict over Inequity   One of the most prevalent sources of conflict in the groups we have observed is perceived **inequity** in the group: group members do not seem to have equal workloads and/or do not make equal contributions to the group. Inequity reduces satisfaction with the group and is associated with high levels of conflict.[31] In our Speaker Series Committee, Kevin's work and contributions to the group were perceived as inadequate. Although Lori rode Kevin the hardest about his lack of commitment to the group, Chris, Deidre, and even Tony mentioned Kevin's lack of follow-through and failure to complete assignments for the group. When Kevin was late again, Chris said, "I'm tired of waiting for the jerk. Let's get started," and later Deidre directly confronted Kevin by listing his behaviors that indicated lack of commitment to the group ("You've missed two of the last four meetings, and were late to the ones you did come to."). Kevin's perceived inequity of effort within the group had created serious conflict between him and the other members. Kevin's continued lack of commitment to the group also contributed to Lori's strong feelings of dislike and her constant needling. She scrutinized his contributions more closely than those of the other members and criticized Kevin for statements that she accepted from other people. For example, both Tony and Kevin wanted an entertaining speaker, but Lori singled Kevin out for ridicule about wanting to party more than learn. Because of his inequity of performance, he was being required to measure up more perfectly to the group's performance norms than the others.

Note how easily the stress of inequity can lead to very obvious coalitions which in turn impact the management of group conflict.[32] Coalitions emerge in groups when members with access to few resources, minimal power, or little bargaining leverage seek out other members in an attempt to level the playing field. Group members have also been known to form coalitions when some member comes to identify more with his or her own subgroup than with the group as a whole and when conflict styles tend to be accommodative—those who do more of the accommodating over time may align themselves with others to get the upper hand. Coalitions, although sometimes functional, can also be detrimental. Members may become willing to hurt their own goals in an effort to defeat the most popular member. Groups experiencing a great deal of coalition conflict may leave themselves vulnerable to external threats because their attention is on the conflict. In addition, communication among members may decrease. When members can perceive a common ground of interest many coalitions will disappear.

Although we describe these four types of conflict as though they are distinct, they are not mutually exclusive. One type can easily lead to another. Frequently two or more types blend. In our example this was most clearly seen with Lori, whose dislike of Kevin combined with Kevin's inadequate contribution to the group and his disagreement with her position (Kevin wanted an entertaining speaker, but Lori wanted an educational one). All these conflicts united to intensify Lori's dislike. Lori looked for things over which to be angry with Kevin. She was probably the most relieved member when Kevin eventually left the group.

Managing Conflict

We hope we have convinced you of the value of innovative, opinion deviance and substantive conflict during small group problem solving. Conflict is inevitable when people meet in groups. Avoiding it *circumvents the very reason for engaging in group discussion*—that the thinking of several people is likely to be more valid and thorough than the thinking of one person acting alone. Both the attitudes of group members involved in a conflict and the procedures they use to manage the conflict affect the outcomes. Using further examples of the Speaker Series Committee, we discuss both attitudes and procedures that facilitate productive conflict.

Basic Approaches toward Conflict Management

Most people have a basic attitude or approach toward managing conflict, either *distributive* or *integrative*. The **distributive approach,** also called a *win-lose* attitude, assumes that what one person gains is at another's expense. Thus, there can be only one winning side; the other or others are losers. In the Speaker Series Committee, Tony and Kevin wanted to choose an entertaining speaker and Deidre and Lori wanted an educational one. The distributive orientation assumes that only one faction can win. *Either* Tony and Kevin get their entertaining speaker, *or* Lori and Deidre get their educational one. Whichever wins, the other side loses.

> When you do make a decision, . . . members should believe that they understood the issue; . . . believe that they had an opportunity to provide their arguments for their option that they preferred, their points of view; and . . . if the decision went with them, that they support it.
>
> *J. J., CEO and General Manager, Utility Company*

The **integrative approach** assumes that there is some way to manage the conflict so that all parties can end up winners; in other words, the main concerns of all parties can be integrated into a solution in which all involved receive what is most important to them. Someone with an integrative orientation would assume that a speaker could be found who is *both* entertaining *and* educational; thus, both factions can win. This approach has also been called a *win-win* attitude. A group may not be able to integrate the concerns of *all* members into its final solution or decision. Perhaps members' values are

Distributive Approach

The conflict management approach that assumes fixed resources must be distributed among parties to the conflict; thus, whatever someone wins, someone else loses.

Integrative Approach

The conflict management approach that assumes solutions can be created to satisfy every party to the conflict.

so divergent they cannot be merged, or maybe resources are so scarce that needs cannot be fully met. In such cases, perhaps partial integration—*compromise*—is the best that can be achieved. However, even if a group does not develop a fully integrative solution, it *certainly* will not develop one if members begin with the premise that integration is impossible. Common Ground projects all over the United States, discussed later, show us that even groups made up of members with deeply polarized viewpoints on an issue can find ways to integrate their efforts. Without an integrative orientation, members will not expend their energies to develop creative solutions but will spend time quarreling about the merits of one proposal over another in an attempt to win rather than find the best solution possible.

In a longitudinal study of 11 work groups in large American organizations Kuhn and Poole discovered that the work groups that took the time and energy to create more integrative solutions to their problems compared to those that merely confronted or avoided them produced more effective decisions.[33] In addition, the work groups that used a more integrated conflict style also managed to fulfill other communicative functions effectively. They met the issues head on, worked through obstacles to their problem, and recognized that often they needed collective attention to the problem. These work groups used the difficult task of integration to develop group norms and rules that effectively guided them in future interaction.

Conflict Management Styles and Tactics

Your perception of the conflict situation is a major determinant of how you are likely to deal with the conflict.[34] Elements of the situation include your perceptions about whether the conflict is repetitive, the degree to which you and the other party have mutual goals, how certain you are about how to solve the problem, whether you believe the other party is the source of the conflict, and the degree of negative feelings you have for the other. These combine to influence your desire to cooperate. The specific management style you choose is likely to be a product both of how cooperative and how assertive you are, as illustrated in Figure 13.2.[35]

As you can see each *style* represents a general pattern of behavior developed over time. Specific choices people make in particular situations as they manage conflict will be referred to as conflict *tactics*. The key difference between a style and a tactic is the degree to which a person is aware of his or her behavior.[36] Generally we are less aware of our styles than our tactics. Regardless, competent group members exhibit an awareness of not only their own preferred style and tactics but also those of other group members. This awareness is a key factor in changing unproductive patterns of conflict in a group. As we discuss each of the general conflict styles we will also introduce you to common tactics group members may use relevant to each style. These styles and representative tactics are summarized in Figure 13.3.

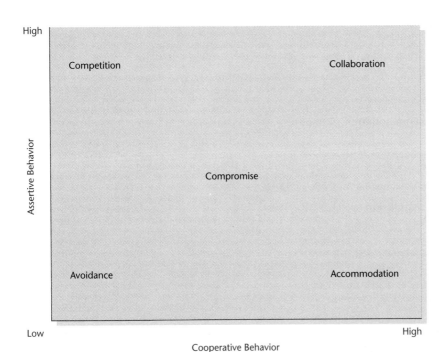

FIGURE 13.2 Your conflict management style depends in part on how assertive and cooperative you are.

Although no conflict style is always best, some conflict styles are perceived as more appropriate in certain circumstances. Canary and Spitzberg found, for example, that the topic of the conflict interacted with the gender of the participants to influence perceptions of both effectiveness and appropriateness.[37] We recommend a contingency view in which the most productive way for settling a conflict depends on time pressures, distribution of information and skills, group member values and needs, and other input variables. For example, two input variables influencing conflict style is the nature of the relationship between the individuals and the type of conflict.[38] Although more collectivist cultures such as Japan may prefer an integrative style that values harmony, preserving the esteem of the others, and relying less on direct confrontation, they may change the style depending on whom the conflict involves and what it concerns. Japanese in conflict over values and opinions tend to be more avoidant with acquaintances than with close friends; they are more integrative with close friends. And if engaged in a conflict of interest, they have no problem being confrontive and dominant with acquaintances compared to close friends.

Whereas each conflict style is appropriate under certain circumstances, having an integrative orientation is always acceptable in problem-solving discussions. The integrative, solution-oriented, and less confrontational styles tend to be associated with group member satisfaction, improved productivity, and increased decision quality.[39]

FIGURE 13.3
Conflict styles and tactics.

Avoidance

Denial
Topic changes
Noncommittal remarks
Irreverent remarks

Accommodation

Giving up/giving in
Disengagement
Denial of needs
Expression of desire for harmony

Competition

Personal criticism
Rejection
Hostile imperatives
Hostile jokes
Hostile questions
Presumptive remarks
Denial of responsibility

Collaboration

Analytic remarks
    Descriptive statements
    Qualifying statements
    Solicitation of disclosure
    Solicitation of criticism
Conciliatory remarks
    Support
    Concessions
    Acceptance of responsibility

Compromise

Appeal to fairness
Suggest a trade-off
Offer a quick, short-term solution

Avoidance

The passive conflict management style that ignores a conflict.

Avoidance   The **avoidance** style is a passive approach in which a participant expends no energy discussing or exploring options. The member who disagrees but says nothing is avoiding conflict. Sometimes called *nonconfrontation*, conflict avoidance reduces satisfaction in groups.[40] Such passive behavior is appropriate only when the problem is unimportant and the risks of making a poor decision are slight. For example, a committee to which one of us belonged was asked to develop a decorating plan for a student lounge/study area. The art instructor on the committee recommended a color scheme not particularly appealing to the chemistry professor on the committee. The students liked the colors, so the chemistry professor kept his objections to himself. He reasoned that because he spent so little time in the lounge, color did not matter much to him.

Individuals avoid conflict by denying, managing the topic, and making noncommittal or irreverent remarks.[41] A group member expresses to you that another member, Kevin, is not doing his fair share of the work and something needs to be done. A response such as, "I do not see that as a problem," can be construed as _denial_. Or you might respond with, "We are winding down our meeting and need to get to the next agenda item," effectively _shifting the topic_ away from the potential issue. A _noncommittal remark_ might look like, "You know that is Kevin being Kevin." Replying with laughter to the concern is considered an _irreverent remark_ that also tries to avoid conflict.

Accommodation   **Accommodation,** also called _appeasement,_ is a highly co-operative but passive approach that occurs when you give in to someone else. It may occur when the issue is not important to you, or when the relationship is more important to you than the outcome. For instance, in the Speaker Series Committee, after a brief discussion about educational versus entertaining speakers, Tony said, "I can go along with an educational speaker. I just want to avoid this arguing." Tony wanted to accommodate in order to end the arguments. Accommodation is appropriate only when the issue is relatively unimportant to you or the other person's needs are genuinely more important to you. Don't accommodate just to end a fight, because the resentment you carry around with you may eventually poison the relationship anyway.

Tony's accommodating tactic is referred as an _expression of desire for harmony_ tactic. Tony goes along with an educational speaker in a personal effort to curtail the arguing. Three other accommodating tactics include variations of _giving up/giving in, disengagement,_ and _denial of needs_.[42] Had Tony responded with, "Have it your way, let's bring in the educational speaker!" he would have given up the conflict. Disengagement would be characterized with a remark like, "You know, I will not even be here for the speaker, so do what you want." Denial of his needs can be found in, "It's okay, go ahead with the speaker you want."

Competition   **Competition** is a highly aggressive, uncooperative style in which one person tries to win over another. Sometimes called _dominating_ or _forcing,_ competition is appropriate when you have strong beliefs about something and you perceive that other approaches will not allow your needs to be acknowledged or accommodated. However, competitive approaches can damage relationships and may end up doing more harm than good. In the Speaker Series Committee, Lori and Kevin competed. Lori threatened to quit the group if only entertaining speakers were chosen, and Kevin told Tony not to accommodate so readily because he, Kevin, had plenty of good arguments left in support of entertaining speakers. Both statements imply that the speaker will do whatever is necessary to get his or her way.

Accommodation

The conflict management style where one person appeases or gives in to the other.

Competition

The uncooperative, aggressive conflict management style where one person attempts to dominate or force the outcome to his or her advantage.

Competitive style tactics include such actions as personal criticism, hostile joking, rejection, and hostile questions.[43] These obviously denote a win-lose orientation and involve one-upping the other party. Lori's *hostile imperative* served as a threat to leave the group if Kevin got his way. Kevin, on the other hand, created a coalition with Tony to gang up on Lori. Competitiveness between Lori and Kevin can be expressed in other ways. Both may have *personally criticized* the other with remarks such as, "Lori, you are so selfish and unconcerned about the rest of us." Kevin could show *rejection* of Lori's hostile imperative by responding to her with, "Go ahead and quit—we don't need you," effectively dismissing her threat and attacking her personally. A *hostile question* that demeans another person could come in the form of a remark from Lori like, "Kevin, who does most of the work for this group?" Kevin on the other hand could attribute feelings to Lori that she has not acknowledged in a *presumptive remark* such as, "Lori, you're just making yourself miserable threatening to quit." Parties in competition also have at their disposal tactics that are designed to *deny personal responsibility* for the conflict. How could Lori deny any personal responsibility for the conflict between her and Kevin?

Collaboration

Collaboration, also called *negotiating* or *problem solving*, is a cooperative and assertive style that stems from an integrative attitude. It encourages all parties to a conflict to work together in searching for a solution that meets everyone's needs. In the Speaker Series Committee, Deidre suggested that the committee look for a speaker who was both entertaining and educational. In doing this, she assumed that both important needs of the factions could be met without either faction having to give up anything, that each faction's "must have" point could be accommodated. Collaborative solutions can be ideal because all members of groups that arrive at collaborative solutions believe they have won without the others' having lost. However, collaboration often takes more time than other approaches and certainly takes more energy.

Compared to competitive tactics, collaborative ones focus on mutual rather than individual concerns and attempt to facilitate gains for all parties involved in the conflict.[44] They are often referred to as integrative because they recognize the interdependence between parties. The first major category of collaborative tactics is *analytical remarks*. These facilitate collaboration by describing and disclosing important information as the parties try to maximize their gains. These kinds of statements are most like the kind you would expect in a supportive versus defensive group climate. Descriptive statements are nonevaluative remarks about events like, "We have confirmed the availability of individual speakers that fit both categories and some that could be both educational and entertaining." Qualifying remarks from group members would define the nature of the conflict between members. For instance, Diedre could say, "Lori and Kevin appear to disagree over the kind of speaker we could get, but I sense that both would entertain the idea of a speaker who could be both

---

Collaboration

The assertive, cooperative conflict management style that assumes a solution can be found that fully meets the needs of all parties to a conflict.

entertaining and educational." Group members can also *solicit both disclosure and criticism* in a nonhostile fashion. Tony could add to the discussion by soliciting from Lori what she meant by saying she would quit. Diedre could also solicit criticism of herself by asking for feedback from the group about her behaviors in the conflict between Lori and Kevin.

The second category of collaborative tactics involves those that are conciliatory; they demonstrate one's role in the conflict and display a willingness to work toward mutual gain.[45] For example, Kevin could back off his attacks of Lori and show *support* for her feelings, "I can see why you would want to quit, Lori." Lori, on the other hand, can reconcile with Kevin by showing a willingness to be flexible, offering a *concession,* rather than threaten to quit if she does not get her way. Important to collaboration is recognizing your role in the conflict and thus being accountable for the nature of the conflict. Kevin could show this *acceptance of responsibility* by acknowledging how he ganged up on Lori in order to win or how he had let the group down by not doing his fair share.

Compromise   A **compromise,** also called a *shared outcome,* assumes that each party to the conflict will have to give up something in order to gain something more important. In the Speaker Series Committee, Chris suggested a compromise when he said; "Maybe we can get two speakers, less expensive, one educational and one entertaining." Each faction would have to agree to give up the idea of bringing in one very well-known speaker. Thus, compromises entail some losses for both parties. For this reason, we recommend attempting to find a collaborative, fully integrative solution when the decision is important to all group members, one in which each member will be responsible for implementing the outcome and the group is not pressed for time.

However, we think compromise should *not* be considered a dirty word! When collaborative resolution is impossible or takes more time than is available, a compromise is a desirable and ethical outcome, especially if each group member feels that what he or she had to give up is fair in comparison with what others had to give up.

Chris's suggestion that they get two speakers by compromising their desires for one well-paid speaker is an example of a *suggested trade-off* tactic common to compromise.[46] He could have also *appealed to fairness* by remarking, "Lori and Kevin you both got what you wanted last time so this time let's go with two speakers." *Offering a quick short-term solution,* "We do not have time to complain about this, let's ask the educational speaker because we can get her immediately," is also an option for the group.

Expressing Disagreement Ethically

Ethical behaviors in conflict situations are those that promote the beneficial outcomes of conflict (e.g., greater understanding of issues, increased cohesiveness) while minimizing the destructive outcomes (e.g., hurt feelings, personal

Compromise

The conflict management style that assumes each party must give up something to get something.

attacks). The following suggestions will help members behave with integrity and sensitivity during conflicts:

1. **Do express your disagreement.**

   We have already noted that not confronting disagreements can reduce satisfaction with the group, and failure to express honest disagreement circumvents the decision-making and problem-solving process in a group. By not speaking up when you disagree, you deprive the group of potentially valuable information. In a sense you deceive, because your silence suggests that you agree.

2. **Stick with the issue at hand.**

   Kreps suggests that when you disagree, you should deal directly with the issue under discussion. Do not bring up side issues or allow hidden agenda items to motivate you.[47] To do so is as unethical as to use irrelevant emotional stories to arouse support.

3. **Use rhetorical sensitivity in expressing your disagreement.**

   Be sensitive and perceptive enough to select words that will not connote negative images. Especially do not try to push others' emotional buttons. Recall from Chapter 6 that this personality trait involves monitoring the effects of your statements on others and adjusting as appropriate. Use persuasion, not threats, to make your points.[48] Being rhetorically sensitive during conflict also means you'll follow the next ethical guideline.

4. **Disagree with the idea but do not ever criticize the person.**

   Express disagreement so that it does not devalue the person with whom you disagree. Members of groups with norms for expressing conflict cooperatively and integratively are more satisfied with the group's process and outcome than members of groups with norms for competitive and distributive (win–lose) expression of conflict.[49] Thus, "One flaw in your proposal to shut down the snack bar is that it does not consider the food service needs of evening students" is far superior to "You inconsiderate bozo! What are the evening students supposed to do?" Above all, no name-calling or personal attacks!

5. **Base your disagreement on evidence and reasoning.**

   Kreps notes that disagreements should be reasonable and substantive, based on evidence and reasoning.[50] They should not be based on rumor, innuendo, unsubstantiated information, or emotionalism. If you have no evidence or your reasoning is shown to be potentially faulty, *agree* instead of quarreling. As much as possible, keep the conflict issue based. This has the added advantage of being more likely to be persuasive.

6. **React to disagreement in a spirit of inquiry, not defensiveness.**

   Alderton and Frey believe that group members' reactions to argument are more important than the arguments themselves in creating group polarization.[51] We mentioned in Chapter 6 that your willingness to communicate must be greater than your need to protect yourself from disagreement or embarrassment. If someone disagrees with you, do not react defensively as though you had been attacked personally. Keep your mind open to others' ideas, evaluations, and suggestions. Listen actively to your fellow member's remarks. Be certain that the person disagreeing has understood your position correctly, then clarify any misunderstandings, and work together to search for the most effective solutions. In this way you can make conflict work *for* rather than *against* the group. This may not be easy! But it will benefit the group and you will have a clear conscience.

> Anybody can get upset, but it takes some effective communication to have something meaningful occur. In my judgment, losing your temper is not one of those things.
>
> *J. R., Lobbyist and former State Legislator*

7. <u>**If someone persists in attacking *you*, stay calm and speak reasonably.**</u>

One of the biggest challenges a group member has is to respond to a personal attack by another. The worst thing you can do is let another's attacks intimidate you into being silent! Instead, confront the attacking member calmly and reasonably, explaining how you feel and what you want the other to do: "I resent your personal attacks, and I think they are inappropriate. I am willing to listen to your objections, but I want you to stop your attacks now." If the attacker was caught up in the heat of the moment, he or she may apologize and calm down. If your initial confrontation doesn't succeed, ask for the *group's* intervention: "Do we all think personal attacks are unacceptable behavior?" The other members, who probably are as uncomfortable as you, will now be encouraged to support you in confronting the attacker.

8. **Use an integrative rather than a distributive <u>approach to solving the conflict.</u>**

Assume that there is a way to satisfy, at least partially, the important needs of all parties to the conflict. Use your energy to search for alternatives that integrate all parties' needs, not to destroy the other party. Act in ways that improve, not damage, the relationship. Remember that a solution satisfying all parties will be more lasting than one leaving one party feeling disgruntled or mistreated. Also, consider the ethics of a person who gains pleasure from beating another in a way that damages the *group!*

Consider This 13.4

Review the eight steps and identify the principles for expressing disagreements ethically. Then ask yourself how each step tries to encourage the principle.

The whole idea that you have to negotiate with people that you have no control over is a very good skill, and I think people need to develop it.

B. H., Director, State-Level Program

No matter how skilled at expressing disagreement and how ethical, group members can still crash on the rocks of conflict if their procedures for handling it are poor. We have selected six procedures for managing stubborn conflicts: *Principled Negotiation, Mediation, Voting, Forcing, Arbitration, and Common Ground approaches.*

Negotiating Principled Agreement

A task-oriented group experiencing a conflict must move toward resolution for the group's goals to be accomplished. There are a variety of techniques designed to help groups resolve conflict. We especially like the *principled negotiation* procedure because it is consistent with all the ethical principles we have outlined above and is an extremely effective procedure that helps a group negotiate consensus from initially divergent points of view. As described by Fisher and Ury, **principled negotiation** is an all-purpose strategy that encourages all participants in a conflict situation to collaborate by expressing their needs and searching for alternatives that meet those needs.[52] It is called "principled" because it is based on ethical principles that encourage users to remain decent individuals and not act in ways that will damage the relationship among them. It puts the integrative approach into action.

Principled negotiation is an efficient and fair way to develop a solution meeting the legitimate needs of all parties; therefore, it is likely to produce lasting solutions. Tutzauer and Roloff say the guidelines in the principled negotiation procedure are consistent with their discoveries about communication behaviors that produce integrative outcomes.[53] They found that exchanging information, asking questions instead of making demands, and foregoing rigid, inflated positions helped bargainers attain integrative outcomes. *Appropriate communication techniques alone* helped bargainers attain integrative outcomes regardless of their initial orientations. In addition, this type of negotiation will not harm the relationship among participants and frequently improves it. We particularly like it because it recognizes the major elements that enter into conflict—perceptions, emotions, behaviors, and interaction among individuals—and acknowledges that each must be considered. The following description of principled negotiation shows how a group can incorporate the communication principles presented throughout this book, including such concepts as rhetorical sensitivity, active listening, and integrative conflict management, into a practical, effective technique for managing conflict. The group leader, an outside consultant, or members themselves can use the procedure. Here are the four steps:

Principled Negotiation

A general strategy that enables parties in a conflict to express their needs openly and search for alternatives to meet the needs of all parties without damaging their relationships.

I've seen cases where <u>people</u> were attacked about their ideas, and I think it's a big mistake. . . . It never works.

J. J., CEO and General Manager, Utility Company

1. **Separate the people from the problem.**

   In most conflicts, the content of the disagreement becomes tangled with the relationship among the participants. Each should be dealt with directly and separately. All parties should be given the opportunity to explain, without interference, how they perceive the conflict and how they feel about it. Parties should share perceptions as they try to put themselves into each other's shoes. If emotions run high, allow them to be vented. Do not overreact to emotional outbursts, but listen actively and show by your actions as well as your words that you care about the needs of the other members with whom your interests conflict. The goal is not to become bosom buddies with the other party to a conflict (although that may happen), but to develop a good working relationship characterized by mutual respect.[54]

2. **Focus on interests, not positions.**

   When group members stake out certain positions ("I insist that we have an educational speaker!"), they become attached to those *positions* rather than the original *needs* the positions were designed to meet. For example, we discussed earlier the committee that debated closing the food service facility at 5 PM. One side's position was that the snack bar must be closed, but the other side's position was that the snack bar must be kept open. These two positions are incompatible, and there is no way to reconcile them—in their present form, one must win and one must lose. However, when group members started to explore the *interests* behind the positions (the desire to save money and the desire to meet needs of evening students), then an avenue opened whereby both parties could have their desires met by finding a way to do *both simultaneously*—provide the students with food without raising costs by expanding the vending service. Rigidly adhering to the initial positions would have precluded the discovery of this solution. Support for this comes from Innami, who discovered that when members stick to their positions, decision quality is impaired, but when they exchange facts and reasons, decision quality improves.[55] Moreover, high-quality arguments are more persuasive and overcome the influence of such factors as status differences.[56]

3. **Invent options for mutual gain.**

   The previous example illustrates how a new option, expanded vending service, was created that had not been apparent when the conflict started. We earlier have suggested separating the invention process from the decision process, and employing techniques like brainstorming. Negotiators should assume that the interests of all parties can be integrated into the group's final solution. The same committee that debated food service options for evening students also discussed how evening students could be served by the bookstore.[57] The evening student adviser on the committee noted that the campus bookstore was open in the evenings only during the first week of the quarter. Many evening students who drove directly to campus from work could not arrive early enough for the bookstore's regular hours, and so were unable to exchange books, purchase supplies, or even browse. The adviser proposed that the bookstore hours be extended to 8 PM every evening. The campus budget officer objected strongly, noting that the proposal would result in cost increases for personnel salaries unlikely to be recovered by purchases made by evening students.

The positions adopted by each person represented attempts to meet the legitimate needs of two important groups: the evening students and the budget watchdogs. However, through open discussion focused on the interests (not the positions) of each, a solution was invented that incorporated both sets of needs. The bookstore would remain open two evenings per week throughout the quarter, and would start business later in the morning the rest of the week. The total number of hours of bookstore operation was the same, so costs were not increased, but the distribution of the hours changed to meet the needs of more students.

4.   **Use objective criteria.**
Negotiations will be perceived as fairer if objective criteria *agreed upon by all parties* are established as the standard for judging alternatives. Group members will profit from establishing such criteria at the beginning of any problem-solving session, but they should *insist* on it in prolonged conflicts because such criteria make negotiation less likely to be a contest of wills and more likely to be settled upon principle instead of pressure. This is an egalitarian approach in that much of the battle for dominance is removed from the negotiation process. For example, many people use the *Bluebook* to determine a fair price for used cars. You may want $5,000 for your 10-year-old Nissan Sentra, and your buyer may want to pay only $100. However, if both of you agree that the *Bluebook* is an appropriate standard and it indicates that a fair price is $1,500 to $2,000, depending on model and condition, this narrows the negotiating range between you and makes reaching agreement more likely.

In another example, the United Way organization of a major midwestern city nearly disintegrated as a result of arguments over which agencies should receive money. Finally, the *ad hoc* committee established a set of cost accounting procedures enabling each agency to determine how many people could be served for what amount. These procedures then served as relatively objective criteria for United Way to use in determining which agencies to fund.

Sometimes, despite a group's best intentions, even principled negotiation fails to bring about consensus, or a group is operating under a time deadline that forces members to use other methods.

When Negotiation Fails: Alternative Procedures

Settlements derived through negotiation by the group itself are preferable to solutions imposed by someone else because they tend to be more acceptable to all members. The first two of the four alternatives presented in the following section involve the group in breaking a deadlock. However, sometimes a group simply is not able to break a deadlock. In that case, when a decision *must* be made, the designated leader has the two remaining options.

Mediation by the Designated Leader If a seemingly irreconcilable conflict emerges over goals or alternatives, the leader might suggest the following procedure, which is an abbreviated form of that used by professional mediators for apparently deadlocked negotiations between a union and management. The procedure represents a last-chance group attempt to arrive at an acceptable decision without resorting to third-party arbitration. If this procedure fails, other alternative procedures can be taken to resolve the conflict issue without producing consensus. Two-sided conflict is assumed for simplicity.

1. Presentation of alternatives.
   a. A proponent of side 1 presents exactly what the subgroup wants or believes and why. Other members supporting the position may add clarifying statements, arguments, evidence, and claims, but proponents of side 2 can say nothing.
   b. Side 2 can now ask for clarification, restatements, explanations, or supporting evidence, but may not disagree, argue, or propose any other alternative.
   c. A spokesperson for side 2 is now required to explain side 1's position to the complete satisfaction of all other group members, both side 1 and side 2. (Note the similarity to active listening presented in Chapter 3.) Only when this person has restated side 1's proposal and supporting arguments to everyone's satisfaction is the group ready to advance to the next step.
   d. Side 2's position is now presented by a spokesperson. Exactly the same procedural rules apply as during presentation and clarification of side 1's position.
2. Charting alternatives.
   a. The designated group leader now writes both positions on a chalkboard or large poster and underneath lists pros (benefits, advantages) claimed by its proponents and evidence advanced in its support. Under the heading cons the leader should list any disadvantages, possible harmful effects, or evidence advanced against the alternative. An example of such a chart is shown in Figure 13.4.
   b. When all positions have been charted, the group may want to see whether there is unanimity about any of the statements on the chart. What, if anything, do members agree upon?

FIGURE 13.4
Example of a chart of pros and cons.

How might accidents be reduced on National Ave?
Construct an overpass

Pro	Con
Would eliminate accidents, if used	Would be expensive
Would not impede traffic flow	Students might not use it (inconvenience)
Would not take long to complete (compared to underground tunnel)	People might throw things at cars below

3. Search for creative alternatives.

   a. The designated leader reviews all elements of common ground shared by all group members, such as shared interest in solving the problem, shared history of the group, and so forth, then urges group members to seek a win–win resolution, an alternative all could accept. The leader may propose such a solution, or

   b. The designated leader asks members to compromise and create an alternative that meets the minimum requirements of both sides.

4. Resolution occurs when and if a consensus or compromise alternative is adopted.

If this procedure is successful, some time should be spent by group members discussing the procedure itself, how they feel about the group and each of the other members, and how the group can manage future conflicts. Generally, when the previously described procedure is followed out of a sincere desire to resolve the conflict, the group will find at least a compromise and will develop increased cohesiveness and team spirit. Lacking a consensus or compromise, other procedures will be needed to reach a decision.

Voting   *Voting* is one such alternative procedure. Naturally, some members are bound to dislike the outcome, but voting may be a necessary step in overcoming an impasse. You may recall the example presented earlier of a faculty subcommittee's presenting a sweeping proposal to the full faculty committee, only to be met with dismay instead of enthusiasm. After repeated attempts to develop an integrative solution failed, the committee took a vote to decide the issue. One danger with voting is that the group may arrive at premature closure on an issue. Be especially careful, if this is the option you select, that the group really is deadlocked.

Forcing   Another option is *forcing*. Here, the leader breaks the deadlock and decides on behalf of the group. For example, in the U.S. Senate the presiding officer can break a tie. As with voting, several members are likely to be disappointed, but in instances in which an outside group, parent organization, or legitimate authority demands a report or when the group faces a deadline, a leader may have little choice.

Third-Party Arbitration *Third-party arbitration* occurs when the group brings in an outside negotiator to resolve its differences. This typically happens with joint labor–management disputes and some court-related cases. Arbitrators often have the power to resolve issues any way they please, from deciding entirely in favor of one party to splitting the difference between them. Sometimes, just the threat of bringing in a third-party arbitrator is enough to force conflict participants to negotiate with each other in good faith. Usually, all parties to the conflict end up feeling dissatisfied. Thus, third-party arbitration should be proposed only when the leader believes the group has reached an impasse and the cost of continuing the conflict, including resentment and the possibility of destroying the group, will exceed the cost of arbitration. Of course, group members must agree to such a resolution procedure.

Sometimes, no resolution about a group's issue is possible, but that does not automatically create a hopeless situation. Even when members cannot agree on basic values or goals, they often can find some areas where they do agree, as with the *Common Ground approaches* we now discuss.

Common Ground Approaches

We began this chapter with a story about Common Ground groups. These kinds of projects have sprung up all over the country.[58] Their purpose is to seek alternative ways to ease tensions surrounding highly contentious and divisive public issues (e.g., abortion, affirmative action, animal testing, biogenetics, bilingual education, immigration). A unique characteristic of these efforts is their common goal: they do not seek to solve the issue or mediate a compromise. Rather, they attempt to create a safe place for dialogue to occur between deeply divided individuals in the hope of finding common ground, thereby easing tensions and perhaps reducing violence. In addition, they attempt to discover and use areas of genuinely shared values between these individuals constructively, something often hidden in contentious debate. **Common Ground dialogue** is a process of constructively managing socially divisive conflict.[59]

You will notice that Common Ground small groups, in their attempt to manage their conflict, are different from those we have focused on in this chapter. We have dealt with groups whose members must manage conflict in their attempts to come to some agreed-upon resolution. Common Ground groups are created with the sole purpose of finding a way to bridge highly divisive viewpoints that can result in violence. So these group members enter their groups already knowing they do not agree and their purpose is not to solve their differences or mediate a compromise. All the above procedures for managing failed negotiation assume a goal of resolution; Common Ground dialogue does not. Yet you will see some, if not all, of the same ethical principles in the rules guiding Common Ground dialogue.

Common Ground Dialogue

A process of constructively managing divisive conflict, in which the participants are unlikely ever to agree, by focusing on the goals and values they *can* share and agree to.

Chasin and Herzig have described several behavioral patterns which occur when individuals get caught up in chronic conflict or stalemated controversy.[60] Often those on one side will not listen to those on the other side; individuals become entrenched in their positions. Questions one side asks the other side clearly have ulterior motives. Members of either side tend to see the members of the other side as all alike. This happens in part because, when confronted, people do minimize their internal differences to appear "together" on the issue. Members of both sides tend to blame the other side for the problem, refuse to see their role in the problem, mind-read the other side, and remain closed-minded about the other side. Attempts by either side to begin a process of conciliation are perceived as propaganda ploys. Finally, members of both sides believe there is value in sticking with the struggle in spite of outsider efforts to break the deadlock. You will see in the following rules of Common Ground dialogue attempts to overcome these behavioral patterns in the pursuit of common ground.

The following is one kind of Common Ground dialogue model applied to the topic of abortion, as in our opening case. You will see that the process is far more involving than you might have expected after reading our case study. This model is comprised of a total of nine steps.[61] Facilitators ensure that both sides of the issue are equally represented and the sessions are held on neutral ground.

Recruitment of Participants

1. Potential participants are identified through informal networks and activist publications, after which Common Ground coordinators make telephone invitations. During these conversations, potential participants are filled in on the Common Ground procedures and answer questions.

2. Follow-up letters are sent to those wishing to participate. The letter details the kind of dialogue that will be facilitated and includes a chart of the dialogue rules. This chart explains the difference between dialogue and debate. Recruits are also given questions to think about before the meeting.

Premeeting Activity

3. Prior to the actual Common Ground dialogue session, participants get acquainted at an informal dinner. They may *not* talk about abortion and may share whatever they wish about themselves as long as they do not reveal which side of the abortion issue they are on. You can see here that the purpose of this step is to help these individuals see each other as *people*, not positions. Sometimes they are also asked to fill out questionnaires the way they think someone from the other side would complete them.

Establishing the Ground Rules for the Dialogue

4. Participants are assigned seats next to someone on the other side of the issue. They are then reintroduced to the dialogue rules and they are asked verbally to agree to them. They must maintain confidentiality, avoid interrupting each other, use respectful speech (e.g., "pro-choice" not "anti-life"), and give each member the right to "pass" if they do not want to respond to a question or comment.

5. The facilitators share with the group their observations of the informal dinner interaction. They point out how much members of each side are in fact more different from each other than the other side assumed.

Rules during the Dialogue

6. Three questions are asked of each member. After a question is read, each member responds in order while everyone else remains attentive and silent. The questions invite members to share a personal experience related to abortion, give what they believe to be the heart of the matter, and identify any gray areas in the abortion issue.

7. Once all three questions are processed, participants are encouraged to ask questions of each other. Participants are encouraged to ask genuine questions of curiosity, not rhetorical ones with hidden agendas. They are reminded not to attempt to persuade but to focus on the member present. "They" and "them" are discouraged so that they do not act as representatives of one side. Active listening is facilitated during discussion.

8. When the dialogue begins to wind down, the facilitators move to end the session. They ask two questions in the same format as the three in step 6. Each member is asked to reflect on what she or he did or didn't do to make the dialogue go as it did. And members are asked to share parting thoughts.

Follow-Up

9. A couple of weeks later, participants are telephoned. They are asked to offer any suggestions for improving the model and how they have taken and will take their experience into their daily lives.

Common Ground dialogue models such as this one are another way to manage failed negotiations and in this case chronic conflict. This model outlines only the general procedures and does not begin to touch on the many rules that guide the actual dialogue. Each step, when applied in actual dialogue, involves extensive mediation by facilitators so that participants can "hear" each other and safely learn where they have common ground. Then, this discovery is used to promote more positive outcomes and possible joint projects by the participants (e.g., reducing teen pregnancy, funding and supporting adoption as a choice) while allowing them to "agree to disagree."

SUMMARY

1. Conflict occurs when interdependent parties perceive incompatible goals, scarce resources, and interference in achieving their goals and express this struggle outwardly. It has perceptual, emotional, behavioral, and interactional dimensions.

2. Although conflict can cause bad feelings, lower cohesiveness, or even group disintegration, it can also stimulate member involvement and understanding, increase cohesiveness, and produce better decisions. An opinion or innovative deviate expresses disagreement and may cause or experience discomfort, but contributes to critical thinking.

3. Types of conflict include substantive (task-oriented), affective (over personality and power differences), procedural (over how the group operates), and inequity (over unequal workloads or contributions by members). One type can lead to another in an actual conflict situation.

4. A distributive orientation to managing conflict assumes winners and losers, but an integrative orientation assumes the possibility of a win–win solution. Degree of cooperation and assertiveness underlie the five common conflict management styles of avoidance, accommodation, competition, collaboration, and compromise, and the tactics used with each style.

5. Ethical principles governing appropriate conflict-managing behavior include expressing one's views sensitively, focusing on the issues, and expressing the disagreement but not attacking another person. Disagreements should be based on substance, not innuendo. Members should respond nondefensively, with a spirit of inquiry, and remain open-minded to contradictory ideas. Finally, members should avoid fight-to-the-death conflict resolution strategies.

6. Group members should try to use procedures such as the principled negotiation procedure that are ethical and help parties find solutions satisfactory to all.

7. If a group cannot achieve consensus, other options include mediation by the leader or voting. Forcing or third-party arbitration, where someone decides for the group, is a last resort.

8. Common Ground dialogue can be used to discuss polarizing public issues, such as abortion, by helping participants discover genuinely shared values that can lessen tension and violence.

KEY TERMS

 Test your knowledge of these key terms by visiting the Online Learning Center website at mhhe.com/galanes11

Accommodation	Competition	Inequity conflict
Affective conflict	Compromise	Integrative approach
Avoidance	Conflict	Principled negotiation
Collaboration	Deviate	Procedural conflict
Common Ground dialogue	Distributive approach	Substantive conflict

EXERCISES

 Go to self-quizzes on the Online Learning Center at mhhe.com/galanes11 to test your knowledge of the chapter concepts

1. Select a group to which you now belong. Try to remember all the recent conflicts or disagreements experienced by the group. On paper, briefly describe each conflict, indicate what type it was, and explain how it was settled. Use the following format:

Description of Conflict	Type of Conflict	How Conflict Was Resolved

2. Think of an extended conflict you observed or were involved in. Analyze it according to the perceptions-emotions-behavior-interaction model.
   a. How did each element of the model affect each other element?
   b. What was the relationship of the conflicting parties to each other at the beginning of the conflict episode and at the end?
   c. What do you conclude about conflict from this?
   d. Would you do anything differently if you were faced with the same situation again?

3. Select a controversial issue for your class about which there are two or more contrasting positions. Form into discussion groups of four or five so that at least two people initially are on each side of the issue. Two classmates should serve as observers for each group of discussants. Discuss the issue and attempt to come to some consensus. Observers should note and report on the following:
   a. What was said about the issue?
   b. How were disagreements expressed?
   c. Were there any ways that disagreement could have been expressed more appropriately? (The observers should pay particular attention to the effect on the receiver of the disagreeing remarks.)

4. Your class should split into dyads with one nonparticipating observer per dyad. One dyad partner should play the role of quality control manager and the other that of production manager in a manufacturing plant. Assume the production manager wants to get the quality control manager to reject fewer items so that production can be increased. Half the groups should be instructed to negotiate with a distributive orientation and half with an integrative one. Observers should note and report exactly what was said in attempting to settle the conflict and what appeared to be the effect. Discuss how you felt in your particular situation. Were there any consistent differences in the feelings of the participants in the two assigned orientations? What did you learn from this activity?

5. Select a controversial public issue with at least two sides. In groups or dyads, explain how you would use the principled negotiation procedure to help the competing sides resolve their differences:
   a. Imagine how people from each side feel about the situation and what their perceptions might be of themselves and people from the opposite side.
   b. First, describe the positions of each side. Then determine what might be the needs or interests behind the positions.
   c. Determine whether there are any interests that might be compatible, and brainstorm options that bring these common interests together.
   d. Determine whether there are any objective criteria that could be used to help the parties resolve their conflict, and show how these criteria might be used.

Discuss your findings and suggestions as a whole class. What did you learn by using the principled negotiation procedure?

BIBLIOGRAPHY

Cathcart, Robert S., Larry A. Samovar, and Linda D. Henman. *Small Group Communication: Theory and Practice*. 7th ed. Dubuque, IA: Brown & Benchmark, 1996, Section 4.

Fisher, Roger, and William Ury. *Getting to Yes: Negotiating Agreement Without Giving In*. New York: Penguin Books, 1983.

Hocker, Joyce L., and William W. Wilmot. *Interpersonal Conflict*. 3rd ed. Dubuque, IA: Wm. C. Brown, 1991.

Pearce, W. Barnett, and Kimberly A. Pearce. "Extending the Theory of the Coordinated Management of Meaning (CMM) through a Community Dialogue Process," *Communication Theory*, 10 (2000): 405–23;

Putnam, Linda L. "Conflict in Group Decision Making." In *Communication and Group Decision Making*. Randy Y. Hirokawa and Marshall Scott Poole, eds. Beverly Hills, CA: Sage 1986, 175–97.

NOTES

1. The primary sources for this case study are Leslie Wirpsa, "Listening Key as Foes Seek Common Goals: Abortion Activists Find Hospitality Helps Melt Barriers," *National Catholic Reporter* (June 28, 1996): 5; and Frederica Mathewes-Green, "Pro-life, Pro-Choice: Can We Talk?" *The Christian Century* (January 3, 1996): 12–15. Other articles providing supporting information are Gene Warner, "Rev. Schenck Joins Common-Ground Camp on Abortion," *The Buffalo News* (March 23, 1999): 4B; Benjamin J. Hubbard, "Room Exists for Discussion on Abortion," *Los Angeles Times* (January 24, 1998): B10; Melodee Hall Blobaum, "Genuine Dialogue Can Bridge the Gap," *The Kansas City Star* (February 20, 1999): 2; and Barbara Brotman, "Both Sides of Abortion Issue Seek Detente; Daylong Session Finds Common Ground," *The Plain Dealer* (December 1, 1998): 6F.

2. Judith Martin and Thomas K. Nakayama, *Experiencing Intercultural Communication: An Introduction* (Boston: McGraw Hill, 2001): 171.

3. Carolyn J. Wood, "Challenging the Assumptions Underlying the Use of Participatory Decision-Making Strategies: A Longitudinal Case Study," *Small Group Behavior* 20 (1989): 428–48.

4. Victor D. Wall, Jr., Gloria J. Galanes, and Susan B. Love, "Small, Task-Oriented Groups: Conflict, Conflict Management, Satisfaction, and Decision Quality," *Small Group Behavior* 18 (1987): 31–55.

5. Kathleen M. O'Connor, Deborah H. Gruenfeld, and Joseph E. McGrath, "The Experience and Effects of Conflict in Continuing Work Groups," *Small Group Research* 24 (August 1993): 362–82.

6. M. R. Shakun, "Formalizing Conflict Resolution in Policy-Making," *International Journal of General Systems* 7 (1981): 207–15.

7. Gordon L. Lippett, "Managing Conflict in Today's Organization," *Training and Development Journal* 36 (1982): 67–75.

8. Joyce L. Hocker and William W. Wilmot, *Interpersonal Conflict*, 3rd ed. (Dubuque, IA: Wm. C. Brown, 1991): 12.

9. Sally M. Vogl-Bauer, "Examining Stress in Small Groups," in *Small Group Communication: Theory and Practice*, 7th ed., eds. Robert Cathcart, Larry Samovar, and Linda Henman (Madison, WI: Brown & Benchmark, 1996): 195–97.

10. Morton Deutsch, "Conflicts: Productive and Destructive," *Journal of Social Issues* 25 (1969): 7–41; Kenneth W. Thomas, "Conflict and Conflict Management," in *Handbook of Industrial and Organizational Psychology*, ed. M. Dunnette (Chicago: Rand McNally, 1976): 890–934; Louis B. Pondy, "Organizational Conflict: Concepts and Models," *Administrative Science Quarterly* 12 (1976): 296–320; Brent D. Ruben, "Communication and Conflict: A System-Theoretic Perspective," *Quarterly Journal of Speech* 64 (1978): 202–12; J. Guetzkow and

J. Gyr, "An Analysis of Conflict in Decision-Making Groups," *Human Relations* 7 (1954): 367–82; and E. P. Torrance, "Group Decision-Making and Disagreement," *Social Forces* 35 (1957): 314–18.

11. Karl Smith, David W. Johnson, and Roger T. Johnson, "Can Conflict Be Constructive? Controversy versus Concurrence Seeking in Learning Groups," *Journal of Educational Psychology* 73 (1981): 654–63.

12. Charles R. Franz and K. Gregory Jin, "The Structure of Group Conflict in a Collaborative Work Group during Information Systems Development," *Journal of Applied Communication Research* 23 (May 1995): 108–27.

13. Ibid.

14. Sue D. Pendell, "Deviance and Conflict in Small Group Decision Making: An Exploratory Study," *Small Group Behavior* 21 (1990): 393–403.

15. Svenn Lindskold and Gyuseog Han, "Group Resistance to Influence by a Conciliatory Member," *Small Group Behavior* 19 (1988): 19–34.

16. Carl L. Thameling and Patricia H. Andrews, "Majority Responses to Opinion Deviates: A Communicative Analysis," *Small Group Research* 23 (1992): 475–502.

17. Kristin B. Valentine and B. Aubrey Fisher, "An Interaction Analysis of Verbal Innovative Deviance in Small Groups," *Speech Monographs* 41 (1974): 413–20.

18. Mark K. Covey, "The Relationship between Social Skill and Conflict Resolution Tactics" (Paper presented at the annual convention of the Rocky Mountain Psychological Association, Snowbird, Utah, 1983).

19. Rick Garlick and Paul A. Mongeau, "Argument Quality and Group Member Status as Determinants of Attitudinal Minority Influence," *Western Journal of Communication* 57 (Summer 1993): 289–308.

20. Renee Meyers, Dale Brashers, and Jennifer Hanner, "Majority-Minority Influence: Identifying Argumentative Patterns and Predicting Argument-Outcome Links," *Journal of Communication* 50 (2000): 3–30.

21. The conflict described in the following episode and used as the extended example here is segment 2 of the videotape ancillary to this text,

Communicating Effectively in Small Groups (Dubuque, IA: Wm. C. Brown, 1991).

22. Guetzkow and Gyr, "An Analysis of Conflict," 367–82.

23. Ibid.

24. Roger C. Pace, "Personalized and Depersonalized Conflict in Small Group Discussions: An Examination of Differentiation," *Small Group Research* 21 (1990): 79–96.

25. Roger Fisher and Scott Brown, *Getting Together: Building a Relationship That Gets to Yes* (Boston: Houghton-Mifflin, 1988): 16–23.

26. Linda L. Putnam, "Conflict in Group Decision Making," in *Communication and Group Decision Making*, eds. Randy Y. Hirokawa and Marshall Scott Poole (Beverly Hills, CA: Sage, 1986): 175–96.

27. Elizabeth Hobman, Prashant Bordia, Bernd Irmer, and Artemis Chang, "The Expression of Conflict in Computer-Mediated and Face-to-Face Groups," *Small Group Research* 33 (2002): 439–65.

28. Ibid.

29. Ibid.

30. Ibid.

31. Victor D. Wall, Jr., and Linda L. Nolan, "Small Group Conflict: A Look at Equity, Satisfaction, and Styles of Conflict Management," *Small Group Behavior* 18 (1987): 188–211.

32. Renee Meyers and Dale Brashers, "Influence Processes in Group Interaction," in *The Handbook of Group Communication Theory & Research*, ed. Lawrence Frey (Thousand Oaks: CA, 1999): 298.

33. Tim Kuhn and Marshall Scott Poole, "Do Conflict Management Styles Affect Group Decision Making?: Evidence from a Longitudinal Field Study," *Human Communication Research* 26 (2000): 558–90.

34. R. H. Kilmann and K. Thomas, "Developing a Forced-Choice Measure of Conflict-Handling Behavior: The MODE Instrument," *Educational and Psychological Measurement* 37 (1977): 309–25.

35. Hal Witteman, "Analyzing Interpersonal Conflict: Nature of Awareness, Type of Initiating Event, Situational Perceptions, and Management Styles," *Western Journal of Communication* 56 (Summer 1992): 248–80.

36. Larry Erbert, "Conflict Management: Styles, Strategies, and Tactics," in *Small Group Communication: Theory and Practice*, 7th ed., eds. Robert Cathcart, Larry Samovar, and Linda Henman (Madison, WI: Brown & Benchmark, 1996): 213.

37. Daniel J. Canary and Brian H. Spitzberg, "Appropriateness and Effectiveness Perceptions of Conflict Strategies," *Human Communication Research* 14 (1987): 93–118.

38. Martin and Nakayama, *Experiencing Intercultural Communication,* 173–74.

39. Meyers and Brashers, "Influence Processes in Group Interaction," 297.

40. Hal Witteman, "Group Member Satisfaction: A Conflict-Related Account," *Small Group Behavior* 22 (1991): 24–58.

41. William Wilmot and Joyce Hocker, *Interpersonal Conflict,* 5th ed. (Boston: McGraw Hill, 1998): 118.

42. Ibid., 136.

43. Ibid.,123.

44. Ibid.,139.

45. Ibid., 139

46. Ibid.,134.

47. Gary L. Kreps, *Organizational Communication*, 2nd ed. (New York: Longman, 1990): 193.

48. Fisher and Brown, *Getting Together*.

49. Gloria J. Galanes, "The Effect of Conflict Expression Styles on Quality of Outcome and Satisfaction in Small, Task-Oriented Groups" (Unpublished doctoral dissertation, Ohio State University, 1985).

50. Kreps, *Organizational Communication*.

51. Steven M. Alderton and Lawrence R. Frey, "Argumentation in Small Group Decision-Making," in *Communication and Group Decision Making*, eds. Randy Y. Hirokawa and Marshall Scott Poole (Beverly Hills, CA: Sage, 1986): 157–73.

52. Roger Fisher and William Ury, *Getting to Yes: Negotiating Agreement Without Giving In* (Boston: Houghton-Mifflin, 1981; Penguin Books, 1983).

53. Frank Tutzauer and Michael E. Roloff, "Communicative Processes Leading to Integrative Agreements," *Communication Research* 15 (1988): 360–80.

54. Fisher and Ury, *Getting to Yes*.

55. Ichiro Innami, "The Quality of Group Decisions, Group Verbal Behavior, and Intervention," *Organizational Behavior and Human Decision Processes* 60 (December 1994): 409–30.

56. Garlick and Mongeau, "Argument Quality and Group Member Status."

57. A version of the discussion about this issue is depicted on the ancillary videotape, *Communicating Effectively in Small Groups* (Dubuque, IA: Wm. C. Brown, 1991). Segment 3 depicts an ineffective discussion, and segment 4 shows an effective discussion where this major issue of bookstore hours is resolved.

58. The information in this section is taken from Trophy R. Olson, "'Common Ground' Discourse as a Way to Mediate in the Abortion Issue: An Interpretive Analysis" (Unpublished master's thesis, California State University, Fresno, 1997).

59. S. Roth, L. Chasin, R. Chasin, C. Becker, and M. Herzig, "From Debate to Dialogue: A Facilitating Role for Family Therapists in the Public Forum," *Dulwich Centre Newsletter* 2 (1992): 41–48.

60. R. Chasin and M. Herzig, "Creating Systematic Interventions for the Sociopolitical Arena," in *The Global Family Therapist: Integrating the Personal, Professional and Political*, eds. B. Bernina-Gould and D. Hillboe DeMuth (Needham, MA: Allyn & Bacon, 1993): 32–69.

61. This is the Public Conversations Project model. See Olson, "'Common Ground' Discourse," 47–52.

© Jeff Hunter/Getty Images

GROUP DISCUSSION AND OBSERVATION TECHNIQUES

Individuals skilled in a variety of group problem-solving techniques are valued and sought-after members of any organization. So are people who can observe a group discussion, analyze the process, spot the problems, and provide appropriate recommendations for improvement. The final two chapters provide information and techniques to help you put your understanding of small group communication to work for the benefit of any group or organization to which you belong.

SPECIAL DISCUSSION TECHNIQUES AND METHODS FOR FACE-TO-FACE AND COMPUTER-MEDIATED GROUPS

Central Message

Special techniques can be used to improve the regulation of discussion, enhance problem-solving effectiveness, and improve overall teamwork in organizations. For any of these techniques to be effective in face-to-face as well as computer-mediated groups, all members must understand the procedure, adapt it effectively, and may need specialized training.

STUDY OBJECTIVES

As a result of studying Chapter 14 you should be able to:

1. Use the guidelines for committees in *Robert's Rules of Order*.

2. Explain how problem census and RISK techniques can help uncover problems; describe the procedures for each technique.

3. Explain how focus groups and buzz groups can generate information for a variety of uses, and describe the procedures for each technique.

4. Plan and lead brainstorming and synectics sessions to enhance group members' creativity.

5. Explain and use the Program Evaluation and Review Technique.

6. Describe the purpose and procedure for conducting the Nominal Group Technique.

7. Explain what quality circles and self-managed work groups are, how they work, and what is necessary for either method to be productive.

8. Describe such electronic support mechanisms as teleconferencing and Group Decision Support Systems, and explain how groups can benefit from them.

Auniversity music department had experienced a number of problems over the years, including faculty members' lack of support for one another and lack of clarity about their vision for what kind of department they perceived themselves to be. Should they model themselves after music conservatories, where students focus intensely on music to the exclusion of other studies, or should they encourage their students to receive a broad general education that includes many other courses besides music?

The dean of the college where the department was housed led the department in a day-long retreat to get faculty focused in a particular direction. He utilized a number of group techniques to accomplish this. After some icebreaker exercises to remove apprehension and inhibitions, he used a modification of the nominal group technique to help the group identify what their main issues were and how they might address them. The faculty members were first asked to identify, in writing, the most problematic 8 or 10 issues they perceived within the department, and they had to state the problems in a positive way. For instance, they couldn't say, "Faculty meetings are a waste of time because we never know what we're going to be talking about." Instead, they had to restate the issue positively: "Our faculty meetings would be more productive if we had an agenda published in advance and we stuck to the agenda." Once all issues had been posted for everyone to see, the dean led the faculty in a discussion of them and they made decisions about what they would do.

The dean also used the nominal group technique variation to identify the department's considerable strengths. After all the issues and problems had been categorized into five or six main themes, he used a variation of the buzz technique to ensure that all the members of this large department participated. The large group was broken into five smaller groups of four or five members, each of which worked on a particular departmental issue. Unlike the typical buzz technique, the groups were given an hour to work through their particular theme and report to the department as a whole. At the conclusion of the retreat, the department had a plan for the year which all members supported, had functioning committees established to work on particular issues, and felt much better about themselves and their future as a department than they had in a long time.

It has been estimated that there are over a million nonprofit organizations in the United States. There are thousands of governmental groups at all levels: local, county, state, and regional. In 1992, there were over 11 million meetings in the United States *every day*! Imagine the number today. You probably belong to about six organized groups and these do not include the many informal groups you belong to.[1] Think about all the techniques these groups use daily, such as the ones used by the dean and the music department.

In Chapter 14 we shift our focus from small group communication theories and processes to specific group formats and techniques. We have included a variety of techniques that were developed for small groups that are components of larger organizations. These techniques can be modified or combined to serve specific group or organizational purposes. The dean in our story modified the nominal group technique and buzz groups to suit his purpose.

> Team leaders need a broad enough scope of facilitation, understanding principles, and then some tools to use to move a group.
>
> *L. H., Director, State-Level Strategic Planning*

Regulating Group Discussion

Appropriate group regulation gives each participant an equal opportunity to speak and ensures that decisions are made democratically. The larger a group, the more important it is to have formal procedures to regulate interaction so order can be maintained. Many organizations and large assemblies have adopted *Robert's Rules of Order*, Newly Revised as their parliamentary code.[2] Robert also includes a code of rules for board and committee meetings of organizations. When an organization adopts *Robert's Rules of Order*, the committees of that organization are bound to use Robert's rules for committees, which are much less formal and detailed than the parliamentary rules that govern large meetings. These rules make it unnecessary (and undesirable) for members to keep uttering "question," "point of order," or "I move to table the motion."

The bylaws of a parent organization may have special rules governing committees; if at any point these contradict what Robert says, the bylaws prevail. Chairs of committees need to know the organization's bylaws and, if the organization has adopted a parliamentary manual, what that manual says about committee procedures.

We have summarized Robert's rules for committees below for three reasons: first, because Robert is the parliamentary authority adopted by most American organizations; second, so you can know how to act in committees covered by *Robert's Rules*; and third, so you can use these rules properly if you are in the formal role of chair.

Administrative Matters

1. The chair of a committee may be selected in one of three ways: appointed by the parent organization, selected by the committee members, or the first person named to the committee is automatically the chair.

2. A committee meets on call of its chair or any two members.

3. A quorum (minimum number of members needed for the committee to take any legal action) is a simple majority of committee members, unless specified otherwise by the parent organization.

4. Formal reports of committees should contain only what was agreed to by a majority of those present at a regular and properly called (notice given to each member) meeting at which a quorum was present. Usually the

chair makes formal reports from a committee in writing, but reports of less formal action or works in progress may be given orally to a parent organization.

5. If a committee has been unable to reach consensus and a minority of its membership wants to make a report or recommendation to the parent organization different from that of the majority, it is usually permitted to do so as soon as the "majority" committee report has been made. This is not a *right* of a committee minority, but during debate under parliamentary rules the members who did not agree with the majority may speak their opposition. However, no one has the right to allude to what happened during the committee's private discussions unless the entire committee has agreed that this is to be permitted.

Responsibilities of the Chair

6. The chair is responsible for records of the committee but may delegate the work, or a separate secretary position may be created. The chair is still responsible for supervising this process.

7. Unlike *presiding* officers, committee chairs can take stands on issues without leaving the chair position. They can also make motions and vote on all questions, as can all other members of the committee. (In some large committees, it may be decided that the chair will act as if in a large assembly; if so, the chair should do so *at all times*, refraining from participating in the substance of a discussion and voting only to create or break a tie.)

Discussing, Making Motions, and Voting

8. Members do not need the formal recognition of the chair to speak, but may speak whenever they want *so long as they do not interrupt others.*

9. Many of the motions required in an assembly are irrelevant. A member can discuss virtually anything informally in committee sessions, so there is no need for points of order, motions to table, or matters of personal privilege. In short, the bulk of what is called *parliamentary law* is obstructive to committee meetings.

10. Motions do not need a second. A motion is a proposal for the group to take some action.

11. There is no limit to how many times a member can speak on an issue, and motions to limit or close discussion are *not* permitted.

12. Informal discussion is permitted with no motion pending. In a parliamentary discussion, members cannot discuss an issue without a motion, but in a committee meeting no motion is needed until *after* the discussion has indicated that consensus or majority decision has been achieved.

13. A majority of those actually voting is required before any decision can be made. Usually a vote is taken to confirm a decision already sensed by the

group. "Straw" (nonbinding) votes can be taken at any time to determine whether a majority or consensus exists before a binding vote is taken. The leader might say, "I think we have consensus on this. Would all who favor the proposal please raise your right hand?"

14. No motion is needed to record a vote. When a proposal is clear to all members, a vote can be taken and the outcome recorded as a decision.

15. The chair can ask if all members consent or agree with an idea or proposal. If no one objects, the decision is made and reported in the minutes. For example: "It was decided by consent that Jean and Bob should draft a resolution to present at the next meeting of the club."

16. A motion to reconsider a previous vote can be made at any time, with no limit to how many times a question can be reconsidered. Unlike in a parliamentary body, even a person who voted with the losing side can move to reconsider. Thus, a person who was absent or did not vote can ask for reconsideration of a previous decision if the action has not yet been carried out.

17. Motions can be amended in committee, but this is best done informally. If time is available, it is preferable to decide changes by consensus rather than by voting.

In summary, few rules of order and precedence are required in committees of organizations that have adopted *Robert's Rules of Order*. Voting is done to show that a legal majority supported a decision, not to shut off discussion. Any issue within the freedom of the committee can be presented for discussion at any time, and discussion can be quite informal and as lengthy as needed.

In the only study of its kind, Weitzel and Geist examined the use of parliamentary procedure in community groups.[3] Although much has been written about parliamentary procedure, no one has explored how using *Robert's Rules of Order* actually affects group decision making. In Chapter 11, we described Vigilant Interaction Theory, which states that the quality of a group's final product is related to the quality of the communication during problem solving and the degree of vigilance a group employs. Weitzel and Geist wanted to know the relationship between group vigilance, the use of parliamentary procedure, and effective problem solving in real versus experimental groups. What they discovered may surprise you.

They found that the community groups did not display a sophisticated understanding of parliamentary procedure even if members thought they were "experts." Few of the groups selected a parliamentarian, many produced and approved slipshod minutes, and motions often went unseconded and were generally handled in a less than sophisticated manner. But does this mean their communication was terrible and group satisfaction was jeopardized? No. These groups used *Robert's Rules of Order* only when they needed to and their problem-solving communication did not appear to suffer from their selective use of the rules. Weitzel and Geist concluded, from this initial research, that there was no evidence that the quality of the groups' communication was impaired by what some might consider inept use of parliamentary procedure.

What does this mean to you? Do not memorize *Robert's Rules of Order* and go into a group thinking they are essential to effective problem solving. Following *Robert's Rules of Order* does not ensure vigilance. The community group members were concerned more about getting their business done than with strict adherence to parliamentary procedure. When parliamentary procedure *is* used, it does help provide a systematic process of problem solving and decision making while protecting group member interests. Thus, to ensure a good decision, groups should use good judgment rather than mechanically or blindly following a particular set of rules.

Group Techniques for Increasing Problem-Solving Effectiveness

In this chapter we present a selection of small group techniques for improving organizational effectiveness. Knowing when and how to apply these techniques will enhance your value to your group or organization. All the techniques we have selected may be tailored for specific contexts or purposes by modifying them or combining them with other techniques. If you decide to use any of them, make sure you or the group coordinator explains the procedures carefully before the group tries them. Providing participants with a handout or chart will help.

We have classified these techniques by their major function: identifying problems, generating information, enhancing creativity, implementing ideas, and improving problem solving within organizations. However, most fulfill more than one function.

Identifying Problems

People closest to a problem (such as the cooks and wait staff in a restaurant, teachers in a school, or production workers in a factory) are often more aware of difficulties and problems than managers are. The following two techniques help bring out the individual perceptions of *all* individuals in an organization. Making such perceptions widely available can help prevent costly or life-threatening events later on.

Problem Census

A technique in which group members are polled for topics and problems that are then posted, ranked by voting, and used to create agendas for future meetings.

The Problem Census   The **problem census** is a "posting" technique used to identify important issues or problems. It is particularly useful for building an agenda for future problem-solving meetings or discovering problems encountered by organization members. A university department where one of us worked periodically conducted a problem census that developed into an agenda for a series of future meetings. The census first identified the list of problems, then different faculty members assigned themselves to research and present an outline of each of the problems for eventual problem solving by the committee. The following are the steps for conducting a problem census:

1. Seat the group in a semicircle facing a chart or board.

2. Explain the purpose of the technique, which is to bring out all problems, concerns, questions, or difficulties any member would like to discuss.

3. The leader then asks each participant, in round-robin fashion, to present one problem or question. This continues until all problems have been presented.

> I think it's okay, when you're in control of the flipchart, to add your idea as well as somebody else's, but I think you have to be careful that you're not stifling it along the way.
>
> *B. H., Director, State-Level Program*

4. The leader posts each problem as it is presented by writing it clearly on the chart or board. The leader must accept totally whatever is presented, never challenging or disagreeing, but asking for clarification or elaboration as needed. Often, the leader can distill a long problem statement into a concise phrase, but should always ask the speaker if the distillation is accurate before posting it. Each filled page of the chart is fastened to the wall for all to see. (A computer display for doing this is available in some organizations.)

5. The group now establishes a priority order for the entire list, usually by having members vote for their top three or four choices. *All* the problems are retained on the agenda; voting just prioritizes the list.

6. The group may now find that some of the questions can be answered or solved at once by other members to the satisfaction of the presenter. Such questions are removed from the list.

7. Each remaining problem is dealt with in turn, based on the number of votes it received, at this or subsequent meetings. Some issues may call for a factual presentation by a consultant, some may be handled by a brief lecture, and some by distributing printed material. Other problems will require extensive analysis and discussion by the entire group or an *ad hoc* subcommittee.

RISK Technique

A small group procedure for communicating and dealing with all risks, fears, doubts, and worries that members have about a new policy or plan before it is implemented.

The RISK Technique   Once a group has decided on a solution, that solution has to be evaluated carefully. Recall that earlier we talked about second-chance meetings where members can raise last-minute doubts, and we reported Hirokawa's research showing that one crucial function a group should perform is evaluation of negative consequences.[4] The **RISK technique** is designed specifically to allow an organization to assess how a proposed change or policy might negatively affect the individuals and groups involved.[5]

A special task force or selected committee of affected employees can use the RISK procedure to benefit not only themselves but also the entire organization. Suppose the CEO of an organization has tentatively decided to restructure a particular department. The CEO could then ask members of that department to participate in a RISK session to identify possible problems (risks) that the proposed restructuring might cause. Minor concerns can then be dealt with immediately, and possible major problems can be identified and perhaps resolved before they occur. More important, if the proposed plan has a *fatal flaw*, the CEO may decide not to implement it. There are six basic steps in the RISK technique:

1. The leader presents the proposed solution or change in detail, and asks members to think of any risks, fears, or problems with the proposal.

2. Members may either brainstorm as a group to generate problems, or may first work individually using the brainwriting procedure described later.

3. The problems are posted in round-robin fashion on a chart or board. Members then should study the list and add to it any additional concerns that occur to them. It is *absolutely imperative* that the leader be nonjudgmental. If members feel threatened they will not reveal their real concerns. Don't rush this process—often the risks felt to be most serious by some members will be voiced after a considerable lull.

4. After this initial meeting, all risks are compiled into a master list and circulated to all participants, who are asked to add anything else that occurs to them.

5. At a second meeting, additional risks felt by any member are added to the master list. Then members discuss each risk one by one. They decide whether each risk is serious or if there are risks that can readily be resolved and removed from the list. Members should be encouraged to share their feelings—fears, doubts, and concerns—during this interaction.

6. The remaining risks are processed into an agenda and handled the same way as items from the problem census. If the risks cannot be resolved, the proposed plan should be seriously reconsidered and either modified or discarded.

Generating Information and Ideas

Focus Group

A group procedure that encourages unstructured discussion focusing on a specific topic or issue, often used to analyze people's interests and values for market research.

Organizations and groups need information for a variety of purposes. The following two procedures are all-purpose techniques that enable group and organization members to provide information about a number of matters that can later be used in numerous ways.

Focus Groups   Long used in advertising and marketing research, **focus groups** enable an organization to identify problems, interests, concerns of employees and the general public, potential markets, and possible directions for innovation. Focus groups engage in unstructured or loosely structured discussion about a topic presented to them by a facilitator, who often simply announces the topic and lets group members respond freely in whatever way they choose. This free-association discussion is usually tape-recorded for later content analysis. Focus groups are often used to discover what customers look for in a product or how they may react to possible name or design changes. Politicians are well known for using focus groups to discover what voters think about certain issues. Focus groups also have provided information about employee morale, patients' feelings about how they were treated in a medical center, student reactions to the effectiveness of an advisement center, and so on.

Focus groups can be used in varied ways. For example, one of us recently served on a focus group for a lawyer preparing to take a major product liability case to court. In front of two focus groups, he briefly presented both sides of the case by sharing the major evidence and arguments from both sides. After he finished, the focus groups went into separate rooms to talk about the evidence while video cameras recorded the discussion. The focus groups did not have to come to agreement; instead, members were encouraged to talk freely about what was and was not convincing about the evidence. Later, the lawyer and his staff analyzed the videotaped discussion to determine where their case was strong, where it needed bolstering, and what the major issues would be from a potential jury's perspective. They were then much better able to sharpen and focus their arguments during the actual trial, which the lawyer eventually won.

> When you get people in these small groups, you find that they're much more comfortable . . . talking than when they are in the big group. . . . That's really an ideal way to try to get everybody to participate.
>
> *S. P., Vice President, Human Resources, Manufacturing Company*

Buzz Groups   A **buzz group session** is used to organize a large meeting into many small groups that work concurrently on the same question. This permits all participants in the large group to become actively involved in the discussion. Purposes may be to generate questions for a speaker or panel, to identify problems or issues, to compile a list of ideas or possible solutions, and generally to stimulate personal involvement and thinking by members of a large assembly. For instance, one of us participated with 500 educational leaders in Kentucky who met to work out techniques for promoting a Minimum Foundation Program for public education in that state. Organizers sought a favorable vote of taxpayers in a special election to support a state tax for local schools based on need. This meant higher taxes and a flow of money from wealthier to poorer districts. Several times the buzz group technique helped identify specific local problems, inexpensive advertising and promotional techniques, arguments for the program, and so forth. Although the conference was large, every attendee participated actively in discussion, and enthusiasm and involvement were remarkable. The college dean in our chapter-opening

Buzz Group Session

Method whereby attendees at a large group meeting can participate actively; the large meeting is divided into groups that discuss a target question, then report their answers to the entire large assembly.

story used a modified version of a buzz group session to ensure participation by all members. The procedure is as follows:

1. The chair presents a target question—as concise, limited, and specific as possible—to the entire assembly, which may be seated in rows in an auditorium or at small tables. The question should be displayed on a blackboard or handout for all to see. The following are examples of such questions:

   - What techniques could be used to publicize the Minimum Foundation Program to citizens of each county or city?

   - What new projects might local unions undertake to help members with social problems?

   - What are the arguments for (or against) a Materials Recovery Facility (MRF) for Springfield?

Consider This 14.1

Now that you have some idea of the sorts of target questions a chair can pose to a group in a buzz group session, think of some questions that the dean in our opening story could have presented to the music department to get them started.

2. Divide the large group into work groups of five or six by seating them at small tables or, if in a large auditorium, by counting off by three in each row. Then have alternate rows turn to face each other as shown in Figure 14.1. Each group should be given a copy of the target question on an index card.

3. Appoint a recorder–spokesperson for each group based on seating by saying something like: "The person sitting in the forward left-hand seat will be its recorder. The recorder should write down on the card *all* ideas presented, then have the group rank-order them." Assistants should then pass out blank cards.

4. Ask each group to record as many answers to the target question as it can think of in 5 or 10 minutes. Spend one minute evaluating the list to decide whether any items should be eliminated and in what order to present them.

5. When one minute remains, warn the groups. Feel free to allow an extra minute if all seem involved. Then, ask each group to evaluate and rank-order its list.

6. At this point you may do any of several things, depending on group size and overall meeting plan:

   a. Collect the cards and edit them to eliminate duplications. Make a tally of the number of times each item was listed. Duplicate and distribute the total list to the entire group at a subsequent meeting or present it to some special group for processing.

FIGURE 14.1 Buzz group seating in an auditorium.

b. Ask each recorder to report orally from his or her seat, in round-robin fashion, one new item from the card as a secretary records all items on a chart or board in front of the room. Process the list as above or according to the problem census technique described earlier.

c. Each recorder presents the complete list to the speaker or panel.

This versatile technique has many variations. For example, groups may have more than 10 minutes and may even follow a brief outline provided by the leader.

Enhancing Group Creativity

Sometimes, innovation is a group's or organization's main goal. In order for groups to maximize their creativity, they must be allowed to function in an environment in which judgment is eliminated and linear thinking is replaced by holistic, intuitive thinking. Later, at a more appropriate time, critical thinking is reintroduced to evaluate the creative ideas generated by the group. The following techniques help a group enhance its creativity.

Brainstorming   The **brainstorming** technique was developed by an advertising executive who recognized the need for imagination and a spirit of playfulness for successful advertising campaigns.[6] In order for the group's creativity to be released, members must feel safe in a nonthreatening environment that is free of judgment.[7] Because critical evaluation kills creativity, the main principle behind brainstorming is "no evaluation" during the brainstorming process. Evaluation of the ideas takes place *after* the group has listed as many ideas as possible.

Brainstorming

A small group technique for stimulating creative thinking by temporarily suspending evaluation.

> People just kept coming up with these wonderful ideas and we kept following up on their wonderful ideas, and the thing just grew like Topsy.
>
> *P. W., Community Volunteer*

Brainstorming is widely used wherever solution multiplicity is needed. It has been used to solve thousands of problems in such diverse industries as banking, engineering and design, marketing, medicine, decorating, programming, education, government, and food science (to name a few). Brainstorming can be used in conjunction with other techniques; it is often used as the

Brainstorming produces many possible solutions to a problem.
© *Amy Etra/PhotoEdit*

second step in the general Procedural Model of Problem Solving. The basic procedure has four steps and involves four major rules:

1. **The group is given a problem to solve.**

    The problem can vary from quite specific (What shall we name our new soft drink?) to highly abstract (How can we improve living conditions in the residence halls?).

    Problems for brainstorming should have high solution multiplicity, and group members may engage in some preparation prior to brainstorming. In one recent case with which the authors are familiar, a team brainstorming names for a new pudding first ate some of the pudding, then talked about its taste and what it reminded them of in an unstructured focus group discussion. Then they brainstormed more than 500 possible names!

2. **Members of the group are encouraged to generate as many solutions as possible.**

    Four general guidelines are followed during this period of brainstorming:

    a. *No evaluation is permitted.* This means that no criticism of, laughing at, or other negative reactions to any idea are permitted. Trying to think imaginatively while being critical is like trying to accelerate with one foot on the gas pedal and one on the brake.

    b. *Quantity is sought.* The more ideas listed, the better. If there is a lull in ideas the facilitator must encourage more by asking the group to think of ways to modify previously listed ideas, add a few more, or consider other characteristics of the problem.

  c. *Innovation is encouraged.* Members are asked to provide unusual ideas, even those that seem wild and crazy at first mention. Remember, every new idea was unique at its inception.

  d. *Hitchhiking is encouraged.* Members are asked to build on or modify ideas presented by other members of the group. A member with a hitchhiked idea snaps his or her fingers for immediate attention to get the idea charted at once.

3. **All ideas are charted so the entire group can see them.**
   The facilitator writes the ideas on large sheets of plain paper, and then posts the sheets along the walls so everyone can see the ideas. (Computer displays are now available for this.) Looking at the posted ideas often triggers new ideas. The sheets can later be used to write the report of the meeting.

4. **All ideas are evaluated at a different session.**
   After the brainstorming technique has been used to generate a long list of possible solutions, critical thinking is used to evaluate each idea, possibly to modify or improve on some of them, or to select for the solution or policy only those ideas that meet essential criteria such as feasibility, effectiveness, and acceptability. Sometimes a different group evaluates the suggestions. If the same group does the evaluating, it should take a break, even if only a short one.

Staying nonjudgmental is not easy! Members have a natural tendency to comment about the suggestions: "That sounds great!" or "That's a goofy idea!" Several companies have come up with creative ways to remind members not to evaluate, either positively or negatively. For instance, in one company group members take squirt guns to meetings, and whoever criticizes an idea during a brainstorming session gets squirted. In other companies, offending members get nerf balls thrown at them.[8] These responses are lighthearted, but they make their point: criticism stifles creativity, and creativity is what brainstorming is all about.

Brainstorming variations   There are several variations to brainstorming that adhere to the same "no evaluation" theme but are designed to overcome obstacles that sometimes impede creativity. These obstacles can include inhibition of participants, one or two dominant speakers, or fixating on a few ideas.[9] One such variation is brainwriting. **Brainwriting** capitalizes on the fact that group members are sometimes more productive when working alone but in the presence of others. During brainwriting, members are given a specified time limit—10 or 15 minutes—and asked to write down as many ideas as they can generate during that time. They are encouraged to write as fast as they can without stopping and, as with brainstorming, to hitchhike on their own ideas. When the time period has elapsed, members share their ideas, in round-robin fashion, and proceed just as with regular brainstorming.

Brainwriting

Individual brainstorming in writing before group discussion of items.

Electronic
Brainstorming

Brainstorming on
computers linked to
a large screen that
displays all
responses, but no
one knows who
contributed which
items.

Another variation, **electronic brainstorming (EBS),** when used anonymously, capitalizes on the fact that anonymity can remove inhibitions. Members sit at computer terminals and type in their ideas. No member knows who contributed the ideas, which are displayed on a large screen visible to all. Gallupe et al. found that electronic brainstorming groups generated more ideas, and more high-quality ideas, than oral brainstorming groups, in larger groups as well as members acting alone.[10] Members were less fearful of being evaluated, and were more satisfied with electronic brainstorming than oral brainstorming. Anonymous EBS has been found to be a superior way to generate ideas for large groups in particular.[11]

In a laboratory study of different leadership/facilitator behaviors and effective brainstorming in both anonymous and identified EBS groups, Sosik and Avolio discovered just how much facilitator behaviors can help or hinder any group's appropriation of technology.[12] When facilitators tried to intellectually stimulate creativity between group members with comments such as "Remember to be innovative when offering our views" and "Let's understand each other's views" the creativity was actually *negatively* impacted. Sosik and Avolio surmise that the timing and the content of intellectual stimulation, even in anonymous EBS groups, introduced judicial thinking too early in the process, which in turn hurt the generation of ideas. Perhaps trying to stimulate members intellectually inadvertently violated the spirit of EBS, for which the norm is an uncritical flow of ideas. When comments were given in an effort to help creativity, they were instead perceived as judgmental and thus violated the expected use of the EBS. A further implication is that no matter the intention of the facilitator or leader, members have to trust the leader and each other. If they do not, then comments meant to facilitate being considerate of others can be taken negatively. Either way, Sosik and Avolio stress the absolute necessity of carefully training leaders and facilitators in the use of computer technology or run the risk of misusing the technology.

Finally, there are several brainstorming software programs that have been developed to help individuals define problems and enhance their creativity. Each program has different strengths and weaknesses, and most are easy to use. Computer magazines periodically compare and evaluate them so you can choose the best for your purposes.

Metaphoric and Analogic Thinking   Metaphoric and analogic techniques encourage group members to focus on similarities between dissimilar things, thereby hoping to gain fresh perspective on the problem or issue to be solved. For example, we have heard the story about the man who developed Velcro after noticing, when he returned from a hike in the woods, how burrs stuck to his socks and pants. This illustrates how an idea in one domain may help solve a problem or suggest an innovation in another domain.

An example of a technique that encourages metaphoric thinking is **synectics,** developed by William Gordon.[13] It encourages linking apparently unrelated elements so as to gain an unexpected insight into a problem. It

Synectics

A group technique
that encourages
members to use
unusual analogies
and metaphors to
create innovative
solutions to
problems.

starts by having the individual or group identify the essence of the problem, then identifying a metaphor or analogy that captures that essence. Group members are encouraged to search for metaphors that seem unrelated to the problem and to use a different sensory perception. For example, if the problem is visual, group members are encouraged to develop a hearing or touch metaphor. The point is to make the usual seem unusual, thereby opening mental doors for new insights to occur. The final step of the procedure is to force-fit the analogy to the problem under consideration so the way to a solution may be opened.

Harriman provides an example of how this generation of "distant analogies" works.[14] A food science manager had a problem with organic debris floating in flavored syrup, which detracted from consumer appeal. The only method he knew to remove the debris also wasted large amounts of the syrup. Needing a fresh perspective, he prevailed on a nonexpert colleague for help. Together they created several images (analogies or metaphors) of "debris" in nature: raking piles of leaves, roadside litter, logs floating down a stream, a canoe floating toward a dam, and so forth. The canoe image reminded the manager that tidal currents change the characteristics of water's surface tension, which in turn reminded him that he had once helped clean up a harbor by using this principle. These images and recollections suggested that he could change the surface characteristics of the syrup (i.e., make it less "sticky") to make the debris easier to remove without wasting syrup.

Discussing the following techniques, adapted from ones suggested by Miller, can help groups or individuals use analogy and metaphor to arrive at innovative solutions:

1. **Look for a personal analogy.**
   Identify with the object and view the problem from the perspective of the object. For example, if you want to create a safer car, imagine that you are the car and ask, "How could I operate more safely?"

2. **Look for a direct analogy.**
   Look for a direct comparison of events from diverse fields. The earlier Velcro illustration compares something from nature with something *human-made*.

3. **Look for a symbolic analogy.**
   Imagine different ways of identifying the function or purpose of a solution by filling in the following: "How can we invent [something] that [performs a function] like an [analogy]?" For example, you might ask: "How can we invent [a safer car] that [stays on track] like a [train]?"

4. **Look for a fantasy analogy.**
   Use your imagination to ignore objective reality and discover what new ideas you can find. For instance, imagine that you can shrink yourself to take a trip through your veins and arteries to look for new ways of getting rid of cholesterol deposits.[15]

Metaphoric and analogic techniques may sound odd, but they work by forcing individuals out of their habitual thinking ruts so they can perceive a problem from a different perspective. They may feel uncomfortable to group members because they make what seems like a clear-cut problem ambiguous, uncertain, and strange. But that is precisely the point! If habitual ways of thinking could solve the problem, then innovation would not be needed. Analogy-based creativity techniques provide a potentially rich source of solutions.

Consider This 14.2

What do you do when you need to come up with a creative solution for a problem? How could you modify your own personal techniques to help a group become more creative?

Implementing Ideas with PERT

Program Evaluation and Review Technique (PERT)

A procedure for planning the details to implement a complex solution that involves many people and resources.

The **Program Evaluation and Review Technique (PERT)** is helpful during the final stage of problem solving—implementation. Sometimes a solution is highly complicated, involving a variety of materials, people whose work must be coordinated, and steps that must be completed in a specific sequence. Think of what is involved in constructing a large building on campus or making something like the space shuttle. PERT was developed to expedite such detailed operations so they can be done efficiently and so people can keep track of each step of a complex project. The procedure can be simplified to help even a student project group keep track of who will do what by when. Siebold summarized the main points of PERT:

1. Describe the final step (how the solution should appear when fully operational).

2. Enumerate any events that must occur before the final goal is realized.

3. Order these steps chronologically.

4. If necessary, develop a flow diagram of the process and all the steps in it.

5. Generate a list of all the activities, resources, and materials needed to accomplish each step.

6. Estimate the time needed to accomplish each step, and then add all the estimates to get a total time for implementing the plan.

7. Compare the total time estimate with deadlines or expectations and correct as necessary (by assigning more people or less time to a given step).

8. Determine which members will be responsible for each step.[16]

The preceding techniques are for improving group work during specific steps in problem solving. Those that follow use groups to improve the overall performance of organizations in general.

Improving Organizational Problem Solving

Everything we presented in the chapters devoted to problem solving and decision making can be applied to any group in an organization to improve its effectiveness. However, there are a number of specific small group procedures that can be used to tap the personal resources of members for organizational objectives. We have selected the Nominal Group Technique, quality circle, and self-managed team as the procedures you are most likely to use.

The Nominal Group Technique   As we said about brainwriting, often people working individually in the presence of others can generate more ideas for solving problems than the same number of people interacting. Delbecq and Van de Ven developed the **Nominal Group Technique** as an alternative that capitalizes on this while minimizing weaknesses that groups sometimes exhibit. *Nominal* means "in name only"; a nominal group alternates between verbal interaction and individual work in the presence of others.[17] It works better for major problems, like our music department group, and long-range planning than for routine meetings.[18] The Nominal Group Technique helps reduce secondary tension, prevents aggressive conflict, and eliminates the chance for some members to make speeches. In an organization, it allows members to express their concerns without fear of reprisals.[19] This was particularly important for the music department in our opening case, and their dean used this technique to help facilitate discussion. In one recent demonstration of its effectiveness, the Nominal Group Technique was used, in combination with a decision analysis technique, to help a complex organization with many independent divisions select a common integrated computer system.[20] Consensus was achieved and participants were satisfied with the process. On the other hand, the Nominal Group Technique is not by itself a complete problem-solving process, it may reduce cohesiveness, and it can produce less member satisfaction than fully interactive formats.[21]

> **Nominal Group Technique**
>
> A procedure in which group members brainwrite individually to generate ideas, then interact to pool, clarify, and evaluate the ideas until a solution has been accepted by weighted voting.

Essentially, the Nominal Group members (six to nine) individually write their ideas, record them on a chart as a group and clarify them, then evaluate them by a ranking procedure until a decision has been reached. The procedure may vary, but it always involves a cycle of individual work followed by discussion. Following are the steps for the designated leader as outlined by Delbecq:

1. Members are seated at a table facing a chart or board. A large group can be divided into several small working groups, each with a leader.

2. Give the group a clear definition of the problem. At this point, there should be no mention of solutions and no interaction.

3. Allow the group 5 to 15 minutes to brainwrite. Each person is asked to write all ideas for solving the problem that he or she can think of. (The leader also generates a list of ideas.)

4. In a round-robin session that includes the leader, list each new idea on a chart for all members to see.

5. Take the group through the list item by item, for clarification and elaboration, but *not* evaluation. Anyone may ask another person for clarification of an idea on the list. Questions such as "What does number 6 mean?" or "Do you understand item 4?" are now in order for discussion, but no lobbying, criticism, or argument are allowed yet.

6. Give each person the same number of note cards (five or so) on which to write the items he or she most prefers. The person arranges the cards and ranks them according to preference, writing 5 on the top card to 1 on the bottom. Alternatively, each member can be given five or more colored stickers to post by the most preferred items.

7. All cards are collected. The ratings are added for each item, and divided by the total number of people in the group. Most items will have a fractional rating. Items no one rated are removed from the list.

8. Engage in an evaluative discussion of those items with the highest ranks. This should be a full and free discussion with critical thinking, disagreement, and analysis encouraged.

9. If a decision is reached, fine. If not, vote again on the remaining items and discuss further. This process can be repeated several times as needed until a clear synthesis of a few ideas or support for one idea has emerged. The group then takes appropriate action on the results.

Quality Circle (Quality Control Circle)

A group of employees meeting on company time to investigate work-related problems and to make recommendations for solving these problems.

Quality Circles   The name **quality circle** has been given to small groups of employees who meet at regular intervals on company time to discuss work-related matters. We use the term *quality circle* as a generic term referring to any type of committee that meets regularly to improve something. In some companies, such groups are referred to as *work effectiveness teams, continuous improvement teams, cycle time reduction teams*, and other designations. Regardless of what they are called, the ultimate purpose of the quality circle is to increase productivity, improve the quality of what is produced, or enhance employee involvement.[22] Quality circle members share their opinions with management in an attempt to solve all sorts of job-related problems. Quality circle techniques were originally developed jointly by American and Japanese management experts working to help postwar Japan prepare to compete for world markets. The participative nature of quality circles meshed well with Japanese culture, although U.S. managers, who saw quality circles as encroaching on their authority, initially rejected them.

Many American companies have instituted quality circles to help them compete more successfully. Corporations using quality circles or some variation of them include Ford Motor Company, General Motors, Hewlett-Packard, Burlington Industries, Ethyl Corporation, Anchor Hocking, Control Data, Galion, Sheller-Globe, 3M, Dresser Industries, Firestone, W. R. Grace, Sony, Honda, Weyerhaeuser, Northrop, SmithKline Beecham, American Airlines, Dow Chemical, Procter & Gamble, Xerox, and Kraft Foods.[23] Nonprofit organizations like the Red Cross and Boy Scouts and a number of school systems also have quality circles. Workers participating in these groups perceive improvements in their communication with superiors, subordinates, and peers, as well as positive effects on their power and influence.[24]

Employees in a quality circle meet with a team leader, usually a supervisor, on company time to discuss production problems, or to react to problems presented to them by management. Usually they meet for an hour a week, but time varies from company to company. Quality circles may work on any problem, from how a restaurant can serve customers more quickly to how a country can develop its exports. All ideas agreed upon are submitted to management, which must react to every suggestion by adopting it; modifying, and then adopting it; investigating it further; or rejecting it with an explanation why. Many companies combine the quality circle with employee bonus systems, which reward either individuals or groups for profit-making or money-saving ideas. Often, the quality circles are one part of a *total quality management* or *continuous improvement program* instituted throughout a company. You will note that any of the techniques discussed thus far—standard decision-making and problem-solving methods, the RISK technique, brainstorming, the Nominal Group Technique, and so on—can be used as needed by the quality circle to enhance its effectiveness.

Although quality circles can be quite effective, merely instituting them in a company will not guarantee success. Sometimes unions see them as a ploy to increase production without improving benefits (perhaps a valid criticism in some cases), and occasionally managers implement quality circle programs without having enough foresight into how the programs will work within that company's culture. Potential problems include middle managers who feel threatened and resist the ideas presented, failure to implement ideas, groups becoming discouraged by management's failure to respond, and management's failure to reward groups financially for their contributions.[25] For quality circles to work, management must be strongly committed to the quality circle program, the program must be part of a long-range plan for organizational development, and participants must be adequately trained in small group dynamics and participative problem solving.[26] Employees must know that their ideas for increasing efficiency will not ultimately cost them jobs or earnings. They must know that their ideas will be respected and dealt with and that they will share in the tangible benefits, such as cost savings, their ideas bring. The employees must have a commitment to the company, but must also be assured of the company's commitment to them. If they are used as a trick to squeeze every ounce of work possible out of employees without rewarding them, quality circles won't work.

Self-Managed Work Groups   **Self-managed work groups,** also called *autonomous work groups*, are teams of peers who determine their own work schedules and procedures within prescribed limits. Sometimes the groups have considerable freedom, even up to the point of hiring and firing team members. Self-managed work groups eliminate many traditional supervisory positions and

Self-Managed Work Group

A small group of peers who determine within prescribed limits their own work schedules and procedures.

reduce the number of middle managers. The team performs such management functions as deciding which member will perform which job, what supplies to order, and what the work schedule will be. Members are cross-trained so that each member can perform several or all of the jobs needed by the team. For example, the custom-order team for one office furniture manufacturer originally included a salesperson skilled at pricing, a furniture designer, a craftsperson who could create specialized parts, and three skilled assemblers. Members cross-trained each other so now the whole team goes to a prospective client's office to listen and offer suggestions. This team's success has contributed significantly to the company's profits.[27] The fact that members of a self-managed work group are cross-trained provides the team tremendous flexibility to deal with absent workers. Members are less likely to become bored or frustrated, and they are more likely to help each other out than in traditional assembly line organizations. Self-managed work teams are used in such companies as Volvo, Saturn, Sherwin-Williams, and Procter & Gamble. As you may surmise, before a self-managed work program can be installed, workers and managers must undergo extensive training in group attitudes, techniques, and procedures.

A self-managed work group usually elects its own leader, who is *not* a supervisor, but a coordinator with legitimate authority from the group. The company's management establishes the work group's area of freedom and assigns what must be produced, but the work group has considerable latitude to decide everything else. Some self-managed work groups establish their own annual budgets, prepare reports, develop specifications for jobs, and solve technical problems that arise in the course of completing jobs. They may even bid for new company business.

Many of the same concerns about quality circles hold for self-managed work teams. Middle managers and unions often feel threatened by them. However, companies using this technique report a 20 to 40 percent increase in production over traditional work organizations.[28] The self-managed work teams require less supervision time, produce higher-quality products, have less absenteeism, and generally have higher morale and job satisfaction than employees under traditional line supervision.

Using Technology to Help a Group

In the last decade, technological hardware and software we could recently only dream about are now affordable and available to help groups. These range from simple systems to highly complex ones. For instance, conference calls use existing telephones and phone lines. Electronic mail (e-mail) lets group members use their personal computers to communicate with each other asynchronously, whenever it is convenient for the individual member.[29] We discussed some of the rules for effective use of e-mail in Chapter 4.

Instant messaging (IM) is fast becoming the way for employees to connect with each other in the corporate world. IM allows for rapid-fire messages compared to e-mail and telephone voice mail that often builds up. Users in possession of any number of other individual's IM handles click on the name to begin an immediate chat session. People who use IM like how quickly they can access others, but the jury is out on the impact of IM on worker productivity.[30] Some systems permit members to coordinate their calendars electronically and more easily find convenient times for meetings. Group writing systems permit multiauthored document writing, in which members create, analyze, edit, and revise a single document simultaneously.[31]

Asynchronous electronic bulletin boards (BBS) and synchronous chat environments like the Internet Relay Chat (IRC) are becoming more and more popular in classrooms.[32] These forms of computer-mediated communication (CMC) are used by instructors to facilitate classroom learning. CMC, as you are aware, lets teachers and classmates talk to each other when it is convenient, may equalize participation, can increase learner self-responsibility, allows learners to see different perspectives, gives them time to think how best to give a message, and prepares them for CMC in their future professions.[33]

Pena-Shaff and associates studied both BBS and IRC in the classroom and their findings have important implications for BBS and IRC use in small groups. Electronic bulletin boards allow group members to post asynchronous messages to each other.[34] These discussions are particularly useful when the group wishes to promote critical thinking and reflection. You can expect group discussions using BBS to be structured, reflective, focused on the task and the topic. The downside to BBS is that it does not promote collaboration and social interaction. Group members also need to be motivated to use it. The synchronous character of text-based "talk," however, does promote collaboration and works well for brainstorming.[35] CMC is more informal and members feel more pressure to reach consensus, yet find it difficult to do so. The freewheeling nature of chat rooms, while helping members initially explore issues, also allows members to get off track easily. Once off track, it is hard to get the discussion back on track. So although chat rooms allow for interaction in real time and immediate feedback, similar to face-to-face interaction, the talk can also be confusing, with the content and flow reflecting "messy" thinking.

Practically speaking, your group first needs to decide whether you want to use an electronic bulletin board service or a chat room—do you want freewheeling discussion that explores ideas or time to critically reflect on issues? Either way you need to consider the following guidelines.[36]

1. Make sure all group members know where the chat room is located and that all members have access to the chat room.

2. Guarantee that the chat room is a private room or you might have your group's discussions interrupted by outsiders.

3. Select a group member as moderator to facilitate clear discussion, motivate discussion, and ensure more equal participation. Reviewing an agenda prior to discussion can help. Group members may rotate who is the moderator for different discussions.

4. Moderators and group members should motivate each other to contribute and collaborate. This is harder in real time, but can be fostered.

5. Use emoticons with reservation. Emoticons can be misread or misunderstood if group members don't know each other.

6. Remember that instant message chatting can easily become derailed and, before you know it, the day has passed and nothing has been accomplished.

As you can see, CMC that helps problem solving takes several forms with different advantages and disadvantages, introduced to you in Chapter 3. These pros and cons need to be weighed against the type of group you are in, the task you face, the nature of your leadership, and member characteristics. We will next discuss two key ways technology can help groups: teleconferences and group decision support.

Teleconferences

Teleconference

A meeting of participants who communicate via mediated channels such as television, telephone, or computer rather than face-to-face.

Teleconferences are electronically mediated meetings that allow members of a group to meet, even though they may be far apart from each other geographically, like the virtual groups we have mentioned previously. Companies can save travel time and money, because face-to-face meetings can be expensive if members have to travel long distances to attend. Teleconferences or net conferencing, as you will recall, can be *videoconferences*, which let members see and hear each other; *audioconferences*, which let members hear but not see each other; and *computer conferences*, which allow members to send messages to one another that are displayed on computer monitors—like the IRC used in classrooms. Chapter 4 discussed the peculiar message characteristics of these conferences, which we touch on again here.

Videoconferences are expensive for most companies, but audioconferences, including telephone conference calls, are routine. Computer conferences are becoming increasingly sophisticated and accessible. A number of companies already are developing their own specialized computer software for employees linked to a network to work simultaneously on a variety of tasks. Recent studies have shown that decisions made by computerized conference groups were just as good as ones made by face-to-face groups, but computer groups were less likely to reach agreement.[37] The *type* of computerized technique appears to make a difference. Murrell found that using the window method, which permits each participant to see the responses of all other participants at once, produced higher decision quality than a message system requiring participants to complete a message before they interact.[38] Some studies have found that computer conferences can provide some advantages over face-to-face meetings. Dubrovsky et al. discovered that inequalities that are due to status and expertise were minimized with electronic mail conferences.[39] Hiltz et al. suggest that computer programs permitting anonymity may help create greater and more equal participation.[40] On the other hand, computer-mediated group decision making leads to more delays, more outspoken advocacy, and more extreme or risky decisions, along with more equal participation, than face-to-face meetings.[41]

From the more than 100 studies of teleconferencing, we can develop practical guidelines for making electronic meetings productive.[42] For audioconferencing, speakerphone equipment is readily available, is relatively inexpensive, and requires no special studios. It can be set up in any office. However, audioconferences lack "social presence."[43] The sense of sharing, belonging, and recognition of each other as individuals can be low. Many key nonverbal cues are absent, and electronic equipment can fail at the most inopportune times. On the other hand, the potential for *greater* equality of opportunity to participate exists in the control equipment used by conference leaders.

For teleconferencing to work best, Johansen et al. recommend that the participants hold an extended face-to-face conference beforehand to form a sense of "groupness."[44] A post-teleconference meeting can be useful as well. It seems that for complex tasks, face-to-face meetings are still preferable, with teleconferences well suited to routine meetings.

Several factors can improve routine teleconferences. A trained moderator is essential, all participants should be aware of the rules and guidelines for speaking, and all speakers should abide by specified time limits.[45] Electronic meetings are not qualitatively different from face-to-face ones, but additional coordination efforts are required because less information (e.g., nonverbal cues) is exchanged. At present, teleconferences are usually recommended for routine meetings and information sharing. For more complex tasks in which the likelihood of disagreements increases, face-to-face meetings are still preferable. As travel costs skyrocket and technological limitations decrease, the need for teleconferences to replace both routine and significant meetings will increase. Several up-and-coming computer-related innovations promise to increase the utility and effectiveness of mediated meetings, even those involving more complex tasks. And it goes without saying that to effectively use these kinds of conferences members need to know how to use them. Any number of texts are now available that give specific instructions on how to effectively set up the conference and optimize the conversation and the collaboration between members.[46]

Group Decision Support Systems

Group Decision Support Systems (GDSS) are the computer-based hardware and software systems designed to improve the quality and speed of group problem solving, especially group idea generation, information organization, evaluation of options, and decision making we discussed in Chapter 11.[47] They are sometimes called *groupware computer-supported cooperative work (CSCW), electronic meeting systems (EMS)*[48] or *group support systems (GSS)*. The development of such systems has been encouraged by the proliferation of personal computers and interconnected computer systems.

Group Decision Support Systems

Computer-based hardware and software systems designed to help groups improve a variety of group outcomes, such as creativity, problem solving, and decision making.

Different GDSS address different decision-making processes. For example, some focus on the idea generation step of brainstorming. Others attempt to improve the entire decision-making process by providing the structure that groups often need but don't otherwise receive. GDSS are usually used in conjunction with face-to-face meetings and may require specialized training of the meeting leader and the members.

GroupSystems and Software Assisted Meeting Management (SAMM), mentioned in Chapter 11, are two of the more commonly known support systems. They include modules to help groups in every area of problem solving, such as helping group management, brainstorming, analysis, policy formation, evaluation and voting, exchanging comments on topics, and so forth. Many find them most helpful during the evaluation of solutions because their procedures are designed to help members react honestly to each other's suggestions and ideas. In 1992 there were over 400 such software programs and they change daily as their developers learn more about their effectiveness.[49]

GDSS are fairly new, so you may not have seen one in operation. The following example should help you picture what some sophisticated systems can do. We recently attended a meeting of a local school board that had been having trouble achieving closure on agenda items at its regular meetings. Members found themselves wandering off track, going in a completely different direction from that provided in the agenda. They accepted the offer made by university faculty members to help them by using GDSS technology. The school board members met in a room specially designed to accommodate GDSS meetings. The room had 12 individual computers linked to each other. The computers were configured in a U shape, with a large overhead projection system, visible to all, at the open end of the U. One faculty member served as a group facilitator by organizing the discussion of the two agenda items the school board president most wanted to complete: deciding what communication issues to emphasize and what promotional strategies to use in the upcoming school bond levy. He stood under the projection screen at the open end of the U. The other faculty member served as the chauffeur, running the computer system for the meeting. He, too, was visible behind the operating desk at the top right of the U. Both the facilitator and chauffeur had specialized training in how to use the system.

At their individual computer stations, group members brainstormed about their first item, the issues to be addressed in the campaign. Each member worked alone; then, when all were ready, they sent their suggestions to the central computer with a keystroke. The master list then appeared on the overhead. No one knew who had made which suggestion. The facilitator and chauffeur clarified vague items and combined like items. Group members were then given the chance to make comments, again anonymously, and send them to the screen. With the help of the facilitator, face-to-face discussion occurred concerning several items. Finally, members ranked all the items and sent them to the system, which automatically tallied the rankings and provided an overall ranking and rating of each item. The rankings and ratings were displayed in numerical and bar graph form, which provided visual reinforcement for the members' opinions. Face-to-face discussion followed, with members easily coming to consensus (or realizing that they already had achieved consensus). They addressed the second issue in the same way.

Reaction of the members was highly positive. The school board president noted that the visual display of ratings and rankings emphasized to some of the long-winded members that consensus had already been achieved; so further discussion was not needed. Both the facilitator and chauffeur reminded the school board that the system was designed to *support*, not replace, effective group discussion. GDSS helps groups do what they *should* do, but often don't do, without computer support: analyze carefully, evaluate thoroughly, and give everyone a chance to participate. They also make record keeping easy because the computer provides an automatic history of all the items that were listed, the comments made about each, and the rankings and ratings of each.

Recent research suggests that GDSS is effective. Olaniran reported that computer-mediated groups produce more ideas than face-to-face groups.[50] However, they take a longer time to come to consensus. Decision quality seemed to be highest when groups used a combination of computer-mediated and face-to-face discussion, as did the school board we just described. Poole and his associates, who have studied GDSS extensively, noted several benefits.[51] Using computer support systems seems to focus members' attention on decision-making procedures and improves organization of the decision-making process. It also sparks insight into the decision process, although it does take time for members to learn the system and orient themselves to it. Jessup and Valacich, in their extensive review of GDSS research, concluded that computer-supported decision making is as good or better than traditional decision making, that members of large groups, especially, are more satisfied because participation can be equalized, that time spent in group meetings can actually be reduced with GDSS, and that such systems help members stay on task.[52]

Whether GDSS improves decision making or not depends on a variety of factors. One of the most important of these is the level of GDSS support, which refers to how sophisticated a system is and how much intervention into the group's natural decision-making process GDSS provides. Benbasat and Lim found that more sophisticated level 2 support produced better decisions and higher satisfaction than level 1 support.[53] This is consistent with the findings of Sambamurthy et al., who concluded that simpler is not always better.[54] The particular mediated system used must be well matched to the task, according to Farmer and Hyatt.[55] For example, some complex tasks require information to be processed via many channels, including audio, video, and screen sharing. However, for other tasks, having an audio channel alone might be sufficient.

Familiarity with the system is another factor influencing GDSS effectiveness. Hollingshead et al. observed that computer group members' poor initial performance seemed to be related to their unfamiliarity with using computer support, but that most of the differences disappear over time.[56] They also noted that face-to-face groups are likely to outperform computer-mediated groups on intellective tasks, where there is a correct answer, and negotiation tasks, where members must reconcile their competing interests. These researchers warn managers planning to institute computer-mediated work groups that there may be initial declines in performance and dissatisfaction until members become comfortable with the technology. GDSS effectiveness is also a function of how tightly it might structure group interaction and some managers themselves may not use these procedures because they do not want their employees to have full access to the information and benefits of computer technology.[57]

> The people that are really good . . . whether or not they've been to formal training, they have good facilitation skills.
>
> *L. H., Director, State-Level Strategic Planning*

The presence of a facilitator also affects GDSS performance. Poole et al. were surprised by their findings that, although groups using GDSS exhibited more organized decision processes, they did not demonstrate improved critical thinking or more thorough evaluation of options.[58] These authors noted that the groups they studied had no facilitator support, and they postulate that this, along with the level of GDSS support as discussed earlier, may have been a key factor hampering GDSS effectiveness. Ideally, a facilitator should have a strong conceptual understanding of the technology and its capabilities, be able to make members comfortable with the technology and help them understand it, select the right technological system for the group, and have it prepared properly.[59] This was a factor in the success of the school board meeting we described earlier. Scott et al. caution that facilitators need to understand the difference between *faithful* use of GDSS procedures—using them as they were intended—and *ironic* use of GDSS—using GDSS contrary to their purpose or spirit. Scott et al. note that it can be very hard to predict how any GDSS will *actually* be utilized because GDSS implementation is a dynamic adaptation between the user and the GDSS technology.[60] Generally speaking; GDSS is designed to promote anonymity, equalize participation, and balance member influence. But some groups used GDSS in a way that was not faithful to these intentions.

Scott et al. found that GDSS users exhibited a strong need to figure out the sources of messages. Over time, members could figure out the styles of different users. Sometimes users follow the rules of the program at the expense of good decision making. For instance, they change their message style frequently without concern for message effectiveness. Equal influence was also hard to achieve even with GDSS use. Users agree with their own comments, use forms of emphasis, and repeat themselves to assert their opinions. Some users played with the rankings of alternatives in an attempt to manipulate the outcome of votes. Users often felt powerless because they discovered that others did not read their messages. Whereas equal participation is easier to facilitate with GDSS use, as compared to anonymity and equal influence, it may encourage social loafing. Finally, users also indicated little commitment to the group's decision. The GDSS benefits declined over time.

As you can see, these computer technologies do not determine themselves how group members appropriate them. Instead group members interact with the technology negotiating the spirit of the technology with their own expectations as evidenced in the above discussion of equal influence and GDSS use. Men and women in enduring task groups utilizing computer-mediated communication use different strategies to respond to the technology's anonymity.[61] They try either to preserve or to eliminate the anonymity, consistent with their status outside the group. In other words, some male and female group members manipulate the technological environment in ways that enhance or preserve their status. Males, who generally have higher status in the general society, try to preserve that status by making the CMC more like FTF (i.e., less anonymous). They do this in part by offering social cues that reveal their sex. In contrast, females reduce social cues they offer, which serves to maintain the anonymity and helps them acquire greater influence in the group. In addition, males in anonymous computer group interaction have not been found to cross sex lines, whereas some females do. Although the research is new and needs to be read with caution, Flanagin et al. point out that users of CMC in groups acknowledge the equalizing potential of this technology and use the technology to benefit themselves, either by preserving or avoiding anonymity.[62] Their research leaves us with interesting questions. How much is CMC use due to a member's identification with his or her sex and understanding of how sex-based norms work, a desire for control, or an attempt to make sense of the technology?

Group Decision Support Systems are much more common now than they were even a couple of years ago. We expect more and more organizations to invest in this technology in the future. Despite widespread research on its use in organizations, few generalizations can be made about the influence of GDSS on group problem solving because these programs are changing daily. GDSS seem to be beneficial for certain kinds of tasks, such as generation and decision making.[63] Face-to-face groups remain better for negotiation and complex, cognitive tasks. As we mentioned above, an important factor in GDSS effectiveness seems to be user familiarity and facilitator knowledge and skill in GDSS use. Groups utilizing GDSS appear to make better decisions, generate more alternatives to problems, and have more even group member participation. However, these groups can take longer to reach decisions, experience less consensus, and are less satisfied than their face-to-face counterparts.[64]

To summarize, no matter how much these systems grow, we remind you that they are designed to *support*, not *replace*, traditional group decision-making and discussion processes. The most we can say is that they are generally good for groups, although not useful in every circumstance.[65] As long as

GDSS procedures are used consistently with their intentions, they can be very effective, but GDSS does not eliminate the need for group members who understand group processes, nor is their use an excuse to slack off on using good communication skills. In fact, GDSS should help focus members' attention on those processes. Knowledgeable individuals who know how to operate the computer support systems as they are intended and who understand groups will always be needed.

Consider This 14.3

You have been asked to help a group use a new GDSS program for problem solving. Given your understanding of the advantages and disadvantages of GDSS, create a list of guidelines you would use if you were to act as facilitator for this group

SUMMARY

1. Leaders of committees created by organizations governed by *Robert's Rules of Order* should know and follow Robert's rules for committees, which are simpler and less formal than parliamentary rules.

2. Two techniques are useful to help members identify problems. The problem census uses a polling–posting method to help a group build an agenda for future problem solving, and the RISK technique spots unforeseen negative reactions to a proposed change of policy or procedure.

3. To generate information, focus groups, unstructured group meetings that can be recorded and content-analyzed, provide a wealth of information for numerous applications. Buzz groups allow every member of a large group to participate.

4. Creativity can be enhanced by brainstorming, including its written and electronic variants, which defers judgment, and

synectics, which seeks unusual analogies to generate a sudden insight into a problem.

5. PERT can be used to work out how to implement a complex solution by breaking it down into sequential, organized steps.

6. Organizations can be enhanced through the Nominal Group Technique, which helps groups reach solutions with a minimum of secondary tension; quality circles, which meet to improve the quality and quantity of products and the work climate; and self-managed work groups of cross-trained members who manage the details of their own work.

7. Various technologies can help groups. Members who cannot meet face-to-face may use teleconferences. Group Decision Support Systems, which are computer-based hardware and software systems, support traditional group decision making in a number of ways.

KEY TERMS

 Test your knowledge of these key terms by visiting the Online Learning Center website at mhhe.com/galanes11

Brainstorming	Nominal Group Technique	RISK technique
Brainwriting	Problem census	Self-managed work groups
Buzz group session	Program Evaluation and Review	Synectics
Electronic brainstorming (EBS)	Technique (PERT)	Teleconferences
Focus groups	Quality circle	
Group Decision Support Systems (GDSS)		

EXERCISES

 Go to self-quizzes on the Online Learning Center at mhhe.com/galanes11 to test your knowledge of the chapter concepts

1. Conduct a problem census focusing on the question, "What topics should our class select for discussion that would be intrinsically interesting and involve the whole class?" Use the rank-ordered topics in future exercises.

2. Select a topic from your problem census and use the Nominal Group Technique to discuss the problem. Your instructor will coordinate and time the exercise, but students should lead each of the groups.

3. Prepare and follow a PERT plan for a major group project. Each member must sign acceptance of the PERT plan.

4. As a whole class or in subgroups of 6 to 12 each, participate in a formal brainstorming session considering questions such as, "What use might Goodwill Industries make of the thousands of used belts donated in collection boxes?"

5. With the instructor's blessing, form a quality circle of volunteers to meet every two weeks to discuss problems in the class and what might be done to solve them, and other ways the class could be made more interesting. The quality circle should give consensus recommendations to the instructor. The instructor should make some reaction to each suggestion at the next class meeting by either incorporating it or explaining why the suggestion was declined.

BIBLIOGRAPHY

Adams, Tyrone, and Normal Clark. *The Internet: Effective Online Communication*. Ft. Worth, TX: Harcourt, 2001.

Baird, John E., Jr. *Quality Circles: Leader's Manual*. Prospect Heights, IL: Waveland Press, 1982.

Jessup, Leonard M., and Joseph S. Valacich, eds. *Group Support Systems: New Perspectives*. New York: Macmillan, 1993.

Johnson, Craig E., and Michael Z. Hackman. *Creative Communication: Principles and Applications*.

Prospect Heights, IL: Waveland Press, 1995, especially Sections 3, 4, and 5.

Krueger, Richard A. *Focus Groups: A Practical Guide for Applied Research*. Newbury Park, CA: Sage, 1988.

McGrath, Joseph E., and Andrea Hollingshead. *Groups Interacting with Technology*. Thousand Oaks, CA: Sage, 1994.

Robert, Henry M. *Robert's Rules of Order*. Newly Revised. Glenview, IL: Scott, Foresman, 1990.

Siebold, David R. "Making Meetings More Successful: Plans, Formats, and Procedures for Group Problem Solving." In *Small Group*

Communication: A Reader. 6th ed. Robert S. Cathcart and Larry A. Samovar, eds. Dubuque, IA: Wm. C. Brown, 1992, 178-91.

NOTES

1. M. H. Butcher, ed., *Fundamentals of Parliamentary Law and Procedure*, 2nd ed. (Dubuque, IA: Kendall/Hunt, 1992).

2. Henry M. Robert, *Robert's Rules of Order*, Newly Revised (Glenview, IL: Scott, Foresman, 1990): 471-521.

3. Al Weitzel and Patricia Geist, "Parliamentary Procedure in a Community Group: Communication and Vigilant Decision Making," *Communication Monographs* 65 (September 1998): 244-59.

4. Randy Y. Hirokawa, "Discussion Procedures and Decision-Making Performance: A Test of a Functional Perspective," *Human Communication Research* 12 (1985): 203-24.

5. Norman R. F. Maier, *Problem-Solving Discussions and Conferences: Leadership Methods and Skills* (New York: McGraw-Hill, 1963): 171-77.

6. Alex Osborn, *Applied Imagination*, rev. ed. (New York: Scribner, 1975).

7. Paul Kirvan, "Brainstorming: It Is More than You Think," *Communication News* 28 (1991): 39-40.

8. Michael Schrage, "Meetings Don't Have to Be Dull," *The Wall Street Journal* (April 29, 1996): A22.

9. Graham Hitchings and Sara Cox, "Generating Ideas Using Randomized Search Methods: A Method of Managed Convergence," *Management Decision* 30 (1992): 58.

10. R. Brent Gallupe, Alan R. Dennis, William H. Cooper, Joseph S. Valacich, Lane M. Bastianutti, and Jay F. Nunamaker, Jr., "Electronic Brainstorming and Group Size," *Academy of Management Journal* 35 (June 1992): 350-70.

11. See also Joseph S. Valacich, Alan R. Dennis, and T. Connolly, "Idea Generation in Computer-Based Groups: A New Ending to an Old Story," *Organizational Behavior and Human Decision Processes* 57 (1994): 448-68.

12. John Sosik and Bruce Avolio, "Inspiring Group Activity: Comparing Anonymous and Identified Electronic Brainstorming," *Small Group Research* 29 (1998): 3-31.

13. Russell L. Ackoff and Elsa Vergara, "Creativity in Problem Solving and Planning," in *Handbook for Creative and Innovative Managers*, ed. Robert L. Kuhn (New York: McGraw-Hill, 1988): 77-90.

14. Richard A. Harriman, "Techniques for Fostering Innovation," in *Handbook for Creative and Innovative Managers*, 136-37.

15. William C. Miller, "Techniques for Stimulating New Ideas: A Matter of Fluency," in *Handbook for Creative and Innovative Managers*, 124.

16. David R. Siebold, "Making Meetings More Successful: Plans, Formats, and Procedures for Group Problem Solving," in *Small Group Communication: A Reader*, 6th ed., eds. Robert S. Cathcart and Larry A. Samovar (Dubuque, IA: Wm. C. Brown, 1992): 187.

17. Andre L. Delbecq, Andrew H. Van de Ven, and David H. Gustafson, *Group Techniques for Program Planning: A Guide to Nominal Group and Delphi Processes* (Glenview, IL: Scott, Foresman, 1975): 7-16.

18. Ibid., 3-4.

19. Alan Honeycutt and Bill Richards, "Nominal Group Process in Organizational Development Work," *Leadership & Organization Development Journal* 12 (October 1991): 24-28.

20. James B. Thomas, Reuben R. McDaniel, Jr., and Michael J. Dooris, "Strategic Issue Analysis: NGT + Decision Analysis for Resolving Strategic Issues," *Journal of Applied Behavioral Science* 25 (May 1989): 189-201.

21. Andre L. Delbecq, "Techniques for Achieving Innovative Changes in Programming" (Presentation at the Midwest Regional Conference of the Family Service Association of America (Omaha, NE, April 20, 1971).

22. June P. Elvins, "Communication in Quality Circles: Members' Perceptions of Their Participation and Its Effects on Related Organizational Communication Variables," *Group & Organization Studies* 10 (1985): 479–507.

23. William V. Ruch, *Corporate Communications* (Westport, CT: Quorum Books, 1984): 205–19.

24. Elvins, "Communication in Quality Circles," 479–507.

25. E. Lawler and S. Mohrman, "Quality Circles after the Fad," *Harvard Business Review* 63 (January–February 1985): 65–71.

26. Gerald M. Goldhaber, *Organizational Communication*, 4th ed. (Dubuque, IA: Wm. C. Brown, 1986): 283.

27. Thomas Owen, "Self-Managing Work Team," *Small Business Reports* (February 1991): 53–65.

28. Henry P. Sims, Jr., and James W. Dean, Jr., "Beyond Quality Circles: Self-Managing Teams," *Personnel Journal* (1985): 25–32.

29. Sue Barnes and Leonore M. Greller, "Computer-Mediated Communication in the Organization," *Communication Education* 43 (April 1994): 129–42.

30. Mathew Schwartz, "The Instant Messaging Debate," *Computerworld* 36 (January 7, 2002): 40.

31. Annette C. Easton, Nancy S. Eickelmann, and Marie E. Flatley, "Effects of an Electronic Meeting System Group Writing Tool on the Quality of Written Documents," *Journal of Business Communication* 31, no. 1 (1994): 27–40.

32. Judith Pena-Shaff, Wendy Martin, and Geraldine Gay, "An Epistemological Framework for Analyzing Student Interactions in Computer-Mediated Communication Environments," *Journal of Interactive Learning Research* 12 (Spring 2001): 41–62.

33. Ibid.

34. Ibid.

35. Ibid.

36. Tyrone Adams and Norman Clark, *The Internet: Effective Online Communication* (Fort Worth, TX: Harcourt, 2001): 105–7.

37. Starr Roxanne Hiltz, Kenneth Johnson, and Murray Turoff, "Experiments in Group Decision Making: Communication Process and Outcome in Face-to-Face versus Computerized Conferences," *Human Communication Research* 13 (1986): 225–52.

38. Sharon L. Murrell, "The Impact of Communicating through Computers" (Unpublished doctoral dissertation, State University of New York at Stony Brook, 1983).

39. Vitaly J. Dubrovsky, Sara Kiesler, and Beheruz N. Sethna, "The Equalization Phenomenon: Status Effects in Computer-Mediated and Face-to-Face Decision-Making Groups," *Human Computer Interaction* 6 (1991): 119–46.

40. Starr Roxanne Hiltz, Murray Turoff, and Kenneth Johnson, "Experiments in Group Decision Making, 3: Disinhibition, Deindividuation, and Group Process in Pen Name and Real Name Computer Conferences," *Decision Support Systems* 5 (June 1989): 217–32.

41. Sara Keisler and Lee Sproull, "Group Decision Making and Communication Technology," *Organizational Behavior and Human Decision Processes* 52 (June 1992): 96–123.

42. Robert Johansen, J. Vallee, and K. Spangler, *Electronic Meetings: Technical Alternatives and Social Choices* (Reading, MA: Addison-Wesley, 1979): 2.

43. John A. Short, E. Williams, and B. Christie, *The Social Psychology of Telecommunications* (London: Wiley, 1976).

44. Johansen et al., *Electronic Meetings*, 113–15.

45. Larry L. Barker, Kathy J. Wahlers, Kittie W. Watson, and Robert J. Kibler, *Groups in Process: An Introduction to Small Group Communication*, 3d ed. (Englewood Cliffs, NJ: Prentice Hall, 1987): 208.

46. Read for example, Adams and Clark, *The Internet: Effective Online Communication*, 105–7.

47. Marshall S. Poole, Michael Holmes, and Gerardine DeSanctis, "Conflict Management in a Computer-Supported Meeting Environment," *Management Science* 37 (August 1991): 926–53; Leonard M. Jessup, Terry Connolly, and David A. Tansik, "Toward a Theory of Automated Group Work: The Deindividuation Effects of Anonymity," *Small Group Research* 21 (August 1990): 333–48; Hiltz et al., "Experiments in Group Decision Making."

48. Noshir S. Contractor and David R. Siebold, "Theoretical Frameworks for the Study of Structuring Processes in Group Decision Support Systems: Adaptive Structuration Theory and Self-Organizing Systems Theory," *Human Communication Research* 19 (June 1993): 528–63.

49. Joseph E. McGrath and Andrea B. Hollingshead, *Groups Interacting with Technology* (Thousand Oaks, CA: Sage, 1994).

50. Bolanle A. Olaniran, "Group Performance in Computer-Mediated and Face-to-Face Communication Media," *Management Communication Quarterly* 7 (February 1994): 256–81.

51. Marshal Scott Poole and Michael E. Holmes, "Decision Development in Computer-Assisted Group Decision Making," *Human Communication Research* 22 (September 1995): 90–127; Marshall Scott Poole, Michael Holmes, Richard Watson, and Gerardine DeSanctis, "Group Decision Support Systems and Group Communication: A Comparison of Decision Making in Computer-Supported and Nonsupported Groups," *Communication Research* 20 (April 1993): 176–213.

52. Leonard M. Jessup and Joseph S. Valacich, eds., *Group Support Systems: New Perspectives* (New York: Macmillan, 1993).

53. Izak Benbasat and Lai-Huat Lim, "The Effects of Group, Task, Context, and Technology Variables on the Usefulness of Group Support Systems: A Meta-Analysis of Experimental Studies," *Small Group Research* 24 (November 1993): 430–62.

54. V. Sambamurthy, Marshall Scott Poole, and Janet Kelly, "The Effects of Variations in GDSS Capabilities on Decision-Making Processes in Groups," *Small Group Research* 24 (November 1993): 523–46.

55. Steven M. Farmer and Charles W. Hyatt, "The Effects of Task Language Demands and Task Complexity on Computer-Mediated Work Groups," *Small Group Research* 25 (August 1994): 331–66.

56. Andrea B. Hollingshead, Joseph E. McGrath, and Kathleen M. O'Connor, "Group Task Performance and Communication Technology: A Longitudinal Study of Computer-Mediated versus Face-to-Face Work Groups," *Small Group Research* 24 (August 1993): 307–33.

57. S. Opper and H. Fresko-Weiss, *Technology for Teams: Enhancing Productivity in Networked Organizations* (New York: Van Nostrand Reinhold, 1992).

58. Poole et al., "Group Decision Support Systems and Group Communication."

59. Victoria K. Clawson, Robert P. Bostrom, and Rob Anson, "The Role of the Facilitator in Computer-Supported Meetings," *Small Group Research* 24 (November 1993): 547–65.

60. Craig R. Scott, Laura Quinn, C. Erik Timmerman, and Diana M. G. Barrett, "Ironic Uses of Group Communication Technology: Evidence from Meeting Transcripts and Interviews with Group Decision Support System Users," *Communication Quarterly* 46 (Summer 1998): 353–74.

61. Andrew Flanagin, Vanessa Tiyaamornwong, Joan O' Connor, and David Seibold, "Computer-Mediated Group Work: The Interaction of Member Sex and Anonymity," *Communication Research* 29 (February 2002): 66–93.

62. Ibid.

63. Hollingshead et al., "Group Task Performance and Communication Technology."

64. Benbasat and Lim, "The Effects of Group, Task, Context, and Technology Variables."

65. Poppy McLeod, "New Communication Technologies for Group Decision Making: Toward an Integrative Framework," in *Communication and Group Decision Making*, 2nd ed., eds. Randy Y. Hirokawa and Marshall Scott Poole (Thousand Oaks, CA: Sage, 1996): 426–61.

15

OBSERVING AND EVALUATING GROUP DISCUSSIONS

Central
Message

Observers and consultants, including students, who understand group communication processes can use a variety of techniques and instruments to help groups evaluate and improve their performance.

STUDY OBJECTIVES

As a result of studying Chapter 15 you should be able to:

1. Explain the benefits of having a consultant observe and work with a group.
2. Prepare an observation guide appropriate for observing a small group.
3. Report observations to groups in ways that are helpful to the group members.
4. Devise and use instruments to assess verbal participation, obtain members' reactions to a meeting, and evaluate both individual members and groups.

Sam, the CEO of a small plant that manufactured specialized circuit boards, decided to hire a consultant to help his executive committee overcome several problems. The committee met weekly and consisted of the department managers: Roger, manufacturing; Elgin, quality assurance; Angela, sales and marketing; and Frank, the comptroller. The team had made several costly mistakes in the past several months, which Sam thought were caused by misunderstandings between members, on top of the pressures caused by an expanding business. In one instance, Angela had promised an early delivery to a customer on the basis of what she thought Roger had said, but the circuit boards weren't ready and the company lost the customer. Things didn't seem to be improving, and Sam didn't know whether the problems were due to his leadership style, the competence of the members, ineffective communication at the weekly meetings, or something else. He needed an objective, informed opinion.

Enter Susanna, organizational trainer and consultant who specialized in team performance and teambuilding. First, she gathered all the information she could about the team by interviewing Sam and reading the group's memos and minutes. This didn't take her long because committee minutes were kept sporadically. She observed three meetings, which highlighted to her what some of the problems might be, and took extensive notes so she could provide specific examples to the members. As a last step, she interviewed each of the group members to gain their perspectives on the meetings and their own performance.

Susanna prepared her feedback for the group. She had a long list of things she could mention, but she didn't want to overwhelm or demoralize the team. She selected the few she thought were most problematic, beginning with "housekeeping." The team did not operate with an agenda, nor was anyone regularly assigned to take notes. She noted that the team met in an employee break room that had snacks handy, but because other employees wandered in and out, the room was noisy and distracting. She observed that at each meeting, nearly every member was called away at least once by a secretary or subordinate to answer a question or take a phone call.

In her report, Susanna recommended that Sam provide members with an agenda at least a day or two before the meeting, and that if members didn't want to rotate the job of taking minutes, Sam's secretary could attend the meetings specifically for that function. She suggested that members find another place to meet—even if that had to be away from the plant, at a private meeting room in a restaurant over breakfast, for example. She also recommended that members not allow their secretaries or subordinates to interrupt the meeting, except for a dire emergency.

> When I'm in a group, I'm always watching, how's the leader doing this and this and this, because I think I learn a lot through example.
>
> *M. K. S., Vice President, Investor Services Firm, retired*

The next recommendations concerned the process of discussion itself. Susanna praised the group for their obvious dedication to the company and their creativity in solving problems. She noted, however, that because there had been several costly misunderstandings, members exhibited signs of distress and distrust, which she thought they could overcome. Susanna gave the group several examples of how their discussion was disorganized, with members jumping from one topic to another without concluding a topic. At any given moment, there could be three different topics under discussion, and it was easy to mishear or misunderstand information. She affirmed that their problems were solvable and gave them several suggestions for how the group could monitor its own discussion process. She spoke privately with Sam about his somewhat lax leadership style and recommended that he keep firmer control of the meetings.

Finally, Susanna designed a training program for the group, to take place during a weekend retreat. The program succeeded in improving the members' basic communication skills and featured several teambuilding activities to help the group begin to recover some of the trust eroded by recent mistakes.

As a member of a group, it's important for you to observe the group communication process while you participate in it. However, you cannot both observe and participate at the same instant. Rather, your attention shifts back and forth between observing and participating, which means that you may miss something. Sometimes you see clearly what your group needs and can supply it (the completer function), but sometimes you can't tell what's missing, what's wrong, or what's needed—or even that there is anything wrong at all! The most skillful participant among us can become so engrossed in discussing an issue we care about that we lose the observer perspective. That was Sam's situation.

That's when a **consultant,** an observer who does *not* participate in the group's discussion, can be of real assistance in identifying what is going wrong and helping the group correct its problems. Evaluation of group processes has been shown to be beneficial to both small groups and the organizations that created them.[1] Feedback from a consultant can help an entire group, including the discussion leader. A consultant does not need to be a professional—our students can and have served as consultants to a number of groups and organizations. Don't underestimate what you already know from having studied small group communication. In many cases, your academic training in small groups is more than most group members and leaders have received! One of our students included in her job portfolio a copy of the small group consulting project she completed as a class assignment. One potential employer, whose organization wanted to move to more group- and team-based work, recognized her potential value to the company and offered her a job on the strength of that class consulting project.

We have two main purposes in this chapter: first, we explain the functions consultants can perform and how they perform them; second, we present

Consultant

A nonparticipant observer who works with a group to determine what it needs, then helps by providing information, special techniques, and procedures.

examples of several types of instruments that both participant-observers (group members) and consultants can use to gather information and feed it back into the group for improvement of future discussion. Included among these instruments are interaction analysis diagrams, member and observer rating scales, postmeeting reaction questionnaires, and content analysis schemes.

Roles of Observers and Consultants

Every student of group communication should spend time observing interaction of discussion groups. As many of our students have remarked, "It looks different when you are sitting outside the circle." We have witnessed the "Ah-ha!" reactions of student observers who finally *saw* a phenomenon that previously had been only an abstract idea.

Preparing to Consult

At this point, you have enough academic knowledge to be helpful. Ideally, though, you should spend some time observing different kinds of groups before you begin to consult. You will be more confident and knowledgeable as a consultant if you have experience as an observer and as a small group member. There are many groups you can observe in their natural settings, such as any small group meeting legally declared open to the public, as are most meetings of boards, councils, and government committees for whom a "sunshine" law exists. Many groups will open their meetings to you if they know you are a student and you promise to maintain the confidentiality of the group's private business. Our students have observed meetings of groups such as church study-discussion classes, project groups in college classes, student activity committees, executive committees of sororities and fraternities, teaching teams, department managers, management executive staffs, task forces, school boards, university boards of regents, quality circles, and self-help groups such as Adult Children of Alcoholics.

Observing as part of a team will increase your learning. A team can take in more than an individual, and team members learn a lot from sharing and discussing their individual insights. An observation team may be able to arrange a fishbowl setup, with observers sitting in a circle outside the discussion group. Sometimes, all observers will focus on the same aspects of group discussion, such as leadership sharing; at other times, each member watches for and reports on a different phenomenon (e.g., Martha observes leadership sharing, Xiuchen focuses on nonverbal signals, Anthony concentrates on how the group uses information). Sometimes, each observer is assigned to watch the behavior of a specific group member, then later shares those observations with the rest of the observation team.

Consultants generally provide three functions for the groups they consult for: they *remind* a group of techniques or principles of discussion it has overlooked, they *teach* a group new procedures and techniques to improve the

The fishbowl is an excellent arrangement for training observers.
© James L. Shaffer

group's performance, and they *critique* a group's performance. Sometimes, consultants do all three of these at once.

Reminding   Often group members need only to be reminded of principles and techniques they already know but have temporarily overlooked in the excitement of a lively argument. When the consultant notices some difficulty with the group's communication process, he or she may remind the group of the principles or techniques that have temporarily been overlooked. A reminder is like a coach during pauses in a football game. Having a reminder can improve a group's decision quality. Schultz et al. trained certain group members to serve as reminders, intervening whenever they observed symptoms of defective group decision making.[2] The reminders were instructed not to be aggressive but to remind the group by providing timely questions and suggestions: "Maybe we shouldn't make our final choice until we've looked at all the alternatives." Reminders, particularly those who were regular group members and not the emergent leaders of their groups, significantly affected decision quality. These researchers suggest appointing a member to serve as a reminder. It is also useful to rotate this reminder role among the members so each has the chance to develop skills without any one person being left out of the discussion for too long. In addition, group members themselves should feel free to function as reminders when they notice something going astray. Whether you are a consultant or participant-observer, here are guidelines to help you *remind* in a sensitive and helpful way:

1. First, give the group a chance to correct itself before you intervene. Interrupt discussion only when you think the group will not become aware of a problem until it has wasted a lot of time or created harmful quarrels out of what could be productive argument. Allow a little frustration to motivate change, but not enough to lower morale or produce severe secondary tension.

2. Focus on communication process and procedures, not on issues and content of the discussion.

3. Don't give orders or force the group to change. Keep in mind that the group is responsible for its own changes—your job is to remind and suggest. Phrase most of your remarks in the form of descriptions of what you have observed, questions, and suggestions. Susanna did this for the executive team: "Did you notice that in the space of only four minutes, the team has discussed _____, _____, and _____?" and "I wonder if Angela and Roger understood each other's proposals?" or "Some members do not appear to have much chance to be heard. Does the group want to do more gatekeeping to ensure that such members' contributions are not missed?" Comments phrased in these ways remind the group of principles of effective discussion without criticizing specific members and possibly arousing defensiveness.

4. Focus on trends and tendencies, as a rule, rather than singling out individual members for comment, unless it is to praise someone.

Teaching Sometimes a consultant can be a helpful teacher by providing basic information about small group processes. Remember, many of the people who participate in groups of all kinds have never studied small group communication and don't know what is normal and what isn't. They need information to know how to resolve relational and procedural difficulties. Just by taking a small group communication course, you are ahead of many group leaders, facilitators, and managers, who may have been thrown into a group with no training.

A teaching consultant can also provide specialized information in the form of procedures and techniques designed to solve specific group difficulties. With the advent of quality circles and self-managed work teams, workers who select coordinator-leaders from their own ranks need both basic and specialized information you may have that is not readily available to most workers.

To serve as a teaching consultant, you will need a thorough grasp of small group communication and a working knowledge of a variety of techniques and procedures, along with a number of observational, feedback, and evaluation instruments. Examples are presented later in this chapter, and there are others available in resources you should know if you plan to serve as a consultant. Here are guidelines for making your remarks as a consultant more acceptable and effective with the people you advise:

1. First, stress the positive; point out what a leader and group are doing well.

2. Focus on the most important things; don't overwhelm a group with more advice and suggestions than it can handle at one time.

3. Don't argue. Present your observations, opinions, and advice; be sure they are understood as you intend; then leave group members free to decide whether or how your evaluations and advice will be used. You are not an umpire with authority to stop the game or throw players out.

4. Don't interrupt a meeting if you need to give advice to the designated leader. If possible, whisper or write suggestions to the leader.

5. Give advice as precisely, clearly, and briefly as possible when you are asked. If the group asks for an explanation or demonstration of some technique or competency, prepare it carefully.

6. Make critical comments in private to a leader (or any member), so the person will not appear to be under attack or lose face with other members.

7. Don't bluff. If a group asks for information or procedures with which you are not familiar, admit you aren't familiar with them and explain that you'll research them for the group. Then feel free to consult print resources or other experts who can help you.

Critiquing   Many consultants, teachers, and trainers provide a group with **critique,** a descriptive analysis and evaluation of the group's strengths and weaknesses. Communication specialists on corporate training and development staffs are often called on to provide evaluations of both groups and individual members to managers, but even students can provide thoughtful critique. Fandt demonstrated that accountability of managerial personnel led to higher levels of performance, higher satisfaction with both process and product, and higher cohesiveness in groups evaluated than in groups not being evaluated to superiors.[3] Greenbaum and associates claim that failure to evaluate adequately the procedures and output of the quality circles is often a major factor in the demise of quality circle programs.[4]

> **Critique**
>
> Analysis and criticism of something, such as identification of strengths and weaknesses in a small group's process and interaction.

> I want to know how the group's perceiving how things go. That's the only way that I can get better with groups.
>
> *M. K. S. Vice President, Investor Services Firm, retired*

In general, a consultant's critique should cover at least four aspects of a group's discussion processes and culture: (1) inputs to and content of the problem-solving discussion; (2) the group process, including patterns of verbal interaction, member roles (including any ego-centered behavior and ethical lapses), communication process, decision making, and problem solving as a whole; (3) the group product, including how well it has been evaluated by the group, how appropriate it is to the goals or problem described by the group, and how committed members seem to be to making it work; and (4) leadership, especially the role of the designated leader and the sharing of leadership functions.[5] When you critique, make sure you use criteria appropriate to the group—a learning group's discussion shouldn't look or sound the same as a problem-solving group's.

Ethical Principles for Consultants

After observing a discussion, a consultant usually makes a detailed feedback statement to the group, describing selected aspects of the discussion and expressing opinions about strong and weak points. While doing so, respect both the individual members and the group as an entity. Consultants should behave so that the group will welcome other observers and consultants in the future. The ethical standards that apply to critic observers are analogous to those that universities use when faculty and students conduct research involving human subjects. Group members being observed are similar to research participants and deserve the same type of protections. These ethical standards also are similar to those for group members that we presented in Chapter 1. We propose that, as consultant, you adhere to the following standards of personal conduct:

1. Do not harm group members either physically or psychologically by your observation and feedback. Don't knowingly cause embarrassment, emotional upset, physical danger, and so forth. For example, it *would* be unethical for a consultant to make fun of a group member in front of the rest of the group, but it *would not* be unethical to speak with that member privately to describe the effect of the offending behavior on the group.

2. Tell the truth. It is unethical to tell a group that a critique will not be given to a superior when in fact it *will*. It is also unethical to tell a group that you think its decision-making procedures are vigilant when in fact you think they are sloppy.

3. Make your criticism constructive. When you point out a problem, you should also suggest what to do to correct it, as Susanna did when she recommended that the group find a different meeting room, that Sam provide an agenda, and that his secretary take minutes. You are there to help, not to judge. You will be more helpful if you present positive evaluations before talking about what needs to be changed: "I like . . . , but you could improve. . . ."

4. Respect the privacy and confidentiality of group members at all times. It is not ethical to share with outsiders what you have observed in a specific group unless: (1) you told the group you were going to do so before observing and the group granted you permission to do so; or (2) you so thoroughly disguise the identity of the group and its members (as in a statistical summary) that no one can possibly identify the group and members in your report. In addition, it is not ethical to receive confidential information from one member and share it with another without permission. Finally, unless a group meeting has been legally declared open to the public, you should not report details or the substance of group business to outsiders.

When the purpose for which you are observing includes reporting findings (for instance, reporting your observations to your teacher or class), you will need to get permission to do so from the group members *before* you do your observing. The persons to be observed may be more willing to let you report if you offer to use pseudonyms instead of real names. In general, treat observed persons just as you would want to be treated if your roles were reversed.

Planning the Consultation

When you first consult for a group, you may feel overwhelmed by all that goes on. Planning your observation and consultation in advance will help you focus on variables most important to your purposes and functions as a consultant. You may first want to talk with the group's leader or the person responsible for the group's output for background material about the group, such as what its purpose is, the history of the group, how effective it is perceived to be, and so forth. One way to cope with information overload is to record the group's discussion on audio- or videotape (but only after obtaining permission from the group) for more detailed analysis at a later time. That way, you will worry less about missing something important and can make notes about parts of the discussion to review later. Before trying to observe systematically, we suggest you practice observing discussions, including videotaped ones, for which you do not need to make any reports. Practice using the sorts of observational instruments and techniques you intend to use as a consultant. As with any skill, most of us need a lot of practice on an instrument before we are ready to perform.

You can use the questions in Table 15.1 as a general guide from which to select a more limited list of questions for a specific observation. If you have been asked to observe interaction as a consultant (or even as a participant-observer), this list can help you decide which processes are going well and then focus on characteristics that group members may want to change.

Obviously, you cannot consider all these questions at the same time. Concentrate on the one or two factors that seem most important to understanding your particular group or that seem most problematic for the group. With increased experience you will discover that you can pay attention to more

Group Purpose/Goals
What is the group's purpose?
Do members clearly understand and accept the group's purpose?
Has the committee achieved a clear understanding of its charge?
Do members seem to know and accept limits on their area of freedom?
Can members describe what sort of output is needed?
Setting
How adequate are meeting facilities, such as seating arrangement, privacy, and comfort?
How adequate are facilities for recording and displaying group progress (information, ideas, evaluations, decisions, and so on)?
Communication Skills and Network
How competently do members encode verbally and nonverbally?
How carefully are members listening to understand each other?
How equally is participation spread among the members?
Is the network of verbal interaction all-channel or unduly restricted?

TABLE 15.1
Questions to help guide your observation.

(continues)

TABLE 15.1
Concluded

Group Culture, Norms, and Communication Climate

To what degree is the group climate characterized by openness, trust, and teamwork?

What attitudes toward each other and the content of information and ideas are members manifesting?

Are cultural, work style, or personality differences interfering with the group's effectiveness?

Are any self-centered hidden agenda items interfering with progress toward the goal?

Are any norms interfering with cohesiveness and progress?

Are arguments being expressed sensitively and being managed to test ideas and achieve consensus, or to win?

Role Structure

Is there a designated leader?

If so, how well is this person performing the role? With what style? Are others encouraged to share in leader functions?

If not, how is leadership distributed? Are any needed services missing?

Are all necessary functional roles being provided?

Are there any ego-centered behavioral roles?

Problem-Solving and Decision-Making Procedures

How vigilant are the group's problem-solving procedures?

Do members seem to be adequately informed or are they planning how to get needed information before reaching decisions?

Are information and ideas being evaluated thoroughly for effectiveness and possible negative consequences, or accepted without question?

Are criteria shared by all group members, or explicitly discussed and agreed upon?

Are there any tendencies toward groupthink?

Has some procedure or agenda for the discussion been accepted by the group? If so, how adequate is it and how well is it being used?

Are information, interpretations, proposals, and decisions being recorded?

Are these provided in some record visible to the entire group?

How creative is the group in finding alternatives?

How frequently are summaries being made and used to focus and move discussion toward the goal?

How are decisions being made?

If needed, is the group making adequate plans to implement its decisions? To evaluate the adequacy of its actual solution(s), and possibly make changes later?

Might procedural changes or special techniques such as brainstorming, committee procedural rules, Nominal Group Technique, or computer charting be beneficial to the group?

factors, or rapidly scan what is happening and then decide where to focus your attention.

Instruments for Observing and Evaluating Discussions

Just as athletic teams, music groups, and actors need regular evaluations and advice to perform optimally, so do task forces, standing committees, boards, quality circles, and self-managed work teams. Any group can benefit from periodic evaluation. Regular reviews should be scheduled, whether or not aided by a consultant. For instance, Hill's "Learning Thru Discussion" procedure includes an evaluation of the discussion as part of each meeting of a learning group.[6] If "How are we doing?" sessions are not scheduled, too often no group evaluations occur, or evaluation takes the form of gripe sessions among a few members with little benefit to the group system.

> With our staff, we do that a lot. At different meetings, we'll do sort of a post-mortem, what did we all think of this meeting.
>
> *L. O., CEO, Health Care Collaborative*

This final section of Chapter 15 is devoted to instruments and techniques for observing and evaluating groups and their members. They can be used by observers or by group members or leaders themselves as part of a group's self-assessment. Feel free to use the instruments as presented or adapt them to suit particular situations and needs.

Verbal Interaction Analysis

A diagram of a **verbal interaction analysis** made by an observer reveals much about relationships among members of a group. The diagram in Figure 15.1 shows relationships among a team called the G.E. Tigers—who talks to whom, how often each member participates orally, and whether the group has members who do not speak up or who dominate the discussion. Notice the information at the top of the figure that identifies group, time, and persons involved. The names of the participants are located around a circle according to seating during the discussion. Each time a member speaks, an arrow is drawn from the person's position toward the person to whom the remark was addressed, or a longer arrow is drawn toward the center of the circle when a member speaks to the entire group. Subsequent remarks in the same direction are indicated by short cross marks on the shaft of the arrow.

For ease in interpreting a verbal interaction diagram, numbers and percentages can be displayed in charts like the ones in Figures 15.2 and 15.3. Judging from the numbers shown in this example, who do you think was discussion leader of the G.E. Tigers? Are there any other reasoned inferences you can make about this group from the data? You could modify this procedure and instrument to capture the frequency of some nonverbal behaviors such as eye contact and body angles.

Verbal Interaction Analysis

An analysis of who talks to whom and how often during a discussion.

FIGURE 15.1
Verbal interaction
diagram.

Group _____G.E. "Tigers"_____

Time_____

Begin ____1:03_____

End ____1:54_____

Place ____Conf. Rm. 14____

Observer __Snow_____

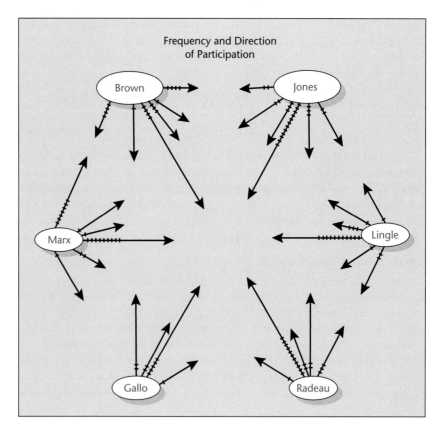

	TO:							
FROM:	**Brown**	**Jones**	**Lingle**	**Radeau**	**Gallo**	**Marx**	**Group**	Total Percent
Brown	–	5	2	4	2	5	5	23 / 16.1
Jones	3	–	3	4	4	3	13	30 / 21
Lingle	2	2	–	3	2	4	12	25 / 17.5
Radeau	3	3	4	–	0	2	12	24 / 16.8
Gallo	3	3	2	0	–	0	6	14 / 9.8
Marx	8	2	2	3	2	–	10	27 / 18.9
Total number / percent	19 / 13.3	15 / 10.5	13 / 9.1	14 / 9.8	10 / 7	14 / 9.8	58 / 40.6	143 / 100

Group __G.E. "Tigers" Q.C.__   Place __Conf. Rm. 14__
Observer __Snow__   Date __11-5-02__
Beginning time __1:03__   Ending time __1:54 pm__

FIGURE 15.2
Displaying data from a verbal interaction diagram.

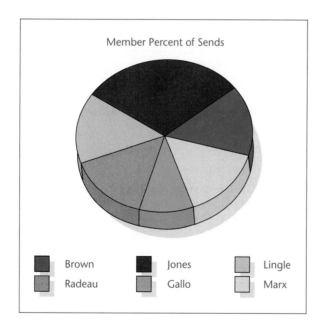

Member Percent of Sends

Brown   Jones   Lingle
Radeau   Gallo   Marx

FIGURE 15.3
Another way to display data from a verbal interaction diagram.

Content Analysis

Content Analysis

An analysis of the content (topics, behaviors, specific words or ideas, fantasy themes, etc.) of a group's discussion.

Content analysis procedures examine the actual content of remarks (topics, types of remarks, fantasy theme structure, etc.) made during a discussion. One type of content analysis focuses on who performs what behaviors and how often. From such a descriptive analysis, members' roles can be described. The examples in Figures 15.4 and 15.5 classify members' behaviors according to the functions they carry out during the observed discussion. Specific behavioral functions are listed along the left side of the chart, and the participants' names in the cells at the head of each column. Each time a member speaks, the observer judges the functional meaning of that statement to the group and places a tally mark in the appropriate cell of the chart. After the discussion the tally marks are converted to numbers and percentages, as shown in Figure 15.5. They can also be converted to pie charts such as the one shown for Jodi in Figure 15.6. From this analysis, can you tell who is probably task leader of this group? Who is the social or maintenance leader? Do any individuals seem to be interfering with the group's progress toward its goal?

A content analysis form could be developed for virtually any set of categories into which observable member behaviors could be classified, such as types of statements, functional stage in problem solving, kinds of questions, ways of expressing inferences, and so on. You might use verbal interaction analysis to trace development of fantasy chains, the progression of an idea from initial introduction through its final form and disposal by the group, types of conflicts, or how information is used by a group. One thing that matters is that the observer is able to classify the remarks consistently, identifying approximately the same behaviors and classifying them about the same way as another independent observer, or with oneself at two different times (using a recording of the discussion).

Questionnaires and Rating Scales

Rating Scale

A pencil-and-paper instrument to measure quantitatively some factor involved in a discussion.

Postmeeting Reaction Form (PMR)

A form, completed after a discussion, on which group members evaluate the discussion, the group, and/or the leader.

Many different types of questionnaires and observer forms have been prepared for evaluating and improving small group interaction. Some of these use open-ended or multiple-response questions; some use rating scales. **Rating scales** contain items that ask a respondent to render a numerical evaluation of some characteristic. You are probably familiar with the 0 to 10 scale used by judges of some Olympic competitions and the scales by which consumer products are rated in magazines. In Chapter 8 we introduced you to SYMLOG, a rating technique in which behaviors of group members are rated on three major dimensions; these ratings are then entered in a three-dimensional chart to describe group-level characteristics and problems. The scales and other forms that follow are provided for your use and to give you ideas about creating others for specific purposes.

Postmeeting reaction forms (PMRs) are questionnaires given to participants at the end of a meeting to get objective feedback for improving future discussions by the group. Because they are anonymous, participants are likely to be candid and honest in their comments and ratings. A PMR form may be

Group _____ Place _____ Observer _____

Date _____ Beginning time _____ Ending time _____

Participants' Names

Behavioral Functions						
1. Initiating and orienting						
2. Information giving						
3. Information seeking						
4. Opinion giving						
5. Opinion seeking						
6. Clarifying and elaborating						
7. Evaluating						
8. Summarizing						
9. Coordinating						
10. Consensus testing						
11. Recording						
12. Suggesting procedure						
13. Gatekeeping						
14. Supporting						
15. Harmonizing						
16. Tension relieving						
17. Dramatizing						
18. Norming						
19. Withdrawing						
20. Blocking						
21. Status and recognition seeking						

FIGURE 15.4
Content analysis of behavioral functions of members.

FIGURE 15.5
Displaying data from analysis of behavioral functions of members.

Group __EXECUTIVE COMMITTEE__				Place __CU LOBBY__		
Observer __ANDY__				Date __11-14-02__		
Beginning time __4:30 P.M.__				Ending time __6:30 P.M.__		

Participants' Names

Behavioral Functions	Mary	John	Edna	Dave	Jodi	Total number / percent
1. Initiating and orienting	5	3				8 / 5.7
2. Information giving	6	5		2	3	16 / 11.4
3. Information seeking			3			3 / 2.1
4. Opinion giving	8	8	4	2	1	23 / 16.4
5. Opinion seeking			2			2 / 1.4
6. Clarifying and elaborating			3			3 / 2.1
7. Evaluating	2	4			1	7 / —
8. Summarizing	2					2 / 1.4
9. Coordinating	8					8 / 5.7
10. Consensus testing				3		3 / 2.1
11. Recording			5			5 / 3.6
12. Suggesting procedure	3		6			9 / 6.4
13. Gatekeeping			1	5		6 / 4.3
14. Supporting	2		2	6		10 / 7.1
15. Harmonizing				3	2	5 / 3.6
16. Tension relieving					6	6 / 4.3
17. Dramatizing		5			3	8 / 5.7
18. Norming				4		4 / 2.9
19. Withdrawing		1				1 / —
20. Blocking	2	5				7 / 5
21. Status and recognition seeking		4				4 / 2.9
Total number / percent	38 / 27.1	35 / 25	26 / 18.6	25 / 17.9	16 / 11.4	140 / 100

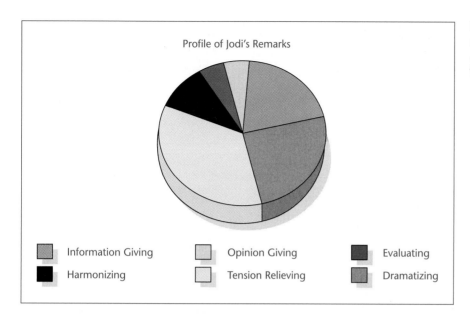

Profile of Jodi's Remarks

- Information Giving
- Harmonizing
- Opinion Giving
- Tension Relieving
- Evaluating
- Dramatizing

FIGURE 15.6 Pie chart displaying Jodi's behavioral functions.

planned by an entire group, a leader, an instructor, a consultant, organizers of a large conference, or by a student of small group communication. The questionnaires are distributed, completed, and collected after a discussion. Responses should be tallied and reported back to the group as soon as possible on a duplicated summary sheet or wall chart. If a group has access to group decision support software, the ratings can be entered and tallied simultaneously. The chart provides the basis for an evaluation discussion and planning changes in group procedures.

The last agenda item is to evaluate the meeting.

L. O., CEO, Health Care Collaborative

Questions and scales should be tailored to fit the purposes and needs of the person(s) preparing the questionnaire. Questions can be about any aspect of group discussion: the substance of the discussion, interpersonal relations, procedures, and techniques. Several types of questions may be mixed on a questionnaire, depending on what the preparer of the questionnaire wants to learn. Two examples of PMR forms are shown in Figures 15.7 and 15.8. Although both are designed to be completed anonymously, it is also possible for groups to set aside the last five or so minutes of a meeting for an open postmeeting discussion about how members felt about the meeting. Figure 15.8, in particular, can guide such a discussion.

Rating scales can be mixed with open-ended questions to assess any aspect of the group and its discussion, including group climate, norms, structure, interpersonal relationships, speaking, listening, content of remarks, and so on. The set of scales in Figure 15.9 was developed by Larkey to evaluate

FIGURE 15.7
Postmeeting
reaction (PMR) form.

Instructions: Check the point on each scale that best represents your honest judgment. Add any comments your wish to make that are not covered by the questionnaire. Do not sign your name.

1. How clear were the *goals* of the discussion to you?

   _____

   very clear   somewhat vague   muddled

2. The *atmosphere* was

   _____

   cooperative and cohesive   apathetic   competitive

3. How well *organized and vigilant* was the discussion?

   _____

   disorderly   just right   to rigid

4. How effective was the *leadership* supplied by the chairperson?

   _____

   too autocratic   democratic   weak

5. *Preparation for this meeting* was

   _____

   thorough   adequate   poor

6. Did you find yourself *wanting to speak* when you didn't get a chance?

   _____

   almost never   occasionally   often

7. How satisfied are you with the *results* of the discussion?

   _____

   very satisfied   moderately satisfied   very satisfied

8. How do you feel about *working again* with this same group?

   _____

   eager   I will   reluctant
   Comments:

FIGURE 15.8
Postmeeting
reaction (PMR) form.

1. How do you feel about today's discussion?

   excellent _____ good _____ all right _____ so-so _____ bad _____

2. What were the strong points of the discussion?

3. What were the weaknesses?

4. What changes would you suggest for future meetings?

(You need not sign your name.)

Postmeeting reaction (PMR) sheets can help a group diagnose its own problems.

© John Davis/ImageState-Pictor/PictureQuest

how members of a diverse work group evaluate how well that group manages its diversity.[7] The composite scale in Figure 15.10, based on a similar one developed by Patton and Giffin, may be used to identify deficiencies in problem-solving procedures.[8]

Almost any characteristic of individual behavior can be evaluated with an appropriate scale. Figure 15.11 shows a simple rating form that can be completed by an observer and given to each participant; alternatively, participants can complete these scales anonymously about each other, and then distribute them to the persons rated. Versions of this form (originally devised by a group of students for their own use) have been used extensively by one of the authors. It is easy to understand, can be completed quickly, and focuses on some of the most important variables of a participant's behavior. Figure 15.12 is similar in purpose but more comprehensive. Figure 15.13 is useful for rating the level of assertiveness of participants, while indicating whether nonassertive participation was evaluated as passive or aggressive.

The previous forms can be used as presented or modified to rate designated leaders, but Figures 15.14 and 15.15 were devised specifically to rate leaders. Exceptionally comprehensive, Figure 15.14 has been modified substantially over the years from one originally devised for rating Air Force personnel as discussion leaders. Figure 15.15 is designed to help a leader engage in introspective self-evaluation after a discussion, identifying specific successes and failings, and then providing an overall rating.

FIGURE 15.9
Workplace diversity
questionnaire.

Instructions: Answer each question on the basis of what you have observed and experienced in your workgroup.

	Agree				Disagree

Inclusion

1. If someone who is not included in the mainstream tries to get information or makes a request, others stall or avoid helping them out in subtle ways.   5 4 3 2 1

2. It seems that the real reason people are denied promotions or raises is that they are seen as not fitting in.   5 4 3 2 1

3. I have to prove myself more and work a lot harder to get into that next position because of my gender or ethnic background.   5 4 3 2 1

4. It's hard to get ahead here unless you are part of the old boys' network   5 4 3 2 1

Ideation

5. When people from different backgrounds work together in groups, some people feel slighted because their ideas are not acknowledged.   5 4 3 2 1

6. People are reluctant to get involved in a project that requires them to balance ideas from different gender and racial points of view.   5 4 3 2 1

7. Individuals with different backgrounds have a difficult time getting their ideas across.   5 4 3 2 1

8. Individuals in our group have a difficult time really listening with an open mind to the ideas presented by those of another culture or gender.   5 4 3 2 1

Understanding

9. When people who are culturally different or of different genders work together in our group, there is always some amount of miscommunication.   5 4 3 2 1

10. Women and people of color are interpreted differently than White males, even when they say the same thing.   5 4 3 2 1

11. Whenever I've confronted someone for giving me a hard time because of my race or gender, they have denied the problem.   5 4 3 2 1

Treatment

12. Some people in our group are "talked down to" because they are different.   5 4 3 2 1

13. People's different ways of talking or acting cause them to be treated as less competent or smart.   5 4 3 2 1

14. Performance evaluations seem to be biased against those who are different, because supervisors focus on very traditional ways of getting work done.   5 4 3 2 1

15. You can just feel a difference in the way some people are treated or talked to because they are different.   5 4 3 2 1

Instructions: On the basis of behaviors and interaction you observed, rate the degree to which the group measured up to each criterion.

Poor 1		Fair 2		Average 3	Good 4	Excellent 5

1   2   3   4   5   **1.** Concerns of all members were established regarding the problem.

1   2   3   4   5   **2.** Components of the undesirable situation and obstacles to change were clearly described.

1   2   3   4   5   **3.** The goal was clearly defined and agreed upon by all members.

1   2   3   4   5   **4.** Possible solutions were listed and clarified before extensive evaluation of them.

1   2   3   4   5   **5.** Criteria for evaluation were previously understood and accepted, or discussed and agreed upon by all members.

1   2   3   4   5   **6.** Based on facts and reasoning, predictions were made regarding the probable effectiveness and possible negative consequences of each proposed solution.

1   2   3   4   5   **7.** Consensus was achieved on the most desirable/acceptable solution.

1   2   3   4   5   **8.** A realistic plan was developed for implementing the solution and, if appropriate, for evaluating its effectiveness.

1   2   3   4   5   **9.** Overall, the problem-solving process was thorough, vigilant, and systematic.

FIGURE 15.10
Problem-solving procedure scale.

FIGURE 15.11
Participant rating scale.

Date _____
Observer _____

_____
(Name of participant)

1. Contributions to the *content of the discussion* (relevant information, issue-centered arguments, adequate reasoning, etc.).

5	4	3	2	1

   outstanding in
   quality and quantity   fair share   few or none

2. Contributions to *efficient group procedures* (agenda planning, responding to prior comments, summaries).

5	4	3	2	1

   always relevant,   relevant, no   sidetracked,
   aided organization   aid in order   confused group

3. Degree of *group orientation and cooperation* (listening to understand, responsible, agreeable, group centered, open-minded).

5	4	3	2	1

   very responsible   self-centered
   and constructive

4. *Speaking competency* (clear, to group, one point at a time, concise).

5	4	3	2	1

   brief, clear,   vague, indirect,
   to group   wordy

5. *Overall value* to the group.

5	4	3	2	1

   most valuable   least valuable

Suggestions:

Participant's name _____

Instructions: Circle the number that best reflects your evaluation of the discussant's participation on each scale.

Superior   Poor

1   2   3   4   5   **1.** Was prepared and informed.

1   2   3   4   5   **2.** Contributions were brief and clear.

1   2   3   4   5   **3.** Comments relevant and well timed.

1   2   3   4   5   **4.** Spoke distinctly and audibly to all.

1   2   3   4   5   **5.** Willingness to communicate.

1   2   3   4   5   **6.** Frequency of participation [if poor, too low( ) or high( )].

1   2   3   4   5   **7.** Nonverbal responses were clear and constant.

1   2   3   4   5   **8.** Listened to understand and follow discussion.

1   2   3   4   5   **9.** Open-mindedness.

1   2   3   4   5   **10.** Cooperative, team orientation.

1   2   3   4   5   **11.** Helped keep discussion organized, followed outline.

1   2   3   4   5   **12.** Contributed to evaluation of information and ideas.

1   2   3   4   5   **13.** Respectful and tactful with others.

1   2   3   4   5   **14.** Encouraged others to participate.

1   2   3   4   5   **15.** Overall rating as participant.

Comments: Evaluator _____

FIGURE 15.12
Discussion participant evaluation scale.

FIGURE 15.13 Assertiveness rating scale.

Discussant _____ Date _____
Observer _____ Time _____

The check mark on each scale indicates my best judgment of your degree of assertiveness as a participant in the discussion.

	Nonassertive	Assertive	Aggressive
Behavior			
Getting the floor	yielded easily	usually refused to let others take over or dominate	interrupted and cut others off
Expressing opinions	never expressed personal opinion	stated opinions, but open to others' opinions	insisted others should agree
Expressing personal desires (for meeting times, procedures, etc.)	never, or did so in a pleading way	stated openly, but willing to compromise	insisted on having own way
Sharing information	none, or only if asked to do so	whenever information was relevant, concisely	whether relevant or not; long-winded, rambling
Manner			
Voice	weak, unduly soft	strong and clear	loud, strident
Posture and movements	withdrawn, restricted	animated, often leaning forward	unduly forceful "table pounding"
Eye contact	rare, even when speaking	direct but not staring or glaring	stared others down
Overall manner	nonassertive	assertive	aggressive

Date _____ Leader _____
Time _____ Observer _____

Instructions: Draw a line through any item not applicable to the discussion you have just observed. Use the following scale to evaluate the designated leader's performance as discussion leader.

5—superior   4—above average   3—average   2—below average   1—poor

Personal Style and Communicative Competencies

To what degree did the leader:
_____ Show poise and confidence in speaking?
_____ Show enthusiasm and interest in the problem?
_____ Listen well to understand *all* participants?
_____ Manifest personal warmth and a sense of humor?
_____ Show an open mind toward all new information and ideas?
_____ Create an atmosphere of teamwork?
_____ Share functional leadership with other members?
_____ Behave democratically?
_____ Maintain perspective on problem and group process?

Preparation

To what degree:
_____ Were all needed physical arrangements cared for?
_____ Were members notified and given guidance in preparing to meet?
_____ Was the leader prepared on the problem or subject?
_____ Was a procedural sequence of questions prepared to guide discussion?

Leadership Techniques

To what degree did the leader:
_____ Put members at ease with each other?
_____ Equalize opportunity to speak?
_____ Introduce and explain the charge or problem so it was clear to all?
_____ Control aggressive or dominant members with tact?
_____ Present an agenda and/or procedural outline for group problem solving?
_____ Encourage members to modify the procedural outline?
_____ State questions clearly to the group?
_____ Guide the group through a thorough analysis of problem before discussing solutions?
_____ Stimulate imaginative and creative thinking about solutions?
_____ Encourage the group to evaluate all ideas and proposals thoroughly before accepting or rejecting them?
_____ See that plans were made to implement and follow up on all decisions?
_____ Keep discussion on one point at a time?
_____ Rebound questions asking for a personal opinion or solution to the group?
_____ Provide summaries needed to clarify, remind, and move group forward to next issue or agenda item?
_____ Test for consensus before moving to a new phase of problem solving?
_____ Keep complete and accurate notes, including visual chart of proposals, evaluations, and decisions?
_____ If needed, suggest compromise or integrative solutions to resolve conflict?
_____ (Other—please specify_____)

FIGURE 15.14
Comprehensive leader rating scale.

FIGURE 15.15
Discussion leader self-rating scale.

Instructions: Rate yourself on each item by putting a check mark in the "Yes" or "No" column. Your score is five times the number of items marked "Yes."
Rating: *excellent,* 90 or higher; *good,* 80–85; *fair,* 70–75; *inadequate,* 65 or lower.

	Yes	No
1. I prepared all needed facilities.	___	___
2. I started the meeting promptly and ended on time,	___	___
3. I established an atmosphere of supportiveness and informality by being open and responsive to all ideas.	___	___
4. I clearly oriented the group to its goal and area of freedom.	___	___
5. I encouraged all members to participate and maintained equal opportunity for all to speak	___	___
6. I listened actively, and (if needed) encouraged all members to do so.	___	___
7. My questions were clear and brief,	___	___
8. I saw to it that unclear statements were paraphrased or, otherwise clarified.	___	___
9. I used a plan for leading the group in an organized consideration of all major phases of problem solving and all components of vigilant interaction.	___	___
10. I saw to it that the problem was discussed thoroughly before solutions were considered.	___	___
11. I actively encouraged creative thinking.	___	___
12. I encouraged thorough evaluation of all proposed solutions, both for effectiveness and negative consequences.	___	___
13. I integrated related ideas or suggestions and urged the group to arrive at consensus on a solution.	___	___
14. I prompted open discussion of substantive conflicts.	___	___
15. I maintained order and organization, promptly pointing out tangents, making transitions, and keeping track of the passage of time.	___	___
16. I saw to it that the meeting produced definite assignments or plans for action, and that any subsequent meeting was arranged.	___	___
17. All important information, ideas, and decisions were promptly and accurately recorded.	___	___
18. I was able to remain neutral during constructive arguments, and otherwise encourage teamwork.	___	___
19. I suggested or urged establishment of needed ethical standards and procedural norms.	___	___
20. I encouraged members to discuss how they felt about group process and procedures.	___	___

SUMMARY

1. Consultants who observe but do not participate in a group's discussion can help a group by reminding members of principles they have forgotten, by teaching members procedures and techniques, and by critiquing a group's performance. Students who have taken a course in small group communication can be effective consultants; their skills are enhanced through observation and practice.

2. Because it is impossible to keep track of all variables at once, consultants should plan their observations by focusing on the most important or most problematic aspects of a group's interaction.

3. Consultants report their findings to groups honestly and constructively, always respecting members' confidentiality.

4. Many different kinds of prepared observation forms and questionnaires can help consultants (and also group members) gather information about a group to assess the group's performance. The forms included in the chapter can serve as models for describing a group's verbal interaction, analyzing the members' behaviors and discussion content, providing postmeeting evaluations to group members, and rating many other aspects of groups.

KEY TERMS

Test your knowledge of these key terms by visiting the Online Learning Center website at mhhe.com/galanes11

Consultant	Critique	Rating scales
Content analysis	Postmeeting reaction forms (PMRs)	Verbal interaction analysis

EXERCISE

Go to self-quizzes on the Online Learning Center at mhhe.com/galanes11 to test your knowledge of the chapter concepts

Divide your class into project groups of five or six members. Each group should select an existing small group to observe and evaluate. You may want to check your student activities office or similar office for lists of on-campus organizations or groups whose meetings you might observe. Class members may have special access to groups in local business or government organizations.

This project will last for the entire term. Although you may be given some time in class for

meetings, expect that you will have to schedule numerous meetings outside class time.

You will need to decide which group to observe, on which aspects of the group to focus (e.g., leadership, roles, decision-making procedures and effectiveness, conflict management, problem-solving procedures, collection and use of information, etc.), and which observation techniques and/or forms to use. Then you will carry out your observations and prepare a report of your findings to the rest of the class, using appropriate visual and other aids. You may also be asked to serve as a consultant to the group you observe and present an oral or written report to the observed group.

BIBLIOGRAPHY

Schwarz, Roger M. *The Skilled Facilitator: Practical Wisdom for Developing Effective Groups*. San Francisco: Jossey-Bass, 1994.

Wheelan, Susan A. *Creating Effective Teams: A Guide for Members and Leaders*. Thousand Oaks, CA: Sage, 1999.

NOTES

1. Patricia M. Fandt, "The Relationship of Accountability and Interdependent Behavior to Enhancing Team Consequences," *Group & Organization Studies* 16 (1991): 300–12; Harold H. Greenbaum, Ira T. Kaplan, and William Metlay, "Evaluation of Problem-Solving Groups," *Group & Organization Studies* 13 (1988): 133–47.

2. Beatrice Schultz, Sandra M. Ketrow, and Daphne M. Urban, "Improving Decision Quality in the Small Group: The Role of the Reminder," *Small Group Research* 26 (November 1995): 521–41.

3. Fandt, "The Relationship of Accountability," 305–7.

4. Greenbaum et al., "Evaluation of Problem-Solving Groups."

5. Ibid., 137–39, 145.

6. W. Fawcett Hill, *Learning Thru Discussion* (Beverly Hills, CA: Sage, 1977): 30–31.

7. Linda K. Larkey, "The Development and Validation of the Workforce Diversity Questionnaire: An Instrument to Assess Interactions in Diverse Work Groups," *Management Communication Quarterly* 9 (February 1996): 296–337.

8. Bobby R. Patton and Kim Giffin, *Problem-Solving Group Interaction* (New York: Harper & Row, 1973): 213–14.

Making Public Presentations of the Group's Output

Often groups must make public presentations of their output, which may take the form of a report, a set of findings or recommendations, and so forth. The group's leader or selected representatives may present a report from the group to the parent organization, a political body, an open meeting of interested community representatives, or another type of public gathering. The members of the audience at such public gatherings may themselves become participants who will discuss the report of the group. The following information presents formats for a variety of public discussion sessions in which group members may find themselves participating.

Panel Discussion

A **panel discussion** is a public presentation in which a small group of people representing varying perspectives informally discusses issues relevant to an important question in front of a listening audience. For example, a panel might discuss abortion laws, solutions to congested parking on campus, what might be done to solve a community's solid waste problem, or the responsibility of society to the victims of crimes. A panel format is sometimes used with a group of aspirants for political office.

> **Panel Discussion**
> A small group whose members interact informally for the benefit of a listening audience.

Groups may participate in panel discussions in a variety of ways. A group may be asked to plan and conduct an entire panel discussion, in which case the entire group must research and present fairly all relevant points of view about the issue. More typically, a group known to support a particular point of view will be asked to supply a representative to serve as a panelist with other panelists who represent different viewpoints. The **moderator** of a panel coordinates the discussion so it does not ramble and so all viewpoints are represented. Participants need to be both knowledgeable about the question under discussion and articulate in expressing their, or the group's, opinions. Panelists generally have an outline of questions to follow, but their speaking is relatively impromptu. Panelists need not agree on anything except which issues to discuss; the lively argument that often ensues can make for an intellectually stimulating program. The panel format is excellent for presenting an overview of different points of view on an issue of public concern. CNN and C-SPAN often include such discussions in their programming.

> **Moderator**
> A person who controls the flow of communication during a public presentation such as a panel or forum discussion.

Preparing for Panel Discussions

Panel and other public discussions call for special physical arrangements and other preparations. First, all discussants should be able to see each other and the audience at all times to facilitate direct interaction. Seat panelists in a semicircle in front of the audience with the moderator either at one end or in the center; thus, panelists have eye contact with each other and the audience. Second, panelists should be seated behind a table, preferably with some sort of cover on the front. Two small tables in an open V make an excellent arrangement. Third, a large name card should be placed in front of each panelist. Fourth, microphones, if needed, should be plentiful enough and unobtrusive. In a large assembly, if a floor mike is required for questions from the audience, it should be placed strategically and audience members instructed in its use. Finally, visual displays of the topic or question under consideration help keep the discussion organized. A chalkboard or easel can be used for this purpose.

The discussion outline for a panel discussion can follow one of several formats. The one described here is common. The moderator should ask panelists in advance to suggest questions and subquestions for the discussion. After these are compiled into a rough outline the moderator intends to use, panelists should receive a copy in advance so they have a chance to investigate and think of possible responses to each question.

The moderator prepares a special outline and uses it during the panel discussion. The outline has an introduction, sequence of questions to be raised, and a planned conclusion format. The moderator acts as a conversational traffic officer directing the flow of the discussion. Moderators ask questions of the group of panelists, see that each panelist has an equal opportunity to speak, and clarify ambiguous remarks or ask panelists to do so. They do not participate directly in the arguments. They summarize each major topic or have the panelists do so and keep the discussion moving along the major points of the outline. A moderator's outline might look like this:

Introduction   "What should be the law governing abortions in the United States?"

  I. Ladies and gentlemen, the question of what the law should be governing abortions in the United States has been a subject of heated argument, physical confrontation, intensive lobbying, court cases, sermons, and pamphlets—and far too little calm, thoughtful discussion.

 II. Today we are fortunate to have a panel of thoughtful experts who represent all major points of view on this subject.

   A. Father Jon McClarety has made an intensive study of the Catholic theology and arguments underlying the church's stand against legalized abortions. He is a member of the Department of Philosophy and Theology of Holy Name Academy.

   B. Robert Byron is an attorney for the Legal Aid Society who has served his society in appeals to the Supreme Court that led to the current legal status of abortions.

    C. Ms. Martine Giles, founder and director of the Adoption Alternatives Agency, has helped arrange more than 300 private adoptions nationally.

    D. Ms. Dorothy Mankewicz, a social worker and volunteer lecturer for Zero Population Growth, has assisted many women who wanted abortions.

    E. Professor Maya Kasakrim is historian of ethical and social values at Western State University and author of two books dealing with the abortion law controversy.

III. Our panelists have agreed to discuss four specific issues that are part of the question you see on the poster before you. "What should be the law governing abortions in the United States?"

    A. When does a human life begin?

    B. Who has the right to decide whether or not a woman should be allowed to have an abortion?

    C. What would be the effects of greater restriction on the right of choice to have an abortion?

    D. Under what conditions, if any, should abortions be legal?

IV. Each panelist will give a brief statement of his or her position on each issue and the reasoning behind it; then the panelists will question and debate their positions informally. After 50 minutes, the floor will be opened for questions from you, our listening audience. While discussion is proceeding, you may want to jot down questions as they occur to you so you can remember them for the forum period (described later).

Body of the Discussion

    I. "When does a human life begin?"

        A. Father McClarety: _____

        B. Ms. Mankewicz: _____

        C. Professor Kasakrim: _____
        and so on.

    (All four issues are discussed, with the moderator summarizing; seeing that each panelist gets an opportunity to present a position on each issue, and question, support, or argue with the others; and moving the group to the next major question at a prearranged time.)

Conclusion

    I. Let's see if we can summarize what we have learned about each other's positions. I'd like each of you to summarize in a minute or less your position and arguments. (Often the moderator does the summing up, with panelists being free to correct or supplement.)

    II. I believe all of us in this room are now better prepared to cope with this vital issue. We now understand each other's positions as well as possible, and the values and beliefs supporting them.

III. Now I wonder what questions our listeners have for the panel? Please raise your hand if you want to ask a question, and wait for me to recognize you by pointing. I will give each person a chance to ask one question before allowing anyone to ask a second question. Your questions can be directed to a particular panel member to answer or to the entire group. If you want a particular panel member to answer, state that person's name. Okay, what's our first question? The lady to my right wearing the maroon blazer—please state your question loudly enough for all present to hear. (Suggestions for conducting a successful forum discussion are provided later in this appendix.)

Public Interviews

Public Interview

One or more interviewers asking questions of one or more respondents for the benefit of a listening audience.

The leader or selected members of a group may be asked to participate in public interviews about the group's work. A **public interview** may be conducted by one or more interviewers of one or more interviewees at a time. *Meet the Press* and *This Week with George Stephanopoulos* are examples of this format, as are press conferences and some political candidate debates. Interviewers and interviewees may agree in advance on a list of major questions or topics to be discussed and on the range of topics for discussion, or the program may be entirely spontaneous. The interviewer's responsibility is to represent the audience by asking questions the audience most wants or needs to have answered, and to help the interviewees clarify their responses. The interviewee's responsibility is to present fairly and clearly the point of view of the group represented.

Forum Discussions

Forum Discussion

A large audience interacting orally, usually following some public presentation.

Sometimes when a group presents a report to a large gathering, members of the audience are permitted to ask questions or express opinions about the group's work. **Forum discussion** refers to this period of verbal interaction during which audience members interact in an organized way with the presenters. The term *forum* also refers to a discussion held by a large gathering of people, such as a university faculty meeting or a town meeting. Frequently a forum follows a panel or interview presentation. Audience members should be told in advance that a forum will follow the public presentation so that they can think of questions or comments. Microphones often are set up at strategic places for audience members to use. Sometimes, audience members are asked to supply their questions or comments in written form to a moderator, who reads them aloud for the entire gathering, followed by responses from panelists or interviewees.

Strict procedural control is needed for a successful forum. The moderator should control the forum so the discussion is interesting and fair to all participants. The following are guidelines to ensure fairness without letting the discussion bog down on one issue:

1. During the introduction to the panel or other program, announce that there will be a forum or question and answer period. This allows listeners to be thinking of questions and remarks.

2. State whether only questions or both questions and comments will be permitted.

3. Just before the audience participation segment, announce definite rules to assure equal opportunity for all to speak, such as:

   a. Raise your hand and wait to be recognized before speaking.

   b. No one may speak a second time until each person who wants the floor has had it once.

   c. Comments or questions should be addressed either to a specific panelist by name or to the entire panel.

   d. Remarks must be limited to not more than _____ seconds.

   e. Speak loudly enough to be heard by everyone or go to the floor microphone.

4. Tell the audience whether there will be a definite length of time for the forum and stick to the time.

5. If the audience is large, recognize people from various parts of the room in a systematic pattern.

6. Encourage different points of view by asking for them: "Does anyone want to present a *different* point of view from that we have just heard?"

7. If a question cannot be heard by all, restate it.

8. If a question is unclear or long, paraphrase it to the originator's satisfaction.

9. When the allotted time is nearly up, state that there is just enough time for one or two more questions or comments.

10. If no one seeks the floor, wait a few seconds, then thank the panel and audience for their participation and either dismiss the meeting or go on to the next item on the agenda.

Informational Resources for the Small Group

B

A group's output can be only as good as its input and throughput allow. No matter how committed members are to the group and how skilled they are at the process of discussion, critical thinking will be impaired if members don't have accurate, relevant, valid, and complete information with which to work. Groups that gather as much relevant information as possible *before* they begin their problem-solving or decision-making procedures will produce better outputs—decisions, solutions, reports, recommendations— than groups whose inputs are inadequate.

Appendix B is designed to help you improve your input resources by assessing the information you have, deciding what additional information you need, and then obtaining it, evaluating it, and organizing it for easy referencing by the group. The four steps, in order, are (1) review and organize your present stock of information and ideas, (2) gather needed additional information, (3) evaluate all the information and ideas you have collected, and (4) organize the information and ideas into a tentative outline. This comprehensive information-gathering procedure is especially useful for important problems and decisions when making a mistake would be costly or worse. In such cases, the search for information should be exhaustive and the evaluation thorough. For problems with little danger of causing a costly mistake, the group can adapt the procedure or focus on just those steps that are most relevant.

Review and Organize Your Present Stock of Information and Ideas

You probably already have some information about the subject. Taking a systematic inventory of the information you currently have saves time and makes it easier for you to recall what you have when you need it.

1. **Place the problem or subject in perspective.**
   To what is it related? What will it affect, and what affects it? For example, when the church board mentioned in Chapter 2 decided on a new location for the church, it had to consider the financial condition of the church, long-range plans, the availability of public transportation and parking facilities, types of activities planned for the church, and so forth.

2. **Make an inventory of information you have about the subject.**
Each member should contribute what he or she knows, similar to the mapping procedure described in Chapter 11. This should be a fairly unstructured, freewheeling process. All this information should be written down.

3. **Organize the information into a rough draft of a problem-solving outline.**
Look over the information for main issues, topics, or questions about the problem. You may want to use the guidelines suggested in Chapter 11.

4. **Look for deficiencies.**
The rough draft will reveal where the group has gaps in its information and will suggest specific information to gather and opinions or ideas that need to be supported.

Gather Needed Information

You are now ready to plan how to correct the gaps in your knowledge and thinking. *Planning* is important; otherwise, haphazard information gathering produces "garbage in" that results in "garbage out" conclusions.

You cannot expect to deal with all this information in a single meeting. Even if members are familiar with the topic in advance, you need time to think about the information and spot gaps. This usually takes two meetings, often more. The following two-step procedure helps ensure that the group overlooks nothing important:

1. **The group should identify and list all the major issues or topics, along with subtopics, that it needs to explore further.**
These issues were suggested by the rough outline produced during step 1 above. Add additional topics or deficiencies as they occur to you. Produce a list of all additional information needed.

2. **The group should assign research responsibilities to individual members.**
Distribute items from the list produced in step 1 equitably to the members and establish deadlines to complete the research. This increases individual responsibility and involvement. Ideally, members can choose voluntarily the topics of most interest to them. A group secretary or chair should keep track of who has agreed to undertake what research.

As a general rule, all members should do some common background study, with two or more of you examining each major source on the topic. This helps offset individual perceptual biases and helps prevent the group from relying on one "specialist" for each topic.

Ways of gathering information are suggested below. Because this information is likely to have been covered in previous communication and composition classes, we review it only briefly.

Note Taking

Information and ideas slip from memory or become distorted unless we make accurate and complete notes. Saying that a key piece of information appeared "in a book by some DNA researcher" is useless because fellow members cannot evaluate the credibility of the information or the source. The best system of note taking is to record each bit of information or data on a separate index card or directly into a database via a laptop computer, along with the topic heading and the full bibliographic reference, as shown in Figure B.1.

Note cards and databases provide both accuracy and flexibility. They can be arranged in groups to help synthesize and interpret the evidence collected. They can be sorted in a variety of ways and consulted with ease during a discussion without having to leaf through a disorganized notebook.

Three important sources for gathering information useful to problem-solving discussions are direct observation, reading, and interviews.

Direct Observation

Many times, needed information can come only from firsthand observation by group members, and often only direct observation can breathe life into a table of statistics or survey results. For example, a group of students trying to improve conditions in a self-service coffee shop of a student union spent time observing and recording how many customers did and did not bus their waste materials, the kinds of litter on the floor and tables, and placement and condition of waste containers.

Self-Monitoring	Why related to leadership emergence

Robert J. Ellis and Steven F. Cronshaw, " Self-Monitoring and Leader Emergence: A Test of Moderator Effects," in *Small Group Research*, 23(February 1992): 113–29.

"It is possible that low and high self-monitors are equally effective at identifying the needs of a group, but only high self-monitors are proficient at modifying their behavior to respond to such needs." p. 124

FIGURE B.1 A note card listing a topic heading, a specific subject, and exact details of the source.

Reading: Print and Electronic Sources

For many topics and problems, the major source of information will be books, journals, newspapers, government documents, and other printed materials, whether in hard copy or online through the Internet. First, it is important to narrow down the print sources likely to yield relevant information. To do that, you need to compile a **bibliography,** which is a list of published sources on a particular topic or issue. Although ideally you would like to locate and evaluate all recent printed information on your topic before making any final decision, that is not always possible. Internet sources are especially helpful here. Be sure, however, that you do not limit yourself to only one or two sources or to sources that support only one point of view. This will produce a bias in your information with no way to cross-check validity.

Bibliography

A list of sources of information about a topic; usually includes books, journal or magazine articles, newspaper stories, interviews, and so forth.

To compile your bibliography as efficiently as possible, first prepare a list of key terms—descriptors—on the topic. For instance, a group investigating, "What type of lottery should our state conduct?" might use the following descriptors: *lottery, sweepstakes, gambling, crime, revenue*, and *betting*. Once you start your search, you may encounter additional terms, such as *victimless* or *wagering*. A reference librarian's help is indispensable in using printed sources of all kinds, including *Sociological Abstracts, Psychological Abstracts, ERIC, Facts on File*, and others. The abstract sources are significant time savers because they provide brief summaries of articles or books so you can determine whether you should read the entire publication for details.

Most such sources are now accessible by computer. Computerized databases such as *ComAbstracts, InfoTrac, PsychInfo, EBSCOhost*, and *Lexis-Nexis* can be invaluable in locating information about a topic. Although some of these databases may entail a fee, they make it extremely easy for you to locate relevant items quickly, so they are usually worth the money. The list of descriptors your group generates provides a starting point for a computer file search.

Most of the electronic databases work the same way. Once you enter the database, often from your university or public library, you can search the database by key word, title, or author. For instance, in gathering information about capital punishment, key words such as *capital punishment, death penalty, death row, lethal injection*, or *electric chair* might be entered. If you know that John Smith has written a number of articles about capital punishment, you could search by author name, *John Smith*. Generally, this search will produce a list of articles pertinent to your topic. If your list is too long, you can refine it by adding additional key words: *capital punishment* and *Missouri*, for example. Sometimes, in addition to the article's title, you can see an abstract, or summary, of the article. More and more often, articles are available full text online. Utilizing electronic search help can save you a lot of time.

Search Engine

Software that allows you to search the Web for items related to key words you enter.

Even if you do not have access to electronic databases, the World Wide Web itself serves as a giant electronic database. By using a **search engine** such as Yahoo.com, Netscape.com, AltaVista.com, or Infoseek.com, you can search the Web for items related to key words you enter. Many search engines attempt to rank-order the items they send you, so that the ones that seem most relevant appear first, but this process is not foolproof, so you may end up with information overload. Even so, you will want to try this to see what you do get.

In addition, seeking out the home page of organizations relevant to your topic can be both efficient and helpful. For instance, if your group is investigating the effects of drinking and driving, you may want to type into your search engine *Students Against Drunk Driving* to see what hits you get. If you do that, you will find that the first website listed is called *Students Against Destructive Decisions*, which is the name for SADD. On that site are several buttons linking you to specific information helpful to your research.

Remember that when you cite research you obtained from the Web, you must provide the reader with enough information to locate the website you used. That means you need, at minimum, the Universal Resource Locator (URL) for the site, any links you clicked to get deeper into the site, and the specific paragraph from which you obtained your specific information or your quoted material.

A good library manual, available at virtually every college or university library, helps in building a bibliography and locating print materials. Also helpful are bibliographies of bibliographies, such as *A World Bibliography of Bibliographies and Bibliographic Sources* and *Bibliographic Sources*. Bibliographies are also found at the end of most books, doctoral dissertations, and research articles. Do not overlook indexes to periodicals, such as *The Readers Guide to Periodical Literature*, *The New York Times Index*, and *Education Index*. Federal and state government publications, in special sections of many libraries, also contain vast amounts of information. The *Monthly Catalog of U.S. Government Publications* and the *Monthly Checklist of State Publications* will help you locate relevant information in these publications. Other useful sources include the *Congressional Quarterly Weekly Report* and the *Congressional Digest*. Many of these, such as *CQ Weekly*, are now online.

Even while you start to compile a bibliography, you can begin reading. A good strategy is for all members of the group to read some of the same things to provide a common background, then divide up the rest of the bibliography. When you evaluate a book for usefulness, read the index and table of contents for clues. Skim rapidly until you find something pertinent to your group, then read carefully. Take notes of the most important ideas and facts, and make copies of particularly valuable information for the rest of the group.

For controversial problems or topics, read as many contrasting interpretations and viewpoints as possible. For example, before developing a campus policy regarding use of laboratory animals for research, study the writings of those who favor and oppose using animals. Although it is easier to remember opinions that support your own, making an effort to understand other points of view is essential for effective group discussion and problem solving. Doing that will also help you increase your level of cognitive complexity.

Interviews

Sometimes you need firsthand information or explanations by a knowledge-able individual; interviews can help you obtain information you cannot get in other ways. Members of the group described earlier that observed the operation of the campus coffee shop also interviewed a number of customers to determine how they felt about its condition and to ask their reasons for not busing their wastepaper and leftovers. They also interviewed the manager to determine why materials that contributed to litter were being used. Most people are flattered to be asked for their information and opinions, but remember that your interviewees are busy and would prefer that you read first, then interview them for clarification.

Interview questions may be open-ended ("Why do you eat in the snack shop?") or closed-ended ("If trash containers were more conveniently located, would you use them? Yes ——— No ———"). In-depth interviews using open-ended questions often yield unexpected information and provide richer data. However, answers to open-ended questions are more difficult and time-consuming to tally. In contrast, closed-ended questions can be asked of many people quickly and are easily tabulated if formulated properly. You may want to use both.

It is invalid to generalize findings from a casual or haphazard sample to a larger population. For example, interviews about location of a new sanitary landfill with 50 people who happen to enter a particular door of city hall will not provide an accurate picture of the beliefs of residents of that city, or even of people who go to city hall. A scientifically designed sample (a *representative* sample) must be taken if results of interviews are to be generalized to members of a larger population. Unless some member of your group has been trained as a survey researcher or you can get such a person to help you, *student groups should generally not undertake a sample survey*.

Other Information Sources

Useful information may crop up anywhere, anytime. You may hear something relevant to your topic or problem while listening to the radio or watching television. Some televised material, such as the program content of C-SPAN, is cataloged and available for purchase or rent. Lectures or public speeches are another source of information. An idea may occur to you when you are not consciously thinking about the group's problem—for example, while riding to school, jogging, or talking with friends. Most of us find it helpful to keep a small notepad or a few note cards with us so we can jot down ideas when they occur, lest we forget or distort them. The important thing is to be alert to unexpected information and record it promptly.

Evaluate the Information and Ideas You Have Collected

The information and ideas you have gathered must be evaluated for accuracy and credibility. Many of your ideas may collapse in the presence of contradictory information, or some of your information may be spurious, from suspect sources, in direct contradiction to other evidence, or irrelevant. Now is the time for the group to cull the misleading, unsubstantiated, or wrong information so your decision or solution will not be faulty.

In Chapter 12 we discussed ways you can evaluate information and reasoning, including information you get from the World Wide Web. In particular, examine the following questions:

1. **Are the sources believable?**
   Is the person a recognized expert? Is there anything—vested interest, known bias—that could have biased his or her opinion? For instance, ideas about medical care in the United States from representative physicians, insurance agents, and pharmaceutical salespeople are likely to be biased in different ways.

2. **Is there a clear distinction made between facts and inferences?**
   Are opinions stated as though they are facts? Can the facts be verified by independent credible sources?

3. **Are statistical data validly gathered, analyzed, and explained?**
   Was the sample representative? Were appropriate statistical procedures used to analyze the data? Are the results appropriately generalized, or overgeneralized?

4. **Are conclusions (inferences) supported by good reasoning?**
   Are there any fallacies that call the conclusions into question? Can you draw different but equally valid conclusions from the same set of evidence?

Organize Your Information and Ideas

The most efficient way to organize the group's information is to write a tentative outline based on a P-MOPS or Single Question sequence for problem solving (see Chapter 11). Ask yourself, "What are the questions that must be answered by our group to arrive at a full understanding of the problem or subject?" Your answers can serve as tentative main points in your outline.

Once you have decided on some tentative major issues or topic areas, you can arrange your notes into piles, one per issue or outline item. Some of the piles can be further divided into subheadings. For example, information concerning the nature of the problem might be arranged under such subheadings as "who is affected," "seriousness of the problem," "contributing causes," "previous attempts to solve the problem," and so forth. Organizing your information like this makes it easier for you to locate pertinent information when a topic arises during group discussion, helps you prepare questions the group needs to consider, and generally helps you and the group conduct an orderly and comprehensive discussion of a complex topic.

When you prepare for a problem-solving discussion, your outline is likely to contain some possible solutions you have found or thought of. You may have evidence or reasoning that shows how similar solutions were tried on a similar problem or even some suggestions about how to implement a plan. However, such thinking and planning should be *tentative*. It is easy to become dogmatic about an issue after you have spent hours preparing to discuss it, but it is absolutely essential that your mind be open. It is inappropriate and harmful to the group for members to come to a discussion prepared to defend their solutions against all comers. Remember that experts at the cutting edge of their fields are usually less dogmatic and sure of themselves than people who know much less.

We emphasize again that the information-gathering strategies we have suggested here can be modified to suit the particular needs of the group. For consequential decisions that will affect many people, something like this full procedure should be used. However, for relatively minor problems with few risks of making a mistake, the group can focus on the parts of this procedure most relevant to the group's problem.

Glossary

A

Abstract General, nonspecific, or vague.

Acceptance requirements The degree to which the solution for a given problem must be accepted by the people it will affect.

Accommodation The conflict management style, high in cooperativeness and low in assertiveness, where one person appeases or gives in to the other.

Action-oriented listener A listener who focuses on the task, remembers details and prefers an organized presentation.

Active listening Listening with the intent of understanding a speaker the way the speaker wishes to be understood and paraphrasing your understanding so the speaker can confirm or correct the paraphrase.

Activity group A group formed primarily for members to participate in an activity such as bridge, bowling, hunting, etc.

Activity orientation The extent to which a culture emphasizes doing or being, taking charge or going with the flow.

***Ad hominem* attack** An attack on a person rather than his or her argument, often involving name-calling; distracts a group from careful examination of an issue or argument.

Adaptive structuration The version of structuration theory that examines how the structures of computer technology get used during group decision making.

Administrative duties One of the major categories of responsibility of a designated leader; includes planning, sending meeting notices, keeping written records, and other administrative functions.

Affective conflict Conflict resulting from personality clashes, likes, dislikes, and competition for power.

Agenda A list of items to be discussed at a group meeting.

Aggressiveness Behavior designed to win or dominate that fails to respect the rights or beliefs of others.

Ambiguous A characteristic of any word or statement that can reasonably be understood in more than one way.

Antecedent phase The preliminary phase in group socialization where individual member characteristics influence member readiness and ability to engage in effective group socialization.

Anticipatory phase The phase in group socialization where members form initial expectations about each other and the socialization process

Area of freedom The scope of authority and responsibility of a group, including limits on the group's authority.

Assembly effect A type of group synergy or nonsummativity whereby the decision of group members collectively is superior to adding together (summing) the wisdom, knowledge, experience, and skills of the members individually.

Assertiveness Behavior that manifests respect both for your own and others' rights as opposed to aggressiveness and nonassertiveness.

Assimilation phase The phase in group socialization where the member and the group have worked out a comfortable fit.

Attitude A network of beliefs and values, not directly measurable, that a person holds toward an object, person, or concept; produces a tendency to react in specific ways toward the object, person, or concept.

Authoritarianism Tendency to accept uncritically the information, ideas, and proposals of authority figures such as a high-status group member or leader; produces preference for strong leaders and subservience as a follower.

Autocratic leader A leader who tries to dominate and control a group.

Avoidance The passive conflict management style that ignores a conflict.

B

Backchannel Nonverbal vocalizations such as mm-hmm and uh-huh that are uttered while another is speaking; partly determined by one's culture, can indicate interest and active listening.

Behavior Any observable action by a group member.

Behavioral function The effect or function a member's behavior has on the group as a whole.

Bibliography A list of sources of information about a topic; usually includes books, journal or magazine articles, newspaper stories, interviews, and so forth.

Boomer generation Individuals born from 1946 to 1964; key experiences include the Vietnam war, the civil rights movement, and Watergate.

Boundary spanner A group member who monitors the group's environment to import and export information relevant to the group's success.

Brainstorming A small group technique for stimulating creative thinking by temporarily suspending evaluation.

Brainwriting Individual brainstorming producing a written list.

Builder generation Individuals born before 1945; key experiences include the Great Depression and World War II.

Buzz group session Method whereby attendees at a large group meeting can participate actively; the large meeting is divided into groups of about six persons each who discuss a target question for a specified time, then report their answers to the entire large assembly.

Bypassing A misunderstanding that results from two people not realizing they are referring to different things by the same words, or who have the same referent for different words.

C

Charge The assignment or goal given to a group, usually by a parent organization or administrator of the parent organization.

Closed system A system, such as a small group, with relatively impermeable boundaries, resulting in little interchange between the system and its environment.

Co-culture A grouping that sees itself as distinct but is also part of a larger grouping.

Cognitive complexity The personal trait that refers to the level of development of a group member's construct system for interpreting signals; cognitively complex individuals are able to synthesize more information and think in more abstract and organized terms than are cognitively simple individuals.

Cohesiveness The degree of attraction members feel for the group; unity.

Collaborating group A group whose members come from different organizations to form a temporary alliance for a specific purpose.

Collaboration The assertive, cooperative conflict management style that assumes a solution can be found that fully meets the needs of all parties to a conflict; a problem-solving conflict management style.

Collectivist culture A culture in which the needs and wishes of the group predominate over the needs of any one individual; the idea of an individual following a path separate from the group is inconceivable.

Committee A small group of people given an assigned task or responsibility by a larger group (parent organization) or person with authority.

> **Ad hoc or special committee** A group that goes out of existence after its specific task has been completed.

> **Conference Committee** A group composed of representatives from two or more groups; members' responsibilities are to represent the interests of their constituents.

> **Standing Committee** A group given an area of responsibility that includes many tasks and continues indefinitely.

Common Ground dialogue A process of constructively managing divisive conflict where the participants are unlikely ever to agree, by focusing on the goals and values they can share and agree to.

Communication A process in which signals produced by people are received, interpreted, and responded to by other people.

Communication apprehension (CA) Anxiety or fear of speaking in a variety of social situations; reticence; shyness.

Communication network The interpersonal channels open for interaction; collectively, who talks to whom.

Communicative competencies The communication-related skills and abilities of members that help groups achieve their goals.

Competition The uncooperative, aggressive conflict management style where one person attempts to dominate or force the outcome to his or her advantage.

Compromise The conflict management style that assumes each party must give up something to get something; a shared solution to a conflict situation.

Computer-mediated communication (CMC) Using computers to interact with others.

Concrete words Low-level abstractions referring to specific objects, experiences, and relationships.

Conflict The expressed struggle that occurs when interdependent parties (including group members) perceive incompatible goals or scarce resources and interference in achieving their goals.

Conformity Following groups norm and not deviating from them.

Conjunctive task A type of group task where each member possesses information relevant to the decision, but no one member alone has all the needed information, thus requiring a high level of coordination among members.

Consensus decision A choice that all group members agree is the best one that they all can accept.

Consultant A nonparticipant observer who works with a group to determine what it needs, then attempts to help by providing inputs, such as special techniques, procedures, and information.

Content analysis An analysis of the content (topics, behaviors, specific words or ideas, fantasy themes, etc.) of a group's discussion.

Content-oriented listener A listener who enjoys analyzing information, dissecting others' arguments; can be seen as overly critical.

Contingency approaches The study of leadership that assumes the appropriate leadership style in a given situation depends on factors such as members' skills and knowledge, time available, the type of task, and so forth.

Control touches Gentle, positive touching of another person in an effort to get that person's attention or request compliance.

Cooperative requirements The degree to which members' efforts need to be coordinated for a group to complete its task successfully (see also Conjunctive task).

Criteria Standards for judging among alternatives; may be absolute (must) or relative.

Critical thinking The systematic examination of information and ideas on the basis of evidence and logic rather than intuition, hunch, or prejudgment.

Critique Analysis and criticism of something, such as identification of strengths and weaknesses in a small group's process and interaction.

Cultural identity The identification with and acceptance of a particular group's shared symbols, meanings, norms, and rules for conduct.

Culture The patterns of values, beliefs, symbols, norms, procedures, and behaviors that have been historically transmitted to and are shared by a given group of persons.

D

Decision making Choosing from among a set of alternatives.

Defensive listening Thinking of how to defend some aspect of one's self-image while appearing to listen to what another is saying.

Democratic leader An egalitarian leader who coordinates and facilitates discussion in a small group, encouraging participation of all members.

Designated leader A person appointed or elected to a position as leader of a small group.

Deviate A group member who differs in some important way, such as degree of participation, values, or opinions, from the rest of the group members; opinion or innovative deviates help groups examine alternatives more thoroughly by expressing opinions different from those held by the majority, thus forcing the group to take a closer look.

Dialect A regional variation in the pronunciation, vocabulary, and/or grammar of a language.

Discussion (small group discussion) A small group of people communicating with each other to achieve some interdependent goal, such as increased understanding, coordination of activity, or solution to a shared problem.

Disjunctive task A type of group task in which members work on parts of the group problem independently, with little or no coordination of effort through discussion needed.

Distributed leadership The concept that group leadership is the responsibility of the group as a whole, not just the designated leader; assumes all members can and should provide needed leadership services to the group.

Distributive approach The approach to managing conflict that assumes there are fixed resources to distribute among parties to the conflict; thus, whatever someone wins, someone else loses.

Dogmatism A tendency to hold rigidly to personal beliefs; closed-mindedness to evidence and reasoning contrary to one's beliefs.

E

Egalitarianism Belief in the equality of all people, resulting in the preference for participation in problem solving by all group members rather than by just a few high-status members.

Electronic brainstorming (EBS) Brainstorming on computers linked to a large screen that display all responses, but no one know who contributed which items.

Emergent leader Member of an initially leaderless group who, by virtue of information and communication competencies, rises from within the group to enact leadership functions and is viewed as the leader by all or most members.

Emoticon Typographical symbols used in computer-mediated communication to convey emotions in regular text, such as the smiley face :-) .

Emotive words Words that evoke specific emotions, connote more than they denote, and serve as triggers for recalling pleasant or unpleasant experiences.

Encounter phase The phase in group socialization where members' expectations meet with the actual behaviors and member and group goals become negotiated.

Environment The context or setting in which a small group system exists; the larger systems of which a small group is a component.

Ethics The rules or standards that a person or group uses to determine whether conduct or behavior is right and appropriate.

Ethnocentrism The belief that one's own culture is inherently superior to all others; tendency to view other cultures through the viewpoint of one's own culture.

Exit phase The phase in group socialization where the group disbands or a member leaves and the group must adapt.

Extraversion-introversion dimension The Myers-Briggs Type Indicator™ dimension concerned with whether one's focus is the external world (extraversion) or one's internal, subjective landscape (introversion).

F

Fact A verifiable observed event; a descriptive statement that is true.

Fallacy A reasoning error.

False dilemma Either-or thinking that assumes, incorrectly, that only two choices or courses of action are possible.

Fantasy A statement not pertaining to the here and now of the group that offers a creative and meaningful interpretation of events meeting a group's psychological or rhetorical need.

Fantasy chain A series of statements by several or all group members in which a story is dramatized to help create a group's view of reality.

Fantasy theme What the content of the dramatization of a fantasy or fantasy chain is about; the manifest theme is the overt, surface content, and the latent theme is the hidden, underlying meaning.

Faulty analogy An incomplete comparison that stretches a similarity too far; assuming that because two things are similar in some respects, they are alike in others.

Feedback A response to a system's output; it may come in the form of information or tangible resources and helps the system determine whether or not it needs to make adjustments in moving toward its goal.

Femininity (as applied to culture) The quality of cultures that value nurturing and caring for others.

Focus group A special group procedure that encourages freewheeling discussion focusing on a specific topic or issue, often used to analyze people's interests and values for market research.

Formation phase The stage in the development of a group during which relationship issues predominate as members work out their relationships with each other.

Forum discussion A large audience interacting orally, usually following some public presentation.

Functions approach The study of functions performed by leaders; the theory that leadership is defined by the functions a group needs and can be supplied by any member.

G

Gatekeeper Any member of a small group controlling who speaks during a discussion; any controller of the flow of messages among members.

Gender Learned and culturally transmitted sex-role behavior of an individual.

Goal The desired outcome a group works to achieve.

Group Three or more people with an interdependent goal who interact and influence each other.

Group charter A written document that describes the purpose of the group, its specific charge, area of freedom, membership, deadlines, and required output.

Group climate A group's emotional and relational atmosphere.

   Defensive climate   An atmosphere characterized by mistrust, in which members tear each other down.

   Supportive climate   An atmosphere of respect, in which members feel valued and appreciated.

Group culture The pattern of values, beliefs, and norms shared by group members, developed through interaction and incorporating members' shared experiences in the group, patterns of interaction, and status relationships.

Group Decision Support Systems (GDSS) or group support systems (GSS) Computer-based software and hardware systems designed to help groups improve a variety of group outcomes, such as creativity, problem solving, and decision making.

Grouphate The feeling of antipathy and hostility many people have against working in a group, fostered by the many ineffective, time-wasting groups that exist.

Group polarization The tendency for group members to make decisions that are more extreme (more risky or cautious) than they would make individually.

Group socialization The process of learning to become part of a group, which involves reciprocal influence among members and between members and the group

Groupthink The tendency of some cohesive groups to fail to subject information, reasoning, and proposals to thorough critical analysis leading to faulty decisions.

H

Hidden antagonizer An unintentional trigger word, not intended to offend, that does in fact provoke an emotional reaction.

High-context communication Communication wherein the primary meaning of a message is conveyed by features of the situation or context instead of the verbal, explicit part of the message.

High-level abstraction A word, phrase, or statement commonly used to refer to a broad category of objects, relationships, or concepts; typically refers to intangibles such as love, democracy, etc.

I

Idiosyncracy credit Additional leeway in adhering to group norms, given to a member for valuable contributions to the group.

Individualistic culture A culture in which the needs and wishes of the individual predominate over the needs of the group.

Individual-level variables Characteristics of the individual members of a group that affect the group's interaction, such as traits, attitudes, values, beliefs, and skills.

Inequity conflict Conflict about perceived unequal workloads or contributions to the group effort.

Inference A statement that includes more than a description of some event, thus going beyond fact; an inference involves some degree of uncertainty or probability and cannot be checked for accuracy by direct observation.

Input variables The energy, information, and raw material used by an open system, which is transformed into output by throughput processes.

Integrative approach The approach to managing conflict that assumes that solutions can be found to satisfy every party to the conflict.

Interaction Mutual influence by two or more people through the communication process.

Intercultural communication Interaction between and among individuals from different cultures or subcultures.

Interdependence The property of a system such that all parts are interrelated and affect each other as well as the whole system.

Interdependent goal An objective shared by members of a small group in such a way that one member cannot achieve the goal without the other members also achieving it.

Intracultural communication Interaction between and among individuals from the same culture or subculture.

Intrinsic interest Extent to which the task itself is attractive and interesting to the participants.

Intuitive problem solvers People who size up a situation, then arrive at a solution without consciously following any perceptible procedure.

K

Kinesics Study of communication through movements.

L

Laissez-faire leader A do-nothing designated leader who provides minimal services to the group.

Leader A person who uses communication to influence others to meet group goals and needs; any person identified by members of a group as leader; a person designated as leader by election or appointment.

Leader as completer A leader who determines which functions or behaviors are most needed for a group to perform optimally, then supplies them or encourages others to do so.

Leader-Member Exchange (LMX) model The leadership model based on the finding that supervisors develop different kinds of leadership relationships with their subordinates, depending on characteristics of both the leader and members.

Leadership Influence exerted through communication that helps a group achieve goals; performance of a leadership function by any member.

Leadership emergence The process by which someone emerges as the leader of an initially leaderless group in which all members start out as equals.

Learning group (study group) A group conducting a learning discussion.

Least-sized group The principle that the ideal group contains as few members as possible so long as all necessary perspectives and skills are represented.

Liaison Communication between or among groups; interfacing; a person who performs the liaison function.

Listening Receiving and interpreting oral and other signals from another person or source.

Low-context communication Communication wherein the primary meaning of a message is carried by the verbal or explicit part of the message.

M

Maintenance functions Relationship-oriented member behaviors that reduce tensions, increase solidarity, and facilitate teamwork.

Majority decision Decision made by vote, with the winning alternative receiving more than half the members' votes.

Masculinity (as applied to culture) The quality of cultures that value assertiveness and dominance.

Meeting notice A written message providing the time, place, purpose, and other information relevant to an upcoming meeting.

Message Either a set of signals from one person to others or interpretation/response of a listener to a set of signals.

Minutes A written record of every relevant item dealt with during a group meeting, including a record of all decisions.

Moderator A person who controls the flow of communication during a public presentation such as a panel or forum discussion.

Multiple causation The principle that each change in a system is caused by numerous factors.

Myers-Briggs Type Indicator™ A personality measure based on the work of Carl Jung that categorizes individuals on the basis of how they relate to the world around them.

N

Net conference A meeting that is electronically mediated by networked computers.

Net generation Individual born from 1977 to 1997; the first truly "wired" generation, comfortable with technology in all forms.

Noise Interference in the communication process; can occur at any step in the process, from the sender's original encoding of the message to the receiver's decoding of it.

Nominal Group Technique A special procedure in which group members brainwrite to generate ideas, then interact to pool, clarify, and evaluate these ideas until a solution has been accepted by weighted voting.

Nonsummativity The property of a system that the whole is not the sum of its parts, but may be greater or lesser than the sum.

Nonverbal signals Messages other than words to which listeners react.

Norm An unstated informal rule, enforced by peer pressure, that governs the behavior of members of a small group.

O

Obstacle Something that interferes or stands in the way of solving a problem, such as lack of information or resources, or attitudes of people who must support the solution.

Open system A system with relatively permeable boundaries, producing a high degree of interchange between the system and its environment.

Output variables Anything that is produced by the throughput processes of a system, such as a tangible product or a change in components of the system; in a small group, outputs are such things as reports, resolutions, changes in cohesiveness, and attitude changes in members.

Overgeneralizing Assuming that because something is true about one or a few items, it is true of all or most items of the same type.

P

Panel discussion A small group whose members interact informally and in impromptu manner for the benefit of a listening audience.

Paralanguage Nonverbal characteristics of voice and utterance, such as pitch, rate, tone of voice, fluency, pauses, and variations in dialect.

Paraphrase Restatement in one's own words of what one understood a speaker to mean.

Participant-observer An active participant in a small group who is at the same time observing and evaluating its processes and procedures.

Passiveness Nonassertive behavior that allows one's own rights and beliefs to be ignored or dominated, often to avoid conflict, even at the expense of good decision making.

People-oriented listener A listener who is sensitive to others, nonjudgmental, and concerned about how his/her behavior affects others; can become distracted from task by others' problems.

Perceiving-judging dimension The Myers-Briggs Type Indicator™ dimension concerning how people organize the world; perceivers are spontaneous and flexible whereas judgers are decisive and sure.

Personal growth group A group of people who come together to develop personal insights, overcome personality problems, and grow personally through feedback and support of others.

Phasic progression The movement of a group through fairly predictable phases or stages, each of which is characterized by specific kinds of statements.

Population familiarity The degree to which members of a group are familiar with the nature of a problem and experienced in solving similar problems or performing similar tasks.

Postmeeting reaction (PMR) form A form, completed after a discussion, on which group members evaluate the discussion, the group, and/or the leader; PMR responses are usually tabulated and reported back to the group.

Power The potential to influence behavior of others, derived from such bases as the ability to reward and punish, expertise, legitimate title or position, and personal attraction or charisma.

Power distance The degree to which a culture emphasizes status and power differences among members of the culture; in low power-distance cultures, status differences are minimized, but in high power-distance cultures, they are highly emphasized.

Preference for procedural order A trait characterized by need or desire to follow a clear, linear structure during problem solving and decision making.

Primary group A group whose main purpose is to meet members' needs for inclusion and affection.

Primary tension Tension and discomfort in members that stems from interpersonal (i.e., primary) sources, including the social unease that occurs when members of a new group first meet or during competition for power among members.

Principled negotiation A general strategy that enables parties in a conflict to express their needs openly and search for alternatives that will meet the needs of all parties without damaging the relationship among parties.

Problem The difference between what actually happens and what should be happening; components include an existing but undesired state of affairs, a goal, and obstacles to achieving the goal.

Problem census A technique in which members of a small group are polled for topics and problems that are then posted, ranked by voting, and used to create agendas for future meetings.

Problem question A question calling the attention of a group to a problem without suggesting any particular type of solution in the question.

Problem solving A multistage procedure for moving from some unsatisfactory state to a more satisfactory one, or developing a plan for doing so.

Problem-solving group A group that discusses to devise a course of action to solve a problem.

Procedural conflict Conflict resulting from disagreement about how to do something.

Procedural Model of Problem Solving (P-MOPS) A five-step general procedure, based on the scientific method, for structuring problem-solving discussions; P-MOPS is adaptable to any type of problem.

Production phase The stage in the development of a group during which task concerns predominate after a group has reached some socioemotional maturity.

Program Evaluation and Review Technique (PERT) A procedure for planning the details to implement a complex solution that involves many people and resources.

Proxemics The study of uses of space and territory between and among people.

Pseudolistening Responding overtly as if listening attentively, but thinking about something other than what the speaker is saying.

Public interview One or more interviewers asking questions of one or more respondents for the benefit of a listening audience.

Q

Quality circle (quality control circle) A group of employees meeting on company time to investigate work-related problems and to make recommendations for solving these problems.

R

Rating scale A pencil-and-paper instrument to measure quantitatively some factor involved in a discussion.

Referent Whatever is denoted by a symbol or statement.

Regulator Nonverbal signal used to control who speaks during a discussion.

Rhetorical sensitivity Speaking and phrasing statements in such a way that the feelings and beliefs of the listener are considered; phrasing statements so as not to offend others or trigger emotional overreactions.

RISK technique A small group procedure for communicating and dealing with all risks, fears, doubts, and worries that members have about a new policy or plan before it is implemented.

Role A pattern of behavior displayed by and expected of a member of a small group; a composite of a group member's frequently performed behavioral functions.

Rule A statement prescribing how members of a small group may, should, or must behave, which may be stated formally in writing, or informally as in the case of norms.

S

Search engine Software that lets you search the Internet using key words.

Secondary group A group whose major purpose is to complete a task, such as making a decision, solving a problem, writing a report, or providing recommendations to a parent organization.

Secondary tension Tension and discomfort experienced by group members that stem from task-related (i.e., secondary) sources, including conflicts over values, points of view, or alternative solutions.

Self-centered functions Actions of a small group member, motivated by personal needs, that serve the individual at the expense of the group.

Self-managed work group A small group of peers who determine within prescribed limits their own work schedules and procedures.

Self-monitoring The extent to which someone pays attention to and controls his or her self-presentation in social situations; high self-monitors are able to assess how others perceive them and adapt their behavior to elicit a desired response.

Sensing-intuiting dimension The Myers-Briggs Type Indicator™ dimension concerned with the type of information individuals use; sensers prefer facts and figures whereas intuiters prefer to dream about possibilities.

Sex Biologically determined femaleness or maleness.

Sidetracking A poor listening habit whereby one group member spins off on a private reverie unrelated to what another group member has said, or whereby one group member moves the conversation in a direction completely different from what was being discussed.

Sign A signal that has an inherent relationship with what it represents, such as a blush or scar.

Signal Any stimulus a person can receive and interpret, including both signs and symbols.

Single Question format A special procedure for structuring problem-solving discussions that facilitates critical thinking and systematic problem solving, but is more suitable for members low in preference for procedural order than more highly structured linear procedures.

Small group A group of at least three but few enough members for each to perceive all others as individuals, who meet face-to-face, share some identity or common purpose, and share standards for governing their activities as members.

Small group communication The scholarly study of communication among members of a small group, among two or more groups, and between groups and larger organizations; the body of communication theory produced by such study.

Small group discussion (see Discussion)

Social loafer A person who makes a minimal contribution to the group and assumes the other members will take up the slack.

Social presence The extent to which participants perceive that a communication medium is like face-to-face communication emotionally and socially.

Solution multiplicity Extent to which there are many different possible alternatives for solving a particular problem.

Solution question A question directed to a group in which the solution to a problem is suggested or implied.

Status The position of a member in the hierarchy of power, influence, and prestige within a small group.

Ascribed status Status due to characteristics external to the group, such as wealth, level of education, position, physical attractiveness, and so forth; status given on the basis of a member's input characteristics.

Earned status Status earned by a member's valued contributions to the group, such as working hard for the group, providing needed expertise, being especially communicatively competent, and so forth; status that comes from performance during a group's throughput processes.

Structuration The concept that a group creates and continuously re-creates itself through members' communicative behaviors; the group's communication both establishes and limits how the group develops.

Structure Organization; arrangement of parts of a system; steps in a procedure.

Styles approach The leadership approach that studies the interrelationship between leader style and member behaviors.

Substantive conflict Conflict resulting from disagreements over ideas, information, reasoning, or evidence.

Symbol An arbitrary, human-created signal used to represent something with which it has no inherent relationship; all words are symbols.

Symbolic convergence The theory that humans create and share meaning through talk and storytelling, producing an overlapping (convergence) of private symbolic worlds of individuals during interaction.

SYMLOG System for the Multiple-Level Observation of Groups, both a theory about member characteristics and effects on group interaction, and a methodology that produces a three-dimensional "snapshot" of a group at a given point in time.

Synectics A special group technique that encourages members to use unusual analogies and metaphors to create innovative solutions to problems.

System An entity made up of components patterned in interdependent relationship to each other, requiring constant adaptation among its parts to maintain organic wholeness and balance.

Systematic problem solvers Organized problem solvers who follow a definite series of steps or sequence, such as those provided by P-MOPS.

System-level variables Features or characteristics of the group as a whole, such as cohesiveness, interaction patterns, norms, roles, and so forth, that affect the group's interaction.

T

Task difficulty Degree of problem complexity and effort required.

Task functions Task-oriented member behaviors that contribute primarily to accomplishing the goals of a group.

Teambuilding A set of planned activities designed to increase teamwork, cohesiveness, or other aspects of group performance.

Technical requirements The degree to which the solution for a given problem is technically feasible or must meet standards of technical excellence.

Teleconference A meeting of participants who communicate via mediated channels such as television, telephone, or computer rather than face-to-face.

Thinking-feeling dimension The Myers-Briggs Type Indicator™ dimension concerned with how individuals prefer to make decisions; thinkers are objective and fact based whereas feelers are subjective and emotion based.

Throughput variables The actual functioning of a system, or how the system transforms inputs into outputs.

Time-oriented listener A listener sensitive to time; may be impatient or try to move group prematurely to closure.

Trait Relatively enduring, consistent pattern of behavior or other observable characteristic.

Traits approach The approach to leadership that assumes leaders have certain traits that distinguish them from followers or members of a group.

U

Uncertainty avoidance The degree to which members of a culture avoid or embrace uncertainty and ambiguity; cultures high in uncertainty avoidance prefer clear rules for interaction, whereas cultures low in uncertainty avoidance are comfortable without guidelines.

V

Variable An observable characteristic that can change in magnitude or quality from time to time.

Verbal interaction analysis An analysis of who talks to whom and how often during a discussion.

Vigilant Interaction Theory The theory that suggests that group members not only must have expertise about a problem, but must also be knowledgeable about the process of problem solving, especially to ensure that all aspects of the problem have been examined and that the pros and cons of all the alternatives have been thoroughly assessed.

Virtual team A group in which the members' interactions take place primarily through some combination of electronic systems, such as computers, telephones, and videoconferences, instead of face-to-face.

W

Worldview One's beliefs about the nature of life, the purpose of life, and one's relation to the cosmos.

X

X generation Individuals born from 1965 to 1976; key experience includes divorce on a massive scale.

Author Index

Subject Index